Emerging Maritime Security Strategies of Global Powers

Kiet Hoang Le
https://orcid.org/0009-0002-9968-1952
Yersin University, Vietnam

Hiep Xuan Tran
University of Science and Education, The University of Da Nang, Vietnam

IGI Global
Scientific Publishing
Publishing Tomorrow's Research Today

Vice President of Editorial Melissa Wagner
Director of Acquisitions Mikaela Felty
Director of Book Development Jocelynn Hessler
Production Manager Mike Brehm
Cover Design Jose Rosado

Published in the United States of America by
IGI Global Scientific Publishing
701 East Chocolate Avenue
Hershey, PA, 17033, USA
Tel: 717-533-8845 | Fax: 717-533-7115
Website: https://www.igi-global.com E-mail: cust@igi-global.com

Library of Congress Cataloging-in-Publication Data

LCCN: 2025038132 (CIP Data Pending)
ISBN13: 9798337344706
Isbn13Softcover: 9798337344713
EISBN13: 9798337344720
British Cataloguing in Publication Data
A Cataloguing in Publication record for this book is available from the British Library.

Table of Contents

Detailed Table of Contents

trends, power balance shifts, and domestic policy drivers. Analysis reveals that while China's economic rise and military modernization enable greater SCS assertiveness, the US maintains technological superiority and alliance advantages. Under Trump's second administration, characterized by transactional diplomacy yet bipartisan anti-China consensus, Washington will likely deepen regional engagement through traditional allies and expanded partnerships. China is projected to intensify gray-zone tactics, maritime presence, and infrastructure development while pursuing economic diplomacy to fragment ASEAN unity. The study concludes that through 2028, the SCS will remain a contested flashpoint marked by persistent tensions and strategic competition, though direct military confrontation remains unlikely due to mutual restraint and crisis management capabilities between both powers.

This chapter examines the South China Sea as a pivotal strategic space in Republic of Korea (ROK)–ASEAN relations since the early twenty-first century. Rather than focusing solely on sovereignty disputes, it conceptualizes the South China Sea as a multi-layered power structure where maritime economic interests, sea-lane security, and great-power competition intersect. The analysis explores how ASEAN employs international law, multilateral institutions, and functional cooperation to manage conflicts and preserve regional centrality, while the ROK, as a middle power, pursues calibrated engagement through ASEAN-led mechanisms to safeguard maritime interests without escalating strategic confrontation. This study positions the South China Sea as an illuminating case for understanding indirect middle-power engagement in regional security governance amid intensifying geopolitical pressures.

This chapter examines China's maritime security strategy in the South China Sea under President Xi Jinping, analyzing its transformation from measured assertiveness to aggressive power projection. While China has achieved significant territorial gains through island construction and enhanced military presence, this strategy faces substantial challenges including coordinated resistance from Southeast Asian states, sustained US commitment to regional allies, and erosion of China's diplomatic credibility. The analysis reveals inherent strategic limitations: gray-zone tactics cannot compel decisive outcomes, military infrastructure remains vulnerable during high-intensity conflict, and prolonged competition imposes mounting economic costs. The chapter forecasts continued low-intensity confrontation characterized by tactical probing, escalating naval competition, and diplomatic stalemate, with the South China Sea remaining a critical flashpoint in US-China strategic rivalry for the foreseeable future.

This chapter systematically analyzes multidimensional challenges confronting China's South China Sea strategy through realism international relations theory. Despite substantial territorial gains via grey-zone tactics and island militarization, China's strategy encounters formidable resistance across five dimensions: determined ASEAN opposition employing collective balancing, intensified US-led containment through alliance consolidation, inherent PLA limitations in combat experience and expeditionary logistics, escalating inadvertent conflict risks, and legitimacy deficits following the 2016 PCA ruling. While offensive realism explains China's expansionist motivations, defensive realist dynamics—particularly balance of power and security dilemma mechanisms—impose structural constraints on Beijing's ambitions. Findings reveal that material superiority alone cannot guarantee strategic success against coordinated multilateral resistance anchored in international legal frameworks, offering critical insights for Asia-Pacific regional stability and conflict prevention.

This chapter examines China's comprehensive strategy in the SCS through the theoretical lens of realism in international relations. Employing qualitative document analysis, the research identifies four integrated strategic pillars: incremental "salami slicing" tactics that gradually alter the status quo without triggering military confrontation; unprecedented artificial island construction and militarization establishing strategic outposts; systematic deployment of coast guard and maritime militia forces operating in legal gray zones; and legal-diplomatic strategies linked with the Belt and Road Initiative. The findings reveal that China's actions exemplify revisionist power behavior in an anarchic system, utilizing coordinated instruments to maximize national interests while avoiding direct conflict. This analysis provides crucial insights for policymakers regarding the multidimensional nature of great power competition and the necessity for comprehensive, long-term regional response strategies.

This chapter analyzes Vietnam's role in the South China Sea maritime system during the 17th-18th centuries—a critical period for contemporary maritime sovereignty formation. Examining the Nguyen Lords' regime in Dang Trong, it demonstrates how Vietnamese polities organized, controlled, and defended maritime space amid regional trade fluctuations and international interactions. Using Vietnamese and international historical sources, the chapter explores three areas: (1) coastal port organization and foreign vessel control, including merchant management and taxation; (2) maritime security through anti-piracy operations and trade route protection; (3) sovereignty practices at SCS islands and archipelagos. The chapter argues that Vietnam actively established regional maritime order rather than remaining passive. These historical practices secured economic-security interests while establishing legal and organizational foundations for modern Vietnamese maritime policy. Examining this maritime heritage is essential for understanding continuity in Vietnam's contemporary maritime strategy.

This chapter examines China's gray zone strategy in the South China Sea and its implications for Vietnam. Through documentary analysis and case study methodology, it demonstrates how China employs paramilitary forces, legal warfare, economic coercion, and information operations to incrementally alter the maritime status quo while remaining below the threshold of armed conflict. The study traces the evolution of Chinese tactics through three distinct phases (2009-2020), revealing increasing sophistication in coordination across military, legal, and diplomatic domains. Vietnam's response combines firm diplomatic protests, adherence to UNCLOS, defense modernization, and "bamboo diplomacy"—flexible yet principled engagement balancing cooperation and resistance. The chapter concludes with policy recommendations emphasizing ASEAN unity, maritime capacity-building, economic diversification, and multilateral cooperation to enhance Vietnam's resilience against gray zone pressures while preserving regional stability.

This chapter examines Vietnam's maritime security strategy in Southeast Asia, analyzing how a middle power navigates complex regional dynamics amid intensifying great-power competition. The study reveals Vietnam's sophisticated "bamboo diplomacy"—a hedging strategy balancing accommodation of China's interests, defense modernization, and strategic partnerships with the US, India, Japan, Australia, and South Korea. Despite lacking an official maritime security definition, Vietnam pursues a three-pronged approach: adherence to UNCLOS and international law, sustained military modernization with significantly increased defense expenditure, and comprehensive strategic partnerships supporting capacity-building and technology transfer. However, structural constraints including power asymmetry with China, substantial economic interdependence, and ASEAN's consensus-based limitations challenge Vietnam's maritime security ambitions while shaping its pragmatic, autonomy-preserving engagement in the contested South China Sea maritime domain.

This chapter examines Australia's strategic posture toward the South China Sea disputes (1996-2013), arguing that national identity shifts fundamentally shaped foreign policy. Employing constructivist, realist, and liberal frameworks, the research traces Australia's identity transformation through three phases: Keating's "part of Asia" aspiration, Howard's "in Asia but not of Asia" realism, and Rudd-Gillard's "bridge between East and West" synthesis. This evolution drove strategic shifts from engagement to US bandwagoning, culminating in sophisticated hedging through diversified partnerships. The Australia-Vietnam security relationship demonstrates how the "bridge" identity enabled complex middle-power diplomacy—maintaining economic ties with China while strengthening regional security cooperation. This research proves national identity constitutes an active variable, not rhetorical backdrop, in maritime strategy formulation.

This chapter examines ASEAN's traditional security cooperation mechanisms in the South China Sea (SCS) from 2000 to 2025, focusing on Vietnam's role in regional maritime security governance. The SCS hosts critical shipping lanes facilitating over one-third of global maritime trade, yet faces escalating tensions from overlapping territorial claims and great power competition. ASEAN has developed multilateral frameworks including the Declaration on the Conduct of Parties, Code of Conduct negotiations, and specialized forums such as the ASEAN Maritime Forum and ADMM+ to manage disputes peacefully. Despite constraints from divergent national interests and consensus-based decision-making, these mechanisms have contributed to regional stability. Vietnam has emerged as a proactive architect of cooperation frameworks, leveraging multilateral institutions to enhance national security while strengthening ASEAN's collective capacity in addressing maritime security challenges.

India's naval nuclearization, particularly through Arihant-class ballistic missile submarines (SSBNs), has fundamentally altered South Asia's strategic landscape. This development disrupts traditional land-based deterrence equilibrium, compelling Pakistan to recalibrate its maritime defense posture despite fiscal and technological constraints. The chapter examines how India's sea-based nuclear capabilities exacerbate regional security dilemmas, increase crisis escalation risks, and complicate command-and-control architectures. Pakistan's response options include developing asymmetric deterrence through submarine-launched cruise missiles, implementing Anti-Access/Area Denial strategies, and strengthening naval partnerships with China. Naval nuclearization threatens regional stability through heightened miscalculation risks in opaque maritime environments while challenging global non-proliferation norms. Sustainable deterrence requires multidimensional responses combining selective modernization, doctrinal adaptation, and proactive diplomacy to prevent an unmanageable arms race.

Foreword

The role of maritime security in strategy has never been greater than it is at present. The oceans have emerged as the centre of geopolitical rivalry and cooperation, as the world's superpowers jostle for control over more and more disputed maritime routes to secure their dominance and influence over key energy resources that have become strategic assets in geopolitics. *Emerging Maritime Security Strategies of Global Powers* offers a timely and detailed analysis of how nations worldwide are redefining their maritime security policies amid shifting political trends, emerging technologies, and evolving power structures.

The book is a valuable source of information on the intricate interrelations between maritime security, international law, geopolitics, and the projection of power. The text draws on the contributions of prominent experts and scholars in international relations, political science, and maritime law, thereby offering an analysis of a wide range of security strategies employed by some of the world's most formidable forces. The book provides valuable information on the future of world maritime governance, where competition, policy, and legal grounds intersect.

The most remarkable aspect of this volume is the range of perspectives, from the rise of middle powers such as France and India to the intricate Sino-Russian naval partnership in the Indo-Pacific. These case studies provide invaluable insight into how the new maritime powers are asserting their interests, ensuring security, and formulating the rules that govern the seas. In addition, the book emphasises the need to work in partnership with international organisations and through multilateral participation, especially in areas such as the South China Sea, where tensions are high.

For policymakers, academics, and practitioners of maritime security and international relations, the book will provide theoretical and practical insights into the drivers of maritime security in an increasingly multipolar world. Given the ongoing strategic environment, awareness of the new maritime security policies of world powers will be invaluable for addressing the emerging challenges and opportunities.

With the world becoming increasingly interconnected and the primary trade and power routes of the world, particularly those concerning maritime security and state control, the book is a treasure trove for the academic community, as it illuminates how the global powers are aligning to define the future of maritime security and governance.

Mohamad Zreik
School of International Studies, Institute of International and Regional Studies, Sun Yat-sen University, China

Preface

The Indo-Pacific maritime domain has emerged as the epicenter of twenty-first-century geopolitical competition, where the convergence of economic vitality, territorial disputes, and great power rivalry shapes the contours of global order. As approximately 80% of global maritime trade traverses these contested waters, maritime security in this region transcends traditional naval concerns to encompass energy security, economic connectivity, international law, and the fundamental principles governing state behavior in the international system. This volume, *"Emerging Maritime Security Strategies of Global Powers"*, offers a comprehensive examination of how states across the power spectrum—from great powers to middle powers—are formulating, implementing, and adapting their maritime security strategies in response to rapidly evolving regional dynamics.

This region currently constitutes a multidimensional strategic ecosystem where diverse security paradigms overlap and compete. China's assertive maritime expansion, particularly in the South China Sea, has fundamentally altered the balance of power, triggering coordinated responses from both traditional powers and regional states. The United States, while maintaining its commitment to freedom of navigation and alliance obligations, faces the challenge of sustaining effective deterrence amid competing global strategic priorities. Notably, middle powers such as India, France, Australia, South Korea, Japan, and Vietnam are increasingly asserting their agency. Rather than serving as passive objects in great power competition, they are actively shaping regional security architecture through innovative diplomatic initiatives and defense modernization.

This transformation reflects broader shifts in the international system. The rules-based order anchored in the United Nations Convention on the Law of the Sea (UNCLOS) faces unprecedented challenges from revisionist strategies that exploit legal ambiguities and operate in gray zones below the threshold of armed conflict. Traditional alliance structures are being supplemented—and in some cases superseded—by flexible minilateral frameworks such as the QUAD and AUKUS, which combine normative influence with hard power capabilities. Simultaneously, regional organizations like ASEAN navigate the delicate balance between maintaining strategic autonomy and addressing collective security threats, demonstrating the enduring relevance of inclusive multilateralism even amid intensifying bipolarity.

This volume is designed to serve multiple constituencies within the international relations and security studies communities. Academic researchers specializing in Indo-Pacific security, maritime strategy, and international law will find rigorous theoretical frameworks and empirical analysis that advance scholarly debates on power transitions, regional order formation, and the efficacy of various strategic approaches. Policymakers and defense analysts will benefit from the volume's practical insights into state behavior, strategic calculations, and the operational dimensions of maritime security cooperation and competition. Graduate students and advanced undergraduates studying international relations, strategic studies, or Asian security will discover accessible yet sophisticated analyses that bridge theoretical concepts with real-world applications.

The book's interdisciplinary approach, drawing on realism, constructivism, liberalism, and geopolitical analysis, ensures that readers from diverse intellectual traditions can engage meaningfully with the material. By incorporating perspectives from scholars based in Vietnam, India, Pakistan, Iran, and Poland, the volume transcends Western-centric analytical frameworks and offers genuinely global insights into regional maritime security dynamics.

CHAPTER OVERVIEW

The volume opens with France's maritime security strategy, demonstrating how a European middle power leverages territorial presence across seven overseas territories and approximately 7,000 deployed military personnel to uphold UNCLOS-based regional order. The chapter reveals France's dual approach of protecting sovereign interests while promoting rules-based international order through naval power projection and strategic partnerships with India, Japan, and ASEAN nations. Despite resource constraints and geopolitical challenges including AUKUS, France's inclusive, multilateral strategy positions it as a balancing force in the region. The second chapter examines the EU's approach, revealing how energy security imperatives drive engagement through green transition initiatives and ocean governance frameworks. With critical maritime routes such as the Strait of Malacca and South China Sea handling the majority of EU trade flows and energy transportation, the chapter analyzes how Brussels elevates its status as a strategic actor while contributing to sustainable governance and compliance with international law.

India's balancing role receives comprehensive treatment in chapter three, analyzing how New Delhi employs soft balancing strategies through QUAD participation and bilateral partnerships while managing significant gaps between strategic ambition and operational capacity. The chapter examines the evolution from SAGAR to MAHASAGAR doctrine and reveals how India successfully positions itself as a responsible regional actor and norm-setter, even as naval modernization faces delays and budgetary constraints limit fleet expansion. The analysis demonstrates that realizing India's Indo-Pacific vision requires bridging capability gaps through increased naval investment and indigenous defense production.

Chapter four examines intensified Sino-Russian naval cooperation from 2021 to 2025, demonstrating that Western pressure has accelerated bilateral coordination without producing formal alliance. The study reveals mounting coordination manifested in increased joint exercises across the Bering Sea, Sea of Okhotsk, and Arctic waters, yet this cooperation remains strategically calibrated rather than alliance-based, constrained by mutual sovereignty concerns and divergent long-term interests. Regional responses demonstrate varied approaches, with U.S. exclusionary mechanisms inadvertently reinforcing Sino-Russian alignment while ASEAN's inclusive strategy preserved strategic autonomy.

Comparative analysis of QUAD and AUKUS in chapter five illuminates how soft and hard power approaches produce synergistic outcomes. The chapter demonstrates that QUAD employs soft power through UNCLOS advocacy, maritime domain awareness, and capacity-building to foster rules-based cooperation, while AUKUS deploys hard power via nuclear-powered submarines and advanced military technologies to provide credible deterrence. The analysis reveals that QUAD surveillance capabilities inform AUKUS enforcement operations, while AUKUS military assets secure QUAD infrastructure investments, arguing that effective maritime security requires balanced integration of normative influence with deterrent capabilities.

Chapter six forecasts South China Sea dynamics in US-China relations through 2028, employing qualitative document analysis to examine geopolitical trends and power balance shifts. The analysis reveals that while China's economic rise enables greater assertiveness, the US maintains technological superiority and alliance advantages. Under Trump's second administration, characterized by transactional diplomacy yet bipartisan anti-China consensus, Washington will likely deepen regional engagement. The study concludes that through 2028, persistent tensions and strategic competition will continue, though direct military confrontation remains unlikely due to mutual restraint and crisis management capabilities.

ASEAN-ROK maritime cooperation, examined in chapter seven, reveals calibrated middle power engagement through multilateral mechanisms. Rather than focusing solely on sovereignty disputes, the chapter conceptualizes the South China Sea as a multi-layered power structure where maritime economic interests, sea-lane security, and great-power competition intersect. The analysis explores how ASEAN employs international law and functional cooperation to manage conflicts, while

South Korea pursues engagement through ASEAN-led mechanisms to safeguard maritime interests without escalating strategic confrontation.

Chapters eight through ten collectively analyze China's maritime strategy from multiple theoretical perspectives. Chapter eight examines the transformation from measured assertiveness to aggressive power projection under President Xi Jinping, revealing substantial challenges including coordinated resistance from Southeast Asian states and erosion of diplomatic credibility. Chapter nine systematically analyzes multidimensional challenges through realism theory, demonstrating that material superiority alone cannot guarantee strategic success against coordinated multilateral resistance anchored in international legal frameworks. Chapter ten employs realism to identify four integrated strategic pillars: incremental "salami slicing" tactics, artificial island construction and militarization, systematic deployment of coast guard and maritime militia forces, and legal-diplomatic strategies linked with the Belt and Road Initiative.

Chapter eleven provides crucial historical context by examining Vietnam's maritime governance practices during the seventeenth and eighteenth centuries under the Nguyen Lords' regime in Dang Trong. Using Vietnamese and international historical sources, the chapter explores coastal port organization, maritime security through anti-piracy operations, and sovereignty practices at South China Sea islands and archipelagos. The analysis argues that Vietnam actively established regional maritime order rather than remaining passive, with these historical practices securing economic-security interests while establishing legal and organizational foundations for modern Vietnamese maritime policy.

Chapters twelve and thirteen analyze Vietnam's contemporary response to Chinese gray zone tactics through "bamboo diplomacy"—sophisticated hedging combining UNCLOS adherence, defense modernization, and strategic partnerships to preserve autonomy. Chapter twelve demonstrates how China employs paramilitary forces, legal warfare, economic coercion, and information operations to incrementally alter the maritime status quo while remaining below the threshold of armed conflict, tracing the evolution through three distinct phases revealing increasing sophistication. Chapter thirteen examines Vietnam's three-pronged approach of international law adherence, sustained military modernization with increased defense expenditure, and comprehensive strategic partnerships supporting capacity-building, while acknowledging structural constraints including power asymmetry and economic interdependence with China.

Australia's strategic evolution in chapter fourteen demonstrates how national identity shifts fundamentally shape maritime policy through constructivist, realist, and liberal frameworks. The chapter traces Australia's identity transformation through three phases: Keating's "part of Asia" aspiration, Howard's "in Asia but not of Asia" realism, and Rudd-Gillard's "bridge between East and West" synthesis, driving strategic shifts from engagement to US bandwagoning and culminating in sophisticated hedging through diversified partnerships. The Australia-Vietnam security relationship demonstrates how the "bridge" identity enabled complex middle-power diplomacy maintaining economic ties with China while strengthening regional security cooperation.

Chapter fifteen examines ASEAN's traditional security cooperation mechanisms from 2000 to 2025, focusing on Vietnam's role in regional maritime security governance. Despite constraints from divergent national interests and consensus-based decision-making, ASEAN has developed multilateral frameworks including the Declaration on the Conduct of Parties, Code of Conduct negotiations, and specialized forums such as the ASEAN Maritime Forum and ADMM+ to manage disputes peacefully. Vietnam has emerged as a proactive architect of cooperation frameworks, leveraging multilateral institutions to enhance national security while strengthening ASEAN's collective capacity.

The volume concludes with chapter sixteen examining naval nuclearization in South Asia, where India's Arihant-class ballistic missile submarines have fundamentally altered the strategic landscape. The chapter analyzes how India's sea-based nuclear capabilities exacerbate regional security dilemmas, increase crisis escalation risks, and complicate command-and-control architectures, while examining Pakistan's response options including developing asymmetric deterrence through submarine-launched cruise missiles and implementing Anti-Access/Area Denial strategies. The analysis reveals that naval nuclearization threatens regional stability through heightened miscalculation risks in opaque maritime environments while challenging global non-proliferation norms.

CONCLUSION

This volume makes several significant contributions to maritime security scholarship and policy discourse. First, it demonstrates that effective maritime security strategies in the Indo-Pacific require multidimensional approaches integrating military capabilities, diplomatic engagement, legal frameworks, and economic instruments. No single tool of statecraft proves sufficient; sustainable security emerges from coordinated application of multiple instruments adapted to specific strategic contexts. The comparative analyses across chapters reveal that successful strategies combine deterrence with reassurance, coercion with cooperation, and unilateral action with multilateral coordination.

Second, the book challenges simplistic binary frameworks that reduce Indo-Pacific dynamics to US-China competition. While great power rivalry undeniably shapes the regional security environment, middle powers exercise genuine agency through innovative strategies that preserve autonomy, advance national interests, and contribute to regional stability. France, India, Australia, South Korea, Vietnam, and other middle powers are not merely objects of great power competition but active architects of regional order whose collective actions significantly influence strategic outcomes.

Third, the volume highlights the enduring relevance of international law and multilateral institutions even amid intensifying power politics. UNCLOS, ASEAN-led mechanisms, and various minilateral frameworks provide essential infrastructure for managing disputes, building confidence, and constraining unilateral actions. While these institutions face significant challenges and cannot guarantee compliance, they establish normative standards that shape state behavior and provide focal points for coordinated responses to revisionist strategies.

Fourth, the book reveals both the potential and limitations of gray zone tactics. While such approaches enable incremental gains without triggering direct military confrontation, they cannot compel decisive strategic outcomes, risk inadvertent escalation, impose mounting economic costs, and erode diplomatic credibility over time. Understanding these dynamics proves essential for both offensive and defensive strategic planning in contemporary maritime competition.

Finally, this volume demonstrates that historical context matters profoundly for contemporary maritime security. Long-established patterns of territorial governance, resource management, and regional interaction inform current sovereignty claims and strategic behavior. Effective policy formulation requires deep understanding of how historical legacies shape contemporary strategic cultures and constrain available options.

As maritime security challenges in the Indo-Pacific continue evolving, this volume provides both rigorous analysis of current dynamics and conceptual frameworks for anticipating future developments. By bringing together diverse theoretical perspectives, empirical case studies, and policy insights from scholars across multiple countries and disciplines, "*Emerging Maritime Security Strategies of Global Powers*" advances our collective understanding of how states navigate one of the most consequential strategic domains of the twenty-first century. The insights contained within these chapters will prove invaluable for scholars, policymakers, and strategic analysts seeking to comprehend and shape the future of Indo-Pacific maritime security.

Kiet Hoang Le
University of Social Sciences and Humanities, Vietnam National University, Hanoi, Vietnam

Hiep Xuan Tran
The University of Da Nang, University of Science and Education, Vietnam

Acknowledgment

This book represents the culmination of extensive research, collaboration, and unwavering support from numerous individuals and institutions whose contributions have been invaluable to its completion. While our names appear as editors, this work is truly the product of collective effort and dedication from many quarters.

First and foremost, we extend our deepest gratitude to our families for their constant encouragement and understanding. Their support has nurtured our academic interests from the earliest stages of our careers, creating an environment where intellectual curiosity could flourish. Throughout the countless hours spent researching, writing, and coordinating with contributors across multiple time zones, their patience never wavered. This book would not have been possible without their love and sacrifice.

We are profoundly grateful to the chapter authors from Vietnam, India, Pakistan, Iran, and Poland whose scholarly rigor and empirical insights have enriched this volume immeasurably. Their commitment to producing work of the highest quality and their willingness to engage across disciplinary boundaries have been instrumental in creating a comprehensive examination of Indo-Pacific maritime security dynamics.

We acknowledge with gratitude the institutional support provided by our home universities and research institutes. Colleagues who engaged in discussions about Indo-Pacific security dynamics contributed significantly to refining the conceptual frameworks employed throughout this volume.

Special thanks are due to the peer reviewers whose careful reading and constructive criticism strengthened each chapter considerably. Their expertise helped ensure theoretical coherence across diverse analytical approaches.

We are grateful to IGI Global for recognizing the importance of this topic and providing a platform for disseminating this research to global audiences. The editorial and production teams demonstrated professionalism throughout the publication process.

Any errors or shortcomings in this volume remain our responsibility alone. It is our sincere hope that this book contributes meaningfully to ongoing conversations about maritime security and regional order in the Indo-Pacific.

Chapter 1
France's Maritime Security Strategy in the Indo-Pacific:
Middle Power's Approach to Regional Order

Duc Minh Dang
https://orcid.org/0000-0002-7441-202X
Institute for European and American Studies, Vietnam Academy of Social Sciences, Vietnam

Dung Thi Phuong Nguyen
https://orcid.org/0009-0006-6095-7762
Institute of European and Americas Studies, Vietnam Academy of Social Sciences, Vietnam

Anh Thi Van Hoang
University of Warsaw, Poland

ABSTRACT

This chapter examines France's maritime security strategy in the Indo-Pacific, analyzing how a middle power leverages territorial presence and strategic partnerships to shape regional order. France maintains sovereign interests through seven overseas territories, contributing to its 11 million km² exclusive economic zone, and deploys approximately 7,000 military personnel across the region. Through documentary analysis, the study reveals France's dual approach: protecting national interests while promoting a rules-based international order grounded in UNCLOS. France employs naval power projection, strategic partnerships with India, Japan, and ASEAN

DOI: 10.4018/979-8-3373-4470-6.ch001

nations, and active participation in multilateral forums to counter unilateral actions and maintain freedom of navigation. Despite resource constraints and geopolitical challenges including AUKUS, France's inclusive, multilateral strategy positions it as a balancing force, demonstrating how middle powers can meaningfully contribute to Indo-Pacific stability through legal frameworks and coalition-building.

1. INTRODUCTION

In the past decade, the concept of the Indo-Pacific has emerged as a crucial geostrategic space of the 21st century. This vast region, spanning from the eastern coast of Africa across the Indian Ocean to the Western Pacific, encompasses dynamic economies and critical sea lanes for global trade. The Indo-Pacific is now widely regarded as the "new global center of gravity," accounting for approximately 60% of the world's GDP and home to nearly 4.5 billion people (Ministère de l'Europe et des Affaires étrangères, 2023a).

This area handles up to 90% of global goods traffic and is a theater for escalating tensions, including great-power competition, territorial claims such as China's assertions over Taiwan and the South China Sea, and a range of traditional and non-traditional security challenges, including arms smuggling, illegal, unreported, and unregulated (IUU) fishing, and climate change (Institut de Recherche Stratégique de l'École Militaire, 2022). The prosperity and stability of the region are decisive for the rules-based international order, as transnational challenges from climate change to global health security are particularly pronounced here (Ministère de l'Europe et des Affaires étrangères, 2023b). For many nations, especially those in Europe, their interests are deeply intertwined with the region. For instance, approximately 40% of the European Union's foreign trade passes through the South China Sea (Ministère de l'Europe et des Affaires étrangères, 2023a).

France is one of the few European nations with a historical presence and direct interests in the Indo-Pacific. Seven of its thirteen overseas territories are located in this region, stretching from the Indian Ocean (Réunion, Mayotte, the Éparses Islands) to the Pacific Ocean (New Caledonia, French Polynesia, Wallis-et-Futuna). These territories are home to approximately 1.6 million French citizens and contribute to France's 11 million km^2 exclusive economic zone (EEZ) (Perrin et al., 2023). This makes France the only EU nation with sovereign territory in the Indo-Pacific. This presence concerns not only French influence but also the maintenance of military and geopolitical balance in a strategically vital area. Thanks to these overseas entities, France considers itself a genuine "Indo-Pacific nation" with sovereign interests and a direct responsibility for regional security and stability. France maintains a permanent military presence of approximately 7,000 personnel at bases and fleets dispersed throughout the Indo-Pacific, in addition to around 700 rotating naval officers (Ministère des Armées, 2018).

The geostrategic shift toward the Indo-Pacific has been accompanied by complex security fluctuations. Intensifying great-power competition, particularly between the United States and China, has made this region the main arena for global strategic rivalry. In recent years, China has increased its military and paramilitary activities and employed "gray-zone" tactics to enforce its territorial claims in the South and East China Seas, directly challenging the rules-based maritime order (Prashanth, 2025). The United States and its allies and partners have responded by enhancing their presence and security partnerships, notably through the formation of new alliances and security dialogues such as the QUAD between the United States, Japan, India, and Australia. Concurrently, many Southeast Asian nations face a multitude of traditional and non-traditional maritime security issues, from territorial disputes and exploitation of marine resources to cybersecurity and transnational crime. These developments have made the regional maritime security landscape more multi-layered and unpredictable than ever before.

In this context, France has proactively recognized the strategic importance of the Indo-Pacific and has shaped its own maritime security strategy for the region. As early as 2018, President Emmanuel Macron initiated the development of France's Indo-Pacific strategy, emphasizing the country's role as a balancing force to maintain an "open and free" regional space based on international law and multilateral cooperation. France's role in the South China Sea is demonstrated through multilateral cooperation within the framework of the EU, NATO, and the QUAD, as well as through bilateral partnerships with regional nations such as Vietnam. The aim is to ensure freedom of navigation and to oppose unilateral actions that violate international law. Strengthening defense and security cooperation with France, leveraging its international commitments under the United Nations Convention on the Law of the Sea (UNCLOS) and its agreements with ASEAN, contributes to the shared goal of maintaining peace and stability in the South China Sea, aligning with the long-term strategic interests of both sides.

This chapter analyzes the geopolitical context and France's maritime security strategy in the Indo-Pacific. It examines France's strategic ambitions and interests, the tools and mechanisms it deploys to implement its strategy, the challenges it faces, and its policy for upholding the rules-based international order.

2. GEOPOLITICAL AND MARITIME SECURITY CONTEXT IN THE INDO-PACIFIC REGION

Strategically, the Indo-Pacific is viewed as a continuous entity, connected via the Strait of Malacca, the primary trade route linking the two oceans. Two main factors account for the Indo-Pacific's strategic importance: first, China's growing footprint across the region; and second, the relative weakening of the U.S. alliance system and its subsequent efforts to revitalize it (Das, 2019). The sea lanes in the Indian Ocean play a crucial role in the global transport of oil, gas, and goods from the Middle East to Australia and East Asia. This is also a notoriously unstable region, plagued by piracy and terrorism. Therefore, ensuring the security of this economic lifeline is of paramount concern to nations worldwide.

While past competition centered on military objectives, strategic bases, and control of sea lanes, today nations are also increasingly competing for economic interests and marine resources. The "sea power" doctrine of Alfred T. Mahan, a leading American naval strategist, provided the theoretical underpinning for nations to pursue maritime strength: "Let us start from the fundamental truth, warranted by history, that the control of the seas, and especially along the great lines drawn by national interest or national commerce, is the chief among the merely material elements in the power and prosperity of nations" (Mahan, 1897, p. 54). Consequently, maritime security in the Indo-Pacific region has become a central and pressing issue on the foreign policy agenda of major powers.

To ensure maritime security, many countries—including the United States, China, Russia, Japan, Australia, India, the European Union, and ASEAN—have proposed their own connectivity strategies for the Indo-Pacific region in recent years. These nations view the maritime domain as an integral part of their connectivity strategies and have adjusted their approaches to increase influence and protect their interests in the region. The Indo-Pacific is currently a locus of profound geopolitical shifts, shaped by the rise of Asian powers and the strategic recalibration of the United States and its allies. The regional security order is being reconfigured under the impact of increasingly intense U.S.-China rivalry.

China, with its status as a global superpower, cannot ignore a region of such strategic importance as the Indo-Pacific. China has continued to increase its presence through its Belt and Road Initiative (BRI) and the "String of Pearls" strategy to expand China's economic influence and infrastructure investment throughout the Indian Ocean, alongside an increase in naval and maritime militia power to enforce its illegitimate sovereign claims, such as the "nine-dash line" in the South China Sea. China has conducted large-scale island-building and militarization of disputed features in the South China Sea, using its coast guard and "maritime militia" vessels to harass the oil and gas and fishing activities of smaller nations—actions that constitute "gray-zone coercion" and directly challenge international maritime law (Prashanth, 2025). China's BRI prioritizes the maritime domain by proposing a "21st Century Maritime Silk Road" to connect seaports, one of the two main connections between China and Europe (Kuo & Kommenda, 2018). The BRI serves strategic political, security, economic, and territorial objectives, aiming to build a new framework for regional and global governance in which China plays a leading role (Tran, 2017). Concurrently, through its "Two Oceans" strategy, China is strengthening its naval presence in the Indian Ocean, having established its first overseas naval base in Djibouti, East Africa, in 2017, and expanding its influence to Indian Ocean island nations.

The United States has issued its "Free and Open Indo-Pacific" (FOIP) strategy, which aims at maintaining a balance of power and protecting strategic sea lanes. The U.S. has strengthened existing military alliances with Japan, South Korea, and Australia while also expanding security cooperation with new partners, including India, Vietnam, and Taiwan. The QUAD, an informal security dialogue between the U.S., Japan, India, and Australia, emerged as a mechanism demonstrating a shared commitment to a free, open, and rules-based region. It also serves to contain and deter China's rise, aiming to secure control over the entire region and thus maintain the U.S.'s economic interests, political power, military strength, and diplomatic influence (Pham & Vu, 2020). In addition to the QUAD, on September 15, 2021, the U.S., the UK, and Australia officially announced the establishment of a trilateral security partnership in the Indo-Pacific (AUKUS). This confirms that AUKUS is a new security-oriented "triangle" structure in the Indo-Pacific aimed at protecting and maintaining the common interests of the parties in the region (Binh et al., 2024).

With the adoption of the EU Strategy for Cooperation in the Indo-Pacific by its 27 member states in April 2021, the bloc took a major step toward participation and increased presence in this geostrategic region. The EU identified seven priority areas in its strategy to enhance its economic, political, and military presence in the Indo-Pacific. This strategy also demonstrates the EU's increased concern for maritime and non-traditional security issues. Accordingly, the EU will promote an open and law-based regional security architecture, including freedom of navigation, capacity building, and strengthening the presence of member states' navies in the Indo-Pacific. It will also enhance dialogue with regional partners on security and defense, support the capacity of regional partners to ensure maritime security, and conduct joint exercises and port calls in the region to protect freedom of navigation (Minh & Trang, 2021, p. 134).

On March 10, 2023, the EU announced its new Maritime Security Strategy, an updated and enhanced version of its first maritime strategy from 2014. This new version reflects and responds to increasing maritime security challenges. The most notable change is the document's greater focus on the Indo-Pacific region, showing a broader ambition to position the EU as a global security provider by engaging in the maritime security domain (Mishra & Yan, 2023). The UK and other European countries have also increased their engagement. The UK deployed its HMS Queen Elizabeth carrier strike group to Asia in 2021 and has maintained two permanent patrol vessels in the Pacific since 2021 (Pajon, 2023b). The European Union launched its Coordinated Maritime Presences initiative in the Indian Ocean. All these actions affirm the vital interests of the West in the security and stability of the Indo-Pacific seas.

In addition to U.S.-China competition, the Indo-Pacific is marked by the persistence of high regional tensions and increasing instability in the regional security structure. This is reflected in unprecedented military spending and the rising status of many parties in the region. The Indo-Pacific is characterized by a number of crisis hotspots, often resulting from unresolved territorial and maritime disputes. These hotspots are also interconnected due to alliance networks and the risk of spillover from one crisis to another, posing the risk of simultaneous conflicts (Ministère de l'Europe et des Affaires étrangères, 2025). These developments are taking place against a backdrop of multilateral system erosion, which is particularly concerning in a region with a lack of robust security architecture. International law is frequently violated: the law of the sea and freedom of navigation are being challenged by unilateral interpretations contrary to UNCLOS, and some arbitration rulings are being openly disregarded. Furthermore, nuclear non-proliferation sanctions decided by the Security Council are being openly ignored (Ministère de l'Europe et des Affaires étrangères, 2025).

These issues make the need for multilateral cooperation to govern the seas based on common laws—especially UNCLOS of 1982—an urgent matter. UNCLOS establishes a comprehensive legal framework to delimit maritime rights and resolve disputes. Adherence to UNCLOS and international legal mechanisms such as the 2016 South China Sea Arbitral Ruling is fundamental to maintaining a stable and equitable maritime order. Maritime security in the Indo-Pacific region will be a key factor in the development of many nations. However, it remains a major regional concern due to increasing non-traditional security threats in addition to maritime border disputes. In particular, events in the South China Sea will continue to attract regional and international attention and could undermine the ability of regional and international stakeholders to sustainably and effectively maintain peace, security, and stability in the region.

It is within this complex strategic context that France emerges as an active party shaping the security balance in the Indo-Pacific through its own approach. For France, participation in ensuring regional security stems not only from its duty as a permanent member of the UN Security Council but also, first and foremost, from its own vital national interests. Instability in the Indo-Pacific—from a crisis in the

Strait of Hormuz to conflict in the South China Sea—could directly impact French citizens, territories, and economic interests. Therefore, France's Indo-Pacific strategy is shaped by integrating national interests with the responsibility to contribute to shared peace and stability, while affirming France's role and influence as a global power with a presence in the region.

3. FRANCE'S STRATEGIC AMBITIONS AND MARITIME SECURITY INTERESTS IN THE INDO-PACIFIC

As the first European country to announce its Indo-Pacific Strategy in 2018, France aims to protect its sovereign interests, particularly in its overseas maritime territories, and to enhance its international standing. In this context, France emphasizes the role of international law and multilateral cooperation to counter unilateral actions that threaten regional stability and to promote a stronger European presence in the region. France's Indo-Pacific maritime security strategy adopts an "inclusive, multilateral" approach, seeking to transcend U.S.-China competition and "maintain a rules-based order" while strengthening strategic partnerships with the U.S., India, Japan, and others to balance China's influence. Confronted with the risk of establishing coercive spheres of influence in the Indo-Pacific as well as in Europe, France is promoting an alliance of independent nations in the form of a sovereignty partnership between these two spaces (Ministère de l'Europe et des Affaires étrangères, 2025). France's Indo-Pacific strategy is driven by two main sets of motivations: (i) protecting national interests from geopolitical shifts in the region; and (ii) affirming France's status as a global power in the future international order.

First, regarding interests, China's rapid rise and the escalating U.S.-China rivalry pose direct challenges to France's sovereign and economic interests in the region. France is concerned that China's expansionist behaviors, such as the illegal "nine-dash line" claim in the South China Sea, could threaten freedom of navigation and access to international waters—conditions vital for trade and connectivity to France's overseas territories. France's Indo-Pacific strategy has evolved into a coherent and assertive policy based on values, presence, and partnerships. It offers an alternative to "binary" competition without being naive about neutrality, by reinforcing multilateral cooperation and upholding legal norms through both diplomacy and action (Niquet, 2025). The delicate balance in decision-making within its "allied but not aligned" stance led to the launch of a France-U.S. dialogue on the Indo-Pacific in 2024, focusing on maritime security, humanitarian and disaster response, the fight against climate change, and critical infrastructure development (Bouffaron & Blandin, 2025, p. 4).

Simultaneously, escalating great power competition risks eroding international law if "the law of the jungle" prevails over "the rule of law," which runs counter to the interests of France—a middle power that relies heavily on the multilateral system to protect its rights. This context has spurred France to act to "defend its interests against China's ambitions and U.S.-China competition" (Pajon, 2023b). On the other hand, under President Macron, France aspires to restore its global influence and standing, emerging as a shaper of the new international order. Macron sees the Indo-Pacific strategy as an opportunity for France to "regain its position as a major power" on the international stage by taking a leading and balancing role in a key region of the 21st century (Pajon, 2023b). At Shangri-La 2025, President Macron reaffirmed that France does not seek alignment with any great power but wishes to act with and through a coalition of like-minded nations committed to sovereignty, multilateralism, and a stable international order (Niquet, 2025).

France sees itself as having a special role and responsibility in the Indo-Pacific based on its unique geographical and historical presence among EU countries. As mentioned, with 1.6 million citizens and the majority of its exclusive economic zone located in the region, France considers itself a "resident power" of the Indo-Pacific (Pajon, 2023b). This gives France a high degree of legitimacy when speaking on regional issues and participating in security-shaping mechanisms. President Macron has repeatedly affirmed that France wants to be a "balancing and stabilizing force" in the Indo-Pacific, promoting the values of freedom, the rule of law, and multilateral cooperation (Pajon, 2023a).

Unlike the confrontational alliance-based approach of AUKUS or the QUAD, France advocates for an "inclusive" strategy, ready to cooperate with all parties based on respect for international law, thereby minimizing the risk of conflict due to great power competition (Ministère de l'Europe et des Affaires étrangères, 2023b). While not targeting any specific country, France's strategy "naturally takes into account the issues posed by China's assertive rise, including in the military domain" (Ministère de l'Europe et des Affaires étrangères, 2023b). France and other EU countries have a common approach to China based on a "three-in-one" perspective: China is an essential partner for cooperation on global challenges (such as climate change and health), an economic competitor that requires a balanced relationship, and also a "systemic rival" with a different model and vision for the world order, especially regarding human rights (Ministère de l'Europe et des Affaires étrangères, 2023b).

Therefore, France determines that it must maintain dialogue and cooperation with China in mutually beneficial areas while resolutely defending its legal principles and core interests when they are challenged. Maritime interests require maritime assets to protect and maintain. For Paris, it is essential to ensure that France has a strong military presence in the Indo-Pacific to protect its people in the event of a crisis and to demonstrate its presence in the region, especially to maintain France's autonomous operational capability while also ensuring that French vessels can freely enter the Indo-Pacific and protect the country's sovereignty (Valori, 2025). The French Navy is the only European navy, along with the British Royal Navy, to possess a full range of capabilities, including nuclear-powered submarines, surface combatants, amphibious ships, maritime patrol aircraft, and an aircraft carrier (Scott, 2025). In addition, based on its Indo-Pacific strategy, France considers its overseas territories to be at the heart of its strategy (Valori, 2025). French territories in Oceania (New Caledonia, Wallis and Futuna, French Polynesia, and Clipperton Island) are located more than 15,000 km from the mainland. France is leveraging its dual status as a resident power and a permanent member of the UN Security Council to affirm a consistent and reliable diplomatic presence in the region (Bouffaron & Blandin, 2025, p. 3).

A concrete manifestation of France's strategic ambitions is its effort to lead a common European approach to the Indo-Pacific. France was the first EU country to devise an Indo-Pacific strategy (2018) and successfully lobbied for the EU to adopt the EU Strategy for Cooperation in the Indo-Pacific in September 2021 (Ministry for Europe and Foreign Affairs, 2021). During its presidency of the Council of the EU in the first half of 2022, France promoted the Indo-Pacific agenda, notably by hosting an Indo-Pacific Ministerial Forum in France (February 2022) that brought together 27 EU member states, around 30 Indo-Pacific countries, and representatives of regional organizations from the Indo-Pacific, thereby affirming Europe's commitment to the region. This pioneering role helps France increase its influence while mobilizing additional resources from the EU to realize its strategic priorities in the Indo-Pacific—tasks that would exceed France's own capabilities if it were to rely solely on national resources.

In summary, France's strategic ambitions and interests in the Indo-Pacific intertwine both "defensive" elements (protecting sovereignty and interests against new security threats) and "proactive" elements aimed at expanding influence and demonstrating its role as a global power. This combination has shaped France's modus operandi: on the one hand, it remains firm on legal principles and core interests; on the other hand, it flexibly cooperates with all parties to maintain strategic balance and avoid confrontational polarization.

4. TOOLS, MECHANISMS, AND CHALLENGES FOR IMPLEMENTING FRANCE'S MARITIME STRATEGY IN THE INDO-PACIFIC

To realize its Indo-Pacific strategy, France mobilizes a wide range of comprehensive tools, from military power and defense partnerships to diplomatic, economic, and cultural initiatives.

The most crucial pillar is the permanent military presence and expeditionary power projection capability of the French Navy. As stated, France maintains around 7,000 military personnel across five joint command headquarters in the region, including three garrison forces in French Indo-Pacific territories: FAZSOI (Indian Ocean), FANC (New Caledonia), and FAPF (French Polynesia); and two forces present in Abu Dhabi and Djibouti (Ministère des Armées, 2018). These forces, which include warships, maritime patrol aircraft, marine units, and air force elements, are capable of performing a variety of missions, from territorial defense and search and rescue to maritime security patrols. These garrisons, along with sovereign forces stationed in Réunion, French Polynesia, and New Caledonia, operate along an "S-axis." This axis connects the metropolitan center with overseas territories through a network of strategic allies and partners, including the United Arab Emirates, India, Singapore, Indonesia, and Australia, as well as Vietnam, South Korea, and Japan. With some of these countries, France has established innovative strategic defense dialogues, such as the trilateral strategic dialogues "France-UAE-India" and "France-India-Australia" (Blandin, 2024).

In addition to its fixed regional forces, France regularly deploys metropolitan fleets to operate in the Indo-Pacific on a rotational basis. For example, in 2019, France deployed the Charles de Gaulle carrier strike group through the Indian Ocean to participate in the "Varuna" exercise with the Indian Navy in the Arabian Sea (GMA News, 2020). In 2021, France sent its nuclear attack submarine Émeraude and a support vessel to patrol the South China Sea, demonstrating its capability to operate in distant waters. In early 2023, for the first time since the 1960s, a French nuclear-powered aircraft carrier strike group completed a journey from the Indian Ocean all the way to the Western Pacific (Léonie, 2025), visiting and conducting exercises with navies from various countries in the region. These naval presences send a clear message that France is committed to maintaining a long-term presence and is ready to contribute to regional stability (Léonie, 2025), as well as to fulfill its strategic intent to secure a foothold in the political dynamics of the Asia-Pacific region.

Alongside its military presence, France is strengthening its footprint in the region through diplomatic engagement with island nations. France involves its overseas territories in the strategy and ensures they benefit from it. The French government is working to ensure that overseas territories are more involved in the formulation and implementation of the Indo-Pacific Strategy while ensuring that France's foreign policy is coherent (Marc, 2025). This is why France actively supports their participation in regional organizations such as the Pacific Community (SPC), the Indian Ocean Community (IOC), and the Pacific Islands Forum (PIF). France is also enhancing its training capabilities within the framework of the Indian Ocean Academy in Réunion, aiming to support the Red Cross Indian Ocean Regional Intervention Platform (PIROI) and, along with Madagascar, the activities of the Indian Ocean Rim Association (IORA) on humanitarian assistance and disaster relief (HADR) (Ministère de l'Europe et des Affaires étrangères, 2025). Within the framework of the Pacific Academy, located in New Caledonia, France implements a training program on civil security.

The network of security-defense partnerships is another key tool in France's strategy. France has built extensive strategic partnerships with many key countries in the Indo-Pacific. Prominent among these are long-standing traditional partners such as India (1998) and Japan (1995), along with Southeast Asian partners such as Indonesia (2011), Singapore (2012), and Vietnam (2013) (Ministère de l'Europe et des Affaires étrangères, 2023b). Cooperation focuses on maritime security, ranging from high-level strategic dialogues and maritime intelligence sharing to bilateral and multilateral exercises.

(i) Partnership with India: France and India have had a strategic and maritime partnership since the early 1980s. The two countries maintain an annual defense dialogue, the annual Varuna naval exercise, and defense cooperation that has expanded into the industrial sector. India has purchased 36 Rafale fighter jets and 6 Scorpène-class submarines manufactured in France. In 2023, France and India signed a Joint Vision on the Indo-Pacific, reaffirming their special defense partnership and close coordination on regional issues (Léonie, 2025). The strategic convergence between the two is reflected in a joint statement acknowledging a common interest in freedom of navigation and the need to "advocate for free and safe access to sea lanes" at the 7th India-France Maritime Cooperation Dialogue held in New Delhi in January 2025 (Scott, 2025).

(ii) Partnership with Japan: France and Japan share a convergence of values and security interests. Both countries are committed to international law, regional stability, and strategic autonomy (Niquet, 2025). They have strengthened defense relations through joint exercises, technological cooperation, and ministerial-level dialogues. France signed a new Defense Cooperation Roadmap in 2023 to increase joint exercises and enhance the interoperability of the two armed forces (Léonie, 2025). The two sides conducted a bilateral amphibious exercise on Japanese territory for the first time in 2021, as well as a joint amphibious exercise in New Caledonia in 2023.

(iii) Relations with Australia: After a period of estrangement due to the AUKUS event (2021), relations are also being gradually restored. In early 2023, France and Australia signed a Reciprocal Access Agreement (RAA) that provides a legal framework for the rotation of military forces and equipment through each other's territories (Léonie, 2025). The two countries also continue to cooperate on humanitarian assistance and disaster relief, exemplified through the trilateral FRANZ mechanism with New Zealand that helped distribute aid in Tonga (2022) and Vanuatu (2023). While France continues to participate in exercises and coordinate with Australia on maritime security in the South Pacific, the strategic relationship once promised by the submarine contract has not been fully restored (Niquet, 2025).

(iv) Southeast Asian Partnerships: Strengthening ties with Southeast Asian countries is a crucial part of France's strategy to diversify partners and enhance security through joint naval activities, training programs, and arms transfers. After the setback when Australia canceled a major submarine deal to switch to purchasing nuclear-powered submarines under the AUKUS treaties in 2021, Southeast Asia, with its increasing defense budgets and investments to cope with a deteriorating security environment, has become a launchpad for arms exports. With Indonesia, several major contracts have been signed, most notably the purchase of 42 Dassault Rafale fighter jets in 2022 and two Scorpène-class submarines (Pajon, 2025b). The Philippines purchased 6 French-built offshore patrol vessels (OPV) for the first time in 2022 (Léonie, 2025). This shows that French defense technology is attractive and helps create a bond of security interests with countries in the region.

France promotes initiatives to support maritime security in Southeast Asia, such as the CRIMARIO program (improving maritime situational awareness for Indian Ocean countries), the ESIWA project (Enhancing Security Cooperation In and With Asia), and the SAFE SEA project (supporting maritime law enforcement in Southeast Asia), with the aim of equipping navies and maritime agencies in the region with a platform for exchanging maritime situational information (IORIS) and promoting bilateral maritime diplomacy. The France-ASEAN partnership is also a key focus: in 2020, ASEAN and France upgraded their relationship to a Development Partnership, providing a basis for France to support ASEAN on non-traditional security issues and promote adherence to UNCLOS in the South China Sea. With the EU becoming an ASEAN Strategic Partner from December 2020, France is in an even better position to embed its security priorities into broader EU-ASEAN cooperation, thereby indirectly promoting a rules-based order in the region.

Multilateral mechanisms and regional security forums are also utilized by France as tools for strategic implementation. France carries a message of support for multilateralism, which is described as a "principle of action," a "tool for peace," and sometimes "the only solution" for global challenges (Duchâtel, 2023). France is an active member of regional organizations it is eligible to join: the Indian Ocean

Rim Association (IORA) as its 23rd full member; the Indian Ocean Commission (IOC) as a member territory (Réunion Island), with France serving as its chair in 2026-2027; the Indian Ocean Naval Symposium (IONS) as an Indian Ocean littoral state; and the Pacific Islands Forum (PIF) as a dialogue partner. In Oceania, France is a founding member of the Pacific Community (SPC). Additionally, France participates in the ASEAN Regional Forum (ARF), the Shangri-La Dialogue, and the Seoul Defense Dialogue as a guest/partner. In 2024, France was granted observer status in the ADMM+ (ASEAN Defence Ministers' Meeting Plus) working groups on maritime security and Humanitarian Assistance and Disaster Relief (HADR) for the 2024-2027 term.

France consistently declares its absolute respect for UNCLOS 1982 and opposes any unilateral claims that violate the law of the sea. In 2016, in a speech at the Shangri-La Dialogue, then-Defense Minister Jean-Yves Le Drian proposed coordinating an EU fleet to conduct freedom of navigation operations (FONOPs) in the South China Sea, while maintaining a "permanent and visible presence" in the region (An, 2016). In January 2025, on the occasion of the La Perouse 25 exercise, which involved naval forces from nine Indo-Pacific countries including Australia, Canada, India, Indonesia, Malaysia, Singapore, the United Kingdom, and the United States, Vice Admiral Jacques Mallard once again affirmed that the French Navy, along with its partners, wants to create a "free, open, and stable" Indo-Pacific region and is ready to cooperate with all allies to enhance interoperability and joint operational capabilities (Scott, 2025). Thus, France has deployed various coordinated patrol activities with major powers and has stated its readiness to intervene if necessary to protect its overseas territories in the region. Through both political statements and practical operations such as FONOPs, exercises, and multilateral patrols, France actively participates in maintaining security and freedom on strategic sea lanes, especially in the South China Sea.

The momentum for regional cooperation is being enhanced through the activation of small multilateral formats, particularly trilateral dialogues. The France-India-Australia dialogue, launched in 2020, is based on a shared vision of respect for international law. This is demonstrated through joint projects on maritime security, the environment, and coordinated actions in multilateral forums. In 2023, a trilateral dialogue was launched between France, India, and the United Arab Emirates. This initiative is based on a common desire to promote stability in the Indian Ocean, paving the way for cooperation in areas such as climate change, biodiversity protection, emerging technologies, research, and culture (Ministère de l'Europe et des Affaires étrangères, 2025). Within the framework of the European Union, the French Navy participates in EU operations (Atalanta, Aspides, Agenor) and actively contributes to the protection of shipping lanes through the regular deployment of key naval assets (carrier strike groups, nuclear submarines, helicopter landing docks, multi-mission frigates) to defend freedom of navigation and adherence to UNCLOS, including in tense areas such as the Taiwan Strait, the East China Sea, and the South China Sea (Marc, 2025).

Despite considerable progress, France's Indo-Pacific strategy continues to face significant challenges while also presenting new opportunities.

Challenge 1: The fundamental challenge is the gap between France's ambition and its available resources. Céline Pajon points out that while France declares the Indo-Pacific a priority, its defense budget and deployed forces are limited, making it difficult to cover such a vast region (Pajon, 2023b). Maintaining just 7,000 permanent troops and a few warships at such a long geographical distance places France under immense strain if crises were to erupt simultaneously in both Europe and Asia. The outbreak of the war in Ukraine in 2022 further created pressure to divert resources, forcing France and Europe to increase defense spending closer to home rather than spreading it to East Asia. The United States—France's key ally—has also shown signs of wanting its European allies to bear more of the burden in their own region, thereby freeing up the U.S. to pivot toward Asia (Léonie, 2025). This places France in a difficult position: it must ensure European security and contain Russia while simultaneously pursuing its ambitions in the Indo-Pacific, all without a commensurate increase in resources.

Challenge 2: The establishment of the AUKUS trilateral security partnership by the U.S., UK, and Australia in 2021 dealt a heavy blow to France's strategic interests and trust: the multi-billion-euro submarine contract with Australia was canceled, and France was temporarily sidelined from a new security structure in the South Pacific. The prior France-Australia submarine deal was expected to anchor France's presence in the Indo-Pacific for decades, and its collapse meant France lost a crucial strategic foothold (Léonie, 2025). While France quickly mended ties with Canberra and pivoted to strengthening relations with India, Japan, and ASEAN countries (Léonie, 2025), the AUKUS incident exposed a reality: the interests of Western powers are not always aligned, and France risks being outmaneuvered if it does not establish an irreplaceable position. Australia remains an essential partner, but also a reminder that geopolitical alignments can be superseded by other options (Niquet, 2025). Furthermore, China's sustained rise with a defense budget many times that of France, along with its firm stance, raises questions about the effectiveness of France's "balancing and inclusive" approach. China might even seek to neutralize France's influence, for example, by backing sovereignty claims that run counter to French interests, as seen in China and Russia's support for Comoros's claim to the French island of Mayotte (Léonie, 2025). This is a reminder that France also has vulnerable points that rivals can exploit in the regional competition for influence.

Challenge 3: A challenge stems from France's sovereignty over disputed overseas territories that could be exploited by competing powers. France's sovereignty is contested in New Caledonia (which held its third referendum on self-determination in 2021) and, to a lesser extent, in French Polynesia. Meanwhile, Comoros maintains a claim to Mayotte, with support from South Africa, China, and Russia; and Mauritius and Madagascar dispute France's sovereignty over Tromelin Island and the scattered islands, respectively, both of which are part of the French Southern and Antarctic Lands (Grare, 2020). The loss of all or part of these territories would undoubtedly weaken France's position in the region. As evidence, in 2022, China proposed a multilateral data and cybersecurity cooperation agreement with Pacific island nations. Although the deal was not finalized, it demonstrated China's desire to dominate the region's intangible space. Members of the Chinese diaspora and friendship groups have been active in New Caledonia and French Polynesia, notably in promoting economic projects that would facilitate access to critical raw materials or fishing rights (Léonie, 2025).

Challenge 4: While France gains diplomatic leverage by representing Europe in the Indo-Pacific, it also risks isolation if other EU nations do not achieve a comparable level of commitment or choose to emphasize different priorities (Niquet, 2025). For instance, coordinating multilateral naval missions often requires French initiative and resources. France continues to encourage broader European participation, but its position remains fundamentally national in nature (Niquet, 2025).

Alongside the challenges, there are also positive opportunities and prospects for France's Indo-Pacific strategy.

Opportunity 1: The growing international interest in the region—evidenced by Germany, the Netherlands, the UK, and the EU all publishing their own Indo-Pacific strategies—creates an environment for France to act as a central coordinator. With its pioneering position, France can lead joint cooperation initiatives, leveraging resources from European partners to compensate for its own limitations (e.g., deploying European ships for a joint presence, collaborating with Germany on maritime security training for ASEAN). The EU has approved a €10 billion investment for projects in the Indo-Pacific by 2027; if it plays its cards right, France could direct a portion of this toward maritime security and sustainable development projects that align with its interests.

Opportunity 2: Many regional countries are seeking reliable partners outside the sphere of the superpowers to diversify their relationships—this creates an opening for France to expand its influence. Countries such as India, Vietnam, and Indonesia welcome France's presence as a balancing third party, offering an alternative for defense technology, investment, and a voice for upholding international law. For example, India views France as a leading strategic partner outside the U.S. alliance system, with high trust in weapon transfers (Rafale, Scorpène) without the risk of sanctions as when purchasing from Russia (Léonie, 2025). After purchasing a squadron of Rafale jets, Indonesia elevated its relationship with France to a Strategic Partnership (2021). Vietnam also recently agreed to elevate its relations with France to a Comprehensive Strategic Partnership (2023)—Vietnam's highest level of relations—reflecting high expectations for future cooperation. These are all signals that the door for France to increase its role in the region remains wide open.

Opportunity 3: The very actions of China and Russia create opportunities for France to strengthen its alliances with concerned nations. China's implicit support for Russia in the war in Ukraine and its increased military presence have made many East Asian countries wary. France, with its dual status as a Euro-Atlantic and Pacific power, can play a bridging role to link European and Asian security. The interconnectedness of the Ukrainian and Indo-Pacific theaters (such as China assisting Russia, or Russia's military cooperation with Myanmar) brings European and Asian allies closer to counter common threats. This provides a basis for France to promote inter-regional multilateral cooperation mechanisms, such as a Europe-Asia Security Dialogue, or to expand NATO's interaction with its Asian partners (Japan, South Korea, Australia). France supported inviting the leaders of these countries to the 2022 NATO Summit, implying that European and Asian security are inextricably linked.

Opportunity 4: There is the possibility of cooperation with the QUAD and AUKUS on France's deployments in the region. France is fully committed to pursuing effective multilateralism, based on respect for the UN Charter and the rule of law. France supports regional organizations in managing common challenges and, in a complementary manner, encourages smaller forms of multilateral cooperation. These flexible, targeted, and affinity-based frameworks help to reinforce regional momentum based on convergence (Ministère de l'Europe et des Affaires étrangères, 2025). France's active participation in the QUAD between the U.S., Australia, India, and Japan, as well as in the AUKUS security partnership between Australia, the UK, and the U.S., is crucial; a presence that will help consolidate France's influence in this sensitive region of the world (Valori, 2025). Although not a formal member of the QUAD, France skillfully leverages this alliance to enhance its regional presence (Huger & Raj, 2021). France has a strategic interest in keeping international sea lanes open for Europe's economic and commercial security. Therefore, France's policy is committed to international law and freedom of navigation, a key reason why it participates in naval exercises alongside other members of the QUAD (inside and outside the group's formal structure). Furthermore, France is also diplomatically and strategically cooperating with all four members. France has cultivated close ties with the U.S. (specifically through NATO), as well as solid relationships with India and Japan.

The prospects for France's Indo-Pacific strategy will depend on its ability to maintain a long-term commitment and adapt flexibly to change. As Céline Pajon suggests, France should adjust its ambitions to be more realistic, shifting from the ambitious role of a "balancing power" (puissance d'équilibre) to a "constructive and pragmatic stakeholder" (stakeholder constructif et pragmatique) in the region (Pajon, 2023b). Instead of spreading itself thin, France can focus on areas of strength such as maritime security, climate change, and humanitarian relief—areas that both meet regional needs and enhance France's image. At the same time, being more sincere about its colonial past and increasing development cooperation with small island nations will help France overcome skepticism and enhance its legitimacy as a partner for the common good (Bachelier & Pajon, 2023). With the diverse partnerships it has built and the political will maintained under future administrations, France has an opportunity to consolidate its role as a positive security actor, contributing to peace and the rules-based order in the Indo-Pacific in the coming years.

In summary, France flexibly combines various tools—from hard military power to soft power partnerships and multilateral channels—to implement its Indo-Pacific strategy. The simultaneous deployment of deterrent power (such as naval presence and exercises), cooperative power (strategic partnerships, capacity-building support), and institutional power (active participation in multilateral frameworks) helps France maximize its influence and affirm its role in the region. The next section will delve into France's approach to protecting the international rules-based order—a consistent centerpiece of France's maritime strategy.

5. POLICY OF UPHOLDING THE INTERNATIONAL RULES-BASED ORDER IN FRANCE'S INDO-PACIFIC STRATEGY

Freedom of navigation in the Indo-Pacific is a particular concern, as a disruption of critical shipping lanes there would have serious consequences for the economic and commercial security of all of Europe (Pajon, 2024). In the context of the Indo-Pacific, where the risk of "the law of the jungle" emerges through unilateral actions, France increasingly emphasizes the principle of the rule of law as the foundation of the regional order.

France's maritime policy consistently emphasizes adherence to international law, especially UNCLOS 1982. In its strategic documents, France affirms its commitment to "acting for freedom of movement" based on a "commitment to defending the rules-based order" and promoting "democratic values and respect for international law" within a multilateral framework (Délégation à l'information et à la communication de la défense, 2019, p. 7). France's policy revolves around defending and promoting the international rules-based order, which is manifested in three ways: (i) promoting the global legal framework (especially UNCLOS) and multilateral institutions; (ii) speaking out and acting decisively against violations of international law in the region; and (iii) supporting the capacity-building of partner countries in maritime law enforcement.

France considers UNCLOS 1982 to be the core legal foundation governing all maritime issues. France repeatedly emphasizes the message that all maritime claims must be consistent with and resolved peacefully in accordance with UNCLOS (GMA News, 2020). In a speech at the Shangri-La Dialogue in 2016, then-Defense Minister Jean-Yves Le Drian stated: "If the law of the sea is not respected today in the South China Sea, it will be threatened tomorrow in the Arctic, the Mediterranean, or anywhere else" (Duchâtel, 2023). In September 2020, along with Germany and the United Kingdom, France submitted a diplomatic note to the United Nations affirming that China's "historical rights" claims in the South China Sea were legally unfounded and violated UNCLOS, while reiterating that the ruling of the Arbitral Tribunal in the Philippines v. China case (July 2016) had clearly confirmed this point (GMA News, 2020). This unprecedented move demonstrated the unified and strong stance of European powers in rejecting China's illegal claims in the South China Sea, thereby indirectly supporting Southeast Asian countries, especially Vietnam and the Philippines, in their persistent legal struggle.

France also called for the creation of an effective and legally binding Code of Conduct (COC) in the South China Sea, consistent with UNCLOS and without prejudice to the rights of third parties. France's vast exclusive economic zone of 10.2 million km^2 in the Indo-Pacific leads France to view the naval programs of certain countries in the region and policies that call UNCLOS into question as potential threats (Duchâtel, 2023). Protecting France's maritime space against illegal activities, particularly illegal economic activities within its exclusive economic zone (EEZ), logically leads to a vision of an international maritime order based on the strict application of UNCLOS. Therefore, France's initial approach focused on issues of naval power and maritime law (Duchâtel, 2023).

In the field, the French Navy actively conducts Freedom of Navigation Operations (FONOPs) to challenge illegal claims or restrictions. Although not as public as the United States, French warships have made their presence felt in sensitive waters on numerous occasions. In April 2019, the French frigate Vendémiaire transited the Taiwan Strait, a rare move for a European navy, showing that U.S. allies are becoming bolder in affirming freedom of navigation on international sea lanes near China (Ali & Stewart, 2019). China reacted strongly, canceling an invitation for France to attend a naval parade and sending a diplomatic protest note, accusing the French vessel of "illegal entry" despite the strait being an international shipping lane (Ali & Stewart, 2019). Despite the pressure, France maintains a firm, law-based stance: in 2021, Minister of the Armed Forces Florence Parly stated, "The South China Sea cannot be the private pond of any single country" and affirmed that France would fly, sail, and operate wherever international law allows (Dang, 2021). This position is consistent with the spirit of UNCLOS Article 87 on the freedom of the high seas and Article 17 on the right of innocent passage in the territorial sea (United Nations, 1982).

France has also repeatedly sent ships to participate in joint exercises for freedom of navigation, for example, with U.S. and UK warships through the South China Sea or the Taiwan Strait, demonstrating a united Western front on upholding the rule of law at sea. Similarly, an exercise with the Philippine Navy took place in the South China Sea off the coast of West Luzon within the Philippines' EEZ. This was a deliberate signal sent to China and also a form of support for the Philippines, a country facing increasing pressure from China regarding the South China Sea in 2024 (Scott, 2025). The joint patrol between France and the Philippines in February 2025 held significant symbolic meaning. It demonstrated that France's freedom of navigation operations are not merely unilateral assertions of sovereignty but are part of a network of partnerships. France acted alongside a claimant country in the region, reinforcing both the sovereignty of the Philippines and the principle that the South China Sea is not a closed body of water (Niquet, 2025). In this context, France's naval deployments and presence in the Indo-Pacific are not merely power projection exercises—they are an expression of a political and legal principle: that law, not might, should determine international outcomes (Niquet, 2025).

In addition to the South China Sea, France also focuses on defending the legal order in other parts of the Indo-Pacific. In the Indian Ocean, France supports East African countries in their fight against piracy in accordance with UN Security Council resolutions (French naval vessels participate in Operation Atalanta in the Gulf of Aden). In the South Pacific, France cooperates with Australia and New Zealand in joint patrols against IUU fishing (Operation Tui Moana). In the Northern Indian Ocean, France promotes the Colombo Initiative for maritime transparency. In other maritime and island disputes (for example, among ASEAN countries), France maintains a neutral stance, calling for peaceful resolution based on international law. This impartial approach helps France build an image as a fair and reliable party, basing its actions on law rather than great power interests.

Finally, an important aspect of France's policy is to support the capacity-building of partner countries in maritime law enforcement, thereby indirectly strengthening the rules-based order. Many Southeast Asian countries have limited resources and experience in maritime security management—for example, difficulty in monitoring vast maritime areas or a lack of equipment and training to effectively deal with increasingly complex challenges such as modern piracy, smuggling, IUU fishing, and oil spills. Recognizing this, France offers to share its expertise in "State Action at Sea" (Action de l'État en mer – AEM), a field in which France is strong due to its effective inter-agency coordination model.

Initiatives include: training programs for naval and coast guard commanding officers and leaders; sharing experience in building maritime law enforcement forces; and training on search and rescue, oil spill response, and anti-smuggling and illegal fishing operations. France is willing to assist in training commanders and leaders for the navies and coast guards of Southeast Asian countries, helping them enhance their patrol and law enforcement capabilities at both the basic security level, such as anti-piracy and IUU fishing, and higher military capabilities such as anti-submarine warfare, air defense, and anti-mine warfare (Bachelier & Pajon, 2023). This capacity building helps regional nations become more confident in protecting their legitimate maritime rights and interests under UNCLOS, reducing the risk of being bullied or coerced.

Similarly, France promotes the sharing of maritime information (establishing maritime security information fusion centers) and cooperation between EU and ASEAN maritime law enforcement forces, in order to effectively detect and respond to violations of the law at sea. France initiated the Pacific Coast Guard Network (2021), which meets annually in French Polynesia or New Caledonia. Within the FRANZ mechanism, France coordinates relief efforts in the event of natural disasters with Australia and New Zealand. France supports the increased participation of island nations in the management of this mechanism while ensuring proper coordination with the Pacific Humanitarian Warehouse Program (PHWP), to which France also contributes (Ministère de l'Europe et des Affaires étrangères, 2025). France supports capacity-building initiatives aimed at structuring and modernizing the armed and security forces of partner nations. The Regional Maritime Research Center (CREM), a bilateral project between France and Sri Lanka established in 2024, aims to train civil and military agents from partner countries on the challenges of maritime defense operations, from maritime surveillance and anti-trafficking to marine environmental protection (Ministère de l'Europe et des Affaires étrangères, 2025).

In summary, defending the international rules-based order is the common thread running through France's maritime strategy in the Indo-Pacific. From the diplomatic front to operations at sea, France persistently promotes the principles of UNCLOS and international law, viewing them as the best shield against great power politics. This approach not only serves France's interests but is also welcomed by many countries in the region that share the need to maintain a stable and equitable maritime order.

6. CONCLUSION

France's maritime security strategy in the Indo-Pacific reflects the efforts of a European power to adapt to the rapidly changing geopolitical environment of the 21st century. With the advantage of territorial presence and direct interests in the region, France has proactively put forward its own strategic vision, which reconciles the protection of national interests with contributions to the common good. Strategic ambitions and interests—from protecting territorial sovereignty, citizens, and resources to affirming its role as a global power—have guided France's actions. To implement this strategy, France uses a coordinated combination of multiple tools, most notably naval power, an extensive network of strategic partners, and an active role in multilateral institutions. Above all, France consistently places emphasis on maintaining the international rules-based order, viewing it as the most effective line of defense against lawlessness and great power politics.

After more than seven years of implementation, France's strategy has achieved some notable results: its presence in the region has been strengthened; relations with key partners (India, Japan, ASEAN, Australia, Vietnam) have been enhanced; and its voice on issues such as the South China Sea and freedom of navigation is respected on the international stage. However, the road ahead remains challenging. France must balance its resources across multiple security priorities, overcome internal limitations, and adapt to the new strategic landscape (post-AUKUS, post-Ukraine). To continue implementing a more effective maritime strategy, France may need to flexibly adjust its approach—focusing on areas with unique added value, coordinating more closely with the EU and its allies, and upholding its legal principles and inclusiveness. France's credibility in the region will increasingly depend on the consistency of its message and the clarity of its commitments. If Paris succeeds in combining its discourse and strategic capabilities, including financial capacity, with sustainable action, it will consolidate its role as a stabilizing power in the Indo-Pacific while leveraging its position as a permanent member of the United Nations Security Council.

France's Indo-Pacific strategy is a testament to the fact that middle powers can also shape the regional order if they cleverly combine their unique advantages and leverage the international legal system. In a rapidly changing and uncertain region, France's presence and contribution—though modest compared to the superpowers—remain important for maintaining an open, stable, and equitable maritime order based on the rule of law. The success or failure of this strategy will not only affect France's interests but will also be a test of Europe's role in the future security architecture of the Indo-Pacific.

FUNDING

This article is the research result of the National Scientific Project: "Adjustments in Major Powers' Foreign Policies from February 2022 to 2030 and the Responses of Vietnam"; Code: KX06.01/21-30.

REFERENCES

Ali, I., & Stewart, P. (2019). Exclusive: In rare move, French warship passes through Taiwan Strait. *Reuters*. https://www.reuters.com/article/world/exclusive-in-rare-move-french-warship-passes-through-taiwan-strait-idUSKCN1S0276/

An, B. (2016). Bien Dong: nguoi Phap dang den [South China Sea: The French are coming]. *To Quoc Newspaper*. https://toquoc.vn/bien-dong-nguoi-phap-dang-den-99151985.htm

Bachelier, J., & Pajon, C. (2023). France in the Indo-Pacific: The need for a pragmatic strategic posture. *Institut français des relations internationales*. https://www.ifri.org/en/studies/france-indo-pacific-need-pragmatic-strategic-posture

Binh, N. T., Hiep, T. X., Co, D. N., & Vuong, N. (2024). The strategic adjustments of China, India, and the US in the Indo-Pacific geopolitical context. *Journal of Liberty and International Affairs*, *10*(1), 173–191. DOI: 10.47305/JLIA24101171n

Blandin, B. (2024). Que pèse la France en Indo-Pacifique? [What weight does France carry in the Indo-Pacific?]. *La Tribune*. https://www.latribune.fr/opinions/tribunes/que-pese-la-france-en-indo-pacifique-995439.html

Bouffaron, P., & Blandin, B. (2025). L'avenir de l'influence européenne dans l'Indopacifique [The future of European influence in the Indo-Pacific]. *Fondation Robert Schuman*. https://www.robert-schuman.eu/questions-d-europe/786-l-avenir-de-l-influence-europeenne-dans-l-indopacifique

Dang, N. (2021). Tau chien chau Au don dap vao Bien Dong [European warships rush into the South China Sea]. *Tuoi Tre Newspaper*. https://tuoitre.vn/tau-chien-chau-au-don-dap-vao-bien-dong-20210313101215098.htm

Das, U. (2019). What is the Indo-Pacific? *The Diplomat*. https://thediplomat.com/2019/07/what-is-the-indopacific/

Délégation à l'information et à la communication de la défense. (2019). *France's defence in the Indo-Pacific*. Paris: Asia-Pacific Center for Security Studies.

Duchâtel, M. (2023). *La crédibilité de la France dans l'Indopacifique: Premières pistes* [France's credibility in the Indo-Pacific: Initial approaches]. *Institut Montaigne*. https://www.institutmontaigne.org/ressources/pdfs/publications/la-credibilite-de-la-france-dans-lindopacifique-premieres-pistes-note-denjeux.pdf

Grare, F. (2020). France, the other Indo-Pacific power. *Carnegie Endowment for International Peace.* https://carnegieendowment.org/2020/10/21/france-other-indo-pacific-power-pub-83000

Huger, B., & Raj, M. (2021). France: A balancing force in Quad and the Indo-Pacific. *Diplomatist.* https://diplomatist.com/2021/05/21/france-a-balancing-force-in-quad-and-the-indo-pacific/

Institut de Recherche Stratégique de l'École Militaire. (2022). *Preventing and combating trafficking of conventional weapons: Challenges and lessons learnt in the Indo-Pacific region.* https://www.irsem.fr/storage/file_manager_files/2025/03/livret-g-n-ral-en.pdf

Kuo, L., & Kommenda, N. (2018). What is China's Belt and Road Initiative? *The Guardian.* https://www.theguardian.com/cities/ng-interactive/2018/jul/30/what-china-belt-road-initiative-silk-road-explainer

Léonie, A. (2025). Deciphering French strategy in the Indo-Pacific. *War on the Rocks.* https://warontherocks.com/2025/03/deciphering-french-strategy-in-the-indo-pacific/

Mahan, A. T. (1897). *The interest of America in sea power, present and future.* Little, Brown & Company.

Marc, A. (2025). The geopolitics of the Indo-Pacific: France's strategy. *Geopolitique.* https://geopolitique.eu/en/2025/02/27/the-geopolitics-of-the-indo-pacific-frances-strategy/

Minh, P. Q., & Trang, N. T. T. (2021). *Quan he quoc te o khu vuc An Do Duong – Thai Binh Duong tu do va rong mo* [International relations in the Free and Open Indo-Pacific region]. The Gioi Publishing.

Ministère de l'Europe et des Affaires étrangères. (2023a). *EU strategy for cooperation in the Indo-Pacific.* https://www.diplomatie.gouv.fr/en/country-files/regional-strategies/indo-pacific/the-european-union-in-the-indo-pacific/

Ministère de l'Europe et des Affaires étrangères. (2023b). *Indo-Pacific: 8 questions to understand France's regional strategy.* https://www.diplomatie.gouv.fr/en/country-files/regional-strategies/indo-pacific/indo-pacific-8-questions-to-understand-on-france-s-regional-strategy/

Ministère de l'Europe et des Affaires étrangères. (2025). *La stratégie indopacifique de la France* [France's Indo-Pacific strategy]. https://www.diplomatie.gouv.fr/IMG/pdf/strate_gie_indopacifique_de_la_france_2025_cle0bc96b.pdf

Ministère des Armées. (2018). *Stratégie française en Indopacifique* [French strategy in the Indo-Pacific]. https://www.defense.gouv.fr/dgris/enjeux-regionaux/strategie-francaise-indopacifique

Ministry for Europe and Foreign Affairs. (2021). *France's Indo-Pacific strategy: Summary*. https://www.diplomatie.gouv.fr/IMG/pdf/en_a4_indopacifique_synthese_rvb_cle068e51.pdf

Mishra, R., & Yan, L. (2023). 'Same, same but different': Assessing ASEAN's and the EU's maritime strategies. *The Strategist*. https://www.aspistrategist.org.au/same-same-but-different-assessing-aseans-and-the-eus-maritime-strategies/

News, G. M. A. (2020). *UK, France, Germany say China's claims in South China Sea violate law, UNCLOS*. https://www.gmanetwork.com/news/topstories/nation/756104/uk-france-germany-say-china-s-claims-in-south-china-sea-violate-law-unclos/story/

Niquet, V. (2025). France in the Indo-Pacific: Between strategic autonomy and regional engagement to support shared values, rule of law and territorial integrity. *The Japan Institute of International Affairs*. https://www.jiia-jic.jp/en/policybrief/pdf/5d450dde0e60b6e18e2b4537f115905a88013d0a.pdf

Pajon, C. (2023a). France's Indo-Pacific approach: Salvaging the rules-based order and staying relevant. In *Indo-Pacific strategies: Navigating geopolitics at the dawn of a new age* (pp. 65–74). Springer., DOI: 10.1007/978-981-99-4729-4_6

Pajon, C. (2023b). France's Indo-Pacific strategy: From a balancing power to a constructive stakeholder. *Institut français des relations internationales*. https://www.ifri.org/en/external-articles/frances-indopacific-strategy-balancing-power-constructive-stakeholder

Pajon, C. (2024). La stratégie indopacifique de la France [France's Indo-Pacific strategy]. *Institut français des relations internationales*. https://www.ifri.org/fr/publications-exterieures/la-strategie-indopacifique-de-la-france

Pajon, C. (2025a). France's contributions to Pacific maritime governance. *East-West Center*. https://www.eastwestcenter.org/publications/frances-contributions-pacific-maritime-governance

Pajon, C. (2025b). France seeks third way between US and China in Southeast Asia. *Lowy Institute*. https://www.lowyinstitute.org/the-interpreter/france-seeks-third-way-between-us-china-southeast-asia

Perrin, C., Temal, R., Saury, H., Le Nay, J., Gattolin, A., & Guerriau, J. (2023). La stratégie française pour l'Indopacifique: Des ambitions à la réalité [France's strategy for the Indo-Pacific: From ambitions to reality]. *Sénat*. https://www.senat.fr/rap/r22-285/r22-285_mono.html

Pham, T. T. B., & Vu, N. Q. (2020). Chien luoc "An Do Duong – Thai Binh Duong" tu do va rong mo cua Hoa Ky: Vai tro va phuong phap thuc hien [The United States' "Free and Open Indo-Pacific" strategy: Role and implementation methods]. *Communication Review*, *938*, 102–106.

Prashanth, P. (2025). Southeast Asia maritime security and Indo-Pacific strategic competition. *Wilson Center.* https://www.wilsoncenter.org/article/southeast-asia-maritime-security-and-indo-pacific-strategic-competition

Scott, D. (2025). French maritime strategy: Carrier-led and Indo-Pacific focused. *Center for International Maritime Security*. https://cimsec.org/french-maritime-strategy-carrier-led-and-indo-pacific-focused/

Tran, V. T. (2017). Belt and Road: Towards the "Chinese Dream". *Communication Review*, *895*, 100–105.

United Nations. (1982). *United Nations Convention on the Law of the Sea (UNCLOS)*. https://www.un.org/depts/los/convention_agreements/texts/unclos/unclos_e.pdf

Valori, G. E. (2025). Le rôle croissant de la marine française dans l'Indo-Pacifique [The growing role of the French Navy in the Indo-Pacific]. *World Geostrategic Insights*. https://www.wgi.world/le-role-croissant-de-la-marine-francaise-dans-lindo-pacifique/?lang=fr

Chapter 2
Securing Energy Supply Through Maritime Security:
The European Union's Strategic Approach in the Indo-Pacific Region

Nhung Hong Nguyen
https://orcid.org/0009-0000-7647-0373
Van Hien University, Vietnam

ABSTRACT

The Indo-Pacific region is increasingly playing a strategic role in the global energy supply chain, particularly for EU. In the context of critical maritime routes such as the Strait of Malacca and the South China Sea handling the majority of trade flows and energy transportation, the EU regards maritime security in this region as a prerequisite for ensuring energy security and maintaining economic connectivity with the area. From the perspective of geopolitics and green politics, this chapter analyzes the EU's strategic approach to securing energy supply through safeguarding maritime security in the Indo-Pacific. This study focusing on the relations between the EU and regional states and multilateral organizations. The research findings indicate that, by promoting the green transition, strengthening ocean governance, and enhancing maritime security cooperation, the EU not only protects its energy interests but also elevates its status as a strategic actor, thereby contributing to reshaping the regional order toward sustainable governance and compliance with international law.

DOI: 10.4018/979-8-3373-4470-6.ch002

1. INTRODUCTION

Classical geopolitical approaches identify geography as a foundational factor shaping foreign policy, power potential, and national positioning. Control over geographical areas equates to access to resources, maintenance of transportation routes, and resource distribution systems, thereby conferring global strategic advantages (Conant & Gold, 1976). Building on this foundation, Alfred Thayer Mahan's Sea Power theory (1890) emphasized that national strength and prosperity are intrinsically linked to maritime control, including the use of seas for peacetime trade and wartime route control to protect national interests (Manship, 1964). Control over strategic maritime routes represents "long-term global power," as nations achieving this maintain sustainable geostrategic advantages. The significance of seas and oceans has been further extended in modern geopolitical theories, where blue geopolitics expands the approach to reveal the oceans' increasing role in national power. Blue geopolitics positions oceans at the center of environmental issues, ecological security, migration, and climate change, demonstrating a shift from land-based to ocean-based perspectives and expanding maritime geography's scope regarding national security, including economic, social, and environmental dimensions of maritime space. All geopolitical spaces—maritime, terrestrial, and atmospheric—are interconnected, each influencing and being influenced by the others through countless flows, exchanges, and linkages (Jones, 2024). Consequently, control over oceans and the capacity to exploit and protect marine energy resources significantly determine the balance of international power, climate change adaptation capacity, and the green economy transition process (Jones, 2024).

Additionally, Green Politics theory demonstrates that humans are no longer the absolute center but exist in relational interconnection with nature, future generations, and non-human beings. Environmental concerns have fostered cooperative efforts among states, leading to the formation and implementation of international agreements and conventions on environmental protection and pollution control, becoming a driving force in global politics closely tied to national interests (Nam, 2015). The environment has become the paramount concern in international relations theory and practice, driving the vigorous expansion and development of Green Theory since the 1990s. For states pursuing development, the environment cannot be separated from the space of existence; it cannot be regarded as a sphere detached from human action, ambition, and needs, nor defined as a concept separate from humankind (Malnes, 1993).

Prominent Green Theory representatives such as Robert E. Goodin, John Barry, Andrew Dobson, Robyn Eckersley, Hugh Dyer, and Peter Christoff have expanded various dimensions of this theory within international relations scholarship. Robert Goodin established the foundation for normative political arguments and green moral values, while John Barry developed the green political economy model and the concept of ecological citizenship associated with regenerative democracy. Andrew Dobson emphasized the distinction between conventional environmental politics and "genuine" green politics grounded in ecology and ecological justice. Robyn Eckersley pioneered the concepts of the green state and ecological sovereignty in the globalization context, while Hugh Dyer introduced green politics into the international relations theoretical system, thereby broadening Green Theory's application scope. This perspective contrasts with traditional international relations theoretical models (realism, constructivism), which focus on human positions and interests as the developmental foundation (Dyer, 2018). This approach is also termed "ecocentrism"—a central characteristic of green thought (Gökpınar, 2019). Although sharing some common themes, Green Theory addresses them from a unique perspective; moreover, concepts such as security, states, and economy—core to classical international relations theories—continue to be discussed in Green Theory but are reinterpreted based on prioritizing ecosystems, ecological ethics, sustainability, and intergenerational responsibility. These elements have established a solid and distinctive theoretical foundation widely agreed upon by scholars of this school.

This study employs geopolitics and Green Politics theoretical frameworks as the conceptual basis for analyzing the relationship between maritime security and the European Union's energy supply in the Indo-Pacific region. Maritime security constitutes part of the EU's overarching strategy for ensuring Union security and neighboring area security, providing support for energy-supplying partners and partners located along energy transit routes. Additionally, the climate-energy nexus has become a driving force promoting sustainable development values, green transition, and regional cooperation initiatives. The EU extends its transition model to neighboring regions by fostering collective awareness of green security, green transition, and environmental responsibility. Within this context, the Indo-Pacific Strategy delineates the EU's area of interest and expands this model through policies such as the European Neighbourhood Policy (ENP) and the Global Gateway, aiming to strengthen EU presence and shape regional order based on sustainable development.

2. THE EU'S STRATEGY IN THE INDO-PACIFIC TO SECURE ENERGY SUPPLY THROUGH MARITIME SECURITY

2.1. Characteristics of the EU's Energy Transition Policy Since 2015

Since 2015, the European Union's energy policy has increasingly constrained national autonomy while strengthening the EU's role. As common EU standards on energy efficiency, low-carbon technologies, system interconnection, supply security, and related domains have been codified into law, member states' capacity to exercise independent domestic policymaking has gradually narrowed—particularly for countries highly dependent on traditional energy sources or those whose interests diverge from the EU's energy transition trajectory. This dynamic reflects a condition of "sharing but not fully ceding" authority (LaBelle, 2024). Consequently, energy policy decisions at the EU level began being adopted through the ordinary legislative procedure (qualified majority voting) rather than the traditional unanimity requirement for sensitive sovereignty-related matters, signaling a decline in member-state veto power. Member states are therefore obliged to comply with emission-reduction pathways, raise targets for energy and carbon efficiency, and expand cross-border infrastructure connectivity.

This shift simultaneously reinforces cohesion and collective capacity—particularly for import-dependent states—while generating tension among those with entrenched reliance on fossil fuels or seeking to retain high levels of discretion in national energy policies. It enhances the EU's substantive enforcement power and significantly reduces "national derogation" within internal legislation (Besnier, 2023; Bettzüge, 2015). Although certain innovations improve coordination, alignment, and the "politicization" of energy policy at the EU level, rigid sovereignty constraints continue to limit the Union's ability to advance deeper federalization in this domain. For member states, the Lisbon Treaty reforms initiated a more forceful authority transfer to the EU in the energy field through common objectives and policy instruments codification and standardization. While several "sovereignty brakes" remain in place, the post-2015 deepening of integration has strengthened cohesion and enhanced the Union's "collective action capacity," yet has also intensified internal tensions, interest competition, and unity challenges—especially during crises.

External shocks such as Paris Agreement commitments (2015) and the energy crisis stemming from Russia-Ukraine relations have become sufficiently large exogenous drivers to induce decisive and comprehensive adjustments in EU energy policy orientation (Powell & Bromley, 2015). One primary implementation instrument of this strategic shift was the National Energy and Climate Plans (NECPs) launch, requiring member states to formulate specific targets for renewable energy development, energy efficiency improvements, and greenhouse gas reduction for 2021-2030. The Governance Regulation of the Energy Union and Climate Action (Regulation EU 2018/1999) use represents a clear indication of increased legal bindingness of the EU's common energy policy from this phase onward (European Commission, 2020). A critical turning point occurred with the European Green Deal introduction in 2019 and the European Climate Law adoption in 2021, through which the EU—for the first time—established legally binding objectives of reducing greenhouse gas emissions by at least 55% by 2030 and achieving carbon neutrality by

2050. Parallel to this were the Fit for 55 package and the REPowerEU, designed to reduce dependence on imported energy from high-risk countries, expand renewable energy deployment, and modernize Europe's energy infrastructure.

Overall, the EU's policy clusters focus over the past two decades has centered on two groups: (i) policies promoting energy efficiency (reducing energy intensity), and (ii) policies generating demand for low-carbon technologies and products (reducing carbon intensity). By constructing "a unique cooperation model that inspires others," imposing new models on regions across the world while attempting to develop a trade policy that is "strong, ambitious and balanced," the EU seeks to become a global leader in the green economy, "a frontrunner in the fight against climate change and in sustainable development" (Council of the European Union, 2019). This orientation has driven the EU to expand its energy relations to reduce dependence on Russia, but it has also affected power equilibria in regions with high levels of geopolitical competition with the United States, China, and Russia, such as Africa, the Middle East, and the Mediterranean. Through seeking reliable suppliers, the EU promotes cooperation on clean energy development—including green hydrogen, biomethane, renewable energy technologies, and critical raw materials. In doing so, it has exerted far-reaching influence on trade, partnerships, pricing, and the medium- and long-term strategies of many countries in their investments in global supply chains for emerging energy sectors, while simultaneously accelerating the shift toward clean energy globally (Sarno & Colantoni, 2023).

A significant shift in the European Union's foreign policy has been the integration of energy transition into the core of its external and security strategy. With the European Green Deal adoption (2019), the EU "internationalized" this objective, turning it into the foundation for new diplomatic, economic, and security initiatives through a foreign policy framework known as Green Deal Diplomacy (GDD) (College of Europe, 2023). Additionally, the Global Gateway—Europe's new strategy launched in 2021 to promote smart, clean, and secure links in the digital, energy, and transport sectors, while strengthening health, education, and research systems worldwide—has mobilized more than €306 billion in investment to support sustainable projects, meet partner countries' needs, and ensure long-term benefits for local communities (European Commission, n.d.). By fostering neighboring countries' social and economic development, the EU gradually connects them to its new development model standards.

The External Energy Strategy issued in 2022, as part of the REPowerEU Plan, guides the EU's global energy cooperation by "systematically promoting and advocating the worldwide shift to non-fossil-fuel energy systems before 2050 and the phase-out of environmentally harmful fossil fuel subsidies" (European External Action Service, 2025). The European Neighbourhood Policy (ENP) has also been supported through the Neighbourhood, Development and International Cooperation Instrument (NDICI – Global Europe), with a total allocation of approximately €79.462 billion (in 2021), of which €19.3 billion was designated for the ENP for the 2021-2027 period (European Commission, 2025a). Therefore, to ensure successful EU energy transition implementation, the Indo-Pacific Strategy operates as a complementary tool to strengthen connectivity between neighboring regions and the EU by prioritizing cooperation, resilience, and sustainability across the region.

2.2. The Role of the Indo-Pacific in the EU's Energy Policy

The European Union's energy security remains heavily dependent on oil, natural gas, and raw materials imports transported through maritime routes and pipeline networks connecting the EU with neighboring regions. In the current context, as energy policy is being adjusted to diversify supply sources to reduce dependence on Russia and advance a full-scale green transition across the EU, the expansion of partnerships with energy suppliers in Africa and Asia has become crucial. Although the green transition constitutes a central objective of EU energy policy, the Union's overall dependence on imported energy remains extremely high, with over 90% of its crude oil and natural gas supply coming from external sources (Eurostat, 2025). In practice, the regions encompassing the EU's strategic partners under the ENP framework for diversifying raw material supply—including South Africa, Ukraine, the Western Balkans, and the Southern Neighbourhood—play a vital role (European Commission, 2025a). Therefore, maritime security has become an indispensable pillar in EU energy strategies. This is particularly significant in the Indo-Pacific region, where key maritime routes and oil and gas pipeline systems connecting EU energy partners are concentrated. Enhancing maritime and ocean awareness, along with the capacity to protect and ensure these sea lanes' safety and continuity, will directly determine the EU's ability to meet its energy objectives and reinforce its regional presence. Within this study's scope, the author focuses on analyzing the role of safeguarding maritime security in supporting the EU's energy policies.

a) The Indo-Pacific as a Critical Maritime Energy Corridor

The Indo-Pacific represents an economic and strategic center of gravity for the world, accounting for more than 60% of the global population, generating 60% of global GDP, and contributing two-thirds of global growth (European Commission, 2021). The region provides substantial economic benefits and constitutes the EU's foremost area of interest, with bilateral trade between the two regions reaching record levels, representing 37% of EU imports and 25% of EU exports in 2022 (Eurostat, 2024). Conversely, more than 40% of EU exports in optical instruments, aircraft, and spacecraft are absorbed by Indo-Pacific markets (Observatory of Economic

Complexity [OEC], 2023). In the medium value-added goods group, the region supplies over 40% of the EU's demand for imported plastics and organic chemicals. Simultaneously, the Indo-Pacific constitutes a major consumption market for EU products exports to China, Japan, India, South Korea, and Saudi Arabia, alongside significant trade in ores, precious metals, and steel—materials essential for industrial production and high-tech goods manufacturing (OEC, 2023).

Particularly, the region contains maritime energy corridors vital to the European Union. These corridors link the EU with energy-supplying countries and traverse key transit states: major energy suppliers (Russia, Algeria, Norway, Qatar) and energy transit states (Ukraine, Belarus, Turkey, Georgia, and several African countries) (European Union, 2007). Among these routes, 22% of EU imports, 8% of LNG, and 10% of crude oil typically pass through the Red Sea and the Suez Canal. Imported petroleum and natural gas products from the Persian Gulf are transported either through the Suez Canal or via the Bab el-Mandeb Strait and the Strait of Hormuz (U.S. Energy Information Administration [EIA], 2024a, 2024b; European Commission, 2021).

Alongside these maritime corridors, the EU is connected to neighboring regions through an extensive oil and gas pipeline network. Notable examples include pipelines from Algeria: two systems running to Spain (Pedro Duran Farell [GPDF] and MEDGAZ) and one pipeline reaching Italy (Enrico Mattei [GEM]), as of 2014 (EIA, 2016; Grigorjeva, 2016). Other key infrastructures include the Druzhba pipeline from Belarus, as well as pipelines crossing Turkey from the Caucasus, the Eastern Mediterranean, the Middle East, and Central Asia into Europe, such as the Trans-Caspian and Black Sea–Southern Europe routes (the Baku–Tbilisi–Ceyhan [BTC] pipeline), the South Caucasus Pipeline (also known as the Baku–Tbilisi–Erzurum/BTE/Shah Deniz pipeline), TANAP, and TAP.

However, the uninterrupted flow of these goods has been, and continues to be, threatened by specific risks such as great-power competition, maritime territorial disputes, internal instability, piracy, trafficking of illicit substances, arms smuggling, kidnapping, terrorist attacks, and increasingly severe climate-related hazards. Any disruption along one of the critical maritime routes in the Indo-Pacific could result in direct revenue losses, indirect impacts on production, and threats to the EU's energy security and competitiveness. Ensuring maritime security in the region, therefore, means "protecting open access to sea lines of communication (SLOCs)" for the European Union (Pacheco Pardo & Leveringhaus, 2022).

b) Maritime Security as the Safeguard of the EU's Energy Supply in the Indo-Pacific

Since the political and social upheavals of the Arab Spring in 2011, the Middle East and North Africa have remained engulfed in cycles of instability, conflict, and humanitarian crises. This series of events has compelled both regional states and external powers to reconfigure their positions and strategies in the region (Hien, 2017). Competition among major powers—primarily the United States and China—has intensified substantially. China has expanded its economic and military influence through the Belt and Road Initiative (BRI), the "string of pearls" strategy, and its "nine-dash line" claims in the South China Sea, which generate tensions with Southeast Asian countries, alongside its activities in the East China Sea that provoke frictions with Japan and Taiwan. It has also broadened its footprint in Africa through new security commitments under the Global Security Initiative (Anh, 2022; Nantulya, 2025; Girardi et al., 2023). The United States, in turn, has advanced an expanded Indo-Pacific Strategy and strengthened the informal QUAD alliance to mitigate risks posed by China as the common strategic challenger. Russia, meanwhile, has increased its presence in the region since 2022, with its energy trade relations with India, China, and several other Indo-Pacific countries showing upward trends, thereby consolidating Russia's interests in the area (An, 2024). Although China does not currently pose a direct military threat to Europe, the EU remains concerned about "fierce competition" and "significant military build-up that could directly affect Europe's security and prosperity" (European Commission, 2021).

Additionally, regional security has become increasingly unstable due to internal conflict in Yemen—most notably the Iran-aligned Houthi movement—alongside the activities of terrorist groups such as al-Qaeda and the United Arab Emirates' attempts to exert control over Perim Island, which have often led to confrontational rather than cooperative relations, particularly regarding authority over maritime security in the area (Alexandre, 2021). Since late 2023, Houthi forces in Yemen have intensified attacks on vessels, especially those bound for Israel, in an effort to pressure an end to the conflict in Gaza (Lahiri & Waterson, 2025). Compounding this situation are Yemen's internal instability, coastal competition between Iran and Saudi Arabia, piracy in the Gulf of Aden, and the military presence of multiple major powers (the United States, France, the United Kingdom, Japan, China, and Saudi Arabia) in Djibouti, all of which have rendered the Bab el-Mandeb Strait a high-risk chokepoint (Girardi et al., 2023). The Gulf of Guinea remains a hotspot for kidnapping and threats to crew safety, and around the Horn of Africa, at least eight incidents involving the hijacking of fishing vessels and bulk carriers were recorded (International Chamber of Commerce International Maritime Bureau [ICC-IMB], 2024). As a result, major shipping companies such as MSC and Maersk have rerouted vessels around the Cape of Good Hope, adding roughly two weeks to transit time and significantly increasing logistics costs, insurance premiums, and the price of imported goods entering the EU (European Parliament, 2024). The Singapore Strait and the Indonesian archipelago have experienced an increase in armed attacks (involving firearms), crew kidnappings, and disruptions to maritime operations. Notably, the trade route through the Strait of Malacca, which links the South China Sea and the Indian Ocean, constitutes one of the most critical and high-risk energy chokepoints (Pratson, 2022). Thus, strategic competition among major powers, coupled with pervasive non-traditional security threats, may lead to conflict, disrupt trade, and create significant potential consequences for Europe. Given Europe's extensive economic exposure to the region and the benefits it derives from the current international order, the EU seeks to maintain a security presence in the Indo-Pacific to safeguard its interests.

3. THE EU'S ACTIVITIES IN THE INDO-PACIFIC TO ACHIEVE ENERGY OBJECTIVES

In the context in which the EU has shifted its energy focus toward "climate neutrality" and "green industrial transformation" since 2019, climate and environmental considerations have become the central pillars shaping its new development model. These priorities continue to steer energy policy, requiring all energy-related measures to contribute to climate objectives and redefining the Union's overall trajectory.

The EU's Indo-Pacific Strategy is regarded as a strategic guideline through which the EU seeks to strengthen its presence in a critical region to secure economic corridors, supply chains, and the global green transition. By disseminating and elevating collective awareness of ecological and climate security, in line with commitments under the Sustainable Development Goals, the Paris Agreement on Climate Change, and frameworks for partnership-building and rules-based order, the EU promotes sustainable development, connectivity, and maritime security across the region (European External Action Service, 2021a). The maritime security and ocean cooperation approach thus becomes an enabling tool for supporting the EU's energy and climate security objectives in the Indo-Pacific. Through its presence and activities, the EU seeks to affirm its role in maintaining a rules-based international order while demonstrating its commitment to normative values associated with the green transition (Misalucha-Willoughby, 2024).

Alongside the Indo-Pacific Strategy, the Strategic Compass for Security and Defence (2022), the revised EU Maritime Security Strategy (EUMSS) (2023), and the updated ENP further reinforce the protective architecture surrounding Europe. The EUMSS is now considered the EU's most comprehensive and integrated framework, connecting multiple domains and actors to address maritime security issues coherently, including the implementation of international law, freedom of navigation, and the protection of critical infrastructure, transport, natural resources, and the environment (Landman, 2015). These issues play a crucial role in safeguarding the EU's strategic energy supply chains. Through this framework, the EU seeks to protect its maritime interests, values, and economy from challenges arising from illicit activities, geopolitical competition, resource rivalry, and other threats such as cyberattacks and hybrid challenges (European External Action Service, 2024a). Particularly, the Global Gateway functions as a financial toolbox focused on promoting green, modern, and resilient investment across partner regions. Between 2021 and 2024, the Global Gateway mobilized more than €306 million, with the largest share directed to Sub-Saharan Africa, followed by the Middle East and North Africa and the Asia-Pacific (European Commission, n.d.). Thus, the interlinkage between climate law, maritime policy, and these strategic objectives establishes a clear connection between the EU's maritime security strategies in the Indo-Pacific to enhancing maritime activities; cooperating with partners on ocean governance; reinforcing a rules-based international order; addressing global challenges; and laying the foundations for rapid, equitable, and sustainable economic recovery, thereby generating long-term prosperity (European Commission, 2021).

3.1. Strengthening Maritime Activities to Safeguard Maritime Energy Corridors and Critical Infrastructure

Increasing the EU's presence in strategic maritime zones is essential for enhancing interoperability and addressing the growing threats to the Union's maritime security, particularly in areas beyond Europe such as the Gulf of Guinea, the Gulf of Aden, the Strait of Hormuz, the Strait of Malacca, and the South China Sea (European Commission, 2023).

Through the EUMSS and its fourth Action Plan, alongside the Indo-Pacific Strategy, the Global Gateway (2021), and the Common Security and Defence Policy (CSDP), the EU has established frameworks and investment mechanisms to respond to maritime security challenges. In this context, the deployment of European Union Training Missions (EUTM) aims to protect maritime energy corridors, safeguard critical infrastructure, and ensure timely responses to the growing range of threats—including organized crime, piracy, terrorism, unlawful interference by foreign states, and risks linked to climate change and natural disasters—which affect maritime trade and infrastructure (European Commission, 2023).

Counter-piracy strategies have expanded into broader maritime security operations in strategically critical chokepoints such as the Strait of Hormuz (EMASOH), the area around the Bab el-Mandeb Strait, and the Horn of Africa (European Commission, 2023). To support its objectives in these regions, the EU is currently deploying three missions in Somalia under the Common Security and Defence Policy, including the European Union Training Mission focused on the military forces of Somalia and Mozambique (Čok, 2025).

The EU Training Mission in Somalia operates alongside the EU Naval Force ATALANTA, the EU Delegation, the EU Special Representative to the Horn of Africa, EU-funded programs, and Member State initiatives (European External Action Service, 2024a). This constitutes the EU's largest military intervention in a foreign country. These missions aim to train the Somali National Army (SNA), build capacity for local police forces and maritime security units, and counter piracy in and around the ports of Mogadishu, Berbera, and Bossaso—locations with potential to become critical connectors between Africa and Europe (European External Action Service, 2024; Čok, 2025).

The military training mission in Mozambique (EUTM Mozambique) seeks to support the Mozambican armed forces through training and capacity-building for the Mozambique Armed Defence Forces. This mission complements wider EU efforts on peacebuilding, conflict prevention, political dialogue, humanitarian assistance, and development cooperation across the Horn of Africa and adjacent maritime spaces (European External Action Service, 2024b).

Additionally, the Coordinated Maritime Presences (CMP) initiative (2021) serves as a flexible instrument of the Common Security and Defence Policy (CSDP). CMP is a unique form of coordination—not a designated action or mission—based on member states' voluntary participation, making optimal use of their naval and air assets while allowing these assets to operate under the EU flag (European External Action Service, 2024b). The CMP deployment in the region enhances naval operations and maintains a visible European maritime presence in the North-Western Indian Ocean, an area that encompasses two critical maritime chokepoints for European trade (the Strait of Hormuz in the Persian Gulf and the Bab el-Mandeb Strait at the Horn of Africa) (Suri, 2023). From this foundation, the CMP concept has been extended to the broader Indo-Pacific region, with its core objectives being to ensure freedom of navigation and to support merchant vessels transiting through the Red Sea, the Strait of Hormuz, and onward into the Indian Ocean. This is achieved through deployed assets that provide training and capacity-building for coastal states' navies (European External Action Service, 2024c). Furthermore, the EU supports the Jeddah Amendment to the Djibouti Code of Conduct in efforts to address maritime security challenges in the region. Additionally, CMP activities promote cooperation with partners through joint maritime exercises, port visits to Mumbai, and the facilitation of information exchange (European External Action Service, 2024c).

The presence missions under EUTM and the CMP mechanism have contributed significantly to enhancing the EU's visibility and engagement in the areas surrounding the Middle East and the western Indian Ocean. Through extensive activities focused on training soldiers, platoon and company commanders, special units, and instructor trainers—amounting to nearly 7,000 personnel—these efforts were funded through the EU's Athena mechanism with approximately €90 million between 2010 and 2020. EUTM Somalia aims to strengthen the "capacity, effectiveness, reputation and accountability" of Somalia's defense sector, enabling the Somali authorities to assume responsibility for their own security and helping to safeguard the stability of East Africa and the Red Sea region. This, in turn, allows the EU to better protect critical maritime transport routes through the Red Sea and the Indian Ocean, ensuring the safe flow of commercial traffic and the protection of economic interests (Williams & Ali, 2020). Other supporting activities—such as EUNAVFOR ASPIDES, which has increased the escort capacity for commercial vessels in the Red Sea since 2024—have significantly reduced the risks of direct attacks from the Houthi movement. However, training operations in Somalia face limitations due to the EU's lack of full control over trainee selection, which remains dependent on the Somali authorities; insufficient post-training support such as monitoring, equipment, and practical mentorship; rapid personnel turnover within the mission, which complicates efforts to build long-term trust; and inadequate coordination with other EU initiatives in Somalia. Similarly, the ASPIDES mission still lacks a unified EU naval fleet and a fully developed multinational rapid-response capability.

EU initiatives to enhance naval presence in the region—such as the CMP—have expanded the geographic scope of EU maritime deployments and strengthened multilateral cooperation with partners including the United States, Japan, and India in key areas such as the Indian Ocean and the Gulf of Guinea. These efforts contribute to improving the interoperability of European naval forces and affirm the EU's position as a global naval provider. The expansion of this concept also signals the EU's ambition to maintain a naval presence in areas where its vessels may have to operate alongside, and potentially confront, Chinese vessels. However, CMP remains a low-cost tool, centered on consensus among member states rather than a "joint command," and divisions persist within the EU regarding approaches to China and responses to Beijing's territorial ambitions in the Indo-Pacific. Consequently, the EU's role in the region remains limited (Nováky, 2022).

Through the activities of EUTM and CMP, the EU has demonstrated its capacity to provide military capabilities and act as a reliable partner in the region in support of its foreign policy objectives. For regional states, the EU's presence conveys a message of support for key norms and ethical standards in international relations, as well as the core purpose of the EU's green diplomacy: benevolent intent and a willingness to assume regional responsibilities and uphold shared standards (Jansson, 2018). This presence is perceived as more reassuring than the dominant military leadership of the United States or the assertive combination of infrastructure investment and territorial claims promoted by China.

3.2. Cooperation with Partners on Maritime Security

The Indo-Pacific is a central arena of power competition among major global actors, with U.S.-China relations exerting profound influence on regional dynamics. China has increasingly articulated clear ambitions to become "a maritime power," modernizing and expanding the People's Liberation Army Navy (PLAN) from a coastal defense force into a blue-water navy capable of global operations across the deep oceans, thereby laying the foundation for a broader Chinese presence (Grare & Reuter, 2023). Additionally, ASEAN's centrality remains one of the core pillars underpinning regional security (Ngo & Hoang, 2025). Given the Indo-Pacific region's sensitivity, it is highly unlikely that all 27 EU member states would agree to launch a CSDP naval operation there (Nováky, 2022). Although it remains uncertain whether the CMP instrument will be expanded to the entirety of the Indo-Pacific, the region's economic significance for Europe—together with the growing attention it has received from EU member states—has already prompted adjustments to the EU's maritime strategy in the area.

First, the EU has undergone a shift in its perception of the Indo-Pacific's critical maritime routes through the Critical Maritime Routes Indian Ocean (CRIMARIO) initiative, designed to enhance Maritime Domain Awareness (MDA). The program expanded from the Western Indian Ocean (CRIMARIO I, 2015) to South Asia, Southeast Asia, and the Pacific (as of 2022) under CRIMARIO II (2020), with the aim of fostering cross-sectoral, inter-agency, and transregional cooperation to help ensure the safety of maritime lines of communication (Nováky, 2022). Subsequently, the emergence of the EU's Indo-Pacific Strategy, alongside the EU Maritime Security Strategy and its Action Plan (2023), clearly demonstrates the EU's growing engagement in building relationships and cooperation on maritime security with multilateral and regional organizations at both global and regional levels—particularly in the Gulf of Guinea and the Indo-Pacific (European Commission, 2023). The EU and its member states have also advanced international cooperation through bilateral dialogues with Australia, Japan, India, Indonesia, South Korea, Oman, and Singapore, as well as with multilateral organizations including the United Nations (UN), International Maritime Organization (IMO), NATO, the African Union (AU), and ASEAN. These engagements take place through port visits, joint exercises, and operational maritime deployments. The Union's participation with international partners contributes to promoting rules-based maritime governance and upholding international conventions, notably the universal application of the United Nations Convention on the Law of the Sea (UNCLOS).

The key multilateral organizations with which the EU seeks to strengthen relations also include the African Union (AU). Peace and security constitute a central component of all high-level political dialogues between the EU and the AU, in which maritime security is a shared concern. This was highlighted during the AU-EU Maritime Ministerial Conference held in Seychelles at the end of 2015, which helped raise awareness of the threats posed by maritime crime (European External Action Service, 2021a). These actions are carried out in line with the African Integrated Maritime Strategy 2050 and the EU's Integrated Maritime Policy. The African Union established maritime-related priorities in its 2014 African Integrated Maritime Strategy (AIMS 2050) and launched the African Decade of Seas and Oceans (2015-2025). The EU has supported the implementation of the AU's 2020 Integrated Maritime Strategy and the African Charter on Maritime Security, Safety and Development (the Lomé Charter), as well as IGAD's Integrated Maritime Security Strategy (2015-2030) (European External Action Service, 2018). The Horn of Africa is particularly important to EU interests. As geopolitical competition among major powers intensifies in the race for raw materials needed for technological advancement, the region has drawn increasing attention. Many island and coastal states in the Indian Ocean, especially in the Horn of Africa, possess limited economic resources, defense capacity, and naval capabilities to enforce effective maritime control. As a result, they rely heavily on external powers, lacking the means and technical expertise required to secure their waters. For many of these states, exercising control over their territorial seas and Exclusive Economic Zones (EEZs) is therefore an almost impossible challenge (Grare & Reuter, 2023). In the Gulf of Guinea, the EU supports regional organizations and coastal states in implementing their own maritime security strategies, strengthening maritime law enforcement, improving port safety and security, enhancing maritime domain awareness, and facilitating information-sharing.

In the Pacific, the EU and ASEAN share common interests; therefore, maintaining peace, stability, security, and a rules-based maritime order is essential—particularly in "sensitive" areas such as the South China Sea, the Strait of Malacca, the Taiwan Strait, and the waters surrounding Singapore. Both sides articulate principles and positions regarding norms of conduct at sea: the EU bases its approach on upholding a "Rules-Based International Order" as the foundation for ensuring openness and freedom in the region, while ASEAN draws on the "ASEAN Way," which emphasizes consensus-building, non-interference, dialogue, cooperation, and adherence to international law. Consequently, both parties actively promote cooperation in this domain.

The EU has participated actively in the ASEAN Regional Forum (ARF) in discussions and workshops on enhancing maritime security cooperation since 2013 (Piasentini, 2024). From 2018 to 2021, the EU, together with Australia and Vietnam, co-chaired the ARF Inter-Sessional Meeting on Maritime Security, focusing on priority themes such as the implementation of the 1982 United Nations Convention on the Law of the Sea (UNCLOS), strengthening maritime law enforcement cooperation, improving maritime domain awareness, ferry safety, dispute settlement, and the law of the sea (European External Action Service, 2022). The EU has also promoted common maritime domain awareness among ASEAN and South Asian states through CRIMARIO I and II (2015-2024). The 4th EU-ASEAN High-Level Dialogue (HLD) on Maritime Security Cooperation, held in 2017, yielded mutual benefits for ASEAN and EU member states and constructively contributed to maintaining peace and good order at sea (European External Action Service, 2017). The EU has also intensified exchanges of experience with partners on maritime security through the "Enhancing Security Cooperation In and With Asia" (ESIWA) project and through bilateral dialogues, while seeking observer ('dialogue partner') status in the Indian Ocean Rim Association (IORA).

However, although the promotion of maritime security cooperation with the AU and ASEAN through CRIMARIO, the ARF, legal-UNCLOS exercises, and capacity-building programs such as SWAIMS/PASSMAR has produced clear value in enhancing awareness of green security, standardizing behavior based on international law, and strengthening ocean governance, the degree to which these partnerships translate into coordinated operational action remains limited. Most current cooperation focuses on establishing dialogue frameworks, information-sharing mechanisms, and soft-skill capacity-building, whereas joint operational projects or common response mechanisms at key maritime chokepoints continue to occur only sporadically. The effectiveness of these initiatives still depends heavily on partners' absorption capacity and the level of resources the EU is willing to commit in the future. As the EU seeks to expand its influence beyond the Indian Ocean and gradually shift eastward toward the Strait of Malacca, these constraints become increasingly evident.

4. IMPACTS OF THE EU'S MARITIME STRATEGY IN THE INDO-PACIFIC

Since 2015, the EU's energy policy has undergone substantial changes through the legalization of energy-related measures and the stronger transfer of authority to the EU in energy governance. By adjusting the rules of the internal market, establishing production standards, competition law, and tax policy, the EU increasingly demonstrates its capacity to influence global public policy through the scale and complexity of its legal system (Damro, 2012). Energy policy has been complemented by the EU's maritime strategy in the Indo-Pacific and by a range of other instruments that delineate the Union's sphere of interest. These include capacity-building for neighboring regions and enhanced presence in strategic areas to diffuse normative and ethical values.

First, these constitute the foundation of the EU's market power, enabling the Union to shape the "rules of the game," technical standards, environmental norms, and global trade and competition rules according to its economic interests. This demonstrates that energy is understood not merely as an economic sector, but also as a tool through which the EU asserts influence—primarily via the externalization of its policies, standards, and energy market regulations to international partners seeking access to the EU market. The externalization of energy policies is supported by the EU's global initiative strategies, wherein the Indo-Pacific Strategy functions as a spatial framework through which these initiatives are operationalized in ways that advance relations with partners and progressively expand the rulebook for the regional market. In essence, the EU's interest in the region is driven by economic considerations. Both the Indo-Pacific Strategy and the Strategic Compass highlight the region's economic importance, noting that four of the EU's top ten trading partners are located there (European External Action Service, 2021b). This economic attractiveness, however, comes with high levels of risk, as the region remains volatile. Despite its geographical distance from Europe, the indirect risks to the EU are substantial. Maintaining safe, stable, and rules-based freedom of navigation is essential for ensuring uninterrupted supply chains, which in turn underpins the EU's economic strength and its international market power.

Second, this strategy contributes to shaping the EU as a normative model. In a context where the region is facing security instability with serious implications for the "rules-based international order," the EU's rule-based approach has helped construct the image of a reliable power. This stands in contrast to other actors whose policies have generated regional instability. Meanwhile, the rise of China—accompanied by "wolf-warrior diplomacy," an expanded naval presence in flashpoints such as the Taiwan Strait, the South China Sea, the Mediterranean, or the Baltic Sea, and China's ambiguous position on the 2022 Ukraine War—has led the EU to "publicly regard China as a direct economic and political competitor" (Pugliese, 2024). While the United States under Donald Trump's "America First" policy focused primarily on countering China's military expansion, the EU concentrated on trade and investment, climate and biodiversity, emerging technologies, and new security threats (such as climate change, illegal fishing, and piracy). This comprehensive approach underscores Europe's role as a stabilizing force, complementing military deterrence with economic development and support for governance (Bouffaron & Blandin, 2025; European External Action Service, 2021b). Therefore, the EU has leveraged its economic resources and cooperation with regional partners to shape emerging standards, positioning itself as a connectivity superpower both within and beyond.

Third, this strategy influences the regional structure. The shortage of energy supplies resulting from the Ukraine war has compelled the EU to expand its external energy partnerships and to restructure energy supply chains to reduce dependence on Russia. The EU has introduced a roadmap for reducing energy-security risks, together with economic plans outlined in the Competitiveness Compass, the Net-Zero Industry initiative, and the Affordable Energy Action Plan, emphasizing how a cleaner and more autonomous energy system will boost economic performance (European Commission, 2025b). Accelerating the use of cleaner energy requires the EU to advance low-carbon technologies, which are key to achieving energy objectives as well as to the Union's broader global positioning strategy (Lv & Qin, 2016; Dahlström et al., 2023). However, this advantage has not translated proportionally into actual manufacturing capability, as most core clean-technology products (such as solar panels, batteries, and wind-power equipment) continue to be produced outside the EU, especially in China. China holds dominant positions in these stages—exceeding 50 percent in extraction and/or refining—across key metals identified by the European Commission as critical, including gallium and germanium (with 94 percent and 83 percent of global refining, respectively) and rare-earth elements (over 90 percent of processing) (Calcara et al., 2025). In reality, this dependence constitutes a threat to the EU's position in the region, especially given China's growing alignment with Russia to counter the influence of the United States and its allies (Odgaard, 2023). At the same time, the EU faces pressure from the United States to adopt firmer measures against China's penetration of the European market. China's BRI initiative not only undermines internal cohesion within the EU but also threatens the European market, as European companies face heightened competition when accessing markets in both Europe and Asia. Assessments indicate that the effects of the BRI stretch far beyond the European continent and are influencing stability in Asia. Hence, maintaining a rules-based order and ensuring unimpeded trade flows across the Indian and Pacific Oceans are vital to Europe's economic security (Geeraerts, 2019). Yet, the EU has not been reduced to a vulnerable actor in the strategic competition between the United States and China. The Union retains a significant position due to its large market, environmental and climate standards, and regulatory frameworks governing trade, all of which encourage other states and markets to adapt to European rules (Bradford, 2012).

5. CONCLUSION

The EU's Indo-Pacific Strategy demonstrates an increasingly explicit linkage between energy security objectives, the green transition, and the maintenance of a rules-based maritime order in the region. One of the strategy's core priorities is to promote the green transition, a rules-based order, and people-to-people connectivity, thereby linking the region to the EU through the externalization of EU values. Through multilateral cooperation mechanisms, green investment, and the diffusion of governance standards in the maritime and energy domains, the EU gradually shapes a distinctive normative and regulatory position—one that differs from the United States' more military-oriented approach and China's infrastructure-driven, geo-economic strategy. However, the EU's influence remains selective and modest given its limited naval resources, the fragmented policy preferences among member states, and the intensifying competition from major powers. The EU has succeeded in creating normative and connectivity-based spheres of influence but lacks the capacity to reshape regional power balances; its role remains supplementary rather than substitutive vis-à-vis traditional security actors. Looking ahead, the degree to which the EU can expand its influence depends on several key conditions: (i) its ability to strengthen naval deployment capabilities and CSDP coordination beyond the immediate neighborhood; (ii) the progress of the green transition without compromising short-term energy security; (iii) its capacity to compete with China in supply chains for strategic materials and clean-energy technologies; and (iv) its ability to maintain political cohesion within the Union.

A potential policy dilemma may emerge if the goal of thorough decarbonization requires phasing out fossil fuels faster than renewable energy capacity can be scaled up, thereby increasing dependence on imported LNG, critical raw materials, or supplies from high-risk countries. Conversely, if the EU can maintain a balance between the green transition, energy security, and maritime presence, the Indo-Pacific could become a key axis for expanding its strategic influence, enabling the EU to reinforce its role as a "rule-making power" in global ocean governance, trade, and green standards. Overall, the assessment suggests that the EU's strategy presents both opportunities to expand its influence and significant structural constraints. A pragmatic approach—one that combines normative ambition with calibrated material capabilities—will determine whether the EU can transform its current presence into sustainable strategic power in the years ahead.

REFERENCES

Alexandre, A. G. (2021). The Strait of Bab El-Mandeb: Stage of geopolitical disputes. *JANUS.NET e-Journal of International Relations, 12*(2), 58–74. https://doi.org/DOI: 10.26619/1647-7251.12.2.4

An, L. (2024). Russia's foreign policy in the Asia-Pacific region. *Communist Review.* https://tapchicongsan.org.vn/web/guest/the-gioi-van-de-su-kien/-/2018/970502/chinh-sach-ngoai-giao-cua-nga-tai-khu-vuc-chau-a---thai-binh-duong.aspx

Anh, V. V. (2022). China's East Sea policy in the 2009-2021 period. *Vietnam Social Sciences, 7*, 27–38.

Besnier, T. (2023). Repower EU: The authority turn for the EU in energy policies? *Bruges Political Research Papers, 91*. College of Europe. https://coleurope.eu/sites/default/files/research-paper/wp91%20Besnier.pdf

Bettzüge, M. O. (2015). European energy policy: Dogma or strategy? *France Stratégie,* 105–138. https://www.strategie-plan.gouv.fr/files/files/Publications/English%20Articles/Study%20-%20Energy%20Union/fs_study_the_union_of_energy_mobettzuge_16092015_final.pdf

Bouffaron, P., & Blandin, B. (2025). The future of European influence in the Indo-Pacific. *Schuman Paper, 786*. Robert Schuman Foundation. https://www.robert-schuman.eu/en/european-issues/786-the-future-of-european-influence-in-the-indo-pacific

Bradford, A. (2012). The Brussels effect. *Northwestern University Law Review, 107*(1), 1–68. https://papers.ssrn.com/sol3/papers.cfm?abstract_id=2770634

Calcara, A., Drieschova, A., & Cusumano, E. (2025). Technological underpinnings of European autonomy and US-China competition. *Journal of European Integration, 47*(6), 943–963. DOI: 10.1080/07036337.2025.2536828

Čok, C. (2025). *React, rinse, repeat: How Europe can help break Somalia's cycle of conflict*. European Council on Foreign Relations. https://ecfr.eu/publication/react-rinse-repeat-how-europe-can-help-break-somalias-cycle-of-conflict/

College of Europe. (2023). *Reinforcing the EU's Green Deal Diplomacy: Recommendations for the next Commission*. College of Europe Policy Brief. https://www.coleurope.eu/sites/default/files/research-paper/CEPOB%204-23%20final.pdf

Conant, M. A., & Gold, F. R. (1976). *The geopolitics of energy*. Westview Press.

Council of the European Union. (2019). *A new strategic agenda for the EU 2019-2024*. https://www.consilium.europa.eu/en/eu-strategic-agenda-2019-2024/

Dahlström, P., Edlund, P. O., & Guibourg, G. (2023). The EU's competitive advantage in the green transition. *IFN Working Paper, 1483*. Research Institute of Industrial Economics.

Damro, C. (2012). Market power Europe. *Journal of European Public Policy, 19*(5), 682–699. DOI: 10.1080/13501763.2011.646779

Dyer, H. (2018). Introducing green theory in international relations. *E-International Relations*. https://www.e-ir.info/2018/01/07/green-theory-in-international-relations/

European Commission. (2020). *National energy and climate plans*. https://energy.ec.europa.eu/topics/energy-strategy/national-energy-and-climate-plans-necps_en

European Commission. (2021). *The EU strategy for cooperation in the Indo-Pacific* [Joint Communication]. https://www.eeas.europa.eu/sites/default/files/jointcommunication_2021_24_1_en.pdf

European Commission. (2023). *An enhanced EU Maritime Security Strategy for evolving maritime threats* [Joint Communication]. https://eur-lex.europa.eu/legal-content/EN/TXT/HTML/?uri=CELEX:52023JC0008

European Commission. (2025a). *Commission adopts RESourceEU to secure raw materials, reduce dependencies and boost competitiveness* [Press release]. https://ec.europa.eu/commission/presscorner/detail/en/ip_25_1131

European Commission. (2025b). *European Neighbourhood Policy*. https://enlargement.ec.europa.eu/european-neighbourhood-policy_en

European Commission. (n.d.). *Global Gateway*. Retrieved March 15, 2025, from https://commission.europa.eu/topics/international-partnerships/global-gateway_en

European External Action Service. (2017). ASEAN-EU co-chairs joint press release on the 4th ASEAN-EU High-Level Dialogue on Maritime Security Cooperation. https://www.eeas.europa.eu/node/33405_en

European External Action Service. (2018). Horn of Africa-Red Sea: Revised EU Maritime Security Strategy Action Plan, regional and global maritime affairs. https://www.eeas.europa.eu/node/47565_en

European External Action Service. (2021a). *EU strategy for cooperation in the Indo-Pacific*. https://www.eeas.europa.eu/eeas/eu-strategy-cooperation-indo-pacific_en

European External Action Service. (2021b). The European Union and the African Union: Peace & security. https://www.eeas.europa.eu/african-union/european-union-and-african-union-peace-security_en

European External Action Service. (2022). *Maritime cooperation.* https://euinasean.eu/maritime-cooperation-2022/

European External Action Service. (2024a). *Coordinated maritime presences.* https://www.eeas.europa.eu/eeas/coordinated-maritime-presences_en

European External Action Service. (2024b). *EU CSDP missions and operations 2023 annual report.* Publications Office of the European Union.

European External Action Service. (2024c). *Maritime security.* https://www.eeas.europa.eu/eeas/maritime-security_en

European External Action Service. (2025). *Green transition: EU green diplomacy.* https://www.eeas.europa.eu/eeas/green-transition-diplomacy_en

European Parliament. (2024). *Maritime security: Situation in the Red Sea and EU response.* https://www.europarl.europa.eu/RegData/etudes/ATAG/2024/757606/EPRS_ATA(2024)757606_EN.pdf

European Union. (2007). *Renewable energy road map.* https://eur-lex.europa.eu/legal-content/EN/TXT/?uri=LEGISSUM:l27065

Eurostat. (2024). *EU trade with the Indo-Pacific region increased in 2022.* https://ec.europa.eu/eurostat/web/products-eurostat-news/w/ddn-20240201-1

Eurostat. (2025). *Oil and petroleum products: A statistical overview.* https://ec.europa.eu/eurostat/statistics-explained/index.php?title=Oil_and_petroleum_products_-_a_statistical_overview

Geeraerts, G. (2019). Europe and China's Belt and Road Initiative: Growing concerns, more strategy. *Security Policy Brief, 118*, 1–6. Egmont Institute. https://www.egmontinstitute.be/app/uploads/2019/11/SPB118.pdf

Girardi, B., Go, Y., Sweijs, T., & Kertysova, K. (2023). *What the Indo-Pacific means to Europe: Trade value, chokepoints, and security risks.* The Hague Centre for Strategic Studies. https://hcss.nl/wp-content/uploads/2023/11/What-the-Indo-Pacific-means-to-Europe-Trade-Value-Chokepoints-and-Security-Risks-HCSS-2023.pdf

Gökpınar, T. A. (2019). Green theory in international relations. In Gökpınar, T. A. (Ed.), *Theories of international relations II* (pp. 163–178). Anadolu University Press.

Grare, F., & Reuter, M. (2023). *The battle for the Indian Ocean: How the EU and India can strengthen maritime security*. European Council on Foreign Relations. https://ecfr.eu/publication/the-battle-for-the-indian-ocean-how-the-eu-and-india-can-strengthen-maritime-security/

Grigorjeva, J. (2016). *Starting a new chapter in EU-Algeria energy relations: A proposal for a targeted cooperation* (Policy Paper No. 173). Jacques Delors Institute. https://institutdelors.eu/content/uploads/2025/04/eualgeriaenergy-grigorjeva-jdib-sept16-2.pdf

Hien, N. T. (2017). Identifying the new political-security situation in the Middle East and North Africa region. *Social Sciences Information. Information Sur les Sciences Sociales*, *8*, 3–13.

International Chamber of Commerce International Maritime Bureau. (2024). *Maritime piracy dropped in 2024, but crew safety remains at risk*. https://icc-ccs.org/maritime-piracy-dropped-in-2024-but-crew-safety-remains-at-risk/

Jansson, P. (2018). Rhetoric and legitimacy in the European Neighbourhood Policy. *Global Affairs*, *4*(2–3), 317–328. DOI: 10.1080/23340460.2018.1535253

Jones, R. (2024). Political geography I: Blue geopolitics. *Progress in Human Geography*, *48*(5), 615–625. DOI: 10.1177/03091325241271521

LaBelle, M. C. (2024). Breaking the era of energy interdependence in Europe: A multidimensional reframing of energy security, sovereignty, and solidarity. *Energy Strategy Reviews*, *52*, 101314. Advance online publication. DOI: 10.1016/j.esr.2024.101314

Lahiri, A., & Waterson, J. (2025). Egypt's Suez Canal revenue fell sharply in 2024 on regional tensions. *Euronews*. https://www.euronews.com/business/2025/04/17/egypts-suez-canal-revenue-fell-sharply-in-2024-on-regional-tensions

Landman, L. (2015). *The EU Maritime Security Strategy: Promoting or absorbing European defence cooperation?* Clingendael Institute.

Lv, J., & Qin, S. (2016). On low-carbon technology. *Low Carbon Economy*, *7*(3), 107–115. DOI: 10.4236/lce.2016.73010

Malnes, R. (1993). Robert E. Goodin: Green political theory [Book review]. *Scandinavian Political Studies*, *16*(2), 185–187. https://tidsskrift.dk/scandinavian_political_studies/article/download/32772/30993

Manship, H. K. (1964). Mahan's concepts of sea power: A lecture delivered at the Naval War College. *Naval War College Review, 16*(5), 15–30. https://www.jstor.org/stable/45236517

Misalucha-Willoughby, C. (2024). *Mixed messages and the EU's Indo-Pacific strategy*. The Hague Centre for Strategic Studies.

Nam, H. K. (2015). Green politics: An approach in international relations. *Political Theory*. https://lyluanchinhtri.vn/home/index.php/quoc-te/item/1005-chinh-tri-xanh-%E2%80%93-mot-cach-tiep-can-trong-quan-he-quoc-te.html

Nantulya, P. (2025). *China widening its influence in Africa through expanded security engagements*. Africa Center for Strategic Studies. https://africacenter.org/spotlight/china-influence-africa-security-engagements/

Ngo, D. L., & Hoang, H. T. (2025). The emerging Indo-Pacific strategy of the Trump 2.0 administration. *International Studies Review*. https://nghiencuuquocte.org/2025/06/13/chien-luoc-an-do-duong-thai-binh-duong-dang-hinh-thanh-cua-chinh-quyen-trump-2-0/

Nováky, N. (2022). The Coordinated Maritime Presences concept and the EU's naval ambitions in the Indo-Pacific. *European Foreign Affairs Review, 21*(1), 129–148. DOI: 10.1177/17816858221089871

Observatory of Economic Complexity. (2023). *EU*. https://oec.world/en/profile/international_organization/eu

Odgaard, L. (2023). Chinese perspectives on alliance and alignment: Entrapment concerns in China's foreign relations. *Asian Affairs, 54*(3), 432–452. DOI: 10.1080/03068374.2023.2230782

Pacheco Pardo, R., & Leveringhaus, N. (2022). *Security and defence in the Indo-Pacific: What is at stake for the EU and its strategy?* European Parliament Directorate-General for External Policies., DOI: 10.2861/10775

Piasentini, M. (2024). *The EU-ASEAN maritime cooperation: Sailing together to different courses?* Centre on Asia and Globalisation, Lee Kuan Yew School of Public Policy. https://lkyspp.nus.edu.sg/cag/publications/center-publications/publication-article/detail/the-eu-asean-maritime-cooperation-sailing-together-to-different-courses

Powell, W. W., & Bromley, P. (2015). New institutionalism in the analysis of complex organizations. *International encyclopedia of the social & behavioral sciences, 16*, 764-769.

Pratson, L. F. (2022). Assessing impacts to maritime shipping from marine chokepoint closures. *Communications in Transportation Research*, *2*, 100083. Advance online publication. DOI: 10.1016/j.commtr.2022.100083

Pugliese, G. (2024). The European Union and an "Indo-Pacific" alignment. *Asia-Pacific Review*, *37*(1), 17–44. DOI: 10.1080/13439006.2024.2334182

Sarno, G. S., & Colantoni, L. (2023). *A changing energy diplomacy: The external dimension of the REPowerEU plan* (IAI Papers 23|05). Istituto Affari Internazionali.

Suri, M. (2023). *Explaining EU maritime security cooperation through the Coordinated Maritime Presences tool*. FINABEL – The European Army Interoperability Centre.

U.S. Energy Information Administration. (2016). *Algeria energy profile: Leading natural gas producer in Africa – Analysis*. Eurasia Review. https://www.eurasiareview.com/15032016-algeria-energy-profile-leading-natural-gas-producer-in-africa-analysis/

U.S. Energy Information Administration. (2024a). *World oil transit chokepoints*. https://www.eia.gov/international/analysis/special-topics/World_Oil_Transit_Chokepoints

U.S. Energy Information Administration. (2024b). *Amid regional conflict, the Strait of Hormuz remains critical oil chokepoint*. https://www.eia.gov/todayinenergy/detail.php?id=65504

Williams, P. D., & Ali, H. Y. (2020). *The European Union training mission in Somalia: An assessment* (SIPRI Background Paper). Stockholm International Peace Research Institute. https://www.sipri.org/sites/default/files/2020-11/bp_2011_eutm_somalia_0.pdf

Chapter 3
Strategic Stewardship: India's Role in Balancing Maritime Power in the Indo-Pacific Region

Shruti Rathore
https://orcid.org/0000-0002-9132-3977
Christ University, India

Judith Anne Lal
https://orcid.org/0009-0003-7198-8685
Christ University, India

ABSTRACT

This chapter examines India's Indo-Pacific maritime vision through soft balancing theory, analyzing how New Delhi navigates China's regional assertiveness while managing internal capability constraints. India's approach integrates normative leadership through UNCLOS advocacy and the evolution from SAGAR to MAHASAGAR doctrine with strategic partnerships via the QUAD, bilateral engagements with Japan and Australia, and ASEAN-centric diplomacy. These frameworks collectively demonstrate India's commitment to a rules-based, free, and open Indo-Pacific order. However, critical gaps exist between ambition and capability: India's naval modernization faces delays, budgetary constraints limit fleet expansion, and defense-industrial weaknesses persist. The study reveals that while India successfully positions itself as a responsible regional actor and norm-setter, realizing its Indo-Pacific vision requires bridging this capability gap through increased naval investment, indigenous defense production, and sustained strategic partnerships.

DOI: 10.4018/979-8-3373-4470-6.ch003

1. INTRODUCTION

The Indo-Pacific has emerged as a critical strategic theater in the 21st century. Encompassing both the Indian and Pacific Oceans, this vast region has witnessed intensified economic integration, cultural exchange, and strategic competition. The term "Indo-Pacific" has gained considerable traction in recent decades, driven by several converging factors: contemporary maritime security challenges, great power rivalry between the United States and China amid Beijing's expansionist posture, and the growing influence of middle powers such as India, Japan, and Australia (Hiep et al., 2024). The region also contains vital strategic chokepoints—the Straits of Malacca, Hormuz, and Bab-el-Mandeb—through which enormous volumes of global trade transit.

As India positions itself as a key Indo-Pacific actor, it has articulated a maritime vision aligned with its national interests. New Delhi champions a "Free, Open, and Inclusive Indo-Pacific" (FOIIP) in accordance with the United Nations Convention on the Law of the Sea (UNCLOS). This vision was initially conceptualized through the Security and Growth for All in the Region (SAGAR) doctrine, which aimed to advance regional cooperation and security. Subsequently, this was elevated to the Mutual and Holistic Advancement for Security and Growth Across Regions (MAHASAGAR) doctrine, reflecting broader geographic and strategic ambitions.

China's rise presents multifaceted challenges to India's national security. Beijing's assertive infrastructure initiatives—notably the Belt and Road Initiative (BRI) and the String of Pearls strategy—have altered regional security dynamics, particularly in the Indian Ocean Region (IOR), where India is widely acknowledged as a resident power (Kiet et al., 2025a). Evolving security dynamics and non-traditional threats have catalyzed India's proactive regional engagement. India addresses these challenges through external partnerships with like-minded nations, exemplified by the Quadrilateral Security Dialogue (QUAD), aimed at establishing a favorable, rules-based, democratic order in the Indo-Pacific. These issue-based coalitions are interest-driven and provide tangible benefits to regional stakeholders. Beyond minilateral frameworks, India pursues bilateral partnerships—with Japan and Australia, for instance—encompassing strategic, economic, and defense cooperation. The Association of Southeast Asian Nations (ASEAN) occupies a central position in India's Indo-Pacific vision, situated at the intersection of the Indian and Pacific Oceans, with ASEAN Centrality closely aligned with India's Act East Policy (AEP) (Kiet et al., 2025b).

Nevertheless, significant challenges persist. Externally, India confronts an asymmetric power balance with China. Beijing's increasing assertiveness compels India to respond across multiple domains—diplomatic, economic, and military. Internally, however, India's expanding naval capability gap and defense production constraints expose a widening disconnect between ambition and capacity. These dual constraints render India's position fragile. Regional actors perceive India as a resident power capable of counterbalancing Chinese assertiveness in the Indian Ocean. However, to emerge as an indispensable partner, India must narrow this ambition-capability gap.

2. THEORETICAL FRAMEWORK

Soft balancing constitutes a non-military approach to constraining a relatively powerful state by undermining and raising the costs of its unilateral actions, without forming formal alliances (Hiep et al., 2023). Unlike military or hard power balancing, soft balancing relies on economic, institutional, and diplomatic instruments. In the Indo-Pacific context, India exerts diplomatic pressure on China—a comparatively stronger regional actor with expansionist tendencies. India conducts joint naval exercises with partner nations, including the Japan-India Maritime Exercise (JIMEX), AUSINDEX, and MALABAR, to enhance interoperability and operational readiness. India and the United States maintain various defense and security agreements—the Logistics Exchange Memorandum of Agreement (LEMOA), the Communications Compatibility and Security Agreement (COMCASA), and the Basic Exchange and Cooperation Agreement (BECA)—demonstrating deep bilateral cooperation. India adheres to UNCLOS and a rules-based order while explicitly criticizing China's unilateral South China Sea actions as destabilizing. By championing UNCLOS principles, India positions itself as a responsible regional actor and norm-setter committed to a free, open, and inclusive Indo-Pacific.

Regarding institutional balancing, India participates in various security, economic, and developmental frameworks including QUAD, the Indo-Pacific Economic Framework (IPEF), and ASEAN-led forums such as the East Asia Summit (EAS) and the ASEAN Defence Ministers' Meeting Plus (ADMM-Plus). Through these platforms, India advances its Indo-Pacific vision by shaping norms and rules rather than directly countering expansionist powers through hard power. These institutions function as agenda-setting mechanisms where like-minded nations collaborate toward common goals: freedom of navigation, openness, inclusivity, and a rules-based order. QUAD joint statements consistently emphasize freedom of navigation and critique unilateral South China Sea status quo changes, implicitly targeting China's coercive tactics and gray-zone operations. Thus, India leverages institutions and multilateral forums to shape a just order without forming formal alliances, counterbalancing coercion through institutions and norms rather than force.

3. FROM ASIA-PACIFIC TO INDO-PACIFIC: HISTORICAL EVOLUTION, STRATEGIC SHIFTS, AND EMERGING REALITIES

The transition from "Asia-Pacific" to "Indo-Pacific" reflects contemporary strategic realities, with major regional stakeholders incorporating "Indo-Pacific" into official policy documents. The region's growing significance is exemplified by the United States renaming the United States Pacific Command (PACOM) to United States Indo-Pacific Command (USINDOPACOM) in 2018, acknowledging the interconnectedness of the Indian and Pacific Oceans.

3.1. Historical Trajectories of the Indian and Pacific Oceans

The Indian and Pacific Oceans, historically distinct geographical entities, have served as crucial theaters for global commerce, cultural exchange, and strategic competition. The Indian Ocean functioned as an early arena for global maritime exchanges, connecting Africa, the Indian subcontinent, the Arabian Peninsula, and Southeast Asia. This maritime space facilitated trade in spices, textiles, precious metals, and ceramics while serving as a conduit for cultural and religious diffusion—Buddhism, Islam, and Hinduism—as well as ideas, artistic forms, and scientific knowledge. Cities such as Calicut, Aden, Muscat, Malacca, and Zanzibar became cosmopolitan hubs, illustrating the ocean's role in early globalization. The Indian Ocean witnessed naval expeditions and commercial diplomacy by empires including the Cholas, Srivijaya, and later the Sultanates of Oman and the Mughal Empire (Manoharan, 2025).

In contrast, the Pacific Ocean's vast expanse and numerous isolated islands initially limited its integration into global networks. Nevertheless, indigenous navigational cultures, particularly Polynesian seafarers, demonstrated remarkable maritime prowess through long-distance voyages connecting Pacific islands long before European contact (Shaka Tribe, n.d.).

The Pacific Ocean's strategic and historical significance was profoundly shaped by the Manila Galleon Trade (1565–1815). Following Spanish conquest of the Americas, this trans-Pacific route connected Manila with Acapulco in New Spain (present-day Mexico), establishing the first sustained maritime link between Asia and the Americas. This trade route not only became the longest-lasting in history but also embedded the Pacific within the emerging global economy, facilitating cross-cultural contact among Asia, the Americas, and Europe—three continents with vastly distinct belief systems, artistic traditions, and social customs (Fisher, 1988).

Together, the Indian and Pacific Oceans have historically shaped trajectories of empire, warfare, commerce, and culture. Their historical relevance extends beyond their peripheries to their role in structuring world orders across centuries. Understanding their past significance establishes essential groundwork for comprehending their present and future strategic value.

3.2. Shift from Asia-Pacific to Indo-Pacific

During the Cold War, the "Asia-Pacific" construct emerged, encompassing Asian territories bordering the Pacific Ocean—primarily East Asia, Southeast Asia, Oceania, and Pacific Rim economies including the United States and Canada. Asia-Pacific was predominantly an economic rather than security conception, institutionalized through the Asia Pacific Economic Cooperation (APEC) in 1989, comprising 21 economies aimed at leveraging regional interdependence and creating greater prosperity through economic integration (Australian Government: Department of Foreign Affairs and Trade, n.d.). This framework operated on a United States hub-and-spokes model, wherein the United States functioned as the dominant hub projecting power through bilateral relationships (spokes), while the spokes maintained weak or no direct connections, creating a centralized, asymmetric security architecture (Hunt, 2024). This Pacific-centric framework marginalized the Indian Ocean and underplayed South Asia and the Arabian Sea's importance.

The Indo-Pacific as a geopolitical concept emerged in the 21st century, broadly understood as an interconnected space linking the Indian and Pacific Oceans. Different nations define the region's geographical expanse differently: the United States delineates it from India's west coast to the United States Pacific shores, while India extends it from the western American coast to the Middle East and eastern Africa. Unlike the Asia-Pacific frame that placed India peripherally, the Indo-Pacific construct positions India centrally at the Indian Ocean's midpoint, situating it at the heart of a key 21st-century geostrategic and geoeconomic domain (Ladwig, 2024).

The Indo-Pacific's recent prominence reflects recognition that the Indian and Pacific Oceans constitute linked strategic theaters—a single geopolitical continuum shaped by trade flows, naval power projection, and critical infrastructure development (Medcalf, 2019). Emerging geopolitical realities—particularly China's rise (challenging United States hegemony), India's ascent, and the securitization of Sea Lines of Communication (SLOCs)—underscore the Indo-Pacific's 21st-century importance. Unlike the Asia-Pacific framework emphasizing economic and continental dimensions led by United States bilateral security alliances, the Indo-Pacific shifts focus toward maritime multipolarity, issue-based coalitions, and networked security.

3.3. The Indo-Pacific Construct

The term "Indo-Pacific" traces its origins to the early 20th century, first used by German geopolitical scholar Karl Haushofer in the 1920s ("Indopazifischen

Raum") and later referenced by Indian historian Kalidas Nag in the 1940s (Pulipaka & Musaddi, 2021). Captain (Dr.) Gurpreet Khurana's 2007 article "Security of Sea Lines: Prospects for India-Japan Cooperation" in the IDSA journal Strategic Analysis marked a precursor to Indo-Pacific concept acceptance and maritime domain significance. This notion was strengthened by Japanese Prime Minister Shinzo Abe's August 2007 Indian Parliament speech, "Confluence of the Two Seas," advancing the connected Indian-Pacific Ocean region concept. Abe remarked

> *"Now, as this new 'broader Asia' takes shape at the confluence of the two seas of the Indian and Pacific Oceans, I feel that it is imperative that the democratic nations located at opposite edges of these seas deepen the friendship among their citizens at every possible level," highlighting the region's growing strategic and economic significance (Ministry of Foreign Affairs of Japan, 2007).*

The region is a global trade hotspot, with an estimated two-thirds of global energy flows and over 90 percent of international trade by volume traversing its sea lanes (Baruah et al., 2023). This economic centrality makes SLOC security a universal concern, as trade disruptions negatively impact states. The region contains several critical maritime chokepoints functioning as lifelines for global trade and energy security.

Strait of Malacca: Considered the most strategically important chokepoint in global geopolitics and international trade, the Strait of Malacca runs between Sumatra (Indonesia) to the west and peninsular Malaysia and southern Thailand to the east, covering approximately 25,000 square miles (65,000 square km). It constitutes the main shipping channel between the Indian and Pacific Oceans and the shortest route for Middle Eastern oil and natural gas supplies to East and Southeast Asia. As of 2023, the strait handled 23.7 million barrels per day (b/d) of oil flow and managed approximately 100,000 vessels annually, underscoring its strategic relevance (United States Energy Information Administration, 2024).

Strait of Hormuz: The most important oil chokepoint, facilitating 20.9 million b/d (2023)—roughly 20 percent of global petroleum consumption. Located between Oman and Iran, it connects the Persian Gulf with the Gulf of Oman and Arabian Sea. The strait's stability is vital for the global economy and energy supply, making it a matter of international concern. Saudi Arabia's East-West crude oil pipeline transports oil to the Red Sea, while the UAE's Abu Dhabi crude oil pipeline routes oil to the Gulf of Oman, both bypassing the strait to reduce dependency, as any blockade or disruption would severely hamper energy trade and security.

Strait of Bab-el-Mandeb: Situated between the Horn of Africa and the Middle East, this chokepoint connects the Red Sea to the Gulf of Aden and Arabian Sea. Its relevance was exemplified during the 2021 Ever Given incident, when a single ship blocking the Suez Canal for six days caused approximately USD 9 billion daily losses in global trade. Most Persian Gulf oil exports through the Suez Canal and

Sumed pipeline must pass through this strait. In the first half of 2023, approximately 9.2 million barrels per day passed through the Suez Canal, accounting for about 9 percent of global demand—a 4.1 percent increase compared to 2021. If the strait were closed, the Sumed pipeline would become the sole oil transportation means for most Persian Gulf exporters (Qiao et al., 2024).

The Indo-Pacific is also characterized by intensifying United States-China geopolitical rivalry amid Beijing's regional expansionism and assertiveness. Launched in 2013, China's ambitious BRI has generated anxieties among regional actors and the United States. The BRI encompasses a vast infrastructure and investment network across Asia, Africa, and Europe. While promoted as fostering economic connectivity and shared prosperity, its dual-use infrastructure investments—ports, railways, and digital networks—are scrutinized for potential military applications that could facilitate People's Liberation Army (PLA) global expansion, create footholds, and blur lines between commercial development and military projection (Russel & Berger, 2020).

Another facet of Chinese expansionism is the String of Pearls strategy, coined in a 2005 United States consultancy Booz Allen Hamilton report predicting China would expand its naval presence throughout the IOR by building maritime civilian infrastructure in friendly regional states. This analytical construct posited China's burgeoning naval presence as strategically located civilian dual-use maritime infrastructure projects across the Indian Ocean—"pearls" ranging from upgraded Hainan Island facilities and artificial South China Sea islands to port developments in Chittagong, Hambantota, Gwadar, and Djibouti, viewed as potential naval outposts providing logistical support and extending China's maritime reach. Despite Beijing's denials and 2013 rebranding as the "21st Century Maritime Silk Road" (part of broader BRI), concerns persisted, particularly for nations like India viewing it as a thinly veiled String of Pearls continuation (Baker, 2015).

China's expansionism constitutes a core reason for creating a counter-narrative to its growing maritime Asian influence. While direct containment is rhetorically denied by several actors, the Indo-Pacific construct provides strategic grammar for balancing through naval posturing, infrastructure finance, and multilateral initiatives without explicitly invoking confrontational logic. Thus, the Indo-Pacific operates as a geopolitically fluid yet strategically disciplined imaginary (Zeng & Zhang, 2021).

The Indo-Pacific's growing economic significance necessitates heightened SLOC security. The region also faces non-traditional security threats ranging from piracy and armed robbery against ships, arms and human trafficking, and narcotics smuggling to Illegal, Unreported, and Unregulated (IUU) fishing, climate change, and natural disasters. The increasing assertiveness of middle powers—India, Japan, and Australia—is also shaping the region. These dynamics highlight the Indo-Pacific's multifaceted security architecture. India's response must be equally multidimensional, engaging proactively in regional frameworks, investing in Maritime Domain Awareness (MDA), and fostering multilateral partnerships. Through such calibrated engagement, India can promote regional stability, economic resilience, and strategic balance in an era of heightened competition and transformation, advancing a free, fair, rules-based order.

4. THE EVOLUTION OF INDIA'S MARITIME STRATEGY: FROM REGIONAL FOCUS TO GLOBAL VISION

Given current realities and geopolitical architecture, India has witnessed an evolution in its maritime vision, transforming from a regional security-driven approach to a more expansive, proactive vision projecting itself as a major Indo-Pacific maritime power, aiming not only to protect its own interests but also to balance power and safeguard other regional actors' interests.

4.1. Foundational Doctrines: From 'Freedom to Use' to 'Secure Seas'

India's maritime vision has undergone profound transformation, evolving from a traditionally conservative posture to a more assertive, expansive vision. The Indian Naval Maritime Doctrine 2015, formally titled "Ensuring Secure Seas: Indian Maritime Security Strategy" (IMSS-2015), represents a significant strategic shift from its predecessor, "Freedom to Use the Seas: India's Maritime Military Strategy" (IMMS-2007). The new doctrine expands India's primary areas of national interest to encompass a larger Indian Ocean portion, explicitly aiming to achieve maritime leadership. This foundational document broadens its scope to address dynamic geopolitical linkages, acknowledging non-traditional threats and organized crime. It formally codifies the Indian Navy's counter-piracy and humanitarian roles, aligning hard-power ambitions with soft-power projection, positioning India as a responsible maritime stakeholder. The doctrine's emphasis on concepts and international law—freedom of navigation and UNCLOS—provides normative foundations for India's strategic vision (Ministry of Defence, 2015).

4.2. The SAGAR and MAHASAGAR Vision: A Conceptual Ascent

Complementing India's maritime doctrine is its IOR vision—the Security and Growth for All in the Region (SAGAR) Doctrine—articulated by Prime Minister Modi on March 12, 2015, during the Mauritius National Coast Guard Ship Barracuda commissioning ceremony. Prime Minister Modi articulated the SAGAR vision as follows

> *"Our vision for the Indian Ocean Region is rooted in advancing cooperation in our region and using our capabilities for the benefit of all in our common maritime home" (Sarangi, 2020).*

The Indian Navy constitutes the most important maritime diplomacy pillar, operationalizing its role through joint exercises, Humanitarian Assistance and Disaster Relief (HADR) operations, and capacity-building measures. India acts as a first responder and net security provider regionally. India's defense exports reached USD 2.76 billion in FY 2024-25, demonstrating upward trajectory and greater geopolitical influence (Chakraborty, 2025). This includes defense equipment exports through grants or defense lines of credit to partner nations upon request. The SAGAR doctrine espouses maritime security cooperation, institutionalized through the Indian Ocean Naval Symposium (IONS), an Indian Navy initiative launched in 2008. IONS is a 25-member voluntary security construct among IOR littoral states' navies and maritime security agencies, conducting biennial meetings to discuss regional security issues and promote friendly relations among member states (Durai, 2025). Table 1 summarizes major Indian overseas Indo-Pacific operations, highlighting objectives, engagement regions, and outcomes.

The SAGAR Doctrine was elevated to MAHASAGAR during Prime Minister Modi's 2025 official Mauritius visit. Just as 'Sagar' in Sanskrit means 'sea,' 'Mahasagar' denotes 'ocean.' This shift signifies a significant leap from regional focus to global maritime vision (Chinoy, 2025). The SAGAR-to-MAHASAGAR shift showcases India's growing ambition and Indo-Pacific outreach, aspiring to become a leading power and net security provider while establishing a free, open, inclusive regional order.

Table 1. Major Indian overseas operations in the Indo-Pacific

Operation	Year	Category	Region/Country	Objectives/Outcomes
Operation Cactus	1988	Military/Security	Maldives (IOR)	Foiled coup, restored government
Operation Sukoon	2006	Evacuation (NEO)	Lebanon (WANA link to IOR)	Evacuated 2,280 people (Indians + foreign nationals)
Operation Raahat	2015	Evacuation (NEO)	Yemen	Evacuated 4,640 Indians and 960 foreign nationals from 41+ countries
Operation Sahayata	2019	HADR	Mozambique (Cyclone Idai)	Relief supplies, medical aid, support teams
Operation Vanilla	2020	HADR	Madagascar (Cyclone Diane)	Delivered relief material and medical teams

continued on following page

Table 1. Continued

Operation	Year	Category	Region/Country	Objectives/Outcomes
Operation Samudra Setu	2020	Evacuation (COVID-19)	Multiple IOR/Indo-Pacific ports	Repatriated 3,992 Indians stranded abroad
Operation Dost	2023	HADR	Türkiye & Syria	Earthquake relief: search and rescue, field hospital, relief supplies

Source: Author's compilation from multiple sources

5. THE INTERNAL CALCULUS: A NAVAL CAPABILITY GAP

India's greatest challenge in realizing its growing Indo-Pacific ambitions and balancing role lies in the widening naval capability gap and need for domestic capability rejuvenation. Despite maritime goals outlined in IMSS-2015 and the SAGAR-MAHASAGAR framework, naval modernization delays due to cost overruns or industrial bottlenecks directly challenge this vision. The Indian Navy's goal of becoming a 200-ship force by 2027 was revised in 2019 to 170, citing acute financial constraints (Philip, 2025). The Indian Navy currently operates 130 medium- to large-sized vessels, many aging and requiring replacement (Martin, 2024). This contrasts sharply with China, which operates a 351-ship battle force fleet, surpassing even the United States Navy.

The long-delayed Project-75 India (P-75I), initiated in 1997 for diesel-electric submarine procurement, experiences delays due to program complexities and lengthy construction timeframes. The deal, worth over Rs 71,000 crore (USD 8.2 billion), significantly exceeds the Rs 43,000 crore benchmark initially set by the Ministry of Defense, raising cost overrun concerns. Deliveries will be delayed to the 2030s, years behind schedule (Sagar, 2025). This contradiction between India's forward-looking maritime dominance aspiration and defense-industrial base structural weaknesses highlights its naval buildup fragility.

The submarine fleet represents an even more acute vulnerability. India operates only a limited number of nuclear-powered and conventional submarines, falling far behind China's rapidly expanding undersea fleet, which provides Beijing both deterrence and sea-denial advantages. Compounding this challenge is India's dependence on foreign suppliers for critical technologies, with indigenous shipbuilding programs frequently delayed and over budget. Although India has strengthened MDA through initiatives like the Information Fusion Centre–Indian Ocean Region (IFC-IOR), persistent gaps remain in long-range surveillance, anti-submarine warfare capabilities, and satellite coverage.

Logistical constraints further limit India's credible blue-water navy function. Recent logistics-sharing agreements—LEMOA and BECA with the United States, and similar arrangements with France and Australia—have expanded operational reach. However, these remain modest compared to China's expanding overseas basing infrastructure, which already includes facilities in Djibouti, Gwadar, and Hambantota. Budgetary limitations exacerbate challenges: the Navy continues receiving only 15-16 percent of India's overall defense budget, curbing modernization and force expansion investment (Jha, 2023).

The technological deficit adds another capability gap dimension. Indigenous development of critical platforms—nuclear attack submarines (SSNs), carrier aviation technologies, and advanced missile systems—lags considerably, maintaining India's reliance on foreign imports. This dependence affects operational readiness, with spare parts shortages, maintenance backlogs, and overstretched deployments undermining sustained frontline warship and aircraft availability. These limitations collectively highlight the widening disparity between India's maritime aspirations and naval capabilities, complicating its ability to assume a central Indo-Pacific security role. This gap constitutes a primary threat to India's long-term strategic balancer role fulfillment, as robust diplomatic frameworks require credible military backing.

6. ANCHORING THE RULES-BASED ORDER: INDIA'S ADHERENCE TO UNCLOS

Given emerging maritime complexities, security challenges, and capability gaps, UNCLOS serves as the foundational legal framework facilitating state behavior and maritime cooperation.

6.1. UNCLOS as a Foundational Framework

Regarded as the "constitution of the oceans," UNCLOS provides foundational principles for oceanic use, defining rights and obligations in specified maritime zones. Signed in 1982 and entering force in 1994, the treaty has been ratified by 169 countries, with India ratifying it on June 29, 1995 (Marine Insight, 2024). UNCLOS delineates distinct maritime zones with specific rights and jurisdictions, measured from a country's baseline—typically the low-water line along the coast (see Table 2).

Table 2. Maritime zones under UNCLOS

Maritime Zone	Distance from Baseline	Sovereignty/Jurisdiction	Coastal State Rights
Internal Waters	Landward side of baseline	Full sovereignty, same as land territory	Complete control over laws, resources, and access
Territorial Sea	Up to 12 nautical miles (nm)	Sovereignty extends to airspace, seabed, and subsoil	Right to enforce laws, regulate use, and exploit resources; foreign ships have innocent passage right
Contiguous Zone	12–24 nm	Limited jurisdiction	Can enforce laws relating to customs, immigration, sanitation, and taxation
Exclusive Economic Zone (EEZ)	12–200 nm	Sovereign rights (not full sovereignty)	Right to explore, exploit, conserve, and manage natural resources (fisheries, oil, gas, wind energy)
Continental Shelf	Natural land territory prolongation (can extend beyond 200 nm)	Sovereign rights over seabed and subsoil for resource exploitation	Rights to explore and exploit seabed and subsoil mineral and non-living resources
High Seas	Beyond EEZ (beyond 200 nm)	No state sovereignty; open to all states	Freedoms of navigation, overflight, fishing, scientific research, and laying submarine cables/pipelines

Source: Author's compilation based on UNCLOS (1982)

With an EEZ of approximately 2.37 million square kilometers (18th largest globally), India's jurisdiction surpasses its surveillance and enforcement capacity (National Centre for Polar and Ocean Research, n.d.). As Table 2 depicts, territorial seas equate to sovereignty, while EEZs equate to sovereign rights (not full sovereignty). India's EEZ encompasses the Lakshadweep Islands (Laccadive Sea) and Andaman and Nicobar Islands (Bay of Bengal and Andaman Sea), representing two of the most strategically important IOR maritime areas. These strategic Indian maritime areas lie in zones where international law rather than national jurisdiction takes precedence. This constitutes an important reason for India championing UNCLOS, aiming to establish a rules-based order in its maritime sphere dependent on collective security and shared norms enshrined in its charter. This serves dual purposes: first, establishing a just order in its EEZ and overall regional peace and security; second, complementing its material limitations and capability gaps by being a norm-setter and rules-based maritime order champion.

6.2. India's Principled Stance: Freedom of Navigation as a Diplomatic Tool

India's UNCLOS adherence constitutes a central statecraft and balancing strategy pillar. By consistently invoking UNCLOS, India frames its own actions and partnerships as legitimate and internationally law-based, while implicitly casting China's unilateral South China Sea actions as illegal and destabilizing. This represents powerful soft-power balancing, building a support coalition among rules-based order-committed nations, providing common ideological foundations for strategic partnerships.

India's South China Sea stance can be understood through law-centric balancing. India has reaffirmed support for freedom of navigation and overflight in South China Sea maritime waters. India firmly anchors its position under UNCLOS, operationalizes that stance in maritime waters, then institutionalizes it in bilateral texts, thereby undercutting China's "no third party" narrative.

In the 2016 Permanent Court of Arbitration ruling in Philippines v. China, the court ruled in the Philippines' favor regarding China's expansionist claims, including its nine-dash line, land reclamation activities, and activities in Philippine waters. China declared the ruling null and void, stating the United Nations holds no position on the case or disputed claims (Campbell & Salidjanova, 2016). This sheer arbitration ruling dismissal constituted a direct liberal institutional order challenge. Regarding this case, India's Ministry of External Affairs (MEA) stated it had "noted the Award" and "reiterates the importance of freedom of navigation, overflight, and unimpeded commerce, as reflected notably in UNCLOS," framing India's interest as rule-of-law-based, not claimant-specific (Ministry of External Affairs, 2016).

India and the Philippines conducted their first joint South China Sea sail and naval drill on August 3-4, 2025, involving INS Delhi, INS Kiltan, and INS Shakti alongside the Philippines' BRP Miguel Malvar and BRP Jose Rizal, demonstrating India's legal position transcending into reality and interoperability (Aljazeera, 2025). China protested, reviving its "third-party interference" line (Gomez, 2025). When pressed on the exercise, MEA Secretary (East) P. Kumaran publicly restated India's doctrine

> *We support freedom of navigation and legitimate commerce through the waters of the South China Sea. India has an abiding interest in peace and stability in the region. Our position is based on the UNCLOS. India also believes that any differences between the parties concerned should be resolved peacefully, without resorting to threat or force." This ties Indian activity directly to UNCLOS and not bloc politics (The Telegraph, 2025).*

The Philippines President H.E. Mr. Ferdinand R. Marcos Jr.'s August 4-8, 2025 state visit marked a pivotal milestone when India-Philippines ties were elevated to a strategic partnership, aiming at political cooperation; defense, security, and maritime cooperation; economic, trade, and investment cooperation; science and technology cooperation; connectivity; consular cooperation; mutual legal and judicial cooperation; culture, tourism, and people-to-people exchanges; and regional, multilateral, and international cooperation. The MEA declaration contended full UNCLOS adherence, respecting freedom of navigation and overflight and rule of law. The statement further noted the 2016 Philippines v. China arbitration as final and binding—an important milestone in resolving maritime disputes peacefully according to international law (Ministry of External Affairs, 2025a; Ministry of External Affairs, 2025c).

India-Philippines diplomatic relations were established in 1949, with 2024 marking 75 years of bilateral ties. The Philippines became the first Southeast Asian nation receiving India's BrahMos cruise missiles, with two batches dispatched in 2024 and 2025, and the final batch anticipated by end-2025, completing the USD 375 million defense contract signed in 2022 (Patel, 2025). This deal benefits both nations: enhancing Philippine Marine Corps advanced coastal defense capability while expanding India's defense and diplomatic Southeast Asian reach (complementing India's Act East Policy and MAHASAGAR vision). Diplomatically, India-Philippines ties strengthened with the Philippines introducing visa-free entry for Indian tourists and India extending free e-visa facilities to Filipinos. Although India-Philippines bilateral trade remains modest at USD 3.3 billion in 2024-25, efforts are underway to elevate the relationship, helping India advance Indo-Pacific strategic objectives and supporting Philippine diplomatic and strategic partnership diversification (Mishra, 2025).

7. THE ARCHITECTURE OF BALANCING: CASE STUDIES IN MARITIME DIPLOMACY

While UNCLOS provides India a stronghold as norm-setter and rules-based order advocate in the Indo-Pacific, India's partnerships with like-minded nations are equally important for establishing an inclusive, prosperous regional order while facilitating India's balance of competing strategic pressures.

7.1. Balancing Through Partnerships: India and the QUAD's Maritime Architecture

The QUAD, comprising four democracies—India, Japan, Australia, and the United States—was catalyzed as a response to the Indian Ocean earthquake-triggered tsunami. QUAD owes its origin to the Tsunami Core Group, a multilateral disaster relief and humanitarian assistance informal alliance announced by United States President George W. Bush on December 29, 2004, to deliver coordinated tsunami-hit area responses. Seen as having non-military genesis, QUAD continues influencing its "public goods" focus. The group was subsequently disbanded, only to return to prominence in 2007 with Japanese Prime Minister Shinzo Abe's Indian Parliament address titled "Confluence of the Two Seas," wherein he reflected on the Indian and Pacific Ocean confluence, viewing them as "seas of freedom and prosperity." Unfortunately, QUAD 1.0 failed to sustain as comprehensive partnership for reasons attributed to Japanese and Australian leadership changes (Shinzo Abe resigned, and Australian Prime Minister John Howard lost his seat to Kevin Rudd, who avoided antagonizing China due to huge economic dependency), United States Afghanistan-Pakistan region investment, China's uneasiness (equating QUAD with Asian NATO), and lack of strong leadership (Choudhury, 2021).

QUAD was revitalized in 2017 (QUAD 2.0) to build and sustain a favorable, rules-based, democratic Indo-Pacific order based on shared values. China's maritime coercive activities necessitated QUAD nation collaboration to address shared challenges and defend freedom of navigation, regional peace, and stability. However, while the United States initially viewed QUAD as a potential military grouping, India carefully maintained strategic autonomy. New Delhi consistently resisted framing QUAD as a military alliance, instead positioning it as a platform for dialogue, cooperation, and issue-based alignment without compromising independent foreign policy choices.

QUAD focuses on building collaboration in non-traditional security areas, with working groups including the Working Group on Counterterrorism, the QUAD Vaccine Partnership, and the QUAD Climate Working Group. The Indo-Pacific Partnership for Maritime Domain Awareness (IPMDA), introduced at the 2022 Tokyo Summit, aims to monitor dark shipping and create more comprehensive, precise real-time maritime overviews of partner nations' waters. The QUAD Partnership for Cable Connectivity initiative pools resources for resilient subsea cable networks, reducing regional dependence on Chinese-operated vessels. These initiatives highlight that collaborative frameworks can be built on comprehensive, issue-specific cooperation rather than strictly military alignments, reinforcing QUAD's character as a flexible, interest-driven partnership rather than formal alliance. This focus on practical, non-military cooperation provides tangible benefits to all Indo-Pacific nations, building interdependence and trust webs that attract nations wary of choosing sides in great power rivalry, ultimately broadening the rules-based order coalition (Financial Express, 2024).

7.2. Bilateral Pillars: Japan and Australia

India's strategic balancing extends beyond multilateral frameworks to bilateral partnerships, notably with QUAD counterparts Japan and Australia. These partnerships expand India's options and bargaining power by ensuring its Indo-Pacific security and influence do not depend on a single country or alliance. Instead, India creates overlapping relationship networks that collectively act as regional instability deterrents. By strengthening these bilateral pillars alongside multilateral commitments, India maintains decision-making independence while contributing to wider Indo-Pacific cooperation and trust architecture. Table 3 elucidates key bilateral partnerships between India and major Indo-Pacific stakeholders—Japan and Australia.

Table 3. Key bilateral partnerships strengthening India's Indo-Pacific strategy: Japan and Australia

Partner	Key Frameworks/Agreements	Major Exercises/Initiatives	Strategic Significance
Japan	India and Japan elevated relations to a "Special Strategic and Global Partnership" in 2014, signaling long-term economic, defense, and strategic interest convergence. The partnership was strengthened by the "Acquisition and Cross-Servicing Agreement" (2020), promoting active defense cooperation and providing military logistics support—including supplies and services—to each other's armed forces during joint exercises, training, and UN peacekeeping operations.	Defense cooperation manifests through regular engagements such as the Japan–India Maritime Exercise (JIMEX), which has grown in scope and complexity, and the annual Dharma Guardian military exercise focusing on joint urban warfare and counter-terrorism drills under UN mandate. Japan participates in the MALABAR naval exercise alongside the United States and Australia, strengthening interoperability and joint operational planning at the multilateral level.	These initiatives reflect a shared "Free and Open Indo-Pacific" vision, enhance operational synergy across land and maritime domains, secure critical sea lanes underpinning regional trade, and counterbalance China's assertive East and South China Sea posture. For India, Japan is also a trusted economic and technological partner, linking strategic cooperation with infrastructure and supply chain resilience.
Australia	India and Australia elevated ties to a "Comprehensive Strategic Partnership" in 2020, underpinned by the "Mutual Logistics Support Agreement" (2020), enabling reciprocal military base and logistics access, and supported by the institutionalized 2+2 Ministerial Dialogue providing strategic guidance across defense and foreign policy domains. The partnership has expanded from primarily maritime focus to comprehensive security relationships covering land, sea, air, cyber, and emerging technologies.	This growing cooperation is demonstrated through the AUSINDEX naval exercise enhancing maritime security and cooperation; the annual AUSTRAHIND military exercise since 2022 enhancing interoperability in conducting joint subconventional operations in semi-urban/semi-desert terrain environments under Chapter VII UN mandate; and participation in Australia's Pitch Black air exercise, where India deploys frontline aircraft alongside other Indo-Pacific partners. Additionally, India and Australia conduct coordinated Indian Ocean patrols, collaborate in MALABAR naval exercises, and have increased joint participation in India's MILAN multilateral naval exercise, reflecting converging regional roles.	These initiatives collectively expand India's strategic Pacific footprint, establish genuine tri-service interoperability across army, navy, and air force, and strengthen logistical and operational synergy. They also deepen mutual QUAD trust, reinforce shared maritime security commitments, and help India diversify its security architecture beyond United States-centric approaches, making Australia a pivotal Indo-Pacific strategy partner.

Source: Author's compilation based on multiple sources

7.3. The ASEAN Nexus

India's ASEAN engagement constitutes a foundational Indo-Pacific vision pillar, deeply shaped by the Act East Policy launched in 2014. India's ASEAN engagement is crucial for counterbalancing China, as it advocates the ASEAN Outlook on the Indo-Pacific (AOIP), which aims to ensure an open, inclusive, rules-based regional order. India-ASEAN relations have grown rapidly from sectoral dialogue partnership in 1992 to full-fledged dialogue partnership in 1996. The India-ASEAN Free Trade Agreement (FTA) was signed in 2009, with the FTA in services signed in 2014. India and ASEAN collaborate on broader security domains—counter-terrorism, cybersecurity, disaster relief, and climate resilience—through platforms like the ASEAN Regional Forum (ARF) and ADMM-Plus. These mechanisms enhance India's Southeast Asian engagement as a regional security partner without undermining ASEAN Centrality (Ministry of External Affairs, 2025b).

During Singapore Prime Minister Mr. Lawrence Wong's official September 2-4, 2025 India visit, a new Comprehensive Strategic Partnership (CSP) roadmap was announced aimed at advancing collaboration in: (i) Economic Cooperation; (ii) Skills Development; (iii) Digitalization; (iv) Sustainability; (v) Connectivity; (vi) Healthcare and Medicine; (vii) People-to-People and Cultural Exchanges; and (viii) Defense and Security Cooperation. An important development was Singapore's "acknowledgement with appreciation" of India's interest in the Malacca Straits Patrol (Ministry of External Affairs, 2025d). The strait is a vital Chinese chokepoint, as over 70 percent of China's petroleum and Liquified Natural Gas (LNG) imports pass through it, making it critical to China's energy and trade security (Paszak, 2021). Beijing remains acutely sensitive to this maritime chokepoint disruptions, fearing potential United States or Indian Navy blockades cutting vital supplies. This strengthens India's regional position, capable of countering China's naval presence while demonstrating India's intent and capability to influence this critical chokepoint and reinforce regional stability commitment.

8. THE CHINA CHALLENGE: A "NOOSE" OF DUAL-USE PORTS

Despite India's strategic Indo-Pacific vision, it confronts rising China and its deepening 30-year naval modernization, which has transformed China's navy into a much more modern, capable force. The People's Liberation Army Navy (PLAN) is the world's largest navy in vessel terms, conducting growing numbers of operations within China's near seas, further extending to Indian and Pacific Oceans and throughout Europe, causing anxieties among nations (Congressional Research Service, 2024).

China's BRI and String of Pearls represent calculated Chinese power projection with significant Indian national security architecture implications. Together, they exemplify strategic fusion of geoeconomic investments and geostrategic imperatives, altering Indo-Pacific—particularly IOR—regional security dynamics, wherein India traditionally asserts primacy. Commercial projects developed under these frameworks create dual-use facilities possessing logistical capabilities supporting naval operations, blurring economic-strategic intent lines. Gwadar Port in Pakistan and Hambantota Port in Sri Lanka exemplify this strategy. Gwadar Port's strategic location, just 70 kilometers from the Strait of Hormuz, provides China a vantage point over the world's most important oil artery and chokepoint. Hambantota Port, leased to China for 99 years after debt default, is often cited as a cautionary example. The PLAN vessel Yuan Wang 5's docking at Hambantota (August 2022), despite Indian diplomatic protests, reaffirmed PLA growing blue-water ambitions, raising alarm bells in New Delhi and reinforcing "pearls" perception as a strategic "noose" around India (Tan, 2022).

India shares an asymmetric power balance with China. China's strategy is not direct military confrontation but an approach blending economic leverage with military capability. Research indicates approximately 80 percent of China's government or government-supported loans are directed toward countries already experiencing some debt distress form, with over half of these loans now in repayment periods, leading to intensified debt trap diplomacy concerns. Estimates suggest China's total outstanding loans exceed USD 1.1 trillion (Green, 2024). China then uses this economic heft to influence strategic footholds—a tactic forcing India to respond on multiple fronts (diplomatic, economic, and military)—highlighting purely military counter limitations. This asymmetric challenge compels India not only to build credible naval deterrents but also to offer compelling, rules-based alternatives to China's model.

9. CONCLUSION

India's Indo-Pacific vision has positioned it as a responsible regional actor—an assertion accepted by regional players. However, this normative leadership will not materialize if India neglects its naval capability gap. Without credible hard power, India's balancing role—whether internal or external—lacks operationality. India should maintain strategic balance by expanding maritime capabilities while simultaneously promoting cooperative frameworks to sustain a rules-based Indo-Pacific order. The FY 2024-25 defense budget was 6.21 lakh crore, of which the Indian

Navy received the smallest share (18.9 percent). The Indian Navy requires new ships and submarines, but with reduced budgetary allocation, projects like P-75I, the second indigenous aircraft carrier (IAC-2), and additional frigates/destroyers remain stalled (Chawla, 2024).

Even with increased Indian Navy budget allocation, India lacks capacity to develop and manufacture advanced weapons and submarines due to defense-industrial challenges. Technologically, India lacks capacity to design or manufacture major systems and critical parts, raw materials, and components, which are ultimately imported from other nations (Behera, 2024). Efforts should be made to scale up the defense industry and promote initiatives like Make in India and Atmanirbhar Bharat to boost India's internal calculus. If India overcomes these internal contradictions, it will not merely balance China but emerge as a leading power shaping Indo-Pacific order. If India neglects this, its vision will remain aspirational, leaving maritime Asia's future to be defined by others.

REFERENCES

Aljazeera. (2025). *Philippines, India hold first joint naval drill in disputed South China Sea.* https://www.aljazeera.com/news/2025/8/4/philippines-india-hold-first-joint-naval-drill-in-disputed-south-china-sea

Australian Government: Department of Foreign Affairs and Trade. (n.d.). *Asia-Pacific Economic Cooperation (APEC).* https://www.dfat.gov.au/trade/organisations/apec/asia-pacific-economic-cooperation-apec

Baker, B. D. (2015). Where is the 'String of Pearls' in 2015? *The Diplomat.* https://thediplomat.com/2015/10/where-is-the-string-of-pearls-in-2015/

Baruah, D. M., Labh, N., & Greely, J. (2023). Mapping the Indian Ocean Region. *Carnegie Endowment for International Peace.* https://carnegieendowment.org/research/2023/06/mapping-the-indian-ocean-region?lang=en

Behera, L. K. (2024). India's defence industry: Achievements and challenges. *Observer Research Foundation.* https://www.orfonline.org/research/india-s-defence-industry-achievements-and-challenges

Campbell, C., & Salidjanova, N. (2016). South China Sea arbitration ruling: What happened and what's next? *United States-China Economic and Security Review Commission.* https://www.uscc.gov/sites/default/files/Research/Issue%20Brief_South%20China%20Sea%20Arbitration%20Ruling%20What%20Happened%20and%20What%27s%20Next071216.pdf

Chakraborty, A. (2025). India's rise in global defense exports and the way forward. *South Asian Voices.* https://southasianvoices.org/def-f-in-n-india-defense-exports-09-15-2025/

Chawla, A. K. (2024). Defence budget 2024-25—An analysis. *SP's Naval Forces.* https://www.spsnavalforces.com/story/?id=874&h=Defence-Budget-2024-25-andmdash;-An-

Chinoy, S. (2025). How shift from SAGAR to MAHASAGAR doctrine signals India's outreach to larger Global South. *Firstpost.* https://www.firstpost.com/opinion/how-shift-from-sagar-to-mahasagar-doctrine-signals-indias-outreach-to-larger-global-south-13881010.html

Choudhury, S. R. (2021). Quad: Origin and evolving dynamics. *Journal of Global Strategic Studies, 1*(2), 6–29. https://www.researchgate.net/publication/357413837_Quad_Origin_and_Evolving_Dynamics Congressional Research Service. (2024). *China naval modernization: Implications for United States Navy capabilities—Background and issues for Congress*. https://sgp.fas.org/crs/row/RL33153.pdf

Durai, S. (2025). India's maritime vision: From SAGAR to Indo-Pacific to MAHASAGAR. *Embassy of India*. https://www.indembassydili.gov.in/section/articles-commissioned-by-xpd-division/india-s-maritime-vision-from-sagar-to-indo-pacific-to-mahasagar-by-amb-suchitra-durai/

Financial Express. (2024). *Explainer: Quad a strategic alliance for stability and progress in Indo-Pacific*. https://www.financialexpress.com/business/defence-explainer-quad-a-strategic-alliance-for-stability-and-progress-in-indo-pacific-3616538/

Fisher, A. S. (1988). Manila Galleon trade textiles: Cross-cultural influences on New World dress. *Textile Society of America Symposium Proceedings*, Article 636. https://digitalcommons.unl.edu/cgi/viewcontent.cgi?article=1635&context=tsaconf

Gomez, J. (2025). India and the Philippines stage joint naval drill in the disputed South China Sea. *AP Newsroom*. https://apnews.com/article/india-philippines-south-china-sea-joint-sail-eecfaa6056d71937716fb4dc22f52b8a

Green, M. A. (2024). Debt distress on the road to "Belt and Road". *Wilson Center.* https://www.wilsoncenter.org/blog-post/debt-distress-road-belt-and-road

Hiep, T. X., Hoan, T. Q., & Kiet, L. H. (2024). Free and Open Indo-Pacific strategy: Competitive Opinions and Trends. *Vestnik of Saint Petersburg University -. International Relations*, *17*(3), 242–259.

Hiep, T. X., Kiet, L. H., & Yen, P. T. H. (2023). Strategic Hedging in Southeast Asia: ASEAN Member States' Policy Responses to China's Growing Economic Influence. *Contemporary Chinese Political Economy and Strategic Relations*, *9*(2/3), 404–438.

Hunt, E. (2024). Building out the US hub-and-spoke empire in the Indo-Pacific. *CounterPunch*. https://www.counterpunch.org/2024/10/24/building-out-the-us-hub-and-spoke-empire-in-the-indo-pacific/

Jha, M. K. (2023). Why India's navy budget needs a big push. *Financial Express*. https://www.financialexpress.com/budget/why-indias-navy-budget-needs-a-big-push-2964769/

Kiet, L. H., Binh, N. T., & Hiep, T. X. (2025a). From border conflicts to maritime competition: Driving forces behind the power rivalry between India and China in the Indian Ocean region. *Australian Journal of Maritime and Ocean Affairs*, **•••**, 1–25. DOI: 10.1080/18366503.2025.2492438

Kiet, L. H., Tam, L. T. T., & Hiep, T. X. (2025b). Caught between dragon and elephant: Vietnam's strategic balancing act in the Sino-Indian rivalry. *China Quarterly of International Strategic Studies*, *11*(2), 99–128. DOI: 10.1142/S237774002550006X

Ladwig, W. (2024). The Indo-Pacific in Indian foreign policy. *The Royal United Services Institute for Defence and Security Studies.* https://www.rusi.org/explore-our-research/publications/policy-briefs/indo-pacific-indian-foreign-policy

Manoharan, N. (2025). Nautical tigers: Contributions of Cholas to India's maritime tradition. In Raju, A. S., & Srinivasan, R. (Eds.), *The Routledge handbook of maritime India* (pp. 19–28). Routledge., DOI: 10.4324/9781003607434-3

Marine Insight. (2024). *Nautical law: What is UNCLOS?* https://www.marineinsight.com/maritime-law/nautical-law-what-is-unclos/

Martin, G. (2024). From the magazine: Indian Navy growing in size and reach. *Asia-Pacific Defence Reporter.* https://asiapacificdefencereporter.com/from-the-magazine-indian-navy-growing-in-size-and-reach

Medcalf, R. (2019). Mapping a multipolar future: The contest for the Indo-Pacific. *Global Asia: A Journal of the East Asia Foundation, 14*(4), 58–69. https://www.globalasia.org/v14no4/feature/mapping-a-multipolar-future-the-contest-for-the-indo-pacific_rory-medcalf

Ministry of Defence. (2015). *Ensuring secure seas: Indian maritime security strategy.* https://bharatshakti.in/wp-content/uploads/2016/01/Indian_Maritime_Security_Strategy_Document_25Jan16.pdf

Ministry of External Affairs. (2016). *Statement on award of arbitral tribunal on South China Sea under Annexure VII of UNCLOS.* https://www.mea.gov.in/press-releases.htm?dtl/27019/statement+on+award+of+arbitral+tribunal+on+south+china+sea+under+annexure+vii+of+unclos

Ministry of External Affairs. (2019). *Humanitarian assistance and disaster relief to Mozambique—Operation Sahayata 2019.* https://www.mea.gov.in/press-releases.htm?dtl/31174/Humanitarian+Assistance+and+Disaster+Relief+to+MozambiqueOperation+Sahayata+2019

Ministry of External Affairs. (2023). *India–Australia bilateral relations.* https://www.mea.gov.in/Portal/ForeignRelation/Aus-brief-2023.pdf

Ministry of External Affairs. (2023). *Operation Dost*. https://www.mea.gov.in/press-releases.htm?dtl/36209/Operation_Dost Ministry of External Affairs. (2025c). *Declaration on the establishment of a strategic partnership between the Government of the Republic of India and the Government of the Republic of the Philippines*. https://www.mea.gov.in/bilateral-documents.htm?dtl%2F39939%2FDeclaration_on_the_Establishment_of_a_Strategic_Partnership_between_the_Government_of_the_Republic_of_India_and_the_Government_of_the_Republic_of_the_=

Ministry of External Affairs. (2025a). *Overview of ASEAN-India relations*. https://www.mea.gov.in/Portal/ForeignRelation/BRIEF-ON-ASEAN-INDIA.pdf

Ministry of External Affairs. (2025b). *India-Japan bilateral relations*. https://indconosaka.gov.in/pdf/bilateral_Brief.pdf

Ministry of External Affairs. (2025d). *India Singapore joint statement*. https://www.mea.gov.in/bilateral-documents.htm?dtl/40094/India_Singapore_Joint_Statement_September_04_2025

Ministry of Foreign Affairs of Japan. (2007). *Confluence of the two seas: Speech by H.E. Mr. Shinzo Abe, Prime Minister of Japan at the Parliament of the Republic of India*. https://www.mofa.go.jp/region/asia-paci/pmv0708/speech-2.html

Ministry of Foreign Affairs of Japan. (2020). *Signing of the agreement between the Government of Japan and the Government of the Republic of India concerning reciprocal provision of supplies and services between the Self-Defense Forces of Japan and the Indian Armed Forces*. https://www.mofa.go.jp/press/release/press4e_002896.html

Mishra, R. (2025). India-Philippines ties now strategic partnership on upward trajectory. *The Diplomat*. https://thediplomat.com/2025/08/india-philippines-ties-now-strategic-partnership-on-upward-trajectory/

National Centre for Polar and Ocean Research. (n.d.). *Survey of the EEZ*. https://ncpor.res.in/pages/researchview/7

Paszak, P. (2021). China and the "Malacca dilemma". *Warsaw Institute*. https://warsawinstitute.org/china-malacca-dilemma/

Patel, R. (2025). India prepares to deliver 3rd and final consignment of BrahMos missiles to Philippines by year end. *Defence.in*. https://defence.in/threads/india-prepares-to-deliver-3rd-and-final-consignment-of-brahmos-missiles-to-philippines-by-year-end.16131/

Philip, S. A. (2025). From competing to beating US in numbers and tonnage, here's how China built its shipping empire. *The Print*. https://theprint.in/defence/from-competing-to-beating-us-in-numbers-and-tonnage-heres-how-china-built-its-shipping-empire/2546925

Press Information Bureau. (2006). *Operation Sukoon for the evacuation of Indian nationals from Lebanon*. https://www.pib.gov.in/newsite/erelcontent.aspx?relid=20224

Press Information Bureau. (2020). *Indian Navy completes "Operation Samudra Setu"*. https://www.pib.gov.in/PressReleasePage.aspx?PRID=1637314

Press Information Bureau. (2020). *Indian Navy launches 'Operation Vanilla' to provide humanitarian assistance and disaster relief at Madagascar*. https://www.pib.gov.in/PressReleasePage.aspx?PRID=1600896

Press Information Bureau. (2024). *India–Australia joint military exercise AUSTRA-HIND commences in Maharashtra*. https://www.pib.gov.in/PressReleasePage.aspx?PRID=2071767

Press Information Bureau. (2024). *India-Japan joint exercise 'Dharma Guardian' commences in Rajasthan*. https://www.pib.gov.in/PressReleaseIframePage.aspx?PRID=2008775

Pulipaka, S., & Musaddi, M. (2021). In defence of the 'Indo-Pacific' concept. *Observer Research Foundation*. https://www.orfonline.org/research/in-defence-of-the-indo-pacific-concept

Qiao, J., Li, Y., & Huang, M. (2024). The geopolitical importance of Bab el-Mandeb Strait: A strategic gateway to global trade. *Middle East Political and Economic Institute*. https://mepei.com/the-geopolitical-importance-of-bab-el-mandeb-strait-a-strategic-gateway-to-global-trade/

Russel, R. R., & Berger, B. H. (2020). Weaponizing the Belt and Road Initiative. *Asia Society Policy Institute*. https://asiasociety.org/sites/default/files/2020-09/Weaponizing%20the%20Belt%20and%20Road%20Initiative_0.pdf

Sagar, P. R. (2025). Navigating uncertainties, India's biggest submarine hunt reaches critical stage. *India Today*. https://www.indiatoday.in/india-today-insight/story/navigating-uncertainties-indias-biggest-submarine-hunt-reaches-critical-stage-2685298-2025-02-25

Sarangi, S. (2020). Unpacking SAGAR (Security and Growth for All in the Region). *USI Occasional Paper*. https://www.researchgate.net/publication/347497121_Unpacking_SAGAR_Security_and_Growth_for_All_in_the_Region

Shaka Tribe. (n.d.). *The art of Polynesian navigation: Exploring ancient seafaring techniques.* https://shakatribeshop.com/pages/the-art-of-polynesian-navigation-exploring-ancient-seafaring-techniques

Tan, Y. (2022). Chinese 'spy ship' Yuan Wang 5 docks in Sri Lanka despite Indian concern. *BBC.* https://www.bbc.com/news/world-asia-62558767

The Telegraph. (2025). *'We support freedom of navigation': India reaffirms South China Sea stance amid Beijing's objection.* https://www.telegraphindia.com/gallery/we-support-freedom-of-navigation-india-reaffirms-south-china-sea-stance-amid-beijings-objection-photogallery/cid/2116566?slide=3

United States Energy Information Administration. (2024). *World oil transit chokepoints.* https://www.eia.gov/international/analysis/special-topics/World_Oil_Transit_Chokepoints

Zeng, X., & Zhang, S. (2021). From "Asia Pacific" to "Indo Pacific": The adjustment of American Asia Pacific strategy from the perspective of critical geopolitics. *East Asian Affairs, 1*(2), 2150009. Advance online publication. DOI: 10.1142/S2737557921500091

Chapter 4

Sino-Russian Naval Cooperation in the Indo-Pacific:

Strategic Convergence, Regional Responses, and Security Implications (2021-2025)

Ha Thi Minh Tran
Hue University, Vietnam

Thao Thi Bui
Hue University, Vietnam

Trang Ngo Huyen Le
Hue University, Vietnam

Phuong Duong Anh Vo
https://orcid.org/0009-0000-7168-9042
Hue University, Vietnam

Ly Thi Khanh Nguyen
https://orcid.org/0009-0006-1201-2369
Hue University, Vietnam

ABSTRACT

This chapter examines the intensification of Sino-Russian naval cooperation in the Indo-Pacific from 2021 to 2025, analyzing its strategic drivers, operational patterns, and regional implications. The study reveals that mounting Western pressure has

DOI: 10.4018/979-8-3373-4470-6.ch004

accelerated bilateral maritime coordination, manifested in increased joint exercises across sensitive areas including the Bering Sea, Sea of Okhotsk, and Arctic waters. However, this cooperation remains strategically calibrated rather than alliance-based, constrained by mutual sovereignty concerns and divergent long-term interests. Regional responses, assessed through Evelyn Goh's framework of comprehensive engagement and balanced influence, demonstrate varied approaches: while U.S. exclusionary mechanisms inadvertently reinforced Sino-Russian alignment, ASEAN's inclusive strategy preserved strategic autonomy without direct confrontation. The chapter concludes with policy recommendations emphasizing multilateral engagement and confidence-building measures to mitigate security dilemmas and maintain regional stability.

1. INTRODUCTION

The Indo-Pacific has emerged as the principal arena of strategic competition in the 21st-century international system, characterized by intensifying multidimensional power rivalries, strategic realignments, and the restructuring of regional order (He & Li, 2020). In response to China's rapid ascent and its growing challenge to the US-led liberal international order, Washington has actively promoted the "Free and Open Indo-Pacific" (FOIP) strategy while simultaneously consolidating and expanding its network of alliances and partnerships with Japan, South Korea, Australia, and other regional actors (Hiep et al., 2024).

Within this context, the strategic repositioning of the US and its allies has generated significant security adjustments across the Indo-Pacific. Naval cooperation has emerged as a particularly critical indicator, reflecting not only military capabilities but also the degree of convergence in strategic interests, foreign policy orientations, and visions of regional order among major powers. Against this backdrop, Russia and China have increasingly demonstrated a convergence of interests as both seek to expand their strategic space, mitigate isolation, and signal alignment within an increasingly fluid and contested regional order (Wilson, 2002). Notably, the period from 2021 to 2025 witnessed a marked intensification of naval cooperation between Russia and China in the Indo-Pacific in terms of both geographic scope and operational coordination.

The significance of this study is underscored by three key developments. First, major-power competition in the Indo-Pacific is becoming increasingly systemic, with naval power playing a central role due to its close association with freedom of navigation, sea lane control, and the capacity to shape regional order. Second, Russia's "special military operation" in Ukraine since 2022 has accelerated Moscow's strategic pivot toward the Asia-Pacific, while China has sought to diversify its security partnerships in response to mounting strategic pressure from the West. Third, the deepening naval cooperation between Russia and China poses direct challenges to existing regional security governance mechanisms, compelling regional actors—including Vietnam—to recalibrate their strategic approaches to preserve stability.

2. METHODOLOGICAL FRAMEWORK

This study primarily employs qualitative research methods, including document analysis, comparative analysis, and theoretical forecasting. Naval cooperation between Russia and China in the Indo-Pacific is examined as a central case study to elucidate the dynamics of cooperation, patterns of interest convergence, and structural constraints shaping this relationship. By conceptualizing naval cooperation as an analytical entry point, the study clarifies the strategic adjustments undertaken by Russia and China amid US-China competition and broader transformations of the international order, while also providing an analytical foundation for assessing the implications of this cooperation for regional security. The research offers policy-relevant insights for key regional and extra-regional actors, including the US, ASEAN, the QUAD, and AUKUS, in their efforts to manage strategic balance and regional integration.

First, this study employs document analysis as its primary research method, examining official statements, policy documents, diplomatic communications, and academic literature produced by both Russia and China. Data sources are drawn from authoritative government publications, international relations research institutes, peer-reviewed academic articles indexed in SCOPUS and ISI databases, and reputable international news organizations. Through systematic document analysis, the study synthesizes policy positions and assesses patterns of naval cooperation between Russia and China based on their shared strategic interests in the Indo-Pacific region.

Second, a comparative analytical approach is integrated to examine how Russia and China design and implement strategies to enhance naval cooperation. This approach facilitates the identification of converging security interests between the two countries in the Indo-Pacific, particularly in the context of heightened uncertainty within the international system and the continued strategic predominance of the US.

Third, the study applies Evelyn Goh's theoretical framework of "comprehensive engagement, balanced influence, and hierarchical order" to analyze and evaluate regional responses—particularly those of Vietnam and Southeast Asian countries—to Russia-China naval cooperation in the Indo-Pacific. According to Goh, Southeast Asia's regional security strategy rests on three interrelated pillars: (1) comprehensive engagement through bilateral relations and multilateral institutions involving multiple major powers, including the US, China, and India; (2) the pursuit of balanced influence, whereby Southeast Asian states utilize economic, diplomatic, and institutional instruments to derive benefits from multiple powers rather than directly counterbalancing any single actor; and (3) the maintenance of a hierarchical regional order aimed at ensuring long-term stability without fostering domination or empire, in which the US functions as the predominant global superpower, China as the leading regional power, followed by Japan, India, and South Korea, with ASEAN occupying the foundational tier of the regional order (cited from Kiet et al., 2025b).

3. NAVAL COOPERATION BETWEEN RUSSIA AND CHINA IN THE INDO-PACIFIC REGION (2021-2025)

3.1. Phase One: Restart and Institutionalization (2021-2022)

During 2021-2022, Russia and China initiated a process of restarting and institutionalizing naval cooperation in the Indo-Pacific region. The political and strategic context of this period created structural conditions that incentivized both countries to accelerate military cooperation, particularly in the naval domain. Unlike earlier phases, when bilateral naval cooperation was largely exploratory, ad hoc, and symbolic, this stage marked a qualitative shift toward deeper coordination driven by an increasing convergence of strategic interests under mounting international and regional pressures.

One of the primary drivers of this shift was the intensification of strategic competition between the US and China, which exerted growing pressure on China's maritime security environment. From 2021 onward, the US FOIP strategy entered a phase of intensified implementation, reflected in the increased frequency of Freedom of Navigation Operations (FONOPs), the expansion of multilateral naval exercises, and enhanced operational coordination among key US allies, notably Japan and Australia (Roy-Chaudhury & Sullivan de Estrada, 2022). Simultaneously, the elevation of the QUAD from a consultative dialogue mechanism to a framework for substantive cooperation on maritime security, together with the establishment of AUKUS in 2021, signaled the progressive militarization of strategic competition in the region (Zhang et al., 2021). Within this evolving security landscape, China faced the growing risk of maritime strategic encirclement, compelling Beijing to seek external military partners capable of mitigating this disadvantage.

Concurrently, from 2022 onward, Russia experienced a significant contraction of its strategic space, most notably in Europe following the launch of its "special military operation" in Ukraine. The prolonged confrontation between Russia and NATO, combined with the expansion and intensification of Western sanctions, severely constrained Moscow's access to advanced technology, international markets, and established security mechanisms (Choonara, 2022). Under these conditions, the Asia-Pacific—and by extension the Indo-Pacific—emerged as an alternative strategic arena through which Russia could preserve its status as a major military power and avoid comprehensive isolation within the international system.

Importantly, the convergence of Russian and Chinese interests during this period did not arise from a full alignment of long-term strategic objectives but rather from overlapping defensive imperatives in response to external pressure. For China, Russia represented a rare strategic partner possessing substantial naval capabilities and a demonstrably confrontational posture toward the US, thereby helping Beijing reduce the risks associated with strategic isolation. Conversely, for Russia, China functioned not only as a crucial economic partner but also as a strategic gateway enabling Moscow to sustain a visible military presence in the Indo-Pacific at a time when its resources were increasingly absorbed by the European theater (Chabarovskaya, 2025).

Figure 1. Number of joint military exercises conducted by Russia and China (2003-2024)

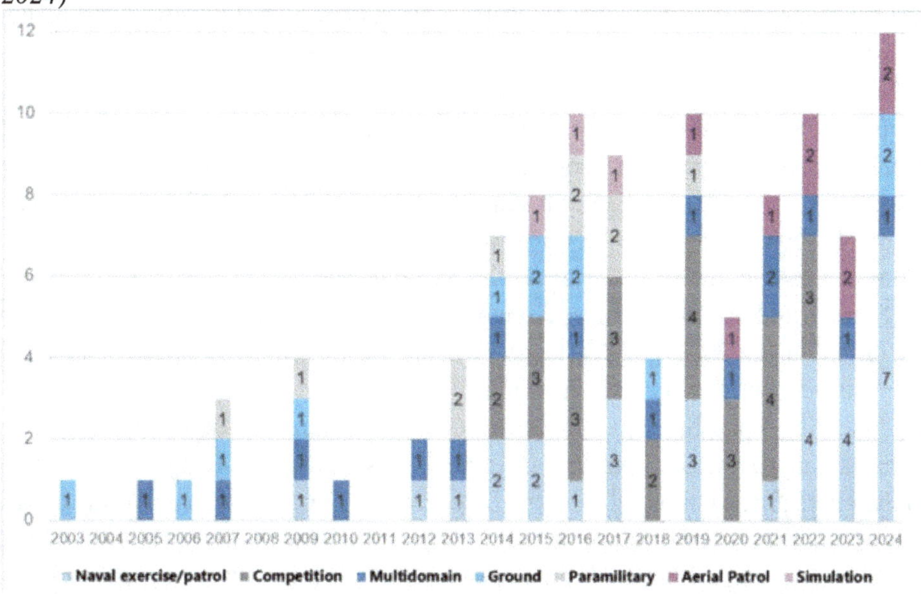

Against this political backdrop, the data presented in Figure 1 indicate that the period 2021-2022 constituted a critical turning point in the process of restarting and institutionalizing naval cooperation between Russia and China, as reflected in both the frequency and nature of joint exercises. From a quantitative perspective, the number of joint exercises conducted in 2021 and 2022 remained consistently high relative to earlier periods. Approximately eight joint exercises were recorded in 2021, rising to ten in 2022—figures that significantly exceed the annual average of one to three exercises observed during the 2003-2013 period.

More importantly, the qualitative transformation of exercises during 2021-2022 underscores a shift from single-domain cooperation toward more complex and multidimensional forms of military coordination, with naval forces assuming a central role. As shown in Table 1, joint naval exercises and maritime patrols accounted for a substantial proportion of overall activities, alongside a growing number of multi-domain operations integrating naval and air forces, joint air patrols, simulation-based drills, and other combined combat elements. The repeated conduct of joint sea and air patrols within relatively short timeframes suggests that Russia-China cooperation has moved beyond technical training or ad hoc exchanges of operational experience toward the standardization of coordinated military presence. This emerging model enables both sides to sustain synchronized operations in sensitive maritime areas, thereby enhancing deterrence, signaling strategic resolve, and complicating the security calculations of external actors in the region.

A longer-term comparison further highlights the structural evolution of Russia-China military cooperation. Prior to 2014, joint exercises were largely experimental in nature and primarily served confidence-building purposes. By contrast, from 2021 onward, bilateral military cooperation—particularly in the naval domain—has exhibited clear signs of institutionalization, manifested in the repeated execution of exercises and the expansion of operational content. The ability to conduct multiple types of exercises within the same year indicates that both sides have developed a relatively flexible coordination framework capable of adapting to shifting strategic requirements without formalizing a military alliance.

From a strategic perspective, the increased frequency and elevated level of cooperation during 2021-2022 reflect a growing convergence of defensive strategic interests between Russia and China in response to mounting pressure from the US and its allies. For China, joint naval exercises and patrols with Russia contribute to mitigating maritime strategic constraints and signal that Beijing is not isolated in the intensifying competition in the Indo-Pacific. For Russia, maintaining a high tempo of military activities in the region allows Moscow to reaffirm its status as a non-Western military power, even as a significant portion of its strategic resources has been absorbed by the conflict in Ukraine since 2022.

Overall, the 2021-2022 period demonstrates that Russia-China naval cooperation has evolved beyond symbolic or superficial interaction toward a more sustained pattern characterized by high-frequency engagement, diversified operational content, and expanded deployment space. These developments laid the foundation for calibrated intensification of naval cooperation during the 2023-2025 period while simultaneously contributing to the growing complexity of the security environment in the Indo-Pacific region.

3.2. Phase Two: Strategic Expansion and Geographic Diversification (2023-2025)

Naval cooperation between Russia and China expanded significantly in scale and strategic scope during the 2023-2025 period. This period marks a substantial increase in the scale, frequency, and geographical reach of Russia-China naval cooperation in the Indo-Pacific region, reflecting a shift from institutionalized cooperation to strategic deployment cooperation. The principal impetus for this expansion stems from the increasingly clear convergence in both countries' strategic understanding regarding a multipolar international order and the necessity of countering mounting pressure from the US and its allies.

Politically, President Xi Jinping's visit to Russia in March 2023 and his statements emphasizing "substantive multilateralism" and "a multipolar world" demonstrate that China and Russia openly share a similar perspective on the challenges posed by the US-led unipolar order (Enkhbat, 2025). In this context, joint naval exercises and patrols become crucial strategic tools, both strengthening bilateral military relations and sending clear political and security signals to the international community. Data indicate that during the period 2021–2024 alone, 16 joint exercises and patrols in the field of naval security took place, with the majority concentrated after 2022.

In terms of operational structure, Russia-China military cooperation during this period was not limited to traditional bilateral exercises but expanded to multilateral and multi-domain exercises, including frameworks such as the Shanghai Cooperation Organization's "Peace Mission" series, Russia's annual strategic exercises (Zapad, Vostok), and increasingly frequent joint naval and air force exercises and patrols. Although not yet fully encompassing emerging domains such as space or cyber warfare, these activities demonstrate a high level of military integration, especially between the navy and air force, aimed at enhancing interoperability and coordinated combat capabilities (Enkhbat, 2025).

For China and Russia, multi-domain exercises have primarily focused on integrating traditional branches of the military—army, air force, and navy—rather than fully expanding into new operational domains such as cyberspace, space, or cognitive warfare. This suggests that bilateral military cooperation, while expanded in scale and intensity, remains cautious and controlled, reflecting both limitations on the extent to which sensitive capabilities can be shared and a lack of readiness for a full-fledged military alliance.

However, within traditional domains—particularly the navy and air force—the frequency and complexity of coordinated operations have increased significantly over the past decade. Joint maritime and air patrols are becoming more frequent and diverse, indicating that Russia-China cooperation has moved beyond mere technical training to establish recurring models of coordinated military presence. This development is closely linked to the modernization of the Chinese military, in which Beijing's leadership, particularly under Xi Jinping, views enhancing the combat capabilities and operational range of its navy as a cornerstone for protecting its expanding strategic interests at sea. In this context, China's increasing participation in bilateral and multilateral naval exercises—both in the near seas surrounding the First Island Chain in the Western Pacific and in distant waters such as the Mediterranean, the Gulf of Oman in the Indian Ocean, and even off the coast of South Africa—reflects a shift from coastal defense to long-range operational capabilities (Kiet et al., 2025a). Cooperation with Russia, a naval power with experience in deploying expeditionary forces, has enabled China to test and expand the operational range of its navy in an increasingly complex strategic environment.

Since their first bilateral naval exercise in the Gulf of Aden in 2009, Russia and China have conducted more than 20 joint exercises, with over half taking place after 2022. This surge, particularly following Russia's military campaign in Ukraine, reflects a convergence of strategic interests amid increasing pressure from the West on both sides. While China avoids openly displaying military support for Russia, the expansion of joint exercises demonstrates Beijing's willingness to provide indirect strategic backing, thereby helping Moscow alleviate its sense of isolation on the international stage.

A core objective of Russia-China joint exercises is to enhance operational interoperability, from command and control and information sharing to fire coordination and force maneuvering. Through these activities, the two countries' militaries have significantly improved their coordination capabilities in simulated battlefield environments. However, the level of interoperability remains far behind highly institutionalized military alliance structures such as NATO (Ditrych & Ekman, 2024). This reflects the "flexible approach" of Russia-China relations, in which cooperation is expanded to counter external pressure while avoiding rigid commitment agreements.

By 2024, Sino-Russian military cooperation saw a notable increase in intensity with 12 joint exercises in a single year, including highly symbolic strategic activities such as the first coast guard patrol in the Arctic and air patrols near Alaska passing through the US Air Defense Identification Zone. Notably, approximately two-thirds of bilateral naval exercises and strategic air patrols were conducted in the Pacific region, indicating a clear shift in the focus of cooperation toward the Indo-Pacific space. The increased frequency of these activities reflects China's growing readiness to strengthen its military partnership with Russia in the region—not to establish a formal alliance but to enhance deterrence capabilities, send strategic signals, and complicate the security calculations of the US and its allies.

3.3. Key Operational Theaters

a) The Bering Sea: Strategic Signaling Near US Territory

The Bering Sea has emerged as a prime deployment space where Sino-Russian naval cooperation is used to operationalize the strategy of expanding presence and indirect deterrence against the US. In early August 2023, a joint Sino-Russian fleet of 11 warships conducted naval patrols near Alaska and moved close to the Aleutian Islands (Al Jazeera, 2023). The choice of this area was not purely for combat purposes but primarily served the goal of strategic signaling, as the two sides coordinated military operations in an area adjacent to the US' "backyard."

From Russia's perspective, these activities can be seen as part of a strategy to divert the attention and resources of the US in the context of Moscow facing increased military pressure from NATO in Europe following the Ukraine conflict. By expanding the space for military interaction into the Pacific and Arctic regions, Russia is forcing the US to consider the possibility of multi-theater confrontation rather than focusing solely on the European theater. For China, participating in patrols in the Bering Sea with Russia allows Beijing to expand its presence beyond the First Island Chain while leveraging bilateral cooperation to mitigate political risks when deploying forces near US territory, thereby enhancing deterrence effectiveness at a relatively low commitment cost.

This trend was further reinforced on July 25, 2024, when China and Russia conducted their first joint strategic air patrol in the Bering Sea, involving two Chinese H-6 bombers and two Russian Tu-95 strategic bombers escorted by Russian Su-30SM and Su-35S fighter jets. The formation flew through the US Air Defense Identification Zone (ADIZ) near Alaska before being tracked and intercepted by the North American Aerospace Defense Command (NORAD) (Mahdzir, 2024). This marked the eighth joint strategic air patrol between the two countries since 2019 and represented an unprecedented expansion of deployment space in Sino-Russian air force cooperation.

The expansion of strategic patrols into the Bering Sea demonstrates that Sino-Russian military cooperation is shifting from symbolic displays of capability to establishing a selective presence at points of direct contact with core US security interests (Enkhbat, 2025). For China, participation in these activities not only helps expand the operational range of its air and naval forces beyond the First Island Chain but also allows Beijing to share the costs of deterrence with Russia, thereby increasing strategic pressure on the US without unilaterally escalating confrontation.

b) Joint Exercises in the Arctic

China's geopolitical competition with the West is rapidly expanding into new domains that Beijing identifies as crucial to its strategic ambitions: outer space, polar regions, cyberspace, and deep seas. As these areas become more accessible, Beijing is expanding its dual-use presence on its path to becoming a global power—and it is not doing so alone. Russia has become a key partner for China's ambitions in space and the Arctic as Europe and other Western nations reduce cooperation with Beijing (Legarda, 2025).

The concept of "new strategic fronts" is a Chinese framework focused on Beijing's interests and goals (Legarda, 2025). However, pursuing these objectives in those domains requires cooperation with external partners to compensate for shortcomings in capacity, know-how, or geographical access. As European partners move toward risk mitigation, restrict technology transfer, withdraw from joint initiatives with China, and impose sanctions on Russia, Moscow is increasingly filling the cooperation gap—albeit with inherent tensions in areas that Russia itself considers strategically important (Legarda, 2025).

Until recently, Europe was China's preferred partner in the Arctic and space. Through science diplomacy, China positioned itself as a potential partner for European nations seeking to build polar and space programs and capabilities. Research cooperation between China and Europe in these areas developed rapidly, often disregarding questions about the inherent risks in this relationship. European nations inadvertently but effectively aided Beijing, allowing and facilitating China's access to more advanced European technology, dual-use know-how, and strategic areas in the Arctic (Legarda, 2025).

However, Europe, the US, and other Western nations have become increasingly cautious about cooperating with China in strategic areas. European nations have shifted from cooperative partnerships to blocking or canceling some Chinese projects on their territory for national security reasons. Examples include China's attempt to purchase an abandoned naval base in Greenland in 2016 (Matzen, 2017), an attempt to purchase a local airport in northern Finland in 2018 (Vanttinen, 2021), and an attempt to acquire land on the Svalbard archipelago in 2024 (Agence France-Presse in Oslo, 2024).

In 2023, the European Space Agency (ESA) announced it no longer planned to send astronauts to China's Tiangong space station (Jones, 2023). Since then, Russia has emerged as Beijing's partner of choice in these new geopolitical competition fronts. Russia's contributions in the Arctic and in space are significant and, in many cases, complement China's capabilities. Russia remains a significant—albeit declining—space power with a well-established space program from which China could benefit. Russia also has sovereign rights over the Arctic, including access to the Northern Sea Route (NSR), and maintains a vast network of Arctic infrastructure and military facilities (Legarda, 2025). Meanwhile, Beijing provides the economic power and technological support Russia needs to counter Western sanctions.

Initially, Russia was reluctant to allow China unrestricted access to Arctic waters, facilities, or trade routes, as well as its space program, fearing competition or interference with its sphere of influence. Moscow initially opposed China's campaign to become an observer state in the Arctic Council and was reluctant to allow Chinese ships free passage on the Northern Sea Route through the Arctic Ocean to Europe and North America (Sun, 2018). In 2021, Russian media reported that the Ministry of Industry and Commerce had blocked Chinese shipyards from winning bids to build new icebreakers for Russia due to concerns about the transfer of underwater designs (Eiterjord, 2023).

In September 2024, the Chinese and Russian Coast Guards conducted their first joint patrol in the Arctic, with the People's Liberation Army operating further north than ever before in the Bering Sea. According to China Daily, this event marked a "historic advance into the Arctic" by the Chinese military, and the Chinese Coast Guard stated that this joint patrol "tested their ability to perform missions in unfamiliar waters" (Wangsh, 2024).

The Northeast Passage, between the Barents Sea and the Bering Sea, is open to maritime activity from July to October (Scott, 2024). The Bering Sea serves as a gateway to the Arctic for China as it expands its presence in the region. In its Arctic Policy White Paper, China declares itself a "near-Arctic nation" and expresses its intention to "build an 'Arctic Silk Road' through the development of Arctic shipping routes" (The State Council Information Office of the People's Republic of China, 2018).

Through joint exercises in the North Pacific, China may be seeking to leverage Russia's presence to bolster its foothold in the region (Williams et al., 2024). However, there is currently no indication that Russia will grant China long-term access to its military facilities in the Arctic.

China's Arctic policy also emphasizes the importance of "maritime security in the Arctic" (Williams et al., 2024). In April 2024 in Murmansk, Russia, the China Coast Guard and the Russian Federal Security Service signed a Memorandum of Understanding on Maritime Law Enforcement Cooperation (Zhuo, n.d.). This indicates that the China Coast Guard is likely to increase its involvement in Arctic affairs, particularly through law enforcement cooperation with Russia in the region.

In 2025, The New York Times obtained an internal FSB planning document detailing Moscow's concerns about Chinese intelligence agents conducting espionage in the Arctic using mining companies and university research centers as fronts (Udah et al., 2025).

Russia's international isolation since the start of the full-scale war in Ukraine has forced Moscow to abandon some of its previous reservations. Western sanctions have narrowed Russia's options in maintaining and expanding its Arctic infrastructure, and its space program has become increasingly outdated. Moscow has clearly decided that it cannot afford to lose China's support, despite the risks. Their cooperation in the Arctic and space is growing wider and deeper, facilitating Beijing's progress in its strategic ambitions. This partnership with Russia is increasing the threat posed by Chinese activities in these areas to European security and interests (Legarda, 2025).

The largest project in space cooperation between China and Russia to date is the plan to develop a joint base on the Moon under the framework of China's International Lunar Research Station (ILRS) initiative. Construction is expected to begin in the 2030s and become fully operational by 2050 (Legarda, 2025). They also recently announced a new agreement to build a nuclear power plant on the Moon to power the research base (Bela, 2025). To date, 13 countries have signed up to participate in ILRS, but Russia remains China's main partner.

China and Russia are also improving the compatibility and interoperability of their BeiDou and GLONASS navigation systems (their alternatives to GPS) (Balazs, 2025). Regular bilateral consultations on the peaceful use of outer space and space security have resulted in commitments to enhance cooperation and jointly develop international space law (Ministry of Foreign Affairs of the People's Republic of China, 2024).

The lack of transparency makes it difficult to assess the details and progress of announced programs. However, the increasing number and importance of space cooperation agreements between China and Russia demonstrate a deepening strategic partnership (Legarda, 2025). Beyond achieving scientific progress, both sides envision a counterweight to US and Western dominance in space (including a space-based economy and rules and norms governing space) and cooperation on space capabilities for military purposes.

Cooperation between China and Russia in the Arctic is becoming increasingly broad and robust. China has invested in numerous mining, energy, and infrastructure projects in northern Russia. A subsidiary of China Poly Group, a state-owned defense corporation, signed an agreement to invest $300 million in a coal terminal in Murmansk (Staalesen, 2017) and to develop a deep-water port at Arkhangelsk on the White Sea, which COSCO reportedly planned to use as its main base for trans-Arctic cargo shipping (TASS, 2017). However, the status of these projects remains unclear. The China Development Bank and the Export-Import Bank are believed to have provided the majority of funding for the development of Russia's Yamal liquefied natural gas project in Western Siberia. In return, approximately 80% of the equipment was manufactured in Chinese and Indonesian shipyards (Karkalanov, 2016). During Vladimir Putin's visit to Beijing in 2023, the two sides also agreed to establish a joint agency to jointly develop the Northern Sea Route and polar shipping technology. This new agency, headed by Aleksei Likhachev, head of Russia's State

Atomic Energy Corporation (Rosatom), and China's Minister of Transport Liu Wei, met for the first time in late 2024 and is expected to facilitate China's access to the Northern Sea Route (Global Times, 2024).

Overall, in the Arctic, the military orientation in Beijing and Moscow's activities is increasingly evident. Although Russia has not yet allowed China to conduct independent military operations in Russian Arctic waters, the two sides have conducted several joint operations in the region in recent years.

c) Joint Exercises in the Sea of Okhotsk

Located between Russia's Far East and the Kamchatka Peninsula, the Sea of Okhotsk plays a crucial role in Russia's defense architecture and serves as a vital sea route to the Pacific Ocean. It is home to important naval bases and is a key area for Russian air defense and submarine operations. The first joint naval exercise between China and Russia in the Sea of Okhotsk was held in 2017 as the second phase of the "Joint Sea" exercise, and the second took place in 2022 as part of Russia's Vostok exercise. While recent naval and air patrol exercises between China and Russia have mostly taken place in the periphery of China's strategic domain, such as the Sea of Japan and the East China Sea, the exercises in the Sea of Okhotsk demonstrate Russia's intention to shift its focus to its own strategic backyard as part of a broader strategy. Furthermore, to enhance its military presence in the Pacific, Russia has been building up its Pacific Fleet, with particular emphasis on modernizing its nuclear-powered ballistic missile submarines. The Sea of Okhotsk serves as a crucial "bastion" for these submarines.

From September 10 to 28, 2024, the Russian Navy and the People's Liberation Army Navy (PLAN) conducted a joint exercise codenamed "North/Interaction-2024" in both the Sea of Japan and the Sea of Okhotsk. Participating ships included the Russian destroyers RFS Admiral Panteleyev (548) and RFS Admiral Tributs (564), as well as the frigates RFS MPK-107 (332), RFS MPK-82 (375), and RFS Smerch (423). On the Chinese side, the fleet included the cruiser CNS Wuxi (104), the destroyer CNS Xining (117), the frigate CNS Linyi (547), and the fleet tanker CNS Taihu (889). The exercise included simulated UAV attacks countered by surface-to-air missiles as well as anti-submarine warfare exercises with a Russian diesel-electric submarine as the target (Mhadzir, 2024). The "North/Interaction" exercise, known as Beibu in Chinese (meaning "north"), is a relatively new annual joint exercise classified as a multi-domain exercise combining joint air and naval drills in the North Pacific.

Russia's strengthening of its Pacific Fleet, along with the gradual expansion of training and exercise areas from the Bering Sea to the Sea of Okhotsk, the Sea of Japan, the East China Sea, and the South China Sea (SCS), could help China shift the maritime balance in the Pacific vis-à-vis the US and its Asian allies. At the same time, this expansion will bolster the Russian naval presence in the region.

Joint naval exercises with Russia in the Sea of Okhotsk allow China to enhance its naval presence and operations in the North Pacific, consistent with its broader Arctic strategy. The Global Times, a Chinese state-run media platform, has emphasized the importance of joint China-Russia exercises in the northern seas, stating that "the North Pacific connects China to shipping lanes in the Arctic, which are becoming increasingly strategically significant due to global warming, so it is important for China to participate in safeguarding the security of these seas" (Xuanzum, 2023).

It appears that Chinese fleets operating in the Sea of Okhotsk will no longer be rare, and this can be seen as China truly accelerating its "long march" northward, with the Sea of Okhotsk and the Bering Sea serving as stepping stones for its future presence in the Arctic via the North Pacific.

d) Joint Exercises in the Sea of Japan and East China Sea

Initially, from 2019 to 2021, joint patrols took place once annually in the Sea of Japan and East China Sea. However, in 2022, two joint air patrols were conducted in these waters. In May 2022, the two countries sent strategic bombers near Japan when leaders of the Quadrilateral Security Dialogue (Australia, India, Japan, and the US)—also known as the Quad—met in Tokyo. Later, in November, Chinese H-6K strategic bombers and Russian Tu-95MS bombers, escorted by Russian Su-30SM and Su-35S fighter jets, flew near Japan and South Korea. The Chinese and Russian aircraft intruded into South Korea's Air Defense Identification Zone with the apparent intention of threatening one of the US' most important allies in the region.

A significant shift occurred in 2023, when the frequency of joint patrols tripled, with two exercises conducted in the Sea of Japan and the East China Sea. The Global Times, as the mouthpiece of the Chinese Communist Party, highlighted the "solid" military cooperation between China and Russia demonstrated through these patrols (Enkhbat, 2024).

The "Joint Sea 2022" exercise took place in the East China Sea in December 2022. According to the official website of the People's Liberation Army (PLA), a senior Chinese naval officer emphasized the importance of these joint exercises, stating that they have developed into a stable platform for cooperation and an important communication channel for the two countries' militaries. The "Joint Sea 2023" exercise, conducted in the Sea of Japan, involved more than 30 naval aircraft, including anti-submarine aircraft, helicopters, and interceptor fighters from both navies. Through these exercises, the two sides demonstrated mutual support as close strategic partners (Enkhbat, 2024).

On November 29-30, 2024, China and Russia conducted their ninth joint air patrol in the Sea of Japan and the East China Sea. During this patrol, China deployed H-6N bombers, marking the first time the People's Liberation Army deployed nuclear-capable bombers in such patrols (Chen, 2024). From China's perspective, these exercises serve a deterrent function by demonstrating Russian support. "Military Strategic Science," a key Chinese publication on military strategy and doctrine published in 2020, emphasizes the role of these exercises in creating confusion and instability. The book asserts that the exercises achieve a deterrent effect by showcasing the PLA's combat capabilities to potential adversaries, inspiring doubt about China's intentions, and causing psychological uncertainty.

e) Joint Exercises in the South China Sea

After an eight-year hiatus, the two countries returned to the region with a joint naval exercise in the SCS in 2024. From July 14 to 17, 2024, the joint naval exercise took place in the SCS, an area where China faces increasing tensions with the Philippines near disputed features. Over the past two years, tensions have escalated as the Chinese Coast Guard used water cannons and rammed Philippine vessels supplying food and water to troops stationed on the BRP Sierra Madre at Second Thomas Shoal (Enkhbat, 2024). Russia's participation in joint naval exercises in the SCS—an area of considerable strategic importance to China—could signal strengthening ties between the two countries' militaries. China sometimes uses military exercises as a warning to rivals that Beijing considers to have engaged in provocative actions. By demonstrating close military ties with Russia, China seeks to deter actions that could undermine its interests or pose a threat to its territorial claims.

In late July 2024, China and Russia held a joint naval exercise near Kaliningrad on the Gulf of Finland. This marks the first time China has participated in a joint naval exercise in a location that could be perceived as provocative to third parties such as Finland. This could be viewed as China's reciprocation to Russia, strengthening the partnership and supporting Russia in the face of NATO expansion. China's rhetoric has generally focused on criticizing the US without directly mentioning NATO as a collective adversary. This action reflects a shift in China's approach to the West, now viewing it as a unified adversary rather than focusing on individual members like the US.

Overall, the frequent joint military exercises between China and Russia serve as a foundation for strengthening the strategic alignment between the two countries. China benefits from a closer military partnership with Russia, which Beijing hopes will serve as an effective deterrent against the US and its allies. China's deterrent intentions through joint exercises with Russia can be inferred from the location, frequency, and type of exercises and patrols conducted.

Joint exercises in sensitive areas such as the SCS and the Gulf of Finland serve as a form of geopolitical messaging. By holding exercises in these areas, Russia and China are signaling to the West their combined military capabilities and willingness to cooperate in areas of mutual interest. Strategic air patrols in the Sea of Japan and the East China Sea often target major US allies in East Asia, such as Japan and South Korea, while joint strategic air patrols and naval exercises near US territory in the Pacific appear aimed at demonstrating capabilities in America's strategic backyard. In the North Pacific, joint coast guard patrols and naval exercises may indicate China's growing interest in strengthening its Arctic presence. However, as China forges military ties with Russia, it must carefully balance this partnership to avoid increasing Russian influence in the Pacific, which could undermine China's own strategic interests. Russia's increasing involvement in East Asian affairs—particularly its influence over North Korea—and its expanding naval presence are likely to complicate China's regional role.

As China and Russia improve interoperability through joint exercises and strategic patrols, as well as increased military cooperation including joint weapons development, NATO will need to closely monitor strategic areas where China aligns military interests with Russia. This alignment could weaken the strategic position of key NATO member states, such as the US, while strengthening the positions of China and Russia. Although the Pacific lies outside NATO's traditional area of focus, any significant military activities in the East are likely to force NATO member states to divert attention from core strategic interests, thus disrupting their ability to concentrate resources effectively.

4. ASSESSING THE TRENDS AND LIMITATIONS IN MILITARY COOPERATION BETWEEN RUSSIA AND CHINA (2021-2025)

Between 2021 and 2025, Sino-Russian naval cooperation in the Indo-Pacific experienced a discernible intensification in both operational tempo and geographical scope, reflecting broader strategic adjustments by both countries in response to a rapidly evolving security environment. This expansion, however, should not be interpreted as evidence of the formation of a military alliance. Instead, it indicates a pattern of selective and carefully calibrated cooperation shaped simultaneously by shared external pressures and by persistent structural constraints within the bilateral relationship.

A central development during this period was the increased frequency of joint naval exercises and patrols. In contrast to earlier phases when bilateral military interactions were primarily symbolic and confidence-building in nature, post-2021 cooperation demonstrated greater regularity and repetition. This shift became more evident after 2022, as Russia faced mounting military and economic pressure from Western states following the conflict in Ukraine, while China encountered a more consolidated US-led security architecture in the Indo-Pacific. Under these conditions, joint naval activities offered both sides a relatively low-cost yet highly visible mechanism for signaling strategic alignment. The rising operational tempo therefore served not only training-related objectives but also a broader communicative function, allowing Moscow and Beijing to complicate the strategic calculations of external actors without incurring the risks associated with formal alliance commitments.

This increase in frequency was accompanied by a gradual expansion in the spatial reach of Sino-Russian naval cooperation. Whereas earlier activities were largely confined to proximate maritime areas such as the East China Sea and the Sea of Japan, the 2021–2025 period witnessed joint operations extending into more distant and strategically sensitive regions. These included the North Pacific, the Bering Sea, the Sea of Okhotsk, the SCS, and parts of the Arctic. Operations conducted near Alaska and the Aleutian Islands were particularly notable, as they signaled an enhanced capacity for joint presence in areas closely connected to core US security interests. At the same time, exercises in the SCS and adjacent waters allowed China to reinforce deterrence in contested maritime spaces while enabling Russia to maintain a visible military profile in the Asia-Pacific despite resource constraints stemming from its commitments in Europe.

Despite these expansions in frequency and geographical scope, Sino-Russian naval cooperation continued to exhibit clear limitations. Most importantly, the relationship has not progressed toward institutionalized military integration. There is no evidence of permanent joint command structures, unified operational doctrines, or binding mutual defense obligations. Even in the Arctic, where cooperation has intensified, Russia has retained strict control over access to key military infrastructure, reflecting enduring concerns over sovereignty and long-term strategic autonomy. These patterns suggest that cooperation remains embedded within a framework of pragmatic caution rather than deep strategic trust.

From China's perspective, cooperation with Russia has facilitated opportunities to operate beyond the First Island Chain and to gain experience in complex maritime environments. Nevertheless, Beijing has consistently avoided entanglement in Russia's core security disputes or any arrangement that might grant Moscow influence over China's maritime priorities, particularly in the SCS. This restraint underscores the extent to which naval cooperation is viewed by China as a supplementary strategic instrument rather than a foundational element of its regional security policy.

Taken together, Sino-Russian naval cooperation in the Indo-Pacific during the 2021–2025 period can be characterized as a process of controlled expansion rather than comprehensive integration. While the frequency and geographical scope of joint activities increased significantly, the depth of cooperation remained deliberately limited. This balance reflects a shared interest in managing external strategic pressure while preserving strategic autonomy. As a result, Sino-Russian naval cooperation is likely to persist as a flexible and instrumental partnership, adapting to shifts in the regional security environment without fundamentally altering the independent strategic trajectories of either country.

5. STRATEGIC RESPONSES TO SINO-RUSSIAN NAVAL COOPERATION: THE US AND ASEAN

5.1. US

Amid the intensification of Sino-Russian maritime security cooperation, countries across the Indo-Pacific have exhibited a wide range of responses shaped by their respective strategic interests and concerns about entanglement in great-power competition. Rather than converging toward a unified regional stance, both states and regional institutions have articulated diverse—and at times contradictory—responses, reflecting variations in national interests, degrees of strategic dependence, and threat perceptions.

Prior to the deepening of Sino-Russian maritime cooperation, the US had already intensified its implementation of the Free and Open Indo-Pacific (FOIP) strategy. This approach involved expanding security alliances and partnerships, notably through frameworks such as the QUAD and AUKUS; increasing the frequency of FONOPs; and strengthening forward military presence via bilateral arrangements, including the Enhanced Defense Cooperation Agreement (EDCA) with the Philippines. Collectively, these measures signaled a discernible shift in US policy away from inclusive balancing toward a more exclusionary model in response to Sino-Russian maritime cooperation. Initially articulated in 2017, the FOIP strategy has been largely sustained and recalibrated under the Biden administration. It continues to rest on three principal pillars:

First, between 2017 and 2022, the US Navy conducted 24 FONOPs in the SCS, marking a substantial increase compared to preceding periods (Storey, 2020). While framed as efforts to uphold international maritime law, these operations primarily function as unilateral assertions of navigational rights rather than as confidence-building measures embedded within bilateral or multilateral institutional frameworks. In contrast to ASEAN's consensus-based approach—particularly through mechanisms such as the ASEAN Defence Ministers' Meeting Plus (ADMM+) aimed at developing shared maritime norms—FONOPs are executed outside regional multilateral arrangements and largely beyond institutional constraints.

This dynamic reveals a strategic paradox. Temporal correlation analysis indicates that despite the escalation of FONOPs, Sino-Russian joint naval exercises increased from two during the 2012–2016 period to approximately six between 2017 and 2022. Notably, the Joint Sea exercises in 2021 and 2022 were conducted in contested maritime areas where FONOPs had also taken place. This overlap suggests that FONOPs may have inadvertently provided a legitimizing rationale for closer Sino-Russian maritime coordination rather than serving as an effective deterrent. Concerns over the deepening of Sino-Russian military cooperation have also been articulated by US strategic analysts, particularly regarding the potential transfer of sensitive submarine technologies from Russia to China. Such cooperation, analysts warn, could significantly alter the regional naval balance. The Commander of US Indo-Pacific Command (INDOPACOM) has similarly expressed apprehension that access to advanced Russian submarine technology could enable China to accelerate its naval modernization and potentially outpace the US in certain capability areas (Wishnick, 2025).

Second, beyond operational measures at sea, Washington has reinforced its regional security architecture through minilateral frameworks such as the Quadrilateral Security Dialogue (QUAD) and AUKUS, alongside an array of bilateral defense agreements. Both the QUAD (US, Japan, India, and Australia) and AUKUS (US, United Kingdom, and Australia) explicitly exclude China and Russia, thereby constituting exclusionary security groupings that, as Evelyn Goh cautions, risk destabilizing the regional order by intensifying bloc-based confrontation.

The QUAD's maritime agenda has focused on enhancing maritime domain awareness (MDA), with increasing emphasis on anti-submarine warfare (ASW), intelligence, surveillance, and reconnaissance (ISR) sharing, as well as capacity-building assistance for smaller coastal states. In their 2023 Joint Statement, QUAD leaders reaffirmed that they "reiterate [their] unwavering commitment to a free, open, inclusive, and resilient Indo-Pacific region" (White House, 2023). Nevertheless, while the QUAD's strengthened MDA and ASW capabilities are clearly aimed at countering China's expanding long-range naval power, the framework itself remains structured as a traditional hub-and-spokes arrangement rather than as an inclusive, multi-centric security architecture aligned with ASEAN preferences.

More broadly, minilateral arrangements such as the QUAD and AUKUS tend to function in a competitive manner that is neither fully supportive of nor complementary to ASEAN-led regional mechanisms. ASEAN's strategic outlook, as articulated in the 2019 ASEAN Outlook on the Indo-Pacific (AOIP), underscores the importance of maintaining strategic balance through cooperation across four priority areas: maritime cooperation, connectivity, implementation of the 2030 Sustainable Development Goals (SDGs), and economic collaboration. Central to the AOIP are principles of inclusiveness, non-alignment, and non-confrontation

(ASEAN, 2019). These principles stand in marked contrast to the structural logic underpinning the QUAD and AUKUS. Whereas the AOIP advocates engagement with all major powers through ASEAN-centered platforms, the QUAD operates as a parallel forum that excludes ASEAN as a collective actor, thereby diluting ASEAN centrality and complicating efforts to sustain a cohesive and inclusive regional security order.

Third, the expansion of military facilities under EDCA in the Philippines—from five designated sites in 2016 to nine in 2023—signals a consolidation of the traditional US-Philippines alliance rather than the flexible and inclusive patterns of interaction emphasized in Evelyn Goh's framework. This development underscores a preference for alliance-based hard balancing over the cultivation of comprehensive and multilateral linkages. According to a detailed report by the Center for Strategic and International Studies (CSIS), in April 2023 the US Department of Defense "announced its intention to allocate an additional US$18 million on top of the US$82 million previously committed to infrastructure investments at existing EDCA sites" (Asia Maritime Transparency Initiative, 2023).

Effectiveness of the US Strategy

Viewed through Goh's theoretical lens, US strategy in the Indo-Pacific has fallen short of achieving the objectives associated with the three strategic pillars, particularly in maintaining an inclusive balance of influence. The expansion of exclusionary alliance mechanisms has reinforced perceptions of "strategic encirclement," a dynamic that Goh identifies as inherently destabilizing to regional order. Within this context, Chinese and Russian leaders have increasingly framed US-led containment efforts as a shared strategic threat, thereby recasting bilateral cooperation as a defensive and adaptive response.

This convergence in strategic outlook is reflected in elite political discourse. In a 2023 speech, President Xi Jinping emphasized "substantive multilateralism" and the pursuit of "a multipolar world," signaling China's alignment with Russia in challenging what both perceive as a US-led unipolar order. Such narratives illustrate how Washington's exclusionary balancing policies have been interpreted in Beijing and Moscow not merely as external pressure but as confirmation of the necessity for deeper strategic alignment.

Empirically, this shift is evident in the frequency and scale of joint Sino-Russian naval exercises, which expanded markedly during the same period in which security mechanisms such as the QUAD and AUKUS became increasingly institutionalized. The Joint Sea exercises, in particular, not only multiplied in number but also broadened substantially in operational scope, extending from nearshore waters to distant maritime theaters, including waters around Japan, the SCS, as well as the Western

Pacific and Arctic regions. This evolution suggests that Sino-Russian naval cooperation represents a deliberate strategic adaptation to mounting pressure generated by US-led exclusionary balancing structures.

Furthermore, exclusionary balancing strategies often generate the very security dilemmas they are intended to mitigate. In this regard, the US "integrated deterrence" strategy, implemented through minilateral mechanisms such as the QUAD and AUKUS, reflects an alliance structure characterized by hub-and-spokes logic with clear lines of alignment. Rather than facilitating inclusive and flexible forms of cooperation, this structure compels regional states to adopt explicit strategic positions. Paradoxically, by framing the Sino-Russian partnership as a unified and enduring strategic threat requiring collective containment, US policy has contributed to solidifying the very image of alliance cohesion that Washington seeks to prevent. This framing risks overstating the durability and systemic nature of Sino-Russian cooperation, which remains largely transactional, adaptive, and notably devoid of formal alliance commitments.

Despite substantial US investment—estimated at approximately US$82 million annually—in infrastructure development under EDCA, the Philippines has been unable to prevent joint Sino-Russian naval activities, including live-fire exercises conducted within its Exclusive Economic Zone (EEZ) in 2023. This outcome underscores the limitations of exclusionary military arrangements in generating effective deterrence absent broader regional legitimacy and acceptance—attributes more commonly associated with inclusive security frameworks. While EDCA enhances US logistical access and deployment flexibility, it lacks credible escalation mechanisms below the threshold of direct military confrontation. Beijing and Moscow are likely cognizant that EDCA-related facilities primarily support surveillance, logistics, and strategic presence rather than sustained combat operations. Consequently, these measures have proven insufficient to deter joint naval exercises in contested maritime spaces.

Moreover, the US faces an inherent tension between security objectives and economic considerations in its sanctions regime targeting Arctic energy projects and the Northern Sea Route. In January 2025, Washington imposed new sanctions on approximately 180 vessels associated with Russia's so-called "shadow fleet," which is frequently employed to circumvent existing sanctions and facilitate Sino-Russian energy cooperation. While these measures aim to disrupt bilateral energy ties, they may simultaneously incentivize Beijing to reinforce its deterrence posture by expanding alternative shipping routes and deepening naval coordination with Moscow. Although such developments could reduce China's reliance on seaborne oil imports, they may also accelerate Beijing's pursuit of greater naval self-reliance and strategic autonomy (Wishnick, 2025).

5.2. ASEAN

ASEAN's response to Sino-Russian maritime cooperation should not be interpreted as strategic indecision but rather as a consistent application of the principles of comprehensive integration and balanced inclusion articulated in Evelyn Goh's theoretical framework. This approach diverges from conventional assessments that evaluate ASEAN's effectiveness primarily in terms of its alignment with US-led deterrence strategies.

The ASEAN Outlook on the Indo-Pacific (AOIP) promotes engagement with all major powers through ASEAN-led mechanisms, including the East Asia Summit (EAS), the ASEAN Defence Ministers' Meeting Plus (ADMM-Plus), and the ASEAN Regional Forum (ARF), rather than through the formation of exclusionary alliances. By prioritizing cooperation in less sensitive domains such as non-traditional maritime security, connectivity, and sustainable development, the AOIP seeks to foster interdependence as a means of reducing incentives for confrontation. Simultaneously, ASEAN implicitly acknowledges existing power hierarchies but endeavors to manage them through its role as an institutional "convenor" rather than attempting either to deny or to submit to hierarchical realities.

ASEAN's rejection of exclusionary balancing thus reflects structural constraints rather than strategic passivity. Varying degrees of economic dependence on China, the continued need for US security guarantees, and selective reliance on Russia in defense and energy sectors render confrontational alliances both impractical and costly for many Southeast Asian states. Within this context, comprehensive integration enables ASEAN to maximize benefits derived from multiple external partners without relinquishing essential strategic access, constituting an optimal strategic choice rather than an act of avoidance.

Accordingly, ASEAN has refrained from entering exclusionary security alignments while maintaining a posture of principled neutrality, thereby safeguarding its collective strategic autonomy. Moreover, despite the intensification of major-power military exercises and naval activities in the region, Southeast Asia has thus far avoided direct military conflict, underscoring the de-escalatory function of ASEAN-led integrative mechanisms. Nevertheless, ASEAN's centrality faces mounting challenges from the proliferation of smaller minilateral security arrangements such as the QUAD and AUKUS, which increasingly divert strategic attention away from ASEAN-centered forums.

Within ASEAN, member states have adopted differentiated yet complementary strategies that reflect the logic of comprehensive integration rather than rigid alignment. The Philippines has established EDCA facilities linked to the US while simultaneously remaining a member of the Regional Comprehensive Economic Partnership (RCEP), participating in Belt and Road Initiative (BRI) projects with

China, and procuring military equipment from Russia. This multi-vector approach enables Manila to secure US security support without forfeiting economic access to China. Vietnam similarly hosts port visits and conducts joint patrols and exercises with the US while sustaining comprehensive strategic partnerships with both Russia and China. Despite experiencing 47 reported incidents of harassment by the Chinese Coast Guard in 2023, Hanoi has continued diplomatic engagement with Beijing, underscoring the premise that comprehensive integration must withstand short-term crises to preserve long-term strategic interaction. Cambodia presents another variant of this adaptive strategy. While facilitating the expansion of China's presence at Ream Naval Base—reportedly supported by approximately US$10 billion in Chinese investment between 2016 and 2024—Phnom Penh has also participated in US-ASEAN joint military exercises and received substantial development assistance from Japan. Notably, when the Philippines raised objections to China's claims in the SCS at the 2024 ASEAN Foreign Ministers' Meeting, Cambodia expressed support for Manila's position, illustrating how economic engagement does not translate mechanically into political subordination. Taken together, these cases demonstrate a pattern of comprehensive and calibrated alignment in which each state balances relations with major powers according to geographical position, economic dependence, historical experience, and defense capacity. This flexibility enhances ASEAN's collective resilience by preventing the crystallization of rigid military blocs.

At the regional level, negotiations over the Code of Conduct (COC) in the SCS can be understood as a form of process-based inclusive balancing. Although the negotiations have yet to yield binding outcomes, sustaining China's participation within a multilateral framework helps constrain unilateral behavior and gradually socialize Beijing into ASEAN-centered diplomatic norms. At the same time, the COC process highlights the limitations of inclusive balancing: while it can manage tensions and mitigate escalation, it does not eliminate coercive practices altogether. As Evelyn Goh emphasizes, the objective of such an approach is not the resolution of great-power rivalry per se but the preservation of strategic autonomy for secondary states within a fluid regional order. Overall, most regional responses to Sino-Russian maritime cooperation have generated only limited tactical effects, which are largely symbolic in nature, while failing to produce meaningful strategic deterrence. In some instances, these responses have even reinforced the dynamics of cooperation between Beijing and Moscow.

6. CONCLUSION

The intensification of Russia-China naval cooperation in the Indo-Pacific from 2021 to 2025 represents a significant evolution in regional security dynamics. This cooperation, driven by converging defensive imperatives rather than full strategic alignment, has expanded both in operational frequency and geographical scope. However, it remains characterized by careful calibration and persistent structural limitations that prevent full military integration. The regional responses to this development—particularly from the US and ASEAN—reveal fundamentally different strategic approaches. The US response, centered on exclusionary minilateral frameworks and increased military presence, may have inadvertently reinforced the very dynamics it seeks to counter. ASEAN's approach, grounded in comprehensive engagement and balanced influence, has preserved member states' strategic autonomy while managing tensions, though it faces ongoing challenges from the proliferation of alternative security arrangements. Looking forward, Sino-Russian naval cooperation is likely to persist as a flexible and instrumental partnership, adapting to shifts in the regional security environment without fundamentally altering either country's independent strategic trajectory. The effectiveness of regional responses will depend on the ability to balance deterrence with engagement, preserve institutional centrality, and maintain strategic autonomy amid intensifying great-power competition.

REFERENCES

Agence France-Presse in Oslo. (2024). Norway blocks sale of last private land on Svalbard after Chinese interest. *The Guardian*. https://www.theguardian.com/world/article/2024/jul/01/norway-blocks-sale-last-private-landsvalbard-china-interest

Al Jazeera. (2023). US deployed warships after China, Russia naval patrol near Alaska: WSJ. https://www.aljazeera.com/news/2023/8/7/us-deployedwarships-after-china-russia-naval-patrol-near-alaska-wsj

ASEAN. (2019). *ASEAN Outlook on the Indo-Pacific*. https://asean.org/wp-content/uploads/2021/01/ASEAN-Outlook-on-the-Indo-Pacific_FINAL_22062019.pdf

Asia Maritime Transparency Initiative. (2023). *More than meets the eye: Philippine upgrades at EDCA sites*. https://amti.csis.org/more-than-meets-the-eye-philippine-upgrades-at-edca-sites/

Balazs, D. (2025). *China-Russia dual-use cooperation stays resilient amid sanctions*. S. Rajaratnam School of International Studies. https://rsis.edu.sg/rsis-publication/rsis/china-russia-dual-use-cooperation-stays-resilient-amid-sanctions/

Bela, V. (2025). China and Russia sign nuclear reactor deal to fuel lunar research station. *South China Morning Post*. https://www.scmp.com/news/china/science/article/3310315/china-and-russia-sign-nuclear-reactor-deal-fuel-lunar-research-station

Chabarovskaya, N. (2025). *Going steady: China and Russia's economic ties are deeper than Washington thinks*. Center for European Policy Analysis. https://cepa.org/comprehensive-reports/going-steady-china-and-russias-economic-ties-are-deeper-than-washington-thinks/

Chen, Y. (2024). PLA steps up security cooperation with Russia in 2024. *The Jamestown Foundation*. https://jamestown.org/program/pla-steps-up-security-cooperation-with-russia-in-2024/

Choonara, J. (2022). The devastation of Ukraine: NATO, Russia and imperialism. *International Socialism, 174*. https://www.researchgate.net/profile/Joseph-Choonara/publication/359585713_The_devastation_of_Ukraine_NATO_Russia_and_imperialism/links/62446cda7931cc7ccf05f724/The-devastation-of-Ukraine-NATO-Russia-and-imperialism.pdf

Eiterjord, T. (2023). Checking back in on China's nuclear icebreaker. *The Diplomat*. https://thediplomat.com/2023/02/checking-back-in-on-chinas-nuclear-icebreaker/

Enkhbat, N. (2024). What China-Russia military exercises portend for Taiwan and beyond. *per Concordiam: Journal of European Security and Defense Issues*. https://perconcordiam.com/joint-implications/

Enkhbat, N. (2025). *Friends with benefits: Assessing Russian–Chinese military exercises* (Research Paper No. 7). NATO Defense College.

Global Times. (2024). China, Russia hold first meeting of subcommittee on Arctic shipping routes cooperation. https://www.globaltimes.cn/page/202411/1323886.shtml

He, K., & Li, M. (2020). Understanding the dynamics of the Indo-Pacific: US–China strategic competition, regional actors, and beyond. *International Affairs*, *96*(1), 1–7. DOI: 10.1093/ia/iiz242

Hiep, T. X., Hoan, T. Q., & Kiet, L. H. (2024). Free and Open Indo-Pacific strategy: Competitive Opinions and Trends. *Vestnik of Saint Petersburg University -. International Relations*, *17*(3), 242–259.

Jones, A. (2023). ESA is no longer planning to send astronauts to China's Tiangong space station. *SpaceNews*. https://spacenews.com/esa-is-no-longer-planning-to-send-astronauts-to-chinas-tiangong-space-station/

Karkalanov, T. (2016). Energy in Russia's foreign policy and EU-Russia relations circumventing sanctions: Yamal LNG becomes a precedent. *Russian International Affairs Council*. https://russiancouncil.ru/en/blogs/tsvetko-karkalanov-en/_2472/

Kiet, L. H., Binh, N. T., & Hiep, T. X. (2025a). From border conflicts to maritime competition: Driving forces behind the power rivalry between India and China in the Indian Ocean region. *Australian Journal of Maritime and Ocean Affairs*, •••, 1–25. DOI: 10.1080/18366503.2025.2492438

Kiet, L. H., Tam, L. T. T., & Hiep, T. X. (2025b). Caught between dragon and elephant: Vietnam's strategic balancing act in the Sino-Indian rivalry. *China Quarterly of International Strategic Studies*, *11*(2), 99–128. DOI: 10.1142/S237774002550006X

Legarda, H. (2025). *The Arctic, outer space and influence-building: China and Russia join forces to expand in new strategic frontiers* (Policy Brief). Mercator Institute for China Studies. https://doi.org/DOI: 10.5281/zenodo.17422312

Mahdzir, D. (2024). NORAD jets intercept joint Russian, Chinese bomber flight near Alaska. *USNI News*. https://news.usni.org/2024/07/25/norad-jets-intercept-joint-russian-chinese-bomber-flights-near-alaska

Matzen, E. (2017). Denmark spurned Chinese offer for Greenland base over security – sources. *Reuters*. https://www.reuters.com/article/world/denmark-spurned-chinese-offer-for-greenland-base-over-security-sourcesidUSKBN1782E1/

Mhadzir, D. (2024). 9 Russian, Chinese warships on joint patrol in the Northwest Pacific after major naval exercise. *U.S. Naval Institute News*. https://news.usni.org/2024/10/01/9-russian-chinese-warships-on-joint-patrol-in-the-northwest-pacific-after-major-naval-exercise

Ministry of Foreign Affairs of the People's Republic of China. (2024). China and Russia hold the first consultation on the peaceful uses of outer space affairs. https://www.mfa.gov.cn/mfa_eng/xw/wjbxw/202408/t20240809_11468731.htm

Roy-Chaudhury, R., & Sullivan de Estrada, K. (2022). India and US FONOPs: Oceans apart. In Sullivan de Estrada, K., & Roy-Chaudhury, R. (Eds.), *Survival* (1st ed., pp. 1–26). Routledge., DOI: 10.4324/9781003422174-11

Scott, M. (2024). When is the Northeast Passage open to ship traffic? *National Snow and Ice Data Center*. https://nsidc.org/learn/ask-scientist/when-northeast-passage-open-ship-trafc

Staalesen, A. (2017). Murmansk counts on Chinese investors. *The Barents Observer*. https://www.thebarentsobserver.com/industry-and-energy/murmansk-counts-on-chinese-investors/135263

Storey, I. (2020). *Southeast Asia and the COVID-19 pandemic: Impact and response*. ISEAS Yusof Ishak Institute.

Sun, Y. (2018). The Northern Sea Route: The myth of Sino-Russian cooperation. *Stimson Center*. https://www.stimson.org/2018/northern-sea-route/

TASS. (2017). Arkhangelsk governor names China as key partner in Arctic projects. https://tass.com/economy/981893

The State Council Information Office of the People's Republic of China. (2018). *China's Arctic policy*. https://english.www.gov.cn/archive/white_paper/2018/01/26/content_281476026660336.htm

Udah, J., Sonne, P., & Troianovski, A. (2025). Secret Russian intelligence document shows deep suspicion of China. *The New York Times*. https://www.nytimes.com/2025/06/07/world/europe/china-russiaspies-documents-putin-war.html

Vanttinen, P. (2021). Finland denied China airbase in the Arctic. *Euractiv*. https://www.euractiv.com/short_news/finland-denied-china-airbase-in-the-arctic/

Wangsh, L. (2024). Chinese Coast Guard conduct joint patrol in Arctic Ocean. *China Daily*. https://global.chinadaily.com.cn/a/202410/02/WS66fce050a310f1265a1c5f6c.html

White House. (2023). *Quad Leaders' Joint Statement*. https://bidenwhitehouse.archives.gov/briefing-room/statements-releases/2023/05/20/quad-leaders-joint-statement/

Williams, H., Bingen, K. A., & MacKenzie, L. (2024). Why did China and Russia stage a joint bomber exercise near Alaska? *Center for Strategic and International Studies*. https://www.csis.org/analysis/why-did-china-and-russia-stage-joint-bomber-exercise-near-alaska

Wilson, J. L. (2002). Strategic partners: Russian-Chinese relations and the July 2001 friendship treaty. *Problems of Post-Communism*, *49*(3), 3–13. DOI: 10.1080/10758216.2002.11655984

Wishnick, E. (2025). The Sino-Russian partnership: Cooperation without coordination. *China Leadership Monitor*. https://www.prcleader.org/post/the-sino-russian-partnership-cooperation-without-coordination

Xuanzum, L. (2023). Russian warships visit China following joint naval patrol in Pacific Ocean. *Global Times*. https://www.globaltimes.cn/page/202308/1296785.shtml

Zhang, T., Zhang, X., & Ke, X. (2021). Quad-FPN: A novel quad feature pyramid network for SAR ship detection. *Remote Sensing (Basel)*, *13*(14), 2771. Advance online publication. DOI: 10.3390/rs13142771

Zhuo, C. (n.d.). Coast Guard, Russia Security Service sign joint MoE. *Ministry of National Defence of the People's Republic of China*. http://eng.mod.gov.cn/xb/MilitaryServices/News_213106/16220829.html

Chapter 5
QUAD and AUKUS: A Smart Power Approach to Indo-Pacific Maritime Security

Jamal Mokhtari
https://orcid.org/0009-0009-8826-453X
Ferdowsi University of Mashhad, Iran

ABSTRACT

This chapter examines Indo-Pacific maritime security through comparative analysis of the QUAD and AUKUS frameworks. The QUAD employs soft power through UNCLOS advocacy, maritime domain awareness, capacity-building, and infrastructure development to foster rules-based cooperation and regional trust. AUKUS deploys hard power via nuclear-powered submarines, advanced military technologies, and joint patrols to provide credible deterrence against coercion. The analysis demonstrates that while each framework operates distinctly, their strategic integration produces synergistic outcomes: QUAD surveillance capabilities inform AUKUS enforcement operations, while AUKUS military assets secure QUAD infrastructure investments. The chapter argues that effective Indo-Pacific maritime security requires balanced approaches combining QUAD's normative influence with AUKUS's deterrent capabilities.

1. INTRODUCTION

The Indo-Pacific region, situated at the crossroads of global trade routes, geopolitical rivalries, and strategic maritime corridors, has emerged as a focal point of 21st-century security dynamics (Hiep et al., 2024). The region confronts complex maritime security challenges, including territorial disputes, freedom of navigation issues, and increasing militarization. Regional and trans-regional actors struggle

DOI: 10.4018/979-8-3373-4470-6.ch005

to balance cooperative diplomacy with military deterrence to maintain maritime stability. China's economic growth and military assertiveness, particularly regarding territorial claims in the South China Sea, have exacerbated tensions and prompted the United States to expand its regional presence to counter Chinese influence (Tertia & Perwita, 2018; Kiet et al., 2025b). Besides, additional threats including piracy, terrorism, and illegal fishing further compromise regional stability (Rahman, 2013).

Comprehensive security cooperation has become essential to address these interlinked threats in the Indo-Pacific. Two distinct frameworks have emerged: the Quadrilateral Security Dialogue (QUAD), comprising Australia, India, Japan, and the United States, and the trilateral AUKUS pact among Australia, the United Kingdom, and the United States. Both the QUAD and AUKUS play significant roles in shaping regional maritime security architecture, particularly in response to China's growing assertiveness (Hiep et al., 2024). While both alliances address common security challenges, they employ fundamentally different approaches. The QUAD emphasizes soft power through multilateral diplomacy and normative influence (Zhang, 2022), whereas AUKUS prioritizes hard power capabilities (Shi, 2022). AUKUS complements the QUAD by providing advanced military technologies, particularly nuclear-powered submarines, which enhance Australia's defense capabilities and strengthen regional deterrence (Lubis et al., 2024).

This study investigates how these contrasting strategies affect maritime security outcomes in the Indo-Pacific. The research question asks: How do the soft power approaches of the QUAD and the hard power of AUKUS influence regional maritime security outcomes, and what impact do these different strategies have on stability and deterrence in the region? Through comparative qualitative analysis of policy documents, joint declarations, and regional security assessments, this study evaluates each framework's effectiveness in addressing threats including maritime disputes, freedom of navigation challenges, and territorial coercion.

The research findings indicate that the QUAD and AUKUS embody complementary yet contrasting roles. The QUAD creates inclusive partnerships to reduce tensions through cooperative engagement in humanitarian assistance and disaster relief (HADR), fostering a rules-based order and promoting democratic values. The alliance established its framework for cooperation through collaborative disaster response to the 2004 tsunami (Lubis, 2022). Concurrently, regional actors including Japan and South Korea have increased defense spending and modernization efforts to counterbalance China's growing assertiveness (Cheng, 2022). AUKUS signals resolve through tangible military capabilities. Their coexistence underscores a broader paradigm shift in regional security that increasingly calls for a hybrid strategy combining diplomatic engagement with credible deterrence.

By bridging debates on the efficacy of soft and hard power, this analysis contributes to scholarly and policy discussions on navigating the complex Indo-Pacific security landscape. It argues for a nuanced approach that balances the normative influence of the QUAD with the deterrence posture of AUKUS, offering insights into maintaining long-term stability amid intensifying great power competition.

2. THEORETICAL FRAMEWORK

This study employs Joseph Nye's smart power theory as its analytical lens to examine how the QUAD and AUKUS employ divergent yet potentially complementary strategies in addressing Indo-Pacific maritime security challenges. Smart power theory provides a conceptually robust framework for understanding how states can strategically integrate coercive capabilities (hard power) with persuasive influence (soft power) to achieve foreign policy objectives more effectively than either approach could accomplish independently.

Joseph Nye introduced smart power in response to observed limitations in traditional single-modality approaches to international relations. His analysis revealed that relying exclusively on military coercion or diplomatic attraction proved insufficient for addressing the complex, multidimensional challenges characterizing contemporary global politics. Nye articulates this insight directly: "The process of converting power from resources to desired outcomes is a sensitive and crucial intermediate variable. The possession of power resources does not guarantee the achievement of desired outcomes in all circumstances. The prerequisite for converting resources into tangible power is an optimal strategy and prudent management" (Nye, 2011, p. 30). This observation forms the conceptual foundation for smart power—the recognition that strategic integration and adaptive application of diverse power instruments determine effectiveness, not merely the quantity of resources possessed. Smart power thus represents a pragmatic synthesis rather than a wholesale rejection of existing theoretical traditions. It acknowledges that different international situations demand different tools, and that rigid adherence to single paradigms constrains strategic flexibility. By advocating context-dependent combinations of coercion and attraction, smart power theory responds directly to the complexity of modern international relations, where purely military or purely diplomatic approaches prove inadequate (Bugulashvili & Scott, 2022).

2.1. Theoretical Foundations: Integrating Realism and Liberalism

Smart power theory draws deliberately from both realism and liberal traditions in international relations, synthesizing their core insights while transcending their limitations. From realism, smart power inherits its focus on hard power—the coercive instruments of military force, economic sanctions, and material capabilities that directly shape adversary behavior through threats or demonstrations of strength (Kiet et al., 2025a). Realism interpretations of military power have evolved beyond crude materialism to recognize intangible dimensions such as technological sophistication, strategic doctrine, and force projection capabilities (Banevičienė, 2021). Smart power incorporates this nuanced realism understanding, acknowledging that military strategies must continuously adapt to changing security environments and evolving perceptions of power. Crucially, smart power retains realism's fundamental commitment to power politics and national interests, rejecting idealistic assumptions that cooperation will spontaneously emerge through shared norms alone. It advocates pragmatic approaches where states judiciously balance military strength with diplomatic engagement to achieve concrete objectives in an anarchic international system (Jansson, 2018). This realism grounding ensures smart power remains attuned to the hard realities of strategic competition and deterrence requirements.

From liberalism, smart power incorporates emphasis on soft power—the capacity to achieve objectives through attraction, persuasion, and institutional cooperation rather than coercion. Soft power operates through cultural influence, diplomatic engagement, normative frameworks, and the projection of values that others find appealing. Liberal theory emphasizes that international institutions, multilateral partnerships, and shared norms can fundamentally shape state behavior by establishing expectations, reducing transaction costs, and creating reputational incentives for compliance (Bugulashvili & Scott, 2022). By integrating these traditions, smart power theory argues that military capabilities and cultural influence, coercion and cooperation, deterrence and engagement are not mutually exclusive but rather complementary tools that, when strategically coordinated, produce synergistic effects unattainable through either modality alone. This integration addresses a critical gap in traditional theories: realism's tendency to underestimate the role of legitimacy and normative influence in shaping sustained outcomes, and liberalism's tendency to underestimate the necessity of credible enforcement mechanisms in deterring aggression.

2.2. Core Principles of Smart Power

Smart power rests on three interrelated principles that guide its application to complex security challenges: pragmatism, multilateralism, and strategic integration.

First, pragmatism constitutes smart power's methodological foundation. Rather than adhering dogmatically to ideological preferences for either coercion or persuasion, pragmatism demands context-sensitive assessment of which instruments are most likely to achieve desired outcomes in specific circumstances (Brynteson, 2014). This principle recognizes that international relations present diverse challenges—some amenable to diplomatic resolution, others requiring credible military deterrence, and many demanding carefully calibrated combinations of both. Pragmatism thus emphasizes strategic adaptability and empirical evaluation of effectiveness, implementing thoughtful and sustainable policies that balance immediate action with long-term governance considerations (Nichols et al., 2021).

Second, multilateralism reflects smart power's recognition that contemporary security challenges transcend the capacity of individual states to resolve unilaterally. Climate change, maritime security, cybersecurity, terrorism, and pandemic disease demand coordinated international responses that pool resources, share information, and establish common normative frameworks. Smart power therefore emphasizes international cooperation, burden-sharing, and institution-building as force multipliers that enhance national influence while distributing costs (Nye, 2008). Multilateral approaches also generate legitimacy—a form of soft power that increases the acceptability of policy initiatives and reduces resistance from other states.

Third, strategic integration represents smart power's defining innovation. Integration refers to the deliberate, synergistic combination of hard power (coercive measures including military force and economic sanctions) and soft power (persuasive instruments including cultural influence and diplomacy) to achieve foreign policy goals more effectively than either could accomplish independently. Nye argues that effective leadership requires combining military and economic coercive strategies with persuasive and attractive approaches to create comprehensive foreign policy strategies (Nye, 2008).

Integration can take multiple forms. Sequential integration involves using soft power to build alliances and establish normative frameworks before employing hard power for collective action, or conversely, conducting military operations followed by soft power-driven post-conflict reconstruction and governance assistance. Simultaneous integration deploys both modalities concurrently—for example, maintaining military deterrence postures while simultaneously engaging in diplomatic negotiations, or providing development assistance alongside security partnerships. Mutually reinforcing integration creates positive feedback loops where soft power initiatives enhance the credibility and acceptability of hard power capabilities, while hard power capabilities provide enforcement mechanisms that give teeth to soft power norms (Bugulashvili & Scott, 2022).

This integration enables more nuanced responses to international problems, recognizing that neither hard power nor soft power alone suffices in today's interconnected world. Military might without legitimacy risks generating counterproductive resistance and coalitional opposition; diplomatic influence without credible enforcement mechanisms risks being dismissed as hollow rhetoric. Smart power seeks the optimal balance and coordination between these modalities.

2.3. Analytical Application to Maritime Security

Smart power theory provides an ideal framework for analyzing the QUAD and AUKUS approaches to Indo-Pacific maritime security because it illuminates both their individual logics and their potential for strategic complementarity.

The QUAD embodies soft power principles through its emphasis on multilateral cooperation, capacity building, normative influence, and voluntary partnerships. By promoting shared values (democracy, rule of law, freedom of navigation), strengthening partner capabilities (maritime domain awareness, disaster relief, infrastructure development), and advocating adherence to international legal frameworks (UNCLOS), the QUAD seeks to shape the regional security environment through attraction and persuasion rather than coercion (Hiep et al., 2024). These initiatives strengthen regional stability by increasing transparency, encouraging cooperation rather than confrontation, and building coalitions around shared interests (Nye, 2010). The persuasive nature of soft power fosters voluntary compliance and long-term partnership, creating durable foundations for regional order.

AUKUS represents hard power's role in maritime security through its focus on advanced military technologies, enhanced deterrence capabilities, and interoperability among defense forces. The provision of nuclear-powered submarines to Australia, development of hypersonic weapons, joint naval patrols, and integrated defense industrial bases signal credible military resolve and impose tangible costs on potential aggressors. These capabilities directly counter regional rivals' assertive actions, providing the deterrence necessary to maintain security when diplomatic persuasion proves insufficient (Han, 2020). Hard power thus supplies the coercive backbone that gives weight to normative commitments and demonstrates willingness to defend core interests.

Critically, smart power theory suggests these approaches are not inherently contradictory but potentially complementary. The QUAD's soft power builds regional legitimacy, establishes normative frameworks, and fosters inclusive partnerships that increase the acceptability and sustainability of security initiatives. AUKUS provides the enforcement credibility and deterrent capabilities that make violations of those norms costly and risky. When strategically integrated, soft power creates favorable diplomatic conditions for hard power deployment, while hard power ensures that soft power norms are taken seriously rather than dismissed as aspirational rhetoric. This synergy—where surveillance capabilities (soft power) inform enforcement operations (hard power), or where infrastructure investments (soft power) are protected by naval patrols (hard power)—exemplifies smart power's core logic.

3. METHODOLOGY

This study employs a structured comparative qualitative analysis to examine the maritime security strategies of the QUAD and the AUKUS alliance in the Indo-Pacific region. The methodological approach is designed to systematically evaluate how soft power and hard power mechanisms shape regional maritime security outcomes, with particular attention to their individual effectiveness and potential synergies. The research is guided by the central question: How do the soft power approaches of the QUAD and the hard power capabilities of AUKUS influence regional maritime security outcomes, and what implications do these divergent strategies hold for stability and deterrence in the Indo-Pacific?

The comparative qualitative approach was selected for its suitability in analyzing complex geopolitical phenomena where causal relationships are multifaceted and context-dependent. Unlike purely quantitative methods, qualitative analysis enables nuanced examination of policy intentions, institutional dynamics, and strategic narratives that underpin maritime security frameworks. The study adopts Joseph Nye's smart power theory as its analytical lens, providing a conceptually rigorous framework for evaluating the integration of soft and hard power instruments in contemporary security strategy. The analysis is structured around three evaluative criteria derived from Nye's theoretical tenets, operationalized to assess both individual alliance effectiveness and their potential for strategic integration. These criteria serve as analytical benchmarks throughout the comparative assessment:

Criterion 1: Institutional Cohesion and Normative Alignment. This dimension examines each framework's capacity to build inclusive partnerships, foster adherence to international legal norms, and generate legitimacy among diverse regional stakeholders. Effectiveness is measured through observable indicators including the expansion of diplomatic partnerships beyond core members, the frequency and substantive depth of joint initiatives with regional organizations such as ASEAN, and the consistency of public discourse supporting rules-based international order. This criterion draws on constructivist insights regarding the role of norms in shaping state behavior while acknowledging realism concerns about material interests (Nye, 2011; Bugulashvili & Scott, 2022).

Criterion 2: Tangible Capability and Deterrent Credibility. This criterion evaluates the deployment of measurable military and technological assets, the enhancement of operational interoperability among alliance members, and the demonstrable impact on adversarial risk calculations. Following Schelling's (1966) conceptualization, deterrence is understood not merely as the possession of military capabilities but as the successful communication of resolve and the credible threat of consequences that alter adversary behavior. Effectiveness indicators include quantitative increases in defense expenditure, concrete technology transfers (such as nuclear submarine acquisitions), the frequency and sophistication of joint military exercises, and observable modifications in adversarial conduct, particularly reductions in gray zone coercion within monitored maritime areas (Jansson, 2018; Han, 2020).

Criterion 3: Strategic Adaptability and Synergistic Integration. Representing the core principle of smart power, this criterion assesses the extent to which soft and hard power instruments are deliberately combined to produce outcomes greater than the sum of their parts. Synergistic integration is evidenced by initiatives where different power modalities reinforce one another—for instance, where maritime domain awareness data (soft power) directly informs and enables naval interdiction operations (hard power), or where humanitarian logistics (soft power) are facilitated through military transport infrastructure (hard power). This criterion emphasizes the adaptive capacity of security frameworks to respond to evolving threats through flexible deployment of complementary tools (Brynteson, 2014; Nichols et al., 2021).

The selection of the QUAD and AUKUS as primary case studies is justified by their prominence as the most significant minilateral security frameworks in the contemporary Indo-Pacific, explicitly designed to address maritime security challenges arising from regional power transitions. Both frameworks emerged in response to similar threat perceptions—particularly China's expanding maritime assertiveness—yet they embody fundamentally different strategic philosophies and operational modalities. This divergence provides analytical leverage for comparative assessment of soft versus hard power approaches. The QUAD, comprising Australia, India, Japan, and the United States, represents a diplomatic coalition emphasizing normative influence, capacity building, and multilateral cooperation. Its origins in the 2004 tsunami relief efforts and subsequent evolution into a comprehensive partnership centered on a "Free and Open Indo-Pacific" (FOIP) reflect conscious prioritization of soft power instruments. Conversely, AUKUS—a trilateral pact among Australia, the United Kingdom, and the United States announced in 2021—explicitly foregrounds military technology sharing, particularly nuclear-powered submarines, signaling a hard power-centric deterrence posture. The contrasting memberships, institutional structures, and strategic objectives of these frameworks make them ideal candidates for structured comparison within a smart power analytical framework.

The empirical foundation of this study rests on systematic triangulation of primary and secondary sources, enhancing analytical rigor and mitigating potential biases inherent in any single data type. Primary sources constitute the core evidence base and include official policy documents, joint communiqués, defense white papers, and bilateral or multilateral agreements issued by member governments. These documents provide authoritative statements of strategic intent, policy commitments, and institutional arrangements. Key primary sources examined include the QUAD Leaders' Joint Statements (2021–2024), the AUKUS partnership announcement and subsequent ministerial declarations, national security strategies of member states, and official defense budget allocations. Secondary sources complement primary materials by offering analytical perspectives, contextual interpretation, and empirical data on implementation and outcomes. These include peer-reviewed academic journal articles providing theoretical frameworks and empirical analyses, regional security assessments from established research institutions such as the Lowy Institute, Stimson Center, and Stockholm International Peace Research Institute (SIPRI), and credible news reports from international media outlets documenting real-time developments in regional maritime security. The integration of scholarly analysis with policy documentation enables examination of both stated intentions and observed practices, facilitating assessment of gaps between rhetoric and reality.

Data analysis proceeded through systematic thematic coding aligned with the theoretical framework's three evaluative criteria. All collected materials were reviewed and coded according to their relevance to institutional cohesion, tangible capability, or synergistic integration. This process involved identifying specific initiatives, policies, or actions attributable to either the QUAD or AUKUS, then categorizing these activities according to their power modality (soft, hard, or hybrid) and assessing their observable impacts on maritime security outcomes. Comparative analysis was conducted through structured paired comparison, examining how the QUAD and AUKUS address similar maritime security challenges through different strategic means. For each major security issue—including maritime disputes, freedom of navigation, capacity building, and deterrence—the study analyzed the specific approaches adopted by each framework, their implementation mechanisms, and their measurable or observable effects. This comparative lens illuminated both complementarities and contradictions between soft and hard power strategies, providing empirical grounding for theoretical arguments about smart power integration. To ensure analytical transparency and replicability, the study employed explicit coding criteria and maintained clear chains of evidence linking empirical observations to theoretical claims. Where quantitative data were available (such as defense spending increases, numbers of joint exercises, or incident frequencies), these were incorporated to substantiate qualitative assessments. However, recognizing the inherent limitations of available data in security studies—particularly regarding classified information and attribution challenges in gray zone activities—the analysis maintains appropriate epistemic humility, clearly distinguishing between established facts, plausible inferences, and speculative interpretations.

To ensure analytical precision, this study operationalizes core theoretical concepts in measurable or observable terms. Maritime security outcomes are defined as changes in four dimensions: (1) the frequency and intensity of maritime incidents and territorial disputes; (2) the security and reliability of sea lines of communication (SLOCs) against both traditional military threats and non-traditional challenges such as piracy and illegal fishing; (3) the capacity of coastal states to effectively monitor and enforce sovereign rights within their Exclusive Economic Zones (EEZs); and (4) the stability of the regional balance of power, measured through changes in military postures, alliance configurations, and patterns of strategic competition. Deterrence, following Schelling's (1966) foundational work, is conceptualized not as the mere possession of military capabilities but as the successful persuasion of potential adversaries that the costs of specific prohibited actions will exceed any anticipated benefits. Operationally, deterrence effectiveness is assessed through observable modifications in adversarial behavior—such as reduced frequency of coercive actions in monitored zones, altered patterns of military deployments, or demonstrated restraint in territorial assertiveness—rather than through capability inventories alone. This behavioral focus acknowledges that deterrence is ultimately a psychological and communicative phenomenon requiring adversary perception and belief, not simply material superiority. Soft power encompasses non-coercive instruments of influence including diplomatic engagement, capacity building assistance, normative advocacy through international institutions, economic incentives and partnerships, and the projection of attractive values and governance models. Hard power refers to coercive or deterrent capabilities including military force projection, advanced weapons systems, defense technology transfers, and economic sanctions. Smart power integration, the study's central analytical concept, denotes the strategic and synergistic combination of these modalities, where their coordinated deployment produces outcomes unattainable through either approach in isolation.

4. QUAD'S SOFT POWER APPROACH TO MARITIME SECURITY

The QUAD, consisting of the United States, Japan, India, and Australia, pursues a soft power approach to maritime security in the Indo-Pacific using non-coercive strategies to promote stability, cooperation, and compliance with international norms (Hiep et al., 2024). This multifaceted approach focuses on economic cooperation, capacity building, and rules-based order. The QUAD's soft power utilizes collective resources, shared democratic values, and multilateral partnerships to comprehensively address maritime security challenges. Focusing on self-determination, rule of law, and sustainable development, the QUAD supports a free, open, and inclusive Indo-Pacific, addressing challenges through cooperation rather than coercion. This strategy complements but does not replace hard power deterrence, reflecting a comprehensive vision for regional stability.

Frist, the QUAD's support for the United Nations Convention on the Law of the Sea (UNCLOS) underscores the importance of collective approaches to maritime sovereignty, particularly regarding South China Sea disputes. This framework is essential for maintaining order and stability in regions characterized by competing territorial claims and resource exploitation. International law, particularly UNCLOS, is increasingly recognized as essential for promoting regional peace and stability, providing frameworks for equitable resource distribution and conflict resolution (Sherwin, 2017). The QUAD's UNCLOS advocacy represents strategic efforts to counter unilateralism and strengthen rule of law in maritime sovereignty. UNCLOS promotes common approaches to maritime security, managing regional tensions through dialogue and shared governance (Singh, 2022). However, this advocacy's diplomatic impact requires scrutiny against tangible outcomes. While the QUAD's consistent invocation of UNCLOS strengthens normative frameworks, its effectiveness in curbing assertive behavior remains contested. Reports indicate over 2,000 instances of Chinese militia operations in contested EEZs in 2023, highlighting ongoing violations of international norms (Tahir & Amin, 2023). This suggests that while the QUAD's soft power fosters favorable diplomatic environments, it lacks coercive mechanisms to directly enforce compliance, highlighting potential space for smart power complement with AUKUS capabilities. This analysis demonstrates that QUAD UNCLOS advocacy strongly aligns with Criterion 1 (Institutional Cohesion and Normative Alignment) but reveals critical shortfalls in Criterion 2 (Tangible Capability and Deterrent Credibility) through inability to singularly alter adversarial behavior. UNCLOS enforcement mechanism limitations restrict effectiveness in curbing aggressive actions by states like China (Nafilla, 2025). China's gray zone tactics exploit legal ambiguities, complicating responses from other nations (McLaughlin, 2022).

Second, the QUAD promotes diplomatic engagement through multifaceted approaches emphasizing shared values, humanitarian cooperation, and climate diplomacy. Bringing together the United States, Japan, Australia, and India, the QUAD aims to promote a FOIP while countering China's assertive regional policies. This cooperative framework enhances security and facilitates dialogue and cooperation among member states and other regional actors. The QUAD serves as a platform for humanitarian assistance and disaster relief (HADR) initiatives, enabling member states to engage in joint operations enhancing regional cooperation (Stevenson & Envall, 2019). This practical engagement is politically neutral, making it an effective diplomatic tool even amid tensions. Collective commitment to democratic values strengthens diplomatic relations and promotes unified responses to regional challenges. This multilateral framework has evolved significantly since its 2017 revival, focusing on inclusivity and cooperation with regional institutions such as ASEAN, critical for maintaining stability facing rising tensions, particularly with China (Jaishankar, 2023). The QUAD relies on diplomatic solutions to conflicts consistent with ASEAN principles of non-interference and peaceful negotiation (Ulis, 2022), aiming to reduce tensions in disputed areas such as the South China Sea.

Third, the QUAD's infrastructure initiatives and maritime security efforts together strengthen Indo-Pacific stability and offer alternatives to China's influence, particularly vis-à-vis the Belt and Road Initiative (BRI). Infrastructure development enhances surveillance and response capabilities against maritime threats in the Indian Ocean Region (IOR). The QUAD significantly promotes infrastructure development through joint initiatives and investment strategies, aiming to improve regional connectivity, economic growth, and maritime security. It has initiated projects in digital technology and supply chain resilience to reduce dependence on China (Shekhar, 2022). For example, Japan and India are developing the Colombo Port Terminal in Sri Lanka and Mataram Port in Bangladesh, offering alternatives to Chinese-funded projects. Australia's investment in Pacific island infrastructure strengthens regional resilience to Chinese influence and ensures safe sea lanes. The Palau submarine cable exemplifies joint QUAD projects. In 2023, the QUAD announced new initiatives for clean energy infrastructure and undersea cables, including funding for a $600 million undersea cable connecting Palau to global telecommunications networks, reducing dependence on Chinese infrastructure. Submarine cables are essential for nearly all voice and internet traffic, including military and financial communications, making them critical to national security, maritime security, and economic stability (Clark, 2016). Infrastructure support for nations like the Solomon Islands similarly aims to reduce dependence on China, enhancing surveillance and response capabilities to maritime threats in the IOR.

Fourth, the QUAD supply chain resilience Initiative aims to increase supply chain resilience, indirectly strengthening maritime security by reducing vulnerabilities in global trade routes. Vulnerabilities in maritime supply chains, particularly between ports of origin and foreign ports, can be reduced through improved security measures and risk management strategies (Young & Gordon, 2020). By diversifying supply sources and reducing reliance on single vulnerability points, the initiative strengthens overall maritime supply chain resilience, increasing security against disruption. By strengthening intermodal transportation options, the initiative reduces reliance on sea routes often vulnerable to piracy and congestion (Zhang et al., 2024). Countries involved in the QUAD Initiative work to diversify supply chains and reduce dependence on weak points such as specific ports or shipping routes. Technology integration offers solutions to supply chain resilience. Advanced technologies such as blockchain and artificial intelligence increase transparency and risk management, making maritime operations safer and more efficient (Ameh, 2024). The QUAD has identified semiconductor supply chains, heavily concentrated in East Asia (e.g., Taiwan, South Korea), as significant vulnerabilities. More than 60% of the world's semiconductors are produced in Taiwan, most shipped through the South China Sea and Strait of Malacca. By localizing production in India, the QUAD would reduce reliance on these strategic waterways, potentially decreasing shipment volumes through these straits and thereby mitigating exposure to piracy and maritime terrorism, growing concerns in these regions (Pulungan, 2021). Furthermore, creating alternative production sites in India and Australia (e.g., Lynas Rare Earths processing) would reduce dependence on East Asian sea routes and decentralize critical trade flows. Strengthening India's role as semiconductor manufacturer would boost intra-QUAD trade, utilize safer Indian Ocean routes, and reduce pressure on traditional maritime bottlenecks.

Fifth, the QUAD nations face increasing competition, particularly from China, necessitating enhanced MDA to safeguard national interests in the Pacific region (Péron-Doise, 2024). The QUAD launched the Indo-Pacific Maritime Domain Awareness Initiative (IPMDA) to share satellite data and technology with regional partners, enabling real-time monitoring of illegal fishing, piracy, and unauthorized maritime activities. IPMDA integrates data from commercial satellites (e.g., HawkEye 360, Capella Space) to monitor "dark shipping" (vessels disabling transponders), often linked to illegal fishing or unauthorized transfers. Therefore, MDA enhances partners' ability to secure their Exclusive Economic Zones (EEZs). Assessing IPMDA effectiveness requires empirical indicators. While direct causal links are complex, regional data suggests progress. The Food and Agriculture Organization (FAO) has noted declining trends in reported illegal, unreported, and unregulated (IUU) fishing incidents in the Indian Ocean since IPMDA's launch. Furthermore, partners like Indonesia have credited shared MDA data with facilitating seizures of vessels engaged in illegal fishing. For example, in late 2023, the Indonesian Ministry of Maritime Affairs and Fisheries reported a 15% increase in successful interdictions in its EEZ, attributing this to enhanced domain awareness from partnerships like the QUAD (Péron-Doise, 2024). The IPMDA initiative thus represents a potent tool for Criterion 1 (Institutional Cohesion) by building cooperative partnerships, while resulting increases in interdictions provide measurable, albeit indirect, indicators of progress toward Criterion 2 (Tangible Capability) by enhancing partners' enforcement capacity. QUAD partners deploy Automatic Identification Systems (AIS), satellite radar, and AI to monitor fishing vessels. India's Information Fusion Centre (IFC-IOR) collaborates with QUAD navies to track shipping lanes and piracy threats. MDA tools like satellite imagery and joint drills (e.g., Exercise Samudra Shakti) improve disaster response efficiency in the Indian Ocean and Pacific. MDA is essential for understanding threats to maritime security, including illegal fishing and smuggling (Bueger & Bergin, 2018), enabling countries to detect anomalies in maritime traffic and intervene in timely manners (Hutchins et al., 2008).

Finally, the QUAD emphasizes collaborative training programs enhancing maritime security capabilities among member states, focusing on both conventional and non-conventional threats (Bateman, 2005). These programs include joint exercises, information sharing, and best practices to improve operational readiness and response to maritime security challenges. QUAD training programs, particularly in HADR, play important roles in improving regional cooperation and maritime security in the Indo-Pacific. This cooperation includes Japan's capacity-building initiatives in Southeast Asia and India's leadership role in the Indian Ocean Rim Association (IORA) focusing on hydrographic support and disaster response training. The Japan Coast Guard (JCG) has implemented extensive capacity-building programs aimed at improving maritime safety and law enforcement in Southeast Asia. These initiatives bolster regional maritime security and align with Japan's broader diplomatic strategy of promoting a FOIP (Furuya, 2022). India has taken leadership roles in IORA, providing hydrographic support and disaster response training to member states, enhancing their capabilities to manage maritime challenges (Monahan et al., 2005).

5. AUKUS HARD POWER STRATEGIES

The AUKUS alliance, formed by Australia, the United Kingdom, and the United States, aims to enhance security cooperation in the Indo-Pacific region, primarily to counter China's growing influence, representing a significant shift in hard power dynamics. This partnership focuses on sharing advanced military technology, particularly nuclear-powered submarines. AUKUS formation is driven by several strategic motivations, including the need for the U.S. to reinforce its Indo-Pacific position, the UK's desire to assert global influence post-Brexit, and Australia's aim to bolster defense capabilities and political ties with key allies (Shi, 2022). AUKUS hard power mechanisms are based on military capabilities.

First, the AUKUS alliance focuses on strengthening collective hard power through military and technological cooperation. A central pillar is equipping Australia with nuclear-powered submarines (SSNs), significantly enhancing its maritime capabilities and deterrent posture against potential adversaries, particularly China (Childs, 2023). This initiative will substantially impact Indo-Pacific maritime security. Australia plans to acquire three to five Virginia-class submarines from the United States by the early 2030s. These acquisitions are central to building Criterion 2 (Tangible Capability) through enhanced interoperability and demonstrated military presence. Furthermore, the UK and Australia are jointly developing the SSN-AUKUS, a new submarine class combining British design and U.S. technology, scheduled to be operational in the 2040s. These submarines will be capable of carrying Tomahawk cruise missiles, significantly enhancing Australia's offensive capabilities. This partnership has prompted neighboring countries such as South Korea and Japan to consider acquiring similar technologies, dynamics that could lead to increased regional tensions, insecurity, and potential arms races (Lubis et al., 2024). Empirical evidence substantiates this concern. Following the AUKUS announcement, regional defense budgets and modernization plans accelerated notably. According to the SIPRI, Japan's defense budget for 2024 increased by 16.5%, the largest jump in decades, explicitly citing regional security concerns. Similarly, South Korea's Defense Acquisition Program Administration (DAPA) fast-tracked its own KSS-III Batch III submarine program, while Indonesia recently concluded negotiations for Scorpène-class submarines from France. This correlation does not imply sole causation but indicates clear regional trends of military modernization that AUKUS has undoubtedly intensified (Cheng, 2022; SIPRI Yearbook, 2024). While this unequivocally strengthens Criterion 2 (Tangible Capability and Deterrent Credibility) for AUKUS members, triggering regional military modernization simultaneously risks undermining Criterion 1 (Institutional Cohesion and Normative Alignment) by fueling security dilemmas and alienating partners like those in ASEAN.

Second, the AUKUS partnership significantly increases member states' production capacities for advanced munitions, emphasizing development of critical modern military technologies, including hypersonic missiles and autonomous weapon systems, to enhance deterrence strategies in the Indo-Pacific region. AUKUS focuses on developing hypersonic weapons capable of traveling at speeds exceeding Mach 5, providing strategic advantages in deterrence and rapid response scenarios (Dolan, 2024). The partnership aims to strengthen integrated deterrence, enabling coordinated military responses among the three countries and thereby improving regional security dynamics (Gumantiara et al., 2024). However, China views this alliance as provocation intensifying the regional security dilemma (Li, 2024). Besides, the AUKUS partnership enhances maritime security through joint exercises and patrols, which improve interoperability, readiness, and collective response capabilities for missions ranging from search and rescue to disaster relief. For example, in April 2024, the three navies conducted a joint submarine and surface ship exercise in the Philippine Sea involving the UK's HMS Anson, Australia's HMAS Farncomb, and the USS Mobile. This follows earlier collaborative efforts, including the 2023 AUKUS Advanced Warfare Trial Event with integrated naval operations, joint anti-submarine warfare training in the Pacific in 2022, and a 2023 joint patrol in the Indo-Pacific involving the permanently stationed British offshore patrol vessels HMS Tamar and HMS Spey alongside U.S. and Australian naval units.

Third, the AUKUS partnership significantly impacts Australia's military infrastructure, primarily through development of the East Coast Submarine Base in Brisbane and upgrades to the Osborne Shipyard in Adelaide. These projects aim to enhance Australia's naval capabilities by supporting construction and maintenance of nuclear-powered submarines, specifically the future SSN-AUKUS class, with expertise from the United States and United Kingdom. The new East Coast Submarine Base in Brisbane is a $10 billion facility that will host nuclear-powered submarines from the early 2030s, enabling sustained operations of submarines designed for long-range stealth, significantly extending Australia's military reach in the Indo-Pacific region (Idris et al., 2022). Concurrently, the Osborne Shipyard in Adelaide is being upgraded to build SSN-AUKUS submarines, with technical advisors from the U.S. and U.K. embedded on site (Lubis et al., 2024). Besides, this initiative includes training Australian personnel at the U.S. Naval Nuclear Training Command in Charleston and the Royal Naval Academy at HMNB Clyde in the U.K., aimed at building skilled workforces capable of operating advanced military technologies. Joint training ensures Australian forces can effectively collaborate with U.S. and U.K. naval operations, enhancing collective security in the Indo-Pacific region (Hall, 2022). The agreement also encourages personnel exchanges, allowing military members to gain firsthand experience in allied operations, fostering deeper understanding of strategic objectives and operational tactics, thereby enhancing collective maritime security efforts (Shi, 2022).

Fourth, the AUKUS partnership emphasizes advanced cybersecurity and information sharing as critical components of its trilateral security framework. This focus is essential for ensuring interoperability and resilience against increasingly sophisticated and pervasive cyber threats. AUKUS not only facilitates nuclear submarine technology sharing but also promotes collaboration in advanced defense technologies, including artificial intelligence and cybersecurity. These capabilities are vital for effective information sharing and operational synergy among partner nations. A key objective is enhanced integration of secure networks such as SIPRNet and MODNET to streamline communication and operational efficiency, thereby creating more unified and resilient operational environments (The United States, Australia, and the United Kingdom, 2022). Besides, defense industry integration under the AUKUS partnership will significantly enhance maritime security in the Indo-Pacific region. One primary mechanism is joint research and development, facilitating shared technological advancements in critical defense systems, including hypersonic technology (Khan, 2022). For example, partner nations are making joint investments to standardize production of submarine components such as propulsion systems and sensors. Collaboration in component production, particularly through partnerships like that between Rolls-Royce and BWX Technologies, aims to enhance SSN-AUKUS program capabilities. These investments are critical to modernizing submarine fleets and ensuring operational readiness in the Indo-Pacific. This technological integration seeks to create robust defense industrial bases capable of responding effectively to emerging regional threats, thereby strengthening deterrence against adversaries. The alliance's focus on integrated deterrence strategies is expected to reshape regional security architecture and potentially shift the balance of power in favor of AUKUS members (Shi, 2022). On the other hand, the AUKUS partnership significantly enhances secure transportation in the Indo-Pacific through deepened military cooperation and technology sharing. It facilitates movement of sensitive components such as highly enriched uranium via dedicated military channels, including use of C-17 Globemaster aircraft under strict security protocols. This method ensures safe and rapid transport of nuclear materials while minimizing exposure to potential threats during transit.

6. COMBINED AND BALANCED APPROACH TO MARITIME SECURITY: INTEGRATING QUAD AND AUKUS STRATEGIES

The complex Indo-Pacific security landscape necessitates hybrid strategies integrating the QUAD's soft power diplomacy with AUKUS hard power deterrence. Balanced approaches leverage normative influence of multilateral cooperation while ensuring credible military deterrents against aggression. This integration aligns with Joseph Nye's smart power theory, which advocates strategic combination of coercion and persuasion. As Nye suggests, neither soft power nor hard power alone is sufficient; their strategic integration is key to addressing 21st-century security challenges.

First, launched in 2022, the QUAD's Indo-Pacific Maritime Domain Awareness (IPMDA) initiative uses satellite technology and artificial intelligence to monitor illegal fishing, piracy, and illicit maritime activities across the Indian and Pacific Oceans. By sharing real-time data with regional partners, it increases transparency and empowers coastal states to secure their Exclusive Economic Zones (EEZs). However, surveillance alone cannot deter aggressive actors such as China, whose gray zone tactics often involve non-military coercive measures. AUKUS hard power mechanisms address this gap. For example, joint AUKUS maritime patrols such as the 2023 deployment of HMS Tamar and Spey with U.S. and Australian partners could leverage IPMDA intelligence to intercept illegal fishing vessels or prevent unauthorized intrusions. Nuclear submarines to be deployed under AUKUS would increase reach, persistence, and deterrent effects of such operations. This combination ensures surveillance (soft power) translates into credible enforcement (hard power), enabling regional partners to better protect their EEZs and fostering collective security environments (Zhang, 2022). This synergy exemplifies Criterion 3 (Strategic Adaptability and Synergistic Integration), where QUAD surveillance assets and AUKUS enforcement capabilities combine to create outcomes neither could achieve alone.

Second, the Palau Submarine Cable Project (2023), a $600 million initiative funded by the QUAD, connects Palau to global telecommunications networks and reduces dependence on Chinese infrastructure. While QUAD investment strengthens digital resilience and builds trust through economic partnerships, security of these cables in disputed waters requires robust military support. AUKUS members have conducted joint patrols near critical submarine cables in the Pacific to protect these assets from sabotage or espionage. For example, U.S. Navy cable repair ships and Australian Collins-class submarines (soon to be replaced by AUKUS SSNs) patrol high-risk areas such as the South China Sea, ensuring QUAD infrastructure investments remain operational despite rising tensions. Submarine cables are essential for global telecommunications, supporting finance, trade, and military communications (Morel, 2016). The South China Sea is a critical maritime route for these cables, making it a focal point for security concerns (Pandey & Bhushan, 2023). This model perfectly illustrates smart power balance: the QUAD's infrastructure project builds normative influence and economic resilience (Criterion 1), while AUKUS patrols provide tangible security (Criterion 2), resulting in integrated and secure outcomes (Criterion 3).

Third, integration of Humanitarian Aid and Disaster Relief (HADR) with AUKUS logistical capabilities can enhance operational efficiency while fostering regional goodwill through QUAD soft power. The 2004 Indian Ocean tsunami exemplified the necessity for coordinated disaster response, leading to QUAD formation, which has since evolved to address various regional challenges including HADR. This collaboration can be further strengthened by leveraging AUKUS military logistics capabilities, ensuring more effective disaster responses. In 2024, AUKUS countries conducted joint HADR exercises in the Philippines, simulating disaster response by deploying American C-17 Globemasters to rapidly deliver relief supplies and Australian Navy ships to provide coastal support. Such initiatives demonstrate how soft power (disaster relief) builds regional goodwill while hard power (military logistics) ensures operational efficiency. Military logistics can significantly enhance humanitarian efforts, providing essential resources and infrastructure during crises (Yuste et al., 2019).

Fourth, the integration of cybersecurity strategies within AUKUS and the QUAD reflects multifaceted approaches to addressing both state-sponsored and non-traditional threats in the maritime domain. AUKUS focuses on enhancing deterrence against cyberattacks through secure communication networks like SIPRNet, fortifying critical infrastructure against hybrid threats. Conversely, the QUAD emphasizes digital connectivity and resilience in supply chains, particularly in semiconductors, to combat issues such as piracy and illegal fishing using advanced technologies like AI and blockchain. These overlapping efforts reveal significant synergies in enhancing maritime security. Both AUKUS and the QUAD highlight the importance of collaborative, multisectoral approaches to cybersecurity, integrating efforts across governmental and private sectors (Marullo, 2022).

Fifth, the QUAD and AUKUS frameworks employ hybrid approaches to ensure freedom of navigation operations in the Indo-Pacific, combining military presence, strategic partnerships, and diplomatic engagement. Both utilize signaling and tactical hedging to convey intentions and build trust among allies, crucial for maintaining regional stability without escalating tensions. These frameworks also address non-traditional security issues such as climate change, which can indirectly support FONOPs by fostering broader cooperation among regional nations (Mafuang, 2024).

Sixth, the QUAD and AUKUS can collaborate to address climate-related maritime challenges including rising sea levels, ocean acidification, and extreme weather events threatening coastal states and critical infrastructure. QUAD soft power could facilitate multilateral agreements on sustainable fishing and marine conservation, while AUKUS hard power capabilities such as advanced naval vessels and surveillance systems could monitor illegal resource extraction and enforce environmental regulations. For instance, QUAD-led initiatives like IPMDA could track environmental degradation, while AUKUS patrols deter illegal activities such as coral reef destruction or unregulated deep-sea mining. This hybrid approach aligns ecological preservation with security, fostering regional trust while deterring exploitation. Such partnerships can improve resilience against climate change and resource exploitation, fostering shared responsibility among regional states (Vitous, 2023).

Seventh, establishing collaborative innovation hubs blending QUAD civilian technological expertise (e.g., AI, renewable energy) with AUKUS defense-industrial capabilities could accelerate advancements in dual-use maritime technologies. For example, QUAD-funded research on autonomous underwater drones for oceanographic studies could be adapted by AUKUS for mine detection or submarine tracking. Similarly, AUKUS cybersecurity frameworks could protect QUAD-backed smart port initiatives in Southeast Asia. These hubs would create pipelines for cutting-edge solutions serving both economic and security goals, exemplifying smart power's integrative pragmatism. Smart port development can create economic hubs attracting investment and innovation while simultaneously fortifying regional security against cyberattacks (Saxena, 2024).

Finally, coordinated narrative strategies could amplify legitimacy of QUAD and AUKUS initiatives. QUAD soft power could emphasize transparency, inclusivity, and adherence to international law through public diplomacy campaigns, while AUKUS military exercises and patrols could symbolically reinforce these narratives. For instance, joint QUAD-AUKUS humanitarian drills in the South China Sea could highlight their commitment to regional stability, countering adversarial propaganda about militarization. By synchronizing messaging and actions, the alliances would strengthen normative influence while deterring coercive tactics through visible resolve. Coordinated actions and communications among QUAD and AUKUS members can strengthen their collective narrative, emphasizing shared values and regional security goals (Sharma, 2010).

While hybrid smart power approaches are theoretically compelling, their practical implementation is fraught with tensions that risk undermining both frameworks' legitimacy. A critical counterargument, often voiced from constructivist perspectives, is that AUKUS's exclusive, hard-power-centric nature directly undermines the QUAD's narrative of inclusive, rules-based partnership. Frist, the complementarity claim is viewed with skepticism in parts of Southeast Asia. ASEAN states, operating on consensus-based models, are wary of being caught in great power contests (Kiet et al., 2025b). AUKUS formation was met with official concern from Indonesia and Malaysia, who fear it could provoke regional polarization and arms races, thereby destabilizing the very environment the QUAD seeks to stabilize (Li, 2024). This creates strategic contradictions: QUAD soft power diplomacy emphasizing ASEAN centrality is potentially hollowed out when its key members simultaneously pursue military pacts perceived by ASEAN as undermining that centrality. Second, does India's participation in the QUAD, which dialogues with China in other forums, become less credible when its QUAD partners are embedding Australia in deeply confrontational military pacts with the UK and US? This duality risks painting the QUAD as a veneer for more aggressive containment strategies, complicating its ability to act as honest broker in regional diplomacy. The paper's advocacy for hybrid models must therefore explicitly acknowledge that trust built by QUAD soft power is inherently fragile and can be eroded by perceptions of AUKUS as provocative, exclusionary alliances. Truly smart strategies must not only combine instruments but also manage these perceptual and diplomatic contradictions.

7. CONCLUSION

The Indo-Pacific's maritime security landscape demands nuanced strategies harmonizing the QUAD's soft power diplomacy with AUKUS hard power deterrence. This study demonstrates that while the QUAD fosters regional trust, inclusivity, and adherence to international norms through economic partnerships, capacity-building, and multilateral engagement, AUKUS strengthens deterrence against coercive threats via advanced military technologies and interoperability. These frameworks, though contrasting, are complementary: the QUAD's emphasis on rules-based order and humanitarian cooperation mitigates tensions, while AUKUS tangible capabilities counterbalance aggression, particularly China's assertiveness.

Joseph Nye's smart power theory underpins the necessity of integrating both approaches. Case studies examined throughout this paper, from IPMDA and joint patrols to secured infrastructure, consistently demonstrate that the QUAD and AUKUS are most effective when their respective strengths in Institutional Cohesion (Criterion 1) and Tangible Capability (Criterion 2) are strategically integrated to achieve Synergistic Effects (Criterion 3). The PMDA and joint AUKUS patrols illustrate how surveillance (soft power) and military enforcement (hard power) synergize to secure critical maritime zones. Similarly, QUAD-funded infrastructure projects like the Palau Submarine Cable, safeguarded by AUKUS patrols, exemplify the hybrid model's efficacy in balancing resilience with deterrence.However, AUKUS risks fueling regional arms races, while overreliance on QUAD normative influence may lack enforcement credibility. Thus, policymakers must prioritize adaptive strategies blending diplomatic engagement with credible military readiness, ensuring stability amid intensifying great-power competition. Ultimately, the Indo-Pacific's security hinges on pragmatic equilibrium, leveraging QUAD soft power to build enduring partnerships and AUKUS hard power to deter aggression. Only through such holistic approaches can the region navigate its complex challenges and sustain long-term peace and stability.

REFERENCES

Ameh, B. (2024). Advancing national security and economic prosperity through resilient and technology-driven supply chains. *World Journal of Advanced Research and Reviews*, *24*(3), 483–500. DOI: 10.30574/wjarr.2024.24.3.3723

Banevičienė, A. Ž. (2021). Interpretation of military power in the context of realism paradigm. *Politologija*, *102*(2), 38–74. DOI: 10.15388/Polit.2021.102.2

Bateman, S. (2005). Capacity building for maritime security cooperation: What are we talking about? *University of Wollongong Research Online*. https://ro.uow.edu.au/cgi/viewcontent.cgi?article=1433&context=lawpapers

Brynteson, D. W. (2014). Smart power: The United States, Iran, and a nuclear deal. *Defense Technical Information Center.* https://apps.dtic.mil/sti/pdfs/AD1003796.pdf

Bueger, C., & Bergin, A. (2018). Uniting nations: Developing maritime domain awareness for the "Blue Pacific." *Cardiff University.* https://orca.cardiff.ac.uk/111371/

Bugulashvili, M., & Scott, J. G. (2022). Getting smarter with Joseph Nye. *Journal of Humanity*, *11*(1). Advance online publication. DOI: 10.31578/hum.v11i1.479

Cheng, M. H. A. (2022). AUKUS: The changing dynamic and its regional implications. *European Journal of Development Studies*, *2*(1), 1–7. DOI: 10.24018/ejdevelop.2022.2.1.63

Childs, N. (2023). The AUKUS anvil: Promise and peril. *Survival*, *65*(5), 7–24. DOI: 10.1080/00396338.2023.2261239

Clark, B. (2016). Undersea cables and the future of submarine competition. *Bulletin of the Atomic Scientists*, *72*(4), 234–237. DOI: 10.1080/00963402.2016.1195636

Dolan, C. (2024). Perspective chapter: AUKUS Pillar 2—Technology, interoperability, and advanced capabilities in the evolving trilateral security partnership. In *Advances in National Security Studies*. IntechOpen. DOI: 10.5772/intechopen.1005189

Furuya, K. (2022). Japan's Coast Guard diplomacy through capacity building in the Indo-Pacific. In *Maritime Security and Japan* (pp. 120–134). Routledge., DOI: 10.4324/9781003216766-9

Gumantiara, M. I., Haqqi, H., & Murdani, A. D. (2024). Regional security complex analysis in Australia, United Kingdom, and United States (AUKUS) viewpoint to the rivalry between United States and China in Taiwan. *Formosa Journal of Sustainable Research*, *3*(3), 541–554. DOI: 10.55927/fjsr.v3i3.8144

Hall, I. R. (2022). AUKUS and Australia–UK strategic reconvergence. *RUSI Journal*, *167*(6–7), 34–42. DOI: 10.1080/03071847.2022.2159514

Han, J. (2020). A vanguard of foreign policy over maritime claims: Naval power rather than national power. *Korean Journal of Defense Analysis*, *32*(2), 311–329. DOI: 10.22883/KJDA.2020.32.2.008

Hiep, T. X., Hoan, T. Q., & Kiet, L. H. (2024). Free and Open Indo-Pacific strategy: Competitive Opinions and Trends. *Vestnik of Saint Petersburg University -. International Relations*, *17*(3), 242–259.

Hutchins, S. G., Gallup, S. P., MacKinnon, D., Schacher, G., Miller, S., Freeman, J., Dunaway, D., & Poeltler, B. (2008). Enhancing maritime domain awareness. *Defense Technical Information Center.* https://apps.dtic.mil/sti/pdfs/ADA486840.pdf

Idris, A. M., Sasongko, N. A., & Kuntjoro, Y. D. (2022). AUKUS cooperation in the form of Australian nuclear submarine technology for stability in Indo Pacific region. *International Journal of Research and Innovation in Social Science*, *6*(2), 745–750. Advance online publication. DOI: 10.47772/IJRISS.2022.6237

Jaishankar, D. (2023). India, the QUAD, and the liberal international order. In *India's Foreign Policy* (pp. 75–81). Springer. DOI: 10.1007/978-981-99-4729-4_7

Jansson, P. (2018). Smartness as prudence: Smart power and classical realism. *Journal of Political Power*, *11*(3), 341–358. DOI: 10.1080/2158379X.2018.1523317

Khan, S. A. (2022). The AUKUS alliance and its implications on the Non-Proliferation Treaty. *BTTN Journal*, *1*(2), 83–94. DOI: 10.61732/bj.v1i2.26

Kiet, L. H., Binh, N. T., & Hiep, T. X. (2025a). From border conflicts to maritime competition: Driving forces behind the power rivalry between India and China in the Indian Ocean region. *Australian Journal of Maritime and Ocean Affairs*, •••, 1–25. DOI: 10.1080/18366503.2025.2492438

Kiet, L. H., Tam, L. T. T., & Hiep, T. X. (2025b). Caught between dragon and elephant: Vietnam's strategic balancing act in the Sino-Indian rivalry. *China Quarterly of International Strategic Studies*, *11*(2), 99–128. DOI: 10.1142/S237774002550006X

Li, Y. (2024). Analysis of the security impact of AUKUS on the South China Sea: Based on defensive realism analysis. *Lecture Notes in Education Psychology and Public Media*, *63*(1), 77–82. DOI: 10.54254/2753-7048/63/20240938

Lubis, L. A. (2022). The QUAD's role in Indo-Pacific maritime security. *Journal of International Relations*, *14*(2), 45–67.

Lubis, L. A., Perwita, A. A. B., & Hadisancoko, R. E. (2024). The role of AUKUS in Australia's military capacity building strategy. *EAJMR East Asian Journal of Multidisciplinary Research, 3*(8). Advance online publication. DOI: 10.55927/eajmr.v3i8.10608

Mafuang, S. (2024). Signaling and tactical hedging as political tools in the formation of minilateral security coalitions: QUAD and AUKUS in the Indo-Pacific region. *World Politics, 4*(4), 30–40. DOI: 10.25136/2409-8671.2024.4.72184

Marullo, F. (2022). *Applying resilience to hybrid threats in infrastructure, digital, and social domains using multisectoral, multidisciplinary, and whole-of-government approach.* NATO Science for Peace and Security Series., DOI: 10.3233/NICSP220017

McLaughlin, R. L. (2022). The law of the sea and PRC gray-zone operations in the South China Sea. *The American Journal of International Law, 116*(4), 821–835. DOI: 10.1017/ajil.2022.49

Monahan, D., Angwenyi, C., Montoro, H., Morishita, T., Mustapha, A., Peralta, W. R., Sharma, S., & Karlapati, S. (2005). *Multi-dimensional, multi-national, multi-faceted hydrographic training: The Nippon Foundation GEBCO training program at the University of New Hampshire*. University of New Hampshire. https://scholars.unh.edu/cgi/viewcontent.cgi?article=1348&context=ccom

Morel, C. (2016). Menace sous les mers: Les vulnérabilités du système câblier mondial. *Hérodote, 163*(4), 33–43. DOI: 10.3917/her.163.0033

Nafilla, A. (2025). International legal implications of the North Natuna maritime dispute: A review of Indonesia–China tensions in the past two years. *International Journal of Social Science and Human Research, 8*(9). Advance online publication. DOI: 10.47191/ijsshr/v8-i9-10

Nichols, T. P., Edgerton, A. K., & Desimone, L. (2021). "Smart power" in standards implementation after No Child Left Behind. *American Journal of Education, 128*(1), 147–169. DOI: 10.1086/716463

Nye, J. S. (2008). Smart power. Great leaders know when hard power is not enough. *Harvard Business Review, 86*(11), 55–59. https://www.ncbi.nlm.nih.gov/pubmed/18972718 PMID: 18972718

Nye, J. S. (2010). Soft power and American foreign policy. In *The Future of American Foreign Policy* (pp. IX–XIII, 127–147). Public Affairs.

Nye, J. S. (2011). *The future of power*. Public Affairs.

Pandey, S. K., & Bhushan, A. (2023). Submarine cables: Issues of maritime security, jurisdiction, and legalities. *European Journal of Theoretical and Applied Sciences*, *1*(4), 117–132. DOI: 10.59324/ejtas.2023.1(4).13

Péron-Doise, M. (2024). La quête de la maritime domain awareness (MDA) dans le Pacifique insulaire. *Revue Défense Nationale*, *872*(7), 44–50. DOI: 10.3917/rdna.872.0044

Pulungan, R. W. (2021). Enhancing maritime security in the Malacca Strait: Cooperation against piracy and maritime terrorism. *Indonesian Journal of International Law*, *7*(2), 39209. DOI: 10.17304/ijil.vol7.2.220

Rahman, C. (2013). The geopolitical context. *University of Wollongong*. https://ro.uow.edu.au/cgi/viewcontent.cgi?article=1977&context=lhapapers

Saxena, P. S. (2024). Cybersecurity issues and solutions for smart power networks. In *Advances in Cybersecurity* (pp. 36–48). CRC Press., DOI: 10.1201/9781003486930-6

Schelling, T. C. (1966). *Arms and influence*. Yale University Press.

Sharma, A. (2010). The QUADrilateral Initiative: An evaluation. *South Asian Survey*, *17*(2), 237–253. DOI: 10.1177/097152311201700204

Shekhar, V. (2022). Rise of QUAD as a 'premier regional grouping.'. *Journal of Global Strategic Studies*, *2*(2), 37–60. DOI: 10.36859/jgss.v2i2.1287

Sherwin, S. L. (2017). Can international law make a difference? UNCLOS and the South China Sea. *Defense Technical Information Center*. https://apps.dtic.mil/sti/pdfs/AD1037983.pdf

Shi, X. (2022). Beyond AUKUS: The emerging grand maritime alliance. *China International Strategy Review*, *4*(2), 248–267. DOI: 10.1007/s42533-022-00123-0

Singh, A. K. (2022). UNCLOS: Facilitating ocean governance and maritime security. *Maritime Affairs*, *18*(1), 72–90. DOI: 10.1080/09733159.2022.2097643

Stevenson, K., & Envall, H. D. P. (2019). The "QUAD" and disaster management: An Australian perspective. In *Regional Security Cooperation* (pp. 13–23). Stimson Center. DOI: 10.26181/6005120FAB69E

Tahir, H., & Amin, F. (2023). Assessing the effectiveness of QUAD in maritime containment of China in the Indo-Pacific region. *South Asian Economic Studies and Research*, *6*(4), 1–6. DOI: 10.36902/sjesr-vol6-iss4-2023(1-6)

Tertia, J., & Perwita, A. A. B. (2018). Maritime security in Indo-Pacific: Issues, challenges, and prospects. *Journal of International Relations*, *14*(1), 77–95. DOI: 10.26593/jihi.v14i1.2795.77-95

The United States. (2022). The United States, Australia, and the United Kingdom Announce "AUKUS" Alliance Focused on Indo-Pacific Security. *The American Journal of International Law*, *116*(1), 164–170. DOI: 10.1017/ajil.2021.69

Ulis, P. (2022). QUAD HADR strategy for the Indo-Pacific. In *Humanitarian Assistance and Disaster Relief in the Indo-Pacific* (pp. 124–135). Routledge., DOI: 10.4324/9781003278719-11

Vitous, C. A. (2023). Dynamics of environmental security in the Indo-Pacific. In *Environmental Security in Asia* (pp. 222–247). Routledge., DOI: 10.4324/9781003336143-15

Yearbook, S. I. P. R. I. (2024). Armaments, disarmament and international security. *Stockholm International Peace Research Institute*. https://www.sipri.org/databases/milex

Young, R. R., & Gordon, G. A. (2020). Intermodal maritime supply chains: Assessing factors for resiliency and security. *Journal of Transportation Security*, *13*(3), 231–244. DOI: 10.1007/s12198-020-00224-0

Yuste, P., Campbell, J. R., Canyon, D. V., Childers, M., & Ryan, B. J. (2019). Synchronized humanitarian, military and commercial logistics: An evolving synergistic partnership. *Safety (Basel, Switzerland)*, *5*(4), 67. DOI: 10.3390/safety5040067

Zhang, D., Tao, J., Wan, C., Huang, L., & Yang, M. (2024). Resilience analysis of maritime transportation networks: A systematic review. *Transportation Safety and Environment*, *6*(4), tde009. Advance online publication. DOI: 10.1093/tse/tdae009

Zhang, K. (2022). Signals, deterrence, and the QUAD. *Asia Policy*, *29*(4), 43–48. DOI: 10.1353/asp.2022.0069

Chapter 6

The South China Sea in US-China Relations: Development Trends and Strategic Forecasts Toward 2028

Hieu Bach Tran
Thai Binh University, Vietnam

Nhi Tran Yen Dinh
Diplomatic Academy of Vietnam, Vietnam

Duc Trung Nguyen
https://orcid.org/0009-0006-9364-069X
University of Social Sciences and Humanities, Vietnam National University, Hanoi, Vietnam

Kiet Hoang Le
https://orcid.org/0009-0002-9968-1952
University of Social Sciences and Humanities, Vietnam National University, Hanoi, Vietnam

ABSTRACT

This chapter forecasts South China Sea (SCS) dynamics in US-China relations through 2028, employing qualitative document analysis to examine geopolitical trends, power balance shifts, and domestic policy drivers. Analysis reveals that while China's economic rise and military modernization enable greater SCS assertiveness, the US maintains technological superiority and alliance advantages. Under Trump's second administration, characterized by transactional diplomacy yet bipartisan anti-China consensus, Washington will likely deepen regional engagement through traditional allies and expanded partnerships. China is projected to intensify gray-

DOI: 10.4018/979-8-3373-4470-6.ch006

zone tactics, maritime presence, and infrastructure development while pursuing economic diplomacy to fragment ASEAN unity. The study concludes that through 2028, the SCS will remain a contested flashpoint marked by persistent tensions and strategic competition, though direct military confrontation remains unlikely due to mutual restraint and crisis management capabilities between both powers.

1. INTRODUCTION

Rivalry among great powers has long defined international politics throughout world history. In the twenty-first century, strategic competition between the US and China has emerged as the predominant characteristic of global affairs. As the two preeminent powers, Sino-American interactions profoundly shape the Asia-Pacific political landscape and regional order. Since 1972, the US has served as the principal architect of East Asia's political configuration. China, meanwhile, has emerged as a rising power seeking interests commensurate with its growing national strength, making conflicts with the US virtually impossible to avoid. Within this vortex of power competition, the South China Sea (SCS) has become the focal arena where US-China rivalry has reached unprecedented intensity. Samuel P. Huntington once suggested that the SCS may represent a potential flashpoint between two civilizations: one embodied by China—an ancient and once-flourishing civilization—and the other led by the US, representing Western civilization currently dominant on the global stage. Consequently, US-China competition plays a preeminent role in shaping SCS developments.

Since Donald Trump's re-election in early 2025, the world has witnessed assertive measures designed to reaffirm America's position as the foremost global superpower. The SCS has remained a critical testing ground—for China's determination to rise and for US efforts to uphold the existing regional order. Understanding the evolving dynamics of competition between these two major powers has become essential for formulating appropriate policy responses and strategic options, particularly for Vietnam amid ongoing US-China rivalry in this contested maritime domain.

This chapter, entitled "*The South China Sea in US-China Relations: Development Trends and Strategic Forecasts Toward 2028,*" forecasts the likely trajectories of US-China interactions regarding the SCS during President Trump's current administration. The research employs qualitative and analytical approaches rooted in social sciences and international relations. Document analysis serves as the principal method, involving systematic collection and interpretation of secondary sources including academic works, policy documents, and official statements from Vietnamese and international scholars, joint statements, speeches by senior leaders, and verified online data from reputable institutions. The study integrates forecasting techniques to project potential trends through 2028, with complementary methods including comparative and statistical analyses applied as appropriate.

2. GEOPOLITICAL CONTEXT: FOUNDATIONS FOR SCS FORECASTING

2.1. The Asia-Pacific Region: Global Strategic Competition Hub

Compared with other regions that have attained relatively stable structures, the Asia-Pacific region remains in a formative stage characterized by diverse trends and competing strategic calculations (Vietnam Journal of Science and Technology, 2021). This area is marked by numerous disputes and complex disagreements carrying potential for escalation into conflict—including the SCS, the East China Sea, the Taiwan Strait, and the Korean Peninsula—as well as issues of separatism, terrorism with ethnic or religious dimensions, and various non-traditional security challenges such as cybersecurity, climate change, water security, and food security.

The region also concentrates many of the world's strategic interest conflicts among major powers and key international actors. Notable examples include China's Belt and Road Initiative (BRI), the US' Free and Open Indo-Pacific (FOIP) strategy, India's "Act East" policy, Japan's "East-West Connectivity" policy, South Korea's "New Southern Policy," Russia's "Greater Eurasia" strategy, and the European Union's "Asia-Europe Connectivity" framework. Additionally, numerous regional multilateral cooperation and dialogue mechanisms have been established and expanded rapidly, including the Asia-Pacific Economic Cooperation (APEC), the East Asia Summit (EAS), the ASEAN Regional Forum (ARF), the ASEAN Defence Ministers' Meeting Plus (ADMM+), the Shanghai Cooperation Organization (SCO), the Shangri-La Dialogue, and the Beijing Xiangshan Forum, among others. The Asia-Pacific has increasingly become the geopolitical center of gravity of the world—a dynamic arena where strategic competition, economic interdependence, and security concerns intersect in shaping the twenty-first-century regional order.

Given the scale and intensity of existing conflicts—many involving numerous actors and deeply rooted contradictions—the regional situation will likely remain unstable and complex through 2028, with unpredictable developments. Such a volatile political and security environment will undoubtedly pose significant threats to peace, security, and stability at global, regional, and national levels (Vietnam Journal of Science and Technology, 2021). Competition and struggles for influence will continue to center on the Asia-Pacific region, where both superpowers—the US and China—converge alongside other major powers including Japan, India, and Russia, drawing attention from key global actors and institutions. Among these dynamics, US-China rivalry remains the most prominent and influential, shaping the regional landscape across multiple domains: economics, military affairs, defence and security, and advanced technology.

In the coming period, ASEAN is expected to continue serving as a key actor in shaping the regional security architecture and constructing the regional order. The organization will likely maintain its intermediary and mediating role in regional affairs, compelling major power centers to recognize ASEAN's centrality and adjust their policies accordingly. Simultaneously, ASEAN remains a primary target of influence and engagement for various coalitions seeking to consolidate and expand their strategic presence in the Asia-Pacific region (Phan & Nguyen, 2022).

However, recent geopolitical developments indicate an emerging trend toward establishing multilateral mechanisms outside the ASEAN framework. These new forms of cooperation either exclude ASEAN entirely or operate independently of ASEAN-centered mechanisms. In this context, the Quadrilateral Security Dialogue (QUAD) has rapidly risen to prominence as a significant security cooperation framework. The decision by QUAD leaders to convene annual summits marks a new phase of revitalization and institutionalization. Furthermore, the creation of AUKUS in September 2021 and the signing of the Reciprocal Access Agreement (RAA) on defence between Japan and Australia on January 6, 2022, underscore the growing trend toward new regional partnerships, alliances, and cooperative mechanisms beyond ASEAN's traditional framework. According to Patrick Cronin, Director of the Asia-Pacific Security Program at the Hudson Institute, the emerging security architecture of Asia in coming decades will likely rest upon three pillars: ASEAN, QUAD, and AUKUS (Cronin, 2021).

While maintenance of regional security and order increasingly depends on the US and its allies and partners, China's growing economic influence—manifested through implementation of the Belt and Road Initiative (BRI), its leadership in establishing the Regional Comprehensive Economic Partnership (RCEP), and its formal application to join the Comprehensive and Progressive Agreement for Trans-Pacific Partnership (CPTPP)—has created risks that regional economic and trade dynamics may gravitate toward China's orbit. Consequently, a potential scenario could emerge wherein the security environment and regional order are primarily shaped by US-led mechanisms, while the economic landscape of the Asia-Pacific comes increasingly under China's steering and coordination through Beijing-proposed or dominated initiatives and cooperative frameworks (Ngo, 2022).

2.2. The US-China Balance of Power: A Multidimensional Analysis

a) Economic Strength: The Race Between the World's Two Largest Economies

In the second decade of the twenty-first century, China's economy has achieved remarkable accomplishments. Analysis of economic data from 1983 to 2023 reveals that China's average annual GDP growth rate during this period reached 9.78%, whereas the US recorded an average of only 2.8% (Lai, 2023). Forecasts suggest that by the end of the third decade of the twenty-first century, China's GDP may equal or even surpass that of the US. To counterbalance the system of economic and financial institutions established by the US and Western countries, China has successively created its own mechanisms and organizations, including the Asian Infrastructure Investment Bank (AIIB), the BRICS grouping, the New Development Bank (NDB), and the Boao Forum for Asia. As the founding initiator, China contributes over 30% of AIIB's total capital and holds a voting share exceeding 26%, whereas other member states contribute less than 10% each (Inclusive Development International, 2016). This affords China greater voting power than any single country possesses in comparable global financial institutions—by contrast, the US holds 16.8% of voting shares in the International Monetary Fund (IMF) and 16.5% in the World Bank (WB), while the US and Japan each hold 16.5% in the Asian Development Bank (ADB).

China is striving to build a coalition of nations supporting its initiatives to compete with the US-led economic order. Notably, the number of founding members of the Asian Infrastructure Investment Bank increased from 21 to 57, including 17 European countries and all 10 ASEAN member states. Despite US objections, an increasing number of Washington's Western allies have joined this international financial institution. As US Treasury Secretary Jack Lew acknowledged, "Our international credibility and influence are at risk. It is no accident that emerging economies are seeking investment opportunities elsewhere. They are frustrated by the US' delay in reforming the IMF" (Reuters, 2015). Among China's various initiatives, the BRI is regarded as the most effective instrument for constructing a distinct economic order with China at its center—leading and dominating the entire system. Participation of numerous countries in the BRI demonstrates both the initiative's appeal and China's expanding influence in the global economic sphere.

Although China's economic power and influence have increased significantly in recent years, the country simultaneously faces numerous internal and external challenges. China's debt-to-GDP ratio reached a record high in 2023 despite a slowdown in borrowing, reflecting weakening economic growth momentum (Xia

& Han, 2024). One major domestic challenge is the demographic crisis stemming from declining birth rates and an aging population. Since peaking at 925 million in 2011, China's working-age population is projected to decline by 225 million by 2050 (Zhao, 2016). By that time, one in every two working-age individuals will be over 65 years old (China Power Team, 2023). This trend signifies erosion of China's former competitive advantage derived from a large pool of low-cost skilled labor, while simultaneously heightening fiscal pressures associated with growing demand for elderly care and social welfare (Liu, 2023).

The intensifying US-China rivalry, marked by trends of decoupling and confrontation, constitutes perhaps the greatest external challenge to China's economy—both presently and in the foreseeable future. In response to China's expanding economic influence, President Donald Trump oversaw introduction of economic policies triggering the US-China trade war beginning in March 2018, imposing tariffs and non-tariff barriers on Chinese imports. Under President Joe Biden, the US maintained high tariffs on Chinese goods while tightening controls over Chinese acquisitions of key American technology firms. Following this strategic trajectory, the US has also sought to counter China's Belt and Road Initiative by launching the Blue Dot Network (BDN)—an initiative aimed at mobilizing Indo-Pacific countries to participate in developing a sustainable and transparent infrastructure network (Ho, 2022).

b) Military Capabilities: From Defense Spending to Regional Presence

For decades, the US has consistently been the world's largest military spender, maintaining a vast network of military bases spanning multiple continents. In 2022, US defence spending accounted for nearly 40% of total global military expenditures—exceeding the combined spending of the next ten countries according to data published by SIPRI (Stockholm International Peace Research Institute, n.d.). In 2023, the US defence budget reached USD 858 billion, while China's defence budget was approximately USD 225 billion, marking a 7.2% increase from the previous year. Although China's defence spending ranked second globally, it still amounted to only about one-quarter of the US total.

However, the US' enormous defence budget is distributed across multiple regions and commitments, including support for Taiwan, military assistance to Ukraine, and maintenance of its extensive global base network. Consequently, the portion of the US defence budget allocated to the Asia-Pacific—particularly Southeast Asia—is no longer overwhelmingly dominant compared with China's regional spending. By contrast, China's geographical proximity to Southeast Asia provides significant strategic advantage. Its defence budget—largely devoted to upgrading armed forces and military assets—can be concentrated on enhancing combat readiness and operational capabilities of the People's Liberation Army (PLA) in Southeast Asia and adjacent areas. With the advantage of geographic proximity, China can maximize its military strength in the region despite its overall defence budget remaining substantially lower than that of the US (Pham, 2023).

Regarding overall military strength, the 2023 Asia Power Index published by the Lowy Institute—Australia's leading foreign policy think tank—indicates that the US remains the predominant power in the Asia-Pacific region. Specifically, the US leads across most indicators, including defence networks, military capability, and future resources, which measure projected distribution of economic, military, and demographic capacity (Lowy Institute, 2023).

However, according to the 2023 China Military Power Report submitted by the US Department of Defense to Congress in October 2023, China continues to modernize, diversify, and expand its nuclear forces at a rapid pace. As of May 2023, China possessed more than 500 operational nuclear warheads. The report further notes that China seeks to expand its overseas logistics and basing infrastructure to enable the People's Liberation Army to project and sustain military power over greater distances. These emerging global logistical networks could enhance the PLA's capacity to disrupt US military operations worldwide. More specifically, beyond the PLA's existing logistics base in Djibouti, China has reportedly considered and planned construction of new overseas military support facilities to enable more diverse and geographically extensive deployment of its forces. The report also cites a statement from an official of the People's Republic of China confirming that the PLA would gain access to portions of Ream Naval Base in Cambodia. Simultaneously, China is expected to expand its military presence in several other partner countries, including Myanmar, Thailand, and Indonesia in Southeast Asia.

In terms of naval power, the number of warships in China's navy has already surpassed that of the US, with the total projected to reach 435 vessels by 2030 (US Department of Defense, 2023). Currently, China possesses three aircraft carriers—Liaoning, Shandong, and Fujian—and many experts believe the country will likely acquire a fourth, nuclear-powered carrier in the near future (Minh, 2022). However, concerning large surface combatants, the US maintains clear superiority in quantity, technology, and operational experience. For instance, the US Navy currently operates 11 nuclear-powered aircraft carriers, each capable of undertaking longer deployments than conventionally powered carriers. Depending on class, a US carrier can carry 60 or more aircraft (Zhang, 2021). By contrast, analysts forecast that China will require at least two more decades to possess 10 aircraft carriers and a nuclear-capable submarine fleet rivaling that of the US Navy (Trung, 2023). The US also enjoys substantial operational advantage in the SCS owing to its extensive combat experience, interoperability, and dense network of allies and partners. The US military's superior combat proficiency is further demonstrated through joint exercises with Southeast Asian nations. According to Abdul Rahman Yaacob, a researcher at the Australian National University, US joint exercises in Southeast Asia are characterized by greater complexity, involving coordinated command and control as well as high degrees of interoperability (Kong, 2023). Therefore, both presently and in the near future, China remains unable to match the US' overwhelming advantage as the world's preeminent naval power.

c) Technological Competition: The Battle for the Future

The balance of power between the US and China in technology has narrowed rapidly over the past decade. According to a report by the Australian Strategic Policy Institute (ASPI), China now leads the global technology race, surpassing the US in 37 out of 44 critical technologies. These include sectors such as radiofrequency communications (5G and 6G), hydrogen energy, electric vehicle batteries, nanomaterials, advanced coatings, supercapacitors, and hypersonic technologies, among others. Experts assess that in the near future, China could potentially monopolize at least eight of these advanced technologies. China's progress has been particularly striking in emerging industries, most notably green vehicle technologies. In 2022, China accounted for 60% of the global electric vehicle market (Ren, 2023). In the ongoing artificial intelligence race with the US, China's military investment in AI development is estimated at between USD 1.6 billion and USD 2.7 billion annually. By comparison, the US Department of Defense reportedly invested a significantly smaller amount—only USD 800 million to USD 1.3 billion in 2020 (Lew, 2021). Eric Schmidt, former CEO of Google, remarked that AI and other emerging technologies are central to China's efforts to expand its global influence and surpass the US in both economic and military power (Schmidt, 2021). To date, the US remains the global leader in research and development spending, with expenditures exceeding USD 679 billion in 2022 (Statista, 2022). However, projections by R&D World estimate that by 2030, China's R&D budget will reach USD 900 billion, investing at least USD 70 billion more annually than the combined R&D expenditures of all US institutions (R&D World, 2020).

Nevertheless, it remains premature to conclude that China will surpass the US in the technological domain in coming years. Owing to its superiority in foundational and core technologies, the US continues to control key strategic chokepoints in global value chains, thereby constraining China's technological upgrading efforts. In 2017, the US government initiated an investigation into China's unfair trade practices. The Office of the US Trade Representative subsequently released two reports in 2018, alleging that—in addition to providing extensive subsidies—China required foreign firms entering joint ventures with local companies to transfer technology from US intellectual property owners as a condition for market access (US Trade Representative, 2018). Other accusations included state-sponsored industrial espionage and intellectual property theft (US Trade Representative, 2018a).

Consequently, since 2018, US authorities have invoked national security concerns to block numerous strategic investments and acquisitions in high-technology sectors. This has been accomplished through expanded powers of the Committee on Foreign Investment in the US (CFIUS) and imposition of export controls on Chinese firms via the Entity List (Brugnatelli, 2022). The primary objective of these restrictions has been to prevent Chinese companies from replicating or stealing US technologies—whether by transferring intellectual property from the US to China or by sending Chinese personnel to US companies for training purposes (Nguyen & Le, 2020). However, these American measures have also led China to recognize its vulnerabilities and, in turn, accelerated its efforts to achieve technological self-reliance and reduce dependence on the US within its supply chains.

d) Soft Power: Global Influence and Image

The concept of "soft power" was first formally introduced in the early 1990s by Professor Joseph S. Nye, an American scholar and former US Assistant Secretary of Defense. According to Nye, soft power refers to the ability to attract and co-opt rather than coerce—to persuade other countries to voluntarily adjust their behavior and policies in accordance with one's preferences, rather than through use of economic or military force. A nation's soft power typically stems from three primary sources: (i) its cultural values, (ii) its political values, and (iii) its foreign policy conduct (Nye, 2006). History has demonstrated that countries capable of effectively leveraging soft power often gain significant advantages, broaden their global influence, and enhance their international standing.

The US is widely regarded as possessing one of the greatest reserves of soft power. Through diverse means, the US has actively promoted its political, economic, and cultural values worldwide—thereby reinforcing and sustaining its position as a global superpower. However, during the presidency of Donald J. Trump, under the slogan "America First," the US withdrew from several key multilateral institutions and agreements, including the United Nations Human Rights Council (UNHRC), the United Nations Educational, Scientific and Cultural Organization (UNESCO), the Paris Agreement on Climate Change (COP21), and the Joint Comprehensive Plan of Action (JCPOA) on Iran's nuclear program; it also threatened to exit the World Trade Organization (WTO). These withdrawals from major international organizations and multilateral frameworks negatively affected the US's global image and diminished its soft power. According to the 2019 "Soft Power 30" Report published by Portland Communications in collaboration with the University of Southern California, the US' soft power ranking had continuously declined since 2016 (McClory, 2019).

After Joe Biden took office in 2021, his administration made efforts to re-engage with multilateral institutions and address transnational security issues—including climate change—in an attempt to restore global confidence in US leadership. Nevertheless, the process of regaining its former status remains challenging, particularly as other major powers—most notably China—have become increasingly active in expanding their global influence in recent years.

For its part, China has long pursued a strategy to enhance its soft power on a global scale. However, China's soft power strategy began gaining significant momentum after the 19th National Congress of the Communist Party of China, with its ultimate goal being realization of the "Chinese Dream." This vision seeks to project to the world the image of a responsible major power—one committed to international cooperation, harmonious development, and peaceful rise (Nguyen, 2020). China has also seized opportunities created by the Trump administration's withdrawal from multiple multilateral institutions to fill the resulting void, consolidate its soft power, and expand its sphere of influence. The country has made considerable financial and personnel contributions to international organizations to reinforce its image as a responsible global actor. China is currently the second-largest contributor to both the United Nations regular budget and the UN peacekeeping budget, and it contributes more peacekeeping personnel than any other permanent member of the UN Security Council (ChinaPower, 2021). These contributions have enabled China to strengthen its diplomatic and political influence worldwide while simultaneously reinforcing its soft power credentials.

However, China's recent political moves have raised concerns, caution, and even anti-China sentiment across much of the world, particularly due to its territorial expansionist policies as reflected in recent maritime confrontations in the SCS and the East China Sea. In the case of the Belt and Road Initiative, China's neighbors and partners have responded with measured caution. For example, local communities in South and Southeast Asian countries such as Myanmar and Sri Lanka have expressed discontent over China's growing presence. Even in Pakistan, where the China-Pakistan Economic Corridor has been widely endorsed, several lawmakers have voiced concerns that such projects could potentially jeopardize national interests (Hoang, 2021).

According to the 2023 annual survey conducted by the ISEAS-Yusof Ishak Institute in Singapore, nearly half of Southeast Asian respondents (49.8%) reported having little or no confidence in China's contributions to regional peace, security, prosperity, and global governance. Among those distrusting China, 41.4% believed that China's economic and military power could pose threats to their national interests and sovereignty. This sentiment was particularly strong in Vietnam, the Philippines, Cambodia, Malaysia, Indonesia, and Singapore. In contrast, trust in the US increased slightly from 52.8% in 2022 to 54.2% in 2023 (ISEAS-Yusof Ishak

Institute, 2023). Furthermore, the US' liberal values, cultural influence, and non-governmental resources continue to be widely recognized. American corporations such as Facebook, Amazon, Apple, and Microsoft have expanded their global reach and presence, permeating daily lives of people worldwide. As a result, the US' soft power continues to maintain its global appeal.

2.3. Internal Drivers Shaping SCS Policies

a) China: Maritime Power Ambitions and Domestic Pressures

For China, domestic political and economic transformations may continue driving the country toward a more assertive posture in the SCS. Politically, the Report of the 20th National Congress of the Communist Party of China reflects an increasingly determined commitment to advancing the country's maritime power strategy, emphasizing the SCS within the broader elevation of "security" as a central pillar of China's foreign policy agenda. The objective set by Chinese leadership for the period 2020-2050 is to enable the People's Liberation Army Navy to extend its operational control beyond the First Island Chain and toward the Second Island Chain. Economically, China's large population and industrial capacity make its economy heavily dependent on substantial imports of raw materials, energy, and food, most of which are sourced externally. The disputed areas in the SCS, known for their abundant energy reserves, play a critical role in sustaining China's future economic growth. Consequently, without securing these supply routes and resources, China will struggle to address both its domestic and external challenges (Yoon, 2015). Furthermore, the need to stimulate post-COVID-19 economic recovery and to counter the US' "economic de-risking" strategy may prompt China to intensify its exploitation and assertive activities in the SCS (Do, 2023).

A widely shared view within China holds that the SCS disputes concern not merely territory, resources, and energy, but also a rising power's pursuit of strategic space commensurate with its growing capabilities, as well as legitimization of the Chinese political elite's authority (Christensen, 2011; Scobell & Harold, 2013). Many analysts have also argued that China's assertiveness in the SCS can be explained, in part, by a recurring tradition in Chinese politics: when facing domestic instability, Chinese leaders tend to externalize internal tensions by escalating confrontations abroad to consolidate internal unity (Kuik, 2017). A notable example occurred in 2012, when China seized control of Scarborough Shoal, then under dispute with the Philippines, shortly after domestic political turmoil erupted following the Bo Xilai scandal.

Currently, China continues grappling with internal challenges and growing domestic pressures, which may encourage it to adopt a more hardline approach toward neighboring states in managing territorial disputes. Such assertive behavior serves both to reinforce domestic cohesion and to divert public attention from more pressing internal difficulties (Kuik, 2017).

In particular, China's SCS strategy is shaped and driven by the power structure of the Chinese Communist Party and its top leadership. All major foreign policy-making institutions in China operate under the direct authority of the CCP Central Committee, with the General Secretary exercising centralized and comprehensive control (Do, 2013). Since Xi Jinping assumed power in 2012, the CCP's leadership role has expanded even further, accompanied by an unprecedented consolidation of Xi's personal authority. In addition to holding the positions of President of the People's Republic of China, General Secretary of the CCP, and Chairman of the Central Military Commission, Xi also chairs numerous leading small groups composed of his closest political allies. Notably, he has successfully established himself as the "core" leader of the Party and institutionalized the "Two Establishes"—establishing Xi Jinping's core position within the CCP Central Committee and the entire Party, and establishing the guiding role of Xi Jinping Thought on Socialism with Chinese Characteristics for a New Era in the Third Historical Resolution, adopted during his second term (Bich, 2022). By removing the leadership age and term limits introduced under Deng Xiaoping, Xi has effectively ensured the possibility of serving another term as General Secretary after the 20th Party Congress. Consequently, China's future policy in the SCS will continue being shaped by President Xi's determination to transform China into a true maritime power, with the SCS disputes serving as a practical testing ground for achieving that strategic objective.

Complementing this dynamic is the increasing involvement of multiple actors influencing China's policymaking in the SCS. These actors include not only administrative and law enforcement agencies—such as the State Oceanic Administration under the Ministry of Natural Resources, the China Coast Guard (formerly under the SOA following the 2013 reorganization but operationally guided by the Ministry of Public Security), and the Maritime Safety Administration under the Ministry of Transport—but also the People's Liberation Army, local authorities, energy corporations, state-owned enterprises, scholars and researchers, as well as fishermen, netizens, and Chinese media outlets (Zhu, 2012). According to Thomas Christensen, former Deputy Assistant Secretary of State for East Asian and Pacific Affairs and one of the world's leading experts on China, Beijing's increasingly assertive actions in disputed waters have benefited many of these stakeholders. These actors have leveraged central government directives on protecting maritime rights and interests to advance their own agendas, urging senior leaders to approve resource exploration projects, land reclamation initiatives, fishing bases, rescue centers, and legal instruments aimed at codifying China's sovereignty claims in the SCS (Jakobson, 2014). Scholars Michael D. Swaine and M. Taylor Fravel have similarly concluded that the growing prominence of sovereignty issues in the Chinese media has accelerated the speed, scope, and intensity of public scrutiny over territorial disputes—thereby increasing domestic pressure on China's top leadership (Swaine & Fravel, 2011).

b) The US: Foreign Policy Under Trump 2.0

The 2024 US presidential election witnessed former President Donald Trump's decisive victory over Democratic candidate Kamala Harris, paving the way for his return to power in January 2025. Trump's triumph is widely regarded as evidence that his "Make America Great Again" agenda has gained acceptance not only within the Republican Party but also among a significant portion of the American electorate. With this victory, Trump became only the second US president in history to win two non-consecutive terms. Furthermore, following the election, Trump's Republican Party secured a majority in both the House of Representatives and the Senate, thereby creating favorable conditions for the incoming administration to advance its legislative agenda—at least during the first two years of his new term.

Trump's first presidency demonstrated his pragmatic approach to nearly all policy issues, which at times diverged from mainstream Republican orthodoxy. He pursued what he termed "principled realism," prioritizing domestic strength, reducing direct overseas engagement, emphasizing tangible outcomes in relations with allies and partners, and consistently placing US national interests above those of allies—or even of the broader international community. White House policies under Trump's leadership were characterized by a blend of economic protectionism and a transactional approach to diplomacy (Nguyen, 2017). However, the unpredictability of his decisions may undermine consistency and coherence of US foreign policy, compelling other nations to remain constantly adaptive and responsive to Washington's changing positions.

Given the substantial differences in outlook from the Biden administration, the foreign policy of the US under the second term of President-elect Donald Trump is expected to undergo significant adjustments and shifts across a wide range of critical issues—from relations with NATO allies across the Atlantic to dealings with rival major powers such as Russia and China, and particularly in response to large-scale conflicts in Ukraine and the Middle East. These adjustments are certain to exert profound impact on an already complex and unpredictable international landscape.

Nevertheless, despite President Trump's highly personalized and unpredictable style, there exists strong bipartisan consensus in the US Congress on the need to identify and counter China. Even in an era of deep political polarization, both the Democratic and Republican Parties share agreement on adopting tough measures toward China. This bipartisan alignment has enabled China-related legislation to pass with little or no opposition from either party—even amid intense partisan divides.

For instance, although Republicans have opposed the Biden administration on numerous foreign policy issues, the CHIPS and Science Act (commonly known as the CHIPS Act)—introduced to strengthen US competitiveness against China in the semiconductor sector—received broad bipartisan support, including votes from the majority of Republican lawmakers (Chivvis & Miller, 2023).

This trend appears to reflect public opinion in the US. A Pew Research Center survey conducted in July 2020 found that nearly 73% of Americans held unfavorable views of China (Silver et al., 2020). Similarly, a Gallup poll in early 2023 reported that four out of five Americans had unfavorable perceptions of China, while two-thirds viewed China as a "critical threat to America's vital interests" (Brenan, 2023). Moreover, a Bloomberg-Morning Consult survey released in January 2024 showed that 38% of Americans regarded US-China relations as a "very important" issue, and another 40% considered it "important" in influencing their vote in the 2024 presidential election—whereas only 4% said they were unconcerned about the issue (Morning Consult & Bloomberg, 2024). Leading US policy research organizations have likewise emphasized that China poses threats to US national interests and have advocated stronger measures to counter China's rise. Judging from the statements and actions of both the Trump and Biden administrations, it is evident that the approaches and recommendations of these think tanks have influenced the perspectives of US policymakers in shaping responses to China's growing power (Kochegurov, 2022). Accordingly, President Trump is expected to continue engaging actively in SCS affairs as part of efforts to contain China's ambitions—the primary strategic competitor to the US in the struggle for global preeminence. His decision to appoint senior cabinet members known for their hardline views on China further indicates that Beijing will remain at the center of US foreign policy between 2025 and 2028 (Sim, 2024; Betts, 2024). However, the US also has no interest in turning the SCS into a theater of confrontation or conflict with China. In reality, the SCS remains a complex strategic issue for Washington.

On one hand, directly challenging China's sovereignty claims—if not grounded in international legal standards and consistent with US principles—could risk provoking Chinese nationalism and encouraging more aggressive behavior by Beijing in the region. On the other hand, an overly passive US posture could undermine American national interests in the SCS and lead other claimant states, allies, and partners to believe that the US is abandoning its commitments to them (Bader, 2014). Furthermore, US resources are currently overstretched due to ongoing conflicts in Ukraine and Gaza, while a significant portion of the American public has expressed discontent with the country's involvement in both crises. This situation places Washington in a difficult position, forcing it to weigh the risks of deeper engagement in a potential SCS conflict and the possibility of military confrontation with China (Guzman, 2024).

2.4. ASEAN's Role: Between Two Great Power Fires

The policies of ASEAN member states, particularly those directly involved in territorial disputes with China, are expected to influence the behavior of both China and the US in the SCS in the coming period. In recent years, several ASEAN countries have demonstrated significant shifts in their SCS policies.

Under the leadership of incumbent President Ferdinand Marcos Jr., the foreign policy of the Philippines has gradually shifted away from the stance adopted by the Duterte administration, marked by renewed emphasis on the US-Philippines alliance. Less than a year after assuming office, President Marcos authorized four additional sites for US military access under the Enhanced Defense Cooperation Agreement (EDCA)—an accord that had largely stalled under former President Rodrigo Duterte. Furthermore, President Marcos has actively leveraged the US alliance network to strengthen the Philippines' strategic position in the SCS. Beyond deepening ties with Washington, he has repeatedly condemned Chinese activities within the Philippines' exclusive economic zone. Notably, in August 2023, the Philippine Senate adopted a resolution denouncing China for its "persistent harassment" of Filipino fishermen and "incursions" into waters claimed by the Philippines in the SCS. The resolution called upon the Marcos administration to take appropriate measures to assert and defend the nation's sovereign rights, including submitting the resolution to the United Nations General Assembly to urge an end to all Chinese harassment activities targeting Philippine vessels in the West Philippine Sea—the official term used by the Philippines for the SCS (Senate of the Philippines, 2023).

This policy shift stems from President Ferdinand Marcos Jr.'s recognition that the Philippines is situated in one of the most geopolitically complex regions in the world, where the SCS dispute remains a central issue. Even during the administration of former President Rodrigo Duterte, tensions in the SCS did not ease—in fact, they intensified, subjecting him to domestic public pressure that ultimately forced a delay in his plan to terminate the Visiting Forces Agreement and the US military presence in the Philippines.

Public expectations for a leader capable of addressing sovereignty issues were among the key factors propelling Ferdinand Marcos Jr. to the presidency, after he pledged to pursue a more balanced foreign policy if elected. Having declared that the Philippines "will not yield even an inch of its territory," President Marcos has demonstrated his resolve to safeguard national sovereignty and territorial integrity through a series of rapid actions aimed at upgrading defence ties with the US and securing new security assurances.

Meanwhile, Malaysia and Indonesia have also adopted firmer positions in defending their sovereignty—showing greater assertiveness in diplomatic exchanges and enhanced resistance through on-site activities. Malaysia, in particular, has worked to strengthen defence cooperation with the US through arms procurement and naval collaboration. The country has hosted US submarines at its ports (January 2019); participated in bilateral exercises such as Keris Strike, Tiger Strike, and Bersama Warrior; and joined multilateral exercises including Cobra Gold, CARAT, RIMPAC, the Southeast Asia Cooperation and Training (SEACAT) exercise, and the ASEAN-US Maritime Exercise.

In August 2019, Malaysia also conducted joint coast guard exercises with the US and, in April 2021, participated in drills in the SCS alongside the USS Theodore Roosevelt Carrier Strike Group. Additionally, Malaysia purchased 12 US-made ScanEagle drones and signed a security cooperation agreement with Japan, which included approximately USD 2.8 million in maritime security assistance to enhance the country's maritime defence capabilities (Reuters, 2023).

Indonesia has likewise placed emphasis on strengthening defence and security cooperation with the US and has expressed support for the US role and military presence in the region. The two countries have continued to hold the annual large-scale joint military exercise "Garuda Shield" in Indonesia. This exercise is now one of the largest multilateral drills in the region, involving 11 other participating nations, including Australia, Singapore, and Japan. Its primary objectives are to enhance capabilities in addressing security challenges and natural disasters, as well as to carry out humanitarian assistance operations aimed at maintaining stability in the Asia-Pacific region.

Nevertheless, despite their concerns over China's actions in the SCS, these ASEAN states generally seek to avoid direct confrontation, prioritizing diplomatic measures to ease tensions with China—which remains the largest trading partner of the Philippines, Malaysia, and Indonesia alike. A notable example occurred following heightened maritime confrontations between China and the Philippines in 2023. During the eighth meeting of the China-Philippines Bilateral Consultation Mechanism on the SCS (January 2024), both sides agreed to improve maritime communication and manage maritime incidents through friendly consultations, while reaffirming that the SCS disputes "do not constitute the entirety of bilateral relations" (Reuters, 2024). This approach reflects a pragmatic calculation in the foreign policies of these nations, which are acutely aware of the asymmetry in military capabilities with China and the potentially severe consequences that any armed conflict in the SCS could have for national security and regional economic stability. Consequently, by focusing on dialogue, these countries aim to pursue peaceful solutions, prevent escalation, and safeguard their economic interests through continued cooperation with China.

Accordingly, the trend among ASEAN claimant states in the SCS to strengthen security cooperation with the US and seek partnerships with extra-regional actors—as a response to China's actions in the disputed waters—is likely to continue throughout the 2024-2028 period. However, these countries are also expected to maintain their diplomatic and economic relations with China, striving to avoid direct confrontation while continuing to assert their sovereign rights and national interests in the SCS.

3. THE SCS TOWARD 2028: SCENARIOS AND FORECASTS

3.1. Sovereignty Disputes: Escalating Tensions or Strategic Restraint?

It is projected that by 2028, the global geopolitical landscape will continue to undergo profound and far-reaching adjustments. Given its strategic geopolitical significance, the SCS is expected to become an increasingly contested arena, driven by overlapping interests of multiple nations worldwide. Tensions in the SCS in 2024 have primarily revolved around maritime and aerial encounters between the Philippines and China, and between China and the US. What is particularly noteworthy, however, is that the escalating friction between the Philippines and China is reshaping the regional power structure, as the Philippines has granted the US access to four additional military bases and fostered "mini-lateral" security linkages with the US, Japan, and Australia. Given these developments, the SCS's strategic landscape from now until 2028 will likely remain highly complex, marked by heightened risks of confrontation among various parties. The scope and intensity of maritime tensions are expected to expand, accompanied by rising diplomatic frictions among the major stakeholders involved (Ton, 2023).

First, in the coming period, China is likely to adopt countermeasures and intensify its military activities and presence in the SCS, while continuing to oppose the presence of the US and its allies in the area. China's maritime forces are expected to be further strengthened, accompanied by expansion and upgrading of military bases in the SCS, including features that Beijing has illegally occupied. China will also likely increase incursions into the exclusive economic zones of other states to maintain a continuous presence in the disputed waters.

In addition, China may deploy a large number of personnel on the Second Thomas Shoal (Ayungin Shoal) and the Scarborough Shoal, while continuing to employ coercive tactics such as water-cannon attacks, ramming maneuvers, and deployment of floating barriers to prevent the Philippines from re-establishing access to these areas (Hung, 2023). However, China will likely proceed with caution in deploying naval forces in order to maintain the momentum of negotiations on the Code of

Conduct, avoid providing justification for deeper US involvement, and preserve a stable environment conducive to its own development. Beyond military activities, China is also expected to advance civilian initiatives, such as development of tourism projects in the Paracel Islands (Hoàng Sa), accompanied by construction of hotels, airstrips, and related infrastructure. On the propaganda front, China will likely continue to shape public opinion in a manner that frames the US and its allies as the primary sources of instability in the SCS.

In its relations with Southeast Asian countries regarding the SCS issue, China is expected to continue pursuing a strategy of easing tensions through various measures across political, economic, and diplomatic fronts. By doing so, Beijing aims to strengthen the economic dependence of these countries on China, thereby mitigating negative reactions from neighboring states toward its actions in the SCS, and more broadly, to foster divisions within ASEAN. Simultaneously, to improve its international image, China will likely adopt a more conciliatory tone on the SCS issue and demonstrate a proactive attitude in negotiations on the Code of Conduct with ASEAN member states. However, these moves do not signify a fundamental shift in China's overall policy; rather, they represent tactical adjustments intended to manage challenges related to the SCS.

Second, as China continues to take assertive actions in the SCS, the US under President Trump's second administration is expected to deepen its engagement in the region—through continuation of Freedom of Navigation Operations, as well as joint exercises and patrols in the SCS. It is anticipated that, with his re-election, President Trump will persist in advancing his foreign policy doctrine of "peace through strength" (Spirlet, 2024). Specifically, he is likely to continue modernizing the US military, enhance cooperation with key allies and partners, and maintain a robust armed force to safeguard national interests. Strategically, the Trump administration may shift more responsibility onto regional partners, favoring a "leading-from-behind" approach through existing mechanisms such as QUAD and AUKUS. In the coming years, the US will likely expand its engagement not only with traditional allies but also with other regional actors to balance China's growing influence in the Indo-Pacific.

In addition to the US, extra-regional powers such as Japan, India, and Australia are expected to show increasing interest in the territorial disputes in the SCS and to enhance their military presence in these contested waters. These countries may seek to promote defence and security cooperation with ASEAN, as well as to support ASEAN claimant states in strengthening their maritime capabilities through security dialogues, defence equipment transfers, and capacity-building initiatives. The involvement of extra-regional forces in the SCS could help mitigate the imbalance in the regional security structure and collectively constrain China's assertiveness. However, these "third parties" have no interest in escalating instability in the SCS, given that their diplomatic relations with China remain short of confrontation, the vital role of the sea lanes for global trade, and the fact that the SCS does not represent their immediate core interests (Lai, 2024). Consequently, their activities in the region will likely be carefully calibrated to avoid direct confrontation with Chinese forces while maintaining their strategic engagement.

Third, given that none of the claimant states possesses economic or military power comparable to China's, it is likely that ASEAN countries will seek to strengthen relations with extra-regional powers by participating in US- and ally-led security initiatives and by leveraging their influence in multilateral forums to shape China's behavior and policies in the SCS. Meanwhile, ASEAN continues to expand its cooperation with China through joint military exercises and by pursuing negotiations on the Code of Conduct in search of a diplomatic solution to the ongoing disputes. However, given that strategic trust between China and several ASEAN members has significantly eroded due to a series of incidents in the SCS since early 2020, it is difficult to expect any major breakthrough in the COC negotiations in particular, or in the broader ASEAN-China dialogue on the SCS before 2028.

Accordingly, it can be projected that developments in the SCS from now until 2028 will become increasingly complex, with potential for heightened tensions and broader escalation. The resolution of disputes in the SCS will remain highly challenging, constrained by historical, geographical, and political considerations, as well as by growing involvement of external stakeholders with vested interests in the region. Nevertheless, a military escalation of the SCS disputes into open armed conflict would inflict severe consequences on all parties involved. Therefore, while the claimants will continue to strengthen their positions and influence, they will also act with a degree of restraint to prevent tensions from spiraling into open warfare (Koh, 2024). In general, the SCS situation through 2028 is expected to remain tense and unstable, though unlikely to deteriorate to the level of direct conflict or war.

3.2. US-China Relations in the SCS: Between Competition and Crisis Management

The US-China relationship remains one of the most consequential bilateral relationships in the contemporary world and will continue to shape both the global order and the regional architecture of the Asia-Pacific through 2028. Given that the SCS encompasses a concentration of strategic interests and serves as a critical arena of influence competition, the rivalry between Washington and Beijing in this maritime domain will continue to serve as a key litmus test of China's ambitions for great-power resurgence and the US' determination to maintain the regional status quo.

During his 2024 presidential campaign, Donald Trump pledged to reinforce his previous economic policies, including imposition of a 60% tariff on all Chinese imports. Beyond tariff measures, he is also expected to further restrict Chinese technology firms' access to US advanced technologies, particularly in the fields of semiconductors and artificial intelligence, through sanctions and stringent export controls. Consequently, Chinese exports to the US will face higher tariffs, and Beijing is likely to retaliate, possibly by raising import duties on US goods, as it did during previous trade confrontations. The result would be an escalation of the trade war, leading to further deterioration in bilateral relations. However, Tong Zhao, a senior fellow at the Carnegie Endowment for International Peace in Washington, has observed that given China's current economic situation, a renewed trade war would inflict substantial damage on Beijing's economy. As a result, faced with mounting US pressure in the economic and technological domains, China is likely to intensify its control over critical maritime routes in the SCS as a means to safeguard vital resources essential to sustaining its economic growth (Foster, 2022).

Meanwhile, President Trump has yet to articulate a detailed strategy for the SCS during his second presidential term. However, under Trump 1.0, the US adopted a hardline stance toward China on this issue—marked by increased deployment of US naval vessels in the region, rejection of China's territorial claims, and criticism of Beijing's coercive actions in the SCS. Consequently, with Trump's return to office, US-China rivalry will remain the defining dynamic in the SCS, and the intensity of competition is unlikely to diminish in significance.

That said, Trump's transactional approach and preference for personalized diplomacy have led many analysts to predict that he may seek to cultivate a personal relationship with Chinese President Xi Jinping, raising concerns about the consistency and predictability of US foreign policy (Hutagalung, 2024). Conversely, it is also possible that Trump will adopt a more isolationist posture in his second term, reflecting pressure within the Republican Party to reduce US involvement abroad (Huld & Zhou, 2024). For example, Trump has repeatedly criticized NATO and threatened to withdraw from the alliance. In an interview with Bloomberg Businessweek on the sidelines of the Republican National Convention (July 2024), he remarked that Taiwanese officials should pay more for US defensive support—deflecting questions about whether he would defend the island against Chinese military action—while asserting that Taiwan had "stolen" America's semiconductor industry (Bloomberg News, 2024). Similarly, upon returning to the White House, Trump may reassess US engagement in the SCS, particularly regarding the China-Philippines disputes and the expanding US military presence in the Philippines (Ross, 2024).

Therefore, while the strategic objectives of US policy in the SCS are likely to remain consistent, President Trump may adopt a flexible approach, oscillating between assertiveness and conciliation toward China, depending on domestic political conditions and the state of bilateral negotiations (Hutagalung, 2024). A clear illustration of this flexibility can be seen during his first term in office, when Trump reversed his stance on the Chinese telecommunications giant ZTE following phone calls with Chinese political leaders in 2018, and similarly softened his position on Huawei after meeting President Xi Jinping at the G20 Summit in 2019 (Palmer, 2024). Given the current complexities of the international environment, Trump may seek to de-escalate tensions with China in the interest of domestic economic stability and to focus on his "America First" agenda. This approach, however, could create opportunities for China to pursue more assertive measures in advancing its long-term strategic ambitions in the SCS.

Historically, China's strategy has relied on taking incremental yet purposeful actions targeting asymmetric strategic interests that are vital to Beijing but non-essential to Washington—thereby minimizing the risk of provoking a direct military confrontation with the US (Chan, 2024).

In general, from now until 2028, unless a major miscalculation leads to open conflict, it is highly unlikely that the SCS issue in China-US relations will escalate into a direct confrontation. This is because both sides possess sufficient strategic maturity and the capability to manage tensions responsibly, thereby avoiding the outbreak of war (Heydarian, 2023). Both China and the US continue to emphasize dialogue through existing mechanisms, such as the Maritime Military Consultative Agreement, under which the two parties have agreed to maintain communication and avoid misunderstandings or misjudgments in maritime affairs (Phuong, 2024).

That said, the complex dynamics of US-China competition in these waters are unlikely to improve in the near term. From now until the end of 2028, the SCS is projected to remain a flashpoint characterized by persistent disputes and overlapping interests, while also serving as a strategic theater for great-power competition between the US and China. The US-China rivalry over the SCS will, on one hand, intensify regional security tensions, and on the other, compel the affected states to adjust their foreign policies to safeguard national and sovereign interests. In particular, Southeast Asian nations, especially those with territorial claims in the SCS, will be the most directly impacted actors, as they must navigate the shifting dynamics of the two major powers' policies and interactions in this contested maritime domain.

4. CONCLUSION

Based on the analysis of development trends in the Asia-Pacific region, the balance of power between the US and China across the economic, military, technological, and soft power dimensions, as well as the internal factors shaping both countries' policies, it can be projected that from now until the end of 2028, the SCS will continue to serve as a critical testing ground for China's determination to rise as a great power and for Washington's efforts to preserve the regional status quo.

On China's side, in order to realize its "nine-dash line" claims, Beijing is expected to continue employing "gray-zone" tactics while accelerating the modernization of its naval and air forces to ensure greater control over the SCS. Simultaneously, China will likely pursue economic diplomacy—a strategy that has proven relatively effective in recent years—in order to strengthen its influence among regional states.

For its part, the US will not only sustain its engagement in SCS affairs but also intensify efforts to rally both its traditional allies and other regional partners in order to balance China's growing power. Although numerous variables may arise that could reshape the strategic adjustments of all stakeholders, the SCS will remain a flashpoint characterized by persistent disputes and conflicting interests, and will continue to serve as a key arena of strategic rivalry between China and the US through 2028. As such, the complex nature of the competition between the two powers in these waters is unlikely to improve in the foreseeable future. Nevertheless, barring any major miscalculation leading to open conflict, it is highly improbable that the SCS issue in US-China relations will escalate into direct confrontation. Both parties possess sufficient strategic maturity and the capability for responsible crisis management, enabling them to avoid the outbreak of a large-scale military conflict.

REFERENCES

Bader, J. A. (2014). The US and China's nine-dash line: Ending the ambiguity. *Brookings*. https://www.brookings.edu/articles/the-u-s-and-chinas-nine-dash-line-ending-the-ambiguity/

Betts, A. (2024). Trump's early second-term choices fuel fears of extremist agenda. *The Guardian*. https://www.theguardian.com/us-news/2024/nov/13/trump-cabinet-administration-appointments

Bich, T. (2022). The process of reaffirming the 'core leadership' role in China. *Voice of Vietnam*. https://vov.vn/the-gioi/ho-so/qua-trinh-tai-xac-lap-vai-tro-lanh-dao-hat-nhan-cua-trung-quoc-post976223.vov

Bloomberg News. (2024). *Trump suggests Taiwan should pay US for protection*. https://www.bloomberg.com/news/videos/2024-07-16/trump-suggests-taiwan-should-pay-us-for-protection-video

Brugnatelli, N. (2022). The US-China battle for the semiconductors industry. *East Asia Forum*. https://www.eastasiaforum.org/2022/06/04/the-us-china-battle-for-the-semiconductor-industry/

Chan, H. (2024). China's big gamble in the SCS. *The Diplomat*. https://thediplomat.com/2024/01/chinas-big-gamble-in-the-south-china-sea/

China Power Team. (2023). How severe are China's demographic challenges? *China Power*. https://chinapower.csis.org/china-demographics-challenges/

ChinaPower. (2021). *Is China contributing to the United Nations' mission?* https://chinapower.csis.org/china-un-mission/

Chivvis, C. S., & Miller, H. (2023). The role of Congress in US–China relations. *Carnegie Endowment for International Peace*. https://carnegieendowment.org/research/2023/11/the-role-of-congress-in-us-china-relations?lang=en

Christensen, T. J. (2011). The advantages of an assertive China. *Foreign Affairs*, *90*(2), 54–67.

Cronin, P. M. (2021). The 3 pillars of Asia's new security architecture. *The Straits Times*. https://www.straitstimes.com/opinion/the-3-pillars-of-asias-new-security-architecture

Do, H. (2023). The SCS situation in 2023 and forecast for 2024. *SCS Studies Center*. https://nghiencuubiendong.vn/tinh-hinh-bien-dong-nam-2023-va-du-bao-nam-2024.56515.anews

Do, T. S. (2013). *Chinese politics in the process of rising and the issues posed for Vietnam.* Encyclopedia Publishing House.

Foster, S. (2022). China on course to elude US chip-making equipment bans. *Asia Times.* https://asiatimes.com/2022/10/china-on-course-to-elude-us-chip-making-equipment-bans/

Guzman, C. (2024). Why the US faces a delicate balancing act on countering China in the SCS. *TIME.* https://time.com/6960916/us-military-intervention-south-china-sea-philippines-china/

Heydarian, R. (2023). Taiwan, US elections and SCS tensions could make 2024 even more geopolitically perilous. *South China Morning Post.* https://www.scmp.com/comment/opinion/article/3246254/taiwan-us-elections-and-south-china-sea-tensions-could-make-2024-even-more-geopolitically-perilous

Ho, Q. L. (2022). The depth of US–China strategic competition. *People's Army Newspaper.* https://www.qdnd.vn/bao-quan-doi-nhan-dan-xuan-nham-dan/bao-quan-doi-nhan-dan-xuan-nham-dan/chieu-sau-canh-tranh-chien-luoc-my-trung-quoc-684193

Hoang, V. (2021). The true nature of China's 'soft power'. *VietnamNet Online Newspaper.* https://vietnamnet.vn/thuc-chat-quyen-luc-mem-cua-trung-quoc-757240.html

Huld, A., & Zhou, Q. (2024). Trump wins the 2024 US presidential election: Implications for China. *China Briefing.* https://www.china-briefing.com/news/trump-china-us-relations-2024-election-victory-implications-businesses/

Hung, N. (2023). Is China escalating tensions in the SCS to ease domestic pressure? *International Studies Review.* https://nghiencuuquocte.org/2023/10/14/trung-quoc-day-cang-thang-tren-bien-dong-nham-giam-suc-ep-noi-bo/

Hutagalung, S. (2024). Would Trump go soft on the SCS? *Asia Times.* https://asiatimes.com/2024/03/would-trump-go-soft-on-the-south-china-sea/

Inclusive Development International. (2016). *Making inroads: Chinese infrastructure investment in ASEAN and beyond.* https://www.inclusivedevelopment.net/wp-content/uploads/2016/12/2.-Asian-Infrastructure-Investment-Bank-VN.pdf

ISEAS Yusof Ishak Institute. (2023). *The state of Southeast Asia: 2023 survey report.* https://www.iseas.edu.sg/wp-content/uploads/2025/07/The-State-of-SEA-2023-Final-Digital-V4-09-Feb-2023.pdf

Jakobson, L. (2014). *China's unpredictable maritime security actors.* Lowy Institute.

Kochegurov, D. A. (2022). Formation of an anti-Chinese consensus among US 'think tanks': From D. Trump to J. Biden. *Herald of the Russian Academy of Sciences, 93*(7), 601–611. DOI: 10.1134/S1019331622130044

Koh, C. (2024). Muscle and mediation set to continue in the SCS. *East Asia Forum.* https://eastasiaforum.org/2024/01/18/muscle-and-mediation-set-to-continue-in-the-south-china-sea/

Kong, A. (2023). Why are China and the US competing in military exercises in Southeast Asia? *VTC News.* https://vtc.vn/vi-sao-trung-quoc-my-chay-dua-tap-tran-quan-su-o-dong-nam-a-ar797034.html

Kuik, C.-C. (2017). Explaining the contradiction in China's SCS policy: Structural drivers and domestic imperatives. *China. International Journal (Toronto, Ont.), 15*(1), 163–186.

Lai, T. B. (2023). US–China strategic competition and its impact on major powers' policy adjustments. *Communist Review.* https://www.tapchicongsan.org.vn/web/guest/tin-binh-luan/-/asset_publisher/DLIYi5AJyFzY/content/canh-tranh-chien-luoc-my-trung-quoc-va-tac-dong-den-dieu-chinh-chinh-sach-cua-cac-nuoc-lon

Lai, T. T. (2024). What will the situation in the SCS look like if Donald Trump is re-elected as US president? *Strategic Studies.* https://nghiencuuchienluoc.org/the-cuc-bien-dong-se-ra-sao-neu-ong-donald-trump-tai-dac-cu-tong-thong-my/

Lew, L. (2021). Chinese military may have an edge over US on artificial intelligence research, report warns. *South China Morning Post.* https://www.scmp.com/news/china/military/article/3154242/chinese-military-may-have-edge-over-us-artificial-intelligence

Liu, Z. Z. (2023). China's pensions system is buckling under an aging population. *Foreign Policy.* https://foreignpolicy.com/2023/06/29/china-pensions-aging-demographics-economy/

Lowy Institute. (2023). *Asia Power Index 2023 edition.* https://power.lowyinstitute.org/

McClory, J. (Ed.). (2019). The Soft Power 30. *Portland Communications.* https://softpower30.com/wp-content/uploads/2019/10/The-Soft-Power-30-Report-2019-1.pdf

Minh, P. (2022). China's fourth aircraft carrier may be nuclear-powered. *Dan Tri Newspaper.* https://dantri.com.vn/the-gioi/tau-san-bay-thu-4-cua-trung-quoc-co-the-chay-bang-nang-luong-hat-nhan-20221009074630875.htm

Morning Consult & Bloomberg. (2024). *Swing States Tracking Poll*. https://pro-assets.morningconsult.com/wp-uploads/2024/01/Full-Data.pdf

Ngo, C. N. (2022). ASEAN's position and role in the Indo-Pacific region: Opportunities amid challenges. *Political Theory Journal*. https://lyluanchinhtri.vn/home/index.php/quoc-te/item/4261-vi-the-vai-tro-cua-asean-o-khu-vuc-an-do-thai-binh-duong-co-hoi-trong-thach-thuc.html

Nguyen, H. (2020). Soft power in a changing world. *Communist Review*. https://www.tapchicongsan.org.vn/web/guest/quoc-phong-an-ninh-oi-ngoai1/-/2018/815776/suc-manh-mem-trong-mot-the-gioi-dang-thay-doi.aspx

Nguyen, V. L., & Le, T. K. (2020). *US–China technological competition in the era of Industry 4.0*. National Political Publishing House.

Nguyen, V. T. (2017). Some observations on President Donald Trump's policy toward the Asia–Pacific region. *The Americas Today Review*, *4*, 3–11.

Nye, J. S. (2006). Think again: Soft power. *Foreign Policy*. https://foreignpolicy.com/2006/02/23/think-again-soft-power/

Palmer, J. (2024). Where does China stand with the next White House? *Foreign Policy*. https://foreignpolicy.com/2024/11/12/china-policy-trump-white-house-xi-jinping-tariffs-taiwan/

Pham, Q. P. (2023). US–China military competition in Southeast Asia and its implications for Vietnam. *Strategic Studies Review*. https://nghiencuuchienluoc.org/canh-tranh-quan-su-my-trung-quoc-o-khu-vuc-dong-nam-a-va-ham-y-doi-voi-viet-nam/

Phan, T. T., & Nguyen, T. S. (2022). Forecasting the world and Asia–Pacific regional order toward 2030. *Communist Review*. https://www.tapchicongsan.org.vn/web/guest/tin-binh-luan/-/asset_publisher/DLIYi5AJyFzY/content/du-bao-trat-tu-the-gioi-khu-vuc-chau-a-thai-binh-duong-den-nam-2030

Phuong, M. (2024). The US and China agree to manage maritime risks. *Dan Tri Newspaper*. https://dantri.com.vn/the-gioi/my-trung-quoc-nhat-tri-kiem-soat-rui-ro-tren-bien-20240528154317798.htm

R&D World. (2020). *2020 R&D global funding forecast*. https://forecast.rdworldonline.com/product/2020-rd-global-funding-forecast/

Ren, D. (2023). *Chinese EV makers on course to smashing 8.5 million 2023 sales target for mainland, industry players and observers say. South China Morning Post*. https://www.scmp.com/business/china-business/article/3237220/chinese-ev-makers-course-smashing-85-million-2023-sales-target-mainland-industry-players-and

Reuters. (2015). *Stalling of IMF reforms adds to appeal of other institutions – US official.* https://www.reuters.com/article/uk-europe-asia-bank-imf-id UKKBN0MD27G20150317/

Reuters. (2023). Japan and Malaysia sign $2.8m maritime security assistance deal. *Bangkok Post.* https://www.bangkokpost.com/world/2706783

Reuters. (2024). *China, Philippines seek better communication, management of conflicts in SCS.* https://www.reuters.com/world/asia-pacific/china-philippines -agree-improve-communication-manage-conflicts-south-china-sea-2024-01-17/

Ross, R. S. (2024). Trump 2.0 and China: A wild card in East Asia. *ThinkChina.* https://www.thinkchina.sg/politics/trump-2-0-and-china-wild-card-east-asia

Schmidt, E. (2021). The AI revolution and strategic competition with China. *The Wire China.* https://www.thewirechina.com/2021/09/05/the-ai-revolution-and -strategic-competition-with-china/

Scobell, A., & Harold, S. W. (2013). An "assertive" China? Insights from interviews. *Asian Security*, *9*(2), 111–131. DOI: 10.1080/14799855.2013.795549

Senate of the Philippines. (2023). *Senate condemns continued harassment of Pinoy fishermen, illegal Chinese incursion in WPS.* https://legacy.senate.gov.ph/press _release/2023/0801_zubiri1.asp

Silver, L., Devin, K., & Huang, C. (2020). Americans fault China for its role in the spread of COVID-19. *Pew Research Center.* https://www.pewresearch.org/global/ 2020/07/30/americans-fault-china-for-its-role-in-the-spread-of-covid-19/

Sim, D. (2024). How could a hawkish Donald Trump White House team shape US–China ties? *South China Morning Post.* https://www.scmp.com/news/china/ diplomacy/article/3285848/how-could-hawkish-donald-trump-white-house-team -shape-us-china-ties

Spirlet, T. (2024). Trump's first term avoided a fight in the SCS. It's only getting harder. *Business Insider.* https://www.businessinsider.com/trump-harder-time -countering-china-south-china-sea-2024-11

Statista. (2022). *Leading countries by R&D spending worldwide 2022.* https:// www.statista.com/statistics/732247/worldwide-research-and-development-gross -expenditure-top-countries/

Stockholm International Peace Research Institute. (n.d.). *SIPRI military expenditure database.* https://www.sipri.org/databases/milex

Swaine, M. D., & Fravel, M. T. (2011). China's assertive behavior part two: The maritime periphery. *China Leadership Monitor*, *35*, 1–29.

Ton, S. T. (2023). The world in 2023 and prospects for 2024. *Dan Tri Newspaper*. https://dantri.com.vn/the-gioi/buc-tranh-the-gioi-nam-2023-va-trien-vong-nam-2024-20231219182349296.htm

Trung, H. (2023). After 50 years of rise, how does China challenge the power of the US and Japan? Voice of Vietnam. https://vov.vn/the-gioi/ho-so/sau-50-nam-troi-day-trung-quoc-hien-thach-thuc-suc-manh-my-va-nhat-ban-ra-sao-post1020596.vov

US Department of Defense. (2023). *Military and security developments involving the People's Republic of China*. https://media.defense.gov/2023/Oct/19/2003323409/-1/-1/1/2023-MILITARY-AND-SECURITY-DEVELOPMENTS-INVOLVING-THE-PEOPLES-REPUBLIC-OF-CHINA.PDF

US Trade Representative. (2018). *Findings of the investigation into China's acts, policies, and practices related to technology transfer, intellectual property, and innovation under Section 301 of the Trade Act of 1974, March 22*. USTR. https://ustr.gov/sites/default/files/Section%20301%20FINAL.PDF

US Trade Representative. (2018a). *Update concerning China's acts, policies and practices related to technology transfer, intellectual property, and innovation*. https://ustr.gov/sites/default/files/enforcement/301Investigations/301%20Report%20Update.pdf

Vietnam Journal of Science and Technology. (2021). *The regional structure of the Asia–Pacific by 2025 and Vietnam's policy*. https://vjst.vn/vn/tin-tuc/4544/cau-truc-khu-vuc-chau-a---thai-binh-duong-den-nam-2025-va-chinh-sach-cua-viet-nam.aspx

Xia, Y., & Han, W. (2024). China's debt-to-GDP ratio climbs to record 287.8% in 2023. *Nikkei Asia*. https://asia.nikkei.com/Spotlight/Caixin/China-s-debt-to-GDP-ratio-climbs-to-record-287.8-in-2023

Yoon, S. (2015). Implications of Xi Jinping's "true maritime power": Its context, significance, and impact on the region. *Naval War College Review*, *68*(3), 40–63.

Zhang, Z. (2021). US–China rivalry: Who has the stronger military? *South China Morning Post*. https://www.scmp.com/news/china/military/article/3140681/us-china-rivalry-who-has-stronger-military

Zhao, X. (2016). Authorities working on plan to delay retirements. *China Daily*. https://www.chinadaily.com.cn/china/2016-07/23/content_26192140.htm

Zhu, F. (2012). *US rebalancing in the Asia-Pacific: China's response and the future regional order* (Discussion Paper No. 12). Victoria University of Wellington, Center for Strategic Studies.

Chapter 7
The South China Sea in ASEAN–Republic of Korea Relations:
Strategic Interests and Maritime Security Cooperation in Historical Perspective

Phan Thi Anh Thu
https://orcid.org/0009-0003-3788-5244
University of Social Sciences and Humanities, Viet Nam National University Ho Chi Minh City, Vietnam

ABSTRACT

This chapter examines the South China Sea as a pivotal strategic space in Republic of Korea (ROK)–ASEAN relations since the early twenty-first century. Rather than focusing solely on sovereignty disputes, it conceptualizes the South China Sea as a multi-layered power structure where maritime economic interests, sea-lane security, and great-power competition intersect. The analysis explores how ASEAN employs international law, multilateral institutions, and functional cooperation to manage conflicts and preserve regional centrality, while the ROK, as a middle power, pursues calibrated engagement through ASEAN-led mechanisms to safeguard maritime interests without escalating strategic confrontation. This study positions the South China Sea as an illuminating case for understanding indirect middle-power engagement in regional security governance amid intensifying geopolitical pressures.

DOI: 10.4018/979-8-3373-4470-6.ch007

1. INTRODUCTION

Within the Asia-Pacific regional security architecture, the South China Sea has emerged as a multi-layered strategic space where maritime economic interests, maritime security imperatives, and international power competition converge and intersect. Far beyond its function as a vital maritime artery for global trade and energy flows, the South China Sea is increasingly recognized as a "geostrategic node" in the ongoing reconfiguration of regional order—a theater wherein great powers calibrate their spheres of influence through both military deployments and institutional instruments. The strategic sensitivity of these waters stems not solely from protracted sovereignty disputes, but also from the securitization of techno-economic interactions, ensuring that any legal or political volatility in this domain can trigger spillover effects extending far beyond its immediate geographical boundaries.

From a regional governance perspective, the "South China Sea issue" is increasingly conceptualized as a power-structural problem rather than a fragmented collection of bilateral disputes. The prevailing power asymmetry among claimant states, coupled with deepening involvement by major powers, has transformed the South China Sea into a critical test of whether regional mechanisms can effectively manage conflicts and sustain a stable order (Weissmann, 2010). Within this context, ASEAN functions simultaneously as a directly affected actor and as the principal institutional hub for advancing restraint, dialogue, and the development of legal norms. Nevertheless, ASEAN's coordinating role remains constrained by internal dynamics—namely, consensus requirements, divergent national interests, and pressures emanating from great-power competition—which collectively limit its regulatory capacity and practical effectiveness (Amer, 2009).

A notable characteristic of existing scholarship on the South China Sea is its predominant focus on claimant states and the strategic calculations of major powers such as the United States and China. By contrast, the role of extra-regional middle powers is frequently relegated to a secondary analytical tier. This analytical gap has become increasingly conspicuous since the early decades of the twenty-first century, as the Republic of Korea (ROK) has steadily expanded its strategic engagement with Southeast Asia through foreign policy initiatives including the New Southern Policy (NSP) and, subsequently, the Korea–ASEAN Solidarity Initiative (KASI). Alongside the expansion of economic cooperation, the ROK has progressively deepened its involvement in non-traditional security domains, maritime capacity-building programs, and discourse on a rules-based order, thereby establishing an indirect yet consequential presence in the maritime security landscape of the South China Sea without assuming the position of a claimant party (Yoon, 2021).

Integrating both empirical and theoretical perspectives, this chapter situates the South China Sea within the broader evolution of ASEAN–ROK relations, treating it as a strategic space possessing substantial historical depth. It is within this arena that the interests, postures, and policy instruments of a middle power are shaped and recalibrated over time. Rather than concentrating on specific sovereignty disputes, this chapter analyzes the mechanisms through which ASEAN and the ROK identify their interests, formulate policies, and operationalize cooperative frameworks pertaining to the South China Sea against the backdrop of an increasingly fluid regional environment since the early twenty-first century.

The principal academic contribution of this chapter lies in "historicizing" the South China Sea as a variable within the study of ASEAN–ROK relations. The South China Sea is treated not merely as contextual background, but as a testing ground for assessing the degree of interest alignment and policy coordination between a regional mechanism (ASEAN) and an extra-regional middle power (the ROK). Through systematic examination of policy pronouncements, cooperative frameworks, and patterns of bilateral and multilateral interaction over time, the chapter elucidates the mechanisms by which the ROK has engaged in regional security governance in an indirect yet increasingly consequential manner. It also identifies the conditions under which such cooperation expands or becomes constrained by power-structural dynamics and institutional limitations (Swenson & Wacker, 2023).

Building upon this analytical foundation, the chapter proceeds through a structured sequence: it begins by framing the South China Sea as a strategic space shaped by power-structural dynamics (Section 2), before examining the respective interests and positions of ASEAN and the Republic of Korea (Section 3). It subsequently assesses the bilateral and multilateral modalities of cooperation related to the South China Sea (Section 4), and concludes by drawing out the theoretical and policy implications for regional maritime security governance amid intensifying great-power competition (Section 5).

2. THE SOUTH CHINA SEA AS A STRATEGIC ISSUE FOR ASEAN AND THE REPUBLIC OF KOREA

2.1. The South China Sea as a Strategic Space: Resources, Connectivity, and Power

In the evolving regional order, the South China Sea has emerged as a functionally convergent strategic space where commercial flows, energy transit, and military operations intersect within a shared maritime domain, generating increasing interdependence among regional and extra-regional actors. This maritime arena no longer operates merely as "disputed territory," but has evolved into a structural platform through which states organize their interests, allocate resources, and adjust strategic behavior under conditions of intensifying international power competition. In this sense, the South China Sea functions as an intermediary variable that directly links the economic drivers and security logics of the contemporary Asia-Pacific (Chew, 2010).

First, the South China Sea is intrinsically associated with global maritime connectivity. It constitutes one of the world's most critical sea lanes, linking East Asia with the Middle East and Europe, and serving as a vital conduit for international trade and energy flows. According to the Asia Society Policy Institute (2021), more than half of global maritime trade and a substantial proportion of oil and gas shipments destined for Northeast Asia transit through the South China Sea, rendering any disruption capable of generating spillover effects extending far beyond the immediate geographical confines of the region. For economies heavily dependent on trade and imported energy—including the ROK, Japan, and China—the South China Sea holds implications not only for the movement of goods but also for economic security and supply chain resilience.

Beyond its connective function, the South China Sea is also recognized as one of the key strategic resource frontiers of the twenty-first century. Regional scholarship consistently underscores its significance for fisheries production and hydrocarbon potential, not only for coastal states but also for extra-regional economies heavily reliant on imported food and energy resources. As Rosenberg (2009) observes, the South China Sea accounts for a substantial share of global fisheries output and plays an essential role in food security across East Asia, particularly as offshore oil and gas basins in the region continue to attract international energy firms. Consequently, the South China Sea is no longer merely an "extractive space," but a domain embedded with strategic risk, where emerging conflicts over energy and food resources can readily escalate into matters of national and even global security.

Nevertheless, evaluating the South China Sea exclusively through the binary lens of economics and resources falls short of capturing its full strategic significance, particularly as the region has increasingly become a theater for military presence and the norm-shaping endeavors of great powers. Comparative analyses by Houlden, Romaniuk, and Hong (2021) suggest that these waters now function as a "geostrategic node" for Asia-Pacific security. Specifically, the South China Sea has become the direct intersection of two critical axes within the regional security architecture: (1) the axis of maritime presence and power projection, and (2) the axis of rule-making and norm-setting that govern state behavior. When these two axes converge in a space characterized by high-density interaction, tactical maneuvers on the ground cease to be localized events; instead, they become inextricably drawn into broader debates concerning legitimacy and legal norms. In essence, the South China Sea serves simultaneously as both a "deployment platform" and a "testing ground" for the rules-based order, defining what actions are permissible, to what extent, and through which regional mechanisms they are validated.

At the institutional level, the South China Sea has consequently evolved into a primary arena for the direct collision of competing visions for regional order. While the United States and its partners advocate for a rules-based order, freedom of navigation, and the legal primacy of the United Nations Convention on the Law of the Sea (UNCLOS), China adopts a more flexible approach that blends international law with historical-political interpretations of maritime rights. Weissmann (2010) argues that the tension between these two approaches renders the South China Sea a structural issue in China–ASEAN relations, gradually eroding coastal states' capacity to exercise strategic restraint and shape their own security environments.

In essence, the South China Sea issue is fundamentally "structural" rather than "situational." Contemporary disputes in these waters no longer stem primarily from isolated state actions. Ayesh and Askari (2025) observe that U.S.–China competition in the South China Sea is increasingly institutionalized through regional policy frameworks, compelling Southeast Asian nations to calibrate their behavior in alignment with the interests and systemic pressures exerted by these two great powers. This defining characteristic renders the South China Sea a pivotal variable in any regional security calculus. From an academic standpoint, this premise provides the foundation for analyzing the roles, interests, and strategies of ASEAN and the ROK in the forthcoming sections.

2.2. The "South China Sea Problem" as a Power Structure

Viewed through a structural analytical lens, the "South China Sea issue" is best conceptualized as a multi-layered power-structural problem, wherein interest conflicts manifest simultaneously at both regional and global levels. This framework deliberately transcends conventional territorial paradigms, instead situating the South China Sea within the overarching strategic logic of the Asia-Pacific regional order.

At the proximate level, disputes in the South China Sea reflect inherent contradictions concerning sovereignty claims, Exclusive Economic Zones (EEZs), and jurisdictional rights under UNCLOS 1982. However, comparative scholarship suggests that these disputes cannot be resolved solely through legal norms. Given significant power asymmetry, the dominant party can impose its will and exert control, while weaker states lack the leverage to compel compliance. Drawing on this reality, Weissmann (2010) argues that although ASEAN member states primarily rely on diplomatic instruments and international law, China integrates legal frameworks with its material preponderance at sea, thereby undermining the collective enforcement capabilities of regional mechanisms. This dynamic explains why legal foundations—including the 2016 Arbitration Award—despite their normative and principled value, continue to face significant obstacles in achieving practical efficacy.

At the structural level, the South China Sea is defined by great-power competition, particularly between the United States and China. Since 2010, it has served as a central arena wherein both powers test divergent models of influence: one anchored in freedom of navigation and a rules-based order, the other grounded in historical rights and perceived core interests (Ayesh & Askari, 2025). Crucially, this rivalry extends beyond the military domain and has become increasingly institutionalized through policy frameworks and strategic partnerships, transforming the South China Sea into a critical link within the global security architecture rather than an isolated regional dispute.

Compared with other contested maritime spaces in the region, the structural character of the South China Sea is particularly pronounced. In the East China Sea, for instance, tensions remain largely confined to the bilateral relationship between China and Japan and are managed with relative stability through diplomatic channels and mutual deterrence. By contrast, the South China Sea has been subject to a form of "forced multilateralization" due to the overlapping interaction of multiple actors' maritime security policies, the European Union's economic interests, and China's long-term strategic ambitions. As Swenson and Wacker (2023) observe, under such conditions, the South China Sea is no longer a domain solely for coastal states; it has become embedded within a broader network of cross-regional strategic competition.

Another defining characteristic of the power dynamics in the South China Sea is the intricate fusion of material and institutional power. Activities such as Freedom of Navigation Operations (FONOPs), multilateral exercises, and rotational force deployments transcend mere deterrence; they are strategically calculated to establish precedents in the interpretation and application of international law. Beckman (2019) contends that within such a contested environment, legal norms cease to function as neutral arbiters and instead become instruments of power competition, wherein stakeholders strive to "legalize" their respective strategic interests. Consequently, a single maritime action can be subjected to diametrically opposed interpretations—deemed lawful within the logic of one party while branded as a violation within the logic of another.

The power structure in the South China Sea is further reinforced through processes of internationalization and selective security linkages. Following the U.S. "rebalance" strategy initiated in 2011, the South China Sea became a strategic anchor for Washington to expand its security partnership network with Japan, Australia, and India. Simultaneously, China intensified bilateral diplomacy and economic initiatives to increase its influence over individual ASEAN member states. This interplay of alliances, partnerships, and influence competition has transformed the South China Sea into a focal point of "layered security," wherein decision-making in the region is shaped not only by the direct interests of claimant states but also by the strategic calculations of extra-regional great powers (Simon, 2011).

Within this structure, coastal states gradually forfeit the capacity to shape their own security trajectories independently. According to Ibarra (2022), the South China Sea represents one of the few contested spaces where small and middle powers function simultaneously as direct protagonists in the conflict and as subjects of a broader power structure over which they exert minimal influence. This defining characteristic ensures that the South China Sea cannot be effectively managed solely through legal mechanisms or bilateral agreements; rather, it remains inextricably tied to the enduring challenge of balancing strategic engagement with the preservation of autonomy within a fundamentally asymmetric power environment.

Taken together, the "South China Sea issue" is not a sequence of isolated disputes, but an open power structure wherein regional cooperation dynamics are intertwined with global competitive pressures. Within this framework, state behavior is inseparable from the systemic logic of power distribution governing the Asia-Pacific order. It is through this structural lens that the roles and strategic calculations of middle powers—most notably the ROK—can be more comprehensively understood in the sections that follow.

2.3. ASEAN and the ROK: Positions and Strategic Calculations

ASEAN's approach to the South China Sea should be understood as a structural choice rather than a short-term policy response or reactive positioning. As a regional organization governed by consensus, lacking coercive authority, and without hard-security instruments, ASEAN operates within a constrained power environment wherein it is virtually unable to directly influence the behavior of major actors such as the United States and China. Under these conditions, ASEAN's most viable strategy is not to "resolve" the dispute in the sense of achieving final adjudication, but rather to manage it through sustained dialogue and risk mitigation. As Damayanti (2019) observes, ASEAN's persistent prioritization of forums such as the ASEAN Regional Forum (ARF), East Asia Summit (EAS), and ASEAN Defence Ministers' Meeting Plus (ADMM+) reflects a distinct institutional logic: rather than seeking a definitive outcome on sovereignty, ASEAN aims primarily to shape behavior, maintain regular channels of communication, and prevent the breakdown of dialogue processes.

From this perspective, ASEAN's role in the South China Sea is not to determine the final outcome of the dispute, but to reduce the likelihood of unilateral action in an unstable security environment. According to Ibarra (2022), by prioritizing less sensitive areas of cooperation—such as maritime security, search-and-rescue operations, and confidence-building measures—ASEAN can modulate sovereignty disputes while limiting the risk that major powers form competing alliance structures outside ASEAN-led mechanisms. Within this logic, although the 2002 Declaration on the Conduct of Parties in the South China Sea (DOC) lacks legally binding force, it nevertheless establishes behavioral principles among relevant parties, helping to curb escalation and enabling ASEAN to continue functioning as an intermediary amid growing involvement of extra-regional powers in the South China Sea.

Compared to other regional organizations, ASEAN operates through indirect institutional power. Because major powers are compelled to participate in ASEAN-led forums, the Association can steer discussions toward de-escalation and conflict avoidance even when it lacks the capacity to shape final outcomes. This suggests that the South China Sea is not only a security challenge but also a strategic arena through which ASEAN reasserts its centrality in the Asia-Pacific security architecture. Yet ASEAN's strategy is not purely preventive; it also constitutes a form of indirect balancing. By expanding its network of partnerships and encouraging extra-regional actors to engage in cooperative mechanisms, ASEAN can establish a relative equilibrium that limits the ability of any single great power to unilaterally dominate the South China Sea. Within this structure, middle powers such as the ROK are viewed as particularly suitable partners—strong enough to make substantive contributions yet lacking hegemonic ambitions, thereby enabling participation without exacerbating strategic confrontation.

The ROK's position on the South China Sea reflects the strategic thinking and behavior of a middle power operating amid great-power competition. Seoul pursues a strategy of "calibrated engagement": avoiding alignment with any specific claimant while consistently supporting international law, freedom of navigation, and peaceful dispute settlement (Yoon, 2021). Far from signifying passive neutrality, this represents a calculated strategic engagement through which the ROK seeks to safeguard its long-term strategic interests without incurring prohibitive political or security costs.

Comparative studies on middle powers reinforce this interpretation. Teo (2018), as well as Karim and Nabila (2022), argue that the behavior of states such as the ROK, Australia, and Indonesia is better understood as status adjustment rather than order reshaping: they seek to expand national influence through cooperative outcomes, cultivate the image of a responsible partner, and avoid hard-security commitments that could erode strategic autonomy. In the ROK's case, this logic is particularly salient given the imperative to maintain its security alliance with the United States while preserving political and economic stability with China—two actors whose interests and rivalries intersect directly in the South China Sea.

The New Southern Policy (NSP) clearly reflects the ROK's effort to restructure its diplomatic space under these conditions. By deepening engagement with Southeast Asia, the ROK has not only diversified its economic relations but also sought to disperse strategic risk and reduce dependence on any single axis of interaction (Kim & Lee, 2020). Building on this foundation, the Korea–ASEAN Solidarity Initiative (KASI) further institutionalized the ROK's regional role through functional cooperation in areas such as maritime security, enhanced coordination, and capacity-building assistance to ASEAN member states in maritime management and surveillance rather than through direct strategic confrontation. This approach allows the ROK to expand its regional influence while sustaining its image as a constructive and cooperative partner in ASEAN's eyes (Yeo, 2023).

In practice, the ROK refrains from approaching the South China Sea merely as a "military hotspot," treating it instead as a strategic space for operationalizing various modalities of soft engagement. Southeast Asia perceives Seoul as a governance-oriented partner capable of sharing expertise in defense modernization, crisis management, and maritime security cooperation within the context of digital transformation, rather than as an actor embroiled in direct international power competition (Hoo, 2022). This facilitates substantial strategic convergence between ASEAN's regional objectives and the ROK's strategic calculus, as both parties prioritize stability, cooperation, and peace.

From a comparative perspective, the ASEAN–ROK case study illustrates how the South China Sea has become a quintessential testing ground for indirect forms of middle-power engagement. Diverging from the assertive behavior of great powers, the ROK does not pursue a foundational order-shaping role; instead, it focuses on integrating into ASEAN-led multilateral mechanisms, thereby contributing to regional security governance in a decidedly non-disruptive manner. Ultimately, the synergy between a regional mechanism that lacks enforcement instruments but wields significant institutional power, and a middle power that prioritizes soft engagement, has transformed the South China Sea into a distinctive strategic space within the trajectory of ASEAN–ROK relations and cooperation in the twenty-first century.

3. POSITIONS AND INTERESTS OF ASEAN AND THE ROK IN THE SOUTH CHINA SEA

3.1. ASEAN: A Conflict Management-Oriented Position to Maintain Regional Stability and Consolidate ASEAN Centrality

Regarding the South China Sea issue, ASEAN pursues a conflict management-oriented approach through soft mechanisms and flexible modalities. In contrast to great powers capable of leveraging military force and strategic deterrence, ASEAN operates under the consensus principle and lacks coercive instruments, possessing neither a collective military force nor mechanisms to compel compliance with majority decisions. Within this context, ASEAN does not place undue emphasis on adjudicating "right versus wrong," but instead focuses on preventing conflict escalation and maintaining a peaceful, stable environment conducive to the development of its member states.

At the policy level, ASEAN's position is operationalized through three key pillars. First, there is an emphasis on international law and norms of conduct. UNCLOS 1982, the ASEAN Charter, and the Treaty of Amity and Cooperation (TAC) serve as the legal bedrock for all of the Association's official declarations. ASEAN's consistent invocation of international law reflects a strategic choice to leverage soft power, thereby bolstering the legitimacy of the Association's small and medium-sized states amid power asymmetry (Beckman, 2019). Consequently, ASEAN identifies legal frameworks as the primary instrument for diplomatic decision-making.

Second, ASEAN pursues the institutionalization of dialogue through multilateral forums. Rather than engaging in bilateral negotiations with individual great powers, ASEAN proactively integrates South China Sea issues into mechanisms such as the ARF, EAS, and ADMM+. These forums serve to recalibrate diplomatic thinking and conduct, guiding parties to sustain dialogue and acknowledge ASEAN's convening capacity (Damayanti, 2019). In practice, the strategic significance of these multilateral forums is reflected not necessarily in specific negotiated outcomes, but rather in ASEAN's persistent efforts to prevent the disruption of dialogue during periods of heightened tension.

Third, ASEAN promotes the expansion of functional cooperation at sea, particularly in maritime security, search and rescue (SAR), counter-piracy, and marine environmental protection. Agastia (2021) argues that maritime security cooperation within the ASEAN framework functions as a "buffering mechanism" that simultaneously strengthens institutions and maintains intra-ASEAN cohesion amid sharp divergences in member states' sovereign interests. Following this logic, maritime cooperation enhances mutual understanding and shared interests, thereby mitigating the risk of conflict escalating into military confrontation.

Nevertheless, the maritime conflict management approach through soft mechanisms manifests inherent limitations. York (2015) observes that ASEAN's common position typically achieves only a minimum consensus—a level sufficient for maintaining a unified stance, yet one that struggles to translate into collective action when member states are subjected to pressure from great powers. Consequently, ASEAN sustains its centrality not through the capacity to dominate or dictate the ultimate resolution of disputes, but rather through its convening capacity, ensuring that regional security remains anchored in a rules-based maritime order, sustained dialogue, and functional cooperation mechanisms.

3.2. The ROK: A Calibrated Engagement Position to Safeguard Maritime Interests

While not directly bearing the impact of South China Sea disputes in the same manner as ASEAN member states, the ROK approaches the issue from the perspective of an extra-regional middle power. Despite being an external actor, the nation maintains vital maritime interests inextricably linked to maritime security. Given that more than 90% of its trade depends on maritime transport, with the vast majority of these sea lanes traversing the South China Sea, the ROK cannot remain indifferent to developments in this strategic space.

The "calibrated engagement" framework fundamentally defines the ROK's position. Yoon (2021) characterizes the ROK as the archetype of a pragmatic middle power: consistently advocating for international law, freedom of navigation, and peaceful solutions while circumventing any commitments or actions that might be construed as direct confrontation with China. This approach enables Seoul to sustain its status as a responsible partner within the international community while simultaneously prioritizing its relations with great powers.

Historically, "calibrated engagement" emerged and solidified as the underpinning logic of the ROK's foreign policy thinking since its rise as a prominent middle power during the late Cold War era. In contrast to traditional great powers that project military presence or seek to establish regional order, the ROK opts for a "calibrated engagement" strategy predicated on three core principles: (i) active participation in international institutions, (ii) regional cooperation without military confrontation, and (iii) flexibility to adjust the level of engagement in response to adverse shifts in the strategic context. In the context of the South China Sea issue, this position reflects a calculated strategic approach, as the ROK maintains only a sufficient level of engagement to uphold fundamental principles such as international law and freedom of navigation. Consequently, "calibrated engagement" serves as a mechanism for strategic autonomy, manifesting a middle power's capacity to proactively and flexibly modulate its external activities amid asymmetric power competition. This distinguishes the ROK's strategic behavior from both major powers (governed by an order-leading logic) and small states (governed by a dependency logic).

Three distinct historical constraints underpin this cautious position. First, the security alliance with the United States serves as the foundational pillar of national security against the North Korean threat. Second, deep-seated economic dependence on China—the ROK's largest trading partner and a decisive factor influencing peace on the Korean Peninsula—shapes policy considerations. Third, the economic lessons from the Terminal High Altitude Area Defense (THAAD) incident, where Beijing's retaliation forced Seoul to bear significant costs for perceived alignment in strategic competition. Meick and Salidjanova (2017) conclude that the THAAD experience has rendered Seoul increasingly risk-averse regarding regional security issues involving U.S.–China competition.

Learning from these constraints, the ROK has prioritized non-confrontational engagement, particularly through cooperation and capacity-sharing. Initiatives such as the New Southern Policy (NSP) and the Korea–ASEAN Solidarity Initiative (KASI) have enabled the ROK to expand its regional presence in Southeast Asia through functional maritime cooperation, including maritime security, maritime surveillance technology transfer, law-enforcement training, and transnational crime coordination. The Daniel K. Inouye Asia-Pacific Center for Security Studies (2020) observes that security cooperation under the NSP allows the ROK to enhance its regional role while avoiding entanglement in direct military competition. This approach embodies a form of "soft engagement," characterized by proactive involvement rather than passive neutrality.

3.3. Comparing ASEAN and the ROK: Convergence in Principle, Divergence in Engagement

The comparison between ASEAN and the ROK reveals a fundamental alignment in principle: both actors consistently prioritize international law, peaceful solutions, and multilateral forums as the bedrock of their conduct regarding the South China Sea. However, this normative convergence does not stem from identical strategic motives; rather, it reflects two distinct logics of action, inextricably linked to the unique status and interests of each actor within the regional architecture.

For ASEAN, rules and institutional frameworks serve primarily as instruments to sustain ASEAN centrality and its convening capacity in a high-conflict environment. Weissmann (2010) argues that in disputes characterized by significant power asymmetry, Southeast Asian states are compelled to "institutionalize the conflict." This strategy aims to curb unilateral dominance and the imposition of will by great powers, thereby safeguarding ASEAN's collective space for action. Accordingly, ASEAN has consistently promoted legal principles—from the DOC to the ongoing Code of Conduct (COC) process—as tools of conflict management and as mechanisms for safeguarding its coordinating role.

By contrast, for the ROK, legal and institutional instruments are not tools for asserting a coordinating role but means of safeguarding maritime interests and minimizing strategic risks. The Asia Society Policy Institute (2021) emphasizes that economies highly dependent on maritime trade, such as the ROK, have a direct stake in sustaining a stable, rules-based maritime order but lack both the incentive and the capacity to bear the enforcement costs of that order. Consequently, Seoul's diplomatic emphasis on UNCLOS, freedom of navigation, and peaceful solutions reflects a strictly pragmatic choice: a strategy designed to protect economic flows without incurring the risks associated with military confrontation.

This divergence in strategic motivations explains why ASEAN–ROK cooperation has expanded primarily in terms of functional breadth rather than strategic depth. In an environment where the South China Sea has been increasingly "internationalized" by great-power competition, cooperative mechanisms and conflict management-oriented approaches tend to produce more durable outcomes than hard-security commitments, which risk triggering adversarial reactions (Ibarra, 2022). Lee and Park (2020) observe that counter-piracy cooperation between the ROK and ASEAN yields far more substantive results than political declarations. Furthermore, Yoshihara (2015) emphasizes that multilateral maritime security cooperation in East Asia is most effective when focused on supportive and capacity-building tasks rather than alliance-based commitments.

Maritime security assistance from middle powers like the ROK plays a vital role in enabling Southeast Asian states to enhance their maritime conflict management capabilities without generating new strategic tensions or altering the balance of power (Ashley & Fraser, 2023). From this perspective, the ROK is regarded as an "appropriately calibrated partner": a state possessing the requisite capacity for substantive cooperation while exhibiting no ambitions to reorder or dominate the regional order.

The normative convergence between these two positions, despite their divergent motivations and levels of commitment, has established a sufficiently substantive collaborative foundation to sustain mutual strategic interests while remaining flexible enough to avoid altering the power structure in the South China Sea. Consequently, maritime security cooperation between the ROK and ASEAN remains primarily supportive and complementary, aimed at enhancing maritime conflict management capabilities rather than forging deep-seated strategic commitments. The ROK refrains from seeking a leadership role in regional security governance, while ASEAN maintains a vigilant stance toward any partner harboring ambitions to alter the existing balance of power (Laksmana & Mantong, 2021).

4. ASEAN–ROK COOPERATION ON THE SOUTH CHINA SEA

4.1. Political Cooperation on the South China Sea Issue

In the political domain, ASEAN–ROK cooperation on the South China Sea most clearly reflects the institutionalization of dialogue, through which the positions of both sides are embedded within ASEAN-led frameworks such as the ARF, EAS, and ADMM+ (Park & Kim, 2007). Departing from an initial focus on "confidence-building" and the positioning of ASEAN as a primary economic–development partner, Seoul has, since the early 2000s, increasingly leveraged these forums to articulate its maritime strategy. This evolution underscores a commitment to the principles of a "free and rules-based" maritime order within the East Asian theater.

At the institutional level, the mechanism of political cooperation is operationalized across two layers: bilateral engagement with individual ASEAN member states and multilateral coordination with ASEAN as a regional entity. At the bilateral level, Seoul systematically consolidates strategic partnerships with pivotal actors—specifically Vietnam, Indonesia, and the Philippines—manifested through diplomatic upgrades and robust defense and security cooperation. Notably, language directly addressing the South China Sea is frequently institutionalized within normative frameworks, utilizing standard terminology such as "peace, stability, and freedom of navigation" (Yoon, 2015).

At the multilateral layer, ASEAN+1, ASEAN+3, the ARF, EAS, and ADMM+ enable the ROK to articulate its stance on conflict management, emphasizing the pacific settlement of disputes, strict adherence to UNCLOS, and the non-use of force. This strategy empowers the ROK to fulfill its responsibilities as a middle power while avoiding alignment in the intensifying U.S.–China competition (Chung, 2025). In contrast to Japan or Australia, the ROK maintains a more calibrated posture, often eschewing direct criticisms of China; nevertheless, Seoul shares a common strategic logic in leveraging ASEAN-led mechanisms to optimize its maritime security interests.

Regarding content, ROK–ASEAN political cooperation revolves around three primary activity clusters, which, while varying in intensity, remain functionally complementary. First, policy dialogue and knowledge sharing, facilitated through joint research and forums among officials and scholars, enable both parties to cultivate a common strategic vocabulary on maritime security, conflict management, and the primacy of international law. This constitutes the "soft layer" of cooperation, providing a foundational baseline for subsequent functional cooperation.

Second, the ROK systematically prioritizes political consultation within ASEAN-led dialogue frameworks. In these venues, Seoul consistently underscores its support for ASEAN centrality as a prerequisite for regional peace and stability. This methodology manifests a distinct departure from the direct approaches of certain external powers, which frequently instrumentalize the South China Sea issue solely within a strategy of China containment (Park & Kim, 2007).

Third, the ROK proactively supports ASEAN's conflict prevention and management initiatives, including mechanisms such as the ASEAN Institute for Peace and Reconciliation (ASEAN-IPR), in line with recent ROK–ASEAN Action Plans. However, when compared to economic cooperation, the political–security pillar remains dialogue-oriented rather than anchored in hard security commitments (Rosnani et al., 2022).

In terms of progression, following the 2010 ASEAN–ROK Joint Declaration, political cooperation was elevated from general commitments to concrete action plans aligned with the development of the ASEAN Political–Security Community (APSC) (Park & Kim, 2007). Building on this foundation, the ROK intensified its regional presence by appointing an Ambassador to ASEAN in 2012 and operationalizing mechanisms such as the ASEAN–ROK Joint Cooperation Committee and joint security dialogues beginning in 2013. This evolution signifies a decisive shift from broad dialogue relations to an institutionalized dialogue partnership, characterized by a structured agenda and systematic project implementation timelines.

Compared to other dialogue partnerships, such as those with the EU or India, the ROK was relatively late in establishing specialized maritime security mechanisms; however, it has more effectively leveraged ASEAN-led dialogue frameworks to promote maritime safety and protect critical trade routes through the South China Sea. The core of Seoul's political approach to the South China Sea is the prioritization of universal principles—specifically international law, the rules-based order, and freedom of navigation—over direct condemnation of specific disputants. Statements delivered at the ADMM-Plus and EAS consistently underscore the necessity of peaceful dispute settlement, strict adherence to UNCLOS, and the guarantee of freedom of navigation and overflight (Chung, 2025).

This strategy reflects Seoul's maritime strategic culture: a fundamental requirement for a stable environment to secure economic interests tied to sea lines of communication (SLOCs), while simultaneously mitigating the risk of economic retaliation from China and preserving stability on the Korean Peninsula. This approach effectively maintains the ROK's degree of strategic autonomy by avoiding alignment within the broader great-power competition.

From 2017 onwards, ROK–ASEAN political cooperation on the South China Sea became more firmly anchored in new foreign policy frameworks, most notably the New Southern Policy (NSP) and its successor, NSP Plus. The NSP elevates ASEAN to a position of strategic priority, structured around three core pillars: People, Peace, and Prosperity. Within the "Peace" pillar, Seoul specifically prioritizes non-traditional security challenges and the preservation of a rules-based regional order. Compared to India's "Act East Policy," the NSP manifests a more pronounced socio-economic orientation and exerts less emphasis on overt strategic competition, thereby providing the ROK with expanded strategic maneuverability to calibrate its diplomatic relations with both Washington and Beijing (Daniel K. Inouye Asia-Pacific Center for Security Studies, 2020).

Nevertheless, as the ROK remains fundamentally constrained by its economic dependence on China and its strategic prioritization of the Korean Peninsula, the

NSP continues to face challenges in securing substantive commitments regarding a regular naval presence in the South China Sea (European Foundation for South Asian Studies, 2023). Within this context, the elevation of ROK–ASEAN relations to a Comprehensive Strategic Partnership in October 2024 primarily signifies the institutionalization of a new political framework rather than the realization of concrete maritime security commitments, such as mutual defense agreements (Asan Institute for Policy Studies, 2024). Compared to ASEAN's comprehensive strategic partnerships with China or Australia, South Korea's NSP places stronger emphasis on non-traditional security cooperation, the digital economy, and supply chain connectivity, whereas areas such as joint patrols or military presence remain limited.

4.2. ROK–ASEAN Security Cooperation on the South China Sea

In the security domain, ASEAN–ROK cooperation on the South China Sea issue centers on two major areas: maritime security and the defense industry. These two domains vary significantly in sensitivity: maritime security is generally more conducive to cooperation because it is tied to functional tasks and capacity-building, whereas cooperation in the defense industry holds greater potential but is more prone to friction due to issues involving core technologies and the strategic calculations of third parties (Kamaruddin, 2020).

First, maritime security constitutes a highly practical concern for many ASEAN states, encompassing illegal fishing, piracy, smuggling, and transnational crime, as well as maritime safety risks and the downstream consequences of sovereignty disputes (Rosnani et al., 2022). Within this landscape, the ROK occupies a favorable strategic position: the nation maintains no direct sovereignty disputes in the South China Sea while possessing unequivocal interests in safeguarding critical sea lines of communication (SLOCs) that traverse the region (Lee & Yoon, 2021). In terms of capabilities, the ROK possesses competitive strengths in shipbuilding, maritime technologies, and port operations; accordingly, Seoul's contributions have largely focused on technical assistance, information-sharing, and enhancing maritime law enforcement capacity among ASEAN member states.

From the perspective of a middle power, the ROK serves as a quintessential model of a nation that maintains regional security through soft power rather than large-scale military deployments. Murphy and Nagy (2024) asserts that middle powers in the Indo-Pacific, such as the ROK, systematically prioritize capacity-building, information-sharing, and cooperation in technology and non-traditional security over binding hard security commitments. This strategic posture enables the ROK to fulfill its responsibilities toward regional maritime security while simultaneously avoiding alignment in the intensifying great-power competition.

Since the early twenty-first century, ROK–ASEAN maritime security cooperation has primarily been operationalized within ASEAN-led dialogue frameworks, namely the ARF, EAS, and ADMM+. This structural arrangement empowers ASEAN to maintain its centrality while providing the ROK with a platform to intensify its regional engagement while effectively managing political risks. The joint co-chairmanship by Singapore and the ROK of the ADMM-Plus Experts' Working Group on Maritime Security (2017–2020), which promoted operational protocols for unexpected encounters at sea and organized field exercises, demonstrates that cooperation in this domain has moved beyond declaratory diplomacy toward functional and capacity-building coordination at sea (Rosnani et al., 2022).

Entering the 2020s, ASEAN–ROK maritime security cooperation has become more proactive, driven by foreign policy frameworks such as the New Southern Policy (NSP) and NSP Plus. Both NSP and NSP Plus designate ASEAN as a strategic priority, within which maritime security and the protection of sea lines of communication have emerged as key components of political–security cooperation (Daniel K. Inouye Asia-Pacific Center for Security Studies, 2020). Within this context, maritime domain cybersecurity has gained increasing prominence. Contemporary maritime operations heavily depend on digital systems, including port management, logistics data, vessel routing, and maritime supply chains, making the protection of the cyber layer of maritime activities a critical domain of maritime security cooperation. For ASEAN–ROK relations, this constitutes a promising area of functional cooperation, enabling both sides to enhance the protection of maritime-related digital infrastructure in a practical and demand-driven manner, while avoiding the political sensitivities often associated with direct military activities at sea (Daniel K. Inouye Asia-Pacific Center for Security Studies, 2020).

In the second pillar of security cooperation, the defense industry offers substantial opportunities for engagement but is characterized by significantly higher strategic sensitivity. The ROK's defense industry is undergoing rapid expansion and actively seeking to enter Southeast Asian markets—a region with escalating demand for defense modernization. Yet large-scale defense cooperation projects, such as submarine and fighter aircraft collaboration with Indonesia, illustrate inherent structural constraints. A portion of core technologies remains dependent on third-party suppliers, thereby reducing the degree of technological autonomy for both the ROK and ASEAN partners. As a result, projects frequently encounter difficulties related to technology transfer, technical standards, and project implementation timelines.

Cooperation between ASEAN and the ROK on maritime security in the South China Sea must be situated within the broader legal framework of the law of the sea. The 2016 Arbitral Tribunal Award is legally binding and further clarified several key provisions of UNCLOS. However, the extent of its impact depends heavily on whether relevant states choose to acknowledge and implement the ruling (Phan and

Lan, 2018). Consequently, the maritime rule of law transcends the mere preservation of UNCLOS and the 2016 Arbitral Tribunal Award; it increasingly depends on whether states internalize these norms into domestic legislation, demonstrate consistent respect for them, and actively operationalize them through state policy and field-level actions (Sumer, 2025).

While non-compliance by certain major powers poses a significant challenge to dispute settlement mechanisms, it is insufficient to precipitate the collapse of the established legal order so long as the majority of regional actors continue to anchor their claims in UNCLOS and judicial mechanisms (Meick & Salidjanova, 2017). Within this context, it is imperative that the ROK does more than merely declare support for UNCLOS or reference the 2016 Arbitral Tribunal Award. Instead, both parties must transition toward operationalizing concrete cooperation initiatives, including policy dialogue, unification of maritime codes of conduct, enhanced maritime law enforcement capacity, and information-sharing, to ensure that international maritime law is effectively applied in practice. These activities collectively reinforce a rules-based maritime order without necessitating coercive commitments. This approach aligns with the "soft but substantive" strategic orientation favored by both ASEAN and the ROK, as both entities seek to preserve a high degree of strategic autonomy amid evolving regional pressures and great-power competition.

5. CONCLUSION

The analyses presented in this chapter demonstrate that, over the historical progression of ROK–ASEAN relations since the early twenty-first century, the South China Sea has transitioned from a peripheral factor to an increasingly critical strategic theater. This issue does not always manifest through overt political commitments or direct military interventions; rather, it is expressed through the ways in which ASEAN and the ROK define their strategic interests, select policy options, and institutionalize their cooperative frameworks. For ASEAN, the South China Sea serves a dual imperative: it is both a litmus test of the Association's capacity to maintain ASEAN centrality within the regional security architecture and a catalyst that compels the organization to continuously balance the protection of its core interests against the structural pressures of great-power competition.

From the perspective of the ROK, this calibrated approach to the South China Sea reflects the defining characteristics and inherent constraints of a middle power operating in a theater of intense great-power competition. By avoiding alignment with specific disputants while systematically prioritizing international law, peaceful dispute settlement, and freedom of navigation, the ROK maintains the requisite equilibrium in its relations with both the United States and China. Simultaneously,

Seoul continues to play an active role in institutionalizing ASEAN-led dialogue frameworks. This "principled yet non-confrontational" methodology elucidates how the ROK can intensify its political–security presence in the South China Sea without precipitating unnecessary escalation of conflict.

Another salient conclusion is the convergence of interests and strategic postures between ASEAN and the ROK regarding their approach to the South China Sea. Both parties prioritize a rules-based order, uphold the centrality of multilateral institutions, and place high priority on maritime security. This convergence provides a solid foundation for various forms of "soft" cooperation—including political-diplomatic dialogue, confidence-building measures, and maritime security capacity-building—extending even into emerging domains such as maritime domain cybersecurity.

From an analytical standpoint, the South China Sea is not merely a "disputed hotspot," but a historical strategic space wherein indirect modalities of middle-power engagement are formed, tested, and recalibrated over time. On this basis, this chapter contributes to an emerging perspective in regional security studies: that non-great-power actors possess the capacity to actively shape regional order through multilateral institutions, functional cooperation, and information-sharing mechanisms.

At the policy level, the South China Sea is increasingly emerging as a strategic anchor within ROK–ASEAN relations. For ASEAN, the constructive presence of the ROK enhances its strategic maneuverability, enabling diversification of partners and mitigating risks associated with over-dependence on any single major power. For the ROK, deeper engagement with ASEAN on South China Sea security issues serves more than immediate needs for maritime safety, the protection of sea lines of communication (SLOCs), and economic interests. It further positions the ROK as a responsible partner committed to upholding a rules-based regional order, viewed through the longitudinal historical progression of East Asian–Southeast Asian relations.

REFERENCES

Agastia, I. G. B. D. (2021). Maritime security cooperation within the ASEAN institutional framework: Taking stock and looking ahead. *Journal of Asian Security and International Affairs*, *8*(1), 62–86.

Amer, R. (2009). The ASEAN conflict management approach revisited: Will the Charter reinforce ASEAN's role? *ASEAS – Austrian Journal of Southeast Asian Studies*, *2*(2), 6–27.

Asan Institute for Policy Studies. (2024). *ASEAN–Korea comprehensive strategic partnership: Prospects for security cooperation (Asan Issue Brief)*. Asan Institute for Policy Studies.

Ashley, R., & Fraser, J. (2023). Common waters: Japan, South Korea, and maritime security assistance in Southeast Asia. *Asia Policy*, *18*(2), 101–126. DOI: 10.1353/asp.2023.0021

Asia Society Policy Institute. (2021). *The South China Sea: Realities and Responses in Southeast Asia*. Asia Society Policy Institute.

Ayesh, S., & Askari, M. U. (2025). China–ASEAN approaches towards the South China Sea disputes. *Journal of Social Sciences Review*, *5*(1), 150–162. DOI: 10.62843/jssr.v5i1.481

Beckman, R. (2019). Maritime security. In Tan, Hsien-Li (Ed.), The legal authority of ASEAN as a security institution (pp. 112–138). Cambridge University Press., DOI: 10.1017/9781108669511.007

Chew, E. (2010). Singapore's Strategic Involvement in the Indian Ocean. In Bateman, S., & Ho, J. (Eds.), *Southeast Asia and the rise of Chinese and Indian naval power: Between rising naval powers*. Routledge.

Chung, E. (2025). *South Korea, a new key power for maritime security within the Indo-Pacific*. Fondation pour la Recherche Stratégique.

Damayanti, A. (2019). Indo-Pacific maritime cooperation: ASEAN mechanisms on security towards global maritime governance. *Global & Strategis*, *13*(1), 91–102. DOI: 10.20473/jgs.13.1.2019.1-44

Daniel K. Inouye Asia-Pacific Center for Security Studies. (2020). *Republic of Korea – New Southern Policy: Information booklet*. Danie K. Inouye Asia-Pacific Center for Security Studies.

European Foundation for South Asian Studies. (2023). *South Korea's New Southern Policy in Southeast Asia and India: Limitations and Opportunities.* European Foundation for South Asian Studies (EFSAS).

Hoo, C. P. (2022). Southeast Asia's expectations of Korea's middle-power agency in the regional security architecture. In Mantong, A. W., & Kharisma, W. (Eds.), *Navigating uncharted waters: Security cooperation between ROK and ASEAN* (pp. 25–38). Centre for Strategic and International Studies (CSIS) Indonesia.

Houlden, G., Romaniuk, S. N., & Hong, N. (Eds.). (2021). *Security, strategy, and military dynamics in the South China Sea: Cross-national perspectives.* Bristol University Press.

Ibarra, E. J. A. (2022). Issue-based cooperation on conflict resolution in the South China Sea: Exploring roles for ASEAN beyond the Code of Conduct. *Journal of Territorial and Maritime Studies*, *9*(1), 97–115. DOI: 10.2307/48684181

Kamaruddin, N. (Ed.). (2020). *The New Southern Policy – Catalyst for deepening ASEAN–ROK cooperation.* ISIS Malaysia.

Karim, M. F., & Nabila, R. (2022). Role conception of the Asia-Pacific middle powers: Comparative analysis of Indonesia, South Korea, Australia and Vietnam. *Journal of Asian Security and International Affairs*, *9*(2), 231–254. DOI: 10.1177/23477970221098469

Kim, H., & Lee, J. (2020). *The New Southern Policy.* ISIS Focus, 4/2020(14).

Laksmana, E. A., & Mantong, A. W. (2021). Missing pillars of strategic autonomy? Security cooperation between Korea and ASEAN. In Lee, K.-H., & Yoon, J.-R. (Eds.), The New Southern Policy Plus: Progress and way forward (pp. 197–218). Korea Institute for International Economic Policy.

Lee, J., & Park, M. (2020). An analysis of ROK and ASEAN's counter-piracy practices in the Indo-Pacific. *KIMS Maritime Security Series*, *6*(2), 45–68.

Lee, K.-H., & Yoon, J.-R. (Eds.). (2021). *The New Southern Policy Plus: Progress and way forward.* Korea Institute for International Economic Policy.

Meick, E., & Salidjanova, N. (2017). China's response to U.S.–South Korean missile defense system deployment and its implications. *U.S.-China Economic and Security Review Commission.* https://www.uscc.gov/research/chinas-response-us-south-korean-missile-defense-system-deployment-and-its-implications

Murphy, T. J., & Nagy, S. R. (2024). Middle power cybersecurity in the Indo-Pacific and the maritime domain: South Korea's role. *Journal of Intelligence, Conflict, and Warfare, 7(1), 1–24.* https://journals.lib.sfu.ca/index.php/jicw/article/download/6454/5793/23201. DOI: 10.21810/jicw.v7i1.6454

Park, S.-Y., & Kim, D. (Eds.). (2007). *ASEAN–Korea relations: Security, trade and community building*. ISEAS–Yusof Ishak Institute.

Phan, H. D., & Lan, N. N. (2018). The South China Sea arbitration: Bindingness, finality, and compliance with UNCLOS dispute settlement decisions. *Asian Journal of International Law*, *8*(1), 36–50. DOI: 10.1017/S2044251317000121

Rosenberg, D. (2009). Fisheries management in the South China Sea. In Bateman, S., & Emmers, R. (Eds.), *Security and international politics in the South China Sea: Towards a co-operative management regime*. Routledge.

Rosnani, R., Heryadi, D., Yani, Y. M., & Sinaga, O. (2022). ASEAN maritime security cooperation: Drivers and constraints. *TransNav: The International Journal on Marine Navigation and Safety of Sea Transportation*, *16*(3), 511–518. DOI: 10.12716/1001.16.03.01

Simon, S. (2011). US–Southeast Asia relations: Deep in South China Sea diplomacy. *Comparative Connections: A Quarterly E-Journal on East Asian Bilateral Relations, 13*(2), 164-165.

Sumer, M. (2025). The rule of law at sea and the challenge of non-compliance: A decade after the South China Sea arbitration. *The Boğaziçi Law Review*, *3*(2), 190–211. DOI: 10.69800/blr.1780335

Swenson, A., & Wacker, G. (2023). *South Korea's evolving Indo-Pacific strategy (SWP Research Paper 2/2023).* Stiftung Wissenschaft und Politik.

Teo, S. (2018). Middle power identities of Australia and South Korea. *The Pacific Review*, *31*(2), 159–177. DOI: 10.1080/09512748.2017.1371210

Weissmann, M. (2010). The South China Sea conflict and Sino-ASEAN relations: A study in conflict prevention and peace building. *Asian Perspective*, *34*(3), 35–69. DOI: 10.1353/apr.2010.0013

Yeo, J.-Y. (2023). *Indo-Pacific concept and Korea–ASEAN Solidarity Initiative: Regional perspectives (East Asian Institute Policy Brief).* National University of Singapore.

Yoon, S.-J. (2015). Maritime Asia: A South Korean perspective. In Till, G. (Ed.), *The changing maritime scene in Asia: Rising tensions and future strategic stability* (pp. 92–113). Springer.

Yoon, S.-J. (2021). South Korea and the South China Sea: A middle-power model for practical policies? In G. Houlden, S. N. Romaniuk, & N. Hong (Eds.), *Security, strategy, and military dynamics in the South China Sea: Cross-national perspectives* (pp. 347–366). Bristol University Press. DOI: 10.2307/j.ctv1t4m1qr.24

York, M. (2015). ASEAN's ambiguous role in resolving South China Sea disputes. *Indonesian Journal of International Law*, *12*(3), 325–346. DOI: 10.17304/ijil.vol12.3.607

Yoshihara, T. (2015). Maritime multilateral security cooperation in East and Southeast Asia. *Asia-Pacific Review*, *22*(1), 24–47.

Chapter 8
China's Maritime Security Strategy in the South China Sea:
Impact, Challenges, and Prospects

Binh Thi Tran
https://orcid.org/0009-0006-4943-8291
Nghe An University, Vietnam

Uyen Le Phuc Nguyen
University of Warsaw, Poland

ABSTRACT

This chapter examines China's maritime security strategy in the South China Sea under President Xi Jinping, analyzing its transformation from measured assertiveness to aggressive power projection. While China has achieved significant territorial gains through island construction and enhanced military presence, this strategy faces substantial challenges including coordinated resistance from Southeast Asian states, sustained US commitment to regional allies, and erosion of China's diplomatic credibility. The analysis reveals inherent strategic limitations: gray-zone tactics cannot compel decisive outcomes, military infrastructure remains vulnerable during high-intensity conflict, and prolonged competition imposes mounting economic costs. The chapter forecasts continued low-intensity confrontation characterized by tactical probing, escalating naval competition, and diplomatic stalemate, with the South China Sea remaining a critical flashpoint in US-China strategic rivalry for the foreseeable future.

DOI: 10.4018/979-8-3373-4470-6.ch008

1. INTRODUCTION

The South China Sea has emerged as one of the most complex and perilous geopolitical hotspots in the contemporary international system. With its strategic location at the heart of the Asia-Pacific region, this maritime area serves not only as a vital shipping route carrying over \$5.3 trillion worth of goods annually—accounting for nearly one-quarter of global trade—but also as a region containing enormous potential energy resources and holding existential security significance for numerous littoral states (Kang, 2025). This multidimensional strategic importance has transformed the South China Sea into an arena of intense power competition, where national interests intertwine with the geopolitical ambitions of major powers, particularly in the context of deepening US-China strategic rivalry.

Over the past decade, the academic community and policy planners have witnessed a significant transformation in China's approach to the South China Sea. Recent research indicates that under President Xi Jinping, China has abandoned its traditional policy of "hide your strength and bide your time" in favor of a considerably more proactive and assertive maritime security strategy (Chan, 2021; Raymond & Welch, 2022; Kiet et al., 2025). This strategic shift has been manifested through the unprecedented large-scale land reclamation campaign during 2013-2016, the militarization of artificial islands, and the dramatic escalation in both scale and frequency of operations by Chinese coast guard forces and maritime militia in disputed waters (Asia Maritime Transparency Initiative, n.d.). From the perspective of international relations theory, particularly the realism school, these developments reflect the inevitable tendency of a rising power to maximize its relative strength and establish regional hegemony to ensure optimal security within the anarchic international system (Mearsheimer, 2001; Kiet & Tuyen, 2023).

Although considerable scholarship exists on China's maritime strategy and South China Sea disputes, most current research tends to focus on describing specific Chinese actions or analyzing individual countries' responses. What remains absent is a comprehensive and systematic assessment of the actual effectiveness of this new strategy within the dynamic regional context, particularly one that examines simultaneously both initial successes and the serious challenges and inherent limitations China faces. Moreover, previous studies have not adequately clarified the fundamental paradox in Beijing's strategy: why a strategy that appears tactically successful—with expanded territorial control and increased military advantage—simultaneously generates significant diplomatic, legal, and international reputational backlash, leading to increasingly robust and organized resistance from regional states.

To fill this gap, this chapter aims to comprehensively analyze China's new maritime security strategy in the South China Sea under Xi Jinping through three complementary perspectives: (1) assessing the strategy's impact on the regional balance of power and balancing responses from other countries; (2) identifying and analyzing external challenges as well as internal limitations that China encounters in implementing and sustaining this strategy; and (3) forecasting potential trends and scenarios for the near and medium term. By applying a geopolitical lens combined with balance of power theory, this research contributes to illuminating the underlying dynamics, inherent contradictions, and long-term prospects of the ongoing strategic competition in one of the world's most important maritime regions. The research findings hold significance not only academically in better understanding the behavior of rising powers, but also provide practical policy implications for concerned states in adjusting response strategies and managing conflict risks amid intensifying power competition in the South China Sea.

2. THE SHIFTING BALANCE OF POWER IN THE SOUTH CHINA SEA AND STATE RESPONSES

The transformation of China's maritime security strategy under President Xi Jinping represents a critical turning point in the country's foreign policy. From a nation pursuing the principle of "hide and bide"—maintaining a low profile and awaiting opportunities—China has transitioned to a markedly more assertive and proactive strategy in the South China Sea. According to maritime security expert Chan (2025), this shift is reflected not only through increased militarization and coercive measures in disputed waters, but also embodies Beijing's broader ambition to become a global maritime power.

From a realism perspective, these developments can be systematically explained. Mearsheimer (2001) argues that great powers in an anarchic international system invariably seek to maximize their relative power and aspire to regional hegemony to ensure optimal security. Consistent with this theoretical prediction, an increasingly economically and militarily powerful China under Xi Jinping has abandoned its restraint and shifted toward an assertive strategy aimed at reshaping the regional order in favor of its national interests (Raymond & Welch, 2022). According to geopolitical logic, China is predicted to seek to push back US military influence from the Asia-Pacific region, similar to how the United States excluded European powers from the Western Hemisphere under the Monroe Doctrine in the 19th century (Kiet & Tuyen, 2023). Empirical evidence shows that China has identified control of the South China Sea as a "core interest" and is striving to establish a "Beijing-centric" regional order (Le & Tran, 2025).

One of the clearest manifestations of the new strategy is China's bold enhancement of military power and improved capabilities for territorial control in the South China Sea. Between 2013 and 2016, China conducted an unprecedented large-scale land reclamation campaign, constructing seven artificial islands on disputed reefs and coral formations (Asia Maritime Transparency Initiative, n.d.). These facilities are equipped with advanced military infrastructure, including runways capable of accommodating fighter aircraft, naval ports for warship berthing, long-range surveillance radar systems, and anti-aircraft and anti-ship missile installations. According to military analysts, these facilities have extended China's operational radius by approximately 620 nautical miles (nearly 1,000 km), creating the capability to threaten and attack most other claimant states in the region from these new outposts.

This development in military infrastructure has led to a significant shift in the maritime balance of power in the South China Sea, tilting decidedly in China's favor. This has generated deep concerns not only among smaller neighboring countries with direct territorial disputes, but also among extra-regional powers with strategic interests in the area. The construction of military bases on artificial islands has substantially enhanced China's ability to control vital shipping lanes passing through the South China Sea—where approximately $5.3 trillion worth of goods are transported annually, with about one-third of the world's oil shipments and half of global liquefied natural gas passing through these strategic waters (Kang, 2025). These figures raise concerns that if China gains absolute control of the South China Sea, it could threaten freedom of navigation and disrupt international trade, thereby creating significant geopolitical leverage.

Beyond hard military power, China maintains overwhelming dominance in maritime law enforcement forces—a crucial tool in its "gray zone" strategy. The China Coast Guard has now become the world's largest coast guard force by fleet size, with more vessels than the combined equivalent forces of all neighboring countries (Asian Military Review, 2024). This numerical superiority enables China to maintain a constant and overwhelming presence in situations of competition below the threshold of armed conflict, using coast guard and maritime militia vessels to patrol, harass foreign vessels, and assert sovereignty claims without escalating to overt military confrontation.

The inevitable consequence of China's assertive moves is that regional states have responded in diverse but generally power-balancing ways. These responses are gradually reshaping the regional security architecture in new directions. Faced with mounting pressure from China, Southeast Asian nations have accelerated defense modernization and strengthened security relationships with the United States and Washington's allies. A prime example is the Philippines under President Ferdinand Marcos Jr., who has implemented a significant policy shift from his predecessor. After a period of estrangement during President Rodrigo Duterte's term—when a China-leaning policy was pursued—the Marcos Jr. administration has restored and even intensified close military cooperation with the United States. Manila signed an expanded Enhanced Defense Cooperation Agreement, allowing US forces access to additional military bases in the Philippines, particularly those strategically located near the South China Sea and Taiwan Strait (Lendon, 2024). Similarly, countries such as Vietnam, Malaysia, and Indonesia have strengthened bilateral and multilateral security cooperation with extra-regional powers to create balancing mechanisms against China's growing strength (Kiet et al., 2025).

Beyond bilateral responses, new multilateral security structures are emerging, partly in response to China's expanding maritime power. The Quadrilateral Security Dialogue, comprising the United States, Japan, India, and Australia, was revived in 2017 and elevated to the summit level (Wei, 2022). AUKUS—a groundbreaking trilateral security pact, particularly in providing nuclear submarine technology to Australia—is also widely viewed by analysts as a direct response to security challenges posed by China in the Indo-Pacific region. Australia's decision to invest an estimated $248.5 billion in nuclear submarines (Jackson, 2023), and Japan's substantial upgrade of its Self-Defense Forces (Yamaguchi, 2025), both demonstrate that regional powers are preparing for long-term strategic confrontation with what they call China's "wolf warrior diplomacy" and increasing military pressure. It can be affirmed that the South China Sea has become a pivotal arena of geopolitical competition in US-China relations, where one side seeks to consolidate sovereignty claims and expand its sphere of influence, while the other, along with its network of allies and partners, strives to maintain a rules-based order and the existing balance of power. This polarization is increasing the risk of confrontation and instability in the region.

Notably, China's new strategy not only impacts smaller regional states but also directly challenges US security commitments. Hu (2021) points out that China's coercive behavior in the South China Sea is not merely defensive reactions to provocations, but appears to be part of a strategically calculated campaign aimed at targeting the weakest link in the US-led alliance system—specifically the Philippines—to gradually erode the credibility and reliability of Washington's alliance commitments. China's increasingly bold assertive actions place the United States in a difficult dilemma: on one hand, if Washington intervenes forcefully to protect allies like the Philippines, it faces the risk of direct conflict with the nuclear-armed power of China; on the other hand, if it stands idle without action, this would seriously damage the credibility of the entire US alliance system not only in Southeast Asia but in other regions worldwide. This potential impact has compelled successive US administrations to reaffirm their security commitments more explicitly and publicly.

For example, in 2019, the Trump administration clearly declared that the US-Philippines Mutual Defense Treaty (MDT) applies to disputes in the South China Sea, including features currently controlled by the Philippines (O'Rourke, 2025a). Simultaneously, Washington has significantly increased its military deterrence presence through more frequent Freedom of Navigation Operations, joint exercises with regional allies, and coordinated patrol activities. Thus, it is evident that China's assertive strategy has pushed the regional situation into higher confrontation, with the risk that miscalculation by any party could lead to a serious security crisis with far-reaching consequences.

In summary, the direct consequence of China's proactive and assertive strategy is that the security situation in the South China Sea has become significantly more tense and polarized than before. The regional balance of power is shifting unfavorably for smaller states, but has simultaneously triggered strong balancing efforts from neighboring countries and extra-regional powers aimed at containing Beijing's ambitions. The South China Sea has thus become the focal point of a new bipolarity in US-China relations in Asia, where any turbulence has the potential to broadly impact both regional and global security and stability.

3. OBSTACLES IN IMPLEMENTATION: FROM BALANCING RESPONSES TO INTERNATIONAL PRESSURE

Despite achieving significant initial strategic advantages, China still faces a series of serious challenges in implementing and sustaining its proactive maritime strategy in the long term. These challenges come from various sources and have the potential to limit the effectiveness and scope of the new strategy.

First and foremost, the resistance and adaptive capacity of Southeast Asian nations are increasing significantly, making it difficult for China to achieve its goal of monopolizing the South China Sea as easily as anticipated. After more than a decade of enduring continuous pressure, littoral states have gradually developed adaptive mechanisms and their own response strategies to China's increasingly sophisticated gray zone tactics (Jenne, 2017). Evidence shows that many countries are not only refusing to capitulate under pressure but are actively seeking ways to counterbalance Beijing's moves.

The Philippines represents a paradigmatic case of policy transformation. From a nation that appeared hesitant and even leaned toward China under President Duterte (Kiet et al., 2024), the Philippines has shifted to a much harder line under President Marcos Jr. For the first time since 2012—when it lost control of Scarborough Shoal to China—Manila has resumed patrol operations in this area and significantly increased its presence in the Spratly Islands (Indo-Pacific Defense Forum, 2023). Particularly noteworthy, the Philippines has persistently conducted monthly resupply missions to its military outpost on the BRP Sierra Madre—an old warship deliberately grounded at Second Thomas Shoal since 1999—throughout 2023 and early 2024, despite China repeatedly using coast guard and maritime militia vessels to surround, blast with high-pressure water cannons, and even dangerously collide with Philippine vessels.

Even more significantly, the Philippines has succeeded in repairing and reinforcing this aging vessel, forcing China to accept a return to the status quo after tense negotiations, demonstrating unwavering determination to maintain de facto sovereignty. Parallel to these maritime actions, the Philippines has skillfully leveraged pressure from China to consolidate domestic support for hardline policies and upgrade its alliance relationship with the United States to new heights. Manila successfully lobbied for the United States to increase annual military assistance to a record $500 million in 2024 to modernize the Philippines' defense capabilities (Lewis & Lema, 2024). Simultaneously, the Philippines has diversified its security partnerships by signing military access agreements with multiple other countries in the region. Most recently, in July 2024, the Philippines signed a historic Reciprocal Access Agreement with Japan, allowing military forces of both countries to be deployed on each other's territory and participate in joint training activities. Particularly, the Marcos administration has proactively conducted diplomatic campaigns to garner broader international support: the number of countries publicly calling on China to comply with the 2016 Arbitral Tribunal ruling has tripled to 27 countries in 2023—a clear indication that China is increasingly isolated legally and in international public opinion (Asia Maritime Transparency Initiative, 2023).

Malaysia and Indonesia have also demonstrated significantly more resolute attitudes in protecting their legitimate resource interests. Despite continuous harassment from Chinese geological survey vessels and coast guard ships, Malaysia has vigorously increased oil and gas exploration and extraction activities in its exclusive economic zone (EEZ): in 2023 alone, Malaysia drilled a record 25 new wells, and continued drilling an additional 15 wells in 2024 in waters off Sarawak state, completely ignoring diplomatic protests and pressure from China (The Asahi Shimbun, 2024). These decisive moves show that countries are directly challenging China's efforts to unilaterally impose the "nine-dash line" claim and have no intention of relinquishing their legitimate rights to exploit resources in their EEZ despite pressure.

Vietnam has taken even more proactive and counterbalancing steps: Hanoi has quietly but steadfastly expanded and consolidated the features it controls in the Spratly Islands. Over the three-year period from 2021 to 2024, Vietnam accelerated dredging and land reclamation activities on at least seven different reefs, raising the total area of artificial islands created by Vietnam to nearly two-thirds of what China has constructed (Asia Maritime Transparency Initiative, 2025). Particularly noteworthy, at Barque Canada Reef, Vietnam has now formed a runway approximately 8,000 feet (roughly 2,400 meters) long—sufficient for most military and civilian aircraft to take off and land at sea level.

What is remarkable and somewhat paradoxical is that China appears not to have attempted to obstruct Vietnam's artificial island construction activities through military means or even strong coercion, despite the significant scale of these operations. Geopolitical analysts offer several hypotheses to explain China's restraint: (i) Beijing may have suffered considerable international reputational damage and resource depletion from intense confrontations with the Philippines throughout 2023, thus unwilling to simultaneously open another front of tension with Vietnam; (ii) Vietnam-China relations have unique party-to-party communication channels and bilateral diplomatic mechanisms that allow the two sides to negotiate behind the scenes more effectively, thereby avoiding escalation to uncontrollable levels (Hai, 2021); (iii) Vietnam is not a formal US ally, so China may not view Vietnam's actions as posing an equivalent major geopolitical challenge as the Philippines case; and (iv) History shows Vietnam is willing to accept high risks and even casualties to defend its strategic interests in the South China Sea (as demonstrated in conflicts in 1974 and 1988), so China's conventional gray zone measures are unlikely to deter Hanoi's determination unless Beijing is prepared to use direct force. All these cases clearly reflect the limitations in the effectiveness of China's "coercion without escalation" tactics: although Beijing can successfully pressure smaller countries in many specific instances, not everywhere and in every situation do adversaries retreat, especially when these countries have demonstrated clear political will and secured support from the international community.

The second challenge China faces is the steadfast presence and long-term security commitments of the United States along with Washington's network of allies and partners in the region. Not only the United States, but other powers such as Japan, Australia, the United Kingdom, and France have regularly deployed warships and submarines through the South China Sea, conducting freedom of navigation operations and asserting their position of non-recognition of the legality of China's "nine-dash line" claim under international law. This multilateral presence poses a serious strategic challenge for China: if Beijing risks military escalation to prevent or expel these forces, it would face the risk of simultaneous conflict with multiple leading naval powers worldwide—a scenario even a powerful China is unlikely to win decisively; on the other hand, if unable to push back or limit this international presence, China's ambition to completely control the South China Sea will be very difficult to realize. To date, China has still shown restraint, not using lethal force directly against US and allied forces, which partly indicates Beijing's leadership remains concerned about America's superior military strength as well as the unpredictable and potentially uncontrollable consequences of a large-scale military conflict. China's current tactic is to maintain pressure at the "gray zone" threshold with the belief that time and continuous pressure will gradually erode other countries' political will and resources, forcing them to accept the new reality. However, the fact that the United States continues to strengthen and reaffirm security commitments with regional allies and partners shows that China's gray zone strategy is encountering serious obstacles, as adversaries are not only not being subdued but are instead strengthening preparations and coordination to respond more effectively.

The third challenge China faces is the serious loss of credibility and trust from neighboring countries, leading to a significant decline in the country's soft power in the region. Although China consistently proclaims its goal of bringing stability and shared prosperity to the region, its assertive actions often characterized as bullying in the South China Sea have created deep skepticism and growing concern among Southeast Asian nations. Notably, even countries that traditionally have friendly relations and high economic dependence on China remain cautious and vigilant. For example, during President Xi Jinping's visit to Southeast Asia in early 2025, he attempted to promote China's image as a long-term, trustworthy partner committed to peace and common development; however, persistent security and economic challenges continue to make many countries in the region maintain wary and cautious attitudes. Evidence shows that most ASEAN countries are pursuing strategies of diversifying foreign relations to maintain strategic balance, rather than accepting a decisive tilt toward China as Beijing desires (Mingjiang et al., 2025).

China's public rejection of the 2016 Arbitral Tribunal ruling and continued maritime pressure are also seriously eroding trust in efforts to negotiate a Code of Conduct (COC) between China and ASEAN, causing this process to essentially stagnate for over a decade without achieving substantive progress (Kiet et al., 2025). Clearly, China's international reputation has been significantly damaged as it is widely perceived as a country willing to trample international law and civilized norms to achieve its geopolitical objectives. Minjiang et al. (2025) even note that China is aware of this issue and sometimes must exercise greater self-restraint to maintain a relatively positive international image. For instance, after its global reputation suffered severely negative impact during the COVID-19 pandemic, China showed more flexibility and cooperation on certain issues, willing to participate in multilateral negotiations to avoid further isolation from the international community. Thus, the hardline strategy itself also sets limits for China: Beijing wants to assert strength and status, but must simultaneously carefully consider the diplomatic and economic consequences if strongly opposed and boycotted by the international community.

The final but no less important challenge comes from China's own internal limitations in pursuing a long-term and costly maritime strategy. China's economy has recently shown worrying signs of slowing growth and faces serious structural problems: increasing public debt burden, potential real estate bubble burst, rapid population aging, and declining labor force (Miao, 2026). These economic challenges compel Beijing to be more financially cautious when expanding influence and investing in overseas projects. For instance, numerous large-scale Chinese infrastructure projects under the BRI framework in Southeast and South Asian countries such as Indonesia, Thailand, Myanmar, Pakistan, and Nepal have been suspended or significantly adjusted due to capital provision and economic efficiency issues (Bharti & Kumari, 2024). If the domestic economic situation continues to weaken, maintaining a powerful navy and constant presence in the South China Sea will also place considerable burden on the defense budget.

On the other hand, although China's military has made rapid technological and equipment advances in recent decades, its actual combat experience remains significantly limited. China's military has not experienced any major naval conflict or modern warfare since the brief 1979 clash with Vietnam, while potential adversaries like the United States have extensive practical combat experience through various wars and conflicts. Therefore, People's Liberation Army (PLA) leadership may be more cautious and avoid risky military "gambles" that could exceed their capacity to control situations.

In conclusion, it can be affirmed that China is encountering numerous serious and multidimensional challenges in implementing its proactive maritime security strategy: fierce and increasingly coordinated resistance from neighboring countries, the steadfast presence of the United States and its alliance network, declining regional credibility and appeal, and practical limitations in resources and combat experience. These factors are somewhat constraining the effectiveness of the new strategy, forcing China to calculate and consider much more carefully rather than being able to dominate completely as initially expected.

4. STRUCTURAL WEAKNESSES: STRATEGIC LIMITATIONS AND DIPLOMATIC COSTS

Besides challenges from the external environment and responses from other countries, China's new maritime security strategy itself reveals several important inherent limitations and weaknesses. These limitations stem from the very nature and implementation methods of the strategy, potentially reducing long-term effectiveness and even creating counterproductive consequences.

First, this strategy fundamentally does not help China definitively resolve sovereignty disputes, but primarily maintains and prolongs tensions at a certain level. The use of gray zone tactics, while allowing China to avoid triggering a full-scale war—which Beijing wants to avoid—also means it cannot force adversaries to completely capitulate and accept China's claims (McLaughlin, 2022). Regional countries still have sufficient time, strategic space, and capacity to respond forcefully, making China's "nine-dash line" claim difficult to materialize in practice in the near future.

Moreover, the maritime dominance China currently holds is only truly effective during peacetime and in low-intensity competition situations. Should a large-scale open military conflict occur, China's outposts, military infrastructure, and gray zone forces could be quickly neutralized by the superior firepower and technology of adversaries. No matter how well-defended, fixed military infrastructure in the middle of the ocean remains priority targets highly vulnerable to adversary long-range attack capabilities, especially cruise missiles and airstrikes. This would directly and seriously affect China's logistics effectiveness and ability to sustain military operations if a large-scale war actually occurs in the South China Sea. Thus, the current strategy is only truly effective as long as China can maintain conflict at low levels and avoid escalation; it does not guarantee or may not even provide strategic advantage for China if the situation escalates into direct and comprehensive military confrontation.

The second limitation is the high cost in diplomatic, legal, and international reputational terms that China must pay for its hardline strategy. The assertive policy often characterized as aggressive in the South China Sea has caused China to lose much goodwill from the international community and face increasing criticism not only from regional countries but also from many other nations and international organizations (Ho, 2023). China's public rejection and refusal to comply with the 2016 Permanent Court of Arbitration ruling—a decision with high legal value under UNCLOS—has placed the country in a position of being seen as contemptuous of international law and contrary to widely recognized civilized norms of conduct (Whomersley, 2017).

The inevitable consequence is that in regional and international forums, China's voice and arguments on South China Sea issues are increasingly doubted and lack persuasiveness, while other countries have solid legal grounds and stronger international community support when opposing China's unilateral actions. Although China has been trying to promote negotiation of COC with ASEAN as a way to improve its cooperative image and show goodwill, this effort has dragged on for many years without achieving any significant substantive results. The COC negotiation process has gone through three rounds of draft review, but continues to deadlock on key points such as geographic scope of application, legal binding nature of the document, and effective enforcement mechanisms. Even the ASEAN Secretary-General's optimistic forecast that the COC could be completed in 2025 has been assessed by many experts as completely unrealismic and unfounded (Lin & Sothirak, 2025). Clearly, the assertive and sometimes bullying strategy has seriously eroded trust between parties, making even more flexible diplomatic solutions difficult to achieve significant progress due to lack of goodwill and mutual trust—key elements in all negotiations. China thus finds itself in an awkward and contradictory situation: the more it advances with hard power and coercive measures, the more politically and diplomatically isolated it becomes regionally and internationally; but changing its position and complying with international rulings would fundamentally contradict its core strategic objectives and historical sovereignty claims. This is a difficult paradox China must face.

The third limitation is the growing burden of maintaining constant presence and engaging in a prolonged arms race. The new strategy requires China to maintain multiple military and paramilitary assets in the South China Sea on a 24/7 basis year-round—from coast guard patrol fleets continuously stationed at hotspots, maritime militia flotillas anchored for extended periods around strategic coral reefs, to fighter aircraft, missiles, and air defense systems deployed on artificial islands (Kuik, 2017). These activities consume significant and continuous resources (fuel, logistics, maintenance, salaries, training...) over an extended period with no clear endpoint. Simultaneously, other countries in the region are also strengthening their military capabilities in response, making it impossible for China to stop or reduce efforts: for example, Japan is building new modern warships and increasing defense budget to 2% of GDP by 2027, Vietnam is upgrading bases and infrastructure in the Spratlys, and the Philippines is purchasing anti-ship missiles, radar, and patrol vessels from the United States and other partners. Therefore, China has entered a long-term competition of endurance and will, requiring continuous investment of substantial resources to maintain or expand its relative advantage.

Although China's economy and defense budget are among the world's largest, "spreading" strength across multiple directions—maintaining presence in the South China Sea, dealing with tensions in the East China Sea with Japan, and preparing for the Taiwan scenario—may create considerable financial and resource pressure in the long term. Additionally, in this race, the United States and allies also have strong motivation and technological capability to develop new weapons and tactics to counter China's advantages—such as long-range anti-ship missiles, naval unmanned aerial vehicles (UAVs), unmanned warfare systems, and other new technologies—requiring China to continuously adjust and upgrade strategy to avoid being technologically surpassed.

Finally, the proactive strategy risks self-limiting effectiveness due to a fundamental contradiction between China's dual objectives: wanting to assert hard power and maritime hegemony while maintaining a stable international environment conducive to continued economic development. The display of military might and application of coercive measures in the South China Sea have made many of China's important economic partners feel concerned and uncomfortable. For instance, the European Union, Japan, and South Korea are all major trading partners of China, and these economies are highly dependent on shipping routes through the South China Sea for transporting goods and energy. However, these countries have not supported and have even criticized China's unilateral actions violating international law in the South China Sea. In other words, China's current strategy is constrained and limited by the contradiction in its strategic objectives: wanting to become regional hegemon militarily and politically while continuing to benefit from global economic integration and maintain stable trade relations with major partners.

In summary, China's proactive and assertive maritime security strategy, despite significantly increasing pressure on other countries and shifting the regional balance of power favorably for Beijing, is not without important inherent weaknesses and limitations. This strategy cannot and is unlikely to achieve decisive sovereignty victory in the near future, while simultaneously causing significant losses in international image, legal credibility, and potentially long-term financial and strategic burden for China itself. These limitations indicate that China will find it difficult to easily or quickly realize its ambition to control the entire South China Sea as desired, as the costs across multiple dimensions are increasingly high.

5. TREND FORECASTING: LONG-TERM COMPETITION AND ESCALATION POTENTIAL

Looking ahead, the South China Sea situation in the coming period is predicted to remain tense, complex, and uncertain, as concerned countries all have their own strategies and calculations, with no signs that parties are ready to make significant concessions on core issues. Based on analysis of current trends and strategic dynamics of parties, several main scenarios and trends can be identified that are likely to shape South China Sea prospects in the near future.

First, and perhaps the most likely scenario, is that the state of "low-intensity confrontation" will continue for an extended period. The South China Sea region currently lacks an effective conflict management mechanism with legal binding force, so encounters, confrontations, and maritime disputes may occur more frequently and with increasing intensity (Doan, 2024). China will likely continue applying tested gray zone tactics: coast guard vessels will still regularly harass fishermen from other countries, obstruct and pressure legitimate oil and gas exploration activities by Vietnam, Malaysia, and Indonesia in their exclusive economic zones; maritime militia fleets will continue occupying positions around strategically valuable coral reefs and rocks to assert de facto presence and maintain continuous pressure. China may also make new moves to test the resolve and reliability of the US-Philippines alliance: for instance, increasing military and diplomatic pressure at Second Thomas Shoal, or preventing Philippine access to other shoals like Sabina Shoal or even attempting to completely reclaim Scarborough Shoal.

These tactical moves aim not only to expand de facto control scope but also to gauge US response, especially amid America's deeply divided domestic politics.

Depending on the intensity and effectiveness of Washington's and allies' response, China will adjust and decide next steps in its long-term South China Sea strategy. Regardless of approach, the situation will generally continue in tense and potentially dangerous stalemate. Therefore, many geopolitical experts have warned that the South China Sea is now no less dangerous than the Taiwan Strait and could actually become the flashpoint for the next major military conflict between great powers if the situation is not well controlled (Kiet & Tuyen, 2023; Jenne, 2017; Raymond & Welch, 2022). This prospect requires concerned parties to seriously consider establishing "safety guardrails" and escalation prevention mechanisms, but to date no truly effective mechanism has been established.

Second, China's naval power will continue to increase significantly in coming years, but this will be accompanied by corresponding balancing responses from other regional countries. China currently possesses the world's largest navy by number of major warships: approximately 370 ships in 2023, and this number is projected to increase to nearly 400 ships by 2025 and possibly 435 ships by 2030 (O'Rourke, 2025b). China continues building new modern destroyers, aircraft carriers (including carriers with advanced electromagnetic launch systems), nuclear submarines and conventional submarines, while actively training and enhancing blue-water combat capabilities to gradually realize the goal of becoming a "global maritime power" by mid-21st century as President Xi Jinping has outlined.

The South China Sea plays a pivotal role in this long-term strategy as a strategic springboard for China to project naval power further, including the vast Indian Ocean and Pacific regions, protect important sea lanes for energy and trade transport, and gradually challenge the long-standing traditional dominance of the US Navy in the region (Chan, 2021). Therefore, it can be confidently predicted that China will not retreat or reduce ambitions in the South China Sea, but rather tend to consolidate and expand long-term military presence there. For example, China may deploy additional modern fighter jets and long-range strategic bombers to artificial islands in the Spratlys when sufficient logistics infrastructure is available; may unilaterally declare establishment of an Air Defense Identification Zone in the South China Sea if political and military conditions permit; or continue building and expanding bilateral military infrastructure in allied countries like Cambodia to create additional support points for South China Sea operations.

However, the continued expansion in scale and capability of China's navy will certainly trigger an increasingly intense and costly regional naval arms race. Other countries are also strengthening their naval capabilities: the United States and allies will almost certainly increase military presence in the South China Sea in both patrol frequency and quality of deployed weapons and equipment; regional powers like India are actively expanding their fleet and Australia is in the process of acquiring nuclear submarines under the AUKUS agreement will also join the competition with formidable new capabilities (Raymond & Welch, 2022). Therefore, the naval balance of power in the South China Sea in the near and medium term will continue in fierce stalemate and intense competition: China may be overwhelmingly superior to individual opponents in numbers and some technological areas, but will face a powerful and increasingly coordinated collective counterweight network if the situation escalates into large-scale military conflict. Even more dangerous is the risk of triggering an endless arms race in the region, depleting economic resources and creating unpredictable security risks for all parties.

Third, diplomatically and legally, significant positive and sustainable breakthroughs are very difficult without major substantive adjustments from China in its position and policies. The prospect of achieving a truly effective, legally binding and seriously implemented COC in the near future is assessed as very dim (Sakhuja, 2023). China will likely continue the tactic of prolonging COC negotiations to buy time for consolidating territorial control and expanding maritime influence, rather than genuinely accepting a strongly binding COC that could limit freedom of action and narrow strategic space. ASEAN countries also do not want and cannot accept passing a half-baked, weak agreement mainly benefiting China without protecting their legitimate interests, so negotiation deadlock may continue for many years. Meanwhile, the international legal framework continues supporting smaller countries' positions: the 2016 Arbitral Tribunal ruling, though not recognized by China, remains an important legal basis with value for countries to assert their rights under international law and mobilize support from the global community (Whomersley, 2017). If the Philippines or other countries decide to file additional new cases with international courts, China will become increasingly awkward and passive in international reputation and legal standing.

Therefore, unless China makes fundamental and substantive changes in its sovereignty position and approach, South China Sea disputes in the near future will be very difficult to find a clear and sustainable diplomatic solution. Instead, concerned countries may move toward temporary and more situation-specific arrangements rather than comprehensive solutions. A typical example is localized and technical "tension reduction" agreements like the temporary agreement between China and the Philippines on resupply to Second Thomas Shoal in late 2024 (International Crisis Group, 2024). However, such patchwork agreements are usually very difficult to sustain long-term, as the deep roots of the problem—namely irreconcilable and incompatible sovereignty claims—remain intact, with each side only temporarily conceding due to short-term tactical calculations.

Fourth, China's domestic political factors and the nature of US-China relations in the broader context will strongly influence and potentially determine South China Sea developments. If Beijing leadership feels increasing pressure from internal issues—such as prolonged economic stagnation, rising social discontent, or need to mobilize nationalism to consolidate political position—or if US-China strategic competition on other fronts becomes more intense (for example, escalating tensions over trade, high technology, or especially the Taiwan issue), then the South China Sea may be elevated to higher priority in foreign policy as a front for displaying national strength and diverting attention.

Conversely, if the two great powers reach agreements or arrangements to reduce tension at the highest strategic level, the South China Sea situation may correspondingly "cool down" as part of a broader deal. However, current signs indicate that both countries are not yet ready or capable of fundamentally compromising on their core interests in the region. The United States continues to view maintaining freedom of navigation, rules-based order, and protecting ally and partner security in the South China Sea as essential interests for ensuring global superpower status and credibility of security commitments (Jannuzi, 2025). China, conversely, views controlling the South China Sea as an indispensable strategic step toward the "great China dream" and for energy security, territorial security, and regional power status (Kiet & Tuyen, 2023). Therefore, prospects for the two sides to easily overlook or trade interests in the South China Sea in a larger agreement are very low, at least in the medium term. Moreover, some international relations scholars even assess that the South China Sea is "the defining arena of the 21st century"—where the balance of power, regional rules of the game, and possibly even world order for decades to come will be shaped (Kiet et al., 2025; Quyet, 2023; Hai, 2021; Emmers, 2013).

6. CONCLUSION

In summary, the South China Sea in coming years will most likely remain a strategic hotspot with persistent competition, continuous tensions, and serious latent security risks. China's new maritime security strategy has marked an important transformation from the traditional "hide and bide" approach to a much more proactive and assertive offensive strategy, helping China significantly improve its military position and expand de facto control scope in the South China Sea, but simultaneously igniting a much larger struggle of power and will with regional countries and extra-regional powers with strategic interests here.

The regional balance of power is currently in a complex and tense stalemate: on one side, China is striving to increase strength to change the status quo favorably and establish a Beijing-centric regional order; on the other side, the United States along with its network of allies and partners are consolidating links to maintain the rules-based order and the current relative balance of power. Although China has created unprecedented challenges to regional security order through its new strategy, fierce and increasingly coordinated responses from concerned parties show they are not at all ready to passively accept this unilateral change.

Therefore, the most likely scenario in the near and medium term is a state of "controlled instability": parties will continuously challenge, probe, and confront each other with military power, economic pressure, and diplomatic campaigns, but all will try to avoid crossing important "red lines" that could lead to total war—something no one truly wants due to unpredictable consequences. China's significant strategic adjustment under President Xi Jinping has thus both brought Beijing a much more confident and assertive maritime power position, while placing the country before an intensely confrontational, complex, and challenging regional security environment. This will continue to profoundly shape the future of the South China Sea for many years to come, as US-China strategic competition shows no signs of cooling, and regional countries are also increasingly determined to protect their legitimate sovereignty, security, and development interests by all possible means. The South China Sea, with its strategic, economic, and symbolic importance, will continue to be one of the most dangerous and closely watched geopolitical hotspots in the world.

REFERENCES

Asia Maritime Transparency Initiative. (2023). *Arbitration Support Tracker.* https://amti.csis.org/arbitration-support-tracker/

Asia Maritime Transparency Initiative. (2025). *No Islet Left Behind: Vietnam Reclaims Land at Every Remaining Spratly Outpost.* https://amti.csis.org/no-islet-left-behind-vietnam-reclaims-land-at-every-remaining-spratly-outpost/

Asia Maritime Transparency Initiative. (n.d.). *China Island Tracker.* https://amti.csis.org/island-tracker/china/

Asian Military Review. (2024). *Has the China Coast Guard Reached Its Limit?* https://www.asianmilitaryreview.com/2024/01/has-the-china-coast-guard-reached-its-limit/

Bharti, M. K., & Kumari, S. (2024). China's Belt and Road Initiative in Southeast Asia and its implications for ASEAN-China strategic partnership. *Asian Review of Political Economy*, *3*(22), 1–21. DOI: 10.1007/s44216-024-00042-4

Chan, E. S. Y. (2021). *China's Maritime Security Strategy: The Evolution of a Growing Sea Power* (1st ed.). Routledge. DOI: 10.4324/9781003158523

Chan, E. S. Y. (2025). China's Discourse of Maritime Power: A Thematic Analysis. *Journal of Contemporary China*, *34*(153), 432–450. DOI: 10.1080/10670564.2024.2319064

Doan, R. L. (2024). The Conflict of Laws in the South China Sea and Its Threats to the Indo-Pacific Rules-Based Order. *Loyola University Chicago Law Journal, 55*(2), 9-69. https://lawecommons.luc.edu/luclj/vol55/iss5/2?utm_source=lawecommons.luc.edu%2Fluclj%2Fvol55%2Fiss5%2F2&utm_medium=PDF&utm_campaign=PDFCoverPages

Emmers, R. (2013). The South China Sea. In *Resource Management and Contested Territories in East Asia* (pp. 51–74). Springer. DOI: 10.1057/9781137310149_5

Hai, D. T. (2021). Vietnam and China: Ideological bedfellows, strange dreamers. *Journal of Contemporary East Asia Studies*, *10*(2), 162–182. DOI: 10.1080/24761028.2021.1932018

Ho, A. N. (2023). Challenges Toward a Rule-based Order in the South China Sea. *Journal of Asian Security and International Affairs*, *10*(2), 169–189. DOI: 10.1177/23477970231173539

Hu, B. (2021). Sino-US Competition in the South China Sea: Power, Rules and Legitimacy. *Journal of Chinese Political Science*, *26*(3), 485–504. DOI: 10.1007/s11366-020-09716-1

Indo-Pacific Defense Forum. (2023). *Philippines bolsters military presence after 'Chinese activities' near islands.* https://ipdefenseforum.com/2023/01/philippines-bolsters-military-presence-after-chinese-activities-near-islands/

International Crisis Group. (2024). *Riding Unruly Waves: The Philippines' Military Modernisation Effort.* https://www.crisisgroup.org/sites/default/files/2025-08/349-philippines-military-modernisation.pdf

Jackson, L. (2023). Australia's nuclear submarine plan to cost up to $245 billion by 2055 -defence official. *Reuters.* https://www.reuters.com/world/asia-pacific/australias-nuclear-submarine-plan-cost-up-245-bln-by-2055-defence-official-2023-03-13/

Jannuzi, F. (2025). U.S. Interests in the South China Sea: Defending Norms, not Territory. In Hung Son, N., & Thi Lan Anh, N. (Eds.), *The South China Sea: The Geo-political Epicenter of the Indo-Pacific?* Springer., DOI: 10.1007/978-981-97-8209-3_3

Jenne, N. (2017). Managing Territorial Disputes in Southeast Asia: Is There more than the South China Sea? *Journal of Current Southeast Asian Affairs*, *36*(3), 35–61. DOI: 10.1177/186810341703600302

Kang, K. (2025). Strategic importance of the South China Sea: Beyond geography. *Pacific Forum.* https://pacforum.org/publications/yl-blog-98-strategic-importance-of-the-south-china-sea-beyond-geography/

Kiet, L. H., Binh, N. T., & Hiep, T. X. (2024). From Arroyo to Duterte: Two Decades of Philippines' Foreign Policy Navigation between the US and China. *Przegląd Strategiczny, 17,* 133-150. https://www.ceeol.com/search/article-detail?id=1331776

Kiet, L. H., Tam, L. T. T., & Hiep, T. X. (2025). Caught between dragon and elephant: Vietnam's strategic balancing act in the Sino-Indian rivalry. *China Quarterly of International Strategic Studies*, *11*(2), 99–128. DOI: 10.1142/S237774002550006X

Kiet, L. H., & Tuyen, N. V. (2023). Vietnam's geopolitical position with the United States in its strategy to contain China's hegemonic ambitions. *Journal of Science and Technology - Danang University, 21*(8.1), 63-69. https://jst-ud.vn/jst-ud/article/view/8630

Kuik, C. C. (2017). Explaining the Contradiction in China's South China Sea Policy: Structural Drivers and Domestic Imperatives. *China. China*, *15*(1), 163–186. DOI: 10.1353/chn.2017.0009

Le, K. H., & Tran, H. X. (2025). Vietnam's strategic partnership role in India's policy to counter China's hegemonic ambitions in the East Sea. In Güçyetmez, F., & Kahraman, A. (Eds.), *Geopolitics of the SCS: Power struggle in Asia* (pp. 263–284). IGI Global Scientific Publishing., DOI: 10.4018/979-8-3693-8109-0.ch012

Lendon, B. (2024). US gains military access to Philippine bases close to Taiwan and South China Sea. *CNN World.* https://edition.cnn.com/2023/04/04/asia/us-philippines-military-base-access-intl-hnk-ml

Lewis, S., & Lema, K. (2024). US pledges funds to boost Philippine defences amid China disputes. *Reuters.* https://www.reuters.com/world/asia-pacific/us-philippines-engagements-help-with-agile-responses-china-says-marcos-2024-07-30/

Lin, J., & Sothirak, P. (2025). The Elusive Code: Why ASEAN Needs a New Playbook for the South China Sea. *Fulcrum.* https://fulcrum.sg/the-elusive-code-why-asean-needs-a-new-playbook-for-the-south-china-sea/

McLaughlin, R. (2022). The Law of the Sea and PRC Gray-Zone Operations in the South China Sea. *The American Journal of International Law, 116*(4), 821–835. DOI: 10.1017/ajil.2022.49

Mearsheimer, J. J. (2001). *The Tragedy of Great Power Politics.* W.W. Norton & Company.

Miao, H. (2026). The Deflation Doom Loop Trapping China's Economy. *The Wall Street Journal.* https://www.wsj.com/world/china/deflation-doom-loop-china-economy-25b0938a

Mingjiang, L., Hiep, L. H., Bing, N. C., & Chandarith, N. (2025). How Southeast Asia Sees Xi Jinping's Regional Push Amid U.S.-China Tensions. *Carnegie Endowment for International Peace.* https://carnegieendowment.org/research/2025/04/how-southeast-asia-sees-xi-jinpings-regional-push-amid-us-china-tensions

O'Rourke, R. (2025a). U.S.-China Strategic Competition in South and East China Seas: Background and Issues for Congress. *Congressional Research Service.* https://www.congress.gov/crs-product/R42784

O'Rourke, R. (2025b). China Naval Modernization: Implications for U.S. Navy Capabilities—Background and Issues for Congress. *Congressional Research Service.* https://www.congress.gov/crs-product/RL33153#:~:text=The%E2%80%A6%20overall%20battle%20force%20%5Bof,by%20the%20end%20of%20FY2030

Quyet, N. H. (2023). Chinese Strategy in the South China Sea: A Growing Quest for Vital Economic and Strategic Interests. *World Affairs, 186*(3), 687–716. DOI: 10.1177/00438200231181141

Raymond, M., & Welch, D. A. (2022). What's really going on in the South China Sea? *Journal of Current Southeast Asian Affairs, 41*(2), 214–239. DOI: 10.1177/18681034221086291

Sakhuja, V. (2023). Code of Conduct in the South China Sea (COC): Prospects and Challenges. *Centre for Public Policy Research.* https://www.cppr.in/articles/code-of-conduct-in-the-south-china-sea-coc-prospects-and-challenges

The Asahi Shimbun. (2024). *Malaysia says it won't bow to China's demands to halt oil exploration in the South China Sea.* https://www.asahi.com/ajw/articles/15416756

Wei, Z. (2022). The evolution of the 'QUAD': Driving forces, impacts, and prospects. *China International Strategy Review, 4*(2), 288–304. DOI: 10.1007/s42533-022-00119-w

Whomersley, C. (2017). The Award on the Merits in the Case Brought by the Philippines against China Relating to the South China Sea: A Critique. *Chinese Journal of International Law, 16*(3), 387–423. DOI: 10.1093/chinesejil/jmx023

Yamaguchi, M. (2025). Pacifist Japan has slowly transformed from exclusively self-defense to a military buildup. *AP News.* https://apnews.com/article/japan-military-buildup-defense-constitution-us-china-4986b7e36b9bb86355898c6d762084e7

Chapter 9
Can Power Override Justice?
Examining the Challenges to China's South China Sea Expansionism

Hoa Le Quynh Phan
https://orcid.org/0009-0003-5724-898X
Dong A University, Vietnam

Phuc Quang Pham
https://orcid.org/0009-0009-9932-1448
University of Social Sciences and Humanities, Vietnam National University, Hanoi, Vietnam

ABSTRACT

This chapter systematically analyzes multidimensional challenges confronting China's South China Sea strategy through realism international relations theory. Despite substantial territorial gains via grey-zone tactics and island militarization, China's strategy encounters formidable resistance across five dimensions: determined ASEAN opposition employing collective balancing, intensified US-led containment through alliance consolidation, inherent PLA limitations in combat experience and expeditionary logistics, escalating inadvertent conflict risks, and legitimacy deficits following the 2016 PCA ruling. While offensive realism explains China's expansionist motivations, defensive realist dynamics—particularly balance of power and security dilemma mechanisms—impose structural constraints on Beijing's ambitions. Findings reveal that material superiority alone cannot guarantee strategic success against coordinated multilateral resistance anchored in international legal frameworks, offering critical insights for Asia-Pacific regional stability and conflict prevention.

DOI: 10.4018/979-8-3373-4470-6.ch009

1. INTRODUCTION

The South China Sea, covering approximately 3.5 million square kilometers and strategically positioned at the nexus of the Pacific and Indian Oceans, has emerged as one of the world's most complex geopolitical flashpoints in the 21st century. This maritime region is not merely a vital international shipping lane through which over $5 trillion in trade passes annually, but also contains abundant oil, gas, and fishery resources, while holding profound strategic security significance for regional states and global powers alike (cited from Kiet et al., 2025a). Over the past two decades, the region has witnessed a dramatic escalation in tensions due to overlapping sovereignty claims between China and numerous Southeast Asian nations, including Vietnam, the Philippines, Malaysia, Brunei, and Indonesia (Kiet et al., 2024).

Since the early 2000s, China has pursued a systematic expansionist strategy in the South China Sea, characterized by the construction and militarization of artificial islands on submerged reefs, the deployment of maritime militia and coast guard forces to assert permanent presence, and the leveraging of economic power to influence neighboring countries, particularly those in Southeast Asia (Hiep et al., 2023). This strategy has been implemented by China with persistence and flexibility, combining so-called "gray zone tactics"—actions that fall below the threshold of direct military conflict yet exceed normal diplomatic activities (Kiet et al., 2025b). Today, China has transformed numerous submerged reefs into military bases equipped with runways, seaports, and radar systems, creating crucial "strongpoints" in the open sea. However, while China has achieved significant territorial gains, its strategy is encountering strong and increasingly coordinated resistance from multiple quarters. ASEAN nations, particularly Vietnam and the Philippines, have enhanced their military capabilities and actively built security cooperation networks with extra-regional powers (Hiep & Kiet, 2024). The US, recognizing threats to its strategic interests, has implemented a "Rebalance to Asia" strategy with increased military presence and expanded security alliances (Kiet & Tuyen, 2023). The international community has also voiced stronger opposition, particularly following the 2016 Permanent Court of Arbitration (PCA) ruling that rejected China's "nine-dash line" claim (Castro, 2020).

Despite extensive research on the South China Sea dispute, most existing studies focus on analyzing China's strategy and actions from an offensive and expansionist perspective, or examining individual countries' responses in isolation. What remains lacking in current scholarship is a comprehensive and systematic analysis of the multidimensional challenges confronting China's strategy—from regional responses and great power intervention to China's inherent limitations and latent strategic risks. Moreover, many studies tend to either exaggerate or underestimate China's actual power in the South China Sea. Some scholars argue China is on track to achieve absolute regional dominance, while others contend international pressure will force China to retreat. This polarization in academic discourse reflects a critical gap: the absence of a balanced, comprehensive assessment of both the achievements and limitations of China's strategy, considering simultaneously geopolitical, military, economic, legal factors and the risk of conflict escalation. From a theoretical perspective, while realism has been widely applied to explain state behavior in the South China Sea, there remains a shortage of studies that systematically employ this theory to analyze not only expansionist motivations but also structural limits of power. Specifically, concepts such as "balance of power," "security dilemma," and "Thucydides Trap" need to be applied in an integrated manner to illuminate the complex dynamics of ongoing strategic competition.

Research on the challenges facing China's South China Sea strategy holds significant importance on both academic and policy fronts. Academically, this study contributes to enriching international relations theory, particularly realism, by applying theoretical concepts to analyze a complex and evolving concrete case. The research also provides an integrated analytical framework for better understanding power competition dynamics between large and small states in the contemporary international system. Practically, this study offers value to policymakers in countries involved in the South China Sea dispute. For ASEAN nations, understanding the weaknesses and challenges China faces can help them develop more effective response strategies, from strengthening internal solidarity to leveraging international legal mechanisms. For the US and its allies, the research provides deep insights into effective intervention methods that avoid dangerous conflict escalation. For China itself, full awareness of these challenges could help them adjust their strategy more prudently, avoiding risks that could threaten the nation's long-term development goals. Furthermore, in the context of increasingly intense US-China strategic competition and heightened risk of military conflict at flashpoints like the South China Sea, understanding the motivations and limitations of all parties is vital for regional peace and stability. This research helps clarify mechanisms that can lead to conflict escalation or restraint, thereby supporting diplomatic efforts to manage crises and maintain peace.

The overarching objective of this research is to comprehensively and systematically analyze the multidimensional challenges facing China's South China Sea strategy, thereby assessing the actual limits of Chinese power in the context of regional strategic competition. To achieve this objective, the research focuses on answering the following main research question: What challenges are limiting the effectiveness of China's South China Sea strategy, and how do these challenges impact the regional balance of power?

Spatially, the research focuses on the South China Sea region, with particular attention to major disputed areas such as the Spratly Islands, Paracel Islands, and overlapping exclusive economic zones. The main actors analyzed include China, ASEAN claimant states (Vietnam, the Philippines, Malaysia, Brunei) and indirectly affected countries (Indonesia, Singapore), along with extra-regional powers, particularly the US, Japan, Australia, and India. Temporally, the research concentrates on the period from the early 2010s to the present (2024), when China's strategy became more assertive and explicit with the commencement of large-scale artificial island construction. However, the research also provides necessary historical context from the 1990s-2000s to understand the dispute's evolution. In terms of content, the research does not focus on proposing detailed solutions to the South China Sea dispute or suggesting specific policies, but primarily analyzes and assesses the challenges China's strategy faces. The research also does not delve into detailed military technical aspects or specialized legal analysis, but concentrates on strategic, geopolitical, and balance of power factors.

This research is expected to contribute to existing knowledge in three main ways: First, theoretically, the research provides a rich case application of realism theory to analyzing a complex contemporary power competition, in which soft power tools, international law, and global public opinion play increasingly important roles alongside traditional military strength. The research demonstrates that even in the modern era, fundamental realism principles like balance of power retain high explanatory value, though they must be applied subtly and comprehensively. Second, empirically, the research provides a comprehensive and updated analysis of the South China Sea situation, integrating military, political, economic, legal, and strategic psychological aspects into a panoramic view. Unlike many studies focusing on only one or two aspects, this research simultaneously assesses all five major challenges, allowing readers a more balanced and comprehensive perspective. Third, policy-wise, the research provides valuable insights for policymakers. By clarifying the real challenges and limits of China's strategy, the research helps relevant countries better understand their adversary's/partner's strengths and weaknesses, thereby building more effective and balanced response policies—sufficiently firm to protect national interests yet sufficiently prudent to avoid dangerous conflict escalation. In summary, this research aims not merely to describe the status quo but also to explain the deep motivations behind actors' actions and reactions, thereby contributing to a deeper understanding of one of the 21st century's most significant geopolitical challenges.

2. RESISTANCE FROM THE FRONTLINES: ASEAN CLAIMANT STATES' STRATEGIES AGAINST CHINA

Despite the overwhelming power disparity between China and Southeast Asian nations across all dimensions, Beijing's expansionist strategy in the South China Sea has faced strong and persistent resistance from numerous regional countries, particularly those with directly overlapping sovereignty claims. Among ASEAN nations, Vietnam stands out with the most resolute and hardline stance against China's actions in the South China Sea. With its direct geographical proximity and lengthy history of confrontation with China, Vietnam clearly recognizes that defending sovereignty over the Paracel and Spratly Islands is not merely a territorial issue but a matter of national survival. In recent years, Vietnam has proactively and actively pursued a comprehensive military modernization program, particularly focusing on upgrading its naval and air forces to create minimum yet effective deterrence capability against China. Vietnam's defense spending has increased steadily, maintaining around 2.3% of GDP since 2007 (compared to approximately 2% previously), despite numerous domestic economic challenges (Vuving, 2017).

Vietnam has executed a series of significant modern weapons purchases from Russia, including: six Kilo-class diesel-electric submarines (ordered during 2009-2013 and delivered during 2014-2017), making Vietnam the country with the largest submarine fleet in Southeast Asia; along with four Gepard 3.9-class frigates displacing 2,100 tons, and dozens of missile boats and various patrol vessels (Vuving, 2017). Vietnam's air force has also been substantially strengthened with a fleet of approximately 35 Su-30MK2 long-range fighter jets (purchased during 2004-2016), while maintaining an abundant weapons arsenal including anti-ship and air defense missiles. It must be emphasized that these weapons are not intended for direct military confrontation with China, but rather serve strategic deterrence purposes, sending a clear message to Beijing that the price will be extremely high if they choose to use force in the South China Sea.

Alongside military capability enhancement, Vietnam has actively pursued a strategy of diversifying defense and security relationships. Although not participating in any formal military alliance, Vietnam has strengthened security cooperation with multiple powers including the US, Japan, India, and Russia (Kiet & Hiep, 2025). Notably, the US officially lifted its arms embargo on Vietnam in 2016 under President Barack Obama's administration, and since then, US warships and aircraft carriers have regularly visited Vietnamese ports. Japan and India have assisted Vietnam through the transfer of patrol vessels and provision of naval force training programs. Vietnam also proactively participates in numerous regional maritime security joint exercises. Most notably, in August 2024, Vietnamese and Philippine coast guard forces conducted their first joint exercise in the South China Sea to exchange experience and coordinate operational skills (Nguyen, 2024). Furthermore, Vietnam signed an exclusive economic zone delimitation agreement with Indonesia in 2023, aimed at strengthening solidarity within ASEAN and promoting joint maritime patrol initiatives. All these diplomatic and military moves demonstrate Vietnam is pursuing a delicate balancing strategy: cooperating while struggling, maintaining economic and friendly relations with China, but simultaneously resolutely opposing any actions infringing on sovereignty from its northern neighbor.

The Philippines, a long-standing US ally, has exhibited significant policy fluctuations but generally shows an increasingly hardline trend in dealing with China. During 2016-2022 under President Rodrigo Duterte, the Philippines proactively adjusted its policy to move closer to China in exchange for aid and investment, even temporarily setting aside the 2016 PCA ruling with the reasoning it would be "raised at an appropriate time" (Castro, 2020; Kiet et al., 2024). However, this conciliatory policy failed to deliver the results Manila expected. China not only delayed implementing promised projects but continued assertive actions, such as directing fire control radar at Philippine vessels and establishing administrative units to manage the Spratly and Paracel Islands. Domestic public pressure and the Philippine military establishment gradually intensified, with consensus that the soft policy toward China was ineffective. In fact, four years after the ruling, by July 2020, the Philippines issued its first official statement demanding China comply with the 2016 ruling, emphasizing the ruling was "non-negotiable" (Castro, 2020). This move marked the Philippines' strategic readjustment back to its traditional alliance trajectory with the US.

On the ground, the Philippines has also increased patrol capability in the West Philippine Sea (the Philippines' term for the South China Sea) while seeking to consolidate entities under its control. A typical example is the BRP Sierra Madre at Second Thomas Shoal, which, despite severe deterioration, continues to receive regular resupply efforts to maintain garrisoned forces. Recently, under President Ferdinand Marcos Jr.'s leadership, the Philippines has demonstrated a markedly harder stance: continuously protesting through diplomatic channels against Chinese vessel harassment incidents, allowing the US to expand military presence at four additional bases in the Philippines under the Enhanced Defense Cooperation Agreement (EDCA) signed in 2023, and coordinating with countries like Japan and Australia in joint exercises. It can be affirmed that the Philippines is gradually returning to its role as an important link in the US strategy to counter China, while being more proactive in defending its sovereignty. Evidence of this includes the Philippines publicly releasing videos and images accusing Chinese coast guard vessels of water cannon attacks and collisions with Philippine resupply vessels in the Second Thomas Shoal area.

Indonesia, although not a claimant state to the Spratly Islands, has in recent years also displayed a harder attitude due to conflicting interests in waters around the Natuna Islands (southern South China Sea). China has included waters north of Indonesia's Natuna Islands within its "nine-dash line" claiming them as "traditional fishing grounds," provoking resolute opposition from Indonesia. Particularly, incidents of Chinese fishing and coast guard vessels intruding into the exclusive economic zone around the Natuna Islands have led to tense confrontations. In January 2020, dozens of Chinese fishing and coast guard vessels appeared north of Natuna, forcing Indonesia to deploy numerous naval vessels and fighter aircraft to drive them away; Indonesia's then-President Joko Widodo even personally visited forces stationed at Natuna as a strong assertion of sovereignty.

Legally, Indonesia has resolutely affirmed there is no dispute whatsoever with China. In May 2020, Indonesia submitted a note verbale to the United Nations, completely rejecting China's "historical rights" claim, citing the 2016 PCA ruling and the 1982 United Nations Convention on the Law of the Sea (UNCLOS) to affirm China has "no legal basis whatsoever" in the South China Sea (Indonesia, 2020). This step shows Indonesia is willing to stand firm on international law principles, although this country previously often maintained a neutral role in the region. Additionally, Indonesia has strengthened military forces for the Natuna region through deploying additional warships, maritime surveillance aircraft, and upgrading military bases on Natuna Besar island (McBeth, 2019). Despite maintaining good economic relations with China, even strengthening deeper political cooperation by joining BRICS, Indonesia still clearly demonstrates it will respond strongly if China infringes on its maritime interests.

From a broader perspective, ASEAN with its ten member states, while sometimes questioned about solidarity on the South China Sea issue, has found that increasing pressure from China has become a catalyst significantly driving regional cooperation. Countries like Vietnam, the Philippines, Malaysia, and Indonesia, despite differences, are united in opposing the nine-dash line; they have even jointly submitted collective notes verbales to the United Nations in 2020 to refute China's illegal claims. Joint patrol initiatives among South China Sea coastal states have begun to be initiated and implemented. In 2022, for the first time, the ASEAN Summit Joint Statement directly mentioned the importance of UNCLOS in resolving the South China Sea issue. This shows ASEAN is increasingly clearly recognizing the need to maintain law-based order, and is indirectly creating isolation for China's violations. Of course, ASEAN has not yet achieved complete unity (Hiep et al., 2023). However, pressure from China has become an important catalyst pushing ASEAN countries closer together to jointly defend their common interests. This is precisely a major challenge to China's "divide and rule" strategy. As Kiet et al. (2025a) argued: "They will find it difficult to break individual sticks if the entire bundle is being tightened."

These developments vividly illustrate the balance of power doctrine in international relations theory. ASEAN nations, despite being much weaker in actual strength, have not capitulated but chosen to balance China's influence through diverse measures: self-strengthening internally (such as Vietnam modernizing its military), uniting with each other (through joint patrols and collective notes verbales), and relying on external counterweights (the US, Japan, Australia). This explains why most of China's neighboring countries tend to increasingly gravitate toward the US. Because they all share a common perception of China as a direct threat requiring containment. Facing an increasingly powerful and unpredictable China, ASEAN nations have no choice but to strengthen internal solidarity and consolidate external alliances to ensure balance of power. This is a natural response to ensure the survival (self-preservation) of small states in a fiercely competitive environment, completely consistent with realism's premise that when security is threatened, states will act to protect themselves. Some countries may choose "hedging" tactics to avoid excessively provoking China, but in the long term, if China continues advancing, the trend of collective balancing against them will become stronger. The more China pressures them, the more motivation the "ASEAN bundle" has to tighten.

3. THE RETURN OF THE US: RECONSTRUCTING REGIONAL ORDER

China's assertiveness and audacity in the South China Sea has not only raised deep concerns within the region but also posed direct challenges to the core strategic interests of the US—the superpower that has maintained a dominant role in the Pacific region since World War II. In response, the US has deployed the "Pivot/Rebalance to Asia-Pacific" strategy since the Obama administration, and this strategy has continued to be developed under subsequent presidents under different names, such as the Free and Open Indo-Pacific (FOIP) Strategy. Within this overall strategic framework, the US has implemented numerous synchronized measures to affirm its leadership role and contain China's expansion in the South China Sea.

First, the US has significantly increased its military presence in the Asia-Pacific region. Since 2012, the US Department of Defense has announced plans to shift 60% of total naval forces to be stationed in the Pacific region before 2020 (increased from approximately 50% previously) (Alexander, 2012). This means numerous aircraft carriers, submarines, and modern destroyers will have a more permanent presence in the Western Pacific region. The US also rotates deployments of strategic bombers, unmanned reconnaissance aircraft, and increases the frequency of large-scale exercises in the region. Since 2015, the US Navy has conducted "Freedom of Navigation Operations" (FONOP) in the South China Sea with regular frequency, approximately every few months. In these operations, US destroyers and cruisers deliberately sail within 12 nautical miles of disputed features occupied by China (such as Subi Reef, Mischief Reef, the Paracel Islands) to challenge China's illegal sovereignty claims (Lagreone, 2017). Although FONOP missions typically last only a few hours before departing, they carry important symbolic and practical significance: affirming the right to innocent passage under UNCLOS provisions, denying the legal validity of maritime claims from artificial islands constructed by China, and demonstrating US readiness to confront if China attempts to impose prohibited or restricted zones. This military presence somewhat reassures allies and prevents China from advancing further, although it also potentially poses risks of unwanted incidents.

Next, the US has actively consolidated and expanded its network of alliances and partnerships in the region to create a multilayered, comprehensive containment mechanism. For traditional allies like Japan, South Korea, and Australia, the US has encouraged and promoted them to play more active and proactive roles in South China Sea-related issues. For instance, Japan has declared its readiness to provide patrol vessels and training programs for Southeast Asian maritime law enforcement forces, while for the first time deploying the helicopter carrier JS Izumo to the South China Sea to participate in joint exercises with the US Navy (Panda, 2017). Australia has also increased its naval activities in the South China Sea and strongly voiced opposition to China's claims.

Particularly noteworthy, in 2021, the US together with the United Kingdom and Australia established the AUKUS security alliance—in which the US and UK committed to assist Australia in building nuclear submarines and cooperate on advanced defense technology. AUKUS is widely viewed by analysts as a strategic response to China's rise, aimed at significantly enhancing underwater deterrence capability for US allies at the gateway to the South China Sea (Haldar & Gupta, 2025). Alongside this, the "QUAD" four-party security dialogue mechanism comprising the US, Japan, India, and Australia was also revived from 2017 and increasingly consolidated (Kiet et al., 2025c). The QUAD has organized periodic summit meetings, large-scale joint naval exercises, and cooperation across many non-traditional security domains. Although in official statements, the QUAD does not name China specifically, scholars and experts worldwide commonly assess that this grouping's main purpose is to create a multilateral security linkage to counter China's growing influence in the Indo-Pacific region (Rudd, 2021). China has expressed clear concern, calling the QUAD an "Asian NATO" and accusing the US of "forming cliques" to oppose China.

For Southeast Asia, the US has actively courted and strengthened relationships with key partners. Singapore, with its strategically important geographical position, has agreed to allow the US to rotationally deploy littoral combat ships at Changi Naval Base (Burgess, 2021). The Philippines under President Marcos Jr. has fully returned to a pro-US policy, activating the Enhanced Defense Cooperation Agreement (EDCA) allowing the US to use additional strategically located bases in Luzon and Palawan (near the South China Sea). Vietnam upgraded its relationship with the US to a "comprehensive strategic partnership" in 2023. Although Vietnam remains cautious in its foreign policy, it has shown willingness to cooperate on defense to a certain extent with the US, such as purchasing military equipment, receiving used patrol vessels, and welcoming US aircraft carrier visits to ports in 2018 and 2020 (Stone, 2019). Indonesia and Malaysia, despite pursuing balancing policies, also welcome the US Navy presence as a factor contributing to maintaining freedom of navigation in the region.

Overall, the US is weaving a complex and encompassing security network with itself at the center, forming a strategic ring encircling China. This picture is completely contrary to the situation in the 1990s when the US neglected the region and China could freely expand its influence. Now, according to expert assessments, the more China advances in the South China Sea, the more justification it provides for the US to tighten its alliance network in Asia. In fact, the Pentagon itself has acknowledged that China's aggressive behaviors could "help strengthen regional countries' relationships with the US" (Associated Press, 2016).

The US' strong and steadfast strategic commitment has placed China in an extremely difficult and disadvantageous position. Beijing's space for action has been significantly narrowed due to the risk of direct confrontation with US military forces if exceeding acceptable limits. For instance, China's plan to impose an Air Defense Identification Zone (ADIZ) over the South China Sea has not yet been realized, partly because the US and allies have declared they will not recognize it and are ready to challenge if China announces an ADIZ, similar to how they responded in the East China Sea (Shalal, 2016). Such hardline moves force the leadership under Xi Jinping to exercise more self-restraint in actions, because they clearly understand any excessive military move could trigger a direct response from a nuclear superpower.

This is the greatest geopolitical challenge to China's expansionist ambitions: they are not simply facing a few small ASEAN countries, but must confront an entire broad front led by the US, determined to maintain the existing regional order. From a realism theory perspective, the US response is entirely predictable and consistent with international relations patterns. Because China's actions have directly threatened the US' superpower status and strategic interests in a critical region. History shows the US intervened to prevent Japan, Germany, and the Soviet Union in their regional hegemony attempts in the 20th century. Therefore, the US "pivot" back to Asia-Pacific as China rises is only a natural and predictable consequence of balance of power laws in the international system.

4. THE ACHILLES' HEEL: MILITARY AND ECONOMIC LIMITATIONS

Despite China achieving remarkable progress in military strength in recent times, its capability to effectively execute its South China Sea strategy still contains significant inherent limitations. These limitations stem from various factors, including technology, logistics, and actual combat experience.

First, regarding military technology and operational proficiency, the People's Liberation Army (PLA) remains in an inferior position compared to the US military across many important aspects. China currently possesses aircraft carriers, nuclear submarines, anti-ship ballistic missiles, and many other modern weapons, but most of their technology still lags behind the US by approximately one generation technologically. A typical example is the J-20 stealth fighter which has only achieved limited stealth capability, unable to compare with US F-22 or F-35 models; China's navy, while having a large number of warships, still shows clear weaknesses in radar system quality, electronic warfare capability, and anti-submarine warfare capability. Particularly important, the PLA's actual combat experience is virtually zero: the PLA has not participated in any modern war since the 1979 border conflict with Vietnam. That 1979 battle was actually a painful defeat for China (although they claimed to have "completed objectives" upon withdrawal), leaving no small "psychological aftershock" among PLA senior leadership (Heath, 2018). For over forty years, the Chinese military has had absolutely no direct combat experience. Chinese military publications themselves acknowledge the military suffers from "peace disease"—due to years without combat, symptoms have emerged including bureaucratic attitudes, insubstantial training, and low combat readiness levels (Wang, 2018).

Chairman Xi Jinping has launched numerous comprehensive reforms and organized large-scale exercises to enhance the PLA's combat readiness, but nothing can truly replace the scale and intensity of an actual war. PLA commanders at all levels, from senior generals to grassroots soldiers, have never experienced real combat, so no one knows with certainty how they will respond when actually engaging in battle. Many international experts consider this the PLA's "Achilles' heel," which could cause them to face serious confusion and suffer heavy losses if confronting the battle-hardened US military (Heath, 2018). Of course, some opinions argue experience is not everything but rather modern weapons and military discipline are the decisive factors. In any case, the PLA's lack of verification on actual battlefields remains a large and worrying unknown. Until experiencing a serious conflict, the Chinese military's true combat capability remains only on paper and in exercises.

Second, China faces serious challenges regarding logistics and maritime resupply capability at distance. The South China Sea lies far from China's main naval bases in Guangzhou and Sanya (Hainan Island). Maintaining continuous and effective presence in this vast offshore maritime region requires robust sustainment capability, which is not the PLA's traditional strength. True, the artificial islands China has constructed have somewhat compensated for these deficiencies. They provide mooring ports, fuel storage, airstrips for transport aircraft, forming important "transit stations" for Chinese forces operating deep in the Spratly Islands area. However, in the event of military conflict, these forward bases would be very vulnerable to isolation or direct attack. They occupy fixed and predictable positions, while China does not yet have a perfect defense shield against adversaries' precise long-range missiles. Western analysts have extensively debated the actual military value of these artificial islands: one view holds the US has full capability to neutralize these islands within the first few days of war thanks to overwhelming superiority in precise long-range firepower (Dahm, 2020). If that scenario occurs, the PLA would lose crucial logistics support stations, forcing Chinese ships and aircraft to withdraw to mainland bases thousands of kilometers away, thereby significantly reducing geographical advantages in situ.

Additionally, to conduct a sustained military campaign in the South China Sea, China needs a large-scale and efficient maritime resupply system: including a fleet of specialized logistics ships to carry fuel, ammunition, provisions; mobile field bases; secure and seamless communications networks. Currently, the PLA Navy's capability in this regard remains quite limited compared to high-intensity warfare requirements. They have relatively few large replenishment ships compared to needs. If compared with the US Navy, which has operated an effective global logistics chain for decades, the PLA lacks experience in organizing and protecting maritime transport lines. Therefore, although China has regular presence in the South China Sea during peacetime, when serious incidents occur, they will face a difficult problem: how to maintain sustained superiority against a more formidable force capable of intercepting and destroying their supply lines.

Third, China's economic capability and technological foundation are showing signs of slowing, raising serious questions about the long-term sustainability of its expansionist strategy. China's economy during 2022-2023 grew at its slowest rate in decades, achieving only approximately 3-5% annually, due to numerous serious internal problems (rapid population aging, severe real estate market crisis, high local government debt, export enterprises facing many difficulties) (Nouwens & McGerty, 2024). A declining economy will directly and severely impact the defense budget. Although China still steadily increases military spending by approximately 7% annually (in 2023 spending about $225 billion, triple that of 2010), this growth rate has exceeded GDP growth rate, meaning the budget burden is increasingly mounting (Nouwens & McGerty 2024). If the economy continues into stagnation, China may face difficulties maintaining large-scale investment in the navy, missile systems, and modern weapons as in recent years.

Additionally, the South China Sea strategy causes significant indirect economic losses: aggressive behaviors have led the West to tighten investment in China, and many global supply chains are gradually leaving China to move to other countries. This in the long term could seriously erode China's comprehensive strength. Technologically, the US and allies are increasingly restricting exports of high technology, particularly advanced semiconductors, to China to slow the PLA's modernization process. If cut off from critical technology sources, the PLA's military upgrade progress could significantly slow. For instance, ambitions to build nuclear-powered aircraft carrier fleets or develop long-range stealth bombers will become much more difficult without advanced chips for radar, information, and control systems. China has also not completely solved complex technological problems such as reliable jet engines, integrated early warning systems, and many other key technologies. This economic and technological pressure will seriously limit China's long-term arms race capability in the South China Sea.

Although China has "home field" advantage in the South China Sea and has grown considerably stronger in recent years, its strategy execution capability remains untested in actual combat and contains important weaknesses: lack of actual combat experience, limitations in expeditionary logistics capability, and economic-technological obstacles. These weaknesses may not be clearly evident during peacetime but will become major and potentially serious problems if China must confront a strong adversary or prolong a conflict. This is the downside China must carefully consider in each strategic step. The limitations outlined above show the actual balance of forces has not yet clearly tilted toward China as many believe. Currently, the global force balance remains in a state of "equilibrium" favorable to the US: the US defense budget significantly exceeds China's, and this country has the capability to rapidly and effectively deploy military power to any region worldwide. The US maintains numerous military bases and robust forces ready for combat in the Asia-Pacific region, and China currently still has no effective way to prevent or neutralize US military moves. This factor establishes a hard ceiling for China's expansionist ambitions.

Realism points out that national power is not unlimited: if China has not achieved overwhelming economic and military superiority over the US, they will find it difficult to unilaterally impose their will. Conversely, the international system will "punish" those attempting to exceed their actual capability limits. For instance, if China hastily uses force imprudently, they face high risk of suffering serious defeat due to stronger adversary intervention. The PLA's current logistical, technological, and experiential limitations are clear evidence that the actual power gap with the US remains very large. In other words, China cannot yet "defend" and maintain its achievements if directly confronting the US military and its allies. From another aspect, offensive realism might encourage China to continue its expansionist strategy to narrow that power gap, because this school's logic holds that "the stronger one becomes, the safer." However, as defensive realisms in China also note, such efforts could produce counterproductive effects by activating balancing against them from the international community (Raditio, 2015). Excessive and imprudent aggression will encounter strong counterattack—this is the paradox China is and will face in the future. To avoid a situation of "overreach," China perhaps needs to adjust its strategy more prudently and wisely, if unwilling to see inherent limitations turn the South China Sea ambition into a dangerous gamble.

5. THE SECURITY DILEMMA AND THE THUCYDIDES TRAP

A serious yet difficult-to-grasp and unpredictable challenge to China's strategy is the risk of conflict escalation spiraling beyond control in the South China Sea, potentially leading to a large-scale war that neither side genuinely desires. The concept of the "Thucydides Trap" is frequently invoked by scholars to describe situations where a rising power conflicts with an established hegemon due to structural contradictions regarding power distribution within the international system. In the specific context of the South China Sea, many experts and analysts worry that the US and China could fall into this dangerous trap if an unexpected incident escalates beyond the capacity of both sides to restrain.

The South China Sea today can be likened to a "powder keg" with countless close-proximity confrontations between Chinese forces and those of other nations (the US, ASEAN countries). Examples include military aircraft intercepting each other at dangerous distances, warships approaching within just dozens of meters, coast guard vessels deliberately ramming the official vessels of other countries, and numerous other tense situations. A single minor mistake or miscalculation—such as a collision resulting in casualties—could ignite fierce reactions in a chain-reaction effect based on alliance treaties. For instance, if Chinese and Philippine vessels clash seriously, resulting in Filipino casualties, Manila might invoke US support under the Mutual Defense Treaty between the two nations. The US would then face an extremely difficult choice: either intervene to protect its ally and risk war with China, or stand aside and lose credibility and the trust of regional allies. Similarly, encounters between China and Japan in the East China Sea or with India in the Indian Ocean region could spill over into the South China Sea due to the interconnected nature of security fronts (Hiep et al., 2024). Even without deliberate intent, the effects of collective security systems could draw multiple nations into a spiral of conflict. This is precisely the extremely dangerous "new Thucydides" scenario that policymakers fear.

Particularly worrying is that emergency communication channels between China and the US and its allies currently lack effectiveness and remain untested in genuine crisis situations. High-level military hotlines have been established but are sometimes not used at the right moment or do not function as expected. A example occurred when China refused to answer calls from the Pentagon following the 2023 incident of a Chinese spy balloon drifting over US territory. This absence of strategic trust between the two sides significantly diminishes the capacity for coordination to contain crises. Both the US and China fear being trapped or exploited by the other during de-escalation processes, and may therefore choose forceful action to save face, leading to unintended escalation beyond initial intentions. The South China Sea is a region with complex multilateral disputes, with numerous military and paramilitary forces intertwined, making on-site crisis control extremely difficult when incidents occur.

Unlike the Cold War period when the US and the Soviet Union confronted each other in Europe with tacit rules established over time, the South China Sea currently lacks a feasible conflict avoidance framework accepted by both sides. ASEAN and China are in the process of negotiating a Code of Conduct (COC), but progress is slow and specific content remains unclear regarding practical effectiveness. Consequently, the risk of "a small spark igniting a forest fire" is ever-present. For example, in 2001, a mid-air collision occurred between a Chinese fighter jet and a US EP-3 reconnaissance aircraft, leading to a diplomatic crisis lasting many days with serious tensions (Leigh et al., 2020). If a similar incident occurred now in the context of much greater tensions, both sides would very likely react with military measures more quickly and find it difficult to back down easily. This could lead to an extremely dangerous and uncontrollable spiral of retaliation and escalation.

As scholar Graham Allison has warned, the Thucydides Trap is not an unavoidable destiny, but the risk of conflict between the US and China is currently at its highest level in decades. The South China Sea is precisely the most volatile flashpoint in the region, where the distance between peace and war can sometimes be measured in just a few nautical miles at sea or a few seconds of decision-making by a warship commander. For China, this risk constitutes an invisible yet ever-present and threatening challenge. A war with the US would be catastrophic for the peaceful rise strategy China is pursuing. It could overturn all economic achievements accumulated over decades, comprehensively isolate China on the international stage, and even seriously threaten the stability of the internal political regime if China faced defeat. Therefore, Chinese leadership simultaneously seeks to continue advancing to expand interests while constantly worrying about and seeking ways to avoid large-scale conflict scenarios. This represents an extremely difficult and complex art of risk balancing, especially as strategic trust among key parties reaches record lows.

Through the analytical lens of realism, the current situation evokes the classic concept of the security dilemma in international relations theory: each step taken by one side to enhance security is perceived by the other as a threat, prompting corresponding countermeasures and creating an increasingly escalating spiral of tension. China builds artificial islands and deploys aircraft and warships—the US responds by deploying aircraft carriers and strategic bombers—China continues to deploy additional missiles and maritime militia... thus, each action that one side considers reasonable defensively is interpreted by the other as potential offensive intent. The South China Sea today clearly embodies a dangerous security dilemma spiral between the US and China, where goodwill can easily be misunderstood and defensive actions can be viewed as provocative.

6. THE SWORD OF DAMOCLES: PCA RULING AND THE LEGITIMACY CRISIS

China's strategy in the South China Sea faces a "soft" but long-lasting challenge regarding legitimacy and international legal foundations. The 2016 ruling by the PCA created an extremely unfavorable legal precedent for China: their historical claims lack recognition and acknowledgment under international law, and actions such as constructing artificial islands and obstructing the activities of fishermen from other countries are considered serious violations of the UNCLOS. Although China has publicly ignored and refused to comply with this ruling, the legal document remains like a "sword of Damocles" hanging over the legitimacy of the nine-dash line. Whenever China takes actions perceived as arrogant or violating, other nations can invoke the ruling to condemn them for blatantly violating international law.

The clearest consequence is that China is experiencing a severe decline in diplomatic credibility on the international stage. From a previous position where many nations remained ambiguous and lacked clear stances on South China Sea disputes, the vast majority of international opinion now understands that China is the party at fault legally. Countries that previously maintained neutral attitudes, such as Malaysia and Indonesia, have now become much bolder in asserting their legal positions. In 2019, Malaysia submitted a filing on extended continental shelf claims to the United Nations, implicitly rejecting the nine-dash line claim and supporting UNCLOS and the PCA ruling as legal bases (United Nations, 2019). In 2020, Indonesia went further by flatly declaring that there is "no legal basis" for China's claims, and therefore they are "not bound by such unlawful claims" (United Nations, 2020a). Clearly, Southeast Asian nations are increasingly actively using the PCA ruling as a powerful legal shield to diplomatically counterattack against China's actions. Even major powers outside the region have spoken out in support of the rules-based order. Countries such as the United Kingdom, France, and Germany jointly sent a note verbale to the United Nations in 2020, supporting UNCLOS and rejecting claims of "historical rights" without clear legal basis (United Nations, 2020b). This international legal front has created a situation isolating China on the international stage: China stands virtually alone with its position, while the rest of the international community (including Japan, Australia, India, and many other countries) maintains the view that the South China Sea must comply with UNCLOS 1982 and international legal principles (Le & Tran, 2025).

China has attempted to evade mention of the PCA ruling in its official diplomatic documents. They seek to prolong negotiations on the COC with ASEAN to demonstrate goodwill and project an image of cooperation, while simultaneously ensuring that the COC does not specifically reference the PCA ruling or specific provisions of UNCLOS (Kiet et al., 2025a). Nevertheless, the greatest difficulty facing the Chinese government is that the 2016 ruling will exist permanently in international legal history unless another international court issues a ruling negating it—something virtually impossible to occur. The ruling also affirms that many features China currently occupies are merely "low-tide elevations" and therefore have no right to claim territorial seas, making it even more difficult for the artificial islands they have constructed to legitimately claim a 12-nautical-mile zone. This means that: although China controls the terrain through force, legally they remain accused of illegal occupation. In the long term, this profound contradiction between "actual power" and "legal right" seriously disadvantages China on the international public opinion front. They are frequently criticized at international conferences and in United Nations reports, and are losing ground among developing nations that China actively seeks to win over to expand influence (Kiet et al., 2024).

Another important aspect is that China's attitude of disregarding international law has caused many nations to deeply doubt the "responsible power" role that China claims and proclaims for itself. China signed UNCLOS 1982 but refused to accept and rejected UNCLOS's mandatory dispute settlement mechanism when the ruling outcome was undesirable, creating the image of a major nation applying "double standards" in international relations. Moreover, China's militarization of international waters and threats to freedom of navigation run counter to widely recognized international practices and norms, causing them to lose significant standing in relations with many countries. Declining credibility can lead to long-term strategic consequences such as: nations becoming less willing to compromise and make concessions to China, and tending to align more closely with the US to jointly defend the international legal order.

Although challenges regarding legality and international public opinion lack the immediate and tangible power of military strength, they are gradually eroding and weakening China's overall strategic position over time. They may control islands through actual presence, build military bases, and coerce smaller neighboring nations, but they cannot compel the entire world to believe that the South China Sea belongs to their legitimate ownership. As long as the current international order with UNCLOS as its foundation remains maintained and respected, China's ambition to "swallow whole" the South China Sea will never be recognized as legitimate by the international community (Kiet et al.,. 2025a). If one day the balance of power shifts unfavorably for China, the established international legal foundations will become powerful tools for other parties to reverse the situation and demand justice. Understanding this, despite aggressive actions in the South China Sea, China frequently repeats the refrain of "respecting international law" nominally, aiming to avoid complete isolation on the international stage. However, the profound contradiction between words and actual actions only makes China's image increasingly negative and less credible.

Actual power typically determines law (might makes right) rather than the reverse. China is testing this premise in the South China Sea: relying on advantages in actual strength to attempt to override and surpass international legal regulations. However, in the 21st century, international law and global public opinion cannot be completely ignored as in the past (Kiet & Tuyen, 2023). Small nations have skillfully used international law as an effective "soft balancing" tool to constrain China—they lack China's military power, but can leverage international courts, the United Nations, and global media to exert considerable diplomatic pressure (Kiet et al., 2025b). This reveals another important limitation of hard power: if actions lack legitimacy and legal basis, a major power can face opposition from the entire international system in the long term. In other words, justice and law, though seemingly weak, are effective weapons for weaker parties, and in a world order increasingly based on rules and norms, legitimacy and righteousness still carry weight and influence that cannot be underestimated.

In summary, China's strategy in the South China Sea has helped them achieve significant advantages in terms of terrain and military presence through the application of flexible and diverse tools (from "salami-slicing" tactics, artificial island construction, use of maritime militia and coast guard, to implementing their own rules and economic power to exert influence). However, this strategy is encountering strong and multilayered reactions from multiple parties: the increasingly determined sovereignty protection of ASEAN nations, stronger and more persistent US and allied intervention, inherent limitations of China itself regarding enforcement capacity, high risks of unintended and uncontrolled conflict escalation, along with growing pressure from international law and public opinion. These factors compel China to continuously exercise caution and calibrate each step, because a mistaken move could lead to serious consequences far beyond control—from being mired in military conflict and economic collapse to completely losing the "peaceful rise opportunity" they have pursued for decades. The struggle in the South China Sea will therefore continue and become increasingly complex, requiring China to carefully calculate each move, while other nations must also persist, maintain unity, and firmly uphold international legal principles to protect their legitimate interests. The South China Sea currently represents an important and decisive test for the regional order: whether power can completely override justice, and the outcome of this test will profoundly and lastingly affect the balance of power in the Asia-Pacific region throughout the 21st century.

7. CONCLUSION

This research has systematically examined the multidimensional challenges confronting China's expansionist strategy in the South China Sea, revealing a complex geopolitical landscape where raw power alone proves insufficient to guarantee strategic success. Through the analytical lens of realism international relations theory, this study demonstrates that despite China's substantial territorial gains and military modernization over the past decade, its South China Sea strategy encounters formidable resistance across five critical dimensions: determined pushback from ASEAN claimant states, intensified US-led containment efforts, inherent military and economic limitations, escalating risks of inadvertent conflict, and a profound crisis of international legitimacy stemming from the 2016 PCA ruling.

The theoretical contribution of this research lies in its nuanced application of realism principles to contemporary maritime disputes. While offensive realism explains China's expansionist motivations driven by security maximization imperatives, this study reveals how defensive realism dynamics—particularly balance of power mechanisms and the security dilemma—impose structural constraints on Beijing's ambitions. The research demonstrates that even asymmetric power relationships do not preclude effective balancing when smaller states employ strategic hedging, forge external partnerships, and leverage international legal frameworks as "soft balancing" instruments. This finding enriches realism theory by illustrating how normative and legal dimensions interact with traditional hard power calculations in twenty-first-century geopolitical competition, where legitimacy and global public opinion constitute consequential variables that cannot be dismissed as mere epiphenomena.

Empirically, this research provides an integrated assessment transcending single-issue analyses prevalent in existing scholarship. By simultaneously evaluating military, diplomatic, economic, legal, and psychological dimensions, the study offers a comprehensive panoramic view of the strategic environment. The analysis reveals a critical paradox: China's grey-zone tactics have successfully altered territorial realities without triggering direct military confrontation, yet these same achievements have catalyzed precisely the multilateral containment coalition Beijing sought to avoid. This unintended consequence validates the realism proposition that states inevitably provoke balancing behavior when their power accumulation threatens systemic stability, regardless of declared peaceful intentions.

From a policy perspective, this research yields actionable insights for multiple stakeholders. For ASEAN nations, the findings underscore the efficacy of collective approaches—coordinated diplomatic protests, joint maritime patrols, and unified legal positions—in constraining a vastly superior adversary. For the US and its allies, the analysis highlights how sustained strategic commitment and alliance cohesion create credible deterrence, even as it warns against provocative actions that could trigger the very escalation all parties seek to avoid. For China, the research illuminates how pursuit of short-term tactical gains risks long-term strategic isolation, economic costs from supply chain diversification, and potential military overextension given the PLA's untested combat capabilities and logistical vulnerabilities.

However, several limitations warrant acknowledgment. First, the research's temporal scope, while capturing recent developments through 2024, cannot fully account for rapidly evolving dynamics, particularly regarding Taiwan contingencies that could fundamentally reshape South China Sea calculations. Second, the study's emphasis on state-centric realism analysis may underweight non-state actors, including multinational corporations and transnational advocacy networks, whose roles in shaping outcomes deserve deeper investigation. Third, while the research identifies escalation risks, predicting actual conflict probability remains inherently speculative given the multitude of contingent variables and human decision-making uncertainties involved.

Future research should explore several promising avenues. First, comparative analysis examining how China's South China Sea approach differs from its strategies in other contested spaces—the East China Sea, Himalayan borders, or the Indian Ocean—could reveal whether observed patterns represent coherent grand strategy or context-specific responses. Second, investigating domestic political drivers of Chinese assertiveness, including nationalist pressures and civil-military relations, would complement this study's systemic-level analysis. Third, scenario modeling of specific escalation pathways, informed by historical analogues and game-theoretic frameworks, could enhance crisis prevention capabilities.

In conclusion, the South China Sea represents a critical test case for international order in an era of shifting power distributions. This research demonstrates that while China has achieved significant tactical successes, its strategy confronts structural impediments that preclude unilateral imposition of a new regional order. The outcome will depend not on material capabilities alone, but on strategic wisdom, diplomatic finesse, and willingness to accommodate competing interests within a rules-based framework. As tensions persist, the international community must navigate between two extremes: neither appeasing expansionism nor triggering catastrophic confrontation. The challenges identified in this research suggest that sustainable resolution requires not Chinese retreat or American containment alone, but rather negotiated arrangements reflecting both contemporary power realities and enduring legal principles—a delicate equilibrium that remains elusive yet essential for twenty-first-century peace and prosperity in the Asia-Pacific region.

REFERENCES

Alexander, D. (2012). US will put more warships in Asia: Panetta. *Reuters*. https://www.reuters.com/article/world/us-will-put-more-warships-in-asia-panetta-idUSBRE85100Z/

Associated Press. (2016). China has reclaimed 3,200 acres in the South China Sea, says Pentagon. *The Guardian*. https://www.theguardian.com/world/2016/may/13/pentagon-report-china-reclaimed-3200-acres-south-china-sea#:~:text=on%20Friday

Burgess, R. R. (2021). US, Singapore reaffirm LCS, P-8 rotational deployments. *Sea Power*. https://seapowermagazine.org/us-singapore-reaffirm-lcs-p-8-rotational-deployments/?print=pdf

Castro, D. R. C. (2020). After four years, the Philippines acknowledges the 2016 arbitral tribunal award. *Asia Maritime Transparency Initiative*. https://amti.csis.org/after-four-years-the-philippines-acknowledges-the-2016-arbitral-tribunal-award/

Dahm, J. M. (2020). Beyond "conventional wisdom": Evaluating the PLA's South China Sea bases in operational context. *War on the Rocks*. https://warontherocks.com/2020/03/beyond-conventional-wisdom-evaluating-the-plas-south-china-sea-bases-in-operational-context/

Haldar, S., & Gupta, S. (2025). AUKUS under review: What lies ahead for Indo-Pacific security. *Observer Research Foundation*. https://www.orfonline.org/expert-speak/aukus-under-review-what-lies-ahead-for-indo-pacific-security

Heath, T. R. (2018). China's military has no combat experience: Does it matter? *RAND Corporation*. https://www.rand.org/pubs/commentary/2018/11/chinas-military-has-no-combat-experience-does-it-matter.html

Hiep, T. X., Hoan, T. Q., & Kiet, L. H. (2024). Free and Open Indo-Pacific strategy: Competitive Opinions and Trends. *Vestnik of Saint Petersburg University -. International Relations*, *17*(3), 242–259.

Hiep, T. X., & Kiet, L. H. (2024). India's competitive strategy with China in Southeast Asia: An analysis of the case of Vietnam. *Journal of Chinese Studies*, *2*(270), 68–80.

Hiep, T. X., Kiet, L. H., & Yen, P. T. H. (2023). Strategic Hedging in Southeast Asia: ASEAN Member States' Policy Responses to China's Growing Economic Influence. *Contemporary Chinese Political Economy and Strategic Relations*, *9*(2/3), 404–438.

Indonesia. (2020). Note verbale No. 126/POL-703/V/20. *United Nations.* https://www.un.org/Depts/los/clcs_new/submissions_files/mys_12_12_2019/2020_05_26_IDN_NV_UN_001_English.pdf

Kiet, L. H., Binh, N. T., & Hiep, T. X. (2024). From Arroyo to Duterte: Two Decades of Philippines' Foreign Policy Navigation between the US and China. *Przegląd Strategiczny, 17*(17), 133–150. DOI: 10.14746/ps.2024.1.9

Kiet, L. H., Binh, N. T., & Hiep, T. X. (2025c). From border conflicts to maritime competition: Driving forces behind the power rivalry between India and China in the Indian Ocean region. *Australian Journal of Maritime and Ocean Affairs*, •••, 1–25. DOI: 10.1080/18366503.2025.2492438

Kiet, L. H., Nguyen, P. H., Tran, H. X., & Nguyen, B. T. (2025b). Vietnam's balancing strategy in the US-China rivalry in Southeast Asia. In Zreik, M. (Ed.), *Innovations and tactics for 21st century diplomacy* (pp. 271–302). IGI Global., DOI: 10.4018/979-8-3693-6074-3.ch012

Kiet, L. H., Tam, L. T. T., & Hiep, T. X. (2025a). Caught between dragon and elephant: Vietnam's strategic balancing act in the Sino-Indian rivalry. *China Quarterly of International Strategic Studies, 11*(2), 99–128. DOI: 10.1142/S237774002550006X

Kiet, L. H., & Tuyen, N. V. (2023). Vietnam's geopolitical position with the US in its strategy to contain China's hegemonic ambitions. *Journal of Science and Technology - Danang University, 21*(8.1), 63-69. https://jst-ud.vn/jst-ud/article/view/8630

Lagreone, S. (2017). US warship came within 6 miles of Chinese artificial island in toughest challenge yet to Beijing South China Sea claims. *USNI News.* https://news.usni.org/2017/05/25/u-s-warship-came-beijing-south-china-sea-claims

Le, K. H., & Tran, H. X. (2025). Vietnam's Strategic Partnership Role in India's Policy to Counter China's Hegemonic Ambitions in the East Sea. In Güçyetmez, F., & Kahraman, A. (Eds.), *Geopolitics of the South China Sea: Power Struggle in Asia* (pp. 263–284). IGI Global., DOI: 10.4018/979-8-3693-8109-0.ch012

Leigh, K., Martin, P., & Leung, A. (2020). Troubled waters: Where the US and China could clash in the South China Sea. *Bloomberg.* https://www.bloomberg.com/graphics/2020-south-china-sea-miscalculation/

McBeth, J. (2019). Indonesia boosts its military presence in the Natuna Islands. *The Strategist.* https://www.aspistrategist.org.au/indonesia-boosts-its-military-presence-in-the-natuna-islands/

Nguyen, H. (2024). Cooperation and struggle define Vietnam's approach to China. *East Asia Forum.* https://eastasiaforum.org/2024/10/28/cooperation-and-struggle-define-vietnams-approach-to-china/

Nouwens, M., & McGerty, F. (2024). China's defence budget boost can't mask real pressures. *International Institute for Strategic Studies.* https://www.iiss.org/online-analysis/military-balance/2024/03/chinas-defence-budget-boost-cant-mask-real-pressures/

Panda, A. (2017). South China Sea: Japan's Izumo helicopter carrier conducts drill with US Navy carrier. *The Diplomat.* https://thediplomat.com/2017/06/south-china-sea-japans-izumo-helicopter-carrier-conducts-drill-with-us-navy-carrier/

Raditio, K. H. (2015). China's shifting behaviour in the South China Sea: A defensive realism perspective. *American Journal of Chinese Studies*, *22*(2), 53–82. https://www.jstor.org/stable/44289102

Rudd, K. (2021). Why the QUAD alarms China. *Asia Society.* https://asiasociety.org/magazine/article/why-quad-alarms-china

Shalal, A. (2016). US says it will not recognize South China Sea exclusion zone. *Reuters.* https://www.reuters.com/article/world/u-s-says-it-will-not-recognize-south-china-sea-exclusion-zone-idUSKCN0WW1QB/

Stone, M. (2019). US to sell 34 surveillance drones to allies in South China Sea region. *Reuters.* https://www.reuters.com/article/world/us-to-sell-34-surveillance-drones-to-allies-in-south-china-sea-region-idUSKCN1T42SS/

United Nations. (2019). *Commission on the Limits of the Continental Shelf (CLCS) outer limits of the continental shelf beyond 200 nautical miles from the baselines: Submissions to the Commission: Partial submission by Malaysia in the South China Sea.* https://www.un.org/depts/los/clcs_new/submissions_files/submission_mysvnm_33_2009.htm

United Nations. (2020a). *Note verbale No. 126/POL-703/V/20.* https://www.un.org/Depts/los/clcs_new/submissions_files/mys_12_12_2019/2020_05_26_IDN_NV_UN_001_English.pdf

United Nations. (2020b). *Note verbale No. 324/2020.* https://www.un.org/Depts/los/clcs_new/submissions_files/mys_12_12_2019/2020_09_16_DEU_NV_UN_001.pdf

Vuving, A. (2017). Tracking Vietnam's force build-up in the South China Sea. *Asia Maritime Transparency Initiative.* https://amti.csis.org/tracking-vietnams-force-build-south-china-sea/

Wang, G. (2018). Digging into the roots of "peace disease". *Ministry of National Defense of the People's Republic of China.* http://www.mod.gov.cn/gfbw/jmsd/4815790.html

Chapter 10
The Art of Incremental Dominance:
China's Coordinated Power Play in the South China Sea

Yen Thi Hai Hoang
Vinh University, Vietnam

ABSTRACT

This chapter examines China's comprehensive strategy in the SCS through the theoretical lens of realism in international relations. Employing qualitative document analysis, the research identifies four integrated strategic pillars: incremental "salami slicing" tactics that gradually alter the status quo without triggering military confrontation; unprecedented artificial island construction and militarization establishing strategic outposts; systematic deployment of coast guard and maritime militia forces operating in legal gray zones; and legal-diplomatic strategies linked with the Belt and Road Initiative. The findings reveal that China's actions exemplify revisionist power behavior in an anarchic system, utilizing coordinated instruments to maximize national interests while avoiding direct conflict. This analysis provides crucial insights for policymakers regarding the multidimensional nature of great power competition and the necessity for comprehensive, long-term regional response strategies.

1. INTRODUCTION

The South China Sea (SCS), spanning over 3.5 million km^2 and serving as one of the world's busiest maritime routes, has emerged as one of the most complex geopolitical flashpoints in the contemporary international system. This region not

DOI: 10.4018/979-8-3373-4470-6.ch010

only hosts over one-third of global maritime trade, valued at approximately $3.4 trillion annually, but also contains abundant oil, gas, and fishery resources, while occupying a strategic position connecting major economies from Northeast Asia to the Indian Ocean and beyond (Hayton, 2024). In the context of a global power shift from West to East, with China's rise as a major power seeking to reshape the regional order, the SCS has become the primary stage for Beijing to demonstrate its strategic ambitions (Mishra, 2021). The escalating tensions in this region—from large-scale artificial island construction and militarization of geographic features to maritime confrontations between law enforcement vessels and fishermen—have attracted profound attention from both the academic community and policymakers worldwide.

Research on China's strategy in the SCS has garnered significant attention from various analytical perspectives in existing academic literature. Some scholars have focused on analyzing the legal aspects of the disputes, particularly the implications of the 2016 Permanent Court of Arbitration ruling and China's response to international law (Pemmaraju, 2016; Schoenbaum, 2017). Other studies have illuminated the economic motivations behind China's actions, from the need to protect energy routes to marine resource exploitation (Kiet et al., 2025a; Hiep et al., 2024). From a security perspective, numerous works have analyzed the militarization of artificial islands and its impact on the regional balance of power (Hieu et al., 2024; Putra, 2024). Recent studies have also examined the role of coast guard and maritime militia forces as instruments in China's "gray zone" strategy (Sarjito, 2024; Le & Tran, 2025). However, most of these studies tend to focus on individual aspects or analyze isolated events, failing to provide a comprehensive and systematic picture of how China integrates different power instruments—from military, economic, and legal to diplomatic—into a coherent overall strategy.

A critical gap in existing research is the absence of a comprehensive and in-depth analysis of how various instruments and methods are coordinated and mutually reinforcing by China to achieve long-term strategic objectives in the SCS. While many studies have identified individual tactics such as "salami slicing" or the use of coast guard forces, there remains insufficient clarity on how these tools are integrated within a comprehensive strategic framework, as well as the connection between the SCS strategy and China's broader global initiatives such as the BRI. Moreover, existing research often lacks a consistent theoretical lens to explain the deeper nature of Chinese behavior, particularly when situated within the context of realism in international relations—a theory with strong explanatory power regarding power motivations and great power competition in an anarchic system (Kiet & Hiep, 2025).

Therefore, this article aims to fill this critical research gap by providing a systematic and comprehensive analysis of the instruments and implementation methods that China has deployed and continues to deploy in the SCS, while situating them within the theoretical framework of realism. Specifically, the article will elucidate four main strategic instruments: (1) the "salami slicing" tactic and the geopolitical logic behind gradual status quo change; (2) the artificial island construction and militarization campaign aimed at establishing strategic outposts; (3) the use of coast guard and maritime militia forces as power instruments in the legal gray zone; and (4) the legal-diplomatic strategy integrated with the BRI initiative. Through detailed analysis of these instruments and how they interact with each other, the article not only clarifies the nature of China's strategy in the SCS but also contributes to a deeper understanding of the behavior of a rising power in the contemporary international system, thereby providing important implications for policymakers and researchers in the region.

2. THEORETICAL FRAMEWORK AND ANALYTICAL APPROACH

This chapter employs qualitative document analysis as its primary research methodology to systematically examine China's strategic behavior in the SCS. Document analysis, as a well-established research method in international relations scholarship, enables researchers to collect, examine, and interpret textual materials to develop empirical knowledge and theoretical understanding of complex geopolitical phenomena (Bowen, 2009). This methodological approach is particularly appropriate for studying China's SCS strategy, as it allows for comprehensive examination of multiple forms of evidence including official policy documents, government statements, legal instruments, military assessments, scholarly publications, and credible media reports spanning the period from 2012 to 2025.

The analytical framework integrates realism theory as the principal theoretical lens through which empirical evidence is interpreted and evaluated. Specifically, the analysis draws upon both defensive and offensive realism perspectives to explain the underlying motivations and strategic logic driving China's actions in the region. This theoretical grounding provides coherent explanatory power for understanding how China, as a rising power, employs various instruments of national power to maximize its interests within an anarchic international system characterized by the absence of a supreme authority capable of enforcing rules and norms.

Data collection proceeded through systematic review of multiple documentary sources. Primary sources include official Chinese government documents such as policy white papers, legislative acts (including the 2021 Coast Guard Law and provincial fisheries regulations), diplomatic statements, and formal responses to international legal proceedings. Secondary sources encompass authoritative analytical reports from established research institutions such as the Asia Maritime Transparency Initiative, the Center for Strategic and International Studies, and various defense ministries' annual assessments. Additionally, the analysis incorporates peer-reviewed academic articles, credible investigative journalism from reputable international media outlets, and official databases tracking maritime incidents and infrastructure development in the disputed waters.

The analytical process involves several systematic steps. First, relevant documents were identified and selected based on their direct relevance to China's strategic activities in the SCS, including military deployments, civilian infrastructure projects, diplomatic initiatives, legal measures, and economic engagement through the Belt and Road Initiative (BRI). Second, these documents were carefully examined to identify patterns, extract specific factual information regarding Chinese actions and policies, and discern the strategic logic underlying specific decisions. Third, the empirical findings were systematically categorized into four thematic strategic pillars: salami slicing tactics, artificial island construction and militarization, deployment of paramilitary maritime forces, and legal-diplomatic strategies integrated with broader economic initiatives. Finally, these findings were interpreted through the realism theoretical framework to explain how individual tactics contribute to China's comprehensive strategy for altering the regional status quo.

To ensure analytical rigor and validity, this study employs triangulation by cross-referencing multiple independent sources when establishing factual claims about specific incidents, infrastructure developments, or policy measures. Where controversies or conflicting interpretations exist in the documentary record, multiple perspectives are acknowledged and evaluated based on the credibility and corroboration of available evidence. This methodological approach enables the chapter to provide a comprehensive, theoretically grounded, and empirically robust analysis of China's multifaceted strategy in the SCS.

3. INCREMENTAL EXPANSION: THE STRATEGY BELOW THE WAR THRESHOLD

One of the most prominent features of China's strategy in the SCS region is the application of the "salami slicing" tactic—a methodological approach based on the principle of dividing objectives into sequential incremental steps, aimed at avoiding triggering strong reactions from adversaries. Rather than implementing large-scale actions all at once, which could easily lead to the risk of direct military confrontation, China has continuously and persistently carried out seemingly minor changes that, when accumulated over time, create alterations to the status quo favorable to its national interests. An important characteristic of this tactic is that each individual Chinese action is typically designed to be small enough not to cross the threshold that could trigger war, yet when aggregated, these steps produce highly significant strategic achievements. In practice, according to a Pentagon report released in 2016, China is using "coercive measures below the threshold of armed conflict," including deploying maritime law enforcement vessels, to advance sovereignty claims "without crossing the threshold that could ignite conflict" (Associated Press, 2016).

When analyzed through the lens of realism theory in international relations, this "salami slicing" tactic clearly embodies the typical characteristics of a revisionist power operating in an anarchic international system: quietly and patiently eroding adversaries' positions to incrementally accumulate advantages, while carefully avoiding provoking opponents to the point where they must respond decisively. Scholar John Mearsheimer—a prominent representative of offensive realism—has astutely observed that China is seeking ways to gradually alter the regional balance of power to strengthen its own national security, stemming from the basic logic that "security requires power, and the more power one has, the more security one achieves" (Seil, 2024). Therefore, China's persistent implementation of an incremental expansion strategy through small and continuous steps can be logically explained through the realism lens: it represents an effort to maximize national interests and power without risking the outbreak of direct warfare, consistent with the inherent "struggle for survival" nature of states in an anarchic international environment. This tactic clearly demonstrates that China is acting precisely as a rising power should, knowing how to exploit opportunities when the balance of forces is tilting in its favor.

China has applied this tactic flexibly across multiple fronts. Regarding maritime patrol operations, they initially deployed only a limited number of coast guard or fishery administration vessels to disputed areas, then gradually increased both frequency and force scale over time. The strategic objective of this method is to create a new de facto "regular presence," thereby causing opposing parties to gradually accept this presence as part of the status quo. Regarding construction and feature modification, China began with seemingly minor activities such as improving shoals, then progressively upgraded their scale to transform them into permanent fortified structures. A example of this method is the formal establishment of Sansha City in 2012 with the mandate to administer the Paracel Islands, Spratly Islands, and all waters within the "nine-dash line" (Haver, 2021). This can be viewed as an administrative move that appears harmless and technical in nature, but in essence created an important internal legal framework for China to legitimize its presence and management authority over these areas. Similarly, in the case of Mischief Reef in the 1990s, China applied a highly systematic step-by-step scenario: beginning with placing marker buoys, followed by constructing fixed concrete markers, then erecting temporary shelters, and finally building a complete permanent base (Mollman, 2022). Each step in this chain of actions was relatively small in scale and did not attract excessive attention, yet when accumulated and combined, they enabled

China to establish de facto control on the ground without needing to use military force openly.

This "salami slicing" tactic places other nations in an extremely strategic dilemma: if they decide to respond with military measures immediately, it appears to be an excessive reaction to a single small-scale incident; however, if they do not respond, they will gradually lose their position and interests in the long term. It can be assessed that the deeper intention of the Chinese government is to force opposing parties to gradually become accustomed to these changes and ultimately regard the matter as a "fait accompli" that cannot be reversed, thereby enabling China to achieve its strategic objectives without paying the price of a costly war.

4. FROM REEFS TO FORTRESSES: PROJECTING POWER THROUGH RECLAMATION

The clearest and most concrete manifestation of China's ambition to alter the status quo is the unprecedented campaign of reclaiming artificial islands in the Spratly Islands region. Beginning in 2013, China conducted a breakthrough campaign: using modern dredging vessels to transform at least seven initially small natural reef structures into large-scale artificial islands with a total area exceeding 3,200 acres (approximately 1,300 hectares) (Asia Maritime Transparency Initiative, 2013). On these reclaimed structures, China rapidly deployed construction of critical infrastructure including long runways for aircraft, deep-water ports, and installation of various modern military equipment. The three largest and most important outposts, commonly referred to as the "Big Three," include: Fiery Cross Reef, Subi Reef, and Mischief Reef.

Fiery Cross Reef, initially just a small rock formation, saw China complete construction of a 3,125-meter runway at this location by September 2015 (Singh, 2020). This artificial island was expanded to approximately 274 hectares, with sufficient area to accommodate hangars for 24 fighter aircraft along with numerous other fortified structures serving military purposes (Asia Maritime Transparency Initiative, 2024). Similarly, Subi Reef was transformed with an area of approximately 395 hectares and equipped with a runway approximately 3 km long, while Mischief Reef reached 558 hectares with a 2,644-meter runway completed in early 2016. These runways exceeding 3,000 meters in length allow modern fighter aircraft and large transport aircraft to take off and land easily and safely. Beyond these structures, China has also excavated deep-water ports capable of receiving large warships, installed long-range radar systems capable of monitoring a vast area, deployed modern air defense missile batteries, and constructed numerous other supporting infrastructure facilities for military operations on these artificial islands.

The reclamation and militarization of these features has provided the People's Liberation Army with highly significant strategic advantages across multiple dimensions. First, these artificial islands serve as important forward bases, significantly extending the operational range of both China's navy and air force deep into the SCS, allowing fighter aircraft and warships to operate longer in the region without needing to return to mainland bases for refueling and resupply. These outposts, when interconnected, form a network of control points spanning the entire Spratly Islands region, providing superior "maritime domain awareness" capabilities through modern radar systems and various sensors installed on the islands. Second, these military bases establish a permanent and continuous military presence, thereby imposing de facto control over disputed waters. China thus has the capability to closely monitor all movements of vessels or aircraft belonging to other nations in the region, while being able to respond quickly and promptly when situations arise. Third, China has cleverly implemented a strategy of partially "civilianizing" these military outposts to create a layer of legal cover. For instance, China has relocated fishermen to live on the islands and organized tourist tours to visit these islands (Lim, 2013). The civilian presence makes it more difficult for adversaries to take military action targeting these islands, as they would easily face international criticism for endangering innocent civilians. In other words, China is strategically calculating to transform these artificial islands into "inviolable bases" both militarily and politically.

The establishment of fortified outposts in the Spratly Islands region serves as concrete and clear evidence for the realism argument that military power is an indispensable foundational pillar for achieving national strategic objectives. Scholar John Mearsheimer has systematically argued that a rising China will seek every means to "maximize the power gap" between itself and neighboring countries and push American influence out of the region, similar to how the United States applied the Monroe Doctrine in the Western Hemisphere historically. In practice, China views controlling and militarizing geographic features in the SCS as important strategic steps to ensure that no Asian nation has sufficient power to threaten their security, and to gradually "remove American power from their backyard" in the region. On the other hand, when viewed through the lens of defensive realism, China might justify that these forward bases are constructed primarily to enhance defensive security against the dense and continuous military presence of the United States and its allies in the region. Regardless of the interpretation, realism scholars agree that a nation's significant increase in power will inevitably trigger a "security dilemma": neighboring countries will feel threatened and will respond by engaging in an arms race, or by forming alliances with each other or with another major power to rebalance power. This has been and continues to occur clearly in the SCS region—as China becomes more aggressive in island construction, other nations increasingly boost defense spending and actively seek security alliances in response.

5. GRAY ZONE OPERATIONS: PARAMILITARY FORCES AS STRATEGIC INSTRUMENTS

Rather than relying solely on regular naval forces in the traditional manner, China has placed great emphasis on using paramilitary maritime forces, particularly the China Coast Guard (CCG) and maritime militia forces, as important instruments to flexibly and skillfully enforce sovereignty claims.

The CCG was officially established in 2013 through the merger of four previously independent maritime law enforcement agencies, commonly called the "Five Dragons," including: maritime surveillance, fishery administration, maritime police, fishery inspection, and maritime customs. After restructuring and reorganization, the CCG was placed under the direct management of the paramilitary People's Armed Police (PAP), which is commanded by the Central Military Commission, and received substantial investment in both operational budgets and modern equipment. As of now, the CCG has become the world's largest coast guard force by scale, with over 130 large patrol vessels (displacing over 1,000 tons)—double the number from 2010 (China Power, 2020). Many newly commissioned CCG vessels have displacements up to 10,000 tons, such as the Zhaotou-class vessels, larger than many destroyers, and are fully equipped with weapons such as 76mm guns and helicopter landing pads, similar to regular military warships (Business Insider, 2021). This significant increase in scale and operational capability enables the CCG to assert law enforcement across the vast maritime area marked by the "nine-dash line." They regularly conduct patrol operations aimed at driving away fishing vessels from other countries operating in the region, blocking oil and gas exploration and exploitation activities by coastal states, and planting flags to assert presence at disputed hotspots. Statistics clearly show that from 2010 to present, among all serious incidents occurring in the SCS, up to 73% of cases involved the presence and activities of Chinese law enforcement vessels (China Power, 2020). Using coast guard forces under the guise of nominally civilian "law enforcement" helps China create a legal gray zone, making it difficult for adversaries to respond with military measures and forcing them to mobilize similar forces for counterbalance.

Alongside the Coast Guard, the People's Armed Forces Maritime Militia (PAFMM) is another strategic "card" in China's hand. This is essentially a tightly organized network of thousands of civilian fishing vessels organized, trained, and ready to perform tasks serving national interests when required. China's maritime militia is composed of two main components: a professional militia force of over 100 large steel-hulled vessels, newly built with designs disguised as ordinary fishing boats but actually equipped with modern communication equipment and high-pressure water cannon systems; and a much larger force comprising traditional civilian fishing vessels, especially vessels from coastal provinces such as Hainan and Guangdong, mobilized to participate when specific tasks arise for maritime operations. In actual operations, each militia vessel typically has only 5-6 crew members when performing "missions," fewer than the normal complement when actually fishing. They receive fuel subsidies, salaries, bonuses, and other support from the government to remain ready to depart on missions when ordered. China typically maintains a very secretive attitude about this maritime militia force, rarely publicly acknowledging which vessels belong to this component. However, evidence gathered from media sources and official state documents clearly shows that militia vessel fleets receive orders directly from superiors and are considered an "extended arm" of the navy when needed (Davidson, 2024).

In practical deployment, maritime militia forces are used by China as an important supporting force to overwhelm opponents numerically and create irreversible faits accomplis at sea. The most common and effective tactic is the "area saturation" tactic: dozens or even hundreds of Chinese fishing vessels in militia roles swarm to anchor around disputed shoals and small islands to assert de facto sovereignty claims on site. A example: in 2012, hundreds of Chinese fishing vessels conducted a blockade of Scarborough Shoal belonging to the Philippines, coordinating closely with Chinese maritime surveillance vessels, resulting in these forces gaining de facto control of this shoal without firing a single shot (Davidson, 2024). Or in March 2021, approximately 200 vessels identified as belonging to China's "militia" forces concentrated in large numbers at Whitsun Reef in the Spratly Islands region (according to Vietnamese nomenclature), causing serious tensions with the Philippines. China's maritime militia forces also do not hesitate to use aggressive and threatening tactics: direct ramming, spraying high-pressure water cannons at other countries' official vessels to drive them away. They have repeatedly rammed and sunk Vietnamese fishing vessels operating around the Paracel and Spratly Islands. According to statistics published by Vietnam, during the period from 2014 to 2022, a total of 98 Vietnamese fishing vessels were rammed and damaged by Chinese vessels in the SCS (Agence France-Presse, 2022).

The systematic mobilization and use of coast guard and maritime militia forces has provided China with several important strategic advantages. First, this approach continues to allow China to avoid the risk of direct military conflict escalation with adversaries. When maritime collisions occur, China can easily argue that these are merely "civilian law enforcement incidents," thereby reducing the severity of the matter and preventing the United States or other nations from having grounds to intervene militarily. Second, the participation of militia and coast guard forces creates significant legal ambiguity and difficulty in identifying the true nature of these forces, causing opposing parties to fall into confusion about whether to respond with regular military forces or civilian forces, leading to delayed responses. Third, this significantly complicates the international community's ability to respond: other countries face difficulties in applying collective defense mechanisms because the Chinese forces deployed are not nominally regular military forces, while it is also difficult to clearly and irrefutably condemn China for violating international law.

In summary, by effectively leveraging the CCG and maritime militia forces, China has built a complete and effective "three-pronged warfare" in the SCS: (1) Regular military forces standing behind in a strategic deterrence role; (2) Coast guard forces directly conducting law enforcement operations on site; (3) Maritime militia forces providing support with large numerical presence. This triad of forces coordinates harmoniously and mutually reinforces effectively, helping China control vast disputed waters while successfully avoiding large-scale direct military conflict. It can be clearly observed that China is cleverly applying the concept of "smart power" through flexible combination of hard and soft power: using coast guard vessels and militia as frontline forces on the ground instead of the regular navy to avoid crossing the threshold that could trigger war, while still achieving important strategic interests. This tactic reflects an extremely pragmatic "using softness to overcome hardness" mentality that classical strategists like Sun Tzu historically extolled—achieving victory without needing to engage in open combat. When examined from the realism perspective, China is cleverly altering the balance of power in the SCS at a low threshold, making it impossible for adversaries to have legitimate and lawful grounds to use force in response. This can be considered a form of "gray zone power play," where international law remains unclear and specific, and on-the-ground is the decisive factor determining winners and losers.

6. LAWFARE AND BILATERAL LEVERAGE: SHAPING THE NORMATIVE BATTLEFIELD

Regarding legal and diplomatic dimensions, it can be clearly affirmed that China only truly respects and complies with international rules when they serve its national interests; in other cases, the nation will interpret them favorably or simply ignore them when those rules prove disadvantageous. The most and clear example of this attitude is China's complete boycott of the SCS arbitration case initiated by the Philippines and subsequent rejection of the entire ruling issued by the Permanent Court of Arbitration (PCA) in 2016. This historic ruling clearly declared that the "nine-dash line" used by China to assert territorial claims has no legal basis under international law, and that China violated the Philippines' sovereign rights within its exclusive economic zone (Castro, 2020). China immediately issued a firm statement that it "does not accept, does not recognize" this ruling as having legal validity. Instead, China persistently maintains the position that territorial disputes should be resolved through direct bilateral negotiations with each concerned country, while opposing any efforts to "internationalize" the issue or use multilateral settlement mechanisms. After the PCA ruling was announced, China emphasized that it was only willing to negotiate directly with the Philippines, avoiding ASEAN or any third party participation in the resolution process. Philippine President Rodrigo Duterte at that time also decided to temporarily set aside the ruling in exchange for goodwill and substantial economic aid from China. This clearly demonstrates that China's bilateral diplomacy priority strategy has proven somewhat effective for their interests. China has a huge advantage in bilateral negotiations due to the overwhelming power disparity compared to individual disputing nations, whereas in multilateral frameworks, they would easily face pressure from multiple countries united together.

Parallel to avoiding multilateral mechanisms, China also proactively uses law in ways most beneficial to its national interests. China has enacted numerous domestic maritime laws aimed at affirming and consolidating their claims in the SCS. A example is the Coast Guard Law enacted in 2021, authorizing CCG forces to use weapons against foreign vessels deemed to be intruding into waters "under China's jurisdiction" (Business Insider, 2021). This law immediately raised deep concerns among neighboring countries, as China could use it to legitimize the use of force, even opening fire, in disputed areas such as the Spratlys and Paracels. Previously, the Fisheries Law enacted in 2012 by Hainan provincial authorities unilaterally banned foreign fishing vessels from operating in approximately two-thirds of the SCS without obtaining permission from China. Chinese authorities also continuously unilaterally impose summer fishing bans annually across the entire SCS, accompanied by threats of heavy penalties for violators, aimed at consolidating and affirming their sovereignty claims. When other countries voice opposition to these unilateral measures, China often cites marine environmental protection regulations or selectively references certain provisions in UNCLOS (United Nations Convention on the Law of the Sea) to justify their actions. It can be clearly seen that China is completely willing to rely on international law when it benefits them, but does not hesitate to ignore it when it becomes disadvantageous.

Regarding diplomatic strategy, China pursues a tactic called "divide and conquer" toward ASEAN member states. As mentioned in previous sections, China uses its enormous economic power as a strategic lever to influence and impact ASEAN member states, aiming to attract some parties to their side or at least disrupt consensus that might be disadvantageous to China's interests. The most and clear cases are Cambodia and Laos—two countries without direct disputes in the SCS but benefiting greatly economically from Chinese investment and aid, thus tending to support China's position at ASEAN forums. In 2012, when Cambodia assumed the role of ASEAN rotating chair, the nation blocked ASEAN from issuing a joint communiqué on the SCS issue, marking the first time in ASEAN's long history that the bloc could not issue a joint statement due to deep disagreement on this issue.

China also actively deploys investment programs and economic aid to countries with direct disputes such as the Philippines, Malaysia, and Indonesia, aimed at reducing these nations' motivation and determination to confront. For instance, in 2016, immediately after the PCA ruling was announced, China made promises of investments up to a massive $24 billion to the Philippines, causing the Duterte administration in Manila to soften its tone and lower demands for an extended period (Castro, 2020). However, it should be noted that these economic "carrots" are sometimes accompanied by punitive "sticks": when the Philippines makes moves too close to the United States, China is fully prepared to apply implicit economic sanctions. A concrete example is in 2023, when China decided to cut banana imports from the Philippines by up to 50%—a key export commodity of great importance to the island nation's economy (Kelly & Wester, 2025). Similarly, China once applied measures to stop allowing Chinese tourist groups to travel to South Korea in 2017 when Seoul decided to deploy the U.S. THAAD missile defense system on its territory. This economic diplomatic tactic has created deep apprehension and concern among ASEAN countries: many nations fear that opposing China too strongly will cause them to bear serious economic consequences. This has significantly contributed to restraining ASEAN's solidarity and collective action capability in addressing common security challenges in the region.

Realism scholars clearly and profoundly view China's behavior as a and concrete example of the principle that "law of power" is overshadowing "power of law." As historian Thucydides famously recorded in the Melian Dialogue in history: "the strong do what they can, while the weak suffer what they must." China is acting precisely according to the spirit and logic of this principle when they only selectively comply with international rules when they do not obstruct or negatively affect their strategic ambitions. Renowned realism theorist Hans Morgenthau also profoundly emphasized that legal principles and ethics in international relations are frequently bent and shaped by specific national interests and the actual power relationship between parties (Morgenthau, 1948). Indeed, China's disregard for the 2016 PCA ruling clearly demonstrates that a major power is fully prepared to set aside international law when that law becomes disadvantageous to its interests and especially when there is no effective enforcement mechanism to implement that law. Scholar John Mearsheimer has gone even further, calling the liberal international order based on rules merely an "empty promise" with no practical value when lacking the necessary balance of power to enforce it effectively (Rachman, 2017). Contrary to ignoring disadvantageous laws, China is highly knowledgeable about using law in the most favorable direction: enacting domestic laws such as the Coast Guard Law and Fisheries Law to "legitimize" their unilateral actions; while cleverly exploiting gaps and ambiguities in international law to advance claims without being seen as the aggressor or clearly violating international law. All of this demonstrates a purely realism approach: rules are merely tools serving power and national interests, not moral standards capable of limiting a major power's behavior.

7. THE MARITIME SILK ROAD: LINKING COMMERCE TO GEOSTRATEGY

China's strategy in the SCS does not exist separately and independently, but is instead tightly linked with their broader global strategy, most notably the BRI. Within this initiative's framework, the "21st Century Maritime Silk Road" component plays the role of incorporating the entire Southeast Asian region into China's long-term strategic map. The BRI aims to develop a network of port infrastructure and maritime connections from China through Southeast Asia, across the Indian Ocean to regions in Africa and Europe (McBride et al., 2023). Therefore, the SCS region serves as a vital and indispensable link in China's global strategic ambitions.

In 2024 alone, China participated in investing in large-scale infrastructure projects in Southeast Asia with total investment capital reaching approximately $25.1 billion (Wang, 2025), thereby both promoting bilateral trade activities and significantly increasing China's geostrategic influence in the region. Preferential financing with low interest rates and massive infrastructure projects have caused some countries in the region to gradually become economically dependent on China. The most and clear examples include China's participation in constructing and expanding Kuantan Port in Malaysia, financing development of Sihanoukville Port in Cambodia, investing in expanding Kyaukpyu Port in Myanmar, and proposing the ambitious Kra Canal project in Thailand that could change the regional maritime map. According to concerns expressed by Western nations, these ports not only serve purely economic and commercial purposes, but in the long term could also become important stopover points providing logistics for Chinese military vessels. Particularly noteworthy, the case of Ream Naval Base in Cambodia has raised much concern: China generously financed the comprehensive upgrade of this naval base, raising widespread speculation that the People's Liberation Army (PLA) will have the right to use Ream for military purposes in the future. According to sources disclosed by the Wall Street Journal, the two countries even signed a secret agreement allowing the PLA Navy access and use of Ream Base for a 30-year term (Kakkar, 2024). If this information is accurate, this would be China's first overseas military base established in Southeast Asia, marking a significant expansion of the PLA's presence and military power in the Gulf of Thailand and the entire SCS region. However, it should be noted that both the Chinese government and the Cambodian government have firmly denied any intention to militarize this base.

From a strategic analysis perspective, the tight integration between the BRI and China's SCS strategy has provided the nation with more leverage and power to implement its strategic objectives in this region, which can be summarized by the term "two-tier power." On one hand, BRI investment projects help cultivate and consolidate friendly political relations with countries in the region, making them increasingly hesitant and reluctant to directly confront China on SCS issues for fear of losing significant economic benefits from investment and trade. On the other hand, in the long-term future, the widespread network of ports built under the BRI framework could provide important logistics facilities to supply the Chinese navy when necessary to deploy far-from-shore operations. Western analysts and observers have expressed deep concern about the scenario called the "string of pearls," in which China gradually owns a chain of strategic bases and ports extending from the SCS across the Indian Ocean, creating important stepping stones for the navy to protect their vital maritime routes (Runde et al., 2024). China firmly rejects all accusations of militarizing BRI projects, asserting that all ports they construct are entirely for civilian economic and commercial purposes. However, observational evidence shows that many Chinese-invested ports are designed with sufficient water depth to accommodate naval warships, and PLA Navy vessels visiting and using these ports is not overly difficult or impossible to implement.

When analyzed from the realism perspective in international relations, the BRI is viewed not merely as a purely economic initiative, but also as an important geostrategic lever aimed at increasing China's comprehensive power on the international stage. The concept of "string of pearls" originated from Western realism analytical circles, used to describe a network of military bases and commercial facilities that China is gradually building along strategic maritime routes from China through the SCS, across the Indian Ocean to regions in Africa. This strategic network includes important "pearls" such as Gwadar Port in Pakistan, Hambantota Port in Sri Lanka, Kyaukpyu Port in Myanmar, and Woody Island in the Paracel Islands, connected together in a continuous chain on the strategic map (Spinetta, 2006). According to the "string of pearls" strategic hypothesis, China is quietly and patiently establishing strategic stopover points to serve the ambition of developing a powerful blue-water navy, thereby having the capability to significantly limit the United States' and India's ability to intervene and influence in this region (Kiet et al., 2025b). In practice, this approach faithfully reflects classical geostrategic thinking proven through history: Alfred Thayer Mahan—the famous American naval strategist of the 19th century—astutely argued that any nation wishing to become powerful and influential on the international stage must have the ability to control important maritime choke points and vital sea routes for global trade (Mahan, 1893). China is doing exactly that through the BRI initiative: investing in building ports and connecting infrastructure to both promote commercial activities serving their economic interests and create long-term and sustainable presence at strategically important positions. It is not a coincidence that many ports built under the BRI framework coincide with the locations of strategically important straits such as the Strait of Malacca, Strait of Hormuz, Bab-el-Mandeb Strait, and many other positions. Directly or indirectly controlling these strategic points will help China ensure security for the flow of oil and essential goods, while creating important power levers that can be used in relations with competing adversaries.

In summary, it can be affirmed that the SCS region is an extremely important and indispensable link in the "Maritime Silk Road," and conversely, the success of the BRI initiative will contribute to consolidating and enhancing China's strategic position in the SCS region. These two strategies mutually complement and support each other organically and effectively: controlling the SCS ensures security for the BRI's important trade route, while the BRI increases economic and political influence, providing China with additional tools and leverage to more easily dominate and control the SCS region.

8. CONCLUSION

Through detailed analysis of the instruments and implementation methods of China's strategy in the SCS, this article has illuminated a comprehensive picture of how a rising power uses a tightly integrated system of power instruments to achieve its long-term strategic objectives. The main findings show that China's strategy is not a series of isolated and random actions, but a carefully designed overall plan in which four main strategic pillars—"salami slicing" tactics, artificial island construction and militarization, use of coast guard and maritime militia forces, along with legal-diplomatic strategy integrated with the BRI—coordinate and mutually reinforce harmoniously to create synergistic effects far exceeding the value of individual instruments.

When situated within the theoretical framework of realism, China's behavior in the SCS fully embodies the characteristics of a revisionist power seeking to alter the status quo to maximize national power and interests in an anarchic international system. The "salami slicing" tactic allows China to incrementally erode adversaries' positions without crossing the threshold triggering war, reflecting the "struggle for survival" logic that realisms like Mearsheimer have identified. The construction of fortified military outposts affirms the fundamental principle that military power is the foundation for protecting national interests and expanding regional influence. The utilization of coast guard and maritime militia forces demonstrates a "smart power" strategy in the legal gray zone, while selective attitudes toward international law evidence the realism view that "law of power" often overshadows "power of law" when effective enforcement mechanisms are absent. Finally, integrating the SCS strategy with the BRI initiative demonstrates long-term geostrategic vision, reflecting Mahan's classical thinking about the importance of controlling sea routes and maritime choke points.

The practical significance of this research is extremely important for policy-makers in regional countries as well as the broader international community. First, clearly understanding the comprehensive and systematic nature of China's strategy helps concerned countries recognize that effective response cannot focus solely on individual incidents, but requires a comprehensive and long-term response strategy. Second, identifying "gray zone" tactics through the use of paramilitary forces requires countries to develop their own maritime law enforcement capabilities and establish regional coordination mechanisms for effective counterbalance. Third, understanding how China exploits gaps in international law and applies "divide and conquer" tactics in ASEAN emphasizes the importance of strengthening regional solidarity and consolidating the international legal framework. Fourth, the connection between the SCS strategy and the BRI warns countries about the long-term and multidimensional nature of power competition, requiring a balanced approach between economic cooperation and protecting national security interests.

In summary, China's strategy in the SCS represents a case study of how a modern great power utilizes a diverse and tightly integrated toolkit of power to pursue national interests in a competitive environment. Understanding this strategy is not only important for addressing current challenges in the SCS, but also provides valuable lessons about the nature of great power competition in the 21st century.

REFERENCES

Agence France-Presse. (2022). Vietnam fisherman recounts attacks by China coast guard in SCS. *South China Morning Post.* https://www.scmp.com/news/asia/southeast-asia/article/3196026/vietnam-fisherman-recounts-attacks-china-coast-guard-south

Asia Maritime Transparency Initiative. (2013). *China Island Tracker.* https://amti.csis.org/island-tracker/china/

Asia Maritime Transparency Initiative. (2024). *Fiery Cross Reef.* https://amti.csis.org/fiery-cross-reef/

Associated Press. (2016). China has reclaimed 3200 acres in the SCS, says Pentagon. *The Guardian.* https://www.theguardian.com/world/2016/may/13/pentagon-report-china-reclaimed-3200-acres-south-china-sea

Bowen, G. A. (2009). Document analysis as a qualitative research method. *Qualitative Research Journal*, *9*(2), 27–40. DOI: 10.3316/QRJ0902027

Business Insider. (2021). *China's ships are getting bigger and more aggressive and Japan is scrambling to keep up.* https://www.businessinsider.com/chinas-coast-guard-ships-worrying-japan-scrambling-to-keep-up-2021-2

Castro, R. C. D. (2020). After four years, the Philippines acknowledges the 2016 arbitral tribunal award! *Asia Maritime Transparency Initiative.* https://amti.csis.org/after-four-years-the-philippines-acknowledges-the-2016-arbitral-tribunal-award/

China Power. (2020). *Are maritime law enforcement forces destabilizing Asia?* https://chinapower.csis.org/maritime-forces-destabilizing-asia/

Davidson, H. (2024). China's maritime militia: The shadowy armada whose existence Beijing rarely acknowledges. *The Guardian.* https://www.theguardian.com/world/article/2024/jun/13/china-maritime-militia-explainer-south-china-sea-scarborough-shoal

Haver, Z. (2021). China maritime report No. 12: Sansha City in China's SCS strategy: Building a system of administrative control. *CMSI China Maritime Reports.* https://digital-commons.usnwc.edu/cmsi-maritime-reports/12/

Hayton, B. (2024). The SCS: Historical and legal background. *Council on Geostrategy.* https://www.geostrategy.org.uk/research/the-south-china-sea-historical-and-legal-background/

Hiep, T. X., Kiet, L. H., & Yen, P. T. H. (2024). India's Look East Policy: Vietnam's pivotal role amidst China's rising regional influence. *Estudios Internacionales (Santiago)*, *12*(3), 51–73. https://periodicos.pucminas.br/estudosinternacionais/article/view/34606

Hieu, B. T., Cuong, A. N., & Nhi, D. T. Y. (2024). Challenges for Vietnam in protecting SCS sovereignty and interests. *Cogent Social Sciences*, *10*(1), 2401629. Advance online publication. DOI: 10.1080/23311886.2024.2401629

Kakkar, M. G. H. (2024). China's new naval base in Cambodia The Excelsior 18 Oct 2024. *Maj Gen Harsha Kakkar Articles*. https://harshakakararticles.com/2024/10/18/chinas-new-naval-base-in-cambodia-the-excelsior-18-oct-2024/

Kelly, B., & Wester, S. (2025). ASEAN caught between China's export surge and global de-risking. *Asia Society*. https://asiasociety.org/policy-institute/asean-caught-between-chinas-export-surge-and-global-de-risking

Kiet, L. H., Binh, N. T., & Hiep, T. X. (2025b). From border conflicts to maritime competition: Driving forces behind the power rivalry between India and China in the Indian Ocean region. *Australian Journal of Maritime and Ocean Affairs*, •••, 1–25. DOI: 10.1080/18366503.2025.2492438

Kiet, L. H., & Hiep, T. X. (2025). Geopolitical conflict between great powers in the 21st century: An analysis of the Ukraine crisis. *Sovremennaya Evropa*, *129*(1), 121–135. DOI: 10.7868/S3034599525010103

Kiet, L. H., Tam, L. T. T., & Hiep, T. X. (2025a). Caught between dragon and elephant: Vietnam's strategic balancing act in the Sino-Indian rivalry. *China Quarterly of International Strategic Studies*, *11*(2), 99–128. DOI: 10.1142/S237774002550006X

Le, K. H., & Tran, H. X. (2025). Vietnam's strategic partnership role in India's policy to counter China's hegemonic ambitions in the East Sea. In Güçyetmez, F., & Kahraman, A. (Eds.), *Geopolitics of the SCS: Power struggle in Asia* (pp. 263–284). IGI Global Scientific Publishing., DOI: 10.4018/979-8-3693-8109-0.ch012

Lim, B. K. (2013). China to let tourists visit disputed SCS islets. *Reuters*. https://www.reuters.com/article/us-china-seas-tourism/china-to-let-tourists-visit-disputed-south-china-sea-islets-idUSBRE93601720130407/

McBride, J., Berman, N., & Chatzky, A. (2023). China's massive Belt and Road Initiative. *Council on Foreign Relations*. https://www.cfr.org/backgrounder/chinas-massive-belt-and-road-initiative

Mishra, R. (2021). Vietnam's regional security perceptions and priorities: Role of India. *India Quarterly. Journal of International Affairs*, *77*(2), 200–218. DOI: 10.1177/09749284211004983

Mollman, S. (2022). How a "fishermen's shelter" on stilts became a Chinese military base in the SCS. *Quartz*. https://qz.com/863811/mischief-reef-how-a-fishermens-shelter-on-stilts-became-a-chinese-military-base-in-the-south-china-sea

Morgenthau, H. J. (1948). Politics among nations: The struggle for power and peace. *University of California San Diego*. http://slantchev.ucsd.edu/courses/ps240/04%20Conflict%20with%20States%20as%20Unitary%20Actors/Morgenthau%20-%20Politics%20among%20nations%20(selected%20chapters).pdf

Pemmaraju, S. R. (2016). The SCS Arbitration (The Philippines and China): Assessment of the award on jurisdiction and admissibility. *Chinese Journal of International Law*, *15*(2), 265–307. DOI: 10.1093/chinesejil/jmw019

Putra, B. A. (2024). Tread with caution: Vietnam's retaliatory and deference measures vis-à-vis assertiveness at sea. *Asian Journal of Political Science*, *32*(1), 57–76. DOI: 10.1080/02185377.2024.2351390

Rachman, G. (2017). Destined for war? China, America, and the Thucydides trap. *Financial Times*. https://nghiencuuquocte.org/2017/07/03/dinh-menh-chien-tranh-trung-quoc-hoa-ky-va-bay-thucydides/

Runde, D. F., Hardman, A., & Bonin, C. (2024). Responding to China's growing influence in ports of the Global South. *CSIS*. https://www.csis.org/analysis/responding-chinas-growing-influence-ports-global-south

Sarjito, A. (2024). China's gray zone strategy in the SCS: Tactics, objectives, and regional implications. *Indonesian Journal of Multidisciplinary Sciences*, *3*(2), 113–135. DOI: 10.59066/ijoms.v3i2.559

Schoenbaum, T. J. (2016). The SCS Arbitration Decision: The need for clarification. *AJIL Unbound*, *110*, 290–295. DOI: 10.1017/S2398772300009181

Seil, C. (2024). Pragmatic offensive realism in the SCS. *European Guanxi*. https://www.europeanguanxi.com/post/pragmatic-offensive-realism-in-the-south-china-sea

Singh, R. (2020). The fiasco that never ends: SCS. *World Press*. https://ecozhdc.wordpress.com/2020/08/30/the-fiasco-that-never-ends-south-china-sea/

Spinetta, L. (2006). Cutting China's "string of pearls". *U.S. Naval Institute Proceedings*. https://www.usni.org/magazines/proceedings/2006/october/cutting-chinas-string-pearls

Wang, C. N. (2025). China Belt and Road Initiative (BRI) investment report 2024. *Green Finance & Development Center.* https://greenfdc.org/china-belt-and-road-initiative-bri-investment-report-2024/

Chapter 11 Maritime Sovereignty and Governance in Seventeenth–Eighteenth Century Dang Trong: Vietnam's Strategic Role in the South China Sea

Ngoc Phuong Mai
https://orcid.org/0009-0005-1334-3680
Vinh University, Vietnam

Vinh Hong Nguyen
Vinh University, Vietnam

ABSTRACT

This chapter analyzes Vietnam's role in the South China Sea maritime system during the 17th-18th centuries—a critical period for contemporary maritime sovereignty formation. Examining the Nguyen Lords' regime in Dang Trong, it demonstrates how Vietnamese polities organized, controlled, and defended maritime space amid regional trade fluctuations and international interactions. Using Vietnamese and international historical sources, the chapter explores three areas: (1) coastal port organization and foreign vessel control, including merchant management and taxation; (2) maritime security through anti-piracy operations and trade route protection; (3) sovereignty practices at SCS islands and archipelagos. The chapter argues that Vietnam actively established regional maritime order rather than remaining passive. These historical practices secured economic-security interests

DOI: 10.4018/979-8-3373-4470-6.ch011

while establishing legal and organizational foundations for modern Vietnamese maritime policy. Examining this maritime heritage is essential for understanding continuity in Vietnam's contemporary maritime strategy.

1. INTRODUCTION

The South China Sea has long been not merely a resource space but also a strategic commercial axis of Southeast Asia. Located on international maritime routes, this region plays a pivotal role in connecting continental Asia with the maritime world and has become a site of continuous interweaving between trade, security, and regional power structures (Kiet & Tuyen, 2023; Hiep et al., 2024). In this context, Vietnam—with its coastline extending along the western side of the South China Sea—is not simply a coastal area subject to external influences but an active agent in organizing, controlling, and expressing maritime power (see more at Trinh, 2025; Kiet et al., 2025; That et al., 2025).

In research on Vietnamese maritime history, the modern period, particularly from the 20th century onward, has often been analyzed through the lens of international law and geopolitics (Kiet et al., 2025; Trinh, 2025; Hiep et al., 2024). For the medieval period, including the 17th-18th centuries, important works have addressed commercial activities, diplomacy, and East-West contacts (Wheeler, 2006; Vy, 1961; Tana, 1999; Tana, 2024). However, the aspect of maritime power practice and maritime governance mechanisms of Vietnamese polities during this period has not yet been examined in a specialized and systematic manner. During these centuries, the two regions chose different institutional configurations: Dang Ngoai (Tonkin) managed foreign trade through a centralized mechanism with conditional openness, restricting international merchants to designated ports such as Pho Hien and Van Don with strict regulations on seasons, commodities, and residence; meanwhile, Dang Trong developed a more open model, linked to the prosperity of port cities, where Hoi An emerged as a representative center, accompanied by institutional systems ensuring trade and maritime security.

Based on this observation, this chapter selects Dang Trong as a case study to clarify how a pre-modern Vietnamese polity designed, implemented, and expressed power over maritime space in the context of Southeast Asia's rapid transformation in trade and international contacts. The analytical scope is limited to the 17th-18th centuries. The research draws on Vietnamese historical sources such as "Phu Bien Tap Luc" (Records of the Pacified Frontier), "Dai Nam Thuc Luc" (Veritable Records of Dai Nam), "Toan Tap Thien Nam Tu Chi Lo Do Thu" (Complete Collection of Maps and Records of Thien Nam Four Routes), and is cross-referenced with foreign sources, thereby developing three main analytical directions: (i) organization and control of coastal ports; (ii) implementation of maritime security; (iii) sovereignty practices on islands and strategic maritime routes. This approach not only affirms that Dang Trong was an active agent in constructing regional maritime order but also allows for rereading historical sources as products of an indigenous political-administrative thought system. Simultaneously, focusing on the case of Dang Trong provides a foundation for scholarly dialogue with contemporary theories on "performative sovereignty," political space, and maritime power in the Southeast Asian context.

2. LITERATURE REVIEW

Research on maritime sovereignty and Vietnam's maritime role in history has developed strongly over recent decades, forming three main approaches: (i) historical-documentary approach to reconstruct maritime governance activities; (ii) international legal approach to affirm territorial sovereignty; and (iii) historical-social approach with new theoretical frameworks on the sea.

First, Vietnam historical works focus extensively on exploiting documentary sources, maps, court documents, and gazetteers to prove the Vietnamese state's presence at sea. Bang (2011, 2014, 2015, 2016, 2022) stands out with systematic research on defense mechanisms, organization of Hoang Sa teams, and the Nguyen dynasty's maritime governance policy, thereby affirming the depth of maritime thinking in the monarchical state model. Many other authors such as Duc (2015), Son (2016), Nha (2013), Van and Ngoc (2009), and Dau (2013) have enriched the evidence base through Han-Nom maps, court documents, and gazetteers, creating a solid documentary foundation for modern sovereignty arguments. These works have the advantage of rich documentation but generally tend toward description, with little analysis of maritime practice as an endogenous power structure.

Second, legal-international approaches emphasize the continuity of sovereignty according to modern legal standards. Thang (2002) and Chemillier-Gendreau (2011) both use historical documents to compare with principles of international public law, thereby creating a bridge between indigenous evidence and international law. Recently, Cuong (2023) has developed this direction by exploiting works of Vietnamese scholars to prove the legitimacy of Hoang Sa-Truong Sa sovereignty under international law. However, a limitation of this research direction is the tendency to project pre-modern state thinking according to modern standards, overlooking the specific practical logic of the historical context.

Third, in international scholarship, many initial studies still revolve around contemporary legal and political disputes (Chang, 1991; Pedrozo, 2014). However, new approaches have opened up ways of reading Vietnamese history from a maritime perspective. Wheeler (2006) proposes the concept of "littoral society," emphasizing the role of non-central communities in constructing coastal order. Roszko (2022) continues to develop the framework of "performative sovereignty," showing that sovereignty is not only a legal concept but also a process constructed through maps, rituals, and daily practices. Tana (2024) in "A Maritime Vietnam" marks a turning point by restructuring Vietnamese history from a maritime perspective, integrating Vietnamese, Chinese, Japanese, and European sources to prove that the sea is not only a livelihood space but also a factor shaping the nature of the Vietnamese state.

From this review, it can be seen that scholarship has contributed many important documents and analytical frameworks, but most still focus on affirming sovereignty or reconstructing historical events. A major gap lies in the fact that Vietnam's maritime practices have not been analyzed as an organized power model with systemic character linked to indigenous political-administrative thinking. This article aims to fill that gap by selecting the case of Dang Trong in the 17th-18th centuries to analyze how this polity designed, implemented, and expressed maritime power, thereby contributing to scholarly dialogue with contemporary theories on "performative sovereignty" and Southeast Asian maritime history.

3. THEORETICAL FRAMEWORK

The article approaches how 17th-18th century Vietnamese polities organized and implemented power over maritime space from a historical-social perspective rather than a modern legal framework. The focus lies not in determining the legitimacy of sovereignty but in analyzing specific political-administrative practices of the monarchical state, which reflect a system of thinking and organization different from the modern nation-state territorial model. Conceptually, the research uses three main categories: (i) Maritime sovereignty: understood as power expressed and reaffirmed through specific practices in maritime space; (ii) Maritime governance: including mechanisms for organizing, supervising, and protecting maritime space through both administrative institutions and social practices; (iii) Political practices legacy: meaning historical forms of power organization with the capacity to shape how the state handles space in contexts different from contemporary legal models.

Theoretically, the article inherits and adapts the concepts of "performative sovereignty" and "functional sovereignty"—expressed through regular activities of Hoang Sa and Bac Hai teams in resource exploitation, fishermen protection, and maritime route control (Roszko, 2022)—to apply to the medieval context. This approach views sovereignty not as a fixed legal state but as a process maintained and legitimized through symbolic acts: patrolling, erecting markers, mapping, issuing edicts, or recording in administrative documents. These acts are both governance tools and means of expressing legitimate power in maritime space. This approach directly dialogues with Wheeler (2006) on "littoral society"—emphasizing non-central structures—and with Tana (2024), who affirms the sea as a foundation shaping the Vietnamese state.

Based on this, the research assumes that the Vietnamese monarchical state did not manage the sea through permanent presence or fixed boundaries but through a flexible mechanism based on rotational presence, coordination between central and local authorities, and periodic organization of specialized teams for maritime exploitation and control. This method both reflects actual control capacity and reshapes maritime space as an inseparable part of national order. Applying this theoretical framework allows the article to read historical sources not only as historical evidence but as textualized power practices. From there, the research can analyze how Dang Trong under the Nguyen Lords organized ports, maintained maritime security, and practiced sovereignty on islands as expressions of a specific, indigenous maritime governance model in the East Asian-Southeast Asian context.

4. METHODOLOGY

This study employs a historical-qualitative research design grounded in critical source analysis and interpretive contextualization. The methodological framework is structured around three interconnected dimensions: source-based documentary analysis, interdisciplinary theoretical integration, and contextualized historical interpretation. This tripartite approach enables systematic examination of how pre-modern Vietnamese polities conceptualized, operationalized, and legitimized maritime power within their specific institutional and geopolitical contexts.

4.1. Primary Source Analysis and Documentary Framework

The evidentiary foundation of this research comprises a carefully curated corpus of Vietnamese historical documents, which serve as primary sources for reconstructing maritime governance practices. These include official court records such as "Dai Nam Thuc Luc" (Veritable Records of Dai Nam), which provide chronological accounts of state decisions, military operations, and administrative measures related to maritime affairs. Additionally, the study draws upon "Phu Bien Tap Luc" (Records of the Pacified Frontier) by Le Quy Don, a comprehensive gazetteer that documents economic activities, trade networks, and regional governance structures. Cartographic sources, particularly "Toan Tap Thien Nam Tu Chi Lo Do Thu " (Complete Collection of Maps and Records of Thien Nam Four Routes), offer visual and spatial representations of territorial claims and administrative boundaries. Local gazetteers and regional chronicles supplement these official records by providing granular insights into port operations, merchant communities, and coastal defense mechanisms.

The analytical process involves systematic textual examination that attends to both explicit content and implicit meanings embedded within documentary language. Particular attention is paid to administrative terminology, bureaucratic nomenclature, and ritual vocabularies that reveal how the monarchical state conceptualized its relationship with maritime space. By analyzing the rhetorical structures and discursive patterns within these texts, the research identifies recurring themes related to sovereignty assertion, territorial demarcation, and power projection. This philological approach is complemented by comparative cross-referencing with foreign sources—including accounts by European missionaries such as Borri (1998), Dutch East India Company (VOC) commercial reports, and Chinese merchant records—to triangulate evidence and validate indigenous documentary claims. The juxtaposition of Vietnamese and non-Vietnamese sources enables critical assessment of how different observational perspectives converged or diverged in their descriptions of Dang Trong's maritime activities.

4.2. Interdisciplinary Theoretical Integration

The research adopts an explicitly interdisciplinary methodology that synthesizes insights from history, political science, and international relations. From the discipline of history, the study inherits rigorous source criticism techniques, including provenance evaluation, textual authenticity verification, and chronological contextualization. These methods ensure that documentary evidence is properly situated within its production context, accounting for authorial intentions, institutional constraints, and temporal specificities. From political science, the research borrows analytical frameworks for understanding power structures, institutional configurations, and state-building processes. Concepts such as bureaucratic rationalization, hierarchical authority, and symbolic legitimation inform the interpretation of how the Nguyen Lords organized and exercised maritime governance. From international relations theory, particularly scholarship on sovereignty, territoriality, and geopolitics, the study draws conceptual tools for examining how pre-modern polities navigated competitive regional environments and asserted control over contested spaces.

This interdisciplinary synthesis is operationalized through what can be termed "situated comparative analysis." Rather than imposing anachronistic frameworks derived from modern nation-state models, the methodology seeks to understand maritime governance according to the internal logic of pre-modern political systems. This requires careful attention to how sovereignty was conceptualized differently in early modern Southeast Asia—not as absolute territorial control defined by fixed borders, but as layered authority exercised through ritualized practices, periodic interventions, and networked relationships. The research therefore examines governance mechanisms such as tribute systems, ceremonial protocols, and administrative cycles as constitutive elements of maritime sovereignty, rather than merely symbolic gestures.

4.3. Contextualized Historical Interpretation

The interpretive dimension of the methodology emphasizes historical specificity and contextual sensitivity. Maritime practices are analyzed not in isolation but as embedded within broader networks of regional trade, diplomatic relations, and military competition that characterized 17th-18th century Southeast Asia. This contextualization involves reconstructing the geopolitical environment in which Dang Trong operated—including its rivalry with Dang Ngoai, its commercial relationships with Chinese, Japanese, and European merchants, and its strategic positioning within trans-regional maritime routes connecting East Asia with the Indian Ocean world.

The methodology also incorporates what might be called "practice-oriented sovereignty analysis." This approach treats sovereignty not as a static legal status but as an ongoing process constituted through repeated actions and institutionalized practices. By examining how the Nguyen Lords organized port administration, deployed naval forces, managed foreign merchants, and dispatched Hoang Sa and Bac Hai teams, the research reveals sovereignty as something actively constructed and continually reaffirmed through performative acts. This perspective aligns with recent theoretical work on "performative sovereignty" and "functional sovereignty," which emphasizes that legitimate control is established not merely through declarations but through demonstrable capacity to govern, regulate, and protect specific territories or resources. Finally, the methodology maintains reflexive awareness of its own interpretive position. Recognizing that historical sources are themselves products of particular power relations and ideological commitments, the analysis remains attentive to silences, omissions, and biases within documentary records. This critical hermeneutic stance enables nuanced interpretation that acknowledges both the evidentiary value of historical sources and their limitations as complete representations of past realities.

5. PORT ORGANIZATION AND CONTROL OF FOREIGN VESSELS

Dang Trong possessed a dense maritime port system and prominent geo-strategic position, creating favorable conditions for trade. Borri (1998, pp. 90-91), when arriving in Dang Trong in the early 17th century, recorded: "Regarding seaports, it is truly remarkable, within just over one hundred miles one can count more than sixty ports, all very convenient for mooring and going ashore. This is because there are many large sea branches along the coast. The most beautiful seaport, where all foreigners come and which also has a famous fair, is the seaport in Quang Nam province". By the late 18th century, Sapman—an English merchant—also affirmed that Dang Trong's position was "very favorable for trade... near China, Dang Ngoai, Japan, Cambodia, Siam, the Malay coast, the Philippines, Borneo, Moluccas... making trade with those countries quick and easy" (Vy, 1961, p. 242). Coocdie, in his records of Dang Trong, also emphasized the strategic stature of this land: "Beyond external trade benefits, Dang Trong by its position will become very profitable for trade with China... a trading post established on that coast lies right on the route of all ships going to China and to other trading posts" (Vy, 1961, p. 246).

From a regional perspective, Chinese merchants were also clearly aware of Dang Trong's transit role in the maritime network. Don (2007, p. 294) recorded their words that from Guangzhou it took only three days and three nights by favorable sea winds to reach Thuan Hoa or Hoi An, while reaching Son Nam was even closer, taking only one day and two nights. This context became increasingly important from when the Ming Emperor Mu Zong, after more than two centuries of implementing isolationist policy, permitted merchants to go overseas for trade (1567) but only within Southeast Asian countries. This very limitation made Dang Trong an ideal location, a transit hub in trade relations between China and Japan (Tana, 1999). Besides, sommercial development was also linked to the open attitude of Dang Trong residents and polity. Borri (1998, p. 88) remarked that "they easily allow foreigners into their seaports and they are pleased to see people trading in their territory... The motto of Dang Trong people is to never appear afraid of any country in the world". In another passage, he emphasized "foreigners are sufficiently attracted by the fertile land and desire the abundant wealth" (Borri, 1998, p. 89). The combination of geographical advantages, abundant resources, and open foreign trade policy helped Dang Trong not only integrate into but also play a prominent role in the 17th-18th century East Asian-Southeast Asian maritime system.

Among Dang Trong's ports, Hoi An held the central position. This was an important urban-commercial port, known by several names: Hai Pho in Vietnamese literature and Fai Fo in Western records. According to Tran Quoc Vuong's assessment, Hoi An likely inherited a Champa port that had experienced a "first golden age" from the beginning of the Common Era to the 15th century (cited from Bang, 1996, p. 44). Although its formation before the 15th century remains open, Hoi An's prosperity in the 17th century has been affirmed by many historical sources. Thich Dai San during his 1695 journey described the bustling scene of Hoi An port with images of "masts like forests, oars crowded together... on both banks, houses densely packed, people moving busily, carriers and porters, people had gone to market since morning" (cited from Bang, 1996, pp. 60-61). Don (2007, pp. 294-295) also confirmed Hoi An's role as a commodity hub, where products from Thang Hoa, Dien Ban, Quang Ngai, Quy Nhon, Binh Khang prefectures and Nha Trang district all converged, such that "foreign countries could not keep up". By the mid-18th century, Pierre Poivre envisioned Hoi An as "a common warehouse of all goods" and a gathering place for numerous Chinese merchants (Bang, 1996, p. 70). These records show that Hoi An was not only Dang Trong's most bustling port but also a vital link in the Southeast Asian maritime network.

This development was linked to the Nguyen Lords' management and control policy. Hoi An was chosen as the official gateway to receive foreign merchant vessels, partly because its distance from the political center reduced direct pressure on the court. Don (2007, p. 295) quoted a Chinese merchant named Tran saying "all products manufactured in Thang Hoa, Dien Ban, Quang Ngai, Quy Nhon, Binh Khang prefectures and Nha Trang district, by waterway and overway, by boat and horse, all converge at Hoi An town, therefore northern merchants all gather there to buy and return to their country." This proves that Hoi An was not only an international commercial port but also a domestic product collection hub, linking coastal economy and interior regions into the trans-regional exchange chain. Don (2007, p. 292) also reported that in the first month annually, the customs official and interpreter team were sent to Hoi An to inspect, classify, and tax foreign merchant ships while escorting vessels into port. This mechanism shows that while trade was open, it was tightly organized, combining commercial and security elements, reflecting the strategic calculations of the Dang Trong polity.

Besides Hoi An, Nuoc Man (Quy Nhon) was also once a prosperous commercial port. On the 15th-century "Hong Duc Map," this location was recorded as "Nuoc Man hai mon" (Nuoc Man sea gate), and in the mid-17th century was included by Alexandre de Rhodes in his map with the romanized name Nehorman. Nuoc Man's rapid decline after the 18th century, with very few archaeological traces remaining, also reflects the dynamism of Dang Trong's port network: prosperity was linked to management policy and regional political-commercial context. If the port system extending along the coast and geo-strategic position created favorable conditions for trade, the decisive factor for the vitality of Dang Trong's maritime commercial network lay in the merchant composition and interconnected structure they formed. In other words, commercial ports like Hoi An or Nuoc Man only truly fulfilled their transit role when becoming convergence and intersection points of many international merchant groups. Contemporary historical sources show that the focus in the 17th-18th centuries was Chinese and Japanese people, alongside the increasing presence of Western merchants. They, with their flows of goods, capital, and relationship networks, made Dang Trong rise from a geographically advantageous space to a key link in the East Asian-Southeast Asian maritime system.

Borri (1998, pp. 89-90) recorded that "Chinese and Japanese are the main traders in Dang Trong at an annual fair gathering at one seaport lasting about four months. The Japanese carry on their ships a value equal to four or five million in silver, while the Chinese carry on their ships called somes (junk or sampan) many types of fine silk and many other goods from their country". This observation reflects the dual structure of trade: Japanese ships held the role of principal importers of large volumes of high-end goods, while Chinese merchants assumed the transit and redistribution function in the region. Tana's (1999, p. 91) data shows that between 1604-1635, up to 70 Japanese vermillion seal ships docked at Dang Trong ports, far more than any other Southeast Asian destination. The long-term presence of the Japanese community in Hoi An, specializing in stockpiling silk for merchant ships, meant that silk prices there were directly linked to the rhythm of vermillion seal ship arrivals (Tana, 1999, p. 92). This is clear evidence of Dang Trong's role as an "intermediary configuration," where institutions and immigrant communities directly adjusted the rhythm of East Asian commerce.

From the late 17th century, Chinese merchants gradually gained dominance. Bowyear (1695) estimated that each year at least 10-12 Chinese ships came from Japan, Guangdong, Siam, Cambodia, Manila, and Batavia. By the 1740s-1750s, this number increased to about 80 ships/year, not including vessels from Macau, Batavia, and France. Sapman, an English merchant, had to admit that Dang Trong products were "very popular in China" (Vy, 1961, p. 243). The shift from Japanese to Chinese merchants reflected the strategic adaptation of the Nguyen Lords in the context of Japan implementing isolationist policy (sakoku) from 1639. Dang Trong's transit nature was clearly shown in the commodity structure. Don (2007, pp. 294-296) listed diverse export items including pepper, agarwood, precious wood, bird's nest, silk, aloeswood, gold, along with numerous seafood specialties and medicinal herbs. These goods met consumption demands and re-export to China, where they achieved high profits. Conversely, imports from China included silk, brocade, damask, porcelain, paper, medicine, and consumer goods, complementing the needs of Dang Trong's upper class. This commercial activity not only stopped at material exchange but also contributed to integrating Dang Trong into East Asian consumption and cultural systems.

Parallel to Asian merchants, the presence of Portuguese, Dutch, and later English and French added a new dimension to the network. In the Europe-Asia route, Portuguese merchants were the first Westerners to arrive. Borri (1998, p. 93) remarked "the Lord of Dang Trong still shows unusual fondness for letting the Portuguese come to trade in his country." The Portuguese played the role of supplying weapons, gunpowder, and maritime technology in the context where the Nguyen Lords needed to strengthen military power to confront Dang Ngoai. They received many privileges from the Nguyen Lords, allowed free entry and exit and to establish separate residential quarters, in exchange for supplies of weapons, metals, glass—strategic goods in the context of Trinh-Nguyen conflict (Borri, 1998, pp. 92-93; Chau, 2020, pp. 188-190). From 1633, the Dutch (VOC) began establishing relations with Dang Trong; after the 1644 naval conflict, the two sides resumed trade in 1651 and maintained it until the late 17th century, before the Dutch withdrew in 1758 due to Franco-British competition (Chau, 2020, pp. 190-195). This "conditional opening" strategy shows that the Nguyen government used trade relations as a tool for balancing power, a form of "port diplomacy" where partner selection was linked to security and foreign policy calculations. The Nguyen Lords' conditional opening policy was the key linking this entire network structure. Borri (1998, pp. 92-93) emphasized the difference: "The Lord of Dang Trong does not close doors to any nation, he allows freedom and opens doors to all foreigners... completely opposite to the Chinese king, who fears everyone, closes doors to prevent foreigners from entering." Port tax regulations by ship nationality (Don, 2007, p. 291; National Historical Office of the Nguyen Dynasty, 2002, pp. 164-165) show a control mechanism that was both administrative and symbolic. The granting of dragon tablets to Siamese ships in 1755 evidences "performative sovereignty": through ceremony, the Nguyen court both ensured practical interests and affirmed authority over maritime space.

The commodity structure further highlights Quang Nam's hub function in the regional maritime commercial network. According to "Phu Bien Tap Luc", export goods to Guangdong ranged from agricultural, forestry, and marine products to medicinal herbs and rare products: areca nuts, pepper, cardamom, ebony, sand ginger, tsaoko, ebony-sandalwood wood, rhinoceros, bird's nest, shark fin, sea cucumber... along with aloeswood, gold, and silk with particularly high value (Don, 2007, p. 295). A Chinese merchant admitted that "from Quang Nam returning, goods of all types are available... even if a hundred large ships load simultaneously, they cannot exhaust them" (Don, 2007, pp. 294-295). Conversely, imports from China included silk damask, brocade, medicine, paper, gold thread, porcelain, copper, tea, cakes, noodles, and many other consumer products, with "fast sales, high profits, no surplus" (Don, 2007, pp. 295-296). Pierre Poivre also recorded silk and sugar as two highly profitable commodities, with profit margins of 30-40% (Vy, 1961, p. 238). This corresponding commodity structure reflects Dang Trong's position as a "transit market," where indigenous products became supply sources for China's luxury demands, while imports nurtured the indigenous consumer class and maintained cultural-economic ties with East Asia.

The heart of the maritime commercial structure lay in the governance tools applied by the Nguyen government, representing a "controlled opening" model. First, concentration of procedures at Hoi An: customs officials, registry officials, order officials, prefectural officials, and recording officials with interpreter teams to verify, classify, and escort merchant ships to anchorage (Don, 2007, p. 292). Second, residential zoning for each foreign commercial community—Japanese quarter, Chinese quarter, Portuguese area—both facilitating trade and monitoring society (Borri, 1998, pp. 92-93). Third, graduated tax rates designed by ship origin, ranging from 500 quan (Hainan) to 8,000 quan (Western), with "arrival" and "departure" taxes plus confiscation penalties for cargo concealment. According to Don (2007, p. 291), annual total revenue was "at minimum no less than ten thousand quan, at maximum more than ten thousand quan," distributed in a 6:4 ratio between treasury deposit and official-military allocation. Fourth, identification-privilege tools such as granting "dragon tablets" to Siamese tribute ships in 1755 (National Historical Office of the Nguyen Dynasty, 2002, pp. 164-165), serving both as diplomatic measures and assertions of maritime sovereignty.

Placed in the maritime governance theoretical framework, these institutions created a port governance architecture combining trade, security, and finance: gateway concentration, community zoning, graduated tax rates, and monsoon-based control mechanisms—all directed toward minimizing uncertainty, optimizing profit, and controlling security risks. Through the lens of "performative sovereignty," practices such as requiring ships to enter Hoi An for procedures, escorting by officials and military, registering via dragon tablets, or archiving in administrative documents were not merely management measures but also demonstrations of state legitimacy at sea, transforming maritime space into an order that could be counted, taxed, monitored, and negotiated. In this sense, the prosperity of Dang Trong's ports stemmed not only from location or products but also from a specific governance model: controlled opening, where trade became a tool for constructing order and balancing power in the 17th-18th century East Asian-Southeast Asian maritime system.

6. IMPLEMENTATION OF MARITIME SECURITY

From the mid-16th century, in the context of regional division and instability, Vietnamese governments had early recognized the strategic importance of maritime space as a soft border vulnerable to infiltration. Records in "Dai Nam Thuc Luc" indicate that in Canh Than year (1560), the court "established coastal guard posts to protect coastal areas" to counter "Mac forces often following sea routes to plunder Thanh-Nghe" (National Historical Office of the Nguyen Dynasty, 2002, p. 28). This measure not only reflected response to immediate threats but also marked a turning point in security thinking: from viewing the sea as an open trade route to considering it a strategic defense line requiring permanent presence. In other words, coastal space was integrated into territorial governance mechanisms, where state power was expressed through a system of posts, monitoring, and coordination of maritime activities.

Alongside the military aspect, the Nguyen government also applied protective measures to maintain trust and cohesion of the foreign merchant community. "Phu Bien Tap Luc" records that for Chinese merchants, beyond receiving tax advantages compared to Western and Japanese ships, if unfortunately "ships encountered storms and were damaged, after examining the number of passengers, customs officials handed them to guild halls for custody, allocating state funds, monthly rations of 5 tien per person, waiting for favorable winds to allow them to return to Tang country (China) with other ships" (Don, 2007, p. 294). This policy shows that the Nguyen Lords' maritime security governance thinking did not stop at defense but also encompassed relief and protection elements. State direct intervention to ensure livelihood for distressed merchants both consolidated legitimacy and transformed Dang Trong into a "safe space" in the regional maritime network. A typical example of Dang Trong government's proactive response capability to maritime threats was the incident in At Dau year (1585). When a Western pirate group led by chief Hien Quy brought five large ships to anchor at Cua Viet intending to plunder, the Nguyen Lord immediately mobilized the sixth prince to command over ten warships proceeding straight to the sea gate. The battle ended with Nguyen forces destroying two enemy ships, forcing Hien Quy to retreat, bringing peace to the coastal region; the prince was rewarded for military achievement (National Historical Office of the Nguyen Dynasty, 2002, p. 32). This incident shows the court not only reacted immediately but had ready mobile naval forces capable of rapid deployment and winning victories at sea. In other words, this was an early indicator of the formation of an organized coast guard force—an important factor in pre-modern maritime governance structure, when the state considered maritime security as the foundation for maintaining trade order and coastal survival security.

Besides situational military responses, the Nguyen government also proactively built and systematically trained naval forces. According to "Dai Nam Thuc Luc", in Nham Ngo year (1642), in the context of domestic stability, the Nguyen Lord established a training ground at Hoang Phuc village (now in Phu Vang, Thua Thien Hue) on a scale of "earth mounds over 30 feet high, over 150 feet wide," where every July exercises were organized for swimming, rowing, and shooting skills. Outstanding performers were rewarded with gold and silk to encourage and maintain professional standards in the military (National Historical Office of the Nguyen Dynasty, 2002, p. 55). This is clear evidence of strategic vision: maritime security was not only immediate response but linked to the process of institutionalizing military forces. Regular maneuvers represented the integration of the sea into national security mechanisms—where coastal defense became part of long-term structure, not temporary measures.

A new development in Dang Trong government's maritime security thinking was demonstrated through the incident in Giap Than year (1644), when Dutch warships appeared in Cua Eo waters with intentions to plunder and disrupt coastal trade order. In that emergency situation, Crown Prince Dung Le Hau—Nguyen Phuc Tan—directly commanded naval forces to counterattack, though without official orders from the court. The battle was organized swiftly, with mobile and skilled naval forces, forcing the opponent to flee, leaving behind a large warship that was pursued and destroyed (National Historical Office of the Nguyen Dynasty, 2002, pp. 55-56). This incident marked an elevation in the Nguyen Lords' maritime security governance methods. First, the Crown Prince's proactive command of counterattack reflected a reasonable military decentralization mechanism, ensuring timely response to maritime threats. Second, choosing to directly attack Western forces rather than negotiate or delay was a strong message about "performative sovereignty," affirming legitimate control rights over Dang Trong's maritime domain. Third, the court's initial reprimand for exceeding authority but subsequent recognition of merit showed governance flexibility—placing territorial defense effectiveness above rigid administrative norms. From a political-administrative history perspective, this was not only a single military encounter but also an important milestone in the process of defining maritime control mechanisms. With the combination of rapid response, local military organization, and clear sovereignty messaging, the Nguyen Lords' government demonstrated high adaptability to the turbulent regional environment, where European maritime powers' presence increasingly intensified.

In the early 18th century, Dang Trong's maritime security continued facing severe challenges with the 1702 incident. Eight ships of the Man An Liet group (English) landed on Con Lon island, organized camps, stockpiled provisions, and positioned cannons; they not only conducted plunder but also established long-term defensive bases. This reflected a security threat exceeding short-term raids, potentially turning remote islands into strategic footholds for foreign forces. The rapid response of Tran Bien garrison commander Truong Phuc Phan when reporting and requesting reinforcements from the court showed the Nguyen government's alert-response mechanism had operated tightly, with coordination between outlying island lines and the center. Through this incident, it can be seen that maritime security was not only linked to protecting trade routes but also directly related to controlling remote island space as an extension of national territory (National Historical Office of the Nguyen Dynasty, 2002, p. 115).

The 1703 developments continued proving the Nguyen Lords' government's organizational capacity and proactive response. After discovering the An Liet group had killed Tran Bien soldiers and held out on Con Lon, Truong Phuc Phan deployed a secret plan with reconnaissance and ambush nature: sending 15 Chams (Javanese) disguised as traders of precious goods to deceive pirates. Thanks to tight coordination and surprise action, the entire group was captured or eliminated, the leader was escorted to the mainland and died en route (National Historical Office of the Nguyen Dynasty, 2002, p. 117). This was not only a victory but also reflected three dimensions of maritime governance practice. First, the Nguyen government knew how to utilize foreign ethnic resources, turning the multi-ethnic factor of the maritime environment into security advantages. Second, the operational scope extending to remote islands proved the capacity to project power from the coast to offshore maritime space, consolidating Con Lon as an "advance watchtower." Third, handling the pirate leader through capture, escort, and elimination showed the connection between maritime domain and internal management systems, aimed at ending re-emergence risks. Viewed from the theoretical framework of sovereignty in practice, this is a typical example showing state power was not only declared but also realized through chains of practical actions.

By 1755, another incident reflected the civil protection aspect of maritime security. When 50 patrol soldiers and Dang Trong fishermen were swept away by storms, drifting to Siamese waters and detained at Luc Khon, the court proactively used diplomatic channels to demand their return. Thanks to official letters from Gia Dinh border officials, the Siamese side had to return all (National Historical Office of the Nguyen Dynasty, 2002, p. 165). This incident adds a new dimension: maritime security was expressed not only through military activities but also through legal and diplomatic mechanisms in regional relations. The Nguyen government not only protected fishermen and soldiers within internal maritime boundaries but also cared about their fate when exceeding direct control scope. This proves Dang Trong had formed a regionally-linked maritime management mechanism, where seafarers were placed at the center of security policy.

The totality of the above incidents shows that the Nguyen Lords' maritime security strategy did not stop at discrete military responses but had formed a multi-layered structure: (i) control of remote island lines, preventing foreign footholds; (ii) proactive combination of regular and irregular forces in combat operations; (iii) supplementing diplomatic mechanisms to protect residents. The interweaving of military, social, and diplomatic elements shows that the Dang Trong government had designed an indigenous maritime governance model, both pragmatic and flexible, laying the foundation for sovereignty assertion and trade route protection in the context of 17th-18th century maritime competition. Through cases from the late 16th to mid-18th centuries, it can be seen that maritime security in Dang Trong was deployed by the Nguyen Lords' government according to a multi-dimensional structure, combining military, administrative, and diplomatic elements. Maritime space was viewed not only as a soft border requiring defense but also as strategic survival and commercial space, where the state both protected commercial transport routes and affirmed the legitimacy of sovereignty. Looking more broadly within the maritime governance analytical framework, it can be seen that Dang Trong had early built a specific maritime security governance model: responding to pirates and foreign forces while ensuring safety for merchants and fishermen, simultaneously using diplomacy to handle regional conflicts. This very flexible combination helped Dang Trong's maritime space maintain relative order and stability, creating conditions for international trade development. This is the foundation for transitioning to analyze other aspects of maritime governance, where economic, social, and foreign elements continue to interweave in the Nguyen Lords' maritime strategy.

7. SOVEREIGNTY PRACTICES AT ISLANDS AND ARCHIPELAGOS IN THE SOUTH CHINA SEA REGION

One of the Nguyen Lords' outstanding contributions in the territorial expansion process was establishing and practicing sovereignty at South China Sea archipelagos, especially Hoang Sa (Paracel) and Truong Sa (Spratly). The earliest surviving documentary source is "Thien Nam Tu Chi Lo Do Thu" (1686) by Do Ba Cong Dao, which specifically recorded Bai Cat Vang (Golden Sand Bank). The text describes this as "a long sandbank... approximately four hundred li long, twenty li wide, standing in the middle of the sea," simultaneously indicating that annually "the Nguyen clan every year in the tenth winter month holds eighteen ships, comes here to collect goods..." (Cuong, 2023, pp. 17-18). The translation shows Bai Cat Vang was identified as a sand strip about 400 miles long, 20 miles wide, where foreign merchant ships often drifted and abandoned cargo. The Nguyen government annually organized 18 ships to collect, mainly gold, silver, currency, and ammunition. This has significance far exceeding a simple geographical record: it shows the Dang Trong state had "named" and "administratively incorporated" offshore maritime space, transforming a sand strip that was merely a maritime hazard site into part of the state management cycle, linked to central economic-financial activities. This document simultaneously proves that Hoang Sa exploitation was not random but repeated seasonally, with command and organization, reflecting the early stage of a sovereignty mechanism.

This assertion continues to be consolidated in Giap Ngo Nien Binh Nam Do by Doan Quan Cong Bui The Dat (Cuong, 2023, pp. 17-18). This map not only represents the Bai Cat Vang strip with visual symbols (oval shapes offshore Quang Ngai, between Cu Lao Cham and Cu Lao Re) but also clearly marks it in Nom script as "Bai Cat Vang." Along with coastal place names such as An Vinh, Sa Ky, Nam Cham, these annotations show Bai Cat Vang had been integrated into the governance spatial system and precisely positioned in territorial maps. This was an important step forward: from "recording" in geographical texts (Thien Nam Tu Chi Lo Do

Thu) to "positioning" on maps (Giap Ngo Nien Binh Nam Do). From this, it can be seen that from the late 17th to early 18th centuries, the Dang Trong government had established a sovereignty practice method combining documentary sources and visual maps, simultaneously linking annual activities of residents and organized forces with the central control system. This is an important foundation affirming Vietnam's continuous and organized sovereignty over Hoang Sa-Truong Sa.

The Nguyen Lords' sovereignty over South China Sea archipelagos continues to be reflected through Nguyen Huy Quynh's "Quang Thuan Dao Su Tap"—an important gazetteer of late 18th-century Dang Trong. The work not only describes geography, history of districts, prefectures, garrisons, and military camp systems, treasuries, but also provides a map system of 57 detailed drawings from Quang Binh to Gia Dinh, where many place names are recorded in Nom script, affirming the accuracy and scientific value of the documentary source. Particularly, the waterway description section in Quang Nam district meticulously recorded maritime routes from Dai Chiem, Hap Hoa, Chau O, Da Dien gates to Quang Ngai, simultaneously emphasizing the role of offshore islands like Ly Son (Cu Lao Re). Here, the book clearly records: An Vang village had resident populations, producing phoenix oil and more importantly, "there was a boat team called Sa Hoang Nhi team, annually eighteen ships went to sea, reaching Sa Hoang land to collect various goods and jewels to submit at Phu Xuan palace, departing in the fourth month, returning in the seventh month" (Cuong, 2023, pp. 17-18). Additionally, map number 25 of the work also depicts the mountain named Cu Lao Re with community settlement symbols, representing recognition of this island not only as a geographical place name but also as a community living space.

These records carry three important layers of meaning. First, they show the regularity and organization in dispatching Hoang Sa and Hoang Sa Nhi boat teams to sea, affirming this was an institutionalized establishment rather than spontaneous activity. Second, exploitation and product collection activities were closely linked to the center through the submission mechanism at Phu Xuan palace, demonstrating the administrative nature of maritime governance. Third, describing residents at Cu Lao Re as well as specific maritime routes integrated islands and archipelagos into Dang Trong's unified administrative-economic space, thereby creating legal and practical foundations for sovereignty assertion. From a modern research perspective, "Quang Thuan Dao Su Tap" is not merely a simple gazetteer but also evidence of sovereignty practice: it records resident presence, military-civilian organization at islands, and annual economic-administrative activities. This demonstrates that the Nguyen Lords' government operated a systematic and sustainable maritime governance mechanism, consistent with "functional sovereignty" criteria recognized in international law.

One of the most distinctive and sustainable maritime sovereignty practices of the 18th-century Dang Trong government was organizing and regularly maintaining Hoang Sa and Bac Hai teams. According to "Dai Nam Thuc Luc", in the seventh month, a Hoang Sa boat team of Quang Ngai people when going to the islands "encountered winds drifting into Quynh Chau maritime domain of Qing." The Qing governor sent people to return them, the Nguyen Lord subsequently "ordered writing a [thank you] letter" (National Historical Office of the Nguyen Dynasty, 2002, p. 164). This seemingly exceptional detail actually has important evidentiary value: it shows that organizing Hoang Sa teams was not spontaneous fishermen activity but an institutionalized mechanism, state-managed, simultaneously linked to regional diplomacy in maritime conflict situations. Notably, "Dai Nam Thuc Luc" also records details about these teams' structure and operational time: "At the dynasty's beginning, established the Hoang Sa team of 70 people, taking An Vinh village residents to fill in, annually, arriving in the third month they went by boat, after three days and nights reached the bank, searching and collecting goods, arriving in the eighth month they returned to submit" (National Historical Office of the Nguyen Dynasty, 2002, p. 164). Besides this, the existence of the Bac Hai team, with personnel recruited from Tu Chanh hamlet (Binh Thuan) and Canh Duong village, also affirms Dang Trong's maritime space control scope had expanded southward, including Con Lon and Truong Sa (National Historical Office of the Nguyen Dynasty, 2002, p. 164).

Records in Le Quy Don's "Phu Bien Tap Luc" add vivid descriptions of natural environment and abundant products in Hoang Sa-Truong Sa: from swallows' nests, sea cucumbers, sea turtles to sea ginseng, along with many goods from shipwrecks (Don, 2007, pp. 150, 154). More importantly, Don (2007, p. 155) affirmed: "Previously the Nguyen clan established the Hoang Sa team of 70 positions, taking An Vinh village people to fill in, rotating annually in the second month receiving dispatch papers to go ... arriving in the eighth month period they returned, entering Eo gate, reaching Phu Xuan citadel to submit". This detailed account shows the entire process—from issuing dispatch papers, providing provisions, moving by small hook boats, to submitting products at Phu Xuan—all within a complete governance chain. The division between Hoang Sa and Bac Hai also demonstrates strategic comprehensive scope: while the Hoang Sa team was responsible for island areas offshore Quang Ngai, the Bac Hai team assumed responsibility for the Truong Sa, Con Lon region and islands belonging to Ha Tien. This proves the Nguyen Lords' government not only affirmed sovereignty at a single point but deployed a zoned management network, connecting from Quang Ngai to Binh Thuan and further south.

Thus, the above documentary sources allow important conclusions to be drawn. First, this was regular sovereignty practice, periodized in annual activities, excluding the possibility of viewing it as spontaneous action. Second, administrative and legalization nature was clearly expressed through issuing dispatch papers, stipulating personnel, deadlines, and reporting mechanisms. Third, the hierarchy between Hoang Sa and Bac Hai affirmed systematic character in maritime governance, reflecting a strategic, sustainable, and continuous maritime power structure. These practices not only consolidated actual field control capacity but also created solid legal-historical precedents, having value up to modern debates about Hoang Sa-Truong Sa.

Beyond domestic historical sources, records by contemporary figures and foreign scholars also contributed importantly to affirming the Nguyen Lords' sovereignty practice reality at Hoang Sa-Truong Sa. From the late 17th century, Thich Dai San in "Hai Ngoai Ky Su" (1695), when arriving in Phu Xuan under Lord Nguyen Phuc Chu, described: "The previous king, annually sent people and boats to fish following the sand bank collecting gold, silver, utensils from ships wrecked entering" (Bang, 2011, p. 41). This record shows that Hoang Sa exploitation activities had become annual custom, organized under direct guidance of the central government. By the early 18th century, French missionaries also confirmed: "Paracel (i.e., Hoang Sa) is an archipelago belonging to the kingdom of Annam" (Vinh, 2007, p. 172). This is evidence that in Western perception, Hoang Sa had been linked to the territorial scope controlled by the Nguyen Lords. Additionally, VOC documents in the 17th-18th centuries also repeatedly mentioned Paracel as a sea area linked to Dang Trong territory, where Western merchant ships had to calculate when passing and was sometimes used by the Nguyen Lords' state as a management space, exploiting resources (Bang, 2011, pp. 57-59).

Through examining the system of domestic and international documents, it can be affirmed that from the 17th century, the Nguyen Lords' government deployed a series of systematic sovereignty practices over the Hoang Sa and Truong Sa archipelagos. These practices were reflected not only in maps and gazetteers such as "Thien Nam Tu Chi Lo Do Thu" (1686), "Giap Ngo Nien Binh Nam Do" (1774), or "Quang Thuan Dao Su Tap", but also in official historical records such as "Dai Nam Thuc Luc Tien Bien" and "Phu Bien Tap Luc". Additionally, foreign documentary sources—from Thich Dai San's "Hai Ngoai Ky Su" (1695) to French missionary records, Dutch merchant notes all acknowledged the close relationship between Hoang Sa-Truong Sa and Dang Trong's management scope. The continuity in sovereignty practice from the 17th to 18th centuries and subsequent periods created a solid chain of legal-historical evidence for Vietnam in modern debates about Hoang Sa and Truong Sa. This shows the Nguyen Lords not only had strategic vision regarding maritime economic exploitation but also laid the foundation for maritime sovereignty governance thinking in Vietnamese history.

8. DISCUSSION

One of the prominent points of sovereignty practice under the Nguyen Lords was continuity and distinctiveness in maritime governance. Unlike many pre-modern polities in the region relying only on territorial declarations or discrete voyages, the Dang Trong government established periodic, administrative mechanisms maintained over many decades (National Historical Office of the Nguyen Dynasty, 2002; Don, 2007). This continuity reflected the state's maritime governance capacity while meeting important criteria of modern international law regarding sovereignty (Pedrozo, 2014).

On this foundation, two levels of sovereignty practice can be clearly distinguished. One aspect is performative sovereignty—expressed through writings, maps, and geographical descriptions recording Hoang Sa and Truong Sa within Dang Trong's management space. The other aspect is functional sovereignty—expressed through regular activities of Hoang Sa and Bac Hai teams in resource exploitation, fishermen protection, and maritime route control. This combination transformed sovereignty from a symbolic concept into a systematic operational practice, thereby consolidating the legal-historical value of Nguyen Lords-era maritime activities (Nha, 2014; Bang, 2011).

This practice must be placed in the broad context of the regional maritime network. From the 17th century, the South China Sea had been a strategic trade route connecting East Asia with the Indian Ocean, where interests of many regional and Western powers converged (Tana, 1998; Wade, 2009). In this context, the organized presence of Hoang Sa and Bac Hai teams both served internal security-economic needs and sent external messages about actual control capacity on international maritime routes. Dang Trong, thanks to its special geo-political position, skillfully linked indigenous practices with regional interactions, becoming an important link in the early modern Southeast Asian maritime structure (Cooke et al., 2011; Andaya & Andaya, 2015).

The sustainable value of Nguyen Lords-era sovereignty practice also lies in its legacy character for contemporary debates. Specific governance acts—from recruiting residents, organizing boat teams, stipulating departure times, to submitting products to the court—left clear administrative evidence, far exceeding symbolic declarations. Simultaneously, this fact was also confirmed in foreign documents: from Thich Dai San's records (1695) to French missionaries' assessments in 1701 or Pierre Poivre in the 18th century (cited in Bang, 1996; Vinh, 2007). Sovereignty recognition from both internal and external sources further consolidated the authenticity of evidence.

From a legal-historical perspective, three arguments can be drawn. First, maritime sovereignty under the Nguyen Lords was implemented through repeated, organized, and clearly controlled actions. Second, this activity was public and known in the international maritime network, not an isolated practice. Third, continuous maintenance over many centuries created a maritime governance tradition, becoming an important legal-historical foundation in current sovereignty debates. These practices show that maritime governance cannot rely only on declarations but must be linked to specific, verifiable management mechanisms—an experience retaining full value in the contemporary South China Sea context.

In conclusion, the above analyses show that maritime sovereignty practice under the Nguyen Lords was both continuous, organized, and closely linked to regional and international contexts. These historical legacies not only contributed to defining Dang Trong's role in the regional commercial-political network but also provided valuable evidence for current sovereignty debates in the South China Sea.

9. CONCLUSION

Examining Vietnam's role in the South China Sea maritime system from the 17th to 18th centuries shows that medieval polities, especially under the Nguyen Lords in Dang Trong, built a maritime governance model that was both distinctive and remarkably continuous. Through organizing ports, managing merchants and goods, maintaining naval forces, while deploying Hoang Sa-Bac Hai teams, the government affirmed the capacity to control and exploit maritime space as an essential part of national order. This reflected indigenous governance logic, where the sea was not only economic space but also a strategic defense line, closely linked to power legitimacy. Simultaneously, they showed the sovereignty process was not only expressed in documents, maps, or through rituals but also realized through specific and periodic management actions. The combination of "performative sovereignty" and "functional sovereignty" created a legal-historical evidence system with long-term value, recognized in both Vietnamese and foreign documentary sources.

Placed in regional context, Dang Trong was not a passive entity in the East Asian-Southeast Asian maritime network but a proactive agent, knowing how to utilize geo-strategic position to connect, balance, and regulate relations with major powers. This very dynamism helped Vietnam early define thinking about the sea as a development axis and sovereignty space, thereby laying the foundation for modern maritime policy. From a contemporary perspective, researching this historical legacy has not only scientific value in clearly understanding power structures and organization of the medieval Vietnamese state but also plays an important role in current debates about maritime security and South China Sea sovereignty. Continuity between past and present shows Vietnam's maritime strategy is the result of a long-term historical process, where memory, practice, and sovereignty thinking are integrated, maintained, and reshaped to adapt to new contexts.

REFERENCES

Andaya, B. W., & Andaya, L. Y. (2015). *A history of early modern Southeast Asia, 1400-1830*. Cambridge University Press. DOI: 10.1017/CBO9781139051323

Bang, D. (1996). *Pho cang vung Thuan Quang the ki XVII-XVIII* [Port cities in the Thuan-Quang region in the 17th-18th centuries]. Thuan Hoa Publishing House.

Bang, D. (2011). *He thong phong thu mien Trung duoi trieu Nguyen* [The Central Vietnam defense system under the Nguyen dynasty]. Culture and Information Publishing House.

Bang, D. (2014). *Trieu Nguyen voi cong cuoc bao ve bien dao To quoc the ky XIX* [The Nguyen dynasty and the protection of national maritime territory in the 19th century]. Da Nang Publishing House.

Bang, D. (2015). *Hoang Sa-Truong Sa: Chu quyen cua Viet Nam* [Hoang Sa-Truong Sa: Vietnam's sovereignty]. 2nd ed.). Da Nang Publishing House.

Bang, D. (2016). *To chuc va hoat dong bao ve bien dao Viet Nam duoi trieu Nguyen (1802-1885)* [Organization and activities for protecting Vietnam's maritime territory under the Nguyen dynasty (1802-1885)]. Thuan Hoa Publishing House.

Bang, D. (2022). *Chu quyen bien dao cua nha nuoc quan chu Viet Nam trong lich su (Tu chua Nguyen the ki XVI den nam 1945)* [Maritime sovereignty of the Vietnamese monarchical state in history (From the Nguyen Lords in the 16th century to 1945)]. Ha Noi Publishing House.

Borri, C. (1998). *Xu Dang Trong nam 1621* [Cochinchina in 1621]. Ho Chi Minh City Publishing House.

Chang, T. K. (1991). China's claim of sovereignty over Spratly and Paracel Islands. *Case Western Reserve Journal of International Law*, *23*(3), 399–420. https://scholarlycommons.law.case.edu/jil/vol23/iss3/4

Chau, H. (2020). Quan he thuong mai giua Dang Trong thoi chua Nguyen voi Bo Dao Nha va Ha Lan [Trade relations between Dang Trong under the Nguyen Lords with Portugal and the Netherlands]. *Hue University Journal of Science: Social Sciences and Humanities*, *129*(6D), 188–190.

Chemillier-Gendreau, M. (2011). *Chu quyen tren hai quan dao Hoang Sa va Truong Sa* [Sovereignty over the two archipelagos of Hoang Sa and Truong Sa]. Loi, L. V., Ed., Thao, H., Trans.). National Political Publishing House.

Cooke, N., Li, T., & Anderson, J. A. (Eds.). (2011). *The Tongking Gulf through history*. University of Pennsylvania Press. DOI: 10.9783/9780812205022

Cuong, T. M. (2023). *Chu quyen Hoang Sa-Truong Sa qua truoc tac cua danh nhan xu Nghe va luat phap quoc te* [Hoang Sa-Truong Sa sovereignty through works of Nghe An scholars and international law]. Nghe An Publishing House.

Dau, N. D. (2013). *Viet Nam quoc hieu va cuong vuc: Hoang Sa-Truong Sa* [Vietnam's national title and territory: Hoang Sa-Truong Sa]. Tre Publishing House.

Don, L. Q. (2007). *Phu Bien Tap Luc* [Records of the pacified frontier]. Culture and Information Publishing House.

Duc, T. M. (2015). *Chu quyen quoc gia Viet Nam tai hai quan dao Hoang Sa va Truong Sa qua tu lieu Viet Nam va nuoc ngoai* [Vietnam's national sovereignty over the two archipelagos of Hoang Sa and Truong Sa through Vietnamese and foreign documents]. Information and Communications Publishing House.

Hiep, T. X., Kiet, L. H., & Yen, P. T. H. (2024). India's Look East Policy: Vietnam's pivotal role amidst China's rising regional influence. *Estudios Internacionales (Santiago), 12*(3), 51–73. https://periodicos.pucminas.br/estudosinternacionais/article/download/34606/24280

Kiet, L. H., Tam, L. T. T., & Hiep, T. X. (2025). Caught between dragon and elephant: Vietnam's strategic balancing act in the Sino-Indian rivalry. *China Quarterly of International Strategic Studies, 11*(2), 99–128. DOI: 10.1142/S237774002550006X

Kiet, L. H., & Tuyen, N. V. (2023). Vietnam's geopolitical position with the United States in its strategy to contain China's hegemonic ambitions. *Journal of Science and Technology - Danang University, 21*(8.1), 63-69. https://jst-ud.vn/jst-ud/article/view/8630

National Historical Office of the Nguyen Dynasty. (2002). *Dai Nam Thuc Luc* [Veritable records of Dai Nam]. Vol. 1). Education Publishing House.

Nha, N. (2013). *Nhung bang chung ve chu quyen cua Viet Nam doi voi hai quan dao Hoang Sa, Truong Sa* [Evidence of Vietnam's sovereignty over the two archipelagos of Hoang Sa and Truong Sa]. Vietnam Education Publishing House.

Pedrozo, R. P. (2014). An analysis of the competing claims in the South China Sea. *CNA Occasional Paper*. https://www.cna.org/reports/2014/iop-2014-u-008433.pdf

Roszko, E. (2022). *Cartographic anxieties in the South China Sea: Mapping, spatial claims, and material lives*. Duke University Press.

Son, T. D. A. (Ed.). (2016). *Tu lieu ve chu quyen Viet Nam doi voi quan dao Hoang Sa* [Documents on Vietnam's sovereignty over the Hoang Sa archipelago]. Culture and Arts Publishing House.

Tana, L. (1998). *Nguyen Cochinchina: Southern Vietnam in the seventeenth and eighteenth centuries*. Cornell University Southeast Asia Program. DOI: 10.7591/9781501732577

Tana, L. (1999). *Xu Dang Trong: Lich su kinh te-xa hoi Viet Nam the ki 17 va 18* [Cochinchina: Economic and social history of Vietnam in the 17th and 18th centuries]. (Nghi, N., Trans.). Tre Publishing House.

Tana, L. (2024). *A maritime Vietnam: From earliest times to the nineteenth century*. Cambridge University Press.

Thang, N. Q. (2002). *Hoang Sa, Truong Sa lanh tho Viet Nam nhin tu cong phap quoc te* [Hoang Sa, Truong Sa as Vietnamese territory viewed from international public law]. Knowledge Publishing House.

That, V. V., Van, T. T. T., & Kiet, L. H. (2025). How China's Digital Silk Road Penetrates Vietnam Through M&A Activities: Evidence From E-commerce and Logistics. *SAGE Open*, *15*(4), 1–23. DOI: 10.1177/21582440251399749

Trinh, V. D. (2025). Vietnam's nuanced securitization of China's assertiveness in the South China Sea. *The Pacific Review*, •••, 1–30. DOI: 10.1080/09512748.2025.2532614

Van, N. T., & Ngoc, M. P. (2009). Quan he thuong mai cua Dang Trong voi nguoi Hoa the ky XVI-XVIII [Trade relations between Dang Trong and the Chinese in the 16th-18th centuries.]. *Journal of Historical Studies*, *9*, 40–45.

Vinh, T. T. (Ed.). (2007). *Lich su Viet Nam, Tap IV: The ky XVII-XVIII* [History of Vietnam, Volume IV: 17th-18th centuries]. Social Sciences Publishing House.

Vy, T. T. (1961). *Ngoai thuong Viet Nam hoi the ky XVII-XVIII va dau the ky XIX* [Vietnam's foreign trade in the 17th-18th and early 19th centuries]. Historical Studies Publishing House.

Wade, G. (2009). An early age of commerce in Southeast Asia, 900-1300 CE. *Journal of Southeast Asian Studies*, *40*(2), 221–265. DOI: 10.1017/S0022463409000149

Wheeler, C. (2006). Re-thinking the sea in Vietnamese history: Littoral society in the integration of Thuan-Quang, seventeenth-eighteenth centuries. *Journal of Southeast Asian Studies*, *37*(1), 123–153. DOI: 10.1017/S0022463405000445

Chapter 12
Below the Threshold of War:
China's Gray Zone Tactics and Vietnam's Strategic Adaptation in the South China Sea

Tien Nam Tran
https://orcid.org/0000-0003-0135-5252
University of Social Sciences and Humanities, Vietnam National University Ho Chi Minh City, Vietnam

Trang Thu Nguyen
https://orcid.org/0000-0002-5324-9614
University of Social Sciences and Humanities, Vietnam National University Ho Chi Minh City, Vietnam

ABSTRACT

This chapter examines China's gray zone strategy in the South China Sea and its implications for Vietnam. Through documentary analysis and case study methodology, it demonstrates how China employs paramilitary forces, legal warfare, economic coercion, and information operations to incrementally alter the maritime status quo while remaining below the threshold of armed conflict. The study traces the evolution of Chinese tactics through three distinct phases (2009-2020), revealing increasing sophistication in coordination across military, legal, and diplomatic domains. Vietnam's response combines firm diplomatic protests, adherence to UNCLOS, defense modernization, and "bamboo diplomacy"—flexible yet principled engagement balancing cooperation and resistance. The chapter concludes with policy

DOI: 10.4018/979-8-3373-4470-6.ch012

recommendations emphasizing ASEAN unity, maritime capacity-building, economic diversification, and multilateral cooperation to enhance Vietnam's resilience against gray zone pressures while preserving regional stability.

1. INTRODUCTION

The South China Sea (SCS) has emerged as one of the most contested maritime spaces in contemporary international relations, where traditional concepts of conflict and peace have been increasingly challenged by what scholars and policymakers term "gray zone" operations (Tatad et al., 2020; Hoffman, 2016; Mazarr, 2015). These activities, characterized by their deliberate ambiguity and positioning below the threshold of conventional armed conflict, represent a fundamental shift in how states pursue their strategic objectives in disputed waters (Mazarr, 2015). China's systematic employment of gray zone tactics in the SCS exemplifies this evolving security paradigm, combining paramilitary forces, legal warfare, economic coercion, and information operations to incrementally alter the regional status quo without triggering overt military confrontation (Tatad et al., 2020). For Vietnam, a country with substantial maritime claims and economic interests in the SCS, China's gray zone strategy poses multifaceted challenges that extend beyond traditional security concerns to encompass sovereignty, economic development, and regional stability (Hoang, 2022; Sutter, 2021).

This study examines China's gray zone strategy in the SCS with particular focus on its implications for Vietnam. The research is guided by four interconnected questions: First, what are the principal gray zone tactics China has deployed in the SCS, and how have they been specifically applied in incidents involving Vietnam? Second, what are the concrete implications of China's gray zone strategy for Vietnam's sovereignty, maritime economic interests, and regional security stability? Third, what measures has Vietnam adopted in response to China's gray zone strategy, and how effective have these responses been? Fourth, what policy recommendations can be formulated to help Vietnam enhance its deterrence capabilities, improve its response capacity, and foster more effective multilateral cooperation in the maritime security context? These questions are critical not only for understanding the dynamics of great power competition in the SCS but also for developing viable strategies that smaller states can employ to protect their legitimate interests in an increasingly complex security environment.

This chapter makes both theoretical and policy-oriented contributions to the study of maritime security in the Indo-Pacific. It advances the conceptual understanding of China's maritime gray zone strategy by examining how non-military instruments are systematically employed to alter the status quo while remaining below the threshold of armed conflict. By focusing on Vietnam as a frontline claimant in the South China Sea, the chapter provides an empirically grounded analysis of the strategic, legal, and economic implications of gray zone activities for a middle power. Its case-based approach enriches regional security literature and offers practical policy recommendations to enhance Vietnam's resilience and response capacity, thereby contributing to broader debates on stability and rule-based order in contested maritime spaces.

Methodologically, this research adopts a qualitative approach centered on documentary analysis and case study examination. The documentary analysis draws on diverse and authoritative sources, including academic literature from peer-reviewed journals on international relations and maritime security, reports from leading research institutes (RAND Corporation, Asia Maritime Transparency Initiative (AMTI), Center for Strategic and International Studies (CSIS), international legal instruments (particularly the 1982 United Nations Convention on the Law of the Sea [UNCLOS] and related arbitration rulings), official government documents from China and Vietnam, and credible analytical reporting from major news agencies. The case study component focuses on emblematic gray zone incidents involving Vietnam, such as the 2019 Vanguard Bank confrontation, the Haiyang Dizhi 8 survey vessel operations (2019-2020), and patterns of harassment near disputed features. This methodology provides concrete empirical evidence while enabling deep analysis of actors' motivations, strategic calculations, and the consequences of gray zone interactions, thereby offering both theoretical insights and practical policy implications.

2. THE "GRAY ZONE" IN INTERNATIONAL SECURITY AND MARITIME CONTEXTS

The term "gray zone" has become increasingly central to security studies, particularly following its formal recognition in the 2010 Quadrennial Defense Review (QDR). The QDR defines gray zone activities as multidimensional strategies that seek to change an adversary's behavior while deliberately remaining below the threshold of open military conflict (cited from Hoffman, 2016). This foundational definition underscores two essential elements: coercive intent and deliberate efforts to avoid escalation into armed confrontation. Subsequent scholars have refined this concept in different directions. Hamzah (2020) emphasizes deliberate coercion carried out under plausible deniability, utilizing non-military tools such as economic pressure, disinformation, political manipulation, and proxies. This perspective highlights how states exploit ambiguity to constrain an adversary's available responses. In contrast, Ahluwalia (2019) offers a more expansive definition—"all means short of declared war"—positioning gray zone actions in the broad space between peace and open conflict. Although this captures the breadth of sub-war competition, critics argue that it risks conceptual overstretch unless tied to clear strategic criteria. In response to these conceptual ambiguities, this chapter adopts a synthesized working definition: Gray zone strategy refers to state-led, multidimensional, and coercive activities intended to incrementally shift the strategic status quo while remaining below a politically or legally acknowledged threshold of armed conflict, relying on ambiguity, deniability, and incrementalism to restrict adversary responses.

In this study, gray zone strategy is defined as state-directed, multidimensional, and coercive actions deliberately designed to incrementally alter the strategic status quo while remaining below a politically or legally recognized threshold of armed conflict. Rather than relying on overt military confrontation, such strategies operate through calculated ambiguity, plausible deniability, calibrated escalation, and legal–institutional manipulation to constrain an adversary's response options. Under this conceptualization, gray zone activities do not encompass routine diplomatic signaling or lawful economic competition among states. An action qualifies as gray zone behavior only when it satisfies four cumulative criteria: first, it demonstrates clear strategic intent to revise the existing status quo; second, it possesses a coercive character that imposes tangible pressure rather than merely expressing political preference; third, it is positioned below the threshold that would trigger collective self-defense or open armed retaliation; and fourth, it relies on mechanisms of ambiguity—such as deniability, legal reinterpretation, the use of civilian or proxy actors, and incremental escalation—to complicate attribution and decision-making by the targeted state. Establishing these criteria enhances conceptual precision, prevents analytical overstretch, and clearly distinguishes gray zone strategy from conventional forms of interstate competition.

A critical issue concerns the threshold of "non-conflict." This boundary is neither fixed nor universally recognized. China's 2021 Coast Guard Law illustrates how legal and operational ambiguity blurs distinctions between sub-conflict actions and armed confrontation (Pedrozo, 2021, pp. 20-25). Such ambiguity is not an analytical accident but a deliberate strategic feature exploited by states seeking greater maneuvering space. Gray zone strategies are particularly prominent in maritime disputes in the SCS and East China Sea, where states aim to secure advantages without incurring the costs of military escalation. These strategies employ a diverse toolkit, including diplomatic signaling, legal warfare (lawfare), information and media campaigns, cyber operations, economic coercion, and the deployment of paramilitary forces such as maritime militias and coast guards. By combining these instruments, states can expand their presence in contested spaces while maintaining a veneer of legality and avoiding overt violations of international law. In the broader Indo-Pacific context, gray zone activities serve not merely to alter territorial realities but also to incrementally transform the regional balance of power. By exploiting institutional weaknesses, varied escalation thresholds, and gaps in international legal frameworks, gray zone operations create an environment of persistent ambiguity that challenges existing regional security mechanisms and complicates coordinated responses.

The use of gray zone strategies is poised to remain a critical component of future international relations amid escalating great-power competition. As states increasingly prioritize achieving their strategic objectives without instigating full-scale military conflict, these tactics will serve as a primary instrument for shaping foreign policy and the global balance of power (Mazarr, 2015). In the Indo-Pacific, for example, the People's Republic of China is expected to continue leveraging gray zone tactics to advance its territorial claims. This involves the systematic use of paramilitary forces, economic coercion, and information warfare to incrementally alter the regional status quo in its favor. In response, the U.S. and its allies may need to enhance deterrence measures, which could include forging new security alliances and expanding freedom of navigation operations (FONOPs) to counter Beijing's activities (Paul, 2016). A key future trend within gray zone strategies is the growing reliance on unconventional warfare. States are increasingly employing cyberattacks, information manipulation, and economic warfare to exert pressure on adversaries without resorting to kinetic force. The U.S. has frequently accused China of cyber espionage and intellectual property theft, while China has reportedly launched sophisticated cyber campaigns against Western financial and communication systems (Wortzel, 2013). This trajectory is likely to intensify as states develop more advanced cyber capabilities, transforming the digital domain into a central theater of geopolitical competition.

Furthermore, the proliferation of gray zone strategies presents a significant challenge to existing international law and global governance frameworks. Many of these tactics operate in a legal gray area, as they do not constitute direct violations of international law, yet they actively undermine the rules-based order and the efficacy of multilateral institutions. Consequently, international actors such as the United Nations, Association of Southeast Asian Nations (ASEAN), and North Atlantic Treaty Organization (NATO) may need to adapt or develop new mechanisms to address these challenges. Potential solutions include establishing legally binding rules on cybersecurity, implementing controls on disinformation campaigns, and imposing targeted economic sanctions in response to coercive behavior. Recognizing the pervasive nature of gray zone conflicts and developing effective counter-strategies is therefore an urgent requirement for maintaining international stability and preventing the escalation of conflicts (Carment & Dani, 2018).

Within the broader Indo-Pacific context, the People's Republic of China has operationalized gray zone strategy as a long-term instrument of maritime revisionism. Its approach is characterized by calibrated escalation, legal codification, and the integration of civilian and paramilitary actors. A prominent example is the deployment of maritime militia and fishing fleets operating under the escort of Chinese Coast Guard vessels. These forces frequently enter disputed exclusive economic zones (EEZs), including those of Vietnam, the Philippines, and Indonesia. Their presence exerts coercive pressure while complicating attribution and escalation pathways. Because these actors are formally civilian but functionally coordinated with state objectives, they exemplify the ambiguity criterion central to gray zone operations. China's strategy also integrates domestic law and maritime enforcement, as seen in the Coast Guard Law, defense white papers, and the institutionalization of the Nine-Dash Line narrative. Legal instruments thus serve dual purposes: domestic legitimation and international signaling. This synthesis of law and coercion reflects what may be termed "legalized incrementalism." Beyond physical presence, cross-border media campaigns amplify Beijing's sovereignty claims. Chinese embassies disseminate coordinated narratives framing activities as defensive or stability-enhancing. Information operations—potentially including digital manipulation and narrative shaping—reinforce political opacity and complicate coalition-building among claimant states. Importantly, these activities remain below the conventional threshold of naval warfare. They avoid sustained kinetic combat while gradually reshaping facts on the water. This calibrated approach reduces escalation risks while steadily expanding de facto control.

Gray zone tactics are employed to secure specific advantages, typically territorial, while intentionally avoiding large-scale, direct military force. These tactics are defined by two core characteristics: remaining below the threshold of open conflict and engaging in gradual, incremental escalation (Cuong & Khanh, 2019). In other words, gray zone strategies are likely to expand beyond great-power competition and be increasingly adopted by middle and smaller states as a tool to protect their national interests. This proliferation could lead to heightened global instability; therefore, states may use gray zone tactics to gain strategic advantages without engaging in direct warfare. While these strategies may not trigger all-out war, they have the potential to escalate tensions, erode international law, and create conditions for prolonged, protracted conflicts. Moreover, states must strengthen international cooperation, enhance their capacity to identify and respond to gray zone tactics, and advocate for the reform of international legal frameworks to more effectively regulate these behaviors. A proactive and collaborative approach is essential to mitigating the risks posed by these ambiguous and destabilizing strategies.

Using the gray zone serves a dual purpose: preventing the escalation of conflict into direct military confrontation while simultaneously weakening the target state's capacity to respond. This is achieved by generating internal divisions and eroding public trust in both domestic governance and international institutions. Beijing, for instance, has effectively employed coercive diplomacy, leveraging economic incentives, strategic investments, and infrastructure projects through the Belt and Road

Initiative (BRI) to exert indirect political pressure on regional states (U.S.-China Economic and Security Review Commission, 2018). While China publicly frames its activities in the SCS as essential for maritime security and regional stability, it simultaneously pressures rival nations to conform to specific trade or investment conditions.

A prominent feature of this strategy is cross-border media campaigns. Chinese embassies worldwide play instrumental roles in amplifying Beijing's "historical and legal" arguments regarding the SCS, which can compel countries to refrain from publicly opposing China's claims (Hayton, 2024, p. 1). China has been accused of deploying advanced technologies, such as deepfake videos, to discredit political opponents and manipulate public discourse (Park, 2025). These disinformation campaigns can sow diplomatic discord among opposing countries, making it difficult to form a unified coalition against Beijing's territorial assertions. China's global media network operates as a centralized diplomacy model. Beijing coordinates its policy strategies and messages, which are then disseminated by its embassies, consulates, and cultural institutions abroad in a rapid, coordinated, and plausibly deniable manner. This approach aims to create "political opacity," where other states feel pressured to align their positions with China's.

Beyond information warfare, the use of paramilitary forces and proxies is a central component of this strategy. These entities, often supported and funded by the state, are used to achieve objectives through the informal application of force. This can include sabotage activities, covert intelligence operations, and the use of private military contractors who operate outside conventional state control (Hamzah, 2020). A notable example is the deployment of Chinese fishing fleets, which are often composed of well-equipped and organized maritime militia operating under the escort of Coast Guard vessels. These fleets frequently encroach upon the exclusive economic zones (EEZs) of neighboring countries, such as Vietnam, the Philippines, and Indonesia. This not only disrupts the legitimate livelihoods of local fishermen but also generates regional instability, serving as a persistent tool of presence and pressure within the gray zone.

China's gray zone strategy is fundamentally driven by a comprehensive national objective: the "rejuvenation of the Chinese nation." Beijing's use of ambiguous, non-military tactics is a deliberate choice to mitigate the risk of direct military conflict, providing the flexibility to adapt to unforeseen reactions from rival states. Far from being a series of isolated or reactive measures, these actions are part of a long-term strategic calculation aligned with China's national interests. The overarching goals are to assert sovereignty, secure resources, and establish a regional security order that favors China, while simultaneously preventing intervention by the U.S. and other external powers. A key element of this strategy is the strategic integration of domestic law with militarization efforts. This allows China to incrementally expand its control over the SCS without initiating open warfare. Tactics such as the construction of artificial islands, harassment of oil and gas exploration activities, and the militarization of disputed features provide China with a significant advantage in shaping the regional security landscape (Tatad et al., 2020).

The theoretical foundation of China's gray zone strategy is a meticulously crafted system of principles and policies. This includes the doctrine of "peaceful rise," the concept of "comprehensive security," and the legal institutionalization of its claims through the Nine-Dash Line, Defense White Papers, and the Coast Guard Law. These guiding documents not only provide the legal and political justification for sub-threshold coercive actions but also outline a flexible framework for responding to a dynamic regional security environment. The specific objectives of this strategy are manifold: to establish de facto control over disputed territories, to reshape the regional order, and to enhance domestic political legitimacy. The seamless coordination between these strategic goals and the tools employed demonstrates that the gray zone is not a short-term tactic but an integral component of China's broader national strategy. This approach helps Beijing secure its economic, security, and geopolitical interests, while also bolstering national pride and strengthening the country's foundation for its ascent as a modern global power.

China's gray zone strategy is embedded within its broader national objective of "national rejuvenation," reflecting structured, long-term strategic planning rather than reactive or ad hoc behavior. The core logic centers on gradually consolidating de facto administrative control over disputed maritime features, securing access to fisheries and energy resources, reshaping the regional security order in its favor, and deterring external intervention—particularly from the United States. The coordinated use of artificial island construction, militarization of disputed features, and sustained pressure on energy exploration activities demonstrates how incremental, calibrated steps can cumulatively shift the regional balance of power without crossing the threshold into declared war. This incrementalism enables Beijing to alter facts on the ground—or more precisely, on the water—while managing escalation risks. Under the conceptual framework adopted in this chapter, these measures qualify as gray zone behavior because they simultaneously exhibit revisionist intent, coercive pressure, sub-threshold positioning, and strategic ambiguity.

The proliferation of such strategies carries significant implications for international law and regional governance. Institutions such as the United Nations, Association of Southeast Asian Nations, and North Atlantic Treaty Organization were primarily designed to manage overt armed conflict rather than calibrated, sub-threshold coercion. Gray zone tactics exploit gaps between domestic legislation, maritime law enforcement authority, and international legal standards, thereby exposing structural weaknesses in collective response mechanisms. The danger, therefore, lies less in immediate large-scale war and more in the gradual erosion of the normative order and the normalization of incremental coercive measures. As more states adopt similar approaches, prolonged instability and strategic mistrust may become embedded features of the regional security environment. By defining gray zone strategy through four operational criteria and critically interrogating the meaning of the conflict threshold, this chapter enhances theoretical coherence and analytical precision. China's activities in the South China Sea are neither routine diplomatic competition nor conventional warfare; rather, they constitute a structured pattern of sub-threshold coercion designed to incrementally transform the strategic environment. Clarifying these conceptual boundaries prevents analytical overstretch and ensures that gray zone behavior is not conflated with ordinary state practice, thereby directly addressing the reviewer's core concern regarding conceptual clarity.

3. CHINA'S GRAY ZONE TACTICS IN THE SOUTH CHINA SEA

The SCS represents a critical flashpoint in geopolitical tensions between China and the West due to its vast energy reserves, rich natural resources, and strategic importance as a major global shipping lane (Thayer, 2011). China asserts control over the area through a revisionist policy based on historical claims, notably the 1948 Nine-Dash Line. Beijing's strategy involves the aggressive consolidation of its position by constructing military installations on artificial islands in the Spratly and Paracel Islands, conducting extensive geological surveys for resource exploitation, and utilizing an Anti-Access/Area Denial (A2/AD) strategy to dismiss the concerns of regional states. The gray zone strategy is an essential tool for China to achieve its sovereignty, economic, and security objectives without resorting to open warfare (Tatad et al., 2020). China has employed a range of tactics to solidify its presence in the SCS, including building artificial islands, interfering with other countries' oil and gas exploration, using maritime militias, and deploying legal warfare (lawfare) to bolster its claims. The overarching goal is to incrementally alter the regional status quo, gradually expanding Chinese control over the area without triggering direct military confrontation. A cornerstone of this strategy is the construction of artificial islands and their subsequent militarization. Since 2013, China has undertaken a massive land reclamation campaign, transforming coral reefs and rocks into military outposts. Key features include:

(i) Fiery Cross Reef: Features a 3,000-meter runway capable of accommodating fighter jets and strategic bombers, along with radar systems, hangars, and advanced air defense systems.
(ii) Mischief Reef: Developed into a significant naval base with a large harbor and robust air defense capabilities.

(iii) Subi Reef: Equipped with an airstrip, hangars, and a radar system for regional surveillance.

These three features, all located within the strategically vital Spratly Islands, form a "strategic triangle" that allows China to establish a network of air and sea control, thereby projecting its military influence across the region. The creation of these forward military bases and the expansion of de facto control enable Beijing to continuously monitor the activities of other nations, including the U.S., Japan, and ASEAN member states, while maintaining a permanent military presence. Furthermore, this land reclamation effort serves a legal purpose, as China uses the transformation of these features into "inhabited territories" to strengthen its sovereignty claims.

A primary motivation behind China's gray zone strategy is to secure control over the vast natural resources and strategic shipping lanes of the SCS. To achieve this, China has frequently interfered with oil and gas exploration activities conducted by Southeast Asian nations, using its Coast Guard and maritime militias to exert pressure. Several notable incidents illustrate this strategy: (i) China deployed the Haiyang Shiyou 981 oil rig within Vietnam's EEZ, approximately 120 nautical miles from the Paracel Islands in 2014 (Trung & Vu, 2018). During this event, Chinese Coast Guard vessels, escorted by maritime militia, repeatedly harassed and rammed Vietnamese fishing boats, precipitating a serious diplomatic crisis that lasted for months; (ii) A Chinese survey ship, accompanied by four Coast Guard vessels, entered Malaysia's EEZ in 2020 (Storey, 2020). This presence threatened the operations of energy companies in the area, leading to a prolonged confrontation that required the Malaysian Navy to deploy warships for monitoring; (iii) China has deployed hundreds of maritime militia vessels to obstruct legitimate oil and gas exploration activities by the Philippines, particularly at Reed Bank, where the Philippines had planned to partner with international energy companies (Vu, 2024). These coercive actions discourage international energy firms from collaborating with regional states, thereby weakening the region's capacity to exploit its own resources and increasing reliance on China for energy and natural resources.

China's gray zone strategy in the SCS is driven by three interconnected strategic objectives: establishing de facto control, shaping the regional order, and enhancing domestic legitimacy. These goals are pursued through a series of actions that fall below the threshold of conventional warfare, allowing Beijing to advance its interests at minimal strategic cost:

(i) The primary objective is to gain de facto control over disputed territories without provoking a direct military response. China has achieved this by using para-military forces, such as the maritime militia and the Coast Guard, to gradually assert administrative control over contested areas. For example, China's actions to seize Scarborough Shoal in 2012 and maintain pressure at Vanguard Bank in 2019 have effectively created a new status quo on the ground. This incremental approach supports Beijing in establishing a foundation for long-term sovereignty claims despite international objections.

(ii) A second key goal is to reshape the regional order in China's favor by undermining ASEAN unity and limiting the influence of external powers like the U.S. and Japan. According to Fravel (2011), China's gray zone tactics create political and psychological pressure on ASEAN members, forcing them to choose between challenging China's actions or accepting the new status quo. The effectiveness of this strategy was highlighted by internal rifts within ASEAN during conferences on the SCS, notably when Cambodia blocked a joint statement in 2012, reflecting China's success in exploiting internal divisions to reshape the strategic environment.

(iii) Moreover, China uses its actions in the SCS to strengthen its domestic legitimacy. By maintaining a firm stance on its territorial claims—even in the face of the 2016 Arbitral Tribunal ruling that rejected the Nine-Dash Line—the government reinforces its image as a strong and assertive power (Wirth, 2021). The success of controlling territory without resorting to war provides compelling evidence to domestic audiences that the regime is effectively protecting national interests. This alignment of foreign policy with a nationalist agenda helps to secure domestic support.

Hence, China's gray zone strategy in the SCS is a carefully calculated, multi-pronged approach aimed at achieving territorial control, influencing regional dynamics, and bolstering the government's standing domestically. These mutually reinforcing goals allow Beijing to expand its influence and secure its national interests while avoiding significant international backlash.

China's implementation of the gray zone strategy in the SCS has evolved through three distinct stages, reflecting a shift from initial, exploratory actions to a more systematic and assertive approach aimed at consolidating control. This process demonstrates a methodical increase in the scale, intensity, and sophistication of China's tactics, as it has adapted to both international reactions and its own strategic goals.

Phase I: Initial Coercion and Probing (2009–2012)

Phase I marks the inception of China's gray zone strategy in the SCS, coinciding with a more assertive demonstration of its maritime ambitions. Actions were characterized by a gradual increase in various non-military activities, designed to test the reactions of other claimants and the broader international community. This strategic shift was primarily driven by China's formal submission of its Nine-Dash Line claim to the United Nations in 2009. Concurrently, unilateral oil and gas exploration activities by Vietnam and the Philippines prompted Beijing to test new coercive measures. The operational approach during this initial phase was a calculated blend of probing rival nations' reactions and gradual encroachment. As Fravel (2011) notes, China sought to "both strengthen its sovereignty claim and avoid being internationally perceived as escalating militarization." Beijing primarily relied on law enforcement and paramilitary forces to achieve these goals. The China Coast Guard and Fisheries Surveillance vessels increased their patrols in disputed waters, leading to a significant rise in arrests of fishermen from neighboring countries.

An early demonstration of this new assertiveness was the March 2009 incident involving the U.S. naval vessel USNS Impeccable, which China harassed to assert its maritime claims. The tools used during this period were almost exclusively non-military: the Chinese Navy was rarely deployed publicly, while there was dense presence of maritime law enforcement and maritime militia. The key outcome of this phase was China's success in incrementally solidifying its claims on the ground without triggering direct conflict. The most significant victory was the de facto control of Scarborough Shoal following a 2012 standoff with the Philippines. This incident demonstrated the effectiveness of China's gray zone tactics in expanding its control without overt use of naval forces. Tactics included harassment of foreign survey vessels and fishing boats, often carried out by the China Coast Guard and maritime militia.

Phase II: Escalation and Artificial Island Construction (2013–2016)

Phase II represents a significant escalation in China's gray zone activities, distinguished by large-scale land reclamation and island-building. This shift was motivated by new leadership's commitment to transforming China into a "maritime power." Beginning around 2013, China transformed numerous reefs and low-tide elevations in the Spratly Islands into fortified artificial islands, equipped with military infrastructure like runways, harbors, and radar systems. This physical expansion directly altered the geography of the SCS.

The China Coast Guard was reorganized in 2013 and equipped with modern, large patrol vessels, while the maritime militia became better trained and more consistently supported Coast Guard operations at hotspots (Wirth, 2021). A key example is the 2014 Haiyang Shiyou-981 drilling rig incident, where Beijing deployed dozens of Coast Guard ships and militia boats to surround the rig in waters near the Paracel Islands, preventing Vietnamese law enforcement from approaching. Concurrently, China engaged in large-scale land reclamation on seven disputed features in the

Spratly Islands from 2014 to 2015, constructing fortified artificial islands to secure long-term strategic advantages.

Legal and propaganda tools were also heavily utilized. Beijing rejected the jurisdiction of the Arbitral Tribunal in the Philippines' lawsuit while simultaneously propagating arguments of "historical rights" to dismiss the legitimacy of the 2016 ruling. Despite the unfavorable ruling from the Arbitral Tribunal, Beijing maintained de facto control of Scarborough Shoal and completed construction of fortified outposts in the Spratlys. As a RAND study noted, China has "won without fighting" in many situations, achieving its maritime objectives without direct military conflict (Wirth, 2021).

The 2015 Defense White Paper explicitly addressed the task of "protecting maritime rights and interests" and criticized foreign interference and neighboring states' actions regarding China's islands and reefs (State Council Information Office of the People's Republic of China, 2015). In terms of implementation, Beijing expanded its gray zone activities both geographically and qualitatively. Civilian and paramilitary forces were mobilized more extensively. This period also included China's response to the 2016 Permanent Court of Arbitration ruling, which invalidated its Nine-Dash Line claim. China's outright rejection of the ruling, combined with its continued militarization of artificial islands, demonstrated its resolve to ignore international law in favor of its own strategic interests. This phase demonstrated China's ability to use a combination of military, economic, and diplomatic pressure to change facts on the ground.

Phase III: Consolidation and Control (2017–2020)

The final stage is defined by consolidation of China's control over newly created and militarized features. The primary motivation for this phase was the need to secure and maintain gains China had achieved in the SCS, particularly in the aftermath of the 2016 Permanent Court of Arbitration ruling. Beijing sought to preserve the favorable status quo it had created while mitigating the risk of increased intervention from external powers.

By this point, artificial islands were largely complete, allowing China to expand its operational presence and defense capabilities. Beijing focused on regular patrols by its Coast Guard and maritime militia to enforce its claims, effectively turning disputed areas into zones under its administrative control. These activities, coupled with sustained pressure on the EEZs of other claimant states, aimed to normalize China's enhanced control over the region. The culmination of this phase solidified China's strategic advantage, making it increasingly difficult for other nations to challenge the altered status quo.

To achieve this, China shifted its approach toward normalizing its overwhelming presence. The China Coast Guard began conducting regular patrols in and around disputed areas, consistently asserting sovereignty over features held by other nations. China also continued to deploy large-scale maritime militia swarms when a show of force was deemed necessary. In early 2021, approximately 200 Chinese militia vessels gathered at Whitsun Reef in the Spratly Islands, putting significant pressure on the Philippines (Morales & Lema, 2021).

Furthermore, China moved to legalize its gray zone activities through domestic legislation. The Coast Guard Law, which took effect in early 2021, explicitly authorizes the force to "take all necessary measures, including the use of weapons," to prevent what it considers sovereign violations (AMTI, 2019). This legislative action demonstrates Beijing's willingness to create a legal basis for escalating pressure within the gray zone.

The outcome of this phase is that China successfully maintained and strengthened its control without making significant concessions. The 2019 Defense White Paper underscored this resolve by stating that pressure to "safeguard China's territorial integrity and maritime rights and interests is increasing," and revealed that from 2012 to 2018, the country's military conducted "more than 72,000 rights protection and law enforcement missions" in disputed waters (State Council Information Office of the People's Republic of China, 2019). This institutionalization and continued presence align with statements from Chinese leadership, particularly President Xi Jinping's declaration that "China cannot lose even an inch of its territory" (Stewart & Blanchard, 2018). Therefore, the period from 2017 to 2021 marks the consolidation and institutionalization of China's gray zone strategy.

By systematically executing its gray zone strategy over three distinct phases, China has successfully expanded and consolidated its de facto control in the SCS. This approach, characterized by low-intensity but continuous and methodical coercive actions, has enabled Beijing to establish a "new order on the ground" without triggering full-scale military conflict. China has gradually eroded international legal principles, including freedom of navigation and the authority of UNCLOS.

Based on Taffer's (2024) research, China employs a strategic combination of paramilitary activities and sophisticated media campaigns as part of its gray zone tactics in the SCS. Beijing uses its maritime militia, armed fishing boats, and Coast Guard vessels to conduct activities like patrolling and harassing rival vessels. These actions are designed to assert sovereignty claims without triggering direct military conflict. Simultaneously, China deploys a multi-channel propaganda campaign, utilizing state media (e.g., Xinhua, CCTV) and fake social media accounts to spread disinformation and manipulate public opinion. This media campaign emphasizes China's historical claims and provides justification for its paramilitary actions, thereby reducing the likelihood of legal or military responses from affected states. In his

2024 paper, Taffer further highlights how China uses political coercion by closely integrating its media, diplomatic, and economic pressures. China's state media and fake social media accounts are used to promote its "historical sovereignty" claims and ambiguous legal arguments. This media strategy aims to discredit international rulings, such as the 2016 Hague Arbitration Court decision, and to create an information environment where it is difficult for international and regional audiences to distinguish between China's legitimate actions and its coercive ones.

A specific example of this political coercion is China's continuous deployment of its maritime militia and Coast Guard vessels at disputed locations like Second Thomas Shoal. These actions have hindered the Philippines' ability to resupply its outpost and protect its sovereignty. The boundary of sub-conflict activity is fluid and context-dependent. China's 2021 Coast Guard Law, which authorizes the use of weapons under certain circumstances, exemplifies how legal and operational ambiguity can blur the line between law enforcement and armed conflict. In practice, this ambiguity allows states to expand their operational space, conduct coercive activities, and complicate international responses, demonstrating that the gray zone is as much about perception and strategic signaling as it is about military or non-military actions.

China's gray zone strategy in the SCS extends beyond conventional military tactics to include operations in cyberspace and outer space. This approach allows Beijing to secure a strategic advantage without triggering full-scale military conflict. By leveraging these unconventional tools, China can enhance its control over the region while minimizing the risk of strong international response. In the domain of cyber warfare, China has systematically conducted cyberattacks against nations with sovereignty disputes in the SCS, notably Vietnam and the Philippines. These attacks frequently target government systems, defense agencies, and energy companies to exfiltrate sensitive information or sabotage critical digital infrastructure. Furthermore, propaganda and manipulation of public opinion on social media are integral to the gray zone strategy. China utilizes networks of fake accounts to disseminate disinformation, disrupt information flows, and erode public trust in regional governments. This is done to create psychological advantage in sovereignty disputes (Plan, 2019).

China's gray zone strategy in the SCS also leverages space operations to gain decisive advantage without direct military engagement. China's sophisticated satellite systems are crucial for monitoring and tracking maritime and military activities of other nations. According to a report from CSIS (2022), both military and civilian satellites are used to monitor shipping lanes and provide support to the Chinese navy and maritime militia in their efforts to assert territorial sovereignty. Furthermore, Beijing has developed and tested anti-satellite (ASAT) technologies to threaten opponents' space assets and protect its own communication and surveillance systems from external disruption. This capability provides a powerful deterrent and a means to deny adversaries critical information in a conflict. By combining cyber and space operations, China attempts to increase its influence in the SCS without force. This multifaceted approach not only bolsters Beijing's sovereignty claims but also places other countries at a disadvantage, as it is difficult to distinguish between hostile actions and legitimate activities. As the dispute becomes more complex, developing effective countermeasures to China's gray zone strategy—including its use of cyber and space assets—will be critical for maintaining the regional balance of power.

Several critical developments in gray zone strategy have emerged since 2020, reflecting the evolving complexity of maritime competition in the Indo-Pacific: (i) The use of lawfare has intensified, with states leveraging international law, domestic regulations, and maritime claims to assert control over contested areas without triggering overt military confrontation. Legal instruments are increasingly coordinated with diplomatic and informational campaigns, creating a multidimensional pressure framework that complicates adversary responses and international adjudication; (ii) Gray zone tactics now frequently integrate civilian, paramilitary, and military resources in coordinated operations. In the maritime domain, this includes deployment of maritime militias, coast guard units, and civilian fishing fleets to project presence and enforce claims, while formal naval forces remain in reserve. This "tri-layered" approach enhances coercive effect while preserving plausible deniability and avoiding political costs of direct military engagement; (iii) The emergence of intelligentized warfare—a framework combining artificial intelligence, cyber operations, and precision information campaigns—has allowed states to calibrate escalation dynamically. Through predictive modeling, real-time surveillance, and cyber-enabled decision support, gray zone actors can apply pressure incrementally, target vulnerabilities with high precision, and adapt operations to adversary responses, all while avoiding overt conflict; and (iv) Economic instruments have become central to gray zone strategies, particularly in maritime competition. Control over ports, shipping lanes, and EEZs, combined with strategic investments and trade leverage, allows states to coerce or influence regional actors without direct military action. These tools intersect with lawfare and paramilitary operations to form multi-layered coercive strategies that shape both territorial control and regional balance of power.

Collectively, these developments demonstrate that gray zone operations have evolved into highly sophisticated, multidimensional, and integrated strategies. The combination of legal, paramilitary, military, cyber, and economic tools enables states to expand influence, exploit adversary vulnerabilities, and manage escalation risk simultaneously.

China's gray zone operations in the SCS cannot be understood as a uniform or automatically successful strategy. Their effectiveness depends on a combination of structural asymmetry, regional fragmentation, and calibrated escalation management.

The contrasting outcomes at Scarborough Shoal and Second Thomas Shoal illustrate this dynamic. At Scarborough Shoal in 2012, China succeeded in establishing de facto control due to its ability to sustain continuous maritime presence, exploit limited Philippine enforcement capacity, and operate in a context of minimal immediate U.S. intervention. ASEAN disunity further reduced diplomatic costs. By maintaining operations through coast guard and maritime militia forces rather than naval combatants, Beijing avoided crossing the threshold of armed conflict while incrementally altering the status quo. By contrast, at Second Thomas Shoal, Chinese pressure has encountered greater resistance. The Philippines has maintained resupply missions, and intermittent U.S. involvement has increased reputational and escalation risks for Beijing. This comparison demonstrates that gray zone tactics are most effective when adversaries lack sustained maritime capacity, alliance backing, and regional cohesion. Success, therefore, is not predetermined by Chinese capability alone but emerges from the interaction between coercive pressure and the resilience of opposing actors.

Notably, phase transitions in Chinese strategy are shaped by both external shocks, such as arbitration rulings or U.S. policy shifts, and domestic factors, including leadership priorities and strategic learning. Gray zone success also relies on exploiting ambiguity and escalation management. By integrating civil, paramilitary, and military capabilities, coupled with legal and economic instruments, China can apply incremental pressure without triggering conventional conflict. This calibrated approach allows adversaries limited options for direct retaliation, effectively constraining countermeasures while advancing national strategic objectives. Conversely, failures often occur when adversaries demonstrate coordinated resistance, international support, or when strategic overreach provokes backlash that exceeds the carefully maintained gray zone threshold.

The evolution of China's approach from 2009 to 2020 reflects adaptive strategic learning shaped by domestic consolidation and external shocks. The initial probing phase (2009–2012) focused on testing regional responses through calibrated maritime enforcement. The subsequent phase (2013–2016) marked a qualitative shift toward geographic transformation, most notably through large-scale land reclamation and militarization. This escalation was enabled by leadership centralization under Xi Jinping and reinforced by lessons drawn from earlier successes. Following the 2016 arbitral ruling, China moved toward institutionalization and normalization of its gains, strengthening coast guard authority and codifying legal tools to formalize administrative control. These phase transitions indicate that gray zone strategy is not static but evolves in response to shifting risk calculations and international reactions.

4. VIETNAM'S STRATEGIC RESPONSES AND POLICY RECOMMENDATIONS

Vietnam's response strategy, meanwhile, reflects a calibrated effort to enhance resilience without triggering escalation. Through diplomatic protest, legal advocacy grounded in UNCLOS, defense modernization, and diversified external partnerships, Hanoi has sought to raise the costs of coercion while preserving strategic autonomy. However, these measures appear more effective in constraining further deterioration than in reversing established faits accomplis. Diplomatic and legal tools reinforce normative legitimacy but lack direct enforcement capacity, while defense modernization strengthens deterrence over the medium term without preventing sub-threshold pressure. Moreover, Vietnam has adopted a multifaceted response to China's gray zone strategy in the SCS, combining a firm diplomatic stance, adherence to international law, and strategic cooperation. In its diplomatic and legal stance, Vietnam has consistently issued strong diplomatic protests against China's assertive actions, such as obstruction of oil and gas exploration in Vietnam's EEZ and imposition of unilateral fishing bans. These protests are grounded in an unwavering affirmation of Vietnam's sovereignty over its waters and the Paracel and Spratly archipelagos. This approach aligns with a broader strategy of promoting international law, with Vietnam frequently citing UNCLOS in its protests. The political, diplomatic, and military impacts of China's strategy demonstrate its continued ambition to dominate the SCS. Beijing continues to invest heavily in its navy and quietly upgrades infrastructure at outposts in the Paracel and Spratly Islands. These actions, coupled with the lack of an effective enforcement mechanism for international rulings and shifts in policy by other claimant states, have allowed China to regain strategic initiative. A significant challenge for Vietnam is confronting China's gray zone activities, such as its maritime militia, which often operate covertly by turning off their Automatic Identification System (AIS) to evade detection.

Vietnam also faces structural trade-offs. Managing domestic nationalist sentiment preserves escalation control but may signal limited tolerance for risk. Efforts to strengthen ASEAN unity are constrained by intra-bloc divisions and China's economic leverage over certain members. Deepening cooperation with the Us—particularly following the 2023 Comprehensive Strategic Partnership—expands diplomatic and technological space but must be balanced against Hanoi's long-standing "Four Nos" defense policy to avoid perceptions of alignment. Despite tensions, Vietnam has maintained bilateral dialogue channels with China to manage disputes and prevent escalation. While Vietnam engages in these discussions, it holds a different view from China on the necessity of involving other relevant parties in multilateral negotiations concerning the Spratly Islands, a position that has at times limited China's diplomatic leverage. The Vietnamese government has also demonstrated sophisticated ability to manage domestic public opinion. Following serious incidents, leaders have made strong public statements to reassure the populace, while also taking steps to "orient public opinion" and de-escalate protests in accordance with bilateral agreements with China (Thayer, 2011). This reflects Vietnam's awareness of the importance of national unity and control over its internal response to external pressure. In addition to bilateral negotiations, Vietnam has been an active participant in regional forums such as ASEAN, contributing to initiatives to counter China's actions despite the bloc's internal divisions on the issue. Meanwhile, Vietnam has strategic opportunities to strengthen its position. It can enhance its maritime presence through modernization of its navy and maritime militia, creating a more robust deterrent against China's "nibbling" tactics. Furthermore, expanding strategic partnerships with major powers like the U.S. and Japan, as well as with other ASEAN members, can bolster Vietnam's defense capabilities and generate international pressure against violations of international law (Putra, 2023). By adhering to its foreign policy of "cooperation and struggle," Vietnam can transform pressure from China's violations into an opportunity to attract international support, thereby reinforcing regional order and promoting compliance with maritime law. This approach allows Vietnam to turn a significant challenge into a strategic advantage, affirming its sovereignty while promoting sustainable development of its marine economy.

In the face of complex security challenges posed by China's gray zone strategy in the SCS, Vietnam's foreign and defense policies must be carefully adjusted to safeguard national interests and maintain a stable environment for development. Vietnam's approach remains rooted in the principles of independence, self-reliance, peace, cooperation, and proactive international integration. Vietnam's foreign policy is guided by the philosophy of "both cooperation and struggle," a principle repeatedly emphasized by General Secretary Trong (2021). This approach mandates that Vietnam is determined to defend its legitimate maritime rights peacefully through dialogue, negotiations, and multilateral cooperation. This includes leveraging international legal mechanisms, particularly UNCLOS 1982. This consistent policy has garnered international sympathy and support for Vietnam's position, enhancing its credibility and helping to curb China's destabilizing actions. Vietnam's defense policy is centered on the principle of peaceful self-defense and is firmly anchored in the "four no's" policy, as articulated by Prime Minister Chinh: (1) No participation in military alliances, (2) No alignment with one country to fight against another, (3) No allowing foreign countries to set up military bases on Vietnamese territory, (4) No using force or threatening to use force in international relations (Ministry of National Defense of Vietnam, 2019, p. 25).

This policy signals Vietnam's commitment to peace and its desire to avoid being drawn into confrontational alliances, while providing reassurance to regional partners about its transparent military stance (Chinh, 2024). However, the "four no's" do not imply isolation. On the contrary, Vietnam actively expands its foreign and defense cooperation based on mutual respect and shared interests. This involves strengthening defense diplomacy and engaging in multilateral security mechanisms like the ASEAN Defence Ministers' Meeting Plus (ADMM+) and the ASEAN Regional Forum (ARF) to contribute to regional peacekeeping efforts. Furthermore, Vietnam recognizes the importance of modernizing its armed forces. The People's Army, Navy, and Coast Guard are being developed to be "revolutionary, disciplined, elite, and modern," capable of defending the country "early and from afar." Investing in a modern, dual-use, and autonomous defense industry is seen as necessary to enhance defense potential and serve national strategic interests. On the ground, Vietnam must prioritize strengthening its maritime law enforcement capabilities by equipping the Coast Guard and Fisheries Surveillance with more vessels and advanced surveillance technology. This will improve their effectiveness in managing and protecting Vietnam's EEZ against China's sophisticated gray zone tactics. Ultimately, these efforts to develop hard power are intended to deter conflict and avoid confrontation while ensuring the nation can protect itself if necessary.

To navigate the complex security landscape shaped by China's gray zone strategy, Vietnam must enhance its diplomatic efforts on both bilateral and multilateral levels. This is essential for creating a network of intertwined strategic interests with other nations, which will help mitigate risks of isolation or dependency in an era of great power competition (Son, 2025). ASEAN remains a crucial pillar of Vietnam's foreign policy. As an active member, Vietnam should prioritize leading efforts to strengthen solidarity and consensus within the bloc on the SCS issue. A unified ASEAN voice is vital for restraining China's unilateral actions; conversely, a divided ASEAN provides greater opportunities for Beijing's gray zone tactics to succeed. Therefore, Vietnam should proactively collaborate with fellow member states to expedite finalization of a substantive and legally binding Code of Conduct (COC) in the SCS, ensuring it aligns with the principles of UNCLOS 1982.

On the global stage, Vietnam's diplomacy must continue to champion international law and mobilize public opinion to support its position on the SCS. Vietnam can take a leading role in proposing initiatives at the United Nations concerning peace and maritime security. It should also call on the international community to condemn violations of maritime law. By "respecting and listening to the opinions of international partners and friends" and maintaining a principled yet flexible approach, Vietnam can build a reputation as a responsible and well-intentioned nation. This foundation is crucial for securing international support when its legitimate interests are threatened. The fact that many countries and organizations have supported Vietnam's stance "without any conditions" demonstrates the effectiveness of its diplomacy, which is guided by the principle that "Vietnam does not choose sides but chooses justice and reason" (Anh, 2023). To avoid being forced into a position of choosing sides in the U.S.-China rivalry, Vietnam must skillfully continue its policy of "multilateralization and diversification." This requires a delicate balance: maintaining stable and trusting relations with China while simultaneously deepening strategic and comprehensive partnerships with other powers. This balanced approach enables Vietnam to secure a broader range of resources for its development and garner greater support on the SCS issue, thereby mitigating pressure from China. This strategy is rooted in a flexible foreign policy that prioritizes national interests, embodying Ho Chi Minh's philosophy of "responding to all changes with the unchanging." In the contemporary context, Vietnam must continue to refine this diplomatic capability, often characterized by the metaphor of "bamboo diplomacy." This concept, with its distinct Vietnamese identity, represents a strategy of "firm roots, a strong trunk, and flexible branches." It signifies a steadfast core stance combined with adaptable and clever strategies. This "bamboo diplomacy" allows Vietnam to effectively navigate unpredictable changes, ensuring both a firm position and the flexibility needed to handle complex international relations (Hung, 2024).

In the realm of foreign economic relations, the development of economic strength—a key component of hard power—is crucial for supporting Vietnam's strategic objectives. A strong, deeply integrated economy provides the resources necessary for national defense and enhances the nation's position on the international stage. Vietnam's long-standing policy of "building an independent, self-reliant economy associated with proactive, active, deep, substantive and effective international integration" reflects this understanding. To achieve this, Vietnam must maximize benefits of its new-generation free trade agreements (FTAs), such as the Comprehensive and Progressive Agreement for Trans-Pacific Partnership (CPTPP), EU-Vietnam Free Trade Agreement (EVFTA), and Regional Comprehensive Economic Partnership (RCEP). The effective implementation of these agreements will expand export markets, attract foreign investment, and facilitate technology transfer, thereby leveraging external resources for national development.

A key strategy is the diversification of economic partners to reduce over-reliance on any single market or supply source. This involves expanding relationships with countries in Europe, the U.S., Japan, South Korea, and India to access capital and advanced technology. Such a policy helps Vietnam avoid potential economic pressure from China. A prime example of this is the 2023 upgrade of the Vietnam-U.S. relationship to a Comprehensive Strategic Partnership, which has opened new avenues for cooperation in semiconductor and high-tech supply chains, enhancing Vietnam's technological autonomy. Furthermore, Vietnam's strategy includes promoting sustainable marine economic development (Truong, 2012). By investing in modernization of key sectors like the oil and gas industry, offshore fishing, aquaculture, and marine tourism, Vietnam not only contributes to its GDP but also affirms its de facto sovereignty over its sea and islands. Cooperating with reputable foreign oil and gas companies to explore and exploit resources in its EEZ, for example, creates a network of shared interests with third parties, compelling China to reconsider disruptive actions. These efforts serve a dual purpose: they support national development while maintaining political and social stability. A robust and independent economy is a significant asset that supports Vietnam's diplomatic and defense strategies. As Prime Minister Chinh (2024) has stated, deep international economic integration is a vital force for maintaining peace and stability, underscoring that economic strength is a fundamental aspect of national defense in peacetime.

Vietnam's counter-strategy to China's gray zone tactics requires leveraging soft power to create strategic advantages. The primary focus is effective public diplomacy to enhance Vietnam's international image and garner global support. Vietnam can implement a multifaceted approach by organizing cultural events abroad, intensifying information campaigns explaining its South China Sea position in international forums across multiple languages, and leveraging the overseas Vietnamese community as a bridge to amplify its voice. Vietnam's contributions to global issues—UN peacekeeping missions, climate change initiatives, and non-traditional security—enhance its standing as a responsible international actor. These actions collectively increase Vietnam's influence, ensuring its stance is widely heard and respected. When Vietnam's prestige and international friendships are strong, China must consider global reactions before escalating gray zone tactics. This soft power effectively complements hard power in protecting sovereignty, constituting a "smart power" approach that many nations have successfully applied.

Vietnam has adopted measures encompassing diplomatic initiatives, UNCLOS advocacy, defense modernization, and "bamboo diplomacy"—a cautious, incremental approach signaling resolve without provoking escalation. However, critical evaluation reveals ambiguous impact on Chinese behavior. Diplomatic protests and legal actions have elevated international awareness, yet have not demonstrably altered China's operational patterns or restrained paramilitary activities. Similarly, incremental defense modernization strengthens deterrence capacity over the medium term, but efficacy depends on regional security context and China's risk tolerance. Trade-offs warrant careful consideration. Domestic measures limiting public protests, while preventing escalation and preserving bilateral dialogue, may inadvertently signal constraints to China, potentially weakening Vietnam's bargaining position. The ambition to "lead ASEAN" faces structural limitations: enduring divisions, varying strategic priorities, and China's exploitation of ASEAN fault lines complicate collective action. Deeper military cooperation with the U.S. raises difficult questions regarding Vietnam's "four nos" policy and risks Chinese retaliation.

Prioritization based on feasibility, urgency, and risk is essential. Immediate measures include maritime surveillance capacity-building, intelligence-sharing, diplomatic initiatives reinforcing ASEAN unity, and improved transparency in reporting

Chinese activities. Medium-term strategies focus on phased defense modernization emphasizing asymmetric capabilities, selective U.S.-Vietnam military cooperation within "four nos" bounds, strengthening economic resilience, and developing comprehensive maritime domain awareness. Long-term efforts should strengthen legal, economic, and multilateral frameworks constraining Chinese coercion, build institutional capacity for sustained competition, foster regional security architecture preserving strategic autonomy, and cultivate next-generation leadership.

Ultimately, China's gray zone strategy operates within the broader framework of U.S.–China strategic rivalry. Its success depends on the absence of coordinated resistance, limited alliance intervention, and careful calibration below escalation thresholds. Conversely, it may encounter limits where regional actors enhance maritime capacity, external powers sustain credible involvement, and diplomatic cohesion increases the reputational costs of coercion. Vietnam's strategy, while primarily defensive and resilience-oriented, demonstrates that gray zone competition is contingent rather than inevitable. The trajectory of the SCS will therefore be shaped not only by Chinese initiative but by the evolving balance between coercive adaptation and regional countermeasures. Vietnam must develop contingency plans for various scenarios: intensified economic pressure, escalated maritime harassment, increased political pressure on ASEAN, and cyber operations. Success in constraining Chinese coercion depends on ASEAN cohesion, credible U.S. commitment to regional security, sustained domestic stability, and effective mobilization of international support. Vietnam's framework should combine resilience-building measures, calibrated diplomatic and military signaling, and scenario planning to manage uncertainty and preserve strategic flexibility, thereby enhancing both analytical rigor and practical relevance of responses to China's evolving maritime strategy.

5. CONCLUSION

China's gray zone strategy in the SCS is characterized by three key features: flexibility, interwoven measures, and persistence. These traits allow Beijing to expand its influence and control without triggering direct military conflict. This strategy is marked by its adaptable nature, with China carefully adjusting its level of coercion to maximize gains while avoiding strong international backlash. As Grossman (2020) notes, Beijing is highly skilled at "walking the tightrope," applying just enough pressure to achieve its goals without crossing the threshold of conventional warfare. This enables China to gradually expand its presence without provoking military response from other nations. For example, following a period of aggressive action, Beijing may temporarily de-escalate to reassure opponents before resuming its efforts to consolidate gains. Besides, China's gray zone strategy is a complex integration of military, paramilitary, legal, economic, and diplomatic tools. Beijing masterfully coordinates these different elements to create comprehensive advantage. Mazarr (2015) describes this as a "pincer" movement, where forces like the maritime militia and Coast Guard work in tandem with legal maneuvering and economic pressure to force concessions without deploying the navy. On the ground, this translates to a three-tiered force structure: (i) Fishing boats/maritime militia on the front lines; (ii) Coast Guard ships performing law enforcement duties; and (iii The Navy providing deterrence and support from a distance. This multi-layered approach makes it difficult for a targeted nation to respond effectively. If a country uses only civilian measures, it cannot counter the aggressive militia. If it uses military force, China can immediately accuse it of provocation. Parallel to this, China employs legal and propaganda tools to legitimize its actions. The establishment of Sansha City in 2012 and the 2021 Coast Guard Law provide legal cover for its activities. Additionally, Beijing regularly uses state media to assert "indisputable sovereignty" over the SCS, shaping public opinion in its favor.

A defining feature of this strategy is its persistence and use of gradual tactics. China pursues its long-term objectives through a series of small, incremental steps, a strategy often described as "salami slicing." Each individual action—such as repositioning a vessel or building a small structure—is not significant enough to provoke conflict, but the cumulative effect creates overwhelming advantage over time. By wearing down the will of opponents and creating a *fait accompli*, China quietly changes the status quo in its favor. The ambiguity of China's actions also makes it difficult to assign blame. Beijing often uses non-state forces, such as civilian fishing vessels or "spontaneous militias," to conduct intrusions and harassment, allowing it to maintain plausible deniability. When challenged, China can deny involvement, blame "fishermen," and make it difficult for other countries to mount legal or diplomatic responses. To sum up, China's gray zone strategy is a flexible and systematic approach that combines various coercive tools to consolidate its maritime claims. By operating in the space between peace and war, Beijing is able to expand its influence without triggering direct military confrontation, thereby maintaining an image of a "peaceful rise" abroad while altering the reality on the ground. However, this has resulted in a more tense regional security environment and a significant decline in trust between China and its neighbors, forcing other countries to seek new countermeasures.

Vietnam's approach to its relationship with China is a multifaceted and proactive strategic posture, rather than one of passive reaction to external pressures (Hai, 2017, pp. 3-7). This strategic orientation is defined by a dual-track policy that deftly combines peaceful, multilateral foreign relations with continuous development of modern, self-reliant defense capability. This cohesive strategy, as articulated by the Communist Party of Vietnam, is a pre-emptive framework designed to safeguard national interests and sovereignty in a complex geopolitical environment (Vuving, 2006). This approach is often described as "bamboo diplomacy," a term that signifies flexibility, resilience, and firm commitment to national interests while swaying with external forces (Hoang, 2022). This proactive stance is operationalized through synchronized deployment of a full spectrum of national power instruments. Diplomacy plays a pivotal role, serving to build a peaceful regional environment and secure international support by fostering strategic partnerships that can act as a counterbalance to potential threats. Parallel to this, economic development is prioritized to establish a solid material and technological foundation, which underpins both national resilience and capacity for modern defense. The military, in turn, is developed not for aggression but as a credible deterrent force, capable of protecting the country's sovereignty and territorial integrity, particularly in the contested waters of the SCS. Finally, cultural soft power is leveraged to enhance Vietnam's international standing and foster domestic unity by promoting its rich heritage and values.

These integrated efforts are directed toward the fundamental goal of protecting sacred sovereignty while simultaneously maintaining the peace and stability essential for continued national development. This strategy, therefore, embodies a sophisticated and feasible combination of hard and soft power, demonstrating Vietnam's commitment to the principle of "protecting the country before it is in danger" (Sutter, 2021). By proactively managing its external relationships and building its internal strength, Vietnam is effectively defending its national interests and sovereignty in the current era of global integration. This balanced approach is critical for a smaller state like Vietnam, which must navigate a relationship of asymmetry with its powerful northern neighbor (Womack, 2006, pp. 1-5).

The evolving nature of gray zone competition in the SCS demands continuous adaptation and strategic innovation from Vietnam. As China refines its tactics and expands its toolkit, Vietnam must remain vigilant and flexible in its responses. The coming years will likely see intensified competition across multiple domains—maritime, cyber, economic, and informational—requiring Vietnam to develop comprehensive, whole-of-government approaches to gray zone challenges. Success will depend on Vietnam's ability to maintain strategic clarity while preserving tactical flexibility, to build domestic resilience while expanding international partnerships, and to defend its sovereignty while contributing to regional stability. The "bamboo diplomacy" approach—firm in principle yet flexible in practice—provides a conceptual foundation for navigating these complex challenges. However, its effectiveness will ultimately be measured by Vietnam's capacity to translate strategic vision into concrete policies, institutional capabilities, and coordinated actions that can effectively counter China's gray zone strategy while preserving Vietnam's autonomy and development trajectory.

REFERENCES

Ahluwalia, P. (2019). Gray zone conflicts and informationisation in the Indian context: Challenges, capabilities and way ahead. *Centre for Land Warfare Studies.* https://www.claws.in/publication/grey-zone-conflicts-and-informationisation-in-the-indian-context-challenges-capabilities-and-way-ahead/

Anh, T. (2023). Prime Minister Pham Minh Chinh receives US Secretary of State Antony Blinken. *Vietnam News.* https://www.vietnam.vn/en/thu-tuong-pham-minh-chinh-tiep-ngoai-truong-hoa-ky-antony-blinken

Asia Maritime Transparency Initiative [AMTI]. (2019). *Failing or incomplete? Grading the South China Sea arbitration.* https://amti.csis.org/failing-or-incomplete-grading-the-south-china-sea-arbitration/

Carment, D., & Dani, B. (2018). War's future: The risks and rewards of grey zone conflict and hybrid warfare. *Canadian Global Affairs Institute.* https://www.cgai.ca/wars_future_the_risks_and_rewards_of_grey_zone_conflict_and_hybrid_warfare

Center for Strategic and International Studies [CSIS]. (2022). *Eyes on the skies: China's growing space footprint in South America.* https://features.csis.org/hiddenreach/china-ground-stations-space/

Chinh, P. M. (2024). Speech at the opening ceremony of the Vietnam International Defense Exhibition 2024. *Hai Duong Newspaper.* https://baohaiduong.vn/thu-tuong-pham-minh-chinh-du-khai-mac-trien-lam-quoc-phong-quoc-te-viet-nam-2024-400871.html

Cuong, H., & Khanh, T. (2019). China's "gray zone" tactics increase the risk of conflict in the East Sea. *Voice of Vietnam.* https://vov.vn/chinh-tri/chien-thuat-vung-xam-cua-trung-quoc-co-moi-lien-he-voi-su-kien-hoang-sa-909828.vov

Fravel, M. T. (2011). China's strategy in the South China Sea. *Contemporary Southeast Asia, 33*(3), 292–319. https://taylorfravel.com/documents/research/fravel.2011.CSA.china.strategy.scs.pdf. DOI: 10.1355/cs33-3b

Grossman, D. (2020). *Regional Responses to U.S.-China Competition in the Indo-Pacific.* RAND Corporation., https://www.rand.org/pubs/research_reports/RR4412z6.html DOI: 10.7249/RR4412.6

Hai, D. T. (2017). *Vietnam and the South China Sea: Politics, security and legality.* Routledge.

Hamzah, T. (2020). Gray zone conflicts in Asia Pacific. *Modern Diplomacy*. https://moderndiplomacy.eu/2020/08/04/gray-zone-conflicts-in-asia-pacific/

Hayton, B. (2024). The South China Sea: Historical and legal background (China Observatory Explainer. *Council on Geostrategy*. https://www.geostrategy.org.uk/app/uploads/2024/09/No.-2024_27-%E2%80%93-The-South-China-Sea_-Historical-and-legal-background.pdf

Hoang, H. H. (2022). Understanding Vietnam's foreign policy choices amid Sino-US rivalry. *ISEAS Perspective*, *2022*(41), 1–10.

Hoffman, F. G. (2016). The contemporary spectrum of conflict: Protracted, gray zone, ambiguous, and hybrid modes of war. In *Index of U.S. military strength* (pp. 25–36). The Heritage Foundation., https://www.heritage.org/military-strength-topical-essays/2016-essays/the-contemporary-spectrum-conflict-protracted-gray

Hung, N. M. (2024). Foreign affairs school, "Vietnamese bamboo" diplomacy in the Doi Moi era. *Communication Review*, *1038*(6), 64–71.

Mazarr, M. J. (2015). Mastering the gray zone: Understanding a changing era of conflict. *United States Army War College Press*. https://press.armywarcollege.edu/monographs/428/

Ministry of National Defense of Vietnam. (2019). *Vietnam national defense 2019*. National Political Publishing House Truth.

Morales, N. J., & Lema, K. (2021). Philippines says 220 Chinese boats have encroached at disputed reef. *Reuters*. https://www.reuters.com/world/china/philippines-says-220-chinese-boats-have-encroached-south-china-sea-2021-03-21/

Park, M. A. (2025). Marketplace (Failure) of Ideas: Foreign Disinformation Campaigns in an Age of Generative A.I. and a Proportionality Approach to Falsehoods. *North Carolina Journal of Law & Technology*, *26*(1), 45–72. https://scholarship.law.unc.edu/cgi/viewcontent.cgi?article=1488&context=ncjolt

Paul, M. (2016). *The United States, China and the freedom of the seas: Washington's FONOPs conflict with Beijing*. Stiftung Wissenschaft und Politik.

Pedrozo, R. (2021). The China Coast Guard Law (2021): A new tool for intimidation and aggression. *Maritime Security*, *3*(1), 1–44.

Plan, L. (2019). APT40: Examining a China-nexus espionage actor. *Poseidon Trident of Innovation*. https://poseidon-us.com/2019/03/04/apt40-examining-a-china-nexus-espionage-actor

Putra, B. A. (2023). Malaysia's "triadic maritime diplomacy" strategy in the South China Sea. *All-Azimuth: A Journal of Foreign Policy and Peace, 12*(1), 166–192. DOI: 10.20991/allazimuth.1455442

Son, B. T. (2025). Vietnam's foreign affairs in 2024: Actively and proactively contribute to creating momentum to bring the country into a new era. *People's Police Newspaper.* https://cadn.com.vn/tich-cuc-chu-dong-gop-phan-tao-da-dua-dat-nuoc-buoc-vao-ky-nguyen-moi-post306975.html

State Council Information Office of the People's Republic of China. (2015). *China's military strategy.* http://eng.mod.gov.cn/xb/Publications/WhitePapers/4887928.html

State Council Information Office of the People's Republic of China. (2019). *China's national defense in the new era.* https://english.www.gov.cn/archive/whitepaper/201907/24/content_WS5d3941ddc6d08408f502283d.html

Stewart, P., & Blanchard, B. (2018). Xi tells Mattis China won't give up "even one inch" of territory. *Reuters.* https://www.reuters.com/article/world/xi-tells-mattis-china-wont-give-up-even-one-inch-of-territory-idUSKBN1JN06N/

Storey, I. (2020). Malaysia and the South China Sea Dispute: Policy Continuity amid Domestic Political Change. *ISEAS Perspective, 10.* https://www.iseas.edu.sg/wp-content/uploads/2020/02/ISEAS_Perspective_2020_18.pdf

Sutter, R. (2021). Vietnam-China relations in the new context. *Asia Policy*, *16*(2), 221–240.

Taffer, A. (2024). The puzzle of Chinese escalation vs. restraint in the South China Sea. *War on the Rocks.* https://warontherocks.com/2024/07/the-puzzle-of-chinese-escalation-vs-restraint-in-the-south-china-sea/

Tatad, R., Despi, D., & Paculba, M. (2020). Navigating China's gray zone strategy in the South China Sea. *OSSSM Digest*, *25*(4), 1–31.

Thayer, C. A. (2011). Chinese assertiveness in the South China Sea and Southeast Asian responses. *Journal of Current Southeast Asian Affairs*, *30*(2), 77–104. DOI: 10.1177/186810341103000205

Trong, N. P. (2021). Full text of General Secretary Nguyen Phu Trong's speech at the National Foreign Affairs Conference. *Government Newspaper.* https://baochinhphu.vn/toan-van-phat-bieu-cua-tong-bi-thu-nguyen-phu-trong-tai-hoi-nghi-doi-ngoai-toan-quoc-102305526.htm

Trung, N. T., & Vu, T. M. (2018). The 2014 Oil Rig Crisis and its Implications for Vietnam–China Relations. In Le, H. H., & Tsvetov, A. (Eds.), *Vietnam's Foreign Policy under Doi Moi* (pp. 72–95). ISEAS–Yusof Ishak Institute. DOI: 10.1355/9789814818155-009

Truong, N. N. (2012). ASEAN-China and the East Sea 2002—A moment of cooperation. *To Quoc Newspaper*. https://toquoc.vn/aseantrung-quoc-va-bien-dong-2002-mot-khoanh-khac-hop-tac-99112664.htm

U.S.-China Economic and Security Review Commission. (2018). Hearing on China's Belt and Road Initiative: Five years later. *USCC*. https://www.uscc.gov/sites/default/files/transcripts/Hearing%20Transcript%20-%20January%2025%2C%202018_0.pdf

Vu, M. P. (2024). Sitting in silence or standing in protests: Endogenous dynamics behind Vietnam foreign policy and the 2014 oil rig crisis. *The Pacific Review*, *37*(2), 388–418. DOI: 10.1080/09512748.2023.2175897

Vuving, A. L. (2006). Strategy and evolution of Vietnam's China policy: A changing mixture of pathways. *Asian Survey*, *46*(6), 805–824. https://papers.ssrn.com/sol3/papers.cfm?abstract_id=1695196. DOI: 10.1525/as.2006.46.6.805

Wirth, C. (2021). Securing the seas, securing the state: The inside/outside of "Indo-Pacific" geopolitics. *The Asia-Pacific Journal, 19*(3), 137–173. https://apjjf.org/2021/3/Wirth

Womack, B. (2006). *China and Vietnam: The politics of asymmetry*. Cambridge University Press. DOI: 10.1017/CBO9780511610790

Wortzel, L. M. (2013). Cyber espionage and the theft of U.S. intellectual property and technology. *USCC*. https://www.uscc.gov/sites/default/files/Wortzel-OI-Cyber-Espionage-Intellectual-Property-Theft-2013-7-9.pdf

Chapter 13
Flexible Yet Resilient: Vietnam's Bamboo Diplomacy and Maritime Security in the South China Sea Era

Tridib Chakraborti
Adamas University, India

Mohor Chakraborty
https://orcid.org/0000-0003-2082-5088
South Calcutta Girls' College, India

ABSTRACT

This chapter examines Vietnam's maritime security strategy in Southeast Asia, analyzing how a middle power navigates complex regional dynamics amid intensifying great-power competition. The study reveals Vietnam's sophisticated "bamboo diplomacy"—a hedging strategy balancing accommodation of China's interests, defense modernization, and strategic partnerships with the US, India, Japan, Australia, and South Korea. Despite lacking an official maritime security definition, Vietnam pursues a three-pronged approach: adherence to UNCLOS and international law, sustained military modernization with significantly increased defense expenditure, and comprehensive strategic partnerships supporting capacity-building and technology transfer. However, structural constraints including power asymmetry with China, substantial economic interdependence, and ASEAN's consensus-based limitations challenge Vietnam's maritime security ambitions while shaping its pragmatic, autonomy-preserving engagement in the contested South China Sea maritime domain.

DOI: 10.4018/979-8-3373-4470-6.ch013

1. INTRODUCTION

In the domain of global politics, maritime security refers to the safeguarding of seas and oceans within a particular geographical area from threats that could compromise peace, sovereignty, trade, and environmental sustainability. It broadly encompasses the protection of maritime domains against threats to freedom of navigation, national sovereignty, and maritime resources as measures to preserve regional stability. Regional maritime security is increasingly crucial to global trade and development. The threats to maritime security embrace a broad array of challenges, including piracy, illegal fishing, maritime terrorism, trafficking, environmental degradation, interstate territorial disputes, and naval conflicts, which require a combination of legal, cooperative, and human-centered approaches for mitigation. Regional maritime security generally focuses on the collective efforts by a group of states within a defined region to ensure the safety, security, and sustainable use of littoral spaces, involving cooperation, coordination, and diplomatic mechanisms to address shared threats and opportunities in regional waters. The core elements of maritime security consist of sovereignty and jurisdictional integrity, freedom of navigation and safety of sea lanes, protection of marine resources and Exclusive Economic Zones (EEZs), maritime law enforcement, crisis management, and conflict prevention (Till, 2009, p. 10).

In Southeast Asia, maritime security serves as an essential foundation for peace, prosperity, sustainable development, and progress. Given the region's economic dependence on maritime trade, the prevalence of unresolved maritime disputes, and the growing influence of external powers in its waters, ensuring maritime security constitutes both a regional and international priority. These dimensions are deeply interwoven due to the region's unique maritime geography and complex political landscape. Over recent decades, this region has become a center of power struggle among multiple actors, including Brunei, China, Malaysia, the Philippines, Taiwan, and Vietnam, further evolving as a flashpoint of strategic rivalry between the United States (US) and China, as well as among member countries of the Association of Southeast Asian Nations (ASEAN). In 2009, China published a map depicting the controversial "Nine-Dash Line" to the United Nations (UN), projecting its territorial claims in the South China Sea (referred to as the East Sea in Vietnam) and subsequently adopted an increasingly assertive posture regarding its claims in the region. Since China's claims overlap with the EEZs of several Southeast Asian countries, the issue has generated territorial, legal, and security disputes. For Southeast Asia, maritime security encompasses not merely defending borders but also securing a stable future for the region. Among other factors, the South China Sea dispute remains one of the most contentious issues. The South China Sea constitutes one of the most strategically vital and contested maritime zones due to its richness in natural resources such as oil, gas, and fisheries, its hosting of major sea lanes, and its facilitation of over US$3 trillion in trade annually.

Among the countries of Southeast Asia in general and ASEAN member states in particular, Vietnam has emerged as a strategically significant player in the regional maritime security architecture due to its location along the South China Sea. As mentioned by former Vice Minister of Defense Nguyen Chi Vinh, Vietnam perceives the conflict in the South China Sea as "one of the most important problems in the maintenance of independence, sovereignty, unity and territorial integrity of the fatherland" and underscores Chinese activities in the littorals as "violation of its EEZ and continental shelf" (as cited in Hung, 2016, p. 23). As regional tensions rise over this sovereignty dispute, Vietnam navigates a complex web of bilateral and multilateral relationships to safeguard its maritime interests and seeks to defend its sovereignty and maritime rights while promoting a rules-based order through legal and multilateral diplomacy. Besides this, it faces increasing pressure from China's assertiveness in disputed waters, particularly through the use of gray-zone tactics such as maritime militia and coercive diplomacy.

Vietnam's maritime security policy has developed gradually, contingent on its national security, economic growth, and foreign policy imperatives, mainly in the context of growing tensions regarding the South China Sea. Since the late 2000s, the concept of maritime security has gained greater prominence in Vietnamese academic writing, media discourse, and diplomatic statements, largely due to emerging external pressures in the South China Sea (Duong, 2021). Despite this strategic significance, Vietnam has been unable to adopt an official definition of "maritime security" in its foreign policy domain or legal documents. This absence is not unintentional, as it attempts to provide negotiating flexibility with China on the one hand and external strategic posturing or maneuvering space with its partners on the other.

In this context, this chapter examines Vietnam's involvement in maritime security cooperation in the South China Sea, the challenges it faces from the dynamics of regional power politics—especially China's assertiveness—and the opportunities arising from partnerships with its ASEAN counterparts, the US, India, and Japan. It also evaluates Vietnam's naval modernization, legal positioning under the UN Convention on the Law of the Sea (UNCLOS), and analyzes its role in shaping regional maritime norms as it treads a delicate and tenuous line between deterrence, diplomacy, and strategic autonomy.

2. VIETNAM'S MARITIME SECURITY DYNAMICS: THEORY AND PRACTICE

In contemporary regional politics, Southeast Asia stands as one of the world's most strategically significant and contested maritime regions, making maritime security a cornerstone of its political stability, economic growth, and regional cooperation. As a responsible maritime actor in Southeast Asia, Vietnam faces several challenges emanating from regional dynamics as it attempts to navigate the complex matrix of asymmetric relations with China while maintaining the tenuous balance and seeking a peaceful and stable relationship with its formidable neighbor. Notwithstanding its discordant ties with Beijing pertaining to contradictory sovereignty claims in the South China Sea, Vietnam's signing of the Comprehensive Strategic Partnership with Beijing in 2008 and its inclusion as a beneficiary of the Belt and Road Initiative (BRI) in 2017 provide space for cooperation with China, premised on considerations of national interest. This reveals the inherent dilemma in Vietnam's China policy as the former seeks to balance realist considerations with pragmatic national interests (Chakraborty, 2024, p. 41), viewed as a logical culmination of its policy adopted since the onset of the post-Cold War period, which heralded the normalization of Sino-Vietnamese relations following 13 years of hostility. This demonstrates a classical hedging posture as the most rational and viable option toward China while maintaining a cautious distance and limited alignment with it. Several factors beyond a simple adversarial dynamic—such as the asymmetry in levels of economic and military development and capability, economic interdependence, historical animosity, communist ideological affinity, and territorial disputes—have contributed to the development of Sino-Vietnamese relations.

Understanding maritime security and its associated threats through the perspective of international relations theories such as realism, liberalism, constructivism, and securitization provides a deeper conceptual framework for analyzing the issue. There are diverse theoretical approaches to maritime security which, when applied to Southeast Asia, clearly reveal the multifaceted interaction of traditional and non-traditional security concerns. In Southeast Asia, realism suggests that states are the principal actors in an anarchic international system where security and survival are paramount. Regarding implications for maritime security, states focus on naval power, sovereignty, and territorial integrity. Maritime disputes, such as the South China Sea issue, are viewed through the perspectives of power competition and security dilemma, while internal/hard and external/soft balancing strategies—such as naval modernization and military and naval cooperation with like-minded partners—emerge as responses to perceived maritime threats (Storey, 2009, p. 36). Vietnam's military modernization and maritime partnerships are viewed as responses to perceived threats, particularly from China's expansionist behavior, in keeping with the logic of defensive realism.

The theory of liberalism focuses on the utility of international cooperation, interdependence, and institution-building for mitigating conflicts and fostering peace. With respect to maritime security, this theory emphasizes multilateral cooperation and adherence to institutional norms as provided in UNCLOS to ensure unhindered maritime trade and freedom of navigation for the Sea Lanes of Communication (SLOCs), which are global commons requiring collective security, information sharing, joint patrols, and amicable dispute settlement mechanisms (Bateman, 2013). Vietnam, through its adherence to a hedging strategy, seeks to balance China's hegemony by strengthening ties with the US, Japan, India, and other regional actors while defending its sovereignty and deterring aggression without provoking an arms race or conflict. Vietnam's pursuit of multilateralism as it leverages institutional collaboration with ASEAN, ASEAN Regional Forum (ARF), East Asia Summit (EAS), ASEAN Defence Ministers' Meeting (ADMM)-Plus, and other mechanisms promotes cooperation, dialogue, and collective norms to uphold the rule of law, UNCLOS principles, and mechanisms of peaceful dispute resolution (Chakraborti & Chakraborty, 2024, p. 65).

Besides, constructivism highlights that security is socially constructed through norms, identities, and discourse, and competing territorial claims to sovereignty—as in the case of the South China Sea—are shaped by national narratives, historical memory, and identity politics. Security communities like ASEAN may construct shared norms and mechanisms for peaceful resolution of disputes, while threat perceptions stemming from various traditional and non-traditional sources influence policy responses at both multilateral and bilateral levels (Acharya, 2009, p. 16). Vietnam's identity and norms as a sovereign, independent nation with historical experiences of resisting foreign domination shape its policy choices. Furthermore, Vietnam supports ASEAN centrality and regional Code of Conduct frameworks, attempting to shape regional norms around maritime conduct with an outlook of norm promotion.

Finally, securitization theory analyzes the manner in which issues are perceived as security threats, often with significant political consequences. This theoretical approach intersects with regional dynamics, including the rise of China, territorial disputes in the South China Sea, and the prevalence of non-traditional threats such as piracy, illegal fishing, trafficking, and marine environmental degradation, which are used to justify increased surveillance and security measures by littoral states, particularly in coastal areas (Emmers, 2010, p. 421).

3. VIETNAM'S MARITIME SECURITY DISCOURSE

It deserves mention at the outset that there is some degree of ambivalence regarding the existence of Hanoi's officially declared maritime security policy. While it may be argued that Vietnam has no declared official definition of "maritime security" and maritime security policy (Duong, 2021), Vietnam's Defence Policy (2016) generally declared the commitment to defend itself against "all aggression, threat against national security, infringement on its national interests" and underscored that the "preservation of a peaceful and stable environment for economic and social development, the achievement of industrialization and modernization under socialist orientation are the highest national interests" (Huong, 2016, p. 1). In Vietnamese usage, two terms are noteworthy: "An ninh bien," signifying a broader "sea security" concept linked to sovereignty, territorial integrity, and national security; and "An ninh hang hai," more specifically related to shipping, port security, and maritime commerce (Duong, 2021). Moreover, though there are references to maritime security priorities—such as freedom of navigation and peace at sea—in the "Defence White Paper" (2019), any definition of the term is absent. Likewise, the "Vietnam Maritime Code," which includes operational definitions such as security levels for ports and vessels, pertains to specific regulatory mechanisms rather than a comprehensive security concept, thus resulting in conceptual overlap and ambiguity.

Vietnam has been unequivocal regarding the imperative of maritime security, ensuring that its "seas are safe, friendly and strictly controlled," besides observing international law and supporting "the protection of the free trade, freedom of navigation and overflight and peaceful economic activities at sea." The Vietnam Border Guard's official website defines maritime security as "a state of stability, safety and freedom from sea-based or land-based threats that may impede the normal activities of countries, organizations and individuals at sea, or sea-based threats to the normal activities of countries, organizations and individuals on land" (Border Guard: Ministry of National Defence, 2021). This definition implies that Vietnam's notion of maritime security is comprehensive in nature, accounting for both traditional and non-traditional threats, largely shaped by the domestic and external environment. Additionally, several legal documents have provided the basis for Vietnam's maritime security strategy, such as the Statement on the Territorial Sea, Contiguous Zone, Exclusive Economic Zone and the Continental Shelf (1977); Statement by the Government of the Socialist Republic of Vietnam on the Territorial Sea Baseline of Vietnam (1982); Petroleum Law (1993); Law on National Border (2003); Fishery Law (2004); Maritime Code of Vietnam (2005); Law of the Sea of Vietnam (2012); and Law on Vietnam Coast Guard (2018) (Ministry of Foreign Affairs of the Socialist Republic of Vietnam, 2020). Besides, the resolution of the

Fourth Conference of the 10th Party Central Committee of the Communist Party of Vietnam (CPV) determined the general goal of Vietnam's Marine Strategy as:

"By 2020, strive to make our country a strong maritime nation, rich from the sea, firmly ensure national sovereignty and sovereign rights at sea, make an important contribution to the cause of industrialization and modernization, making the country rich and strong. Our Party emphasizes that in the cause of building and defending the Fatherland, developing the marine economy has become an important spearhead in the country's economic development strategy. At the same time, the sea is also an important strategic defense direction of the country" (cited from Khanh, 2021).

The Strategy for the Sustainable Development of Vietnam's Marine Economy by 2030, with a vision to 2045, in its Resolution 36 NQ/TW adopted by the Central Committee of CPV in 2018, emphasized balancing marine economic growth with maritime protection. The Vietnam Maritime Code (2023) specified security planning for ships, seaports, and maritime structures; dissemination of maritime security information; maritime safety assurance systems and communication of sea lanes and navigational routes; and called for peaceful, law-based resolution of maritime disputes, freedom of navigation, and support for UNCLOS and ASEAN Code of Conduct frameworks. In February 2025, Vietnam officially declared a new baseline for its territorial waters in the Gulf of Tonkin, reinforcing its maritime claims under UNCLOS as part of its national security strategy (Anh, 2024; Pham, 2025).

The documents mentioned above, however, do not provide an official definition of "maritime security," and no official document published by the Party, State, or Government of Vietnam elucidates the meaning of "maritime security." However, for several years, Vietnam has not used the term "maritime security" in its foreign and security policy domain, unlike Western countries. The implications of this omission can be explained as follows: First, it may obstruct domestic policy coherence, potentially leading to coordination challenges for multiple agencies, such as the Navy, Coast Guard, fisheries authorities, and maritime administration, which operate with overlapping mandates. Scholars and practitioners of Vietnamese security governance have noted that such vagueness can hinder implementation and strategic planning (Thao, 2025). Second, the absence of conceptual clarity affects Vietnam's external posturing. While it is unwaveringly committed to international law, especially UNCLOS, it does so without articulating how maritime security is defined within its national context (Viet Nam News, 2025). This approach contrasts with that of many other Southeast Asian states that have adopted unambiguous maritime security strategies, which enhance transparency and certainty in regional cooperation (Bradford, 2021). Finally, conceptual ambiguity may limit Vietnam's capacity to counter regional maritime security threats. As Vietnam seeks to pursue a more proactive role within ASEAN and the broader Indo-Pacific domain, the absence of a clearly articulated maritime security concept may constrain its normative way of functioning.

Vietnam's maritime strategy, embedded in several official documents and statements, has addressed the territorial and maritime disputes in the South China Sea, along with other non-traditional security threats, since the security of its land territory has been virtually guaranteed following the delimitation of the common land border with China in the late 1990s. Each of the above legal documents clearly presents a distinctive position on the essence of "maritime security" in Vietnam, which is quite multilayered. For instance, Vietnam's Law of the Sea and the Maritime Code are complementary: while the former refers to the national security aspect of the sea, the latter refers to maritime activities, covering seagoing ships, crew, seaports, and related matters (Duong, 2021).

Despite the ambiguity in terms of having a declared maritime policy, Vietnam ensures the same due to the following reasons: First, its involvement in territorial disputes over the Paracel and Spratly Islands in the South China Sea necessitates protection of its sovereignty and assertion of sovereign rights over these contested territories; Second, Vietnam's reliance on export orientation makes the security of sea lanes and freedom of navigation imperative; Third, Vietnam's dependence on maritime resources for economic activities, such as fishing, aquaculture, and offshore oil and gas exploration, also makes the safeguarding of maritime interests a necessity; and finally, protecting marine biodiversity and coastal habitats is crucial for sustainable development (Tran, 2023, p. 3). Arising from these imperatives, Vietnam's maritime strategy is embedded across several official documents and statements, not based on a standalone decree but rather on a comprehensive strategy reflected in legal codes, resolutions, and official statements. Hanoi has, over the years, published four "Defence White Papers" in 1998, 2004, 2009, and 2019, identifying four major threats to its national security: economic decline and unsustainable development; hostile forces attempting to weaken the CPV's rule; disputes over territorial sovereignty and maritime jurisdiction in the South China Sea; and non-traditional security threats. However, the absence of official interpretation does not imply the de-prioritization of maritime security by Vietnam. Although "maritime security" has not been explicitly mentioned, two of the four threats enumerated above are directly related to this concept. In fact, disputes over territorial sovereignty and maritime jurisdiction in the South China Sea and non-traditional security threats, including maritime crimes such as piracy, illegal migration, arms and drug trafficking, are considered as texts of its maritime security policy and as critical matters of its development policy (Nguyen, 2022, p. 343). Vietnam's "Defence White Paper" (2019), while not using the term "maritime security," has used the term "maritime," thus explaining:

"As a maritime nation, Vietnam always pays special attention to maritime security, ensuring that Vietnam's seas are safe, friendly and strictly controlled. Vietnam always observes international law and supports the protection of free trade, freedom of navigation and overflight and peaceful economic activities at sea" (cited from Tran, 2023, p. 3).

It also emphasizes Vietnam's commitment to ensuring its seas as "safe, friendly, and strictly controlled"; reaffirms respect for international law and adherence to the "Four Nos": no military alliances; no alignment with any country against another; no foreign military bases; and no use or threat of force in international relations (Ministry of National Defence of the Socialist Republic of Vietnam, 2019, p. 23). However, it neither provides a comprehensive definition nor an articulated set of guiding principles for maritime security. The Vietnamese Government ensures the delegation of institutional responsibility among the defense agencies, the Navy, Coast Guard, Fisheries Surveillance, Border Protection, and others, which coordinate through ad hoc rather than centralized maritime authority frameworks. This delegation and dispersed mandate do not dilute the clarity of its maritime strategy.

Vietnam's maritime security approach emerges from consensus-driven policymaking within the CPV framework. The Politburo and Central Committee craft decisions collectively, involving multiple stakeholders, such as the National Boundary Commission, PetroVietnam, fisheries authorities, and scientists. This inclusive yet decentralized process supports maritime stability and security. Therefore, the above-mentioned principles apply broadly to its defense and foreign policies and not uniquely to the maritime security strategy. At sea, Vietnam also follows a "cooperation and struggle" approach through the exercise of peaceful cooperation while asserting sovereign claims under international law. These frameworks implicitly refer to maritime security without a dedicated maritime-focused codification. As Vietnam faces multidimensional challenges, such as territorial disputes, illegal fishing, environmental threats, and China's gray-zone tactics, it lacks a defined strategy to address gray-zone tactics, particularly in scenarios not tantamount to overt confrontation. Such ambiguity is perhaps a deliberate strategy to manage uncertainty, and the absence of clearly articulated principles of maritime security attempts to provide negotiating flexibility with China on the one hand and external strategic posturing or maneuvering space with its partners on the other.

Vietnam's practice of "bamboo diplomacy," characterized by flexible, resilient, and non-aligned engagement with all major powers, ensures regional stability and economic development without resorting to principle-heavy declarations, especially regarding maritime strategy. This strategic ambiguity, representing pragmatic realist hedging under structural constraints, helps Vietnam navigate the delicate balance between resisting external pressure (particularly from China) and avoiding overt confrontation or military entanglement. This may be explained in terms of realism blended with tangible geopolitical imperatives and the constructivist logic of intangibles, represented by images and perceptions such as the Sino-Vietnamese War (1979) and the "security dilemma" emanating from China's hegemonic overtures in the South China Sea in shaping bilateral interactions. It manifests a synergy of history with defensive realism, implying that the means employed by China to enhance its security interests have a disproportionate impact on Vietnam, thereby instilling a threat perception in its psyche regarding the power asymmetry and future intentions of China. Vietnam's defensive realist logic of security maximization seeks to maintain the regional balance of power by adhering to both internal and external balancing mechanisms. Thus, the neoliberal logic of Sino-Vietnamese interactions may be situated within the framework of the interrelation between power and asymmetrical interdependence as a power resource. The primacy of securing Vietnam's national interests and developmental logic, particularly in the context of interdependent globalization and the advantages of BRI membership, has facilitated its "limited alignment" with China (Acharya, 2003-2004, p. 150). On the other hand, Vietnam's resort to "bamboo diplomacy" or external balancing strategy of forging cooperative engagements with "like-minded" partners entails a deterrent effect on China.

However, it deserves mention that the tensions and trade-offs inherent in Vietnam's adoption of a dual strategy with China—as the former seeks to balance realist considerations with pragmatic national interests—emerge from the former's economic dependence on the latter. It requires exercising balance and caution while navigating ideological and economic factors such as the CPV's ideological affinities and party-to-party relations with the Communist Party of China, shared political values, and its dependence on China for trade, investment, and BRI cooperation. This dependence is bolstered by the BRI's synchronization with Vietnam's "Two Corridors, One Economic Circle" framework, which focuses on fast-tracking infrastructure connections, including railways, expressways, and border gates, facilitating connectivity, human resources development, infrastructure, and people-to-people contacts, among others. This has been demonstrated by the steady rise in Sino-Vietnamese trade and investment ties, exploring their structural complementarity and natural geographic advantage in logistics and transportation in various spheres. China has remained Vietnam's largest trade partner for more than two decades, with total bilateral trade exceeding US$260 billion in 2024, and Chinese firms supplying over 50% of imported raw materials for Vietnam's crucial textile and garment industry. China has emerged as the top export destination for Vietnam's agricultural, forestry, and fishery products, providing tangible benefits to Vietnamese farmers. Moreover, as its sixth-largest foreign investor, Chinese Foreign Direct Investment (FDI) in Vietnam totaled US$31.26 billion as of March 2025 (Hanh, 2025). These conditions arising primarily from Hanoi's economic dependence on Beijing might constrain the former's security partnerships with states like the US and India, prompting it to avoid participation in formal military alliances or informal groupings like the Quadrilateral Security Dialogue (QUAD)-plus initiative.

The sustainability of this balancing act has been influenced by the Sino-US rivalry, with China leveraging the consequences of US President Donald Trump's tariff pressure on Vietnam, threatening to impose 20% and 40% tariffs on several Vietnamese goods and goods transshipped through Hanoi from a third country like China, respectively (Hayton, 2025). Although Vietnam is dependent on the US market, prompting it to resort to unilateral negotiations with Washington, the balance is in favor of China, bolstering Hanoi's reliance on support from China, facilitating the "unbalanced" economic pull and greater engagement with it. This will not only foster Beijing's vision of greater economic integration with Southeast Asia and more market access for its companies but also fortify its image as the alternative to American unilateralism and economic coercion (Bland, 2025).

Finally, the absence of a formal and official definition of maritime security and the existence of dispersed legal instruments and agencies prevent unified policy articulation, while consensus-driven governance yields deliberate vagueness over firm statements. While the existing principles like the "Four Nos" are defense-wide rather than specifically maritime-oriented, these are perhaps adapted to the complex, evolving threats such as gray-zone coercion and hybrid conflicts, which resist linear principle-based responses. In summary, strategic ambiguity supports flexibility, despite obscuring clarity in the domain of maritime security.

4. CHALLENGES TO MARITIME SECURITY: IDENTIFYING AND ADDRESSING THE IMPEDIMENTS

Vietnam occupies a central position in the maritime security architecture of Southeast Asia due to its long coastline and strategic location bordering the South China Sea. With over 3,260 kilometers of coastline and more than 3,000 islands and islets (including the disputed Paracel and Spratly Islands), Vietnam's maritime domain is central to its considerations of economic development, sovereignty, and national defense. As a claimant state in the South China Sea dispute, its maritime strategy blends defensive realism, legal diplomacy, and regional/international cooperation and is conditioned by a number of factors such as economic development, sovereignty, national defense, and commitment to protecting maritime rights, securing marine resources, and ensuring peaceful development. While committed to the peaceful resolution of maritime disputes and ASEAN centrality, Vietnam is also steadily upgrading its defense capabilities and enhancing the scope of international partnerships to protect its maritime interests amid rising regional tensions.

In this broad framework, this section identifies the principal challenges to maritime security and integrates them with Vietnam's policy responses to these threats, both traditional and non-traditional in nature.

First, maritime disputes in the South China Sea, particularly with respect to the overlapping sovereignty claims among China, Brunei, Malaysia, the Philippines, Taiwan, and Vietnam, are a major source of concern. China's assertion of the "Nine-Dash Line" overlaps with the EEZs of these states. The situation has been compounded by China's construction and militarization of artificial islands in the disputed space, further threatening regional stability, peace, and order. As one of the first countries to approve UNCLOS, Vietnam ratified the same in 1994, joining the international community "in building a fair legal order that promotes development and cooperation at sea." It affirmed sovereignty over its internal waters and territorial waters, as well as sovereign rights and jurisdiction over the contiguous sea, EEZ, and continental shelf, while strictly calling on other countries to respect its sovereign rights. Besides, Vietnam's adherence to UNCLOS has been the catalyst for its accession to various international conventions on maritime and marine management, such as the UN Agreement for the Implementation of the Provisions of UNCLOS; Agreement relating to the Conservation and Management of Straddling Fish Stocks and Highly Migratory Fish Stocks; in addition to signing nearly 11 conventions of the International Maritime Organization, including the Convention for the Safety of Life at Sea, the Convention for the Prevention of Pollution from Ships, the Convention on Civil Liability for Oil Pollution Damage, the Convention on Facilitation of Maritime Traffic, and the Convention on Maritime Search and Rescue. Furthermore, to comply with UNCLOS principles, Vietnam has adapted its legal system on the seas and oceans, enacting strategies, policies, and plans to ensure the effective and sustainable use of its marine resources (Cuong & Dung, 2024). However, Vietnam's adherence to UNCLOS and adoption of legal strategies in tandem with it may not have the intended effect of constraining China's assertiveness in the region, particularly in the South China Sea. Besides, China's rejection of international arbitration and adjudication—as, for instance, pertaining to the Permanent Court of Arbitration's (PCA) award in favor of the Philippines (2016), citing its right under UNCLOS to opt out of such procedures—exposes the limitations of the legal approach. This calls for Vietnam's coordination with ASEAN and insistence on its organizational leverage to reconcile divergences with China regarding dispute resolution and confidence-building mechanisms. Premised on documents like the Single Draft Negotiating Text (SDNT), such initiatives should focus on removing ambiguities in the Declaration on the Conduct of Parties in the South China Sea (DOC), at least in four areas: geographical scope, legal status (binding or not), efficacy of third-party involvement in dispute settlement, and opening it to accession by other states—such that the impediments to finalizing the Code of Conduct in the South China Sea (COC) may be addressed.

Second, issues related to freedom of navigation and strategic competition further exacerbate regional tensions. The US and its allies regularly conduct Freedom of Navigation Operations (FONOPs) to balance China's hegemonic ambitions and uphold liberal institutionalism in the regional littorals. Simultaneously, the growing presence and involvement of other regional maritime states such as Australia, India, and Japan have the potential for intensified strategic rivalries, which could result in an increasingly volatile maritime environment. Under the circumstances, Vietnam's cooperation with its partners in the defense domain has been encouraged to foster technology transfers, joint ventures, and collaborations in developing weapon prototypes and manufacturing advanced weaponry to build a modern defense industry. While emphasizing coordinated efforts to boost "scientific and technological capabilities, institutional frameworks and human resources," Vietnam's Chief of the General Department of National Defense Industry, Lt. Gen. H Quang Tu n, highlighted the imperative of strategic planning and international partnerships for technology transfer, joint ventures, training cooperation, and branding military and dual-use products for export (as cited in Viet Nam News, 2024). The signing of Comprehensive Strategic Partnership agreements between Vietnam and India (2016), South Korea (2022), Japan (2023), the US (2023), and Australia (2024) not only enhances the space for bolstered defense cooperation to address capacity gaps in defense capabilities and preparedness but also attests to Hanoi's serious resolve to balance China's assertiveness in the region. Vietnam's emphasis on defense modernization has been evident in terms of its weapons procurement, boosted by the signing of agreements with Russia and India since 2000, resulting in several high-value purchases such as Gepard-class frigates, Kilo-class submarines, SIGMA-9814 frigates, Molniya-class guided missile fast attack craft, and Su-30MK2 fighter jets. Since India and Vietnam share ownership and operation of weapons systems of Russian origin, New Delhi has been providing spare parts for some Russian-origin equipment to the Vietnamese Navy, such as the Petya-class warships and OSA-II class missile boats. Besides, systems of Soviet origin in the Vietnamese military, such as T-54/55 main battle tanks and BMP family infantry fighting vehicles, have been upgraded in collaboration with India, thus necessitating cooperation in technology transfer (Chakraborty, 2020, p. 24). Furthermore, following the US's lifting of the arms embargo, Vietnam acquired Hamilton-class cutters, encouraging bilateral negotiations on the purchase of F-16s from Washington and K-9 self-propelled howitzers and related equipment from Seoul.

Third, in addition to traditional security issues, non-traditional security threats, including Illegal, Unreported, and Unregulated (IUU) fishing, piracy, sea robbery, kidnapping for ransom, trafficking of arms, drugs, weapons, and human beings, particularly in strategic chokepoints such as the Strait of Malacca and the Sulu-Celebes Seas, have serious consequences for Vietnam's commercial shipping, endangering seafarers, inflating insurance and shipping costs, and eroding investor confidence. Activities often involving foreign fishing fleets, such as Chinese vessels operating in Vietnamese or Indonesian waters, have led to diplomatic tensions between the stakeholders. Besides, environmental and climate-related challenges emanating from global warming, such as coral reef degradation, marine pollution, and rising sea levels, largely pose another threat to littoral states like Vietnam. Additionally, ocean acidification and overfishing are factors that severely impact marine biodiversity and threaten regional food security. Consequently, the challenges to environmental and food security have emerged as critical components of maritime governance that need to be addressed by Vietnam.

To counter these risks, Vietnam's reliance on regional initiatives such as the Regional Cooperation Agreement on Combating Piracy and Armed Robbery against Ships in Asia (ReCAAP) and the Malacca Strait Patrols (MSP) tends to enhance coordination and maritime security needs to be complemented by stricter norms of maritime governance along with embarking upon means for narrowing significant gaps in capacity and coordination among Southeast Asian states, such as limited naval and coast guard capabilities, insufficient intelligence-sharing mechanisms, and lack of coordinated responses. In this context, Vietnam's adherence to bilateral and institutional mechanisms under the ASEAN framework provides the platform for strengthening maritime cooperation and dialogue to ensure environmental protection, scientific research, Search and Rescue (SAR), and law enforcement to counter the transnational crimes mentioned above. Furthermore, cooperation in the spheres of Blue Economy, development, and preservation of marine ecology provides opportunities for Vietnam, its ASEAN counterparts, other partners, and China in using, managing, and conserving ocean, sea, and marine life and coastal ecosystems. This can be achieved across various sectors, such as fisheries, aquaculture, maritime transport, renewable energy, tourism, climate change, Research and Development (R&D), and the establishment of harmonized common standards in SAR cooperation. Such initiatives would address threats to security and focus on sustainable development of the regional maritime domain. In this respect, diplomatic negotiations embodied in Vision Statements, Plans of Action, and Joint Declarations under the ASEAN rubric—such as the "Joint Declaration on ASEAN-China Strategic Partnership for Peace and Prosperity (2003)," "Plans to Implement the Joint Declaration on ASEAN-China Strategic Partnership for Peace and Prosperity" (2005-2010, 2011-2015, 2016-2020, and 2021-2025), "Declaration for a Decade of Coastal and Marine Environmental Protection in the South China Sea (2017)," and "ASEAN Leaders' Vision Statement on a Cohesive and Responsive ASEAN: Rising Above Challenges and Sustaining Growth (2020)"—have not only outlined hard-core traditional security-related issues but also acknowledged the imperative of addressing non-traditional security threats, which have a direct bearing on sustainable development, marine ecology, biodiversity conservation, and the like. At the bilateral level as well, Vietnam's proposed discussions with China for concluding agreements on cooperation in fishery, release and protection of aquatic resources in the Gulf of Tonkin, in addition to establishing a hotline to deal with unexpected fishery incidents and maritime SAR cooperation (The State Council of the People's Republic of China, 2025), are significant for confidence-building, sustainable joint resources management, and preventive diplomacy.

Finally, while multilateral initiatives within the ASEAN framework, such as the ADMM-Plus, ARF, and EAS, have attempted to build trust and establish cooperative security among member states, progress in this respect has been slow and incremental. ASEAN's consensus-based decision-making model and the disparate levels of threat perceptions among member states often result in fragmented responses, limiting the effectiveness of regional maritime security cooperation. Therefore, it is imperative for Vietnam to address the challenges arising from diverse threats to regional maritime security beyond the traditional factors such as contested claims to sovereignty in the South China Sea to encompass a host of non-traditional components including safeguarding economic interests and resources, environmental sustainability, and regional stability, as discussed above.

5. ENSURING MARITIME SECURITY: VIETNAM'S EMPHASIS ON NAVAL MODERNIZATION AND DEFENSE PARTNERSHIPS

Vietnam's policy regarding the attainment of maritime security in general and in the South China Sea in particular is based on maintaining the regional status quo and preventing Chinese hegemony and encroachment through a three-pronged strategy aimed at accommodating the latter's security interests, enhancing self-defense capacities, and seeking regional and international cooperation. The principal objectives of its maritime security policy are: safeguarding national sovereignty, sovereign rights, and jurisdictional claims over the South China Sea; ensuring safety of sea lanes and freedom of navigation; protecting marine ecosystems and resources, including combating IUU fishing; developing the maritime economy under the blue economy model; and strengthening maritime law enforcement and deterrence capabilities (Huong, 2016, p. 26). Prior to examining Vietnam's maritime security initiatives in Southeast Asia in general and with respect to the South China Sea in particular, it is significant to contextualize the regional initiatives related to maritime domain awareness, maritime law enforcement, and disaster relief. This is based on two principal mechanisms: Vietnam's defense modernization and fostering cooperation with its partners, as discussed in the following subsections. As Vietnam "promotes cooperation with countries inside and outside the region to address common security challenges" (Ministry of National Defence, 2019, p. 32), a comprehensive, rules-based, and multilateral cooperative security approach rooted in the tenets of regionalism and global norms is essential for navigating the complex maritime challenges.

Vietnam's initiatives in addressing the maritime security challenges in the region hinge on its pursuit of hedging as a strategy toward China to produce mutually advantageous effects under situations of high uncertainties, while emphasizing internal/hard balancing by embarking on military augmentation and modernization drives, and external/soft balancing mechanisms by promoting multilateral engagement with like-minded partners. Hedging has emerged as an effective strategy for addressing the security dilemma introduced by China's offensive realist rationale of power maximization, aspiring to regional hegemony. By contrast, following the realist logic of security maximization through deterrence, Vietnam has sought to maintain the regional status quo and balance of power. As China continues its gray-zone tactics of intimidating states like the Philippines and Vietnam, which have commercial stakes and disputes over territorial claims in the South China Sea littorals, international opinion against this unilateral infringement of a state's sovereign rights and jurisdiction, bolstered by voices of like-minded partners such as India and the US, has a deterrent effect on Beijing (Chakraborty, 2024, p. 40).

Thus, Vietnam's policy of self-reliance and investing in the modernization of its military to develop a deterrent capability against China is complemented by its resort to other measures, including soft balancing through international institutions and strengthening its relations with regional states, especially Australia, India, Japan, South Korea, and the US. Nevertheless, in most cases, Vietnam has not been eager to push the relationship with the US so far as to have an unfavorable impact on China, though the only exception in this regard could be in case of Beijing's assertiveness and hegemony in the South China Sea.

5.1. Vietnam's Defense Modernization

The emergence of both traditional and non-traditional security threats in the maritime domain has made defense modernization a sine qua non insofar as Vietnam's defense policy in general and maritime policy in particular are concerned. This has prompted Vietnam to pursue both strategies of internal and external balancing by enhancing its defense expenditure and preparedness on the one hand and fostering strategic and defense partnerships with like-minded regional and extra-regional states such as the US, India, Japan, Australia, South Korea, and ASEAN member states on the other. Vietnam's defense modernization represents a hybrid approach, blending defensive realism and liberalism, manifested in hedging through institutional engagement. In the post-normalization period, Vietnam has pursued this strategy with China to produce mutually advantageous effects while emphasizing internal/hard balancing by embarking on military augmentation and modernization drives, and external/soft balancing mechanisms by promoting multilateral engagement with like-minded partners. Vietnam's military modernization drive, commencing in the post-12th CPV Congress, which had embarked on "gradual" modernization of "several critical services, with the Navy and the Air Force at the forefront," was replaced by the urge for "immediate" modernization as one of its guiding principles in the wake of the 13th CPV Congress, taking cognizance of the threats emanating from the South China Sea dispute. In this trajectory, this CPV Congress was indeed a watershed event, since it unveiled a policy for developing a dual-use defense industry, paving the way for greater private sector participation in the defense-industrial complex. Subsequently, Hanoi undertook a three-pronged procurement strategy premised on diversifying sources of advanced military platforms (Phoung, 2022), with regional states such as India, Japan, and South Korea being identified as potential suppliers; upgradation and modernization of old weapons and systems. The shared ownership and operation of weapons systems of Russian origin by India and Vietnam and the former's provision of spare parts for some Russian-origin equipment to the Vietnamese Navy; and self-reliance and indigenization in defense production, ranging from small and advanced arms to technology-driven high-tech domains, are significant.

In keeping with its modernization drive, increasing the defense budget has focused on facilitating self-reliance in defense production, prioritizing R&D, emphasizing cyber and electronic warfare capabilities, technology transfer, local manufacturing, and international cooperation. An analysis of the trend in Vietnam's defense expenditure reveals a significant rise since 2005, when it spent approximately US$1 billion to US$4.9 billion in 2017, following an all-time high of US$5 billion in 2016 and exceeding US$4.4 billion in 2015. Vietnam's official defense budget demonstrated a remarkable 258% increase within a decade (from US$1.3 billion in 2006 to US$4.4 billion in 2015). Accordingly, its defense spending witnessed an escalation from 2.23% of Gross Domestic Product (GDP) in 2010 to 2.36% in 2018, amounting to approximately US$5.8 billion, in conjunction with the "Overall Strategy for International Integration Through 2020, Vision to 2030, (2016)" (Chakraborty, 2020, p. 23). This Strategy underscored Vietnam's commitment to "enhance and upgrade defense and security relations with partners … deploy seriously and consistently the agreements and programs on defense and security cooperation with big countries like Russia, India, Japan, and some other potential partners like Australia and Israel, and gradually expand the content of defense and security cooperation … within ASEAN … [and] between ASEAN and its partners" (Vietnam Government Portal, 2016).

In addition, the "Defence White Paper" (2019) outlined Vietnam's commitment to "introduce modern equipment" and its determination to build defense and diplomatic ties with the international community. It also prioritized Vietnam's self-reliance by "building and enhancing weapons and equipment" and to provide a level of defense investment that is "in line with the country's economic development" (Ministry of National Defence of the Socialist Republic of Vietnam, 2019, p. 5).

While estimating Vietnam's defense budget from 2003–2018, according to the Stockholm International Peace Research Institute (SIPRI), Vietnam has demonstrated some of the largest increases in military expenditure in Southeast Asia. During the period under review, its military spending increased nearly 700%—from US$841 million in 2003 to US$5.5 billion in 2018—the latter accounting for 8.1% of total government spending and 2.3% of GDP. The SIPRI data also reveals that from 1995 to 2022, Vietnam's arms imports totaled US$9.1 billion, with Russia accounting for US$7.471 billion (81.5%). During 2018-2020, Vietnam's military spending is estimated to have had an annual average increase of 8.78%, according to a report published by the International Institute for Strategic Studies (IISS). The data further illustrates that in 2022, Vietnam planned to allocate US$6.65 billion for recurrent defense expenditure, accounting for 12.3% of state expenditure estimates in 2023. In 2022, Global Data reported that Vietnam's military expenditure for acquisition was estimated to be around US$1.1 billion in 2021 and was projected to grow at 8.1% annually, reaching US$1.8 billion between 2023 and 2027. Regarding total defense expenditure, the report forecasted an increase at 8.5% year-on-year, projected to reach US$8.5 billion in 2027. Vietnam ranked 15th on the list of top global arms importers, while featuring among the top six arms importers in the Asia-Pacific region between 2010 and 2022 (US Department of Commerce, International Trade Administration, 2024). Between 2020-2024, Vietnam's defense acquisition budget has seen a remarkable ascent, with a Compound Annual Growth Rate (CAGR) of 12.6%, forecasting the maintenance of a positive CAGR of 9.4% with a cumulative investment of US$14.1 billion during 2025-2029. Spurred by China's assertive strategies in the South China Sea, Vietnam's defense budget is estimated to increase to US$10.2 billion by 2029, with a CAGR of 5.6% from US$7.8 billion in 2024 (Global Data, 2024). This will facilitate the procurement of fighter and multirole aircraft, armored vehicles, naval vessels, patrol ships, maritime patrol aircraft, and surveillance equipment, in addition to bolstering capabilities in digital battlefield, electronic intelligence, and cybersecurity domains to develop a self-reliant and technologically sophisticated armed force.

5.2. Strategic Cooperation with Regional Partners

Vietnam has established strategic partnerships with 16 countries, comprehensive partnerships with 11 countries, and special strategic relations with Laos and Cambodia. According to the "Defence White Paper" (2019), it has defense ties with over 80 countries and international organizations, in addition to setting up defense attaché offices in 37 countries and in the UN by 2019. On the other hand, 49 countries have established defense and military attaché offices in Vietnam. The "Defence White Paper" highlights that its "national defence policy is peaceful and self-defensive in nature and promotes defence cooperation with countries to improve its capabilities to protect the country and address common security challenges" (Ministry of National Defence of the Socialist Republic of Vietnam, 2019, pp. 23-24).

Vietnam's defense policy has focused on multilateralization and diversification rather than alliance-building or exclusive reliance on a particular state. Its signing of Comprehensive Strategic Partnerships, including the mechanisms of defense dialogues, military exercises, training, capacity-building, and purchase of military equipment and future technological cooperation with various major and regional powers such as the US, Australia, India, Japan, and South Korea, as discussed below, in order to safeguard its sovereignty and national interests, attests to the same.

First, the Comprehensive Strategic Partnership between Vietnam and Australia (2024) provides the foundation for holistic and multifaceted defense cooperation and expansion of defense industry, capacity-building, maritime security, information and intelligence sharing, strengthening maritime cooperation, including sustainable marine resource management; combating IUU fishing; education and training programs, practical exchanges, enhancing cooperation in cybersecurity and critical technology through capacity-building initiatives to address cybersecurity threats associated with hybrid warfare (Office of the Prime Minister of Australia, 2024, Cl. 8).

Second, with respect to India, since the signing of the Comprehensive Strategic Partnership agreement in 2016, Indo-Vietnamese defense collaboration has scaled new heights, adorned by high-level summitry and exchanges, interactions and interoperability of the defense forces, ship visits, port calls, bilateral naval exercises, and the focus on developing defense-industrial cooperation through extension of defense Lines of Credit to Vietnam (Embassy of India in Vietnam, 2016, Cl. 6). The Indian Navy's regular training for Vietnamese submarine crews, visits by Indian naval vessels to Vietnam and vice versa, have strengthened tactical skills and enhanced maritime awareness between them. India has played a prominent role in training Vietnamese military personnel, including in naval and submarine-related capacity building, thereby strengthening its maritime deterrence competencies in the South China Sea (Singh, 2025). India also has sustained Vietnam's military modernization through credit lines for patrol boats, gifting of the missile corvette "INS Kirpan," and training on platforms such as fighter jets and submarines.

Third, the Comprehensive Strategic Partnership agreement between Vietnam and South Korea (2022) provides a blueprint for enhancing cooperation in politics, defense, and security, particularly in the spheres of technology, defense industry, capacity-building, and training (The Ministry of Finance of the Socialist Republic of Vietnam, 2022). Their cooperation can be interpreted in terms of tangible material and strategic gains, prominent in the realm of defense-industrial modernization. The procurement of South Korean military equipment by Vietnam demonstrates tangible benefits, technological progression, and diversification of arms suppliers. This contributes directly to Vietnam's material defense capabilities and reduces reliance on inherited arrangements.

Fourth, the Comprehensive Strategic Partnership agreement between Vietnam and Japan (2023) envisages defense-industrial cooperation, transfer of defense equipment and technology to the Ministry of Defense of Vietnam to facilitate its self-reliant defense capabilities, capacity-building, delegation-level deliberations to maintain and enhance the effectiveness of defense dialogue, information-sharing, coordination and consultation mechanisms. It emphasizes bolstering cooperation in maritime security and safety through joint training, information sharing, and capacity building between the Coast Guards from both sides, as well as exploring opportunities to expand cooperation in response to non-traditional security challenges, such as cybersecurity, economic security, terrorism, and transnational organized crimes (Ministry of Foreign Affairs of Japan, 2023, Cl. 12-14).

Finally, the Comprehensive Strategic Partnership signed between Vietnam and the US (2023) envisions "further cooperation in defense industry and defense trade in accordance with each side's conditions through mutually agreed mechanisms," while also committing to "assist Vietnam to develop its self-reliant defense capabilities in accordance with the needs of Vietnam and established mechanisms" (US Embassy and Consulate in Vietnam, 2024). Since the lifting of the ban on the sale of weapons to Vietnam in May 2016, the US has conducted sales through the Maritime Security Initiative, Cooperative Threat Reduction Program, and Foreign Military Financing. The US delivered T-6C training aircraft in 2024, transferred Hamilton-class Coast Guard cutters in 2017 and 2020 to help improve its maritime law enforcement capabilities, in addition to contributing 24 Metal Shark patrol boats and six ScanEagles to assist in maritime security (US Department of State: Bureau of East Asian and Pacific Affairs, 2025).

These agreements are not only significant in terms of modernizing Vietnam's defense profile and preparedness but also fulfilling the objective of developing a "streamlined and strong Army by 2025, and a revolutionary, regular, advanced and modern People's Army by 2030" (Thayer, 2024). Furthermore, these agreements institutionalize the conduct of bilateral, joint, and multilateral naval and coast guard exercises, thus reflecting Vietnam's strategic diversification in defense partnerships. Spanning a plethora of exercises from bilateral peacekeeping, Humanitarian Assistance and Disaster Relief to enhancing interoperability among the forces, multi-domain operations, and mutual capacity-building, initiatives such as VINBAX with India, MILAN (multilateral), and goodwill exercises with Japan are guided by shared concerns over regional stability and balance, especially in the South China Sea. However, the success of these partnerships for strengthening Vietnam's defense capabilities and strategic weight has been mixed in nature. In this respect, mention may be made of Vietnam's defense cooperation with the US, which has been encumbered by deep-seated historical mistrust, human rights concerns, and the former's acute sensitivity to Chinese reactions. Thus, Vietnam pragmatically evades participation in high-intensity joint exercises or alliance-like arrangements. Despite its strategic potential, the partnership between India and Vietnam is constrained by the latter's non-alignment doctrine, avoiding formal alliance commitments, collective defense obligations, and overtly anti-China posturing, resulting in incremental rather than transformational defense cooperation with New Delhi.

Similarly, Vietnam's partnership with Japan suffers from a lack of operational depth due to the latter's constitutional constraints and Hanoi's sensitivity toward regional power dynamics, which severely limit hard military cooperation. As a result, defense engagement focuses on exchanges and confidence-building measures rather than force projection. While Japan enhances Vietnam's diplomatic leverage, it contributes minimally to Hanoi's immediate military capabilities, thereby constraining the partnership's practical defense utility. Likewise, Australia's engagement with Vietnam is largely confined to non-traditional security fields and capacity-building, with limited contributions to the latter's strategic deterrence or combat readiness. This narrow scope reflects Vietnam's hedging strategy and Australia's preference for low-risk engagement, which has the potential for bolstering Hanoi's long-term institutional capability rather than contributing significantly to immediate, pressing strategic challenges. Finally, Vietnam's defense partnership with South Korea, primarily driven by defense export interests, has been narrow and transactional insofar as broader strategic or operational integration is concerned, thus limiting its contribution to strategic deterrence.

In summary, Vietnam's defense partnerships with the countries discussed above prioritize strategic autonomy over alliance dependence. While the relations have been elevated to the level of Comprehensive Strategic Partnerships, their practical defense outcomes vary in scope, intensity, and strategic impact, revealing both effectiveness and inherent constraints. While India and the US contribute significantly to Vietnam's strategic signaling and maritime security posture, the Vietnam-Australia component prioritizes training and capacity-building. Furthermore, Japan reinforces diplomatic legitimacy and normative support to Vietnam, and South Korea strengthens defense-industrial modernization. Although these partnerships have enhanced Vietnam's strategic autonomy and international standing, their effectiveness is constrained by factors such as Hanoi's commitment to the non-alignment doctrine, interoperability challenges, geopolitical sensitivities, relations with China, and the structural incongruence pertaining to the strategic interests of the stakeholders.

6. CONCLUSION

As a coastal nation strategically located along the South China Sea, Vietnam occupies a pivotal position in the evolving dynamics of regional maritime security. Confronted with increasing geopolitical competition, heightened tensions over territorial claims in the Spratly and Paracel Islands, and the proliferation of non-traditional security threats, Vietnam finds itself navigating a complex landscape of both opportunities and challenges. Its historical experiences of resisting foreign domination, combined with evolving naval capabilities and proactive diplomacy, have positioned the nation as a significant actor in promoting regional stability in accordance with international maritime norms.

Vietnam's maritime security approach embodies a sophisticated balancing act that reflects the principles of "bamboo diplomacy"—flexible, resilient, and pragmatic. While safeguarding its sovereignty and maritime interests, Hanoi pursues a three-pronged strategy: accommodating China's security concerns through economic engagement and the Comprehensive Strategic Partnership signed in 2008; enhancing self-defense capabilities through sustained military modernization; and cultivating strategic partnerships with regional middle powers including Australia, India, Japan, and South Korea, as well as the United States. This hedging strategy enables Vietnam to maintain peaceful relations with China while simultaneously building deterrent capabilities and diversifying its security partnerships to counterbalance potential Chinese assertiveness.

Through diplomatic engagement, legal initiatives supporting UNCLOS, regional cooperation within the ASEAN centrality framework, and comprehensive military modernization, Vietnam has evolved from a reactive to a proactive contributor in the regional security architecture. Its robust defense modernization drive—including the acquisition of submarines, surveillance systems, and coastal defense capabilities—demonstrates commitment to enhancing maritime domain awareness and deterrence. Yet, rather than seeking confrontation, Vietnam emphasizes strategic restraint and multilateralism, actively participating in ASEAN-led mechanisms such as ARF, ADMM-Plus, EAS, and negotiations for a binding Code of Conduct in the South China Sea.

However, Vietnam faces persistent structural challenges that constrain its maritime security ambitions. The power asymmetry with China remains substantial, compounded by ASEAN's internal divisions and consensus-based decision-making that often produces fragmented responses to regional threats. China's continued construction of artificial islands, deployment of maritime militia, and employment of gray-zone tactics in contested waters directly challenge Vietnam's sovereignty claims and undermine the rules-based maritime order. Furthermore, Vietnam's economic dependence on China—with bilateral trade exceeding US$260 billion in 2024—creates inherent tensions in its dual strategy, limiting the extent to which it can align with external powers or participate in overtly anti-China security arrangements.

Looking forward, Vietnam's maritime security trajectory will likely be shaped by its ability to refine its hedging strategy while maintaining strategic autonomy. Under the leadership of CPV General Secretary Tô Lâm, who emphasizes foreign policy as an instrument of national strength rather than ideological alignment, Vietnam may witness gradual shifts toward more assertive positioning. The concept of "optimal positioning"—maximizing freedom of choice while preserving decision-making autonomy—may complement traditional bamboo diplomacy, enabling Vietnam to navigate the intensifying Sino-US rivalry more effectively. Vietnam's role in shaping Indo-Pacific maritime security ultimately hinges on its capacity to balance assertiveness with diplomacy, deterrence with dialogue, and national interests with regional stability. While enduring significant constraints, Vietnam possesses strategic opportunities to lead in norm-building, strengthen multilateral coalitions, and advance a rules-based maritime order. As maritime security becomes increasingly central to Indo-Pacific geopolitics, Vietnam's nuanced navigation of these contested waters will not only determine its own developmental trajectory but also significantly influence the broader architecture of regional peace, stability, and cooperation in Southeast Asia.

REFERENCES

Acharya, A. (2003-2004). Will Asia's past be its future? *International Security*, *28*(3), 149–164. https://www.jstor.org/stable/4137480. DOI: 10.1162/016228803773100101

Acharya, A. (2009). *Constructing a security community in Southeast Asia: ASEAN and the problem of regional order*. Routledge. DOI: 10.4324/9780203939239

Anh, T. N. H. (2024). Assessing Vietnam's maritime governance capacity: Priorities and challenges. *Asia Maritime Transparency Initiative*. https://amti.csis.org/assessing-vietnams-maritime-governance-capacity-priorities-and-challenges/

Bateman, S. (2013). Cooperation or trust: What comes first in the South China Sea? *S. Rajaratnam School of International Studies*. https://rsis.edu.sg/rsis-publication/rsis/2055-cooperation-or-trust-what-com/

Bland, B. (2025). Trump's tariffs will push Southeast Asia uncomfortably close to China. *Chatham House*. https://www.chathamhouse.org/2025/04/trumps-tariffs-will-push-southeast-asia-uncomfortably-close-china

Bradford, J. (2021). Evolving conceptualizations of maritime security in Southeast Asia. *Asia Maritime Transparency Initiative*. https://amti.csis.org/evolving-conceptualizations-of-maritime-security-in-southeast-asia/

Chakraborti, T., & Chakraborty, M. (2024). The reflexive silhouette of China in the Indo-Vietnam mirror: Competition, confrontation and the future. In Ranjan, A., Scott, D., & Chalk, P. (Eds.), *India and China in Southeast Asia* (pp. 63–89). Palgrave Macmillan. DOI: 10.1007/978-981-97-6903-2_4

Chakraborty, M. (2020). Bilateral convergence between India and Vietnam: Defence collaboration and 'Make in India'. *Vietnam Journal for Indian and Asian Studies*, *2020*, 20–27.

Chakraborty, M. (2024). China's soft power diplomacy in Vietnam: Assessing the dynamics and efficacy of Belt and Road architecture. In Zreik, M. (Ed.), *Soft power and diplomatic strategies in Asia and the Middle East* (pp. 36–58). IGI Global. DOI: 10.4018/979-8-3693-2444-8.ch003

Cuong, D. V., & Dung, P. C. (2024). UNCLOS significant to Vietnam's peace, stability, long-term development. *Vietnam Law Magazine*. https://vietnamlawmagazine.vn/unclos-significant-to-vietnams-peace-stability-long-term-development-73173.html

Duong, N. N. (2021). Vietnam's conceptualization of maritime security. *Asia Maritime Transparency Initiative.* https://amti.csis.org/vietnams-conceptualizations-of-maritime-security/

Embassy of India in Vietnam. (2016). *India-Vietnam Comprehensive Strategic Partnership.* https://www.indembassyhanoi.gov.in/docs/1693902939StrategicPartnership.pdf

Emmers, R. (2010). ASEAN and the securitization of transnational crime in Southeast Asia. *The Pacific Review, 23*(4), 419–430. DOI: 10.1080/09512740320000085653

Global Data. (2024). *Vietnam defense market size, trends, budget allocation, regulations, acquisitions, competitive landscape and forecast to 2029.* https://www.globaldata.com/store/report/vietnam-defense-market-analysis/

Guard, B. Ministry of National Defence, People's Army of the Socialist Republic of Vietnam. (2021). *Vietnam's policy on maritime security.* http://bienphongvietnam.gov.vn/chinh-sach-cua-viet-nam-ve-an-ninhbien.html

Hanh, V. N. (2025). Vietnam-China economic partnership: Insights from top Chinese leader's visit. *Vietnam Briefing.* https://www.vietnam-briefing.com/news/vietnam-china-economic-partnership-amid-global-tensions-top-chinese-leaders-visit.html/

Hayton, B. (2025). Vietnam's tariff deal with Trump reflects balancing act between US and China. *Chatham House.* https://www.chathamhouse.org/2025/07/vietnams-tariff-deal-trump-reflects-balancing-act-between-us-and-china

Huong, N. M. (2016). *New context of Vietnam's national security challenges.* ISEAS Publishing. https://bookshop.iseas.edu.sg/publication/2196

Khanh, V. V. (2021). *Vietnam's policy on maritime security.* http://bienphongvietnam.gov.vn/chinh-sach-cua-viet-nam-ve-an-ninh-bien.html

Ministry of Foreign Affairs of Japan. (2023). *Joint Statement on the Elevation of the Japan-Vietnam Relations to a Comprehensive Strategic Partnership for Peace and Prosperity in Asia and the World.* https://www.mofa.go.jp/files/100587102.pdf

Ministry of Foreign Affairs of the Socialist Republic of Vietnam. (2020). *White Paper on the Legal Status of Vietnam's Maritime Zones under the 1982 United Nations Convention on the Law of the Sea (UNCLOS).* https://vietnamlawmagazine.vn/unclos-significant-to-vietnams-peace-stability-long-term-development-73173.html

Ministry of National Defence of the Socialist Republic of Vietnam. (2019). *Vietnam National Defence.* https://s.rfi.fr/media/display/41558134-9451-11ea-b6c6-005056a98db9/2019VietnamNationalDefence.pdf

Nguyen, H. (2022). *Vietnam and the shift towards maritime security cooperation.* Brill. DOI: 10.1163/9789004532847_019

Office of the Prime Minister of Australia. (2024). *Joint Statement on the Elevation to a Comprehensive Strategic Partnership between Vietnam and Australia.* https://www.pm.gov.au/media/joint-statement-elevation-comprehensive-strategic-partnership-between-vietnam-and-australia

Pham, L. (2025). Vietnam's Gulf of Tonkin baseline helps protect sovereignty rights. *Hanoi Times.* https://hanoitimes.vn/vietnams-gulf-of-tonkin-baseline-helps-protect-sovereignty-rights.642354.html

Phoung, N. T. (2022). With arms expo, Vietnam seeks to diversify its defense procurements. *The Diplomat.* https://thediplomat.com/2022/12/with-arms-expo-vietnam-seeks-to-diversify-its-defense-procurements/

Singh, M. (2025). India, Vietnam expand defense ties across land, sea, air domains. *Indo-Pacific Defense Forum.* https://ipdefenseforum.com/2025/05/india-vietnam-expand-defense-ties-across-land-sea-air-domains/

Storey, I. (2009). Maritime security in Southeast Asia: Two cheers for regional cooperation. *Southeast Asian Affairs*, 36–58. https://www.jstor.org/stable/27913377

Thao, T. T. (2025). Maritime security and Vietnamese perspective. *Science Council of Japan.* https://www.scj.go.jp/en/sca/activities/conferences/conf_5_programs/pdf/5thsecuritythao.pdf

Thayer, C. (2024). Australia-Vietnam comprehensive strategic partnership: The defence dimension. *The Strategist.* https://www.aspistrategist.org.au/australia-vietnam-comprehensive-strategic-partnership-the-defence-dimension/

The Ministry of Finance of the Socialist Republic of Vietnam. (2022). *Vietnam and ROK Take Ties to Comprehensive Strategic Partnership.* https://trial.mof.gov.vn/webcenter/portal/btcen

The State Council of the People's Republic of China. (2025). *China, Vietnam Agree to Build All-round Cooperation Pattern.* https://english.www.gov.cn/news/202504/16/content_WS67fef369c6d0868f4e8f1bac.html

Till, G. (2009). *Sea power: A guide for the twenty-first century.* Routledge. DOI: 10.4324/9780203880487

Tran, B. (2023). Vietnam's quest for enhanced maritime domain awareness. *ISEAS – Yusof Ishak Institute.* https://www.iseas.edu.sg/wp-content/uploads/2024/01/ISEAS_Perspective_2023_96.pdf

U.S. Department of Commerce, International Trade Administration. (2024). *Vietnam Country Commercial Guide: Defense and Security Sector.* https://www.trade.gov/country-commercial-guides/vietnam-defense-and-security-sector

U.S. Department of State. Bureau of East Asian and Pacific Affairs. (2025). *Bilateral Relations Fact Sheet: Relations with Vietnam.* https://2021-2025.state.gov/bureau-of-east-asian-and-pacific-affairs/releases/2025/01/u-s-relations-with-vietnam/

U.S. Embassy and Consulate in Vietnam. (2024). *Fact Sheet: One-year Anniversary of the U.S.-Vietnam Comprehensive Strategic Partnership.* https://vn.usembassy.gov/fact-sheet-one-year-anniversary-of-the-u-s-vietnam-comprehensive-strategic-partnership/

Viet Nam News. (2024*). Vietnam modernizes military, strengthens national defense.* https://vietnamnews.vn/politics-laws/1689314/viet-nam-modernises-military-strengthens-national-defence.html

Viet Nam News. (2025). *Vietnam calls for respect for international law to ensure maritime* security. https://vietnamnews.vn/politics-laws/1723311/viet-nam-calls-for-respect-for-international-law-to-ensure-maritime-security.html

Vietnam Government Portal. (2016). *Overall Strategy for International Integration through 2020, vision to 2030.* http://news.chinhphu.vn/Home/Overall-strategy-for-international-integration-through-2020-vision-to-2030/20161/29060.vgp

Xueren, L. (2025). Xi's visit to strengthen China-Vietnam bond, regional growth. *Xinhua.* https://english.cctv.com/2025/04/15/ARTIlLYpl3PF3RPLHDiluXxD250415.shtml

Chapter 14
From "Outsider" to "Bridge": National Identity and Australia's Strategic Evolution in the South China Sea Disputes (1996–2013)

Hiep Xuan Tran
University of Science and Education, The University of Da Nang, Vietnam

Giang Minh Nguyen
https://orcid.org/0000-0002-8336-9991
University of Social Sciences and Humanites, Vietnam National University Ho Chi Minh City, Vietnam

Tam Thi Thanh Le
Dong A University, Vietnam

ABSTRACT

This chapter examines Australia's strategic posture toward the South China Sea disputes (1996-2013), arguing that national identity shifts fundamentally shaped foreign policy. Employing constructivist, realist, and liberal frameworks, the research traces Australia's identity transformation through three phases: Keating's "part of Asia" aspiration, Howard's "in Asia but not of Asia" realism, and Rudd-Gillard's "bridge between East and West" synthesis. This evolution drove strategic shifts from engagement to US bandwagoning, culminating in sophisticated hedging through diversified partnerships. The Australia-Vietnam security relationship demonstrates how the "bridge" identity enabled complex middle-power diplomacy—maintaining

DOI: 10.4018/979-8-3373-4470-6.ch014

economic ties with China while strengthening regional security cooperation. This research proves national identity constitutes an active variable, not rhetorical backdrop, in maritime strategy formulation.

1. INTRODUCTION

The geopolitical architecture of the Indo-Pacific region has undergone profound transformation in the post-Cold War era, characterized predominantly by China's rapid ascent and the consequent intensification of strategic competition among major powers (Tran & Nguyen, 2024). Positioned at the nexus of these shifting dynamics, Australia confronts an increasingly complex and contested regional environment that challenges its traditional strategic calculus. The South China Sea (SCS), a critical maritime corridor and flashpoint for territorial disputes, has emerged as the principal theater where these geopolitical tensions manifest most acutely. For Australia—a middle power with substantial economic ties to Asia and an enduring security alliance with the United States—the SCS disputes represent not merely a distant maritime controversy but a fundamental test of its foreign policy autonomy, national security imperatives, and regional identity (White, 2011).

This research focuses specifically on the critical period from 1996 to 2013, a transformative era that witnessed fundamental shifts in Australia's strategic orientation toward the SCS and the broader Indo-Pacific region. This seventeen-year timeframe encompasses three distinct political administrations—the Howard Coalition government (1996-2007), the Rudd-Gillard Labor governments (2007-2013), and the initial months of the Abbott Coalition government—each of which articulated markedly different conceptions of Australia's national identity and regional role. The period begins with the election of the Howard government in 1996, which marked a decisive departure from the Keating Labor government's "part of Asia" vision, and concludes in 2013 with the release of the Defence White Paper, by which point Australia had firmly established its "bridge" identity and sophisticated hedging strategy.

The selection of this timeframe reflects several critical inflection points in Australia's strategic evolution. The 1997 Asian Financial Crisis tested the new Howard government's regional engagement framework. The September 11, 2001 attacks fundamentally reshaped Australia's security priorities, deepening alignment with the United States. The 2007 election brought Labor back to power under Kevin Rudd, initiating a shift toward creative middle-power diplomacy. China's increasingly assertive posture in the SCS, particularly following its formal submission of the nine-dash line to the United Nations in 2009, created urgent pressures for Australia to refine its strategic approach. By 2012-2013, with the release of the Australia in the Asian Century White Paper and the Defence White Paper, Australia had articulated a comprehensive framework for managing its dual imperatives of economic engagement with China and security cooperation with the United States and regional partners.

The central aim of this article is to investigate the evolution of Australia's strategic posture regarding the SCS disputes between 1996 and 2013, analyzing how these strategic shifts were intrinsically linked to the country's changing diplomatic ideology and its conception of "middle power" diplomacy. Specifically, this research traces the trajectory of Australia's self-identification—from the articulation of being "in Asia but not of Asia" (1996-2007), through the transition period of creative middle-power engagement (2007-2010), to the full articulation of the "bridge between East and West" role (2010-2013)—demonstrating how these identity narratives shaped operational strategies in the SCS.

By correlating domestic identity narratives with external strategic behavior during this timeframe, this research provides a nuanced explanation for Australia's shift from the Howard government's bandwagoning with the United States to the Rudd-Gillard governments' sophisticated strategy of "hedging." Furthermore, this research advances the constructivist argument that national identity constitutes not a fixed variable but a fluid construct that actively shapes, and is shaped by, a state's foreign policy decisions. The examination of the 1996-2013 period captures a complete cycle of identity transformation, allowing for systematic analysis of how identity shifts drive strategic adjustments in middle-power behavior within contested regional environments.

2. LITERATURE REVIEW

A systematic review of existing scholarship on Australian foreign policy reveals a rich and diverse body of work addressing the nation's position in the Asian region. However, close examination of journal articles, conference papers, theses, and dissertations available through major academic databases indicates a distinct research gap in connecting the evolution of Australia's national identity narratives directly to its strategic maneuvers in the SCS.

The foundational literature on Australia's engagement with Asia is extensive. Scholars such as Evans and Grant (1995) provided early, comprehensive analyses of Australia's foreign relations in the immediate post-Cold War landscape. Their work documents the Keating government's vigorous pursuit of regional integration, framing the "part of Asia" narrative as a necessary adaptation to the economic realities of the late twentieth century. This period is often characterized in the literature as one of "enmeshment," whereby Australia sought security in Asia rather than from Asia. Building upon this foundation, Allan and Michael (2007) offer an incisive analysis of the machinery of Australian foreign policymaking. They dissect the "Howard Paradox"—the government's capacity to deepen economic ties with Asia while simultaneously strengthening the US alliance and emphasizing Australia's Western heritage. Their work is crucial for understanding the pivot to the "in Asia" narrative, suggesting that Australia's foreign policy embodies an ongoing tension between its history (Western origins) and its geography (Asian location).

In the realm of national identity and constructivism, scholars have made significant contributions. Elder (2017) argues that Australian national identity constitutes a fluid concept, constantly reshaped by forces of globalization and modernization. Similarly, Pham (2015) posits that identity functions as a compass for foreign policy, defining state goals through self-positioning relative to other nations. These constructivist accounts provide the theoretical foundation for arguing that Australia's behavior in the international arena is determined not solely by material power distribution but by how it perceives its own identity. The concept of "middle power" constitutes another dominant theme in the literature. Ungerer (2007) explores this concept specifically within Australian foreign policy, analyzing how Canberra employs "niche diplomacy" and coalition-building to amplify its influence. This literature suggests that Australia's identity as a responsible middle power compels it to support a rules-based global order—a crucial factor in shaping its SCS stance.

Regarding the SCS and regional security, the literature is equally robust but often operates independently from the identity discourse. Tran (2012) and Huynh (2019) have extensively examined Australia's relations with Southeast Asian nations, particularly Vietnam, and its stance on the SCS. Their works highlight Australia's increasing security contributions and support for freedom of navigation. Nguyen's master's thesis (2025) provides granular examination of the Australia-Vietnam relationship, framing it as a key component of Australia's broader hedging strategy against uncertainty in the Indo-Pacific. This body of work emphasizes the practical aspects of security cooperation—port visits, training exercises, and strategic dialogues—as evidence of Australia's growing commitment to the region.

However, the literature notes a distinct shift following the 1996 election of the Liberal-National Coalition. Key government documents such as the 1997 White Paper In the National Interest highlight a retreat from the "part of Asia" narrative toward a more pragmatic "national interest" approach (Nguyen, 2025). A significant cluster of contemporary research focuses on the terminological and strategic shift from "Asia-Pacific" to "Indo-Pacific." Recent studies identify the 2012-2013 period as a critical juncture where the "Indo-Pacific" construct was adopted not merely as semantic change but as deliberate strategic maneuvering to dilute Chinese centrality by incorporating India and the United States into a single strategic framework (Nguyen, 2025).

Critical review of these disparate strands reveals a missing link. While abundant studies exist on identity politics and separate technical analyses of maritime strategy, there is a paucity of research that systematically integrates these two domains over the extended period from 1996 to 2013. Few studies explicitly trace how the shift from the "part of Asia" narrative to the "bridge" narrative acted as the causal mechanism for the transition from a policy of "engagement" to one of "hedging" in the SCS. Most existing literature treats identity as backdrop rather than as an active variable in maritime strategy formulation. Furthermore, while the "hedging" concept is widely applied to Southeast Asian states, its application to Australia's specific maneuvering between 2009 and 2013—specifically through the lens of its upgraded partnership with Vietnam—remains under-explored in English-language scholarship. This research aims to fill this gap by synthesizing constructivist analysis of identity formation with realism assessment of strategic posture, thereby providing a holistic explanation for the increasing sophistication of Australia's approach to the SCS disputes.

The works of Carlyle Thayer, Rory Medcalf, and Australian scholars such as White (2011) and Beeson (2013) have examined Australia's dilemma between its security ally (the United States) and its economic partner (China). Australia's Defence White Papers of 2009 and 2013 have been thoroughly analyzed to reveal the country's growing concern over China's military modernization. However, a research gap exists in the lack of studies that integrate all three theoretical traditions—realism, liberalism, and constructivism—to systematically explain the specific transformations during the 1996–2013 period. Most studies rely on single-dimensional explanations: either security pressure (realism) or economic interests (liberalism). Few have clarified how the transformation of national identity (from "Outsider" to "Bridge") interacted with strategic decisions in the SCS during the power transition between the Coalition and Labor governments. This article addresses that gap.

3. THEORETICAL FRAMEWORK

To rigorously analyze the evolution of Australia's strategic posture, this article employs a theoretical framework that synthesizes three dominant schools of international relations theory: realism, liberalism, and constructivism. This theoretical eclecticism is necessary because no single paradigm can fully account for the complexity of Australia's behavior.

Realism serves as the foundational lens for understanding the structural pressures of the international system. It explains Australia's acute sensitivity to the shifting balance of power in the Indo-Pacific, particularly the rise of China's military capabilities and the relative uncertainty regarding US hegemonic continuity. From a realism perspective, Australia's deep-seated anxiety about its "northern approaches" and its unwavering commitment to the US alliance (ANZUS) constitute rational responses to ensure survival in an anarchic system. Realism is particularly useful in analyzing the "bandwagoning" tendency observed during the Howard era, where security concerns dictated closer alignment with the global hegemon. Within this framework, Australia operates as a "middle power" under conditions of international anarchy, where survival constitutes the primary goal. The balance of power concept explains Australia's actions as rational responses to the shifting distribution of material capabilities, notably China's rapid military expansion and the relative uncertainty of US hegemonic presence. The "fear of abandonment" by its great power ally drives Australia to engage in "bandwagoning" behavior, deepening the ANZUS alliance to ensure continued US engagement in the region (Nguyen, 2025). Furthermore, the security dilemma illuminates the cycle of action-reaction in the SCS; realism posits that Australia's pursuit of security through mechanisms like AUKUS is interpreted by China as containment, leading to further militarization (Nguyen, 2022).

Liberalism provides explanatory power for Australia's strong advocacy for international law (such as UNCLOS) and its substantial investment in multilateral institutions like ASEAN, APEC, and the East Asia Summit (EAS). This perspective highlights the role of economic interdependence and institutional cooperation in mitigating conflict. It elucidates why Australia, despite security concerns, continues to pursue robust trade relations with China and champions a rules-based order in the SCS. Liberalism explains the "engagement" aspect of Australia's strategy, viewing trade and dialogue as essential tools for regional stability. This theoretical strand clarifies Australia's championship of the Code of Conduct (COC) in the SCS (Huynh, 2018). Additionally, the theory of complex interdependence accounts for the "economic gravity" of China, explaining the "hedging" strategy whereby Australia seeks to maintain robust economic ties with Beijing while securing itself militarily against potential Chinese assertiveness. The tension between liberal economic imperatives and realism security concerns constitutes a central dynamic analyzed in this article (Nguyen, 2021).

Constructivism is central to this research, bridging the gap between structural pressures and specific policy choices. As posited by Alexander Wendt, "anarchy is what states make of it," implying that state behavior is driven by shared ideas, identities, and norms rather than material capabilities alone. Following the insights of Pham (2015) and others, this study treats national identity not as a fixed attribute but as a variable that influences how Australia perceives its interests. Whether Australia conceives itself as an "outpost of the West" or an "integral part of Asia" fundamentally alters how it interprets the threat posed by SCS disputes and defines its role in resolving them. Constructivism allows us to understand the "bridge" narrative not merely as rhetoric but as a cognitive framework that enables Australia to justify its hedging strategy—maintaining Western values while integrating with Asian dynamism. It helps explain the ideological transitions from Keating's "Asian engagement" to Howard's "mateship" with the US, and the subsequent "bridge" narrative under Rudd and Gillard. Constructivism argues that Australia's "interests" in the SCS are constructed through its self-identification as a defender of international law and a "good international citizen."

Furthermore, norm entrepreneurship explains Australia's reliance on norms such as freedom of navigation to constrain great powers, framing its SCS diplomacy as a defense of the normative structure of international society (Nguyen, 2025). This hedging strategy, characterized by deepening security partnerships with regional states like Vietnam and Japan while maintaining economic engagement with China, represents a distinct maturation in Australian statecraft. Understanding this evolution is critical for policymakers and scholars alike, as it illuminates the capacity of middle powers to shape regional order and uphold international law in an era of great power rivalry.

4. METHODOLOGY

This article employs a qualitative research approach, specifically utilizing historical analysis and document analysis methods. The research draws upon a wide range of primary and secondary sources, including Australian government White Papers (1997, 2003, 2012, 2013), official statements, diplomatic speeches, and academic literature. The method of synthesis and qualitative data analysis is applied to these documents to trace the "process of formation and transformation of national identity" and correlate it with foreign policy decisions.

The analysis proceeds chronologically and thematically. First, it examines the text of key policy documents to identify the prevailing identity narrative of each era. Second, it maps these narratives against specific diplomatic and military actions taken regarding the SCS and relations with key regional partners like Vietnam. By triangulating official rhetoric with tangible policy outcomes (e.g., the signing of strategic partnerships, military deployments, aid packages), the research establishes a causal link between identity and strategy. This approach allows for deep reading of how Australia's self-conception as a "responsible middle power" has been constructed and operationalized over time.

The historical method permits examination of policy adjustments in chronological order (1996-2013), revealing the trajectory and continuity of change and identifying key inflection points such as the 1997 Asian Financial Crisis or the 2009 Nine-Dash Line submission (Huynh, 2019). The systemic/structural method situates Australia within the broader Indo-Pacific system, analyzing the interaction between domestic political changes and systemic shifts. Finally, case study analysis uses the Australia-Vietnam relationship to operationalize these theories, synthesizing official government documents, diplomatic statements, and secondary academic analysis to construct a coherent narrative of strategic evolution (Tran & Nguyen, 2024).

5. HOW IDENTITY SHAPED STRATEGY DURING THREE DISTINCT PHASES

Comprehensive analysis of Australia's strategic posture in the Indo-Pacific, specifically concerning the SCS disputes, reveals a distinct and complex evolutionary trajectory that directly mirrors the country's shifting national identity. This historical progression represents not merely a chronological sequence of events but a theoretical evolution wherein each phase is underpinned by a specific diplomatic ideology that dictates strategic behavior. By applying the theoretical lenses of constructivism, liberalism, and realism, one can explicitly analyze how Australia's changing self-conception has actively shaped, and been shaped by, its foreign policy choices and security strategies across three distinct eras.

The first phase, occurring under the Labor government of Paul Keating, was defined by an ambitious constructivist project to fundamentally reshape Australia's national identity. Keating explicitly articulated an aspiration for Australia to be "part of Asia," a narrative designed to overcome the "tyranny of distance" and shed the colonial legacy of being exclusively a Western outpost in an Asian region. From a constructivist perspective, this represented a deliberate attempt to reconstruct the state's identity to align with its geographical reality, positing that Australia's future security depended on its cultural and political acceptance by its neighbors. This new "Asian identity" drove a foreign policy heavily reliant on liberal institutionalism. The strategic logic held that by "enmeshing" itself in the region's political and economic fabric, Australia could guarantee its security through interdependence rather than traditional military balancing. Consequently, Australia's approach to the SCS disputes during this period was characterized by cautious neutrality and a focus on diplomatic engagement. The government prioritized regional stability through institution-building, playing a pivotal role in establishing the Asia-Pacific Economic Cooperation (APEC) and the ASEAN Regional Forum (ARF). These actions operationalized liberalism: the belief that multilateral institutions could socialize rising powers like China and mitigate conflict through dialogue. Driven by liberal institutionalism, Australia placed considerable faith in regional architecture to socialize China and mitigate conflict (Huynh, 2019).

The second phase, emerging with the election of the Howard government and intensifying after the September 11 attacks, marked a sharp pivot toward realism, justified by a nuanced constructivist shift. Rejecting Keating's "Asian identity" as idealistic overreach, Howard posited a new narrative: Australia was "in Asia" but not "of Asia" (Nguyen, 2021). This semantic distinction was profound; it acknowledged Australia's geographical location while aggressively reaffirming its Western cultural and political values. The 1997 White Paper In the National Interest codified this approach, emphasizing bilateral relationships with traditional allies over multilateral enmeshment. Following the events of September 11, 2001, the 2003 Foreign Affairs and Trade White Paper Advancing the National Interest crystallized this new identity: Australia was a country in Asia, but not of Asia (Nguyen, 2025). Through a realism lens, this period represents classic "bandwagoning" strategy. Faced with a volatile global security environment defined by the "War on Terror," Australia prioritized its survival by aligning its security calculus almost entirely with the global hegemon, the United States. The 2003 White Paper reflected this prioritization of global security concerns over regional nuances, often viewing regional stability through the prism of the US alliance. In the context of the SCS, Australia's strategic calculus became synchronized with US hegemonic interests. The "in Asia" identity allowed Australia to act as a "deputy sheriff" in the Pacific—a role that reassured its great power ally but occasionally alienated regional neighbors (McDonald, 2005). This era was defined by the realism imperative of balancing economic opportunism with China against robust traditional security reliance on the US. While economic ties with China expanded substantially, Australia deepened its security cooperation with the US, viewing the American presence as the indispensable realism guarantor of regional order (Korolev, 2023).

However, as the geopolitical landscape grew increasingly complex, a third identity emerged under the Rudd and Gillard governments and was sustained by subsequent Coalition leadership. This phase is characterized by the sophisticated identity of Australia as a "bridge connecting Asia and the West." This narrative, most clearly articulated in the 2012 White Paper Australia in the Asian Century, represents a constructivist synthesis: it positions the nation as deeply integrated into the Indo-Pacific economic and security architecture while maintaining its distinct Western democratic values (Australian Government, 2012). This "bridging" identity facilitated a transition from simple bandwagoning to complex "hedging" strategy. By 2012, the rapid modernization of the Chinese military forced another major recalibration toward the "Indo-Pacific" construct. In this phase, Australia positioned itself as a "bridge connecting Asia and the West," engaging in complex "hedging" to maximize economic benefits from China while actively hardening its security posture (Nguyen, 2021). This hedging strategy represents a masterful blend of realism balancing and liberal engagement.

On the realism dimension, the "bridge" identity allowed Australia to justify deepening defense ties with the US—such as the 2011 announcement of US Marine rotations in Darwin—not as a hostile act against Asia but as a necessary stabilizing measure (Nathan, 2021). Simultaneously, the liberal aspect of hedging was evident in Australia's proactive engagement with ASEAN-led mechanisms like the EAS and ADMM+ to promote a rules-based order. In the SCS context, this manifested in explicit opposition to unilateral actions and diversification of security partnerships. Australia moved beyond simple bandwagoning to cultivating a network of strategic ties with middle powers, operationalizing the "bridge" concept. A prime example was the elevation of relations with Vietnam. In 2009, Australia and Vietnam signed a Comprehensive Partnership, creating a framework for cooperation in defense, security, and trade. This was not merely diplomatic symbolism; it constituted a strategic signal that Australia was building a "coalition of the willing" to maintain the status quo.

During the signing of the Enhanced Comprehensive Partnership in 2015, Prime Minister Tony Abbott explicitly linked this relationship to regional order, stating that both nations deplore any unilateral change to the status quo and support freedom of navigation by air and sea in the SCS (Bloomberg News, 2015). This statement highlights how the bridge identity enables Australia to navigate the security dilemma: by framing its actions as supporting the sovereignty of all nations (a liberal norm), it can pursue realism balancing against Chinese assertiveness without explicitly declaring hostility (Björkdahl et al., 2015). This strategic nuance continued to evolve, demonstrating the flexibility of the bridge identity. By 2019, alignment with the US was reframed through the lens of sovereignty—a concept that resonates with both realism survival instincts and liberal respect for international law. Prime Minister Scott Morrison articulated this distinct Indo-Pacific identity in Hanoi, asserting that Australia's stance was not about choosing sides but about ensuring that each and every nation in this region could have confidence in its own independence and sovereignty, thereby rejecting the notion of Australia acting solely as a US deputy.

The 2013 Defence White Paper explicitly identified the security of Southeast Asia as connecting the Indian and Pacific Oceans, thereby linking Australia's security directly to freedom of navigation in the SCS (Australian Government, 2013). Thus, by 2013, Australia was no longer a passive observer but an active participant in regional security architectures. The bridge identity had successfully empowered Australia to play a dual role: maximizing economic integration with China while simultaneously hardening its security posture through diversified alliances and staunch defense of international law. This trajectory confirms that Australia's strategic behavior in the SCS is not a static response to external pressure but a dynamic output of its evolving national identity, interpreted through the competing and complementary logics of realism, liberalism, and constructivism.

6. OPERATIONALIZING HEDGING: THE VIETNAM CASE STUDY

The trajectory of security relations between Australia and Vietnam from 1998 to 2013 represents one of the most remarkable strategic realignments in the modern history of the Indo-Pacific. Proceeding from a history of conflict and ideological estrangement, the two nations navigated a complex path toward strategic convergence, driven by shared pressures of a changing regional order and the imperatives of middle-power diplomacy. The evolution of security milestones during this fifteen-year period serves as critical markers of this transformation, revealing a shift from tentative confidence-building measures to the institutionalization of deep defense cooperation. This analysis explores the strategic significance of these milestones, demonstrating how they facilitated Australia's transition from viewing Vietnam as an aid recipient to treating it as a pivotal security partner in the face of rising geopolitical tensions in the SCS.

The establishment of the Inaugural Regional Security Dialogue in 1998 serves as the foundational bedrock for the modern security relationship. Occurring just years after the Keating government's push for engagement with Asia, this event marked the first formal acknowledgment that Australia and Vietnam shared security interests beyond the immediate post-war settlement of the Indochina conflicts (Huynh, 2019). From the perspective of liberal institutionalism, this dialogue was significant because it broke the silence on hard security matters that had characterized the bilateral relationship since the end of the Vietnam War. It moved engagement beyond the safe confines of development aid and trade into the more sensitive realm of regional stability, validating the liberal belief that regular communication reduces uncertainty and transaction costs between states. By initiating this dialogue, Australia signaled its recognition of Vietnam not merely as a transitional economy but as a sovereign actor with a legitimate perspective on regional security architecture. This aligned with the broader "Part of Asia" aspiration, where Australia sought to enmesh itself in the political fabric of the region. For Vietnam, participating in such a dialogue with a US ally was a bold step in its own policy of "multilateralizing" foreign relations, signaling willingness to engage with the West to balance its complex relationship with China (Huynh, 2019).

Following closely on this diplomatic breakthrough was the opening of the Australian Defence Attaché Office in Hanoi in 1999, reciprocated by Vietnam in Canberra shortly thereafter. While seemingly a bureaucratic procedure, the establishment of permanent defense presence was a profound indicator of growing trust that can be viewed through the lens of constructivism. The physical presence of uniformed personnel in each capital institutionalized the defense relationship, moving it from sporadic diplomatic talks to continuous, working-level engagement. This milestone allowed for daily management of defense ties, facilitating information exchange and the gradual erosion of historical suspicions. It provided the necessary infrastructure for the "norm-building" phase of the relationship, where military officers from both sides began to understand each other's strategic cultures, doctrines, and threat perceptions. This norm-building culminated in the 2018 elevation of ties, where Prime Minister Malcolm Turnbull announced the "Strategic Partnership" by explicitly linking bilateral cooperation to the maintenance of "peace, stability and respect for international law in the Asia-Pacific region," including freedom of navigation in the SCS (Department of Foreign Affairs and Trade, 2017). From a realism perspective, this was a low-cost, high-value mechanism for "internal balancing," allowing both nations to gain insight into regional military dynamics without formally committing to an alliance.

As the new millennium progressed, the relationship broadened significantly, typified by the 2003 Joint Statement on Development Cooperation. While primarily focused on economic and development aid, the strategic undercurrent of this milestone was the expansion of cooperation into non-traditional security domains, particularly transnational crime. In the aftermath of the September 11 attacks and the Bali bombings, Australia's security calculus shifted heavily toward counter-terrorism and border security. The 2003 agreement, and subsequent cooperation on transnational crime, reflected Australia's "In Asia" strategy, which pragmatically viewed regional partners as essential for Australia's own domestic security. Vietnam, with its long borders and proximity to the Golden Triangle, was identified as a critical partner in combating drug trafficking and people smuggling. The strategic significance of this period lies in the successful compartmentalization of security cooperation; by working together on functionally specific, less politically sensitive issues like transnational crime, the two nations built a reservoir of "strategic trust" that would later prove essential for addressing harder security issues like the SCS disputes. This era demonstrated that security cooperation could deliver tangible benefits to both sides, validating the liberal institutionalist argument that functional cooperation breeds spillover effects into other areas of high politics.

The year 2008 marked a definitive turning point with the announcement of the Australia-Vietnam Joint Statement on Comprehensive Partnership. This event represented the culmination of a decade of trust-building and a qualitative leap in the relationship. By elevating the relationship to Comprehensive Partnership status, both nations formally acknowledged that their interests had converged across a wide spectrum of issues, from trade and education to defense and security. Strategically, this recognition reflected the changing balance of power in the Asia-Pacific. For Australia, securing a comprehensive partnership with Vietnam—a rising middle power with strategic location on the SCS—was a crucial element of its hedging strategy against the uncertainties of China's rise. It allowed Australia to diversify its regional partnerships beyond its traditional Anglosphere alliances. For Vietnam, the partnership with Australia provided a crucial counterweight and a source of diplomatic support in its efforts to integrate into the global economy and security architecture. The "Comprehensive" label signaled that defense ties were no longer an isolated or sensitive pillar but an integral component of the broader national relationship, thereby shielding defense cooperation from potential political shocks.

The institutionalization of defense ties reached a new zenith in 2010 with the signing of the Memorandum of Understanding (MOU) on Defense Cooperation. Signed on the sidelines of the inaugural ASEAN Defence Ministers' Meeting Plus (ADMM+) in Hanoi, this document provided the legal and political framework for practical military-to-military engagement. The strategic significance of this MOU cannot be overstated. It moved the relationship from "dialogue" to "action." The MOU laid the groundwork for cooperation in specific, high-value areas such as maritime security, counter-terrorism, and peacekeeping training. Crucially, it was signed in the same year that tensions in the SCS began to escalate significantly, with China asserting its "nine-dash line" more aggressively. In this context, the MOU constituted a subtle but clear signal of "soft balancing." It allowed Australia to support Vietnam's capacity to resist coercion—through English language training for peacekeepers and maritime capacity building—without explicitly forming an anti-China military pact. This aligns with the constructivist insight that shared norms and identities (in this case, as maritime trading nations committed to a rules-based order) can drive security cooperation even between differing political systems. The 2010 MOU effectively operationalized Australia's desire to be a "security provider" in the region rather than merely a consumer of US security guarantees.

This momentum was sustained and elevated with the establishment of the Strategic Diplomatic-Defense Dialogue in 2012. This "2+2" dialogue mechanism, typically reserved for close allies and partners, brought together senior officials from both the foreign ministries and defense ministries of both countries (Huynh, 2019). The creation of this dialogue mechanism signified a high degree of strategic maturity and trust. It allowed for synchronization of diplomatic and military strategies, ensuring coherence across the policy spectrum. In the context of the Australia in the Asian Century White Paper released the same year, this dialogue was the practical manifestation of the "bridge" strategy. Australia was positioning itself as a conduit between Western security architectures and Asian strategic realities. The 2012 dialogue provided a forum for frank discussions on the SCS, allowing both sides to align their messaging on the importance of international law (UNCLOS) and freedom of navigation. It marked the transition of the relationship from a bilateral focus to a regional strategic partnership, where both nations coordinated their approaches to multilateral forums like the EAS and the ASEAN Regional Forum.

Finally, the sequence of milestones culminates in 2013 with the 40th Anniversary of diplomatic relations and the convening of the first formal Defence Ministers'

Meeting. This event was symbolic of the full normalization and strategic convergence of the two nations. By 2013, the security relationship had evolved from tentative steps to a robust partnership characterized by regular high-level political and defense engagement (Medcalf, 2013). The strategic significance of reaching this point was the confirmation that Australia and Vietnam had successfully navigated the "tyranny of distance" and historical enmity to become "natural partners" in the Indo-Pacific. The regular Defence Ministers' Meeting established a direct line of communication at the highest level of defense decision-making, ensuring that the strategic vision set by political leaders was translated into operational reality. This solidified the "hedging" strategy for both nations; for Australia, Vietnam had become a reliable partner in Southeast Asia that shared its concerns about maintaining a stable maritime order, while for Vietnam, Australia had become a trusted provider of security assistance and a vocal supporter of its sovereignty rights under international law.

Strategic Synthesis of the Vietnam Case

The evolution of security milestones between 1998 and 2013 tells a story of deliberate, incremental, and increasingly sophisticated strategic engagement. The progression from the 1998 Regional Security Dialogue to the 2010 MOU and the 2013 Defence Ministers' Meeting reflects a deepening realization in both Canberra and Hanoi that their national security interests were inextricably linked. This period laid essential groundwork for the subsequent elevation of the relationship to a Strategic Partnership in 2018 and the Comprehensive Strategic Partnership in 2024. The transformation was driven by realism assessment of the shifting balance of power, facilitated by liberal institutionalist mechanisms like the 2+2 dialogue, and cemented by constructivist reshaping of national identities—from former enemies to essential partners in a shared maritime future. These milestones demonstrate that Australia's "bridge" to Asia was not merely rhetorical but was built on the solid foundation of practical defense diplomacy and shared strategic interests with key regional powers like Vietnam.

The regional security structure has witnessed a significant shift in Australia's approach, moving from its past Forward Defense Policy to comprehensive engagement. Australia not only maintains its traditional alliance with the US but also actively participates in and promotes mechanisms such as the Quad, AUKUS, and ASEAN-led forums like ADMM+ and ARF. Australia provides military training to thousands of ASEAN personnel annually. Particularly with Vietnam, Australia supports the transportation of UN peacekeeping forces, demonstrating its proactive role in shaping regional security. Australia has successfully constructed a national identity as an exemplary and responsible global citizen and a bridging middle power. Furthermore, Australia is a staunch supporter of the rules-based order and UNCLOS

1982. The upgrading of relations to Comprehensive Strategic Partnerships with countries such as Singapore, Indonesia (2018), and Vietnam (2024) demonstrates its commitment to strengthening security through a diverse network of alliances to mitigate pressure from China's rise.

Australia acts in its core national interests, as 60% of its goods pass through the SCS (Nguyen, 2025). Strengthening ties with Vietnam—a key player in the SCS—helps Australia contain Chinese interference and ensure freedom of navigation. Australia's identity has evolved from a "white outpost" to part of the "Asian Century." This shift in its perception of its own position (from a traditional middle power to a strategic partner of ASEAN) has prompted Australia to move away from rigidly choosing sides and instead build an inclusive regional security network. Australia's strategic trajectory in the region, particularly its deepening relationship with Vietnam, demonstrates that the country is using its middle-power diplomatic identity to both benefit economically from China and safeguard its security through close engagement with ASEAN and international legal values.

The evolution of Australia's strategic posture serves as a compelling case study for the interplay of structural realism and constructivist identity politics. The transition from "part of Asia" to "bridge" was driven by the structural pressure of China's rise—a realism concern—but the form of Australia's response was dictated by its evolving identity. The "part of Asia" era failed because it denied Australia's history; the "in Asia" era succeeded in security terms but risked isolationism (Nguyen, 2021). The "bridge" identity synthesized these, allowing Australia to leverage its Western heritage (liberal values, US alliance) as an asset in Asia rather than a liability. This enabled the hedging strategy: Australia could economically integrate with China (liberalism) while simultaneously balancing against it through the US alliance and new partnerships with Vietnam (realism). Specifically, the deepening of the Australia-Vietnam relationship illustrates this hedging in action. By 2013, Australia was providing English language training for Vietnamese peacekeepers and conducting joint strategic dialogues. These actions were driven by a shared identity as "middle powers" seeking to preserve their autonomy against great power encroachment (Nguyen, 2021). Australia's support for Vietnam in multilateral forums was a manifestation of its "good international citizen" identity, using norms and institutions to constrain great power aggression in the SCS. Thus, the evolution of Australia's SCS policy was not a linear reaction to external threats but a complex calibration of its national self-conception against the changing realities of the Indo-Pacific order.

In the "Part of Asia" phase, Australia's actions focused on norm-building and Track II diplomacy. However, as realism pressures mounted with China's island reclamation, Australia's actions hardened into explicit opposition to unilateral actions (Nguyen, 2022). The "Bridge" identity drove Australia to deepen security partnerships with key regional states, most notably Vietnam. Both nations share concerns about strategic imbalance, leading to the upgrade of relations to a Strategic Partnership in 2018 and practical defense cooperation in areas like peacekeeping and maritime training (Tran & Nguyen, 2024). This evolution reveals a complex interplay where Australia utilizes minilateral mechanisms like the Quad and AUKUS as operational manifestations of its balancing strategy, while simultaneously employing liberal institutions to keep diplomatic channels open (Nguyen, 2022). Historically, the "Western outpost" identity created a sense of acute vulnerability, necessitating a forward defense mentality. The Howard-era formulation of "In Asia" resolved this tension by allowing Australia to assert its Western values and legitimize a "Deputy Sheriff" role in the region. By 2012, the "Bridge" narrative facilitated a more proactive role, allowing Australia to facilitate the entry of extra-regional powers into the region while explaining Western security concerns to Asian partners. This identity shapes Australia's responsibilities not merely as a protector of trade routes but as a good global citizen defending the global commons and UNCLOS (Nguyen, 2025). This strategic imagination represents a quintessential constructivist act, remapping the region to include India and create a favorable balance of power, thereby positioning Australia as a central Indo-Pacific power rather than a peripheral state (Nguyen, 2021).

The "bridge" identity (2007-2013) unleashed a more proactive and complex set of actions, best described as "hedging." Recognizing the structural pressure of China's rise and the increasing contestation in the SCS, Australia moved to diversify its security portfolio. This involved deepening ties with "middle powers" to create a strategic buffer. The relationship with Vietnam serves as the clearest case study of this evolution. In 2009, Australia and Vietnam signed the "Comprehensive Partnership," which explicitly included cooperation on "defense and security" as a key pillar. This represented a significant departure from the previous era. Action moved beyond rhetoric to substance: Australia began providing English language training for Vietnamese peacekeepers, established a Defence Attaché Office in Hanoi (1999) and reciprocated in Canberra (2000), and initiated annual Strategic Dialogues at the Vice-Ministerial level. By 2010, the two nations signed a Memorandum of Understanding (MOU) on defense cooperation at the ADMM+, formalizing frameworks for maritime security training and intelligence sharing. These actions were driven by a constructivist convergence of identities: both Australia and Vietnam identified as middle powers seeking to uphold international law (UNCLOS) against the coercion of great powers. Australia's support for Vietnam's chairmanship of ASEAN in 2010, a year pivotal for internationalizing the SCS disputes, underscored this strategic alignment. The "bridge" identity allowed Australia to facilitate Vietnam's integration into the global security order while simultaneously signaling to China that unilateralism would be met with a networked regional response.

The shifting narratives of Australian identity have profoundly shaped its perceived role and responsibilities in the region, leading to a more assertive and nuanced foreign policy regarding the SCS. Australia moved from a neutral, self-reliant stance in the mid-1990s toward a more aligned "bandwagoning" approach with the United States in the early 2000s, identifying as "in Asia." Subsequently, by 2012, Australia adopted a proactive, integrating, and hedging strategy, positioning itself as "a bridge connecting Asia and the West" in response to a more contested regional environment. This identity transformation was not merely rhetorical but had tangible strategic consequences. For instance, the 2013 Defence White Paper emphasized Southeast Asia as a "geographic centre" connecting the Indian and Pacific Oceans, reinforcing Australia's commitment to regional security architectures like the EAS and ADMM+. The structuring of this bridging identity is evident in Australia's moves surrounding the SCS issue, where it has sought to cooperate closely with major democracies and middle powers to maintain the status quo and resist coercion. This strategic posture allows Australia to assert its relevance as a "responsible middle power," balancing its history and geography to navigate the complexities of the Asian Century.

Furthermore, the "bridge" identity compelled Australia to invest in the capacity-building of its neighbors. Recognizing that a weak Southeast Asia creates a vacuum for great power competition, Australia ramped up its engagement with ASEAN. The Vietnam case is illustrative: Australia moved from viewing Vietnam merely as an aid recipient to a "strategic partner" in security. By 2013, the two nations were conducting joint strategic dialogues and cooperating on transnational crime and maritime security. This shift was not solely about countering China; it was about empowering middle powers to have a voice in the regional order. The "bridge" role allowed Australia to synthesize the realism need for balance of power with the liberal desire for institutional cooperation and the constructivist goal of identity affirmation. It positioned Australia not as an outsider looking in, or a deputy looking up, but as a central player ("geographic centre") in the Indo-Pacific, actively weaving a fabric of security that could withstand the tensions of the SCS.

7. CONCLUSION

The evolution of Australia's strategic posture in the SCS demonstrates a clear correlation between its domestic national identity narratives and its external diplomatic actions. As Australia transitioned from seeking to be "part of Asia" to positioning itself as a "bridge" between East and West, its foreign policy matured from tentative engagement to a sophisticated hedging strategy. This transformation reflects Australia's adaptation to the structural realities of the Indo-Pacific, specifically the rise of China and the enduring US alliance, while attempting to carve out an independent middle-power role. By employing a constructivist lens alongside realism and liberalism, this research highlights that Australia's security choices are determined not solely by material power but are deeply influenced by its evolving self-conception in the international arena.

Australia's strategic posture regarding the SCS disputes has undergone profound transformation, inextricably linked to the evolution of its national identity. From the idealistic aspiration of the "part of Asia" narrative in the 1990s to the realism retrenchment of "in Asia" in the 2000s, and finally to the pragmatic synthesis of the "bridge" identity in the 2010s, Australia has continuously adapted its foreign policy framework to survive and thrive in a volatile region. This identity evolution has driven a strategic shift from tentative engagement to bandwagoning, and ultimately to a mature hedging strategy defined by proactive middle-power diplomacy.

The emergence of the "bridge" identity has been particularly consequential. It has empowered Australia to act as a stabilizing force in the Indo-Pacific, advocating for a rules-based order in the SCS while actively diversifying its security portfolio through partnerships with nations like Vietnam. This research confirms that for Australia, identity is not merely a domestic cultural question but a central variable in its national security strategy. As the Indo-Pacific continues to be the crucible of twenty-first-century geopolitics, Australia's ability to maintain this "bridging" role—balancing its history with its geography, and its economy with its security—will be the defining feature of its strategic future.

The case of the Australia-Vietnam relationship serves as a powerful illustration of how identity narratives translate into concrete strategic outcomes. The progression from historical adversaries to strategic partners demonstrates that Australia's "bridge" identity is not empty rhetoric but a functional framework that enables complex diplomatic maneuvering. By positioning itself as simultaneously of the West and in Asia, Australia has created strategic space to pursue security cooperation with regional partners while maintaining its core alliance commitments.

REFERENCES

Allan, G., & Michael, W. (2007). *Making Australian foreign policy.* Cambridge University Press.

Australian Government. (1997). In the National Interests - Australia's Foreign and Trade Policy (White Paper). *Department of Foreign Affairs and Trade.* https://catalogue.nla.gov.au/catalog/61954

Australian Government. (2003). Advancing the National Interest: Australia's Foreign and Trade Policy White Paper. *Department of Foreign Affairs and Trade.* https://nla.gov.au/nla.obj-2203648089/view?partId=nla.obj-2204274174

Australian Government. (2012). Australia in the Asian Century White Paper. *Department of the Prime Minister and Cabinet.* https://apo.org.au/node/31647

Australian Government. (2013). Defence White Paper 2013. *Department of Defence.* https://www.defence.gov.au/about/strategic-planning/defence-white-paper

Beeson, M. (2013). The Decline of US Economic Power and Influence: Implications for Australian Foreign Policy. *Australian Journal of Political Science*, *48*(2), 197–207. DOI: 10.1080/10361146.2013.787920

Björkdahl, A., Chaban, N., Leslie, J., & Masselot, A. (2015). *Importing EU norms: Conceptual Framework and Empirical Findings.* Springer. DOI: 10.1007/978-3-319-13740-7

Bloomberg News. (2015). US urges Asean to patrol S. China Sea. *Bangkok Post.* https://www.bangkokpost.com/world/500536/us-urges-asean-to-patrol-s-china-sea

Department of Foreign Affairs and Trade. (2017). *Prime Ministers' Joint Outcomes Statement.* https://vietnam.embassy.gov.au/hnoi/PM2.html

Elder, C. (2017). *Being Australian: Narratives of National Identity.* Allen & Unwin.

Evans, G., & Grant, B. (1995). *Australia's foreign relations in the world of the 1990s.* Melbourne University Press.

Huynh, T. S. (2019). *Australia-Vietnam Relations (1991-2013).* Ho Chi Minh City National University Publishing House.

Korolev, A. (2023). Transition from hedging to balancing in Australia's China policy: Theoretical and empirical explorations. *Australian Journal of International Affairs*, *77*(5), 548–568. DOI: 10.1080/10357718.2023.2274446

McDonald, M. (2005). Constructing Insecurity: Australian Security Discourse and Policy post-2001. *International Relations, 19*(3), 297–320. DOI: 10.1177/0047117805055408

Medcalf, R. (2013). The Indo-Pacific: What's in a Name? *The American Interest.* https://www.the-american-interest.com/2013/10/10/the-indo-pacific-whats-in-a-name/

Nathan, M. G. (2021). *China Geostrategic Relations: the Belt and Road Initiative, Asian Region instability and Australia* [PhD dissertation]. Charles Darwin University.

Nguyen, M. G. (2021). Looking back at Vietnam - Australia relations: Achievements and prospects. *Journal of Science and Technology Development - Social Sciences and Humanities, 5*(3), 1172-1180.

Nguyen, M. G. (2022). Vietnam - Australia Security and Defense Cooperation: Current Situation and Prospects. *Journal of Indian and Asian Studies, 4*(113), 67–76.

Nguyen, M. G. (2025). *Australia's foreign policy towards Vietnam under Prime Minister Scott Morrison's tennure (2018-2022).* Master's Thesis, University of Social Sciences and Humanities, Vietnam National University Ho Chi Minh City.

Pham, T. T. (2015). Constructivism. *Nghiencuuquocte.* https://nghiencuuquocte.org/2015/03/01/chu-nghia-kien-tao/

Tran, N. T. (2012). Asia in Australia's foreign policy - history and present. *Journal of Social Sciences and Humanities, 53*, 16–23. https://www.thuvientailieu.vn/tai-lieu/chau-a-trong-chinh-sach-doi-ngoai-cuaaustralia-lich-su-va-hien-tai-tran-nam-tien-55151

Tran, X. H., & Nguyen, M. G. (2024). Looking back at 50 years of Vietnam - Australia relations (1973 - 2023). In Institute of Southeast Asian Studies (Vietnam Academy of Social Sciences). *Proceedings of the International Conference: 50 years of Vietnam - Australia relations: Looking back and looking forward* (pp. 79-98). Social Sciences Publishing House.

Ungerer, C. (2007). The concept of "middle power" in Australian foreign policy. *The Australian Journal of Politics and History, 53*(4), 538–551. DOI: 10.1111/j.1467-8497.2007.00473.x

White, H. (2011). Power Shift: Australia's Future between Washington and Beijing. *Quarterly Essay.* https://www.quarterlyessay.com.au/essay/2010/08/power-shift/extract

Chapter 15
ASEAN and the South China Sea: Traditional Security Cooperation Mechanisms and Vietnam's Strategic Engagement

Hai Thi Thanh Duong
https://orcid.org/0009-0004-6115-5206
Vinh University, Vietnam

ABSTRACT

This chapter examines ASEAN's traditional security cooperation mechanisms in the South China Sea (SCS) from 2000 to 2025, focusing on Vietnam's role in regional maritime security governance. The SCS hosts critical shipping lanes facilitating over one-third of global maritime trade, yet faces escalating tensions from overlapping territorial claims and great power competition. ASEAN has developed multilateral frameworks including the Declaration on the Conduct of Parties, Code of Conduct negotiations, and specialized forums such as the ASEAN Maritime Forum and ADMM+ to manage disputes peacefully. Despite constraints from divergent national interests and consensus-based decision-making, these mechanisms have contributed to regional stability. Vietnam has emerged as a proactive architect of cooperation frameworks, leveraging multilateral institutions to enhance national security while strengthening ASEAN's collective capacity in addressing maritime security challenges.

DOI: 10.4018/979-8-3373-4470-6.ch015

1. INTRODUCTION

The South China Sea (SCS) stands as one of the world's most strategically significant and contested maritime regions. Connecting the Pacific and Indian Oceans, it hosts critical international shipping lanes that facilitate over one-third of global maritime trade, valued at approximately 5.3 trillion USD annually (Kiet et al., 2025a). This vital waterway's geopolitical and geoeconomic importance extends beyond commerce, encompassing substantial energy resources, rich fishing grounds, and strategic military positions that shape regional power dynamics in the twenty-first century (Koga, 2022).

The contemporary security landscape of the SCS is characterized by overlapping territorial claims, intensifying militarization, and complex great power competition (Yoshimatsu, 2022). China's assertive pursuit of control over the SCS—manifested through its contentious "nine-dash line" claim, extensive island reclamation activities, and military infrastructure development—has fundamentally altered the regional security architecture (Kiet & Tuyen, 2023). These actions directly challenge the sovereignty claims of ASEAN member states, particularly Vietnam, the Philippines, Malaysia, and Brunei, while contravening the 1982 United Nations Convention on the Law of the Sea (UNCLOS). Simultaneously, the United States' Indo-Pacific strategy has designated Southeast Asia as a critical theater for balancing Chinese influence, thereby transforming the SCS into a focal point of Sino-American strategic rivalry (Hiep et al., 2024; Kiet et al., 2025b).

This volatile environment presents ASEAN with both unprecedented challenges and opportunities. Maritime security has evolved from a peripheral concern to a central pillar of national security for all Southeast Asian nations (Thayer, 2018b). Beyond traditional security threats stemming from territorial disputes and military posturing, the region confronts multifaceted non-traditional security challenges including piracy, terrorism, environmental degradation, illegal fishing, and transnational crime (Hiep et al., 2024). The convergence of these traditional and non-traditional threats, compounded by external power interventions, demands robust multilateral cooperation mechanisms (Zhang, 2023). Since the 1990s, ASEAN has progressively developed an intricate web of security cooperation frameworks aimed at managing SCS tensions through peaceful dialogue and multilateral engagement (Yoshimatsu, 2022). These mechanisms—including the Declaration on the Conduct of Parties (DOC) signed in 2002, the ongoing Code of Conduct (COC) negotiations, and specialized forums such as the ASEAN Maritime Forum (AMF), ASEAN Defence Ministers' Meeting Plus (ADMM+), and East Asia Summit (EAS)—represent institutionalized efforts to establish behavioral norms, build strategic trust, and prevent conflict escalation (Zhang, 2023). However, the effectiveness of these mechanisms remains constrained by divergent national interests among ASEAN members, asymmetrical power relations with China, and the organization's consensus-based decision-making culture (Kiet et al., 2025b).

Vietnam occupies a particularly significant position in this regional security dynamic. As both a founding ASEAN member and a principal claimant in SCS disputes, Vietnam has actively championed multilateral approaches to maritime security while simultaneously defending its sovereignty claims. Vietnam's evolving role—from a relatively new ASEAN member to a proactive architect of regional cooperation frameworks—exemplifies how middle powers can leverage multilateral institutions to enhance national security and shape regional order. This study examines the development and effectiveness of ASEAN's traditional security cooperation mechanisms in the SCS during the first two decades of the twenty-first century, with particular attention to Vietnam's contributions in strengthening regional maritime security governance.

2. LITERATURE REVIEW

Maritime security represents a relatively recent concept within the broader field of security studies in international relations. Traditionally, security has been defined from geopolitical perspectives emphasizing deterrence, power balancing, and military strategy (Vo, 2019, p. 25). In contemporary contexts, maritime security has evolved to emphasize maintaining peace and order, ensuring safety for ships, passengers, crews, cargo, and property, as well as marine environmental management for sustainable human development. According to Czeslaw Dyrcz and colleagues, the maritime dimension for nations encompasses safety, security, and defense perspectives (cited from Baruah, 2022). Governed by international, regional, and national laws, regulations, and related guidelines, maritime security is divided into traditional and non-traditional security issues. However, the conceptual demarcation between these categories is fluid, as traditional and non-traditional security elements often interweave in complex ways (Ta et al., 2015, p. 46). Traditional security focuses on issues of external aggression, including maritime disputes, threats to member states' sovereignty, and armed conflicts (Vo, 2019, p. 42). Given regional and global concerns about the SCS due to this maritime region's critical significance for peace, stability, and development in East Asia and throughout the Asia-Pacific, both traditional security issues—such as island disputes and maritime territorial conflicts—and non-traditional security challenges—including piracy and environmental pollution—have received concentrated research attention from international scholars (Yoshimatsu, 2022; Zhang, 2023; Kiet et al., 2025a). This scholarship addresses the strategic importance of the SCS, interests of countries within and outside the region, international legal aspects of disputes, and ASEAN's role in addressing SCS maritime security.

Regarding the SCS's strategic importance, threats, and the role of regional co-operation mechanisms, Alfred Thayer Mahan identified three requirements and six main conditions for sea power: production, transportation, and colonies as requirements; geographical location, physical configuration, territorial scope, population size, national character, and government character as conditions (Mahan, 1987). These characteristics, formulated in the late 19th century, systematized maritime power concepts. Today, for coastal states, these factors constitute important elements supporting comprehensive national strength (Kiet et al., 2025c). However, divergent perceptions among SCS regional countries have led to confrontational behaviors affecting international cooperation. Consequently, some nations have lost strategic direction, bringing substantial instability to regional peace and security—results of prioritizing secondary national interests over fundamental ones (see more at Hu, 2023). Research by Hao (2011) indicates that nations' strategic confrontational actions lead to clear opposition among neighboring countries and tense security situations in the SCS region, thereby weakening mutually beneficial economic cooperation. To ensure economic development and domestic social stability while maintaining regional peace and development, nations should subordinate SCS-related interests to fundamental and long-term strategic objectives. In Hideaki Kaneda's research on "The Strategic Importance of the SCS and Maritime Transportation Routes", the SCS's value is recognized from the maritime transportation network perspective. The research argues that maritime routes connecting the Indian Ocean, Malacca Strait, SCS, and East China Sea constitute the region's "lifeline," as regional development depends on energy sources and commercial transportation. Therefore, protecting these critical maritime routes has become increasingly urgent, especially as China demonstrates hegemonic behavior in the SCS and East China Sea, expressing ambitions to dominate these maritime areas (cited from Quy & Ngoc, 2013, pp. 31-50).

The SCS is analyzed from the perspective of competing national interests and issues related to seas and oceans. Multiple interests of disputing and non-disputing countries are affected, and although parties have made dialogue efforts to reduce tensions and move toward solutions, current developments reveal persistent risks due to the dispute's complex nature and individual nations' strategic calculations (Kiet et al., 2025b). The SCS is often described as a geopolitical competition arena between the US and China in the context of America's Asia-Pacific rebalancing policy and China's rapid military modernization, or as the most complex issue in ASEAN-China relations (Kiet & Tuyen, 2023). This analytical level proves useful in explaining involved parties' overall strategies while predicting behavior through international relations theories. Before addressing daily challenges in this maritime area—such as piracy, natural disasters, environmental pollution, biodiversity decline, and climate change directly affecting regional residents—and based on consensus about the SCS's geopolitical importance, security and safety policies of relevant countries within and outside the region are urgently needed. According to Rear Admiral (Retired) Hideaki Kaneda, Director of the Okazaki Institute, Japan, instability factors in current regional security are divided into two main types: traditional and non-traditional factors.

> *"Traditional factors include residual Cold War confrontation mechanisms, such as tensions on the Korean Peninsula and in the Taiwan Strait, which continue to cast shadows of instability and unpredictability over the region. The second factor is China's rapid military development, primarily in naval and air forces, as well as space and cyber capabilities, which could disrupt the regional military balance. The third factor includes territorial, religious, and ethnic disputes arising from historical controversies, with island disputes potentially escalating into armed conflicts. The fourth factor involves maritime interest confrontations closely related to territorial disputes. All these factors could seriously impact the region's overall security and stability by potentially obstructing the safety of sea lines of communication (SLOC)" (cited from Quy & Ngoc, 2013).*

In summary, maritime security generally and traditional SCS security specifically constitute complex security challenges that the international community and region must address. Particularly given China's increasingly ambitious strategies and actions in the SCS, inter-state conduct issues, regional arms race phenomena, and America's renewed engagement in Southeast Asia, this research examines how ASEAN has developed internal cooperation mechanisms and those involving related parties over the past two decades, along with Vietnam's role.

3. METHODOLOGY

This study employs a comprehensive qualitative research design to analyze the evolution of ASEAN's traditional security cooperation mechanisms in the SCS within the changing geopolitical landscape of the Asia-Pacific region from 2000 to 2025. The research integrates multiple analytical approaches to provide nuanced insights into how ASEAN has developed institutional frameworks for maritime security governance while managing competing interests among member states and external powers.

The methodology combines historical analysis, institutional examination, and policy document analysis. Primary sources include official ASEAN documents—the ASEAN Charter, Community Vision 2025, summit declarations, and joint communiqués from key ministerial meetings (AMF, EAMF, ADMM, ADMM+)—which provide authoritative evidence of institutional structures, strategic priorities, and policy responses. Official statements from dialogue partners including China, the United States, Japan, and other regional powers are analyzed to understand external perspectives and interactions with ASEAN initiatives. Secondary sources comprise peer-reviewed academic journals, policy papers, and scholarly monographs from both Western and Asian researchers, ensuring balanced representation of diverse analytical perspectives on ASEAN's maritime security role.

The study employs a three-tiered analytical framework. At the systemic level, it examines how structural changes in the international system—particularly China's rise and America's rebalancing strategy—have shaped ASEAN's cooperation mechanisms. At the regional level, the research investigates ASEAN's institutional development, including the ASEAN Community, multilateral forums (ASEAN+3, EAS, ARF), and their effectiveness in promoting transparency, monitoring behavior, and building trust among parties involved in SCS disputes. The analysis specifically evaluates the DOC and COC negotiation processes as instruments of conflict management. At the national level, the study examines Vietnam's strategic engagement within ASEAN frameworks, assessing how Vietnam has leveraged multilateral mechanisms to enhance its diplomatic position and influence regional maritime security governance. This multi-level approach enables systematic analysis of the complex interactions between great power politics, regional institutionalism, and national foreign policy strategies that collectively shape maritime security cooperation in the SCS.

4. THE SCS SITUATION AND THE IMPORTANCE OF MARITIME SECURITY COOPERATION MECHANISMS

The SCS constitutes the primary territorial waters of six countries: China, Vietnam, the Philippines, Indonesia, Brunei, and Malaysia (Koga, 2022). In terms of value, the SCS can be compared to a resource-rich arena where all countries prioritize their interests. Currently, most regional countries engage in maritime oil and gas extraction and production, including China, Vietnam, Malaysia, Brunei, Indonesia, and Thailand, with Indonesia being an OPEC member (Yoshimatsu, 2022). In marine economic development such as fishing and aquaculture, the SCS is considered a major fishing ground. Annually, regional countries harvest approximately 7-8% of total global fish catches in the SCS alone (Koga, 2022). Possessing vital transportation routes for the Asia-Pacific region and the world, the SCS occupies a crucial economic position for ASEAN nations. Maritime routes passing through the SCS serve as commercial arteries with trade valued at approximately 5.3 trillion USD annually (Kiet et al., 2025a). According to US Energy Agency statistics, one-third of global crude oil and over half of liquefied natural gas are transported through the

SCS. The volume of crude oil and liquefied gas transported through this maritime area is 15 times larger than that transported through the Panama Canal. Annually, approximately 70% of Japan's imported oil and 45% of its exported goods transit through the SCS (Vietnam New Agency, n.d). China has 29 of its 39 maritime routes passing through this region, with approximately 60% of its import-export goods and 70% of its imported oil transported by sea through the SCS (Vietnam News Agency, n.d). Vietnam, Thailand, the Philippines, Malaysia, Cambodia, Singapore, Indonesia, and Brunei—ASEAN countries with borders adjacent to the SCS—depend heavily on these maritime routes. Southeast Asian nations' goods export volume through the SCS accounts for 55%, newly industrialized countries 26%, and Australia 40% (Vietnam News Agency, n.d.).

China seeks to control the SCS primarily to access natural resources such as oil, gas, and seabed minerals, while ensuring control over important maritime routes and strengthening military influence, thereby expanding political and strategic power in the Asia-Pacific region (Kiet & Tuyen, 2023). In 1958, when promulgating the Territorial Sea Law, China declared sovereignty over the Paracels (Hoang Sa) and Spratlys (Truong Sa) of Vietnam (Nguyen & Tran, 2025). Consequently, two main types of disputes exist in the SCS: territorial sovereignty disputes over the Hoang Sa and Truong Sa archipelagos, and disputes in determining boundaries of overlapping maritime zones and continental shelves among countries with adjacent or opposite coasts when applying 1982 UNCLOS provisions. Disputes in the Truong Sa archipelago area are most complex because they involve multiple parties: Vietnam, China, Taiwan, the Philippines, Malaysia, and Brunei. During the 1970s, coastal SCS states became embroiled in prolonged disputes. China made numerous claims demonstrating tendencies to use coercive diplomacy and force to pursue territorial claims (Nguyen & Tran, 2025). In 1974, Chinese forces expelled South Vietnam from the Hoang Sa archipelago (Kiet & Tuyen, 2023). Subsequently in 1988, Chinese forces expelled Vietnamese troops from Gac Ma Rock after sinking three Vietnamese fishing vessels near Cross Reef (Quy, 2012, p. 65). In the early 1990s, China declared the entire SCS as its territory, arguing that Chinese sovereignty over the SCS had existed for millennia (Koga, 2022). Regarding SCS islands, China claimed to have discovered and developed these islands first. China repeatedly stated that reef reclamation in the SCS is "completely legal" because these reefs lie within the "nine-dash line" over which China asserts sovereignty, though this claim has never been recognized by the international community and has been vehemently opposed (Voice of Vietnam, 2019). This claim not only violates the 1982 UNCLOS but directly infringes upon the exclusive economic zones (EEZ) and continental shelves of many coastal nations, particularly Vietnam, the Philippines, Malaysia, and Brunei (Koga, 2022). In 2002, China and ASEAN reached the DOC when Beijing adopted a softer stance on SCS disputes (Yoshimatsu, 2022). However, from 2007 to 2008, Beijing implemented assertive approaches that heightened tensions. China's unilateral activities have increased the risk of unintended conflict, threatening peace, stability, and freedom of navigation in the region (Thayer, 2018a).

By 2009, China officially revealed its ambitions by submitting to the United Nations the "nine-dash line" map (also called the cow's tongue line), asserting sovereignty claims over approximately 2 million km^2 of sea area and 13 km^2 of land area in the SCS, including the Hoang Sa and Truong Sa archipelagos and Scarborough Shoal (Koga, 2022). Most significantly, China designated the SCS as its "core interest" in 2010 and harassed survey vessels exploring oil and gas in other countries' EEZs in 2011 (Hossain, 2013). The Aquino administration protested at least six incidents of Chinese provocation, including the Scarborough Shoal incident involving China's intrusion into waters within the Philippines' 200 nautical mile exclusive economic zone (Maliwanag, 2011). With increasing naval power, China demonstrated intentions to expand maritime claims by conducting numerous military exercises involving modern surface warships (Koga, 2022). In 2010, China exerted diplomatic pressure on ASEAN countries before the US-ASEAN Summit, with the Chinese Navy conducting its fourth naval exercise in the SCS (Koga, 2022). These actions demonstrate China's assertion of undisputed sovereignty and its rapid development of capability to maintain naval force deployment deep into maritime zones. China's actions in the SCS have been assessed as "examples of Beijing's arrogance" (Quy, 2012, pp. 74-75). China's claims sounded alarm bells not only for ASEAN claimant nations but also for non-claimant nations like Indonesia, Singapore, Japan, the US, and South Korea—all of which depend on unimpeded maritime traffic through the SCS. Most recently, on September 16, 2025, China announced "control measures" for Philippine government vessels; Manila accused Chinese forces of using water cannons that injured sailors and damaged the BRP Datu Gumbay Piang, continuing disputes around unilateral "conservation zone" moves at shoals (Permanent Court of Arbitration, n.d.). These incidents demonstrate escalating risk levels and the increasingly common use of coast guard and maritime militia forces instead of open military confrontation.

Beyond tensions from SCS disputes and China's escalating actions, the SCS faces non-traditional security realities including both violent and non-violent activities. The violent category includes piracy, maritime terrorism, drug trafficking, and human trafficking (Yoshimatsu, 2022). The non-violent category includes activities causing marine environmental pollution, climate change, natural disasters at sea, cyber attacks targeting ships, illegal fishing and marine resource exploitation, and goods smuggling (Kiet & Hiep, 2025). Thus, the SCS—the world's busiest trade route, surrounded largely by Southeast Asian nations, with abundant resources and potential—faces impacts from numerous challenges requiring highly complex international relations management rather than ordinary national conduct (Koga,

2022). Arms race behavior and strengthened law enforcement measures to control maritime zones directly increase armed conflict risks, threaten maritime safety, and endanger fishermen's livelihoods. These behaviors occur due to sovereignty disputes, interest conflicts, and regional nations' competing interests, preventing parties from implementing effective cooperation measures.

ASEAN, established in 1967, initiated alliances and cooperation mechanism development to avoid and limit foreign intervention in internal affairs and avoid being drawn into great powers' geopolitical schemes. At the 25th ASEAN Ministerial Meeting in Manila in July 1992, the "ASEAN Declaration on the SCS" was adopted. This was ASEAN's first document on the SCS, affirming that "all adverse developments in the SCS directly affect regional peace and stability" and emphasizing "the need to resolve all jurisdictional and sovereignty issues associated with the SCS by peaceful means, without using force" (ASEAN, 1992). At the 26th ASEAN Ministerial Meeting, both the 1992 Declaration and 1993 Communiqué requested "all directly involved parties comply with the principles" of the Declaration (ASEAN, 1993). To demonstrate ASEAN's solidarity on the SCS issue, the process of establishing regional conduct rules began in 1999. After three years of dialogue and consultation among ASEAN members and between ASEAN and China, the DOC in the SCS was adopted by ASEAN and Chinese Foreign Ministers in November 2002 in Phnom Penh. In ASEAN's development trajectory, recent charters have emphasized the Association's paramount importance in ensuring security protection, directed toward the goal of "promoting peace, security and stability in the ASEAN region" (ASEAN Charter, Article 1.15). To achieve this, ASEAN commits to maintaining "centrality and proactive role ... as a fundamental dynamic in its relations and cooperation with external partners" (ASEAN, 2025). In this spirit, recognizing the SCS's importance in the contemporary context, ASEAN has actively and proactively participated in promoting cooperation mechanism development, with peaceful solutions as the foundation for participating in resolving sovereignty disputes in the Asia-Pacific region.

5. ASEAN's TRADITIONAL SECURITY COOPERATION MECHANISMS IN THE SCS

According to the 1982 UNCLOS—a comprehensive international legal document encompassing all major contents in international maritime and oceanic law and practice—the Convention is recognized as a maritime constitution with over 300 articles providing comprehensive provisions in maritime management and exploitation fields. Most importantly, it unified methods for determining the scope and legal regimes of maritime zones and continental shelves under coastal states' sovereignty, sovereign rights, and national jurisdiction, clearly stipulating rights and obligations of all states—maritime and landlocked, developed or developing—in numerous fields including security, maritime safety, environmental protection, natural resource exploration and exploitation, transportation and communication, and scientific research (Pýc, 2019). The Convention also established procedures for resolving maritime disputes among nations by peaceful means, utilizing maritime resources based on principles of fairness, sustainability, and mutual respect for sovereignty (United Nations, 1982). From the UN Charter, the ASEAN community drew foundational ideas to become a cohesive community, expanding cooperation while affirming its central role in handling issues and maintaining regional peace, security, and stability. In the context of persistent territorial disputes, jurisdictional rights, and resource exploitation conflicts in the SCS, establishing behavioral expectations through maritime security cooperation mechanisms within the ASEAN framework has become urgent. Since the 1990s, ASEAN has clearly recognized the SCS's strategic role for regional peace, stability, and development, progressively forming dialogue and cooperation frameworks to manage tensions, prevent conflicts, and promote trust among involved parties (Felker, 2001).

Building the ASEAN Community with three pillars, including the ASEAN Political-Security Community (APSC) pillar officially launched in 2003, cooperation responding to maritime security challenges in Southeast Asia has been conducted at various levels. These levels include cooperation within ASEAN frameworks such as the ASEAN Regional Forum (ARF), ADMM+, EAS, along with behavioral orientation agreements such as DOC and the COC negotiation process, establishing institutional foundations for regional maritime security cooperation. With the perspective of being an organization promoting regional cooperation, ASEAN reached consensus and proactively united in conflict management. From the 1992 ASEAN Declaration on the SCS and the DOC signed by China and ASEAN in Phnom Penh on November 4, 2002 commitments related to SCS issues were recorded (ASEAN, 2002). Specifically, parties committed to complying with principles and objectives of the UN Charter, UNCLOS, TAC, five principles of peaceful coexistence, and other universal international law principles; committed to resolving territorial and jurisdictional disputes by peaceful means, without using force or threatening to use force. Among DOC's ten provisions, emphasis was placed on fundamental principles such as: not using or threatening to use force, exercising restraint in actions that complicate or escalate disputes, and resolving disputes through peaceful means consistent with principles of the UN Charter, TAC, and especially the 1982 UNCLOS (ASEAN, 2002). Simultaneously, DOC called for strengthening confidence-building measures and cooperation in less sensitive areas such as marine scientific research, environmental protection, rescue operations, and combating transnational crime.

Although DOC lacks legally binding value, it plays an important role as a normative framework establishing behavioral expectations among parties. DOC acceptance demonstrates a level of political commitment to maintaining stability and handling disputes by peaceful means. In the context of lacking a formal and effective conflict management mechanism, DOC helped reduce the risk of miscalculation, misunderstanding, or unintended collisions, thereby supporting maintenance of a relatively peaceful environment in the SCS for over a decade after signing (Fang, 2015). The DOC has progressively contributed to consideration and formation of a legally binding document on conduct relations among countries both within and outside the region. Principles of democracy, rule of law, governance, and integrity have been disseminated and integrated into ASEAN Community policies and operational practices to gradually narrow differences and increase consensus in perceptions among member states. However, DOC's limitations are also evident: due to lacking implementation and monitoring mechanisms, parties' continued unilateral actions—particularly large-scale construction and militarization activities in the SCS—raised doubts about DOC's practical effectiveness (Hieu et al., 2024). Therefore, the negotiation process to build a more binding COC was initiated in 2013 as a necessary next step to overcome DOC's limitations.

Beyond political frameworks like DOC, the ARF demonstrates its role as an open and comprehensive multilateral security dialogue mechanism, contributing to maintaining peace, stability, and building strategic trust in the region. The ARF, established in 1994 with the spirit of "promoting peace and security through dialogue and cooperation in the Asia-Pacific" (Hong, 2018, p. 73), initiated dialogue and consultation mechanisms on regional security and political issues. ARF is one of few regional mechanisms where all parties directly involved in SCS disputes are present, including ASEAN countries, China, the US, Japan, South Korea, and other partners. Thanks to this inclusiveness, ARF facilitates dialogue, exchange of views, and formation of maritime conduct norms. Although ARF lacks binding enforcement mechanisms, the forum's declarations and activities have helped form positive behavioral expectations, such as not unilaterally changing the status quo, prioritizing peaceful solutions, and promoting transparency in maritime conduct (Katsumata, 2009). In the context of lacking a formal collective security institution in Southeast Asia, ARF still plays a foundational role in regional security governance through soft cooperation and strategic trust building.

After the DOC was signed in 2002, ASEAN entered a new phase, transitioning from political-diplomatic dialogue to institutionalizing maritime security cooperation mechanisms. The regional security context during this period experienced significant fluctuations, with increasing tensions in the SCS. China's rise both economically and militarily, pushing the "nine-dash line" claim and increasing maritime activities, threatened the sovereignty and territorial integrity of coastal countries including Vietnam in 2009. The expansion of extra-regional powers' presence, alongside increasingly prominent non-traditional challenges such as piracy, smuggling, and marine pollution, placed greater demands on ASEAN to focus on building multilayered institutional cooperation networks connecting defense, security, legal, and marine economic sectors. Beyond political frameworks and security dialogue, several specialized co-operation initiatives play practical roles in establishing behavioral expectations and promoting regional stability in the SCS. Notable among these is the ASEAN-China Maritime Cooperation Fund, established in 2011 with an initial budget exceeding 3 billion renminbi sponsored by China. This fund has supported numerous practical cooperation programs including marine scientific research, environmental protection, maritime security, search and rescue, and combating transnational crime. On July 21, 2011, in Bali, Indonesia, within the framework of the 44th ASEAN Ministerial Meeting, ASEAN and China reached the Guidelines for the Implementation of the DOC. This is viewed as involved parties' effort to restrain and manage SCS disputes, which were becoming increasingly tense and attracting special international attention. Additionally, the ASEAN-China Joint Statement on Marine and Coastal Environmental Protection (2017-2027) demonstrated parties' commitment not to commit acts causing environmental damage or harming other nations' legitimate rights and interests, thereby shaping acceptable behavioral boundaries in multilateral maritime activities. Another technically oriented but strategically valuable tool is the ASEAN-China Hotline on Maritime Emergency Response, established in 2016. This mechanism helps strengthen direct communication among high-level diplomats to prevent misunderstandings, reduce miscalculation, and handle crises promptly in unintended maritime situations (Nguyen, 2018).

The AMF, established in 2007 under the Vientiane Action Plan, created a dialogue foundation on issues such as maritime safety, search and rescue, information sharing, and technical cooperation. The first forum organized in 2010 in Indonesia focused on themes from maritime security to environmental protection and sustainable exploitation. The 2012 AMF Chairman's Statement affirmed maritime security's role in all three ASEAN Community pillars, while emphasizing compliance with international law including UNCLOS 1982 and ASEAN documents such as the 1967 Bangkok Declaration, 1976 TAC, and 2002 DOC. From 2012, ASEAN countries along with eight partner countries that are EAS members officially organized the EAMF to expand discussion and cooperation on maritime security. The first EAMF Chairman's Statement affirmed UNCLOS's key role in maritime governance and emphasized regional instruments such as TAC, DOC, and COC. Cooperation areas include connectivity, capacity building, maritime vocational training, environmental protection, and fisheries management. At this forum, the US proposed the ASEAN EAST maritime vocational training program and expressed intention to join the Regional Cooperation Agreement on Combating Piracy and Armed Robbery against

Ships in Asia (ReCAAP) (ASEAN Secretariat, 2010). EAMF has now met nine times, expanding discussion content and exploiting advantages of having partners outside ASEAN participate, who are also important sources of financing, initiatives, and human resources.

Since 2013, ASEAN and China officially launched the negotiation process for the COC in the SCS to institutionalize principles stated in the DOC Declaration (2002) into a framework of rules with greater legal binding force (Quyet & Nguyet, 2023). The momentum for this process largely came from escalating tensions in the SCS following the 2014 HD-981 oil rig incident and China's large-scale island reclamation activities, causing deep concern about regional destabilization risks. After many rounds of consultation, in August 2017, at the ASEAN-China Foreign Ministers' meeting in Manila, parties officially adopted the draft COC framework. This framework is viewed as an initial symbolic step, laying the foundation for a final document capable of establishing conduct rules, crisis management mechanisms, and building trust among parties involved in SCS disputes (VietnamPlus, 2017). According to many scholars' assessments, if COC is completed according to its initial objectives, it will be an important tool for controlling behavior, promoting transparency, increasing strategic predictability, while establishing systematic mechanisms for handling maritime incidents, contributing to maintaining stability and preventing unintended conflicts (Koga, 2022; Fang, 2015; Thayer, 2012). Specifically, in the COC framework, mentioned contents include: "promoting mutual trust," "cooperation obligations," and "self-restraint." In the Joint Statement "ASEAN-China Cooperation toward the 21st Century," ASEAN Leaders and Chinese President Jiang Zemin directly addressed the SCS in Article 8: Recognizing that maintaining regional peace and stability serves all parties' interests, parties commit to resolving differences or disputes through peaceful means, without threatening to use force or using force. Related parties agree to resolve SCS disputes through friendly consultation and negotiation consistent with universal international law principles, including the 1982 UNCLOS. Parties agree to seek cooperative solutions on issues of common concern (ASEAN-China Joint Statement, 1997).

However, the COC negotiation process has encountered significant challenges, including fundamental differences in expectations between ASEAN and China. While ASEAN consistently expected to build a COC with clear legal binding force, including independent monitoring mechanisms and sanctions for violating behavior, the negotiation process has been hindered by China's position (Koga, 2022). Beijing has firmly supported a soft political agreement that is non-binding and avoids intervention in sovereignty issues. This divergence in expectations has led to prolonged stagnation in the COC negotiation process. Many scholars point out that the lack of specific commitments—such as non-militarization, not establishing air defense identification zones, or prohibiting reclamation of features in the SCS—raises fundamental questions about COC's substantive effectiveness (Ayesh & Askari, 2025, pp. 153-154). This suggests China still seeks to maintain flexible strategic space in the region while weakening ASEAN's collective coordination and control capability over unilateral actions in disputed maritime areas. Nevertheless, COC is still viewed as an important diplomatic step forward, demonstrating joint efforts in building a rules-based regional order, at least formally and in terms of conduct norms. Subsequent negotiations, particularly from 2018-2023, saw ASEAN focus on developing a complete COC text, though progress remained slow with considerable uncertainty regarding final content. Reality shows that, like the Declaration, this framework agreement seemingly lacks mechanisms ensuring implementation or sanctions for violating any provisions in the (potential) COC. This apparently suits all parties—countries declare their desire for peace and stability but resist constraints on their freedom of action. This framework allows China to appear cooperative without needing to restrict its behavior, while giving ASEAN officials a sense that their working process is producing results (Nguyen, 2017).

Beyond bilateral and multilateral cooperation mechanisms, ASEAN implements sustained dialogue mechanisms. The ASEAN-China Dialogue plays the role of a formal foundation and stable institution to maintain communication, promote functional cooperation, and—most importantly—build strategic trust between both parties in the context of existing disagreements about the SCS. This mechanism's core objective is directed toward a cohesive, constructive, and comprehensive relationship between ASEAN and China (Hu, 2023). In practice, regular dialogues, particularly Senior Officials' Meeting on DOC (SOM-DOC) and ASEAN-China Joint Working Group meetings, are not only exchange forums but also specific policy and technical cooperation channels. In May 2017, both parties jointly reviewed progress implementing the hotline between Foreign Ministers and applying the Code for Unplanned Encounters at Sea (CUES), measures aimed at reducing collision risks and increasing transparency in emergency situations. Additionally, dialogue also included functional maritime cooperation contents such as marine environmental protection and ensuring maritime safety in the SCS (ASEAN Secretariat, 2017). These advances clearly demonstrate the trust-building role that the ASEAN-China Dialogue mechanism has achieved: not only through rhetoric but through practical coordination mechanisms. Particularly, these dialogues provide the foundation for promoting the negotiation process and institutionalization of the COC in the SCS. Completing discussion of the COC framework in 2017 and forming the Single Draft Negotiating Text (SDNT) in 2018 at SOM-DOC paved the way for the substantive negotiation process (Thayer, 2018b). The SDNT reflected parties' diverse proposals and positions, creating legal and political foundations for the future COC. This SDNT was adopted at the ASEAN-China Post Ministerial Conference (PMC) and ASEAN Summit in 2018, before entering the first reading in 2019 with a target of COC completion in 2021 (ASEAN Secretariat, 2018, 2019). Although the final binding document has not yet been achieved, the dialogue process has demonstrated this mechanism's central role in maintaining contact, minimizing risks, and gradually building trust between ASEAN and China on an inherently sensitive and divisive issue. Rather than avoiding conflict, dialogue provides a stable foundation for parties to seek consensus and strengthen joint commitments to regional peace and stability.

The EAS was designed as a strategic forum to promote political dialogue and security cooperation between major powers and Southeast Asian nations, thereby building trust and promoting regional stability. However, the practical implementation of this role regarding the SCS issue has shown clear limitations. During 2019-2020, US non-participation in high-level EAS under President Donald Trump significantly weakened the forum's effectiveness and influence. However, US positions on the SCS remained unchanged. In 2018, at the EAS Foreign Ministers' Meeting (EAS-FMM), US Secretary of State Mike Pompeo sharply criticized China's militarization behavior in the SCS and expressed deep concern about regional security (Indo-Pacific Defense Forum, 2018). That same year, Vice President Mike Pence also spoke frankly at EAS that "China's actions in the SCS are illegal and dangerous" (White House, 2018). This demonstrates that EAS had become a channel for the US and allies to express tough stances, publicly criticizing China. Simultaneously, China also utilized EAS to refute criticisms and defend its positions. Beijing often expressed satisfaction with the progress of COC negotiations in the SCS, while calling on the US to stop interfering and respect bilateral efforts between ASEAN and China (Zhou & Zhou, 2017). At the 2018 EAS, Foreign Minister Wang Yi publicly affirmed that SCS militarization was undertaken to respond to US actions and for self-defense against threats (Ministry of Foreign Affairs People's Republic of China, 2018). This confrontation somewhat transformed EAS into an arena for influence competition among major powers, reducing space for constructive dialogue. Facing the risk of being drawn into great power competition, some ASEAN countries proactively maintained distance and sought to moderate the SCS issue within the EAS framework. For example, the Philippines once proposed not bringing the SCS into formal discussion due to concerns about causing "fierce confrontation" (Roxas, 2017). Meanwhile, Indonesia at the 2020 EAS-FMM also warned that ASEAN should not be drawn into strategic competition among powers (Federal Government Documents, 2020). It can be assessed that ASEAN countries in EAS in recent years have tended to shift focus from dispute resolution to promoting functional cooperation and building trust at sea. This is clearly reflected in EAS Chairman's Statements from 2017-2020, with similar contents such as: welcoming progress in COC negotiations, noting agreements such as CUES and ministerial hotlines, but simultaneously maintaining cautious and consistent language about "concerns" rather than "condemnation." Therefore, although EAS is a high-level multilateral forum with major power participation, it has gradually been sidelined in direct efforts to resolve SCS disputes, shifting direction to become a foundation for trust building and tension restraint more symbolically than substantively.

Overall, ASEAN mechanisms over the past two decades have progressively and actively developed in both depth and breadth, reducing tensions in SCS disputes. Particularly from 2017 to 2020, ASEAN played an active role in maintaining cooperation mechanisms, dialogue, and building trust among involved parties regarding the SCS issue. Through forums such as ASEAN Summit, ASEAN-China Dialogue, EAS, and Ministerial-level meetings, ASEAN created a stable dialogue space, allowing member countries as well as partners like China and the United States to express viewpoints and promote cooperation in functional areas such as marine environmental protection, maritime safety, and establishing emergency hotlines (Zhang, 2023). Particularly, this process contributed to promoting certain changes in China's positions. If previously Beijing firmly opposed a COC with legally binding force, by 2019 the country demonstrated a more accommodating attitude, publicly supporting an effective and feasible COC. China also reduced the frequency and intensity of criticism of extra-regional countries' presence like the United States, instead proposing to establish notification mechanisms prior to military activities of parties not directly involved in disputes. These shifts demonstrate ASEAN mechanisms' role in forming favorable diplomatic environments, thereby contributing to shaping behavior and strategies of major powers and strengthening internal bloc solidarity to more effectively protect regional interests.

6. VIETNAM'S ROLE IN DEVELOPING TRADITIONAL SECURITY COOPERATION MECHANISMS IN THE SCS

The SCS constitutes Vietnam's strategic space, serving as an international exchange gateway containing conditions and potential for national development, and functioning as a boundary protecting the nation "early and from afar" toward the sea (Thayer, 2018a; Hieu et al., 2024; Kiet et al., 2025a). In the 21st century, seas and islands have become—and continue to become—important factors and conditions governing and shaping Vietnam's future and development trajectory, with the aim of making the country strong through seas and enriched by seas (Kiet & Tuyen, 2023). Therefore, protecting sovereignty and national strategic interests in the SCS has always received special attention from the Communist Party of Vietnam, with the Party's viewpoints and policies on this issue regularly supplemented and developed to meet new situational requirements.

After more than a quarter century of ASEAN membership, Vietnam's position and role have significantly increased. From a new ASEAN member with low regional integration levels, Vietnam has become one of the most proactive, active members in fulfilling ASEAN commitments and participating in building and promoting ASEAN's institutionalization and internal bloc linkage (Chapman, 2017). Vietnam has become a factor creating regional solidarity, promoting completion of ASEAN's expansion process, and contributing to ASEAN's development into a Community of Southeast Asian nations. ASEAN has transformed from a small, loosely cooperative organization in Southeast Asia into a closely cooperative organization with an increasingly complete institutional apparatus and an important partner highly valued by many major countries. In ASEAN's development process, Vietnam plays an increasingly active role in determining the Association's development direction and institutionalization, advocating for ASEAN's correct development trajectory, strategic orientation, and major decisions. Vietnam's imprint in ASEAN has been demonstrated successively through achievements in successfully performing rotating responsibilities, including: (i) Hosting the 6th ASEAN Summit (1998); (ii) Chairman of the ASEAN Standing Committee (2000-2001); (iii) ASEAN Chairman (2010); (iv) Coordinator of relations between ASEAN and important partners including the US, Russia, EU, India, and Japan; and (v) ASEAN Chairman (2020).

In the ASEAN Community building process, Vietnam has consistently played a core role in determining objectives, development directions, and forming major ASEAN decisions, including: (i) ASEAN Vision 2020 (1997); (ii) Vision implementation plans (Hanoi Action Programme 1998 and Vientiane Action Plan 2004); (iii) ASEAN Charter (2007); (iv) ASEAN Community Building Roadmap (2009-2015); (v) ASEAN Community Vision 2025 along with implementation plans for each pillar (2015); and (vi) Master Plan on ASEAN Connectivity (MPAC). Vietnam has made substantial contributions to expanding relations and promoting cooperation between ASEAN and partners, enhancing ASEAN's international role and position, especially its central and leading role in regional forums such as the EAS, ARF, and ADMM+. Particularly, Vietnam has left deep imprints contributing to enhancing the value and operational effectiveness of these forums, notably: (i) Successfully promoting EAS expansion to include Russia and US participation; (ii) Mobilizing and successfully hosting the first ADMM+ in Hanoi; and (iii) Building the Hanoi Action Plan implementing the 2010 ARF Vision Declaration. Vietnam's contributions are also reflected through core roles in the process of building the Work Plan on Maintaining and Enhancing ASEAN's Central Role (2009) and the Revised Work Plan on ASEAN's Central Role (2015), contributing to promoting regional architecture formation based on ASEAN-led processes.

At the 34th ASEAN Foreign Ministers' Meeting organized in Hanoi (2001), in the role of ASEAN Standing Committee Chairman, Vietnam proactively proposed and achieved countries' consensus in adopting the Hanoi Declaration on Narrowing Development Gap for Closer ASEAN Integration. The Declaration aimed to concretize and implement the Initiative for ASEAN Integration (IAI) adopted by the Association's leaders in 2000. Subsequently, in the role of Chairman of the Task Force on IAI, Vietnam promoted ASEAN countries in achieving IAI objectives. These objectives constitute important elements realizing the ASEAN Community generally and APSC specifically, creating frameworks and foundations for the ASEAN Community building and completion process in subsequent periods. It can be said Vietnam participated in the ASEAN Community building process fully from the idea formation stage, through policy formulation to implementing foundational documents, thereby affirming capabilities and progressively enhancing its position in ASEAN (Dang, 2014). Vietnam also plays an active, core role in consolidating and strengthening ASEAN internal solidarity and unity. Vietnam, along with other members, particularly founding members, has skillfully handled differences arising among member countries, promoting common positions and voices on regional issues. Vietnam has made substantial contributions to expanding relations and promoting cooperation between ASEAN and partners, enhancing ASEAN's international role and position, especially its central and leading role in regional forums (Chapman, 2017). These contributions are reflected through core roles in building frameworks that promote regional architecture based on ASEAN-led processes.

In ASEAN's maritime security cooperation mechanisms regarding the SCS, Vietnam has consistently been proactive within ASEAN on SCS issues, viewing ASEAN as a useful channel to protect national sovereignty while responsibly building ASEAN to become more effective. Regarding security, ASEAN cooperation mechanisms and those between ASEAN and partners help Vietnam enhance its position, particularly in issues related to the SCS. ASEAN represents an appropriate force aggregation mechanism helping Vietnam enhance power and strength, gaining additional support and assistance in security and political issues and managing relations with major powers, particularly China and the US. Since 2002, Vietnam chose close integration with ASEAN on SCS issues, jointly signing the DOC, which has contributed significantly to reducing regional tensions and maintaining peace and stability in the SCS. Clearly, when an ASEAN member country integrates its sovereignty commitments or disputes within the organization, that country simultaneously gains a certain degree of sovereignty protection while obtaining security guarantees. Vietnam consistently adheres to the principle of resolving disputes and disagreements in the SCS by peaceful means, based on respecting independence, sovereignty, and legitimate interests of nations, while complying with international law including the 1982 UNCLOS. Besides, China's actions from May to July 2011 in Vietnam's waters seriously violated Vietnam's sovereign rights and jurisdiction over its continental shelf and exclusive economic zone, contravening the 1982 UN Convention on the Law of the Sea and contrary to the spirit and letter of the DOC signed between ASEAN and China in 2002. Vietnam demonstrated measured reaction while upholding viewpoints protecting peace, directing disputes toward common agreements and avoiding conflict. This was proven at the 10th Asia Security Conference (Shangri-La Dialogue 10) in June 2011 in Singapore with the theme "Responding to New Maritime Security Challenges." Vietnamese Defense Minister Phung Quang Thanh delivered an important speech with the assessment:

> *"As a maritime nation, having experienced many wars, we deeply understand the value of peace and stability for national construction and development. Therefore, Vietnam's defense policy is one of peace and self-defense" (Communist Review, 2011).*

Vietnam played an active role with ASEAN countries in building and adopting the Bali Concord II Declaration in Bali, Indonesia (October 2003), establishing strategic directions for ASEAN's development toward building a dynamic, self-reliant, and cohesive ASEAN Community by 2020 (later ASEAN decided on 2015) with three main pillars: (i) ASEAN Security Community (ASC); (ii) ASEAN Economic Community (AEC); and (iii) ASEAN Socio-Cultural Community (ASCC—the concept for this community followed Vietnam's initiative). To build the important document creating legal and institutional frameworks supporting ASEAN in implementing Community building objectives, Vietnam proactively and actively participated in building the ASEAN Charter (2007). Vietnam's active participation in the Charter drafting process contributed significantly to the Charter being completed and signed with basic and comprehensive contents, synthesizing and systematizing ASEAN's existing fundamental objectives, principles, and agreements while updating contents to suit new circumstances. The Charter also demonstrated fairly balanced and harmonized viewpoints and fundamental interests of member countries, reflecting ASEAN's "unity in diversity." Thus, Vietnam more clearly demonstrated its role within the ASEAN framework, strongly shifting from "participating" to "proactively and actively contributing to building" a strong ASEAN in the region, creating consensus and consistency leading to resolving SCS dispute issues in peace and stability, bringing prosperity to Southeast Asian nations.

Beyond strengthening promoting internal bloc cooperation and linkage, Vietnam actively participated in promoting cooperation between ASEAN and external partner countries in many different fields, simultaneously contributing to upholding and maintaining ASEAN's leading role in regional cooperation processes. This is reflected through coordinating and promoting ASEAN's bilateral external relations with strategic dialogue partners such as Japan, Russia, the US, and Australia. In the role of coordinator of dialogue relations between ASEAN and China (2009-2012), EU (2012-2015), India (2015-2018), Japan (2018-2021), and South Korea (2021-2024), Vietnam played the role of active bridge in strengthening relations between ASEAN and partners, including contributing to resolving some difficulties, helping elevate relations between both parties, highly appreciated by both ASEAN and

Dialogue countries. Simultaneously, Vietnam also made positive contributions to maintaining ASEAN's leading role in regional cooperation processes initiated by ASEAN such as ASEAN+1, ASEAN+3, EAS, thereby contributing to promoting and upholding the Association's international role and position.

7. CONCLUSION

It can be said that with important geopolitical and geoeconomic positions, maritime sovereignty disputes among some countries/territories within and outside the region in the SCS area along with maritime sovereignty disputes among some countries over many decades, ASEAN has responded to traditional maritime challenges, rapidly developing cooperation mechanisms to ensure peaceful environments, stability, and development for Southeast Asian regional countries. ASEAN always maintains peaceful cooperation mechanisms, stability, and regional security. The most important cooperation field is ensuring non-use of force or threat of force and resolving SCS disputes among sovereignty-claiming countries by peaceful means.

Accordingly, ASEAN has been widely recognized as an effective tool for member countries to pursue national interests. Maintaining independence, self-reliance, socio-economic development, maintaining political regimes, and preserving national identity have become common denominators for Southeast Asian regional countries to gather together in the ASEAN organization. For this reason, ASEAN had conditions to expand throughout the entire Southeast Asian region in 1999 when all regional countries became Association members. From an Association of five founding countries, ASEAN has developed, expanded membership, and become a cohesive Community of ten Southeast Asian nations. With ASEAN's connecting and cooperation-promoting role, from a region with many conflicts and tensions, Southeast Asia has become a region of peace, stability, and development. From diverse and different countries in many aspects, ten Southeast Asian nations have increasingly unified and united, together consolidating dialogue habits, building consensus, strengthening cooperation to handle common regional issues.

It can be said that after over 50 years of existence and development, ASEAN has become a large, strong, and cohesive political-economic entity with a "central" role for peace and security in Southeast Asia specifically and the Asia-Pacific and Indo-Pacific generally. These are undeniable achievements, making ASEAN one of the world's most successful regional organizations. ASEAN's achieved results in traditional security cooperation mechanisms over the past two decades have created important foundations and further strengthened connectivity and sustainability within the Association of ASEAN nations. ASEAN has become the foremost important factor in maintaining peaceful environments, security, and cooperation for development in Southeast Asia, the Asia-Pacific, and Indo-Pacific, serving as an essential factor providing powerful support for pursuing security, development, and position objectives of both individual member countries and the entire region.

For Vietnam, as an active member of the ASEAN Community, promoting national strength and position as during the Communist Party's leadership: Vietnam always affirms it must firmly protect national sovereignty at sea, resolutely and persistently struggle against all acts violating national territorial sovereignty; resolve disputes in maritime areas with overlapping sovereignty by peaceful means, through diplomacy and legal means; actively negotiate delimitation of maritime boundaries and continental shelves to reduce contradictions; maintain peace, security, freedom, and maritime safety, striving to contribute to making the SCS a safe maritime area complying with international law. Consequently, national sovereignty at sea is firmly maintained, with Vietnam contributing to making the SCS a region of peace, security, and safety for activities, consistent with international law.

REFERENCES

ASEAN. (1992). *Singapore Declaration Of 1992 Singapore, 28 January 1992.* https://asean.org/singapore-declaration-of-1992-singapore-28-january-1992/

ASEAN. (1993). *Joint Press Statement for the Meeting to Explore the Establishment of the Consultative Relationship with the People's Republic of China Beijing, China, 13-14 September 1993.* https://asean.org/joint-press-statement-for-the-meeting-to-explore-the-establishment-of-the-consultative-relationship-with-the-peoples-republic-of-china-beijing-china-13-14-september-1993/

ASEAN. (2002). *Declaration on the Conduct of Parties in the South China Sea.* https://asean.org/declaration-on-the-conduct-of-parties-in-the-south-china-sea-2/

ASEAN Secretariat. (2010). *Chairman's Statement: 1st Expanded ASEAN Maritime Forum, Manila.* https://asean.org/chairmans-statement-1st-expanded-asean-maritime-forum-manila/

ASEAN. (2025). *ASEAN Political-Security Community Strategic Plan.* https://asean.org/asean-political-security-community-strategic-plan/

ASEAN-China Joint Statement. (1997). *Joint Statement of the Meeting of Heads of State/Government of the Member States of ASEAN and the President of the People's Republic of China Kuala Lumpur, Malaysia, 16 December 1997.* https://asean.org/joint-statement-of-the-meeting-of-heads-of-state-government-of-the-member-states-of-asean-and-the-president-of-the-peoples-republic-of-china-kuala-lumpur-malaysia-16-december-1997/

Ayesh, S., & Askari, M. U. (2025). China-ASEAN approaches towards the South China Sea disputes. *Journal of Social Sciences Review*, *5*(1), 150–162. https://www.researchgate.net/publication/390315176. DOI: 10.62843/jssr.v5i1.481

Baruah, D. M. (2022). Maritime competition in the Indian Ocean. *Carnegie Endowment for International Peace.* https://carnegieendowment.org/2022/05/12/maritime-competition-in-indian-ocean-pub-87093

Chapman, N. (2017). Mechanisms of Vietnam's Multidirectional Foreign Policy. *Journal of Current Southeast Asian Affairs*, *36*(2), 31–69. DOI: 10.1177/186810341703600202

Communist Review. (2011). *Stabilizing the South China Sea: Requires cooperation among all parties.* https://www.tapchicongsan.org.vn/hoat-ong-cua-lanh-ao-ang-nha-nuoc/-/2018/13486/on-dinh-bien-dong--can-su-hop-tac-giua-cac-ben.aspx

Dang, C. T. (2014). ASEAN Political-Security Community after 2015 and Vietnam's participation. *Journal of International Students*, *3*(88), 172–177.

Fang, Y. (2015). The South China Sea Disputes: Whither a Solution? In Huang, J., & Billo, A. (Eds.), *Territorial Disputes in the South China Sea* (pp. 164–188). Palgrave Macmillan., DOI: 10.1057/9781137463685_10

Felker, G. (2001). ASEAN Regionalism and Southeast Asia's Systemic Challenges. In: *Twenty-First Century World Order and the Asia Pacific* (pp. 213-253). Palgrave Macmillan, New York. https://doi.org/DOI: 10.1057/9780230107175_8

Hao, S. (2011). China's Positions and Interests in the South China Sea: A Rational Choices in its Cooperative Policies. *Center for Strategic and International Studies.* https://www.csis.org/analysis/chinas-positions-and-interests-south-china-sea-rational-choices-its-cooperative-policies

Hiep, T. X., Hoan, T. Q., & Kiet, L. H. (2024). Free and Open Indo-Pacific strategy: Competitive Opinions and Trends. *Vestnik of Saint Petersburg University -. International Relations*, *17*(3), 242–259.

Hong, P. (2018). *Understanding ASEAN.* National Political Publishing House.

Hossain, K. (2013). The UNCLOS and the US-China hegemonic competition over the South China Sea. *Journal of East Asia and International Law*, *6*(1). Advance online publication. DOI: 10.14330/jeail.2013.6.1.05

Hu, L. (2023). Examining ASEAN's effectiveness in managing South China Sea disputes. *The Pacific Review*, *36*(1), 119–147. DOI: 10.1080/09512748.2021.1934519

Indo-Pacific Defense Forum. (2018). *Congressional ASEAN group wants closer U.S.-ASEAN ties.* https://ipdefenseforum.com/2018/08/congressional-asean-group-wants-closer-u-s-asean-ties/

Katsumata, H. (2009). The Significance of the ASEAN Regional Forum (ARF). In: *ASEAN's Cooperative Security Enterprise - Critical Studies of the Asia Pacific Series* (pp. 16-34). Palgrave Macmillan, London. DOI: 10.1057/9780230277038_2

Kiet, L. H., Binh, N. T., & Hiep, T. X. (2025c). From border conflicts to maritime competition: Driving forces behind the power rivalry between India and China in the Indian Ocean region. *Australian Journal of Maritime and Ocean Affairs*, •••, 1–25. DOI: 10.1080/18366503.2025.2492438

Kiet, L. H., Nguyen, P. H., Tran, H. X., & Nguyen, B. T. (2025b). Vietnam's balancing strategy in the US-China rivalry in Southeast Asia. In Zreik, M. (Ed.), *Innovations and tactics for 21st century diplomacy* (pp. 271–302). IGI Global., DOI: 10.4018/979-8-3693-6074-3.ch012

Kiet, L. H., Tam, L. T. T., & Hiep, T. X. (2025a). Caught between dragon and elephant: Vietnam's strategic balancing act in the Sino-Indian rivalry. *China Quarterly of International Strategic Studies, 11*(2), 99–128. DOI: 10.1142/S237774002550006X

Kiet, L. H., & Tuyen, N. V. (2023). Vietnam's geopolitical position with the US in its strategy to contain China's hegemonic ambitions. *Journal of Science and Technology - Danang University, 21*(8.1), 63-69. https://jst-ud.vn/jst-ud/article/view/8630

Koga, K. (2022). *Managing Great Power Politics: ASEAN, Institutional Strategy, and the South China Sea*. Springer. DOI: 10.1007/978-981-19-2611-2

Mahan, A. T. (1987). *The influence of sea power upon history, 1660-1783* (5th ed.). Dover Publications.

Maliwanag, D. A. (2011). Philippines accuses China of 'serious violations' in South China Sea. *Inquiret.* https://globalnation.inquirer.net/3205/philippines-accuses-china-of-%e2%80%98serious-violations%e2%80%99-in-spratlys

Ministry of Foreign Affairs People's Republic of China. (2018). *Wang Yi's remarks on his attendance at the Foreign Ministers' Meetings on East Asia Cooperation.* https://www.fmprc.gov.cn/eng/gjhdq_665435/2675_665437/2777_663548/2779_663552/202406/t20240607_11413438.html

Nguyen, H., & Tran, T. (2025). China's Lawfare in the South China Sea: An Overview. In: *Lawfulness and Lawfare in the South China Sea* (pp. 41-138). International Law in Asia. Springer, Singapore. DOI: 10.1007/978-981-95-4001-3_2

Nguyen, T. K. P. (2017). Content of the framework agreement on the Code of Conduct in the South China Sea. *International Studies.* https://nghiencuuquocte.org/2017/06/26/thoa-thuan-khung-ve-coc/

Nguyen, T. M. (2018). Building the cooperative mechanism's peace, stability in the East Sea nowadays. *The Journal of Middle East and North Africa Sciences, 4*(8), 20–27.

Permanent Court of Arbitration. (n.d.). *The South China Sea Arbitration (The Republic of Philippines v. The People's Republic of China).* https://pca-cpa.org/cn/cases/7/

Pyć, D. (2019). The Role of the Law of the Sea in Marine Spatial Planning. In Zaucha, J., & Gee, K. (Eds.), *Maritime Spatial Planning* (pp. 375–395). Palgrave Macmillan., DOI: 10.1007/978-3-319-98696-8_16

Pyć, D. (2019). The role of the law of the sea in marine spatial planning. *Maritime spatial planning*, 375-395.

Quy, D. D. (2012). *South China Sea Disputes, Law, Geopolitics and International Cooperation*. World Publishing.

Quy, D. D., & Ngoc, N. M. (Eds.). (2013). *South China Sea geopolitics: Interests, policies and actions of related parties*. World Publishing.

Quyet, V. L., & Nguyet, N. T. A. (2023). U.S.-Vietnam maritime security cooperation in the South China Sea: From the Obama administration to the current Biden administration. *Cogent Arts & Humanities, 10*(1), 2231697. Advance online publication. DOI: 10.1080/23311983.2023.2231697

Roxas, P. A. V. (2017). Philippines leader says sea dispute 'better left untouched'. *Inquirer.* https://globalnation.inquirer.net/161911/duterte-south-china-sea-dispute-china-vietnam-asean-taiwan

Secretariat, A. S. E. A. N. (2017). *Declaration for a Decade of Coastal and Marine Environmental Protection in the South China Sea (2017-2027).* https://asean.org/wp-content/uploads/2017/11/Declaration-for-a-Decade-of-Coastal-and-Marine-Environmental-Protection-in-the-South-China-Sea-2017-2027.pdf

Secretariat, A. S. E. A. N. (2018). *Chairman's Statement of the ASEAN Post Ministerial Conference (PMC) 10+1 Sessions with the Dialogue Partners.* https://asean.org/chairmans-statement-of-the-asean-post-ministerial-conference-101-sessions-with-the-dialogue-partners-and-trilateral-meetings/

Secretariat, A. S. E. A. N. (2019). *Chairman's Statement of the 22nd ASEAN-China Summit.* https://asean.org/chairmans-statement-of-the-22nd-asean-china-summit-2/

Ta, N. T., Pham, T. D., & Doan, M. H. (Eds.). (2015). *Non-traditional security: Theoretical and practical issues*. Political Theory Publishing House.

Thayer, C. A. (2012). ASEAN's Code of Conduct in the South China Sea: A Litmus Test for Commumty-Building? *Asia-Pacific Journal, 10*(34), e4. DOI: 10.1017/S1557466012032998

Thayer, C. A. (2018a). The Evolution of Vietnamese Diplomacy, 1986–2016. In Le, H. H., & Tsvetov, A. (Eds.), *Vietnam's Foreign Policy under Doi Moi* (pp. 23–44). ISEAS–Yusof Ishak Institute. DOI: 10.1355/9789814818155-007

Thayer, C. A. (2018b). A closer look at the ASEAN-China single draft South China Sea Code of Conduct. *The Diplomat*. https://thediplomat.com/2018/03/a-closer-look-at-the-asean-china-single-draft-south-china-sea-code-of-conduct

United Nations. (1982). *United Nations Convention on the Law of the Sea*. https://www.un.org/Depts/los/convention_agreements/convention_overview_convention.htm

Vietnam News Agency. (n.d.). *Freedom of navigation in the South China Sea.* https://vietnam.vnanet.vn/vietnamese/long-form/tu-do-hang-hai-tren-bien-dong-343073.html

VietnamPlus. (2017). *ASEAN and China officially adopt COC framework draft.* https://www.vietnamplus.vn/asean-va-trung-quoc-chinh-thuc-thong-qua-du-thao-khung-coc-post459670.vnp

Vo, X. V. (Ed.). (2019). *Non-traditional maritime security cooperation in Southeast Asia and suggestions for Vietnam's policy*. Social Sciences Publishing House.

Voice of Vietnam. (2019). *Why does China have to push the 'cow's tongue line' claim?* https://vov.gov.vn/vi-sao-trung-quoc-phai-thuc-day-bang-duoc-yeu-sach-duong-luoi-bo-dtnew-122636

White House. (2018). *Prepared remarks for Vice President Pence at the East Asia Summit Plenary Session*. https://trumpwhitehouse.archives.gov/briefings-statements/prepared-remarks-vice-president-pence-east-asia-summit-plenary-session/

Yoshimatsu, H. (2022). ASEAN and Great Power Rivalry in Regionalism: From East Asia to the Indo-Pacific. *Journal of Current Southeast Asian Affairs*, *42*(1), 25–44. DOI: 10.1177/18681034221139297

Zhang J. (2023). Rebuilding strategic autonomy: ASEAN's response to US–China strategic competition. *China International Strategy Review,* 1–17. DOI: 10.1007/s42533-023-00128-3

Zhou, L., & Zhou, V. (2017). Donald Trump's early East Asia Summit exit casts doubt over US ties to Asia. *South China Morning Post*. https://www.scmp.com/news/china/diplomacy-defence/article/2119926/donald-trumps-early-summit-exit-casts-doubt-over-us

Chapter 16

India's Naval Nuclearization and Pakistan's Strategic Response:
Implications for South Asian Stability

Hammad Ahsan
University of Sargodha, Pakistan

Ashfaq Ahmed
https://orcid.org/0000-0001-9238-6024
University of Sargodha, Pakistan

Muhammad Adil Iqbal
https://orcid.org/0000-0001-5777-6131
National University of Sciences and Technology, Pakistan

ABSTRACT

India's naval nuclearization, particularly through Arihant-class ballistic missile submarines (SSBNs), has fundamentally altered South Asia's strategic landscape. This development disrupts traditional land-based deterrence equilibrium, compelling Pakistan to recalibrate its maritime defense posture despite fiscal and technological constraints. The chapter examines how India's sea-based nuclear capabilities exacerbate regional security dilemmas, increase crisis escalation risks, and complicate command-and-control architectures. Pakistan's response options include developing asymmetric deterrence through submarine-launched cruise missiles, implementing

DOI: 10.4018/979-8-3373-4470-6.ch016

Anti-Access/Area Denial strategies, and strengthening naval partnerships with China. Naval nuclearization threatens regional stability through heightened miscalculation risks in opaque maritime environments while challenging global non-proliferation norms. Sustainable deterrence requires multidimensional responses combining selective modernization, doctrinal adaptation, and proactive diplomacy to prevent an unmanageable arms race.

1. INTRODUCTION

South Asia's strategic landscape is characterized by persistent instability rooted in territorial disputes and historical grievances. The India-Pakistan rivalry, particularly over Kashmir, has resulted in multiple wars and continues to shape regional security dynamics (Wueger, 2024). The 1971 conflict, which led to the creation of Bangladesh, exemplifies how Indian military intervention transformed a political dispute between East and West Pakistan into an armed conflict. Many Pakistani strategists argue that nuclear deterrence would have prevented India's intervention in East Pakistan (Zulqarnain et al., 2024). These historical episodes underscore the prevalence of security dilemma dynamics in South Asian geopolitics, where efforts by one state to enhance its security invariably heighten the insecurity of its adversary. Uncertainty about intentions compounds this dilemma, as demonstrated when India capitalized on Pakistan's vulnerability in 1971.

This study addresses three critical questions that animate contemporary strategic discourse: (i) Can Pakistan's traditionally land-centric nuclear posture evolve to credibly deter India's emerging sea-based capabilities without triggering fiscal exhaustion or strategic overreach? (ii) How does the opacity inherent in submarine operations heighten miscalculation risks during confrontations, such as naval blockades or Balakot-type crises? and (iii) What consequences does the unchecked proliferation of naval nuclear weapons hold for global non-proliferation regimes and South Asia's fragile deterrence architecture?

To address these questions, the chapter proceeds as follows. Section 2 establishes the theoretical framework rooted in security dilemma theory and examines the regional security context. Section 3 traces the evolution and strategic motivations behind India's naval nuclear capabilities, including SSBN development and sea-based missile systems. Section 4 analyzes Pakistan's strategic vulnerabilities in the maritime domain and existing naval posture. Section 5 evaluates the strategic implications of India's naval nuclearization for Pakistan across military, economic, and diplomatic dimensions. Section 6 outlines Pakistan's strategic response options, including asymmetric deterrence, A2/AD strategies, and naval diplomacy. Section 7 assesses broader implications for regional stability and the global security architecture. Section 8 concludes with policy recommendations for sustaining deterrence while promoting crisis stability.

2. THEORETICAL FRAMEWORK AND REGIONAL SECURITY CONTEXT

The security dilemma concept, foundational to understanding regional dynamics, was developed by Herbert Butterfield, John H. Herz, and Robert Jervis. Herz first articulated the term "security dilemma" in a seminal 1950 article in *World Politics*, arguing that in anarchic societies—which have existed throughout most of known history—actors become "concerned about their security from being attacked, subjected, dominated, or annihilated" (Herz, 1950, p. 157). In seeking protection from such threats, actors are compelled to accumulate power to escape the influence of others' capabilities. This accumulation, however, increases others' insecurity and compels them to prepare for worst-case scenarios. In such environments, where absolute security remains elusive, power competition becomes endemic, creating self-perpetuating cycles of security and power accumulation.

Butterfield (1951) illustrated how security concerns can drive adversarial states toward war even when neither seeks conflict, asserting that "the greatest war in history can be produced without the intervention of any great criminals who might be out there to do deliberate harm in the world" (p. 19). His work demonstrated that devastating conflicts can emerge between powers genuinely seeking to avoid confrontation. Building on these foundations, Jervis (1978) observed that "many of the means by which a state tries to increase its security decrease the security of others" (p. 169). He further noted that "one state's gain in security often inadvertently threatens others" (p. 169). The essence of Jervis's argument is that in anarchic international systems, one state's enhanced security necessarily produces insecurity in others. This dynamic generates persistent fears of destruction and creates uncertainty. Military miscalculation in such environments can escalate conventional conflicts to the nuclear level, particularly when one state perceives a technological advantage and attempts to capitalize on favorable circumstances through preemptive action.

This theoretical debate centers on identifying the optimal pathway to lasting peace in South Asia through strategic stability. Strategic stability, which ensures credible deterrence, could facilitate enduring peace through dialogue and diplomacy. The central thesis of this work is that India's naval nuclearization heightens strategic instability, undermines Pakistan's maritime defense posture, and necessitates multidimensional strategic responses.

India's naval nuclearization poses significant threats to South Asian strategic stability. In a land war scenario, India possesses the capability to blockade Pakistan's naval routes. Given that Karachi is a metropolitan center housing millions of inhabitants, the threat of Indian nuclear attack creates a chilling strategic environment for Pakistan. Such miscalculations could precipitate nuclear exchanges targeting Pakistan's inland population centers. Even a successful blockade of Pakistan's naval ports would threaten the country's energy security, given its status as a net importer of crude oil and natural gas. Consequently, Pakistan must invest substantially in its naval sector to establish credible deterrence necessary for maintaining lasting peace. India's hegemonic ambitions pose a constant threat to South Asian stability, with historical evidence demonstrating India's pioneering role in introducing nuclear capabilities across South Asia's land, air, and naval domains.

The security dilemma framework best characterizes South Asia's strategic situation, particularly following India's naval nuclearization through its *Arihant*-class ballistic missile submarines (SSBNs). This development has compelled Pakistan to recalibrate its strategic posture to restore deterrence equilibrium. This chapter interrogates the strategic implications of India's naval nuclearization for Pakistan, employing a multi-paradigmatic framework that synthesizes offensive realism, deterrence theory, and constructivist insights to unravel the complex interplay of material power and identity-driven narratives.

The analysis focuses on two contradictory dynamics. India's acquisition of SSBNs potentially stabilizes deterrence through enhanced second-strike capability. Simultaneously, however, this development exacerbates Pakistan's security dilemma, prompting its acquisition of the Babur-3 submarine-launched cruise missile (SLCM). These bilateral tensions create centripetal forces drawing in China and Quad powers, thereby imparting a global dimension to this regional conflict.

3. EVOLUTION AND STRATEGIC MOTIVATIONS OF INDIAN NAVAL NUCLEAR CAPABILITIES

India's progression toward a credible nuclear triad, particularly through the induction of nuclear-powered ballistic missile submarines (SSBNs), has fundamentally altered South Asia's strategic naval domain. While India frames these developments within its doctrine of credible minimum deterrence, Pakistan interprets them as steps toward regional dominance and acquisition of sea-based first-strike capability. India's pursuit of a sea-based nuclear deterrent began with the Advanced Technology Vessel (ATV) program initiated in the late 1980s. This program culminated in India's first indigenously constructed nuclear-powered ballistic missile submarine, INS *Arihant*, commissioned in August 2016 (Ramsay, 2018). The *Arihant*'s commissioning marked India's entry into the exclusive group of nations possessing SSBN capabilities, successfully completing its nuclear triad. The submarine carries the

K-15 Sagarika submarine-launched ballistic missile (SLBM) with an approximate range of 700 kilometers. India has enhanced its second-strike capabilities through the development of the longer-range K-4 missile, with an estimated range of 3,500 kilometers (Ramsay, 2018).

India's second SSBN, INS *Arighat*, represents an advanced platform featuring enhanced stealth characteristics, a larger reactor core for improved endurance, and increased SLBM capacity. Commissioned on August 29, 2024, it now operates alongside *Arihant* in securing the Indian Ocean (Afridi, 2024). India is actively constructing a fleet of four to five SSBNs while simultaneously developing advanced SLBMs including the K-5 and K-6, reportedly possessing ranges of 5,000 and 6,000 kilometers respectively (see Table 1). These developments reflect India's intention to establish a robust and sustainable sea-based deterrent capable of striking adversaries deep within their territories (Kristensen & Korda, 2021).

Table 1. India's indigenous nuclear naval submarines and capabilities (as of 2024)

Submarine	Status	Missiles	Missile Range (km)	Notes
INS *Arihant*	Commissioned (2016)	K-15, K-4	700, 3,500	Operational
INS *Arighat*	Commissioned (2024)	K-4, K-15	3,500, 700	Operational
SSBN-3/4/5	Under Construction	K-4, K-5, K-6	Up to 6,000	Continuous naval deterrence goal

Sources: The authors compiled the data from Esin (2020)

India's SSBN acquisitions suggest three primary strategic rationales. First, India aims to counter Chinese nuclear submarines operating in the Indian Ocean theater. Second, India seeks escalation dominance over Pakistan by diluting Pakistan's nuclear leverage during crises. Third, despite its non-NPT status, India seeks recognition as a "responsible nuclear power" through these acquisitions. Beyond SSBNs, India has pursued aircraft carrier development, including INS Vikramaditya (leased from Russia) and two indigenously constructed carriers intended to establish dominance in the Indian Ocean. India's carrier program includes both conventional and planned nuclear-powered vessels (see Table 2), demonstrating long-term commitment to blue-water naval capabilities.

Table 2. Indian aircraft carrier projects

Aircraft Carrier	Capacity	Specifications
INS *Vikrant*	45,000 tons	Flagship aircraft carrier (commissioned 2022)
INS *Vishal*	65,000-75,000 tons	First nuclear-powered aircraft carrier (projected by 2030)

Sources: The authors compiled the data from International Defence Analysis (2024) and BBC (2022)

India is also developing Visakhapatnam-class destroyers with advanced capabilities, including INS *Surat* (commissioned May 2022) as a stealth guided missile destroyer, INS *Imphal* (commissioned December 2023) equipped with state-of-the-art weapons and sensors, and Project-17A aimed at improving Radar Cross-Section (RCS) and stealth capabilities (Kulkarni, 2025). India's strategic justification for this expansion centers on ensuring survivability and viable second-strike capability within its nuclear deterrence framework, specifically in response to China's and Pakistan's nuclear weapon developments. By deploying SSBNs, India seeks to maintain deterrence stability and protect its nuclear forces against first strikes.

Four mechanisms may result from India's disruption of the mutual vulnerability equilibrium. First, India's disproportionate second-strike capability against Pakistan incentivizes a preemptive posture. Second, Pakistan may face "use-it-or-lose-it" pressure in scenarios involving perceived SSBN attacks. Third, during crises, Pakistan may interpret dual-use assets like *Arihant* as nuclear threats, complicating threat assessment. Fourth, India's Project 75(I) (six AIP-powered attack submarines) and Pakistan's Hangor-class response exemplify action-reaction dynamics.

India's ambitions to dominate the Indian Ocean disrupt the delicate balance toward strategic stability, rendering South Asia increasingly insecure. The Indian Navy's advancing nuclear capabilities demonstrate strategic resolve and technological prowess that neighboring countries feel compelled to emulate. Sea-based deterrence enhances second-strike options by being less vulnerable to preemptive strikes than land-based missiles or air-launched weapons. India's SSBN commissioning forces competitors, particularly Pakistan, to recalculate strategic options. SSBNs' mobility, stealth, and survivability make them ideal platforms for ensuring retaliatory capabilities even following devastating first strikes.

However, India's naval nuclear ambitions face significant challenges. Maintaining and securing nuclear installations at sea requires massive investments in infrastructure, command-and-control structures, and fail-safe protocols. Additionally, India lacks extensive operational experience managing SSBN patrols, potentially resulting in judgment lapses or accidental escalation (Wueger, 2016). Integrating nuclear warheads on mobile maritime platforms raises serious command-and-control questions, particularly during emergencies, potentially destabilizing South Asia's already precarious security situation (Basrur, 2009).

Nevertheless, India continues substantial investment in developing a comprehensive nuclear fleet. India's sea-based deterrent is increasingly viewed as integral to its strategic autonomy and regional influence, intended to balance Chinese power amid intensifying Indo-Pacific geopolitical competition (Pant, 2009), despite concerns among smaller South Asian neighbors. India's MIRVs provide overkill capacity with Pakistan, while joint patrols with Quad partners combined with SSBN deployments send hegemonic signals regionally, particularly to Pakistan. This first-strike potential aligns with Mearsheimer's offensive realism but contradicts Waltz's defensive realism tenets, which advocate minimal deterrence capacity. This theoretical tension characterizes India's regional force posture.

Nonetheless, naval nuclearization exacerbates Pakistan's security dilemma. Pakistan's acquisition of nuclear-capable ballistic missiles in the naval domain has eroded Indian escalation control during potential conflicts. Miscommunication or judgment errors may lead adversaries to target these nuclearized submarines, potentially spiraling out of control. India's pursuit of strategic stability through enhanced deterrence paradoxically risks actual deterrence breakdown due to spiraling action-reaction dynamics within this security dilemma environment. Indian policymakers face a "Goldilocks dilemma": their capabilities lack strategic clarity with China, yet remain significant enough to concern Pakistan. Indian submarines operate under a "bastion strategy" in Bay of Bengal and northern Indian Ocean protected waters. Their Sagarika K-15 missiles with 750-kilometer range pose minimal threat to China but significantly erode Pakistan's strategic position.

India's pursuit of sea-based nuclear deterrence stems from multiple ideological, geopolitical, and strategic considerations extending beyond mere deterrence. These objectives reflect India's broader ambitions to become a significant maritime power capable of shaping Indo-Pacific regional events. Primary incentives driving India toward naval nuclearization include building survivable second-strike forces, countering regional competitors (China and Pakistan), projecting military power throughout the Indian Ocean Region (IOR), and asserting international status. The imperative to develop credible second-strike capability, essential for nuclear deterrence, primarily drives India's naval nuclearization. Nuclear-powered ballistic missile submarines provide superior endurance, mobility, and stealth compared to land-based missiles and air-launched nuclear warheads vulnerable to preemptive attack.

India's No First Use (NFU) doctrine requires assured retaliation capability following nuclear attack. Developing SSBNs such as INS *Arihant* and INS *Arighat* equipped with SLBMs enhances India's strategic resilience by reducing vulnerability to decapitating strikes that could eliminate deterrent forces (Afridi, 2024). China's growing Indian Ocean footprint has profoundly shaped India's maritime security perspective. The Chinese People's Liberation Army Navy (PLAN) has increased submarine deployments in the Indian Ocean, with SSBNs now conducting deterrence patrols from Hainan Island (Rehman, 2024). Beijing's establishment of a military base in Djibouti and its "String of Pearls" infrastructure development from Gwadar to Hambantota signals long-term strategic penetration into the Indian Ocean (Kiet, 2023).

This perceived encirclement motivated India's fleet nuclearization. By maintaining credible sea-based deterrence, India seeks to deny China nuclear supremacy and demonstrate survivability and retaliatory capability even in worst-case scenarios. The K-4 and future K-5/K-6 SLBMs, with ranges from 3,500 to 6,000 kilometers, are designed to ensure Indian SSBNs can strike strategic targets deep within China (Kristensen & Korda, 2021). China possesses continuous sea deterrence capability with advanced Anti-Submarine Warfare (ASW) capabilities and attack submarines. Indian submarines lack advanced stealth capabilities and can be detected through acoustic and digital signatures. China could neutralize these submarines in active hostile environments.

The underlying reality appears to be India's aspiration to become the net security provider in the Indian Ocean—an argument sponsored and supported by the United States (White House, 2025). Approximately fifty percent of global shipments transit these waters. Freedom of navigation requires that no single state dominate these routes. In an anarchic world, such preponderant power over globally significant trade routes threatens international peace and navigation freedom, potentially endangering smaller powers' sovereignty in the Indian Ocean Region. Historical precedents support this concern: U.S. dominance in the Caribbean Sea has resulted in excessive naval power projection to influence smaller Caribbean states' behavior, exemplified most recently by the Trump administration's naval blockade of Venezuela ostensibly targeting illegal drug trade.

Pakistan's advances in tactical nuclear weapons and emphasis on full-spectrum deterrence have prompted India to upgrade its second-strike posture. India seeks dominance in its approach to South Asian neighbors. Despite Pakistan's lack of nuclear submarines, Indian strategists remain concerned about regional nuclear instability. South Asia's short distances and rapid escalation cycles compound these complications (Kapur, 2008). The Indian SSBN fleet provides an escalation control mechanism. Sea-based deterrence could reduce probabilities of rash or accidental launches by introducing complexity and delay into crisis decision-making. Additionally, invulnerable retaliatory forces enable India to absorb first strikes and retaliate precisely, restoring deterrence without immediate escalation (Basrur, 2009).

The Indian Ocean constitutes India's strategic focus. Beyond hosting critical maritime chokepoints such as the Strait of Hormuz and Malacca Strait, it facilitates 80% of global oil trade (Chaturvedi & Rumley, 2015). India aspires to achieve deterrence through dominance and denial in its broader maritime neighborhood, positioning itself as the net security provider. Naval nuclearization forms a core element of this aspiration. SSBNs enable strategic signaling, extended deployment, and sub-surface deterrent patrols that project power beyond Indian shores. This aligns with India's 2015 Maritime Security Strategy, which advocates possessing "credible underwater capability" to "shape a favorable maritime environment" and counter threats (Baruah, 2015).

India's SSBN program reflects its desire for recognition as a responsible and technologically advanced nuclear state. Achieving a complete nuclear triad places India among an exclusive group including the United States, Russia, China, France, and the United Kingdom. This capability enhances India's geopolitical position, supporting its applications for membership in international export control and non-proliferation regimes such as the Nuclear Suppliers Group (NSG). Furthermore, it strengthens India's leadership in international naval alliances, including the Quad alignment with the United States, Japan, and Australia, while enhancing defense diplomacy (Pant & Bommakanti, 2020).

India's strategic community, including military and civil bureaucracy, strongly supports naval nuclearization. The nuclear submarine program sustains itself through long-term financing, prestige, and bureaucratic momentum. The military-industrial complex, particularly the Indian Navy, Bhabha Atomic Research Centre (BARC), and Defence Research and Development Organisation (DRDO), maintains institutionalized stakes in sea-based deterrent development. Moreover, domestic political consensus on strengthening deterrence against Pakistan and China ensures SSBN development consistency across administrations regardless of party affiliation (Perkovich, 2001).

India's naval nuclearization stems from multiple strategic rationales deeply rooted in its security environment, regional geopolitics, and international aspirations. Indian SSBN programs represent strategies integrating deterrence, diplomacy, and growth beyond mere military capability demonstration, enabling India to confront challengers, demonstrate power, and showcase technological superiority. Indian political leadership jealously guards control over nuclear forces. Second-strike capability potency demands nuclear warhead placement aboard SSBNs. Officially, India maintains warheads separate from delivery platforms, consistent with its No First Use doctrine. However, communication breakdowns in the field could result in local military commanders inadvertently employing these warheads, potentially triggering total nuclear war. How Indian policymakers plan to address communication breakdowns and prevent nuclear catastrophe remains unclear. This emerging maritime nuclear strategy presents new regional stability challenges, most significantly for Pakistan.

4. PAKISTAN'S STRATEGIC VULNERABILITIES AND RESPONSE OPTIONS

Pakistan's maritime security policy is shaped by limited naval capabilities, shifting regional imperatives, geostrategic position, and the increasing threat posed by India's naval nuclearization. Pakistan has historically pursued constrained maritime defense relative to its broader land-based security policy. However, Indian Ocean nuclearization and escalating Indian naval assertiveness have compelled Pakistan to reconsider and increasingly enhance its conventional and strategic naval deterrents. Pakistan's approximately 1,046-kilometer coastline along the Arabian Sea includes two critical ports: Karachi and Gwadar. Pakistan's maritime interests encompass protecting Sea Lines of Communication (SLOCs), defending Exclusive Economic Zones (EEZs), securing commercial ports, and defending against naval attacks from adversaries, particularly India. Pakistan's proximity to the Strait of Hormuz creates strategic interests in regional energy routes. Over 60% of global oil transits this chokepoint; any disruption would severely impact Pakistan's economic and energy security (Kiet et al., 2025).

As of 2025, the Pakistan Navy operates 36 active naval units, including 15 frigates, 16 submarines, 16 corvettes, 3 *Munsif*-class countermining vessels, and 85 offshore patrol vessels (Global Military, 2025). Additionally, the navy maintains various smaller vessels including missile boats, coastal defense batteries, and maritime surveillance aircraft (see Table 3). The backbone of Pakistan's underwater capability comprises French-origin Agosta-class submarines, including three Agosta-90B submarines with Air-Independent Propulsion (AIP) systems. These submarines' extended underwater endurance provides Pakistan with a modest but credible underwater deterrent.

Table 3. Pakistan navy key assets (2024)

Platform Type	Number	Key Features
Agosta-90B Submarines	5	AIP-enabled, torpedo and missile-capable
Frigates (F-22P, Type 054A/P)	9	Multi-role, Chinese-origin, surface warfare
Fast Attack Craft (Missile)	8	Anti-ship and patrol roles
Maritime Patrol Aircraft	6+	Sea King, P-3C Orion
Coastal Defense Batteries	N/A	Zarb and Harbah anti-ship missiles

Sources: The authors compiled the data from Nuclear Threat Initiative (2024)

Pakistan is expanding its fleet through Chinese assistance, adding Hangor-class submarines to significantly enhance underwater combat capabilities (Firepower, 2024). India's naval nuclearization now compels Pakistan to consider sea-based nuclear options. Pakistan tested the Babur-3 submarine-launched cruise missile (SLCM) in January 2017, with an approximate 450-kilometer range fired from submerged platforms (Khan, 2017). This nuclear-capable missile aims to provide Pakistan with second-strike capability. Although not yet deployed on nuclear-powered submarines, the Babur-3 represents an experimental sea-based deterrent marking Pakistan's initial attempt to develop survivable nuclear forces at sea. Pakistan will likely depend on conventionally powered submarines for nuclear delivery systems, similar to early Soviet Cold War strategy, unlike India's SSBN-based approach (Kroenig, 2018).

Pakistan's nuclear doctrine emphasizes "minimum credible deterrence," though this has increasingly shifted toward "full-spectrum deterrence" in response to perceived Indian conventional and strategic superiority. This shift involves developing offensive and defensive technologies capable of countering Indian naval superiority in maritime environments, particularly in Pakistan's proximate waters. This doctrinal evolution manifests in coastal defense system deployment, anti-access/area denial (A2/AD) technologies, and sea-launched cruise missiles. Pakistan's Harbah and Zarb anti-ship missiles, launched from land and naval platforms, are designed to deter Indian naval advances near maritime borders (Ali, 2021). Rather than matching Indian Navy tonnage, Pakistan invests in defensive A2/AD technologies protecting its Exclusive Economic Zone and seaports. Pakistan successfully tested its Smash anti-ship ballistic missile on November 25, 2024 (Brahy, 2024).

Gwadar Port development under the China-Pakistan Economic Corridor (CPEC) umbrella has increased Pakistan's maritime strategic depth. Providing deep-sea port access, Gwadar enables Pakistan to extend naval operations westward toward the Gulf of Oman while reducing Karachi dependence. However, Gwadar faces threats from Indian submarine blockades and maritime denial operations. This strategic resource has become simultaneously a leverage point and potential liability, necessitating more robust seaborne defense forces in Balochistan and along the Makran coast (Jabeen, 2024).

Active participation in regional maritime security cooperation forms part of Pakistan's maritime policy. Pakistan conducts and participates in exercises such as AMAN, gathering navies from over 40 countries including China and NATO members. This enhances shared security in the Indian Ocean while supporting Pakistan's image as a responsible maritime power (Ahsan, 2023). Pakistan has advocated for designating the Indian Ocean a "nuclear weapon-free zone," highlighting instability risks from India's SSBN deployments. Through forums such as the United Nations and Indian Ocean Rim Association (IORA), Pakistan promotes diplomatic norms limiting maritime militarization (Zulqarnain et al., 2024).

Despite strategic imperatives, Pakistan faces numerous challenges modifying its naval posture. The primary limitation is constrained financial allocation. The Navy receives only 10-12% of Pakistan's overall defense expenditure, which disproportionately favors the Army and territorial border defense (Hasan, 2015). Second, unlike India, Pakistan cannot indigenously manufacture nuclear submarines or SLBMs, remaining heavily reliant on imports and Chinese assistance. This advanced domestic military-industrial complex deficit may become a critical bottleneck during actual hostilities. Additionally, naval capability concentration near Karachi, as demonstrated during the 1971 war, renders Pakistan vulnerable to blockade or preemptive strikes. These limitations indicate that while Pakistan works to adapt to maritime threats, its sea-based deterrent remains nascent and unlikely to rival India's SSBN program in sophistication or scope for at least another decade.

Pakistan is gradually but steadily shifting its maritime security approach. Islamabad responds to Indian naval nuclearization by combining asymmetric deterrence, conventional naval modernization, and multilateral engagement within limited financial and technological constraints. Effective deterrence can be achieved through upgraded coastal defenses, Babur-3 SLCM deployment, and AIP submarine investment. However, infrastructure, sustainability, and C4ISR (command, control, communications, computers, intelligence, surveillance, and reconnaissance) remain deficit areas requiring continued investment. As India's SSBN fleet expands, Pakistan must balance deterrent requirements, regional stability, and economic interests, particularly concerning CPEC asset and maritime traffic security.

5. STRATEGIC IMPLICATIONS FOR PAKISTAN

India's acquisition of sea-based nuclear capabilities, nuclearizing the Indian Ocean, confronts Pakistan with a complex web of strategic challenges extending beyond military concerns to encompass alliance politics, resource allocation, crisis escalation, deterrence behavior, and strategic stability. As India consolidates its naval nuclear triad, Pakistan assumes a reactive posture attempting to preserve deterrent credibility without strategic overreach. The most immediate consequence of Indian naval nuclearization is bilateral strategic stability erosion. South Asian strategic stability has long relied upon land-based mutual vulnerability concepts. SSBN induction, particularly India's *Arihant*-class, disrupts deterrence symmetry by providing India with survivable second-strike capability. This survivability undermines Pakistan's land-based nuclear deterrent posture. If Indian SSBNs can operate silently and respond following first strikes, Pakistan may feel less constrained from Indian preemptive or punitive actions, particularly given conventional military imbalances.

Despite fiscal and technological constraints, Pakistan must respond by developing nascent sea-based deterrence. Babur-3 submarine-launched cruise missile (SLCM) research, development, and testing reflects strategic movement toward developing initial second-strike capability. Although Indian sea-based deterrence remains more credible than Pakistani capabilities, Pakistan's efforts fulfill deterrence theory's underlying principle of reestablishing mutual vulnerability (Narang, 2016). However, employing conventional submarines for nuclear delivery raises command-and-control challenges. Unlike SSBNs, conventional platforms remain vulnerable because they must surface regularly. Furthermore, deploying nuclear assets at sea complicates Pakistan's traditionally centralized control paradigm (Montgomery & Sagan, 2009), necessitating naval nuclear asset integration into existing command-and-control mechanisms.

India's naval buildup exerts direct operational and psychological pressure on the Pakistan Navy. Countering Indian SSBN patrols, carrier battle groups, and advanced anti-submarine warfare (ASW) capabilities requires diverting scarce resources toward maritime defense from Pakistan's already strained military budget. Pakistan must modernize its naval fleet, acquire new platforms such as Type 054A/P frigates and Hangor-class submarines, and deploy land-based anti-ship missile batteries to counter these threats. However, these initiatives require time and finance that Pakistan must balance against other security and development objectives (Askari & Iqbal, 2023).

Perhaps the most catastrophic consequence of Indian naval nuclearization is heightened crisis escalation and miscalculation likelihood. Deploying nuclear capabilities at sea raises serious concerns during peacetime signaling and wartime operations. Disagreements over platform payloads—whether submarines or warships carry conventional or nuclear weapons—can trigger preemptive attacks based on worst-case analysis during crises. Additionally, SSBNs' strategic sanctuary may embolden India toward greater conventional theater aggression. Conversely, if Pakistan perceives its sea-based deterrent as vulnerable, it could face "use-it-or-lose-it" dilemmas. Miscalculation probabilities increase in this volatile environment, particularly during high-speed naval operations (Kristensen & Korda, 2022).

Strategic implications extend beyond military security. India's expanding sea-control capabilities, underpinned by nuclear-powered submarines and long-endurance systems, directly threaten Pakistan's economic interests, specifically the CPEC. During conflicts, Indian forces could blockade or disrupt Gwadar Port, a critical CPEC node. Moreover, merchant shipping lanes vital to Pakistan's trade and oil imports face risks from Indian SSNs. Economic corridor securitization taxes Pakistan's security establishment, compelling enhanced air and naval surveillance in western maritime domains (Jabeen, 2024).

India's naval nuclearization has significantly increased Pakistan's defense dependence on China, particularly in maritime domains. Beyond cooperating on Hangor-class submarine production and coastal radar networks, China has provided Pakistan with frigates, submarines, and intelligence equipment. While this strategic collaboration enhances Pakistan's capabilities, increased Chinese dependence could constrain Pakistan's policy autonomy during regional conflicts or crises. Additionally,

India perceives China-Pakistan naval collaboration as part of a broader strategy to curtail Indian supremacy in the Indian Ocean (Pant & Bommakanti, 2020).

India's naval nuclearization necessitates doctrinal transformation within Pakistan's Strategic Plans Division (SPD). Pakistan's nuclear command must now incorporate decentralized and mobile nuclear platforms, particularly in maritime domains, whereas it previously focused exclusively on land-based, centralized deterrence. Beyond command-and-control structural adjustments, this doctrinal shift requires institutional learning, coordination, and training across the Pakistan Navy and Strategic Forces Command. In opaque maritime environments where attribution is difficult and communications can be jammed or spoofed, risks of inadvertent launch, misidentification, and command failure increase substantially (Noor, 2023).

India's submarine nuclear deployments have also undermined opportunities for bilateral arms control and naval confidence-building measures (CBMs). While land-based nuclear forces can be verified and capped through dialogue, submarines and sea-launched missiles are inherently stealthy and unverifiable. India opposes Pakistan's frequent appeals to designate the Indian Ocean a nuclear-weapon-free zone. This asymmetry in transparency and restraint complicates efforts to stabilize deterrence through arms limitations or crisis communication channels (Zulqarnain et al., 2024).

India's naval nuclearization represents a profound shift in South Asia's deterrence context with far-reaching implications for Pakistan. Pakistan must balance maintaining deterrence, avoiding escalation, and managing limited resources while strategic stability erodes and credible sea-based deterrence must be developed. Beyond growing security threats, the expanding maritime imbalance compels Pakistan to rely increasingly on external allies, particularly China, to counter Indian capabilities. This situation demands strategic reassessment of Pakistan's procurement strategy, diplomatic engagement, and military doctrine. The absence of arms control regimes governing naval nuclear deployments renders this situation more complex. Without creative diplomacy and regional engagement, the Indian Ocean risks becoming a theater of deterrent instability, trapping Pakistan in perpetual reactive posturing.

6. PAKISTAN'S STRATEGIC RESPONSE OPTIONS

Pakistan must devise a rational, multidimensional strategic response to India's growing naval nuclearization and sea-power aspirations. Due to technological gaps and financial limitations, Islamabad cannot simply mirror India's capabilities. To uphold credible deterrence, defend maritime interests, and ensure regional stability, Pakistan must adopt a hybrid approach incorporating diplomacy, strategic alignments, doctrinal adaptability, and selective modernization. The following response options outline an effective course of action.

First, developing and institutionalizing sea-based second-strike capability, essential for credible minimum deterrence, should constitute Pakistan's highest priority. While SSBNs remain financially and technologically unattainable, Islamabad can employ diesel-electric submarines with nuclear-capable cruise missiles, such as Babur-3, to maintain effective deterrence. China has committed to providing Pakistan with eight Hangor-class submarines between 2023 and 2028, with four constructed in China and four produced locally. These vessels will enhance endurance and survivability in the Arabian Sea through improved stealth and air-independent propulsion (AIP) capabilities (Fretay, 2025). When combined with low-yield nuclear SLCMs, these submarines can offer credible second-strike posture within Pakistan's resource constraints (Narang, 2016). However, this asymmetric deterrence must be doctrinally integrated beyond mere symbolism. It requires robust command-and-control procedures, strategic force training, and secure maritime communications infrastructure to prevent abuse or inadvertent escalation. Additionally, Pakistan should prioritize developing long-range nuclear-capable sea-launched cruise missiles to preclude Indian counterforce temptations. This approach strengthens Pakistan's deterrence posture from secure close-to-shore platforms without matching Indian naval tonnage.

Second, against the backdrop of India's blue-water navy advantage and increasing expeditionary ambitions, Pakistan must develop Anti-Access/Area Denial (A2/AD) strategies to prevent Indian maritime hegemony in Pakistan's littoral regions. This involves deploying a mix of coastal defense batteries, land-based anti-ship ballistic and cruise missile systems, and unmanned platforms. The Harbah anti-ship cruise missile and Zarb coastal missile system, both launched from surface vessels, provide this deterrence layer. Integrating over-the-horizon targeting using drone and satellite-based reconnaissance will further enhance precision strike capabilities (Petrovski & Radovanović, 2021). Developing mobile coastal missile batteries and stationing fast-attack craft at strategic chokepoints such as the Makran Coast and Gwadar approaches must rank among Pakistan's highest priorities. These asymmetrical weapons can inflict significant costs on superior naval adversaries, particularly in constricted spaces like the North Arabian Sea.

Third, although submarines provide stealth and deterrence, Pakistan's surface fleet modernization remains imperative for presence operations, escort duties, and maritime security patrols. Acquiring four Type 054A/P guided-missile frigates from China significantly enhances surface capabilities with modern Anti-Submarine Warfare (ASW) systems, radar, and anti-aircraft weapons. When combined with advanced Azmat-class missile craft and MILGEM-class corvettes co-designed with Turkey, these vessels augment the Pakistan Navy's capability for multi-domain operations and extended presence along strategic sea lanes, particularly near the

Gulf of Oman and Strait of Hormuz (Sabah, 2021). Maritime domain awareness is equally imperative. Augmenting coastal radar networks, employing unmanned aerial vehicles (UAVs) such as ScanEagle, and integrating satellite imagery into naval intelligence can enhance surveillance and early-warning capabilities. Prompt situational awareness underpins both peacetime monitoring and wartime readiness.

Fourth, under the National Command Authority (NCA), Pakistan established the Naval Strategic Forces Command (NSFC) on May 19, 2012, as a dedicated maritime strategic command to augment maritime nuclear capabilities. This organization oversees deployment, coordination, and potential employment of sea-based nuclear forces, providing tactical, operational, and strategic direction for nuclear-capable naval weapons. To ensure survivability, continuity, and control during crises, NSFC must be supported by dual-key authorization procedures, secure communications links (e.g., satellite or very-low-frequency systems), and regular peacetime exercises (Ali & Sidhu, 2022). Developing such architecture requires political will, civil-military coordination, and investment in strategic communications infrastructure.

Fifth, due to maritime limitations, Pakistan must aggressively pursue naval diplomacy and strategic partnerships, especially with China and Turkey. These alliances serve dual objectives: political signaling toward regional adversaries and power multiplication through collective exercises and technology sharing. China's investment in Gwadar Port development and supply of critical naval platforms constitutes a long-term stabilizing factor for Pakistan. Continued cooperative patrols, intelligence sharing, and collaborative naval technology development will enhance deterrence against Indian aggression in the western Indian Ocean (CPEC, 2020). Pakistan may also leverage international forums such as the Indian Ocean Naval Symposium (IONS) to promote standards of responsible maritime conduct and non-nuclearization. Such forums help Pakistan project itself as a responsible regional maritime security actor despite potential Indian opposition.

Sixth, strategic signaling through doctrinal ambiguity and flexibility remains an economical tool in Pakistan's strategic response arsenal. By declining to confirm or deny the nuclear nature of specific platforms, such as Babur-3 or Hangor-class submarines, Pakistan maintains deterrence through uncertainty (Ali & Sidhu, 2022). This stance forces adversaries to account for worst-case possibilities in their planning while preserving escalation control. Uncertainty must be combined with selective disclosures and credible signals to maintain psychological credibility (Montgomery & Sagan, 2009). Pakistan should also consider incremental declaration changes to its nuclear doctrine. Pakistan may emphasize full-spectrum maritime deterrence and reaffirm its ability to retaliate across multiple domains following maritime aggression. Besides, South Asia now faces a dangerous naval security dilemma due to India's naval nuclearization. Pakistan aims to develop a sophisticated, multifaceted, and sustainable strategy ensuring deterrence, safeguarding sea lanes, and preventing escalation without engaging in ship-for-ship or missile-for-missile competition with India. This requires enhancing A2/AD capabilities, modernizing surveillance systems, institutionalizing naval command arrangements, and developing asymmetric sea-based deterrence. Meanwhile, strategic partnerships and naval diplomacy can help Pakistan counterbalance Indian assertiveness while boosting maritime power. Pakistan must exercise prudence and agility in this shifting deterrence theater to protect its economic vitality, naval strategic credibility, and sovereignty.

7. IMPLICATIONS FOR REGIONAL STABILITY AND GLOBAL SECURITY ARCHITECTURE

Beyond bilateral competition, naval nuclear arms emergence in South Asia—primarily through India's maritime-based nuclear deterrent and Pakistan's potential asymmetric response—injects complex strategic implications into regional and global security systems. These developments challenge existing arms control regimes, threaten crisis stability, increase escalation risks, and test Indo-Pacific Theater power balances. Consequently, South Asian naval nuclearization must be viewed against global strategic stability contexts (Kazmi, 2025).

First, India's SSBN and sea-launched ballistic missile deployments, combined with Pakistan's pursuit of nuclear-capable cruise missiles on conventional submarines, generate a perilous second-strike dynamic. Although both countries claim adherence to minimum deterrence theories, the ambiguity of naval nuclear assets substantially complicates crisis signaling and escalation control. Realistic analysis indicates India pursues dominant deterrence strategy, seeking to render Pakistan strategically inconsequential through continuous weapons improvement programs. Underwater deployments are inherently clandestine, with SSBN deployments raising miscalculation probabilities. Rivals' inability to monitor sea-based nuclear stockpiles compounds "use-it-or-lose-it" challenges during crises, particularly amid limited communication or defective early-warning systems. The absence of deconfliction measures, naval incident-specific hotlines, or confidence-building measures (CBMs) at sea within South Asia aggravates this problem (Acton, 2015). Consequently, the regional security environment faces unintentional escalation risks, particularly if one party perceives conventional naval operations as nuclear threat precursors.

Second, naval forces operating through international waterways face greater uncertainty and miscalculation susceptibility than ground forces typically operating within national borders or along fixed boundaries. Nuclear-powered submarine presence or doubts regarding vessels' nuclear capabilities may engender overreaction during potential naval standoffs, particularly amid fog of war. For example, during crises, India may conclude that Pakistan placing a Babur-3-armed submarine on patrol signals nuclear threshold escalation intent. Alternatively, Pakistan may interpret Indian SSBN patrols near its coast as preemptive strike rehearsals. Without checks, such perceptions can accelerate conflict buildup, reduce crisis decision-making windows, and erode strategic restraint (Mian et al., 2019). Additionally, conventional and nuclear capability convergence in naval systems may promote preemptive targeting during warfare. Unclear nuclear warhead deployment status on submarines exacerbates this issue.

Third, South Asian naval nuclearization also influences broader Indo-Pacific strategic calculations. China's increasing maritime presence in the Indian Ocean Region (IOR), comprising port calls, intelligence vessels, and submarine patrols, partially motivates India's SSBN development. Responsively, India seeks to become a regional net security provider, increasingly relying on nuclear-powered secure deterrence. The China-India-Pakistan triangular relationship generates layered deterrence systems. Consequently, actions targeting one actor, such as India's naval posture against China, produce unintended consequences for others, such as Pakistan. The ultimate result is a multilayered deterrent environment with overlapping strategic theaters and blurred threat perceptions (Matamis, 2025). India's Quadrilateral Security Dialogue (QUAD) participation and United States partnership also influences nuclear signaling (Hiep et al., 2024). Washington may inadvertently heighten regional vulnerabilities by encouraging Indian maritime assertiveness through technology transfers, information exchange, and cooperative maneuvers.

Fourth, the naval dimension of nuclear deterrence creates significant challenges for global non-proliferation order, notably the Treaty on the Non-Proliferation of Nuclear Weapons (NPT). India has introduced this variable in the Indian Ocean with proactive U.S. backing. Although neither India nor Pakistan are NPT parties, their actions impact the normative environment and create templates for other potential nuclear states. Mobile nuclear platforms and sea-based delivery systems present greater transparency and verification challenges. Unlike fixed land-based missiles susceptible to satellite monitoring and inspection systems, sea-based nuclear warheads escape such scrutiny. This transparency deficit threatens arms control and may encourage other regional powers, especially in East Asia and the Middle East, to perceive naval nuclear options as viable deterrents (Levesques et al., n.d.). Furthermore, the absence of mutual declarations among China, India, and Pakistan regarding SSBN deployments, hotline communications, or sea-based CBMs represents a significant gap in global strategic governance. This gap increases probabilities of unauthorized launches, nuclear accidents, and maritime security violations.

Fifth, nuclear weapon deployment at sea raises environmental and human safety concerns. Nuclear-armed submarines cruise environmentally sensitive regions such as the Bay of Bengal and Arabian Sea, where accidental explosions, leaks, or sinkings could produce long-term human and marine health impacts. India's and

Pakistan's safety standards, accident preparedness, and disaster response capabilities regarding underwater nuclear activities remain largely unknown. Moreover, during crises, nuclear facility-adjacent naval bases, such as Visakhapatnam or Karachi, face vulnerability to precision attacks or sabotage due to high population densities (Koppe, 2014). In 2018, INS Arihant SSBN suffered major damage from saltwater intrusion (Carlin, 2024). This accident could have ignited catastrophic humanitarian and marine disasters due to nuclear fissile material present in the nuclear reactor submarine. Additionally, naval nuclear exchanges would produce catastrophic humanitarian effects not only for South Asia but also for nearby areas dependent on Indian Ocean fishing and marine trade.

Sixth, Despite risks, South Asian naval nuclearization presents opportunities for regional communication and confidence-building. India and Pakistan can explore bilateral agreements to: (i) Designate the Indian Ocean a nuclear-free zone; (ii) Establish maritime CBM systems, either through SAARC or dedicated Indo-Pacific maritime security forums; and (iii) Exchange notifications of SLBM tests or SSBN patrols and create incidents-at-sea agreements managing inadvertent naval encounters.

Non-political forums must facilitate discussions on safety protocols and crisis management methodologies. These include international naval symposiums, regional think-tank dialogues, and track-two diplomacy. Nuclear-armed submarines' devastating dangers must spur both states to institute safeguards and cultivate cooperative maritime practices despite political animosity. Beyond the India-Pakistan case, South Asian sea-based nuclear capability evolution holds far-reaching implications. It contributes to global non-proliferation norm deterioration, transforms regional deterrence structures, and generates crisis escalation dangers. The Indian Ocean represents a potential nuclear miscalculation hotspot due to strategic maritime relations among Pakistan, China, and India. International and regional stakeholders should prioritize transparency, communication, and moderation to mitigate these dangers. While deterrence remains nuclear strategy's cornerstone, its maritime application necessitates creating new guidelines, doctrines, and safety protocols well-suited to underwater domain complexities.

8. CONCLUSION

India's pursuit of a robust sea-based nuclear deterrent has radically transformed South Asian geopolitics. SSBN operationalization, such as INS Arihant, and induction of long-range submarine-launched ballistic missiles, including K-4 and forthcoming K-6 systems, exemplify Indian ambitions to project power beyond borders and attain credible second-strike capability. From India's perspective, these advancements may enhance deterrence, but they pose formidable strategic challenges for Pakistan, particularly in naval domains. Pakistan, traditionally prioritizing conventional military parity and land-based deterrence, now confronts multifaceted threats, including potentially undetected and robust nuclear capabilities hidden beneath the Indian Ocean surface.

This development complicates Pakistan's deterrence calculus while enhancing crisis instability risks, command-and-control vulnerabilities, and intraregional arms competition. Sea-based nuclear weapons presence in South Asia's relatively shallow and congested waterways heightens misperception, misidentification, and accidental escalation probabilities during heightened tensions. To successfully navigate this emerging security scenario, Pakistan must adopt strategies leveraging asymmetric strengths, emphasizing affordable deterrent systems, and engaging constructively in regional diplomacy. Efforts will focus on fleet modernization, enhancing nuclear-tipped cruise missile technology, and bolstering command-and-control infrastructure while institutionalizing sea-based confidence-building measures and contributing to multilateral security forums.

Besides, Indian Navy nuclearization's broader implications extend beyond South Asia to affect Indian Ocean Region and broader Indo-Pacific strategic equilibria. Growing numbers of nuclear-powered facilities in these waters demand international attention to crisis de-escalation measures, naval governance, and arms control. Against this backdrop, Pakistan's response must address bilateral challenges with India while contributing to broader efforts maintaining peace and preventing nuclear conflict along one of the globe's most strategic sea lanes. Ultimately, South Asia's naval nuclearization trajectory is marked by the critical need for proactive diplomacy, doctrinal coherence, and strategic vision. Deterrence sustainability and regional peace will hinge on Pakistan's ability to contain India's maritime ambitions without initiating an unmanageable arms race.

REFERENCES

Acton, J. M. (2015). Virtual nuclear deterrence and strategic stability. In *Global nuclear disarmament* (pp. 61–74). Routledge.

Afridi, M. (2024). Issue brief on "Commissioning of INS-Arighat: India's growing undersea nuclear capabilities and its implications on deterrence stability in South Asia." *Institute of Strategic Studies.* https://issi.org.pk/issue-brief-on-commissioning-of-ins-arighat-indias-growing-undersea-nuclear-capabilities-and-its-implications-on-deterrence-stability-in-south-asia/

Ahsan, Z. (2023). Issue brief on "Pakistan's Aman exercise." *Institute of Strategic Studies Islamabad.* https://issi.org.pk/issue-brief-on-pakistans-aman-exercise/

Ali, I., & Sidhu, J. S. (2022). Dynamics of Pakistan's nuclear doctrine: Implications for strategic stability in South Asia. *Journal of Asian and African Studies, 57*(4), 856–871. DOI: 10.1177/00219096211039533

Ali, M. S. (2021). Anti-access/area denial strategy for Pakistan Navy. *CISS Insight Journal, 9*(1), 33–51.

Askari, M. U., & Iqbal, M. A. (2023). Pakistan's response to Indian naval strategic vision. *South Asian Studies, 38*(1), 21–36.

Baruah, D. M. (2015). India's evolving maritime strategy. *The Diplomat.* https://thediplomat.com/2015/12/indias-evolving-maritime-strategy/

Basrur, R. M. (2009). *Minimum deterrence and India's nuclear security.* NUS Press.

BBC. (2022). *INS Vikrant: Inside India's newly-commissioned aircraft carrier.* https://www.bbc.com/news/world-asia-india-62749345

Brahy, J. (2024). Pakistan Navy announces successful test of Smash anti-ship ballistic missile. *Army Recognition Group.* https://www.armyrecognition.com/news/navy-news/2025/pakistan-navy-announces-successful-test-of-smash-anti-ship-ballistic-missile

Butterfield, H. (1951). *History and human relations.* Collins.

Carlin, M. (2024). A hatch was left open on a $3,000,000,000 submarine: You know what happened next. *The National Interest.* https://nationalinterest.org/blog/buzz/hatch-was-left-open-3000000000-submarine-you-know-what-happened-next-208923/

Chaturvedi, S., & Rumley, D. (2015). The future for Indian Ocean cooperation. In *Geopolitical orientations, regionalism and security in the Indian Ocean* (pp. 300–314). Routledge. DOI: 10.4324/9781315689487-19

CPEC. (2020). *China's strategic support is vital to CPEC security.* https://cpecinfo.com/chinese-strategic-support-is-vital-to-cpec-security/

Esin, V. (2020). India's nuclear capabilities. *Russia and America in the 21st Century, 3*, Article 11821. https://doi.org/DOI: 10.18254/S207054760011821-0

Firepower, G. (2024). *Global Firepower 2023.* https://www.globalfirepower.com

Fretay, H. (2025). Pakistan strengthens stealth submarine capabilities with launch of second Hangor-class in China. *Army Recognition Group.* https://armyrecognition.com/news/navy-news/2025/pakistan-strengthens-stealth-submarine-capabilities-with-launch-of-second-hangor-class-in-china

Global Military. (2025). *Pakistan Navy.* https://www.globalmilitary.net/navies/pak/

Hasan, S. (2015). Navy gets only 10pc of defence budget. *Dawn.* https://www.dawn.com/news/1217390

Herz, J. H. (1950). Idealist internationalism and the security dilemma. *World Politics, 2*(2), 157–180. DOI: 10.2307/2009187

Hiep, T. X., Hoan, T. Q., & Kiet, L. H. (2024). Free and Open Indo-Pacific strategy: Competitive Opinions and Trends. *Vestnik of Saint Petersburg University -. International Relations, 17*(3), 242–259.

International Defence Analysis. (2024). *Indian naval development – An analysis.* https://internationaldefenceanalysis.com/indias-naval-development-an-analysis/

Jabeen, M. (2024). *Maritime security challenges to Gwadar seaport.* Paper presented at the 3rd International Security Congress, Necmettin Erbakan University, Konya, Turkey.

Jervis, R. (1978). Cooperation under the security dilemma. *World Politics, 30*(2), 167–214. DOI: 10.2307/2009958

Kapur, S. P. (2008). Ten years of instability in a nuclear South Asia. *International Security, 33*(2), 71–94. DOI: 10.1162/isec.2008.33.2.71

Kazmi, Z. (2025). The blind spot in South Asia's deterrence debate. *Strategic Vision Institute.* https://thesvi.org/the-blind-spot-in-south-asias-deterrence-debate/

Khan, B. (2017). Pakistan tests Babur-3 submarine-launched cruise missile. *Quwa.* https://quwa.org/daily-news/pakistan-tests-babur-3-submarine-launched-cruise-missile/

Kiet, L. H. (2023). Some Factors Influencing the Geopolitical Competition Between India and China in the Indian Ocean Region in the 21st Century. *Journal of China Studies*, *6*(262), 69–87.

Kiet, L. H., Binh, N. T., & Hiep, T. X. (2025). From border conflicts to maritime competition: Driving forces behind the power rivalry between India and China in the Indian Ocean region. *Australian Journal of Maritime and Ocean Affairs*, **•••**, 1–25. DOI: 10.1080/18366503.2025.2492438

Koppe, E. V. (2014). Use of nuclear weapons and protection of the environment during international armed conflict. In Bersagel, A. G., Nystuen, G., & Casey-Maslen, S. (Eds.), *Nuclear weapons under international law* (pp. 247–268). Cambridge University Press., DOI: 10.1017/CBO9781107337435.018

Kristensen, H. M., & Korda, M. (2021). Estimating world nuclear forces: An overview and assessment of sources. *Stockholm International Peace Research Institute.* https://www.sipri.org/commentary/topical-backgrounder/2021/estimating-world-nuclear-forces-overview-and-assessment-sources

Kristensen, H. M., & Korda, M. (2022). Indian nuclear weapons, 2022. *Bulletin of the Atomic Scientists*, *78*(4), 224–236. DOI: 10.1080/00963402.2022.2087385

Kroenig, M. (2018). A strategy for deterring Russian nuclear de-escalation strikes. *Atlantic Council, Scowcroft Center for Strategy and Security.* https://www.atlanticcouncil.org/wp-content/uploads/2018/04/Nuclear_Strategy_WEB.pdf

Kulkarni, S. (2025). INS Surat, INS Nilgiri and INS Vaghsheer commissioned: Their features, how they add to Navy's capabilities. *The Indian Express.* https://indianexpress.com/article/explained/ins-surat-ins-nilgiri-and-ins-vaghshee-commissioned-three-cheers-for-indian-navy-9781179/

Levesques, A., Bowen, D., & Gill, J. H. (n.d.). Nuclear deterrence and stability in South Asia: Perceptions and realities. *International Institute for Strategic Studies.* https://www.iiss.org/research-paper/2021/05/nuclear-deterrence-south-asia/

Matamis, J. (2025). Nuclear ambiguity in the Indian Ocean. *Stimson Center.* https://www.stimson.org/2025/nuclear-ambiguity-in-the-indian-ocean/

Mian, Z., Ramana, M., & Nayyar, A. (2019). Nuclear submarines in South Asia: New risks and dangers. *Journal for Peace and Nuclear Disarmament*, *2*(1), 184–202. DOI: 10.1080/25751654.2019.1621425

Montgomery, A. H., & Sagan, S. D. (2009). The perils of predicting proliferation. *The Journal of Conflict Resolution, 53*(2), 302–328. DOI: 10.1177/0022002708330581

Narang, V. (2016). Strategies of nuclear proliferation: How states pursue the bomb. *International Security, 41*(3), 110–150. DOI: 10.1162/ISEC_a_00268

Noor, S. (2023). Pakistan's evolving nuclear doctrine. *Arms Control Association.* https://www.armscontrol.org/act/2023-10/features/pakistans-evolving-nuclear-doctrine

Nuclear Threat Initiative. (2024). *Pakistan submarine capabilities.* https://www.nti.org/analysis/articles/pakistan-submarine-capabilities/

Pant, H. V. (2009). India in the Indian Ocean: Growing mismatch between ambitions and capabilities. *Pacific Affairs, 82*(2), 279–297. DOI: 10.5509/2009822279

Pant, H. V., & Bommakanti, K. (2020). In stand-off, keeping an eye on the nuclear ball. *The Hindu.* https://www.thehindu.com/opinion/op-ed/in-stand-off-keeping-an-eye-on-the-nuclear-ball/article32016062.ece

Perkovich, G. (2001). *India's nuclear bomb: The impact on global proliferation.* University of California Press.

Petrovski, A., & Radovanović, M. (2021). Application of detection reconnaissance technologies use by drones in collaboration with C4IRS for military interested. *International Scientific Journal, 21*(40), 117. https://www.researchgate.net/publication/352481081

Ramsay, R. A. S. (2018). INS Arihant fully operational and raring to go. *SP's Naval Forces.* https://www.spsnavalforces.com/story/?id=582&h=INS-Arihant-Fully-Operational-and-Raring-to-Go

Rehman, H. (2024). India's growing strategic behaviour in the Indian Ocean: Implications for regional strategic environment. *Margalla Papers, 1*, 30–44. DOI: 10.54690/margallapapers.28.1.238

Sabah, D. (2021). Turkey-made corvette tailored for Pakistan Navy launched in Istanbul. *Daily Sabah.* https://www.dailysabah.com/business/defense/turkey-made-corvette-tailored-for-pakistan-navy-launched-in-istanbul

White House. (2025). *United States-India Joint Leaders' Statement.* https://www.whitehouse.gov/briefings-statements/2025/02/united-states-india-joint-leaders-statement/

Wueger, D. (2016). India's Nuclear-Armed Submarines: Deterrence or Danger? *The Washington Quarterly, 39*(3), 77–90. DOI: 10.1080/0163660X.2016.1232636

Zulqarnain, D., Shehwar, D., & Nizamani, S. A. (2024). Power dynamics in Indian Ocean: US Indo-Pacific strategic report and prospects for Pakistan's national security. *Government: Research Journal of Political Science*, *13*, 1–11.

Compilation of References

Acharya, A. (2003-2004). Will Asia's past be its future? *International Security*, *28*(3), 149–164. https://www.jstor.org/stable/4137480. DOI: 10.1162/016228803773100101

Acharya, A. (2009). *Constructing a security community in Southeast Asia: ASEAN and the problem of regional order*. Routledge. DOI: 10.4324/9780203939239

Acton, J. M. (2015). Virtual nuclear deterrence and strategic stability. In *Global nuclear disarmament* (pp. 61–74). Routledge.

Afridi, M. (2024). Issue brief on "Commissioning of INS-Arighat: India's growing undersea nuclear capabilities and its implications on deterrence stability in South Asia." *Institute of Strategic Studies*. https://issi.org.pk/issue-brief-on-commissioning-of-ins-arighat-indias-growing-undersea-nuclear-capabilities-and-its-implications-on-deterrence-stability-in-south-asia/

Agastia, I. G. B. D. (2021). Maritime security cooperation within the ASEAN institutional framework: Taking stock and looking ahead. *Journal of Asian Security and International Affairs*, *8*(1), 62–86.

Agence France-Presse in Oslo. (2024). Norway blocks sale of last private land on Svalbard after Chinese interest. *The Guardian*. https://www.theguardian.com/world/article/2024/jul/01/norway-blocks-sale-last-private-landsvalbard-china-interest

Agence France-Presse. (2022). Vietnam fisherman recounts attacks by China coast guard in SCS. *South China Morning Post*. https://www.scmp.com/news/asia/southeast-asia/article/3196026/vietnam-fisherman-recounts-attacks-china-coast-guard-south

Ahluwalia, P. (2019). Gray zone conflicts and informationisation in the Indian context: Challenges, capabilities and way ahead. *Centre for Land Warfare Studies*. https://www.claws.in/publication/grey-zone-conflicts-and-informationisation-in-the-indian-context-challenges-capabilities-and-way-ahead/

Ahsan, Z. (2023). Issue brief on "Pakistan's Aman exercise." *Institute of Strategic Studies Islamabad.* https://issi.org.pk/issue-brief-on-pakistans-aman-exercise/

Al Jazeera. (2023). US deployed warships after China, Russia naval patrol near Alaska: WSJ. https://www.aljazeera.com/news/2023/8/7/us-deployedwarships-after-china-russia-naval-patrol-near-alaska-wsj

Alexander, D. (2012). US will put more warships in Asia: Panetta. *Reuters.* https://www.reuters.com/article/world/us-will-put-more-warships-in-asia-panetta-idUSBRE85100Z/

Alexandre, A. G. (2021). The Strait of Bab El-Mandeb: Stage of geopolitical disputes. *JANUS.NET e-Journal of International Relations, 12*(2), 58–74. https://doi.org/DOI: 10.26619/1647-7251.12.2.4

Ali, I., & Stewart, P. (2019). Exclusive: In rare move, French warship passes through Taiwan Strait. *Reuters.* https://www.reuters.com/article/world/exclusive-in-rare-move-french-warship-passes-through-taiwan-strait-idUSKCN1S0276/

Ali, I., & Sidhu, J. S. (2022). Dynamics of Pakistan's nuclear doctrine: Implications for strategic stability in South Asia. *Journal of Asian and African Studies, 57*(4), 856–871. DOI: 10.1177/00219096211039533

Ali, M. S. (2021). Anti-access/area denial strategy for Pakistan Navy. *CISS Insight Journal, 9*(1), 33–51.

Aljazeera. (2025). *Philippines, India hold first joint naval drill in disputed South China Sea.* https://www.aljazeera.com/news/2025/8/4/philippines-india-hold-first-joint-naval-drill-in-disputed-south-china-sea

Allan, G., & Michael, W. (2007). *Making Australian foreign policy.* Cambridge University Press.

Ameh, B. (2024). Advancing national security and economic prosperity through resilient and technology-driven supply chains. *World Journal of Advanced Research and Reviews, 24*(3), 483–500. DOI: 10.30574/wjarr.2024.24.3.3723

Amer, R. (2009). The ASEAN conflict management approach revisited: Will the Charter reinforce ASEAN's role? *ASEAS – Austrian Journal of Southeast Asian Studies, 2*(2), 6–27.

An, B. (2016). Bien Dong: nguoi Phap dang den [South China Sea: The French are coming]. *To Quoc Newspaper.* https://toquoc.vn/bien-dong-nguoi-phap-dang-den-99151985.htm

An, L. (2024). Russia's foreign policy in the Asia-Pacific region. *Communist Review.* https://tapchicongsan.org.vn/web/guest/the-gioi-van-de-su-kien/-/2018/970502/chinh-sach-ngoai-giao-cua-nga-tai-khu-vuc-chau-a---thai-binh-duong.aspx

Andaya, B. W., & Andaya, L. Y. (2015). *A history of early modern Southeast Asia, 1400-1830.* Cambridge University Press. DOI: 10.1017/CBO9781139051323

Anh, T. (2023). Prime Minister Pham Minh Chinh receives US Secretary of State Antony Blinken. *Vietnam News.* https://www.vietnam.vn/en/thu-tuong-pham-minh-chinh-tiep-ngoai-truong-hoa-ky-antony-blinken

Anh, T. N. H. (2024). Assessing Vietnam's maritime governance capacity: Priorities and challenges. *Asia Maritime Transparency Initiative.* https://amti.csis.org/assessing-vietnams-maritime-governance-capacity-priorities-and-challenges/

Anh, V. V. (2022). China's East Sea policy in the 2009-2021 period. *Vietnam Social Sciences, 7,* 27–38.

Asan Institute for Policy Studies. (2024). *ASEAN–Korea comprehensive strategic partnership: Prospects for security cooperation (Asan Issue Brief).* Asan Institute for Policy Studies.

ASEAN. (1992). *Singapore Declaration Of 1992 Singapore, 28 January 1992.* https://asean.org/singapore-declaration-of-1992-singapore-28-january-1992/

ASEAN. (1993). *Joint Press Statement for the Meeting to Explore the Establishment of the Consultative Relationship with the People's Republic of China Beijing, China, 13-14 September 1993.* https://asean.org/joint-press-statement-for-the-meeting-to-explore-the-establishment-of-the-consultative-relationship-with-the-peoples-republic-of-china-beijing-china-13-14-september-1993/

ASEAN. (2002). *Declaration on the Conduct of Parties in the South China Sea.* https://asean.org/declaration-on-the-conduct-of-parties-in-the-south-china-sea-2/
ASEAN Secretariat. (2010). *Chairman's Statement: 1st Expanded ASEAN Maritime Forum, Manila.* https://asean.org/chairmans-statement-1st-expanded-asean-maritime-forum-manila/

ASEAN. (2019). *ASEAN Outlook on the Indo-Pacific.* https://asean.org/wp-content/uploads/2021/01/ASEAN-Outlook-on-the-Indo-Pacific_FINAL_22062019.pdf

ASEAN. (2025). *ASEAN Political Security Community Strategic Plan.* https://asean.org/asean-political-security-community-strategic-plan/

ASEAN-China Joint Statement. (1997). *Joint Statement of the Meeting of Heads of State/Government of the Member States of ASEAN and the President of the People's Republic of China Kuala Lumpur, Malaysia, 16 December 1997.* https://asean.org/joint-statement-of-the-meeting-of-heads-of-state-government-of-the-member-states-of-asean-and-the-president-of-the-peoples-republic-of-china-kuala-lumpur-malaysia-16-december-1997/

Ashley, R., & Fraser, J. (2023). Common waters: Japan, South Korea, and maritime security assistance in Southeast Asia. *Asia Policy*, *18*(2), 101–126. DOI: 10.1353/asp.2023.0021

Asia Maritime Transparency Initiative [AMTI]. (2019). *Failing or incomplete? Grading the South China Sea arbitration.* https://amti.csis.org/failing-or-incomplete-grading-the-south-china-sea-arbitration/

Asia Maritime Transparency Initiative. (2013). *China Island Tracker.* https://amti.csis.org/island-tracker/china/

Asia Maritime Transparency Initiative. (2023). *Arbitration Support Tracker.* https://amti.csis.org/arbitration-support-tracker/

Asia Maritime Transparency Initiative. (2023). *More than meets the eye: Philippine upgrades at EDCA sites.* https://amti.csis.org/more-than-meets-the-eye-philippine-upgrades-at-edca-sites/

Asia Maritime Transparency Initiative. (2024). *Fiery Cross Reef.* https://amti.csis.org/fiery-cross-reef/

Asia Maritime Transparency Initiative. (2025). *No Islet Left Behind: Vietnam Reclaims Land at Every Remaining Spratly Outpost.* https://amti.csis.org/no-islet-left-behind-vietnam-reclaims-land-at-every-remaining-spratly-outpost/

Asia Maritime Transparency Initiative. (n.d.). *China Island Tracker.* https://amti.csis.org/island-tracker/china/

Asia Society Policy Institute. (2021). *The South China Sea: Realities and Responses in Southeast Asia.* Asia Society Policy Institute.

Asian Military Review. (2024). *Has the China Coast Guard Reached Its Limit?* https://www.asianmilitaryreview.com/2024/01/has-the-china-coast-guard-reached-its-limit/

Askari, M. U., & Iqbal, M. A. (2023). Pakistan's response to Indian naval strategic vision. *South Asian Studies*, *38*(1), 21–36.

Associated Press. (2016). China has reclaimed 3,200 acres in the South China Sea, says Pentagon. *The Guardian.* https://www.theguardian.com/world/2016/may/13/pentagon-report-china-reclaimed-3200-acres-south-china-sea#:~:text=on%20Friday

Associated Press. (2016). China has reclaimed 3200 acres in the SCS, says Pentagon. *The Guardian.* https://www.theguardian.com/world/2016/may/13/pentagon-report-china-reclaimed-3200-acres-south-china-sea

Australian Government. (1997). In the National Interests - Australia's Foreign and Trade Policy (White Paper). *Department of Foreign Affairs and Trade.* https://catalogue.nla.gov.au/catalog/61954

Australian Government. (2003). Advancing the National Interest: Australia's Foreign and Trade Policy White Paper. *Department of Foreign Affairs and Trade.* https://nla.gov.au/nla.obj-2203648089/view?partId=nla.obj-2204274174

Australian Government. (2012). Australia in the Asian Century White Paper. *Department of the Prime Minister and Cabinet.* https://apo.org.au/node/31647

Australian Government. (2013). Defence White Paper 2013. *Department of Defence.* https://www.defence.gov.au/about/strategic-planning/defence-white-paper

Australian Government: Department of Foreign Affairs and Trade. (n.d.). *Asia-Pacific Economic Cooperation (APEC).* https://www.dfat.gov.au/trade/organisations/apec/asia-pacific-economic-cooperation-apec

Ayesh, S., & Askari, M. U. (2025). China–ASEAN approaches towards the South China Sea disputes. *Journal of Social Sciences Review*, *5*(1), 150–162. DOI: 10.62843/jssr.v5i1.481

Bachelier, J., & Pajon, C. (2023). France in the Indo-Pacific: The need for a pragmatic strategic posture. *Institut français des relations internationales.* https://www.ifri.org/en/studies/france-indo-pacific-need-pragmatic-strategic-posture

Bader, J. A. (2014). The US and China's nine-dash line: Ending the ambiguity. *Brookings.* https://www.brookings.edu/articles/the-u-s-and-chinas-nine-dash-line-ending-the-ambiguity/

Baker, B. D. (2015). Where is the 'String of Pearls' in 2015? *The Diplomat.* https://thediplomat.com/2015/10/where-is-the-string-of-pearls-in-2015/

Balazs, D. (2025). *China-Russia dual-use cooperation stays resilient amid sanctions.* S. Rajaratnam School of International Studies. https://rsis.edu.sg/rsis-publication/rsis/china-russia-dual-use-cooperation-stays-resilient-amid-sanctions/

Banevičienė, A. Ž. (2021). Interpretation of military power in the context of realism paradigm. *Politologija, 102*(2), 38–74. DOI: 10.15388/Polit.2021.102.2

Bang, D. (1996). *Pho cang vung Thuan Quang the ki XVII-XVIII* [Port cities in the Thuan-Quang region in the 17th-18th centuries]. Thuan Hoa Publishing House.

Bang, D. (2011). *He thong phong thu mien Trung duoi trieu Nguyen* [The Central Vietnam defense system under the Nguyen dynasty]. Culture and Information Publishing House.

Bang, D. (2014). *Trieu Nguyen voi cong cuoc bao ve bien dao To quoc the ky XIX* [The Nguyen dynasty and the protection of national maritime territory in the 19th century]. Da Nang Publishing House.

Bang, D. (2015). *Hoang Sa-Truong Sa: Chu quyen cua Viet Nam* [Hoang Sa-Truong Sa: Vietnam's sovereignty]. 2nd ed.). Da Nang Publishing House.

Bang, D. (2016). *To chuc va hoat dong bao ve bien dao Viet Nam duoi trieu Nguyen (1802-1885)* [Organization and activities for protecting Vietnam's maritime territory under the Nguyen dynasty (1802-1885)]. Thuan Hoa Publishing House.

Bang, D. (2022). *Chu quyen bien dao cua nha nuoc quan chu Viet Nam trong lich su (Tu chua Nguyen the ki XVI den nam 1945)* [Maritime sovereignty of the Vietnamese monarchical state in history (From the Nguyen Lords in the 16th century to 1945)]. Ha Noi Publishing House.

Baruah, D. M. (2015). India's evolving maritime strategy. *The Diplomat.* https://thediplomat.com/2015/12/indias-evolving-maritime-strategy/

Baruah, D. M. (2022). Maritime competition in the Indian Ocean. *Carnegie Endowment for International Peace.* https://carnegieendowment.org/2022/05/12/maritime-competition-in-indian-ocean-pub-87093

Baruah, D. M., Labh, N., & Greely, J. (2023). Mapping the Indian Ocean Region. *Carnegie Endowment for International Peace.* https://carnegieendowment.org/research/2023/06/mapping-the-indian-ocean-region?lang=en

Basrur, R. M. (2009). *Minimum deterrence and India's nuclear security*. NUS Press.

Bateman, S. (2005). Capacity building for maritime security cooperation: What are we talking about? *University of Wollongong Research Online.* https://ro.uow.edu.au/cgi/viewcontent.cgi?article=1433&context=lawpapers

Bateman, S. (2013). Cooperation or trust: What comes first in the South China Sea? *S. Rajaratnam School of International Studies.* https://rsis.edu.sg/rsis-publication/rsis/2055-cooperation-or-trust-what-com/

BBC. (2022). *INS Vikrant: Inside India's newly-commissioned aircraft carrier.* https://www.bbc.com/news/world-asia-india-62749345

Beckman, R. (2019). Maritime security. In Tan, Hsien-Li (Ed.), The legal authority of ASEAN as a security institution (pp. 112–138). Cambridge University Press., DOI: 10.1017/9781108669511.007

Beeson, M. (2013). The Decline of US Economic Power and Influence: Implications for Australian Foreign Policy. *Australian Journal of Political Science, 48*(2), 197–207. DOI: 10.1080/10361146.2013.787920

Behera, L. K. (2024). India's defence industry: Achievements and challenges. *Observer Research Foundation.* https://www.orfonline.org/research/india-s-defence-industry-achievements-and-challenges

Bela, V. (2025). China and Russia sign nuclear reactor deal to fuel lunar research station. *South China Morning Post.* https://www.scmp.com/news/china/science/article/3310315/china-and-russia-sign-nuclear-reactor-deal-fuel-lunar-research-station

Besnier, T. (2023). Repower EU: The authority turn for the EU in energy policies? *Bruges Political Research Papers, 91.* College of Europe. https://coleurope.eu/sites/default/files/research-paper/wp91%20Besnier.pdf

Betts, A. (2024). Trump's early second-term choices fuel fears of extremist agenda. *The Guardian.* https://www.theguardian.com/us-news/2024/nov/13/trump-cabinet-administration-appointments

Bettzüge, M. O. (2015). European energy policy: Dogma or strategy? *France Stratégie,* 105–138. https://www.strategie-plan.gouv.fr/files/files/Publications/English%20Articles/Study%20-%20Energy%20Union/fs_study_the_union_of_energy_mobettzuge_16092015_final.pdf

Bharti, M. K., & Kumari, S. (2024). China's Belt and Road Initiative in Southeast Asia and its implications for ASEAN-China strategic partnership. *Asian Review of Political Economy, 3*(22), 1–21. DOI: 10.1007/s44216-024-00042-4

Bich, T. (2022). The process of reaffirming the 'core leadership' role in China. *Voice of Vietnam.* https://vov.vn/the-gioi/ho-so/qua-trinh-tai-xac-lap-vai-tro-lanh-dao-hat-nhan-cua-trung-quoc-post976223.vov

Binh, N. T., Hiep, T. X., Co, D. N., & Vuong, N. (2024). The strategic adjustments of China, India, and the US in the Indo-Pacific geopolitical context. *Journal of Liberty and International Affairs, 10*(1), 173–191. DOI: 10.47305/JLIA24101171n

Björkdahl, A., Chaban, N., Leslie, J., & Masselot, A. (2015). *Importing EU norms: Conceptual Framework and Empirical Findings*. Springer. DOI: 10.1007/978-3-319-13740-7

Bland, B. (2025). Trump's tariffs will push Southeast Asia uncomfortably close to China. *Chatham House*. https://www.chathamhouse.org/2025/04/trumps-tariffs-will-push-southeast-asia-uncomfortably-close-china

Blandin, B. (2024). Que pèse la France en Indo-Pacifique? [What weight does France carry in the Indo-Pacific?]. *La Tribune*. https://www.latribune.fr/opinions/tribunes/que-pese-la-france-en-indo-pacifique-995439.html

Bloomberg News. (2015). US urges Asean to patrol S. China Sea. *Bangkok Post*. https://www.bangkokpost.com/world/500536/us-urges-asean-to-patrol-s-china-sea

Bloomberg News. (2024). *Trump suggests Taiwan should pay US for protection*. https://www.bloomberg.com/news/videos/2024-07-16/trump-suggests-taiwan-should-pay-us-for-protection-video

Borri, C. (1998). *Xu Dang Trong nam 1621* [Cochinchina in 1621]. Ho Chi Minh City Publishing House.

Bouffaron, P., & Blandin, B. (2025). L'avenir de l'influence européenne dans l'Indopacifique [The future of European influence in the Indo-Pacific]. *Fondation Robert Schuman*. https://www.robert-schuman.eu/questions-d-europe/786-l-avenir-de-l-influence-europeenne-dans-l-indopacifique

Bouffaron, P., & Blandin, B. (2025). The future of European influence in the Indo-Pacific. *Schuman Paper, 786*. Robert Schuman Foundation. https://www.robert-schuman.eu/en/european-issues/786-the-future-of-european-influence-in-the-indo-pacific

Bowen, G. A. (2009). Document analysis as a qualitative research method. *Qualitative Research Journal*, *9*(2), 27–40. DOI: 10.3316/QRJ0902027

Bradford, J. (2021). Evolving conceptualizations of maritime security in Southeast Asia. *Asia Maritime Transparency Initiative*. https://amti.csis.org/evolving-conceptualizations-of-maritime-security-in-southeast-asia/

Bradford, A. (2012). The Brussels effect. *Northwestern University Law Review*, *107*(1), 1–68. https://papers.ssrn.com/sol3/papers.cfm?abstract_id=2770634

Brahy, J. (2024). Pakistan Navy announces successful test of Smash anti-ship ballistic missile. *Army Recognition Group.* https://www.armyrecognition.com/news/navy-news/2025/pakistan-navy-announces-successful-test-of-smash-anti-ship-ballistic-missile

Brugnatelli, N. (2022). The US-China battle for the semiconductors industry. *East Asia Forum.* https://www.eastasiaforum.org/2022/06/04/the-us-china-battle-for-the-semiconductor-industry/

Brynteson, D. W. (2014). Smart power: The United States, Iran, and a nuclear deal. *Defense Technical Information Center.* https://apps.dtic.mil/sti/pdfs/AD1003796.pdf

Bueger, C., & Bergin, A. (2018). Uniting nations: Developing maritime domain awareness for the "Blue Pacific." *Cardiff University.* https://orca.cardiff.ac.uk/111371/

Bugulashvili, M., & Scott, J. G. (2022). Getting smarter with Joseph Nye. *Journal of Humanity, 11*(1). Advance online publication. DOI: 10.31578/hum.v11i1.479

Burgess, R. R. (2021). US, Singapore reaffirm LCS, P-8 rotational deployments. *Sea Power.* https://seapowermagazine.org/us-singapore-reaffirm-lcs-p-8-rotational-deployments/?print=pdf

Business Insider. (2021). *China's ships are getting bigger and more aggressive and Japan is scrambling to keep up.* https://www.businessinsider.com/chinas-coast-guard-ships-worrying-japan-scrambling-to-keep-up-2021-2

Butterfield, H. (1951). *History and human relations.* Collins.

Calcara, A., Drieschova, A., & Cusumano, E. (2025). Technological underpinnings of European autonomy and US-China competition. *Journal of European Integration, 47*(6), 943–963. DOI: 10.1080/07036337.2025.2536828

Campbell, C., & Salidjanova, N. (2016). South China Sea arbitration ruling: What happened and what's next? *United States-China Economic and Security Review Commission.* https://www.uscc.gov/sites/default/files/Research/Issue%20Brief_South%20China%20Sea%20Arbitration%20Ruling%20What%20Happened%20and%20What%27s%20Next071216.pdf

Carlin, M. (2024). A hatch was left open on a $3,000,000,000 submarine: You know what happened next. *The National Interest.* https://nationalinterest.org/blog/buzz/hatch-was-left-open-3000000000-submarine-you-know-what-happened-next-208923/

Carment, D., & Dani, B. (2018). War's future: The risks and rewards of grey zone conflict and hybrid warfare. *Canadian Global Affairs Institute.* https://www.cgai.ca/wars_future_the_risks_and_rewards_of_grey_zone_conflict_and_hybrid_warfare

Castro, D. R. C. (2020). After four years, the Philippines acknowledges the 2016 arbitral tribunal award. *Asia Maritime Transparency Initiative.* https://amti.csis.org/after-four-years-the-philippines-acknowledges-the-2016-arbitral-tribunal-award/

Castro, R. C. D. (2020). After four years, the Philippines acknowledges the 2016 arbitral tribunal award! *Asia Maritime Transparency Initiative.* https://amti.csis.org/after-four-years-the-philippines-acknowledges-the-2016-arbitral-tribunal-award/

Center for Strategic and International Studies [CSIS]. (2022). *Eyes on the skies: China's growing space footprint in South America.* https://features.csis.org/hiddenreach/china-ground-stations-space/

Chabarovskaya, N. (2025). *Going steady: China and Russia's economic ties are deeper than Washington thinks.* Center for European Policy Analysis. https://cepa.org/comprehensive-reports/going-steady-china-and-russias-economic-ties-are-deeper-than-washington-thinks/

Chakraborti, T., & Chakraborty, M. (2024). The reflexive silhouette of China in the Indo-Vietnam mirror: Competition, confrontation and the future. In Ranjan, A., Scott, D., & Chalk, P. (Eds.), *India and China in Southeast Asia* (pp. 63–89). Palgrave Macmillan. DOI: 10.1007/978-981-97-6903-2_4

Chakraborty, A. (2025). India's rise in global defense exports and the way forward. *South Asian Voices.* https://southasianvoices.org/def-f-in-n-india-defense-exports-09-15-2025/

Chakraborty, M. (2020). Bilateral convergence between India and Vietnam: Defence collaboration and 'Make in India'. *Vietnam Journal for Indian and Asian Studies, 2020*, 20–27.

Chakraborty, M. (2024). China's soft power diplomacy in Vietnam: Assessing the dynamics and efficacy of Belt and Road architecture. In Zreik, M. (Ed.), *Soft power and diplomatic strategies in Asia and the Middle East* (pp. 36–58). IGI Global. DOI: 10.4018/979-8-3693-2444-8.ch003

Chan, H. (2024). China's big gamble in the SCS. *The Diplomat.* https://thediplomat.com/2024/01/chinas-big-gamble-in-the-south-china-sea/

Chan, E. S. Y. (2021). *China's Maritime Security Strategy: The Evolution of a Growing Sea Power* (1st ed.). Routledge. DOI: 10.4324/9781003158523

Chan, E. S. Y. (2025). China's Discourse of Maritime Power: A Thematic Analysis. *Journal of Contemporary China*, *34*(153), 432–450. DOI: 10.1080/10670564.2024.2319064

Chang, T. K. (1991). China's claim of sovereignty over Spratly and Paracel Islands. *Case Western Reserve Journal of International Law*, *23*(3), 399–420. https://scholarlycommons.law.case.edu/jil/vol23/iss3/4

Chapman, N. (2017). Mechanisms of Vietnam's Multidirectional Foreign Policy. *Journal of Current Southeast Asian Affairs*, *36*(2), 31–69. DOI: 10.1177/186810341703600202

Chaturvedi, S., & Rumley, D. (2015). The future for Indian Ocean cooperation. In *Geopolitical orientations, regionalism and security in the Indian Ocean* (pp. 300–314). Routledge. DOI: 10.4324/9781315689487-19

Chau, H. (2020). Quan he thuong mai giua Dang Trong thoi chua Nguyen voi Bo Dao Nha va Ha Lan [Trade relations between Dang Trong under the Nguyen Lords with Portugal and the Netherlands]. *Hue University Journal of Science: Social Sciences and Humanities*, *129*(6D), 188–190.

Chawla, A. K. (2024). Defence budget 2024-25—An analysis. *SP's Naval Forces*. https://www.spsnavalforces.com/story/?id=874&h=Defence-Budget-2024-25-andmdash;-An-

Chemillier-Gendreau, M. (2011). *Chu quyen tren hai quan dao Hoang Sa va Truong Sa* [Sovereignty over the two archipelagos of Hoang Sa and Truong Sa]. Loi, L. V., Ed., Thao, H., Trans.). National Political Publishing House.

Chen, Y. (2024). PLA steps up security cooperation with Russia in 2024. *The Jamestown Foundation*. https://jamestown.org/program/pla-steps-up-security-cooperation-with-russia-in-2024/

Cheng, M. H. A. (2022). AUKUS: The changing dynamic and its regional implications. *European Journal of Development Studies*, *2*(1), 1–7. DOI: 10.24018/ejdevelop.2022.2.1.63

Chew, E. (2010). Singapore's Strategic Involvement in the Indian Ocean. In Bateman, S., & Ho, J. (Eds.), *Southeast Asia and the rise of Chinese and Indian naval power: Between rising naval powers*. Routledge.

Childs, N. (2023). The AUKUS anvil: Promise and peril. *Survival*, *65*(5), 7–24. DOI: 10.1080/00396338.2023.2261239

China Power Team. (2023). How severe are China's demographic challenges? *China Power*. https://chinapower.csis.org/china-demographics-challenges/

China Power. (2020). *Are maritime law enforcement forces destabilizing Asia?* https://chinapower.csis.org/maritime-forces-destabilizing-asia/

ChinaPower. (2021). *Is China contributing to the United Nations' mission?* https://chinapower.csis.org/china-un-mission/

Chinh, P. M. (2024). Speech at the opening ceremony of the Vietnam International Defense Exhibition 2024. *Hai Duong Newspaper.* https://baohaiduong.vn/thu-tuong-pham-minh-chinh-du-khai-mac-trien-lam-quoc-phong-quoc-te-viet-nam-2024-400871.html

Chinoy, S. (2025). How shift from SAGAR to MAHASAGAR doctrine signals India's outreach to larger Global South. *Firstpost*. https://www.firstpost.com/opinion/how-shift-from-sagar-to-mahasagar-doctrine-signals-indias-outreach-to-larger-global-south-13881010.html

Chivvis, C. S., & Miller, H. (2023). The role of Congress in US–China relations. *Carnegie Endowment for International Peace*. https://carnegieendowment.org/research/2023/11/the-role-of-congress-in-us-china-relations?lang=en

Choonara, J. (2022). The devastation of Ukraine: NATO, Russia and imperialism. *International Socialism, 174*. https://www.researchgate.net/profile/Joseph-Choonara/publication/359585713_The_devastation_of_Ukraine_NATO_Russia_and_imperialism/links/62446cda7931cc7ccf05f724/The-devastation-of-Ukraine-NATO-Russia-and-imperialism.pdf

Choudhury, S. R. (2021). Quad: Origin and evolving dynamics. *Journal of Global Strategic Studies, 1*(2), 6–29. https://www.researchgate.net/publication/357413837_Quad_Origin_and_Evolving_Dynamics Congressional Research Service. (2024). *China naval modernization: Implications for United States Navy capabilities—Background and issues for Congress*. https://sgp.fas.org/crs/row/RL33153.pdf

Christensen, T. J. (2011). The advantages of an assertive China. *Foreign Affairs, 90*(2), 54–67.

Chung, E. (2025). *South Korea, a new key power for maritime security within the Indo-Pacific.* Fondation pour la Recherche Stratégique.

Clark, B. (2016). Undersea cables and the future of submarine competition. *Bulletin of the Atomic Scientists*, *72*(4), 234–237. DOI: 10.1080/00963402.2016.1195636

Čok, C. (2025). *React, rinse, repeat: How Europe can help break Somalia's cycle of conflict*. European Council on Foreign Relations. https://ecfr.eu/publication/react-rinse-repeat-how-europe-can-help-break-somalias-cycle-of-conflict/

College of Europe. (2023). *Reinforcing the EU's Green Deal Diplomacy: Recommendations for the next Commission*. College of Europe Policy Brief. https://www.coleurope.eu/sites/default/files/research-paper/CEPOB%204-23%20final.pdf

Communist Review. (2011). *Stabilizing the South China Sea: Requires cooperation among all parties*. https://www.tapchicongsan.org.vn/hoat-ong-cua-lanh-ao-ang-nha-nuoc/-/2018/13486/on-dinh-bien-dong--can-su-hop-tac-giua-cac-ben.aspx

Conant, M. A., & Gold, F. R. (1976). *The geopolitics of energy*. Westview Press.

Cooke, N., Li, T., & Anderson, J. A. (Eds.). (2011). *The Tongking Gulf through history*. University of Pennsylvania Press. DOI: 10.9783/9780812205022

Council of the European Union. (2019). *A new strategic agenda for the EU 2019-2024*. https://www.consilium.europa.eu/en/eu-strategic-agenda-2019-2024/

CPEC. (2020). *China's strategic support is vital to CPEC security*. https://cpecinfo.com/chinese-strategic-support-is-vital-to-cpec-security/

Cronin, P. M. (2021). The 3 pillars of Asia's new security architecture. *The Straits Times*. https://www.straitstimes.com/opinion/the-3-pillars-of-asias-new-security-architecture

Cuong, D. V., & Dung, P. C. (2024). UNCLOS significant to Vietnam's peace, stability, long-term development. *Vietnam Law Magazine*. https://vietnamlawmagazine.vn/unclos-significant-to-vietnams-peace-stability-long-term-development-73173.html

Cuong, H., & Khanh, T. (2019). China's "gray zone" tactics increase the risk of conflict in the East Sea. *Voice of Vietnam*. https://vov.vn/chinh-tri/chien-thuat-vung-xam-cua-trung-quoc-co-moi-lien-he-voi-su-kien-hoang-sa-909828.vov

Cuong, T. M. (2023). *Chu quyen Hoang Sa-Truong Sa qua truoc tac cua danh nhan xu Nghe va luat phap quoc te* [Hoang Sa-Truong Sa sovereignty through works of Nghe An scholars and international law]. Nghe An Publishing House.

Dahlström, P., Edlund, P. O., & Guibourg, G. (2023). The EU's competitive advantage in the green transition. *IFN Working Paper, 1483*. Research Institute of Industrial Economics.

Dahm, J. M. (2020). Beyond "conventional wisdom": Evaluating the PLA's South China Sea bases in operational context. *War on the Rocks.* https://warontherocks.com/2020/03/beyond-conventional-wisdom-evaluating-the-plas-south-china-sea-bases-in-operational-context/

Damayanti, A. (2019). Indo-Pacific maritime cooperation: ASEAN mechanisms on security towards global maritime governance. *Global & Strategis*, *13*(1), 91–102. DOI: 10.20473/jgs.13.1.2019.1-44

Damro, C. (2012). Market power Europe. *Journal of European Public Policy*, *19*(5), 682–699. DOI: 10.1080/13501763.2011.646779

Dang, N. (2021). Tau chien chau Au don dap vao Bien Dong [European warships rush into the South China Sea]. *Tuoi Tre Newspaper.* https://tuoitre.vn/tau-chien-chau-au-don-dap-vao-bien-dong-20210313101215098.htm

Dang, C. T. (2014). ASEAN Political-Security Community after 2015 and Vietnam's participation. *Journal of International Students*, *3*(88), 172–177.

Daniel K. Inouye Asia-Pacific Center for Security Studies. (2020). *Republic of Korea – New Southern Policy: Information booklet.* Danie K. Inouye Asia-Pacific Center for Security Studies.

Das, U. (2019). What is the Indo-Pacific? *The Diplomat.* https://thediplomat.com/2019/07/what-is-the-indopacific/

Dau, N. D. (2013). *Viet Nam quoc hieu va cuong vuc: Hoang Sa-Truong Sa* [Vietnam's national title and territory: Hoang Sa-Truong Sa]. Tre Publishing House.

Davidson, H. (2024). China's maritime militia: The shadowy armada whose existence Beijing rarely acknowledges. *The Guardian.* https://www.theguardian.com/world/article/2024/jun/13/china-maritime-militia-explainer-south-china-sea-scarborough-shoal

Délégation à l'information et à la communication de la défense. (2019). *France's defence in the Indo-Pacific*. Paris: Asia-Pacific Center for Security Studies.

Department of Foreign Affairs and Trade. (2017). *Prime Ministers' Joint Outcomes Statement.* https://vietnam.embassy.gov.au/hnoi/PM2.html

Do, H. (2023). The SCS situation in 2023 and forecast for 2024. *SCS Studies Center.* https://nghiencuubiendong.vn/tinh-hinh-bien-dong-nam-2023-va-du-bao-nam-2024.56515.anews

Doan, R. L. (2024). The Conflict of Laws in the South China Sea and Its Threats to the Indo-Pacific Rules-Based Order. *Loyola University Chicago Law Journal, 55*(2), 9-69. https://lawecommons.luc.edu/luclj/vol55/iss5/2?utm_source=lawecommons.luc.edu%2Fluclj%2Fvol55%2Fiss5%2F2&utm_medium=PDF&utm_campaign=PDFCoverPages

Dolan, C. (2024). Perspective chapter: AUKUS Pillar 2—Technology, interoperability, and advanced capabilities in the evolving trilateral security partnership. In *Advances in National Security Studies*. IntechOpen. DOI: 10.5772/intechopen.1005189

Don, L. Q. (2007). *Phu Bien Tap Luc* [Records of the pacified frontier]. Culture and Information Publishing House.

Do, T. S. (2013). *Chinese politics in the process of rising and the issues posed for Vietnam*. Encyclopedia Publishing House.

Duchâtel, M. (2023). *La crédibilité de la France dans l'Indopacifique: Premières pistes* [France's credibility in the Indo-Pacific: Initial approaches]. *Institut Montaigne*. https://www.institutmontaigne.org/ressources/pdfs/publications/la-credibilite-de-la-france-dans-lindopacifique-premieres-pistes-note-denjeux.pdf

Duc, T. M. (2015). *Chu quyen quoc gia Viet Nam tai hai quan dao Hoang Sa va Truong Sa qua tu lieu Viet Nam va nuoc ngoai* [Vietnam's national sovereignty over the two archipelagos of Hoang Sa and Truong Sa through Vietnamese and foreign documents]. Information and Communications Publishing House.

Duong, N. N. (2021). Vietnam's conceptualization of maritime security. *Asia Maritime Transparency Initiative*. https://amti.csis.org/vietnams-conceptualizations-of-maritime-security/

Durai, S. (2025). India's maritime vision: From SAGAR to Indo-Pacific to MAHASAGAR. *Embassy of India*. https://www.indembassydili.gov.in/section/articles-commissioned-by-xpd-division/india-s-maritime-vision-from-sagar-to-indo-pacific-to-mahasagar-by-amb-suchitra-durai/

Dyer, H. (2018). Introducing green theory in international relations. *E-International Relations*. https://www.e-ir.info/2018/01/07/green-theory-in-international-relations/

Eiterjord, T. (2023). Checking back in on China's nuclear icebreaker. *The Diplomat*. https://thediplomat.com/2023/02/checking-back-in-on-chinas-nuclear-icebreaker/

Elder, C. (2017). *Being Australian: Narratives of National Identity*. Allen & Unwin.

Embassy of India in Vietnam. (2016). *India-Vietnam Comprehensive Strategic Partnership*. https://www.indembassyhanoi.gov.in/docs/1693902939StrategicPartnership.pdf

Emmers, R. (2010). ASEAN and the securitization of transnational crime in Southeast Asia. *The Pacific Review*, *23*(4), 419–430. DOI: 10.1080/0951274032000085653

Emmers, R. (2013). The South China Sea. In *Resource Management and Contested Territories in East Asia* (pp. 51–74). Springer. DOI: 10.1057/9781137310149_5

Enkhbat, N. (2024). What China-Russia military exercises portend for Taiwan and beyond. *per Concordiam: Journal of European Security and Defense Issues*. https://perconcordiam.com/joint-implications/

Enkhbat, N. (2025). *Friends with benefits: Assessing Russian–Chinese military exercises* (Research Paper No. 7). NATO Defense College.

Esin, V. (2020). India's nuclear capabilities. *Russia and America in the 21st Century*, *3*, Article 11821. https://doi.org/DOI: 10.18254/S207054760011821-0

European Commission. (2020). *National energy and climate plans*. https://energy.ec.europa.eu/topics/energy-strategy/national-energy-and-climate-plans-necps_en

European Commission. (2021). *The EU strategy for cooperation in the Indo-Pacific* [Joint Communication]. https://www.eeas.europa.eu/sites/default/files/jointcommunication_2021_24_1_en.pdf

European Commission. (2023). *An enhanced EU Maritime Security Strategy for evolving maritime threats* [Joint Communication]. https://eur-lex.europa.eu/legal-content/EN/TXT/HTML/?uri=CELEX:52023JC0008

European Commission. (2025a). *Commission adopts RESourceEU to secure raw materials, reduce dependencies and boost competitiveness* [Press release]. https://ec.europa.eu/commission/presscorner/detail/en/ip_25_1131

European Commission. (2025b). *European Neighbourhood Policy*. https://enlargement.ec.europa.eu/european-neighbourhood-policy_en

European Commission. (n.d.). *Global Gateway*. Retrieved March 15, 2025, from https://commission.europa.eu/topics/international-partnerships/global-gateway_en

European External Action Service. (2017). ASEAN-EU co-chairs joint press release on the 4th ASEAN-EU High-Level Dialogue on Maritime Security Cooperation. https://www.eeas.europa.eu/node/33405_en

European External Action Service. (2018). Horn of Africa-Red Sea: Revised EU Maritime Security Strategy Action Plan, regional and global maritime affairs. https://www.eeas.europa.eu/node/47565_en

European External Action Service. (2021a). *EU strategy for cooperation in the Indo-Pacific*. https://www.eeas.europa.eu/eeas/eu-strategy-cooperation-indo-pacific_en

European External Action Service. (2021b). The European Union and the African Union: Peace & security. https://www.eeas.europa.eu/african-union/european-union-and-african-union-peace-security_en

European External Action Service. (2022). *Maritime cooperation*. https://euinasean.eu/maritime-cooperation-2022/

European External Action Service. (2024a). *Coordinated maritime presences*. https://www.eeas.europa.eu/eeas/coordinated-maritime-presences_en

European External Action Service. (2024b). *EU CSDP missions and operations 2023 annual report*. Publications Office of the European Union.

European External Action Service. (2024c). *Maritime security*. https://www.eeas.europa.eu/eeas/maritime-security_en

European External Action Service. (2025). *Green transition: EU green diplomacy*. https://www.eeas.europa.eu/eeas/green-transition-diplomacy_en

European Foundation for South Asian Studies. (2023). *South Korea's New Southern Policy in Southeast Asia and India: Limitations and Opportunities*. European Foundation for South Asian Studies (EFSAS).

European Parliament. (2024). *Maritime security: Situation in the Red Sea and EU response*. https://www.europarl.europa.eu/RegData/etudes/ATAG/2024/757606/EPRS_ATA(2024)757606_EN.pdf

European Union. (2007). *Renewable energy road map*. https://eur-lex.europa.eu/legal-content/EN/TXT/?uri=LEGISSUM:l27065

Eurostat. (2024). *EU trade with the Indo-Pacific region increased in 2022*. https://ec.europa.eu/eurostat/web/products-eurostat-news/w/ddn-20240201-1

Eurostat. (2025). *Oil and petroleum products: A statistical overview*. https://ec.europa.eu/eurostat/statistics-explained/index.php?title=Oil_and_petroleum_products_-_a_statistical_overview

Evans, G., & Grant, B. (1995). *Australia's foreign relations in the world of the 1990s*. Melbourne University Press.

Fang, Y. (2015). The South China Sea Disputes: Whither a Solution? In Huang, J., & Billo, A. (Eds.), *Territorial Disputes in the South China Sea* (pp. 164–188). Palgrave Macmillan., DOI: 10.1057/9781137463685_10

Felker, G. (2001). ASEAN Regionalism and Southeast Asia's Systemic Challenges. In: *Twenty-First Century World Order and the Asia Pacific* (pp. 213-253). Palgrave Macmillan, New York. https://doi.org/DOI: 10.1057/9780230107175_8

Financial Express. (2024). *Explainer: Quad a strategic alliance for stability and progress in Indo-Pacific.* https://www.financialexpress.com/business/defence-explainer-quad-a-strategic-alliance-for-stability-and-progress-in-indo-pacific-3616538/

Firepower, G. (2024). *Global Firepower 2023.* https://www.globalfirepower.com

Fisher, A. S. (1988). Manila Galleon trade textiles: Cross-cultural influences on New World dress. *Textile Society of America Symposium Proceedings*, Article 636. https://digitalcommons.unl.edu/cgi/viewcontent.cgi?article=1635&context=tsaconf

Foster, S. (2022). China on course to elude US chip-making equipment bans. *Asia Times.* https://asiatimes.com/2022/10/china-on-course-to-elude-us-chip-making-equipment-bans/

Fravel, M. T. (2011). China's strategy in the South China Sea. *Contemporary Southeast Asia, 33*(3), 292–319. https://taylorfravel.com/documents/research/fravel.2011.CSA.china.strategy.scs.pdf. DOI: 10.1355/cs33-3b

Fretay, H. (2025). Pakistan strengthens stealth submarine capabilities with launch of second Hangor-class in China. *Army Recognition Group.* https://armyrecognition.com/news/navy-news/2025/pakistan-strengthens-stealth-submarine-capabilities-with-launch-of-second-hangor-class-in-china

Furuya, K. (2022). Japan's Coast Guard diplomacy through capacity building in the Indo-Pacific. In *Maritime Security and Japan* (pp. 120–134). Routledge., DOI: 10.4324/9781003216766-9

Geeraerts, G. (2019). Europe and China's Belt and Road Initiative: Growing concerns, more strategy. *Security Policy Brief, 118*, 1–6. Egmont Institute. https://www.egmontinstitute.be/app/uploads/2019/11/SPB118.pdf

Girardi, B., Go, Y., Sweijs, T., & Kertysova, K. (2023). *What the Indo-Pacific means to Europe: Trade value, chokepoints, and security risks.* The Hague Centre for Strategic Studies. https://hcss.nl/wp-content/uploads/2023/11/What-the-Indo-Pacific-means-to-Europe-Trade-Value-Chokepoints-and-Security-Risks-HCSS-2023.pdf

Global Data. (2024). *Vietnam defense market size, trends, budget allocation, regulations, acquisitions, competitive landscape and forecast to 2029*. https://www.globaldata.com/store/report/vietnam-defense-market-analysis/

Global Military. (2025). *Pakistan Navy*. https://www.globalmilitary.net/navies/pak/

Global Times. (2024). China, Russia hold first meeting of subcommittee on Arctic shipping routes cooperation. https://www.globaltimes.cn/page/202411/1323886.shtml

Gökpınar, T. A. (2019). Green theory in international relations. In Gökpınar, T. A. (Ed.), *Theories of international relations II* (pp. 163–178). Anadolu University Press.

Gomez, J. (2025). India and the Philippines stage joint naval drill in the disputed South China Sea. *AP Newsroom*. https://apnews.com/article/india-philippines-south-china-sea-joint-sail-eecfaa6056d719377l6fb4dc22f52b8a

Grare, F. (2020). France, the other Indo-Pacific power. *Carnegie Endowment for International Peace*. https://carnegieendowment.org/2020/10/21/france-other-indo-pacific-power-pub-83000

Grare, F., & Reuter, M. (2023). *The battle for the Indian Ocean: How the EU and India can strengthen maritime security*. European Council on Foreign Relations. https://ecfr.eu/publication/the-battle-for-the-indian-ocean-how-the-eu-and-india-can-strengthen-maritime-security/

Green, M. A. (2024). Debt distress on the road to "Belt and Road". *Wilson Center*. https://www.wilsoncenter.org/blog-post/debt-distress-road-belt-and-road

Grigorjeva, J. (2016). *Starting a new chapter in EU-Algeria energy relations: A proposal for a targeted cooperation* (Policy Paper No. 173). Jacques Delors Institute. https://institutdelors.eu/content/uploads/2025/04/eualgeriaenergy-grigorjeva-jdib-sept16-2.pdf

Grossman, D. (2020). *Regional Responses to U.S.-China Competition in the Indo-Pacific*. RAND Corporation., https://www.rand.org/pubs/research_reports/RR4412z6.html DOI: 10.7249/RR4412.6

Guard, B. Ministry of National Defence, People's Army of the Socialist Republic of Vietnam. (2021). *Vietnam's policy on maritime security*. http://bienphongvietnam.gov.vn/chinh-sach-cua viet nam ve an-ninhbien.html

Gumantiara, M. I., Haqqi, H., & Murdani, A. D. (2024). Regional security complex analysis in Australia, United Kingdom, and United States (AUKUS) viewpoint to the rivalry between United States and China in Taiwan. *Formosa Journal of Sustainable Research, 3*(3), 541–554. DOI: 10.55927/fjsr.v3i3.8144

Guzman, C. (2024). Why the US faces a delicate balancing act on countering China in the SCS. *TIME.* https://time.com/6960916/us-military-intervention-south-china-sea-philippines-china/

Hai, D. T. (2017). *Vietnam and the South China Sea: Politics, security and legality.* Routledge.

Hai, D. T. (2021). Vietnam and China: Ideological bedfellows, strange dreamers. *Journal of Contemporary East Asia Studies, 10*(2), 162–182. DOI: 10.1080/24761028.2021.1932018

Haldar, S., & Gupta, S. (2025). AUKUS under review: What lies ahead for Indo-Pacific security. *Observer Research Foundation.* https://www.orfonline.org/expert-speak/aukus-under-review-what-lies-ahead-for-indo-pacific-security

Hall, I. R. (2022). AUKUS and Australia–UK strategic reconvergence. *RUSI Journal, 167*(6–7), 34–42. DOI: 10.1080/03071847.2022.2159514

Hamzah, T. (2020). Gray zone conflicts in Asia Pacific. *Modern Diplomacy.* https://moderndiplomacy.eu/2020/08/04/gray-zone-conflicts-in-asia-pacific/

Hanh, V. N. (2025). Vietnam-China economic partnership: Insights from top Chinese leader's visit. *Vietnam Briefing.* https://www.vietnam-briefing.com/news/vietnam-china-economic-partnership-amid-global-tensions-top-chinese-leaders-visit.html/

Han, J. (2020). A vanguard of foreign policy over maritime claims: Naval power rather than national power. *Korean Journal of Defense Analysis, 32*(2), 311–329. DOI: 10.22883/KJDA.2020.32.2.008

Hao, S. (2011). China's Positions and Interests in the South China Sea: A Rational Choices in its Cooperative Policies. *Center for Strategic and International Studies.* https://www.csis.org/analysis/chinas-positions-and-interests-south-china-sea-rational-choices-its-cooperative-policies

Hasan, S. (2015). Navy gets only 10pc of defence budget. *Dawn.* https://www.dawn.com/news/1217390

Haver, Z. (2021). China maritime report No. 12: Sansha City in China's SCS strategy: Building a system of administrative control. *CMSI China Maritime Reports.* https://digital-commons.usnwc.edu/cmsi-maritime-reports/12/

Hayton, B. (2024). The SCS: Historical and legal background. *Council on Geostrategy*. https://www.geostrategy.org.uk/research/the-south-china-sea-historical-and-legal-background/

Hayton, B. (2024). The South China Sea: Historical and legal background (China Observatory Explainer. *Council on Geostrategy*. https://www.geostrategy.org.uk/app/uploads/2024/09/No.-2024_27-%E2%80%93-The-South-China-Sea_-Historical-and-legal-background.pdf

Hayton, B. (2025). Vietnam's tariff deal with Trump reflects balancing act between US and China. *Chatham House*. https://www.chathamhouse.org/2025/07/vietnams-tariff-deal-trump-reflects-balancing-act-between-us-and-china

Heath, T. R. (2018). China's military has no combat experience: Does it matter? *RAND Corporation*. https://www.rand.org/pubs/commentary/2018/11/chinas-military-has-no-combat-experience-does-it-matter.html

He, K., & Li, M. (2020). Understanding the dynamics of the Indo-Pacific: US–China strategic competition, regional actors, and beyond. *International Affairs*, *96*(1), 1–7. DOI: 10.1093/ia/iiz242

Herz, J. H. (1950). Idealist internationalism and the security dilemma. *World Politics*, *2*(2), 157–180. DOI: 10.2307/2009187

Heydarian, R. (2023). Taiwan, US elections and SCS tensions could make 2024 even more geopolitically perilous. *South China Morning Post*. https://www.scmp.com/comment/opinion/article/3246254/taiwan-us-elections-and-south-china-sea-tensions-could-make-2024-even-more-geopolitically-perilous

Hien, N. T. (2017). Identifying the new political-security situation in the Middle East and North Africa region. *Social Sciences Information. Information Sur les Sciences Sociales*, *8*, 3–13.

Hiep, T. X., Hoan, T. Q., & Kiet, L. H. (2024). Free and Open Indo-Pacific strategy: Competitive Opinions and Trends. *Vestnik of Saint Petersburg University -. International Relations*, *17*(3), 242–259.

Hiep, T. X., & Kiet, L. H. (2024). India's competitive strategy with China in Southeast Asia: An analysis of the case of Vietnam. *Journal of Chinese Studies*, *2*(270), 68–80.

Hiep, T. X., Kiet, L. H., & Yen, P. T. H. (2023). Strategic Hedging in Southeast Asia: ASEAN Member States' Policy Responses to China's Growing Economic Influence. *Contemporary Chinese Political Economy and Strategic Relations*, *9*(2/3), 404–438.

Hiep, T. X., Kiet, L. H., & Yen, P. T. H. (2024). India's Look East Policy: Vietnam's pivotal role amidst China's rising regional influence. *Estudios Internacionales (Santiago)*, *12*(3), 51–73. https://periodicos.pucminas.br/estudosinternacionais/article/view/34606

Hieu, B. T., Cuong, A. N., & Nhi, D. T. Y. (2024). Challenges for Vietnam in protecting SCS sovereignty and interests. *Cogent Social Sciences*, *10*(1), 2401629. Advance online publication. DOI: 10.1080/23311886.2024.2401629

Ho, Q. L. (2022). The depth of US–China strategic competition. *People's Army Newspaper*. https://www.qdnd.vn/bao-quan-doi-nhan-dan-xuan-nham-dan/bao-quan-doi-nhan-dan-xuan-nham-dan/chieu-sau-canh-tranh-chien-luoc-my-trung-quoc-684193

Ho, A. N. (2023). Challenges Toward a Rule-based Order in the South China Sea. *Journal of Asian Security and International Affairs*, *10*(2), 169–189. DOI: 10.1177/23477970231173539

Hoang, V. (2021). The true nature of China's 'soft power'. *VietnamNet Online Newspaper*. https://vietnamnet.vn/thuc-chat-quyen-luc-mem-cua-trung-quoc-757240.html

Hoang, H. H. (2022). Understanding Vietnam's foreign policy choices amid Sino-US rivalry. *ISEAS Perspective*, *2022*(41), 1–10.

Hoffman, F. G. (2016). The contemporary spectrum of conflict: Protracted, gray zone, ambiguous, and hybrid modes of war. In *Index of U.S. military strength* (pp. 25–36). The Heritage Foundation., https://www.heritage.org/military-strength-topical-essays/2016-essays/the-contemporary-spectrum-conflict-protracted-gray

Hong, P. (2018). *Understanding ASEAN*. National Political Publishing House.

Hoo, C. P. (2022). Southeast Asia's expectations of Korea's middle-power agency in the regional security architecture. In Mantong, A. W., & Kharisma, W. (Eds.), *Navigating uncharted waters: Security cooperation between ROK and ASEAN* (pp. 25–38). Centre for Strategic and International Studies (CSIS) Indonesia.

Hossain, K. (2013). The UNCLOS and the US-China hegemonic competition over the South China Sea. *Journal of East Asia and International Law*, *6*(1). Advance online publication. DOI: 10.14330/jeail.2013.6.1.05

Houlden, G., Romaniuk, S. N., & Hong, N. (Eds.). (2021). *Security, strategy, and military dynamics in the South China Sea: Cross-national perspectives*. Bristol University Press.

Hu, B. (2021). Sino-US Competition in the South China Sea: Power, Rules and Legitimacy. *Journal of Chinese Political Science*, *26*(3), 485–504. DOI: 10.1007/s11366-020-09716-1

Huger, B., & Raj, M. (2021). France: A balancing force in Quad and the Indo-Pacific. *Diplomatist*. https://diplomatist.com/2021/05/21/france-a-balancing-force-in-quad-and-the-indo-pacific/

Hu, L. (2023). Examining ASEAN's effectiveness in managing South China Sea disputes. *The Pacific Review*, *36*(1), 119–147. DOI: 10.1080/09512748.2021.1934519

Huld, A., & Zhou, Q. (2024). Trump wins the 2024 US presidential election: Implications for China. *China Briefing*. https://www.china-briefing.com/news/trump-china-us-relations-2024-election-victory-implications-businesses/

Hung, N. (2023). Is China escalating tensions in the SCS to ease domestic pressure? *International Studies Review*. https://nghiencuuquocte.org/2023/10/14/trung-quoc-day-cang-thang-tren-bien-dong-nham-giam-suc-ep-noi-bo/

Hung, N. M. (2024). Foreign affairs school, "Vietnamese bamboo" diplomacy in the Doi Moi era. *Communication Review*, *1038*(6), 64–71.

Hunt, E. (2024). Building out the US hub-and-spoke empire in the Indo-Pacific. *CounterPunch*. https://www.counterpunch.org/2024/10/24/building-out-the-us-hub-and-spoke-empire-in-the-indo-pacific/

Huong, N. M. (2016). *New context of Vietnam's national security challenges*. ISEAS Publishing. https://bookshop.iseas.edu.sg/publication/2196

Hutagalung, S. (2024). Would Trump go soft on the SCS? *Asia Times*. https://asiatimes.com/2024/03/would-trump-go-soft-on-the-south-china-sea/

Hutchins, S. G., Gallup, S. P., MacKinnon, D., Schacher, G., Miller, S., Freeman, J., Dunaway, D., & Poeltler, B. (2008). Enhancing maritime domain awareness. *Defense Technical Information Center*. https://apps.dtic.mil/sti/pdfs/ADA486840.pdf

Huynh, T. S. (2019). *Australia-Vietnam Relations (1991-2013)*. Ho Chi Minh City National University Publishing House.

Ibarra, E. J. A. (2022). Issue-based cooperation on conflict resolution in the South China Sea: Exploring roles for ASEAN beyond the Code of Conduct. *Journal of Territorial and Maritime Studies*, *9*(1), 97–115. DOI: 10.2307/48684181

Idris, A. M., Sasongko, N. A., & Kuntjoro, Y. D. (2022). AUKUS cooperation in the form of Australian nuclear submarine technology for stability in Indo Pacific region. *International Journal of Research and Innovation in Social Science*, *6*(2), 745–750. Advance online publication. DOI: 10.47772/IJRISS.2022.6237

Inclusive Development International. (2016). *Making inroads: Chinese infrastructure investment in ASEAN and beyond.* https://www.inclusivedevelopment.net/wp-content/uploads/2016/12/2.-Asian-Infrastructure-Investment-Bank-VN.pdf

Indonesia. (2020). Note verbale No. 126/POL-703/V/20. *United Nations.* https://www.un.org/Depts/los/clcs_new/submissions_files/mys_12_12_2019/2020_05_26_IDN_NV_UN_001_English.pdf

Indo-Pacific Defense Forum. (2018). *Congressional ASEAN group wants closer U.S.-ASEAN ties.* https://ipdefenseforum.com/2018/08/congressional-asean-group-wants-closer-u-s-asean-ties/

Indo-Pacific Defense Forum. (2023). *Philippines bolsters military presence after 'Chinese activities' near islands.* https://ipdefenseforum.com/2023/01/philippines-bolsters-military-presence-after-chinese-activities-near-islands/

Institut de Recherche Stratégique de l'École Militaire. (2022). *Preventing and combating trafficking of conventional weapons: Challenges and lessons learnt in the Indo-Pacific region.* https://www.irsem.fr/storage/file_manager_files/2025/03/livret-g-n-ral-en.pdf

International Chamber of Commerce International Maritime Bureau. (2024). *Maritime piracy dropped in 2024, but crew safety remains at risk.* https://icc-ccs.org/maritime-piracy-dropped-in-2024-but-crew-safety-remains-at-risk/

International Crisis Group. (2024). *Riding Unruly Waves: The Philippines' Military Modernisation Effort.* https://www.crisisgroup.org/sites/default/files/2025-08/349-philippines-military-modernisation.pdf

International Defence Analysis. (2024). *Indian naval development – An analysis.* https://internationaldefenceanalysis.com/indias-naval-development-an-analysis/

ISEAS - Yusof Ishak Institute. (2023). *The state of Southeast Asia: 2023 survey report.* https://www.iseas.edu.sg/wp-content/uploads/2025/07/The-State-of-SEA-2023-Final-Digital-V4-09-Feb-2023.pdf

Jabeen, M. (2024). *Maritime security challenges to Gwadar seaport.* Paper presented at the 3rd International Security Congress, Necmettin Erbakan University, Konya, Turkey.

Jackson, L. (2023). Australia's nuclear submarine plan to cost up to $245 billion by 2055 -defence official. *Reuters*. https://www.reuters.com/world/asia-pacific/australias-nuclear-submarine-plan-cost-up-245-bln-by-2055-defence-official-2023-03-13/

Jaishankar, D. (2023). India, the QUAD, and the liberal international order. In *India's Foreign Policy* (pp. 75–81). Springer. DOI: 10.1007/978-981-99-4729-4_7

Jakobson, L. (2014). *China's unpredictable maritime security actors*. Lowy Institute.

Jannuzi, F. (2025). U.S. Interests in the South China Sea: Defending Norms, not Territory. In Hung Son, N., & Thi Lan Anh, N. (Eds.), *The South China Sea: The Geo-political Epicenter of the Indo-Pacific?* Springer., DOI: 10.1007/978-981-97-8209-3_3

Jansson, P. (2018). Rhetoric and legitimacy in the European Neighbourhood Policy. *Global Affairs*, *4*(2–3), 317–328. DOI: 10.1080/23340460.2018.1535253

Jansson, P. (2018). Smartness as prudence: Smart power and classical realism. *Journal of Political Power*, *11*(3), 341–358. DOI: 10.1080/2158379X.2018.1523317

Jenne, N. (2017). Managing Territorial Disputes in Southeast Asia: Is There more than the South China Sea? *Journal of Current Southeast Asian Affairs*, *36*(3), 35–61. DOI: 10.1177/186810341703600302

Jervis, R. (1978). Cooperation under the security dilemma. *World Politics*, *30*(2), 167–214. DOI: 10.2307/2009958

Jha, M. K. (2023). Why India's navy budget needs a big push. *Financial Express*. https://www.financialexpress.com/budget/why-indias-navy-budget-needs-a-big-push-2964769/

Jones, A. (2023). ESA is no longer planning to send astronauts to China's Tiangong space station. *SpaceNews*. https://spacenews.com/esa-is-no-longer-planning-to-send-astronauts-to-chinas-tiangong-space-station/

Jones, R. (2024). Political geography I: Blue geopolitics. *Progress in Human Geography*, *48*(5), 615–625. DOI: 10.1177/03091325241271521

Kakkar, M. G. H. (2024). China's new naval base in Cambodia The Excelsior 18 Oct 2024. *Maj Gen Harsha Kakkar Articles*. https://harshakakararticles.com/2024/10/18/chinas-new-naval-base-in-cambodia-the-excelsior-18-oct-2024/

Kamaruddin, N. (Ed.). (2020). *The New Southern Policy – Catalyst for deepening ASEAN–ROK cooperation*. ISIS Malaysia.

Kang, K. (2025). Strategic importance of the South China Sea: Beyond geography. *Pacific Forum.* https://pacforum.org/publications/yl-blog-98-strategic-importance-of-the-south-china-sea-beyond-geography/

Kapur, S. P. (2008). Ten years of instability in a nuclear South Asia. *International Security, 33*(2), 71–94. DOI: 10.1162/isec.2008.33.2.71

Karim, M. F., & Nabila, R. (2022). Role conception of the Asia-Pacific middle powers: Comparative analysis of Indonesia, South Korea, Australia and Vietnam. *Journal of Asian Security and International Affairs, 9*(2), 231–254. DOI: 10.1177/23477970221098469

Karkalanov, T. (2016). Energy in Russia's foreign policy and EU-Russia relations circumventing sanctions: Yamal LNG becomes a precedent. *Russian International Affairs Council.* https://russiancouncil.ru/en/blogs/tsvetko-karkalanov-en/_2472/

Katsumata, H. (2009). The Significance of the ASEAN Regional Forum (ARF). In: *ASEAN's Cooperative Security Enterprise - Critical Studies of the Asia Pacific Series* (pp. 16-34). Palgrave Macmillan, London. DOI: 10.1057/9780230277038_2

Kazmi, Z. (2025). The blind spot in South Asia's deterrence debate. *Strategic Vision Institute.* https://thesvi.org/the-blind-spot-in-south-asias-deterrence-debate/

Kelly, B., & Wester, S. (2025). ASEAN caught between China's export surge and global de-risking. *Asia Society.* https://asiasociety.org/policy-institute/asean-caught-between-chinas-export-surge-and-global-de-risking

Khan, B. (2017). Pakistan tests Babur-3 submarine-launched cruise missile. *Quwa.* https://quwa.org/daily-news/pakistan-tests-babur-3-submarine-launched-cruise-missile/

Khanh, V. V. (2021). *Vietnam's policy on maritime security.* http://bienphongvietnam.gov.vn/chinh-sach-cua-viet-nam-ve-an-ninh-bien.html

Khan, S. A. (2022). The AUKUS alliance and its implications on the Non-Proliferation Treaty. *BTTN Journal, 1*(2), 83–94. DOI: 10.61732/bj.v1i2.26

Kiet, L. H., & Tuyen, N. V. (2023). Vietnam's geopolitical position with the United States in its strategy to contain China's hegemonic ambitions. *Journal of Science and Technology - Danang University, 21*(8.1), 63-69. https://jst-ud.vn/jst-ud/article/view/8630

Kiet, L. H., & Tuyen, N. V. (2023). Vietnam's geopolitical position with the US in its strategy to contain China's hegemonic ambitions. *Journal of Science and Technology - Danang University, 21*(8.1), 63-69. https://jst-ud.vn/jst-ud/article/view/8630

Kiet, L. H., Binh, N. T., & Hiep, T. X. (2024). From Arroyo to Duterte: Two Decades of Philippines' Foreign Policy Navigation between the US and China. *Przegląd Strategiczny, 17,* 133-150. https://www.ceeol.com/search/article-detail?id=1331776

Kiet, L. H. (2023). Some Factors Influencing the Geopolitical Competition Between India and China in the Indian Ocean Region in the 21st Century. *Journal of China Studies*, *6*(262), 69–87.

Kiet, L. H., Binh, N. T., & Hiep, T. X. (2024). From Arroyo to Duterte: Two Decades of Philippines' Foreign Policy Navigation between the US and China. *Przegląd Strategiczny*, *17*(17), 133–150. DOI: 10.14746/ps.2024.1.9

Kiet, L. H., Binh, N. T., & Hiep, T. X. (2025a). From border conflicts to maritime competition: Driving forces behind the power rivalry between India and China in the Indian Ocean region. *Australian Journal of Maritime and Ocean Affairs*, •••, 1–25. DOI: 10.1080/18366503.2025.2492438

Kiet, L. H., & Hiep, T. X. (2025). Geopolitical conflict between great powers in the 21st century: An analysis of the Ukraine crisis. *Sovremennaya Evropa*, *129*(1), 121–135. DOI: 10.7868/S3034599525010103

Kiet, L. H., Nguyen, P. H., Tran, H. X., & Nguyen, B. T. (2025b). Vietnam's balancing strategy in the US-China rivalry in Southeast Asia. In Zreik, M. (Ed.), *Innovations and tactics for 21st century diplomacy* (pp. 271–302). IGI Global., DOI: 10.4018/979-8-3693-6074-3.ch012

Kiet, L. H., Tam, L. T. T., & Hiep, T. X. (2025b). Caught between dragon and elephant: Vietnam's strategic balancing act in the Sino-Indian rivalry. *China Quarterly of International Strategic Studies*, *11*(2), 99–128. DOI: 10.1142/S237774002550006X

Kim, H., & Lee, J. (2020). *The New Southern Policy.* ISIS Focus, 4/2020(14).

Kochegurov, D. A. (2022). Formation of an anti-Chinese consensus among US 'think tanks': From D. Trump to J. Biden. *Herald of the Russian Academy of Sciences*, *93*(7), 601–611. DOI: 10.1134/S1019331622130044

Koga, K. (2022). *Managing Great Power Politics: ASEAN, Institutional Strategy, and the South China Sea*. Springer. DOI: 10.1007/978-981-19-2611-2

Koh, C. (2024). Muscle and mediation set to continue in the SCS. *East Asia Forum*. https://eastasiaforum.org/2024/01/18/muscle-and-mediation-set-to-continue-in-the-south-china-sea/

Kong, A. (2023). Why are China and the US competing in military exercises in Southeast Asia? *VTC News*. https://vtc.vn/vi-sao-trung-quoc-my-chay-dua-tap-tran-quan-su-o-dong-nam-a-ar797034.html

Koppe, E. V. (2014). Use of nuclear weapons and protection of the environment during international armed conflict. In Bersagel, A. G., Nystuen, G., & Casey-Maslen, S. (Eds.), *Nuclear weapons under international law* (pp. 247–268). Cambridge University Press., DOI: 10.1017/CBO9781107337435.018

Korolev, A. (2023). Transition from hedging to balancing in Australia's China policy: Theoretical and empirical explorations. *Australian Journal of International Affairs*, *77*(5), 548–568. DOI: 10.1080/10357718.2023.2274446

Kristensen, H. M., & Korda, M. (2021). Estimating world nuclear forces: An overview and assessment of sources. *Stockholm International Peace Research Institute*. https://www.sipri.org/commentary/topical-backgrounder/2021/estimating-world-nuclear-forces-overview-and-assessment-sources

Kristensen, H. M., & Korda, M. (2022). Indian nuclear weapons, 2022. *Bulletin of the Atomic Scientists*, *78*(4), 224–236. DOI: 10.1080/00963402.2022.2087385

Kroenig, M. (2018). A strategy for deterring Russian nuclear de-escalation strikes. *Atlantic Council, Scowcroft Center for Strategy and Security*. https://www.atlanticcouncil.org/wp-content/uploads/2018/04/Nuclear_Strategy_WEB.pdf

Kuik, C. C. (2017). Explaining the Contradiction in China's South China Sea Policy: Structural Drivers and Domestic Imperatives. *China*. *China*, *15*(1), 163–186. DOI: 10.1353/chn.2017.0009

Kuik, C.-C. (2017). Explaining the contradiction in China's SCS policy: Structural drivers and domestic imperatives. *China*. *International Journal (Toronto, Ont.)*, *15*(1), 163–186.

Kulkarni, S. (2025). INS Surat, INS Nilgiri and INS Vaghsheer commissioned: Their features, how they add to Navy's capabilities. *The Indian Express*. https://indianexpress.com/article/explained/ins-surat-ins-nilgiri-and-ins-vaghshee-commissioned-three-cheers-for-indian-navy-9781179/

Kuo, L., & Kommenda, N. (2018). What is China's Belt and Road Initiative? *The Guardian*. https://www.theguardian.com/cities/ng-interactive/2018/jul/30/what-china-belt-road-initiative-silk-road-explainer

LaBelle, M. C. (2024). Breaking the era of energy interdependence in Europe: A multi-dimensional reframing of energy security, sovereignty, and solidarity. *Energy Strategy Reviews*, *52*, 101314. Advance online publication. DOI: 10.1016/j.esr.2024.101314

Ladwig, W. (2024). The Indo-Pacific in Indian foreign policy. *The Royal United Services Institute for Defence and Security Studies.* https://www.rusi.org/explore-our-research/publications/policy-briefs/indo-pacific-indian-foreign-policy

Lagreone, S. (2017). US warship came within 6 miles of Chinese artificial island in toughest challenge yet to Beijing South China Sea claims. *USNI News.* https://news.usni.org/2017/05/25/u-s-warship-came-beijing-south-china-sea-claims

Lahiri, A., & Waterson, J. (2025). Egypt's Suez Canal revenue fell sharply in 2024 on regional tensions. *Euronews.* https://www.euronews.com/business/2025/04/17/egypts-suez-canal-revenue-fell-sharply-in-2024-on-regional-tensions

Lai, T. B. (2023). US–China strategic competition and its impact on major powers' policy adjustments. *Communist Review.* https://www.tapchicongsan.org.vn/web/guest/tin-binh-luan/-/asset_publisher/DLIYi5AJyFzY/content/canh-tranh-chien-luoc-my-trung-quoc-va-tac-dong-den-dieu-chinh-chinh-sach-cua-cac-nuoc-lon

Lai, T. T. (2024). What will the situation in the SCS look like if Donald Trump is re-elected as US president? *Strategic Studies.* https://nghiencuuchienluoc.org/the-cuc-bien-dong-se-ra-sao-neu-ong-donald-trump-tai-dac-cu-tong-thong-my/

Laksmana, E. A., & Mantong, A. W. (2021). Missing pillars of strategic autonomy? Security cooperation between Korea and ASEAN. In Lee, K.-H., & Yoon, J.-R. (Eds.), The New Southern Policy Plus: Progress and way forward (pp. 197–218). Korea Institute for International Economic Policy.

Landman, L. (2015). *The EU Maritime Security Strategy: Promoting or absorbing European defence cooperation?* Clingendael Institute.

Lee, J., & Park, M. (2020). An analysis of ROK and ASEAN's counter-piracy practices in the Indo-Pacific. *KIMS Maritime Security Series*, *6*(2), 45–68.

Lee, K.-H., & Yoon, J.-R. (Eds.). (2021). *The New Southern Policy Plus: Progress and way forward.* Korea Institute for International Economic Policy.

Legarda, H. (2025). *The Arctic, outer space and influence-building: China and Russia join forces to expand in new strategic frontiers* (Policy Brief). Mercator Institute for China Studies. https://doi.org/DOI: 10.5281/zenodo.17422312

Leigh, K., Martin, P., & Leung, A. (2020). Troubled waters: Where the US and China could clash in the South China Sea. *Bloomberg.* https://www.bloomberg.com/graphics/2020-south-china-sea-miscalculation/

Le, K. H., & Tran, H. X. (2025). Vietnam's strategic partnership role in India's policy to counter China's hegemonic ambitions in the East Sea. In Güçyetmez, F., & Kahraman, A. (Eds.), *Geopolitics of the SCS: Power struggle in Asia* (pp. 263–284). IGI Global Scientific Publishing., DOI: 10.4018/979-8-3693-8109-0.ch012

Lendon, B. (2024). US gains military access to Philippine bases close to Taiwan and South China Sea. *CNN World.* https://edition.cnn.com/2023/04/04/asia/us-philippines-military-base-access-intl-hnk-ml

Léonie, A. (2025). Deciphering French strategy in the Indo-Pacific. *War on the Rocks.* https://warontherocks.com/2025/03/deciphering-french-strategy-in-the-indo-pacific/

Levesques, A., Bowen, D., & Gill, J. H. (n.d.). Nuclear deterrence and stability in South Asia: Perceptions and realities. *International Institute for Strategic Studies.* https://www.iiss.org/research-paper/2021/05/nuclear-deterrence-south-asia/

Lew, L. (2021). Chinese military may have an edge over US on artificial intelligence research, report warns. *South China Morning Post.* https://www.scmp.com/news/china/military/article/3154242/chinese-military-may-have-edge-over-us-artificial-intelligence

Lewis, S., & Lema, K. (2024). US pledges funds to boost Philippine defences amid China disputes. *Reuters.* https://www.reuters.com/world/asia-pacific/us-philippines-engagements-help-with-agile-responses-china-says-marcos-2024-07-30/

Lim, B. K. (2013). China to let tourists visit disputed SCS islets. *Reuters.* https://www.reuters.com/article/us-china-seas-tourism/china-to-let-tourists-visit-disputed-south-china-sea-islets-idUSBRE93601720130407/

Lin, J., & Sothirak, P. (2025). The Elusive Code: Why ASEAN Needs a New Playbook for the South China Sea. *Fulcrum.* https://fulcrum.sg/the-elusive-code-why-asean-needs-a-new-playbook-for-the-south-china-sea/

Liu, Z. Z. (2023). China's pensions system is buckling under an aging population. *Foreign Policy.* https://foreignpolicy.com/2023/06/29/china-pensions-aging-demographics-economy/

Li, Y. (2024). Analysis of the security impact of AUKUS on the South China Sea: Based on defensive realism analysis. *Lecture Notes in Education Psychology and Public Media, 63*(1), 77–82. DOI: 10.54254/2753-7048/63/20240938

Lowy Institute. (2023). *Asia Power Index 2023 edition.* https://power.lowyinstitute.org/

Lubis, L. A. (2022). The QUAD's role in Indo-Pacific maritime security. *Journal of International Relations*, *14*(2), 45–67.

Lubis, L. A., Perwita, A. A. B., & Hadisancoko, R. E. (2024). The role of AUKUS in Australia's military capacity building strategy. *EAJMR East Asian Journal of Multidisciplinary Research*, *3*(8). Advance online publication. DOI: 10.55927/eajmr.v3i8.10608

Lv, J., & Qin, S. (2016). On low-carbon technology. *Low Carbon Economy*, *7*(3), 107–115. DOI: 10.4236/lce.2016.73010

Mafuang, S. (2024). Signaling and tactical hedging as political tools in the formation of minilateral security coalitions: QUAD and AUKUS in the Indo-Pacific region. *World Politics*, *4*(4), 30–40. DOI: 10.25136/2409-8671.2024.4.72184

Mahan, A. T. (1897). *The interest of America in sea power, present and future*. Little, Brown & Company.

Mahan, A. T. (1987). *The influence of sea power upon history, 1660-1783* (5th ed.). Dover Publications.

Mahdzir, D. (2024). NORAD jets intercept joint Russian, Chinese bomber flight near Alaska. *USNI News*. https://news.usni.org/2024/07/25/norad-jets-intercept-joint-russian-chinese-bomber-flights-near-alaska

Maliwanag, D. A. (2011). Philippines accuses China of 'serious violations' in South China Sea. *Inquiret*. https://globalnation.inquirer.net/3205/philippines-accuses-china-of-%e2%80%98serious-violations%e2%80%99-in-spratlys

Malnes, R. (1993). Robert E. Goodin: Green political theory [Book review]. *Scandinavian Political Studies*, *16*(2), 185–187. https://tidsskrift.dk/scandinavian_political_studies/article/download/32772/30993

Manoharan, N. (2025). Nautical tigers: Contributions of Cholas to India's maritime tradition. In Raju, A. S., & Srinivasan, R. (Eds.), *The Routledge handbook of maritime India* (pp. 19–28). Routledge., DOI: 10.4324/9781003607434-3

Manship, H. K. (1964). Mahan's concepts of sea power: A lecture delivered at the Naval War College. *Naval War College Review*, *16*(5), 15–30. https://www.jstor.org/stable/45236517

Marc, A. (2025). The geopolitics of the Indo-Pacific: France's strategy. *Geopolitique*. https://geopolitique.eu/en/2025/02/27/the-geopolitics-of-the-indo-pacific-frances-strategy/

Marine Insight. (2024). *Nautical law: What is UNCLOS?* https://www.marineinsight.com/maritime-law/nautical-law-what-is-unclos/

Martin, G. (2024). From the magazine: Indian Navy growing in size and reach. *Asia-Pacific Defence Reporter.* https://asiapacificdefencereporter.com/from-the-magazine-indian-navy-growing-in-size-and-reach

Marullo, F. (2022). *Applying resilience to hybrid threats in infrastructure, digital, and social domains using multisectoral, multidisciplinary, and whole-of-government approach.* NATO Science for Peace and Security Series., DOI: 10.3233/NICSP220017

Matamis, J. (2025). Nuclear ambiguity in the Indian Ocean. *Stimson Center.* https://www.stimson.org/2025/nuclear-ambiguity-in-the-indian-ocean/

Matzen, E. (2017). Denmark spurned Chinese offer for Greenland base over security – sources. *Reuters.* https://www.reuters.com/article/world/denmark-spurned-chinese-offer-for-greenland-base-over-security-sourcesidUSKBN1782E1/

Mazarr, M. J. (2015). Mastering the gray zone: Understanding a changing era of conflict. *United States Army War College Press.* https://press.armywarcollege.edu/monographs/428/

McBeth, J. (2019). Indonesia boosts its military presence in the Natuna Islands. *The Strategist.* https://www.aspistrategist.org.au/indonesia-boosts-its-military-presence-in-the-natuna-islands/

McBride, J., Berman, N., & Chatzky, A. (2023). China's massive Belt and Road Initiative. *Council on Foreign Relations.* https://www.cfr.org/backgrounder/chinas-massive-belt-and-road-initiative

McClory, J. (Ed.). (2019). The Soft Power 30. *Portland Communications.* https://softpower30.com/wp-content/uploads/2019/10/The-Soft-Power-30-Report-2019-1.pdf

McDonald, M. (2005). Constructing Insecurity: Australian Security Discourse and Policy post-2001. *International Relations, 19*(3), 297–320. DOI: 10.1177/0047117805055408

McLaughlin, R. L. (2022). The law of the sea and PRC gray-zone operations in the South China Sea. *The American Journal of International Law, 116*(4), 821–835. DOI: 10.1017/ajil.2022.49

Mearsheimer, J. J. (2001). *The Tragedy of Great Power Politics.* W.W. Norton & Company.

Medcalf, R. (2013). The Indo-Pacific: What's in a Name? *The American Interest.* https://www.the-american-interest.com/2013/10/10/the-indo-pacific-whats-in-a-name/

Medcalf, R. (2019). Mapping a multipolar future: The contest for the Indo-Pacific. *Global Asia: A Journal of the East Asia Foundation, 14*(4), 58–69. https://www.globalasia.org/v14no4/feature/mapping-a-multipolar-future-the-contest-for-the-indo-pacific_rory-medcalf

Meick, E., & Salidjanova, N. (2017). China's response to U.S.–South Korean missile defense system deployment and its implications. *U.S.-China Economic and Security Review Commission.* https://www.uscc.gov/research/chinas-response-us-south-korean-missile-defense-system-deployment-and-its-implications

Mhadzir, D. (2024). 9 Russian, Chinese warships on joint patrol in the Northwest Pacific after major naval exercise. *U.S. Naval Institute News*. https://news.usni.org/2024/10/01/9-russian-chinese-warships-on-joint-patrol-in-the-northwest-pacific-after-major-naval-exercise

Mian, Z., Ramana, M., & Nayyar, A. (2019). Nuclear submarines in South Asia: New risks and dangers. *Journal for Peace and Nuclear Disarmament*, *2*(1), 184–202. DOI: 10.1080/25751654.2019.1621425

Miao, H. (2026). The Deflation Doom Loop Trapping China's Economy. *The Wall Street Journal.* https://www.wsj.com/world/china/deflation-doom-loop-china-economy-25b0938a

Mingjiang, L., Hiep, L. H., Bing, N. C., & Chandarith, N. (2025). How Southeast Asia Sees Xi Jinping's Regional Push Amid U.S.-China Tensions. *Carnegie Endowment for International Peace.* https://carnegieendowment.org/research/2025/04/how-southeast-asia-sees-xi-jinpings-regional-push-amid-us-china-tensions

Minh, P. (2022). China's fourth aircraft carrier may be nuclear-powered. *Dan Tri Newspaper*. https://dantri.com.vn/the-gioi/tau-san-bay-thu-4-cua-trung-quoc-co-the-chay-bang-nang-luong-hat-nhan-20221009074630875.htm

Minh, P. Q., & Trang, N. T. T. (2021). *Quan he quoc te o khu vuc An Do Duong – Thai Binh Duong tu do va rong mo* [International relations in the Free and Open Indo-Pacific region]. The Gioi Publishing.

Ministère de l'Europe et des Affaires étrangères. (2023a). *EU strategy for cooperation in the Indo-Pacific*. https://www.diplomatie.gouv.fr/en/country-files/regional-strategies/indo-pacific/the-european-union-in-the-indo-pacific/

Ministère de l'Europe et des Affaires étrangères. (2023b). *Indo-Pacific: 8 questions to understand France's regional strategy*. https://www.diplomatie.gouv.fr/en/country-files/regional-strategies/indo-pacific/indo-pacific-8-questions-to-understand-on-france-s-regional-strategy/

Ministère de l'Europe et des Affaires étrangères. (2025). *La stratégie indopacifique de la France* [France's Indo-Pacific strategy]. https://www.diplomatie.gouv.fr/IMG/pdf/strate_gie_indopacifique_de_la_france_2025_cle0bc96b.pdf

Ministère des Armées. (2018). *Stratégie française en Indopacifique* [French strategy in the Indo-Pacific]. https://www.defense.gouv.fr/dgris/enjeux-regionaux/strategie-francaise-indopacifique

Ministry for Europe and Foreign Affairs. (2021). *France's Indo-Pacific strategy: Summary*. https://www.diplomatie.gouv.fr/IMG/pdf/en_a4_indopacifique_synthese_rvb_cle068e51.pdf

Ministry of Defence. (2015). *Ensuring secure seas: Indian maritime security strategy*. https://bharatshakti.in/wp-content/uploads/2016/01/Indian_Maritime_Security_Strategy_Document_25Jan16.pdf

Ministry of External Affairs. (2016). *Statement on award of arbitral tribunal on South China Sea under Annexure VII of UNCLOS*. https://www.mea.gov.in/press-releases.htm?dtl/27019/statement+on+award+of+arbitral+tribunal+on+south+china+sea+under+annexure+vii+of+unclos

Ministry of External Affairs. (2019). *Humanitarian assistance and disaster relief to Mozambique—Operation Sahayata 2019*. https://www.mea.gov.in/press-releases.htm?dtl/31174/Humanitarian+Assistance+and+Disaster+Relief+to+MozambiqueOperation+Sahayata+2019

Ministry of External Affairs. (2023). *India–Australia bilateral relations*. https://www.mea.gov.in/Portal/ForeignRelation/Aus-brief-2023.pdf

Ministry of External Affairs. (2023). *Operation Dost*. https://www.mea.gov.in/press-releases.htm?dtl/36209/Operation_Dost Ministry of External Affairs. (2025c). *Declaration on the establishment of a strategic partnership between the Government of the Republic of India and the Government of the Republic of the Philippines*. https://www.mea.gov.in/bilateral-documents.htm?dtl%2F39939%2FDeclaration_on_the_Establishment_of_a_Strategic_Partnership_between_the_Government_of_the_Republic_of_India_and_the_Government_of_the_Republic_of_the_=

Ministry of External Affairs. (2025a). *Overview of ASEAN-India relations*. https://www.mea.gov.in/Portal/ForeignRelation/BRIEF-ON-ASEAN-INDIA.pdf

Ministry of External Affairs. (2025b). *India-Japan bilateral relations.* https://indconosaka.gov.in/pdf/bilateral_Brief.pdf

Ministry of External Affairs. (2025d). *India Singapore joint statement.* https://www.mea.gov.in/bilateral-documents.htm?dtl/40094/India_Singapore_Joint_Statement_September_04_2025

Ministry of Foreign Affairs of Japan. (2007). *Confluence of the two seas: Speech by H.E. Mr. Shinzo Abe, Prime Minister of Japan at the Parliament of the Republic of India.* https://www.mofa.go.jp/region/asia-paci/pmv0708/speech-2.html

Ministry of Foreign Affairs of Japan. (2020). *Signing of the agreement between the Government of Japan and the Government of the Republic of India concerning reciprocal provision of supplies and services between the Self-Defense Forces of Japan and the Indian Armed Forces.* https://www.mofa.go.jp/press/release/press4e_002896.html

Ministry of Foreign Affairs of Japan. (2023). *Joint Statement on the Elevation of the Japan-Vietnam Relations to a Comprehensive Strategic Partnership for Peace and Prosperity in Asia and the World.* https://www.mofa.go.jp/files/100587102.pdf

Ministry of Foreign Affairs of the People's Republic of China. (2024). China and Russia hold the first consultation on the peaceful uses of outer space affairs. https://www.mfa.gov.cn/mfa_eng/xw/wjbxw/202408/t20240809_11468731.htm

Ministry of Foreign Affairs of the Socialist Republic of Vietnam. (2020). *White Paper on the Legal Status of Vietnam's Maritime Zones under the 1982 United Nations Convention on the Law of the Sea (UNCLOS).* https://vietnamlawmagazine.vn/unclos-significant-to-vietnams-peace-stability-long-term-development-73173.html

Ministry of Foreign Affairs People's Republic of China. (2018). *Wang Yi's remarks on his attendance at the Foreign Ministers' Meetings on East Asia Cooperation.* https://www.fmprc.gov.cn/eng/gjhdq_665435/2675_665437/2777_663548/2779_663552/202406/t20240607_11413438.html

Ministry of National Defence of the Socialist Republic of Vietnam. (2019). *Vietnam National Defence.* https://s.rfi.fr/media/display/41558134-9451-11ea-b6c6-005056a98db9/2019VietnamNationalDefence.pdf

Ministry of National Defense of Vietnam. (2019). *Vietnam national defense 2019.* National Political Publishing House Truth.

Misalucha-Willoughby, C. (2024). *Mixed messages and the EU's Indo-Pacific strategy.* The Hague Centre for Strategic Studies.

Mishra, R. (2025). India-Philippines ties now strategic partnership on upward trajectory. *The Diplomat*. https://thediplomat.com/2025/08/india-philippines-ties-now-strategic-partnership-on-upward-trajectory/

Mishra, R., & Yan, L. (2023). 'Same, same but different': Assessing ASEAN's and the EU's maritime strategies. *The Strategist*. https://www.aspistrategist.org.au/same-same-but-different-assessing-aseans-and-the-eus-maritime-strategies/

Mishra, R. (2021). Vietnam's regional security perceptions and priorities: Role of India. *India Quarterly. Journal of International Affairs*, *77*(2), 200–218. DOI: 10.1177/09749284211004983

Mollman, S. (2022). How a "fishermen's shelter" on stilts became a Chinese military base in the SCS. *Quartz*. https://qz.com/863811/mischief-reef-how-a-fishermens-shelter-on-stilts-became-a-chinese-military-base-in-the-south-china-sea

Monahan, D., Angwenyi, C., Montoro, H., Morishita, T., Mustapha, A., Peralta, W. R., Sharma, S., & Karlapati, S. (2005). *Multi-dimensional, multi-national, multi-faceted hydrographic training: The Nippon Foundation GEBCO training program at the University of New Hampshire*. University of New Hampshire. https://scholars.unh.edu/cgi/viewcontent.cgi?article=1348&context=ccom

Montgomery, A. H., & Sagan, S. D. (2009). The perils of predicting proliferation. *The Journal of Conflict Resolution*, *53*(2), 302–328. DOI: 10.1177/0022002708330581

Morales, N. J., & Lema, K. (2021). Philippines says 220 Chinese boats have encroached at disputed reef. *Reuters*. https://www.reuters.com/world/china/philippines-says-220-chinese-boats-have-encroached-south-china-sea-2021-03-21/

Morel, C. (2016). Menace sous les mers: Les vulnérabilités du système câblier mondial. *Hérodote*, *163*(4), 33–43. DOI: 10.3917/her.163.0033

Morgenthau, H. J. (1948). Politics among nations: The struggle for power and peace. *University of California San Diego*. http://slantchev.ucsd.edu/courses/ps240/04%20Conflict%20with%20States%20as%20Unitary%20Actors/Morgenthau%20-%20Politics%20among%20nations%20(selected%20chapters).pdf

Morning Consult & Bloomberg. (2024). *Swing States Tracking Poll*. https://pro-assets.morningconsult.com/wp-uploads/2024/01/Full-Data.pdf

Murphy, T. J., & Nagy, S. R. (2024). Middle power cybersecurity in the Indo-Pacific and the maritime domain: South Korea's role. *Journal of Intelligence, Conflict, and Warfare, 7(1), 1–24.* https://journals.lib.sfu.ca/index.php/jicw/article/download/6454/5793/23201. DOI: 10.21810/jicw.v7i1.6454

Nafilla, A. (2025). International legal implications of the North Natuna maritime dispute: A review of Indonesia–China tensions in the past two years. *International Journal of Social Science and Human Research, 8*(9). Advance online publication. DOI: 10.47191/ijsshr/v8-i9-10

Nam, H. K. (2015). Green politics: An approach in international relations. *Political Theory*. https://lyluanchinhtri.vn/home/index.php/quoc-te/item/1005-chinh-tri-xanh-%E2%80%93-mot-cach-tiep-can-trong-quan-he-quoc-te.html

Nantulya, P. (2025). *China widening its influence in Africa through expanded security engagements*. Africa Center for Strategic Studies. https://africacenter.org/spotlight/china-influence-africa-security-engagements/

Narang, V. (2016). Strategies of nuclear proliferation: How states pursue the bomb. *International Security, 41*(3), 110–150. DOI: 10.1162/ISEC_a_00268

Nathan, M. G. (2021). *China Geostrategic Relations: the Belt and Road Initiative, Asian Region instability and Australia* [PhD dissertation]. Charles Darwin University.

National Centre for Polar and Ocean Research. (n.d.). *Survey of the EEZ*. https://ncpor.res.in/pages/researchview/7

National Historical Office of the Nguyen Dynasty. (2002). *Dai Nam Thuc Luc* [Veritable records of Dai Nam]. Vol. 1). Education Publishing House.

News, G. M. A. (2020). *UK, France, Germany say China's claims in South China Sea violate law, UNCLOS*. https://www.gmanetwork.com/news/topstories/nation/756104/uk-france-germany-say-china-s-claims-in-south-china-sea-violate-law-unclos/story/

Ngo, C. N. (2022). ASEAN's position and role in the Indo-Pacific region: Opportunities amid challenges. *Political Theory Journal*. https://lyluanchinhtri.vn/home/index.php/quoc-te/item/4261-vi-the-vai-tro-cua-asean-o-khu-vuc-an-do-thai-binh-duong-co-hoi-trong-thach-thuc.html

Ngo, D. L., & Hoang, H. T. (2025). The emerging Indo-Pacific strategy of the Trump 2.0 administration. *International Studies Review*. https://nghiencuuquocte.org/2025/06/13/chien-luoc-an-do-duong-thai-binh-duong-dang-hinh-thanh-cua-chinh-quyen-trump-2-0/

Nguyen, H. (2020). Soft power in a changing world. *Communist Review*. https://www.tapchicongsan.org.vn/web/guest/quoc-phong-an-ninh-oi-ngoai1/-/2018/815776/suc-manh-mem-trong-mot-the-gioi-dang-thay-doi.aspx

Nguyen, H. (2024). Cooperation and struggle define Vietnam's approach to China. *East Asia Forum.* https://eastasiaforum.org/2024/10/28/cooperation-and-struggle-define-vietnams-approach-to-china/

Nguyen, H., & Tran, T. (2025). China's Lawfare in the South China Sea: An Overview. In: *Lawfulness and Lawfare in the South China Sea* (pp. 41-138). International Law in Asia. Springer, Singapore. DOI: 10.1007/978-981-95-4001-3_2

Nguyen, M. G. (2021). Looking back at Vietnam - Australia relations: Achievements and prospects. *Journal of Science and Technology Development - Social Sciences and Humanities, 5*(3), 1172-1180.

Nguyen, M. G. (2025). *Australia's foreign policy towards Vietnam under Prime Minister Scott Morrison's tennure (2018-2022).* Master's Thesis, University of Social Sciences and Humanities, Vietnam National University Ho Chi Minh City.

Nguyen, T. K. P. (2017). Content of the framework agreement on the Code of Conduct in the South China Sea. *International Studies.* https://nghiencuuquocte.org/2017/06/26/thoa-thuan-khung-ve-coc/

Nguyen, H. (2022). *Vietnam and the shift towards maritime security cooperation.* Brill. DOI: 10.1163/9789004532847_019

Nguyen, M. G. (2022). Vietnam - Australia Security and Defense Cooperation: Current Situation and Prospects. *Journal of Indian and Asian Studies, 4*(113), 67–76.

Nguyen, T. M. (2018). Building the cooperative mechanism's peace, stability in the East Sea nowadays. *The Journal of Middle East and North Africa Sciences, 4*(8), 20–27.

Nguyen, V. L., & Le, T. K. (2020). *US–China technological competition in the era of Industry 4.0.* National Political Publishing House.

Nguyen, V. T. (2017). Some observations on President Donald Trump's policy toward the Asia–Pacific region. *The Americas Today Review, 4*, 3–11.

Nha, N. (2013). *Nhung bang chung ve chu quyen cua Viet Nam doi voi hai quan dao Hoang Sa, Truong Sa* [Evidence of Vietnam's sovereignty over the two archipelagos of Hoang Sa and Truong Sa]. Vietnam Education Publishing House.

Nichols, T. P., Edgerton, A. K., & Desimone, L. (2021). "Smart power" in standards implementation after No Child Left Behind. *American Journal of Education, 128*(1), 147–169. DOI: 10.1086/716463

Niquet, V. (2025). France in the Indo-Pacific: Between strategic autonomy and regional engagement to support shared values, rule of law and territorial integrity. *The Japan Institute of International Affairs.* https://www.jiia-jic.jp/en/policybrief/pdf/5d450dde0e60b6e18e2b4537f115905a88013d0a.pdf

Noor, S. (2023). Pakistan's evolving nuclear doctrine. *Arms Control Association.* https://www.armscontrol.org/act/2023-10/features/pakistans-evolving-nuclear-doctrine

Nouwens, M., & McGerty, F. (2024). China's defence budget boost can't mask real pressures. *International Institute for Strategic Studies.* https://www.iiss.org/online-analysis/military-balance/2024/03/chinas-defence-budget-boost-cant-mask-real-pressures/

Nováky, N. (2022). The Coordinated Maritime Presences concept and the EU's naval ambitions in the Indo-Pacific. *European Foreign Affairs Review, 21*(1), 129–148. DOI: 10.1177/17816858221089871

Nuclear Threat Initiative. (2024). *Pakistan submarine capabilities.* https://www.nti.org/analysis/articles/pakistan-submarine-capabilities/

Nye, J. S. (2006). Think again: Soft power. *Foreign Policy.* https://foreignpolicy.com/2006/02/23/think-again-soft-power/

Nye, J. S. (2008). Smart power. Great leaders know when hard power is not enough. *Harvard Business Review, 86*(11), 55–59. https://www.ncbi.nlm.nih.gov/pubmed/18972718 PMID: 18972718

Nye, J. S. (2010). Soft power and American foreign policy. In *The Future of American Foreign Policy* (pp. IX–XIII, 127–147). Public Affairs.

Nye, J. S. (2011). *The future of power.* Public Affairs.

O'Rourke, R. (2025a). U.S.-China Strategic Competition in South and East China Seas: Background and Issues for Congress. *Congressional Research Service.* https://www.congress.gov/crs-product/R42784

O'Rourke, R. (2025b). China Naval Modernization: Implications for U.S. Navy Capabilities—Background and Issues for Congress. *Congressional Research Service.* https://www.congress.gov/crs-product/RL33153#:~:text=The%E2%80%A6%20overall%20battle%20force%20%5Bof,by%20the%20end%20of%20FY2030

Observatory of Economic Complexity. (2023). *EU.* https://oec.world/en/profile/international_organization/eu

Odgaard, L. (2023). Chinese perspectives on alliance and alignment: Entrapment concerns in China's foreign relations. *Asian Affairs, 54*(3), 432–452. DOI: 10.1080/03068374.2023.2230782

Office of the Prime Minister of Australia. (2024). *Joint Statement on the Elevation to a Comprehensive Strategic Partnership between Vietnam and Australia*. https://www.pm.gov.au/media/joint-statement-elevation-comprehensive-strategic-partnership-between-vietnam-and-australia

Pacheco Pardo, R., & Leveringhaus, N. (2022). *Security and defence in the Indo-Pacific: What is at stake for the EU and its strategy?* European Parliament Directorate-General for External Policies., DOI: 10.2861/10775

Pajon, C. (2023b). France's Indo-Pacific strategy: From a balancing power to a constructive stakeholder. *Institut français des relations internationales.* https://www.ifri.org/en/external-articles/frances-indopacific-strategy-balancing-power-constructive-stakeholder

Pajon, C. (2024). La stratégie indopacifique de la France [France's Indo-Pacific strategy]. *Institut français des relations internationales.* https://www.ifri.org/fr/publications-exterieures/la-strategie-indopacifique-de-la-france

Pajon, C. (2025a). France's contributions to Pacific maritime governance. *East-West Center.* https://www.eastwestcenter.org/publications/frances-contributions-pacific-maritime-governance

Pajon, C. (2025b). France seeks third way between US and China in Southeast Asia. *Lowy Institute*. https://www.lowyinstitute.org/the-interpreter/france-seeks-third-way-between-us-china-southeast-asia

Pajon, C. (2023a). France's Indo-Pacific approach: Salvaging the rules-based order and staying relevant. In *Indo-Pacific strategies: Navigating geopolitics at the dawn of a new age* (pp. 65–74). Springer., DOI: 10.1007/978-981-99-4729-4_6

Palmer, J. (2024). Where does China stand with the next White House? *Foreign Policy.* https://foreignpolicy.com/2024/11/12/china-policy-trump-white-house-xi-jinping-tariffs-taiwan/

Panda, A. (2017). South China Sea: Japan's Izumo helicopter carrier conducts drill with US Navy carrier. *The Diplomat.* https://thediplomat.com/2017/06/south-china-sea-japans-izumo-helicopter-carrier-conducts-drill-with-us-navy-carrier/

Pandey, S. K., & Bhushan, A. (2023). Submarine cables: Issues of maritime security, jurisdiction, and legalities. *European Journal of Theoretical and Applied Sciences, 1*(4), 117–132. DOI: 10.59324/ejtas.2023.1(4).13

Pant, H. V., & Bommakanti, K. (2020). In stand-off, keeping an eye on the nuclear ball. *The Hindu*. https://www.thehindu.com/opinion/op-ed/in-stand-off-keeping-an-eye-on-the-nuclear-ball/article32016062.ece

Pant, H. V. (2009). India in the Indian Ocean: Growing mismatch between ambitions and capabilities. *Pacific Affairs*, *82*(2), 279–297. DOI: 10.5509/2009822279

Park, M. A. (2025). Marketplace (Failure) of Ideas: Foreign Disinformation Campaigns in an Age of Generative A.I. and a Proportionality Approach to Falsehoods. *North Carolina Journal of Law & Technology*, *26*(1), 45–72. https://scholarship.law.unc.edu/cgi/viewcontent.cgi?article=1488&context=ncjolt

Park, S.-Y., & Kim, D. (Eds.). (2007). *ASEAN–Korea relations: Security, trade and community building*. ISEAS–Yusof Ishak Institute.

Paszak, P. (2021). China and the "Malacca dilemma". *Warsaw Institute.* https://warsawinstitute.org/china-malacca-dilemma/

Patel, R. (2025). India prepares to deliver 3rd and final consignment of BrahMos missiles to Philippines by year end. *Defence.in*. https://defence.in/threads/india-prepares-to-deliver-3rd-and-final-consignment-of-brahmos-missiles-to-philippines-by-year-end.16131/

Paul, M. (2016). *The United States, China and the freedom of the seas: Washington's FONOPs conflict with Beijing*. Stiftung Wissenschaft und Politik.

Pedrozo, R. P. (2014). An analysis of the competing claims in the South China Sea. *CNA Occasional Paper.* https://www.cna.org/reports/2014/iop-2014-u-008433.pdf

Pedrozo, R. (2021). The China Coast Guard Law (2021): A new tool for intimidation and aggression. *Maritime Security*, *3*(1), 1–44.

Pemmaraju, S. R. (2016). The SCS Arbitration (The Philippines and China): Assessment of the award on jurisdiction and admissibility. *Chinese Journal of International Law*, *15*(2), 265–307. DOI: 10.1093/chinesejil/jmw019

Perkovich, G. (2001). *India's nuclear bomb: The impact on global proliferation.* University of California Press.

Permanent Court of Arbitration. (n.d.). *The South China Sea Arbitration (The Republic of Philippines v. The People's Republic of China).* https://pca-cpa.org/cn/cases/7/

Péron-Doise, M. (2024). La quête de la maritime domain awareness (MDA) dans le Pacifique insulaire. *Revue Défense Nationale*, *872*(7), 44–50. DOI: 10.3917/rdna.872.0044

Perrin, C., Temal, R., Saury, H., Le Nay, J., Gattolin, A., & Guerriau, J. (2023). La stratégie française pour l'Indopacifique: Des ambitions à la réalité [France's strategy for the Indo-Pacific: From ambitions to reality]. *Sénat.* https://www.senat.fr/rap/r22-285/r22-285_mono.html

Petrovski, A., & Radovanović, M. (2021). Application of detection reconnaissance technologies use by drones in collaboration with C4IRS for military interested. *International Scientific Journal, 21*(40), 117. https://www.researchgate.net/publication/352481081

Pham, L. (2025). Vietnam's Gulf of Tonkin baseline helps protect sovereignty rights. *Hanoi Times*. https://hanoitimes.vn/vietnams-gulf-of-tonkin-baseline-helps-protect-sovereignty-rights.642354.html

Pham, Q. P. (2023). US–China military competition in Southeast Asia and its implications for Vietnam. *Strategic Studies Review*. https://nghiencuuchienluoc.org/canh-tranh-quan-su-my-trung-quoc-o-khu-vuc-dong-nam-a-va-ham-y-doi-voi-viet-nam/

Pham, T. T. (2015). Constructivism. *Nghiencuuquocte.* https://nghiencuuquocte.org/2015/03/01/chu-nghia-kien-tao/

Pham, T. T. B., & Vu, N. Q. (2020). Chien luoc "An Do Duong – Thai Binh Duong" tu do va rong mo cua Hoa Ky: Vai tro va phuong phap thuc hien [The United States' "Free and Open Indo-Pacific" strategy: Role and implementation methods]. *Communication Review*, *938*, 102–106.

Phan, T. T., & Nguyen, T. S. (2022). Forecasting the world and Asia–Pacific regional order toward 2030. *Communist Review*. https://www.tapchicongsan.org.vn/web/guest/tin-binh-luan/-/asset_publisher/DLIYi5AJyFzY/content/du-bao-trat-tu-the-gioi-khu-vuc-chau-a-thai-binh-duong-den-nam-2030

Phan, H. D., & Lan, N. N. (2018). The South China Sea arbitration: Bindingness, finality, and compliance with UNCLOS dispute settlement decisions. *Asian Journal of International Law*, *8*(1), 36–50. DOI: 10.1017/S2044251317000121

Philip, S. A. (2025). From competing to beating US in numbers and tonnage, here's how China built its shipping empire. *The Print*. https://theprint.in/defence/from-competing-to-beating-us-in-numbers-and-tonnage-heres-how-china-built-its-shipping-empire/2546925

Phoung, N. T. (2022). With arms expo, Vietnam seeks to diversify its defense procurements. *The Diplomat*. https://thediplomat.com/2022/12/with-arms-expo-vietnam-seeks-to-diversify-its-defense-procurements/

Phuong, M. (2024). The US and China agree to manage maritime risks. *Dan Tri Newspaper*. https://dantri.com.vn/the-gioi/my-trung-quoc-nhat-tri-kiem-soat-rui-ro-tren-bien-20240528154317798.htm

Piasentini, M. (2024). *The EU-ASEAN maritime cooperation: Sailing together to different courses?* Centre on Asia and Globalisation, Lee Kuan Yew School of Public Policy. https://lkyspp.nus.edu.sg/cag/publications/center-publications/publication-article/detail/the-eu-asean-maritime-cooperation-sailing-together-to-different-courses

Plan, L. (2019). APT40: Examining a China-nexus espionage actor. *Poseidon Trident of Innovation*. https://poseidon-us.com/2019/03/04/apt40-examining-a-china-nexus-espionage-actor

Powell, W. W., & Bromley, P. (2015). New institutionalism in the analysis of complex organizations. *International encyclopedia of the social & behavioral sciences, 16*, 764-769.

Prashanth, P. (2025). Southeast Asia maritime security and Indo-Pacific strategic competition. *Wilson Center.* https://www.wilsoncenter.org/article/southeast-asia-maritime-security-and-indo-pacific-strategic-competition

Pratson, L. F. (2022). Assessing impacts to maritime shipping from marine chokepoint closures. *Communications in Transportation Research, 2*, 100083. Advance online publication. DOI: 10.1016/j.commtr.2022.100083

Press Information Bureau. (2006). *Operation Sukoon for the evacuation of Indian nationals from Lebanon.* https://www.pib.gov.in/newsite/erelcontent.aspx?relid=20224

Press Information Bureau. (2020). *Indian Navy completes "Operation Samudra Setu"*. https://www.pib.gov.in/PressReleasePage.aspx?PRID=1637314

Press Information Bureau. (2020). *Indian Navy launches 'Operation Vanilla' to provide humanitarian assistance and disaster relief at Madagascar.* https://www.pib.gov.in/PressReleasePage.aspx?PRID=1600896

Press Information Bureau. (2024). *India–Australia joint military exercise AUSTRA-HIND commences in Maharashtra.* https://www.pib.gov.in/PressReleasePage.aspx?PRID=2071767

Press Information Bureau. (2024). *India-Japan joint exercise 'Dharma Guardian' commences in Rajasthan.* https://www.pib.gov.in/PressReleaseIframePage.aspx?PRID=2008775

Pugliese, G. (2024). The European Union and an "Indo-Pacific" alignment. *Asia-Pacific Review, 37*(1), 17–44. DOI: 10.1080/13439006.2024.2334182

Pulipaka, S., & Musaddi, M. (2021). In defence of the 'Indo-Pacific' concept. *Observer Research Foundation.* https://www.orfonline.org/research/in-defence-of-the-indo-pacific-concept

Pulungan, R. W. (2021). Enhancing maritime security in the Malacca Strait: Cooperation against piracy and maritime terrorism. *Indonesian Journal of International Law*, *7*(2), 39209. DOI: 10.17304/ijil.vol7.2.220

Putra, B. A. (2023). Malaysia's "triadic maritime diplomacy" strategy in the South China Sea. *All-Azimuth: A Journal of Foreign Policy and Peace, 12*(1), 166–192. DOI: 10.20991/allazimuth.1455442

Putra, B. A. (2024). Tread with caution: Vietnam's retaliatory and deference measures vis-à-vis assertiveness at sea. *Asian Journal of Political Science*, *32*(1), 57–76. DOI: 10.1080/02185377.2024.2351390

Pyć, D. (2019). The role of the law of the sea in marine spatial planning. *Maritime spatial planning*, 375-395.

Pyć, D. (2019). The Role of the Law of the Sea in Marine Spatial Planning. In Zaucha, J., & Gee, K. (Eds.), *Maritime Spatial Planning* (pp. 375–395). Palgrave Macmillan., DOI: 10.1007/978-3-319-98696-8_16

Qiao, J., Li, Y., & Huang, M. (2024). The geopolitical importance of Bab el-Mandeb Strait: A strategic gateway to global trade. *Middle East Political and Economic Institute.* https://mepei.com/the-geopolitical-importance-of-bab-el-mandeb-strait-a-strategic-gateway-to-global-trade/

Quy, D. D. (2012). *South China Sea Disputes, Law, Geopolitics and International Cooperation*. World Publishing.

Quy, D. D., & Ngoc, N. M. (Eds.). (2013). *South China Sea geopolitics: Interests, policies and actions of related parties*. World Publishing.

Quyet, N. H. (2023). Chinese Strategy in the South China Sea: A Growing Quest for Vital Economic and Strategic Interests. *World Affairs*, *186*(3), 687–716. DOI: 10.1177/00438200231181141

Quyet, V. L., & Nguyet, N. T. A. (2023). U.S.-Vietnam maritime security cooperation in the South China Sea: From the Obama administration to the current Biden administration. *Cogent Arts & Humanities*, *10*(1), 2231697. Advance online publication. DOI: 10.1080/23311983.2023.2231697

R&D World. (2020). *2020 R&D global funding forecast*. https://forecast.rdworldonline.com/product/2020-rd-global-funding-forecast/

Rachman, G. (2017). Destined for war? China, America, and the Thucydides trap. *Financial Times*. https://nghiencuuquocte.org/2017/07/03/dinh-menh-chien-tranh-trung-quoc-hoa-ky-va-bay-thucydides/

Raditio, K. H. (2015). China's shifting behaviour in the South China Sea: A defensive realism perspective. *American Journal of Chinese Studies*, *22*(2), 53–82. https://www.jstor.org/stable/44289102

Rahman, C. (2013). The geopolitical context. *University of Wollongong*. https://ro.uow.edu.au/cgi/viewcontent.cgi?article=1977&context=lhapapers

Ramsay, R. A. S. (2018). INS Arihant fully operational and raring to go. *SP's Naval Forces*. https://www.spsnavalforces.com/story/?id=582&h=INS-Arihant-Fully-Operational-and-Raring-to-Go

Raymond, M., & Welch, D. A. (2022). What's really going on in the South China Sea? *Journal of Current Southeast Asian Affairs*, *41*(2), 214–239. DOI: 10.1177/18681034221086291

Rehman, H. (2024). India's growing strategic behaviour in the Indian Ocean: Implications for regional strategic environment. *Margalla Papers*, *1*, 30–44. DOI: 10.54690/margallapapers.28.1.238

Ren, D. (2023). *Chinese EV makers on course to smashing 8.5 million 2023 sales target for mainland, industry players and observers say. South China Morning Post*. https://www.scmp.com/business/china-business/article/3237220/chinese-ev-makers-course-smashing-85-million-2023-sales-target-mainland-industry-players-and

Reuters. (2015). *Stalling of IMF reforms adds to appeal of other institutions – US official*. https://www.reuters.com/article/uk-europe-asia-bank-imf-idUKKBN0MD27G20150317/

Reuters. (2023). Japan and Malaysia sign $2.8m maritime security assistance deal. *Bangkok Post*. https://www.bangkokpost.com/world/2706783

Reuters. (2024). *China, Philippines seek better communication, management of conflicts in SCS*. https://www.reuters.com/world/asia-pacific/china-philippines-agree-improve-communication-manage-conflicts-south-china-sea-2024-01-17/

Rosenberg, D. (2009). Fisheries management in the South China Sea. In Bateman, S., & Emmers, R. (Eds.), *Security and international politics in the South China Sea: Towards a co-operative management regime*. Routledge.

Rosnani, R., Heryadi, D., Yani, Y. M., & Sinaga, O. (2022). ASEAN maritime security cooperation: Drivers and constraints. *TransNav: The International Journal on Marine Navigation and Safety of Sea Transportation*, *16*(3), 511–518. DOI: 10.12716/1001.16.03.01

Ross, R. S. (2024). Trump 2.0 and China: A wild card in East Asia. *ThinkChina.* https://www.thinkchina.sg/politics/trump-2-0-and-china-wild-card-east-asia

Roszko, E. (2022). *Cartographic anxieties in the South China Sea: Mapping, spatial claims, and material lives.* Duke University Press.

Roxas, P. A. V. (2017). Philippines leader says sea dispute 'better left untouched'. *Inquirer.* https://globalnation.inquirer.net/161911/duterte-south-china-sea-dispute-china-vietnam-asean-taiwan

Roy-Chaudhury, R., & Sullivan de Estrada, K. (2022). India and US FONOPs: Oceans apart. In Sullivan de Estrada, K., & Roy-Chaudhury, R. (Eds.), *Survival* (1st ed., pp. 1–26). Routledge., DOI: 10.4324/9781003422174-11

Rudd, K. (2021). Why the QUAD alarms China. *Asia Society.* https://asiasociety.org/magazine/article/why-quad-alarms-china

Runde, D. F., Hardman, A., & Bonin, C. (2024). Responding to China's growing influence in ports of the Global South. *CSIS.* https://www.csis.org/analysis/responding-chinas-growing-influence-ports-global-south

Russel, R. R., & Berger, B. H. (2020). Weaponizing the Belt and Road Initiative. *Asia Society Policy Institute.* https://asiasociety.org/sites/default/files/2020-09/Weaponizing%20the%20Belt%20and%20Road%20Initiative_0.pdf

Sabah, D. (2021). Turkey-made corvette tailored for Pakistan Navy launched in Istanbul. *Daily Sabah.* https://www.dailysabah.com/business/defense/turkey-made-corvette-tailored-for-pakistan-navy-launched-in-istanbul

Sagar, P. R. (2025). Navigating uncertainties, India's biggest submarine hunt reaches critical stage. *India Today.* https://www.indiatoday.in/india-today-insight/story/navigating-uncertainties-indias-biggest-submarine-hunt-reaches-critical-stage-2685298-2025-02-25

Sakhuja, V. (2023). Code of Conduct in the South China Sea (COC): Prospects and Challenges. *Centre for Public Policy Research.* https://www.cppr.in/articles/code-of-conduct-in-the-south-china-sea-coc-prospects-and-challenges

Sarangi, S. (2020). Unpacking SAGAR (Security and Growth for All in the Region). *USI Occasional Paper.* https://www.researchgate.net/publication/347497121_Unpacking_SAGAR_Security_and_Growth_for_All_in_the_Region

Sarjito, A. (2024). China's gray zone strategy in the SCS: Tactics, objectives, and regional implications. *Indonesian Journal of Multidisciplinary Sciences, 3*(2), 113–135. DOI: 10.59066/ijoms.v3i2.559

Sarno, G. S., & Colantoni, L. (2023). *A changing energy diplomacy: The external dimension of the REPowerEU plan* (IAI Papers 23|05). Istituto Affari Internazionali.

Saxena, P. S. (2024). Cybersecurity issues and solutions for smart power networks. In *Advances in Cybersecurity* (pp. 36–48). CRC Press., DOI: 10.1201/9781003486930-6

Schelling, T. C. (1966). *Arms and influence.* Yale University Press.

Schmidt, E. (2021). The AI revolution and strategic competition with China. *The Wire China.* https://www.thewirechina.com/2021/09/05/the-ai-revolution-and-strategic-competition-with-china/

Schoenbaum, T. J. (2016). The SCS Arbitration Decision: The need for clarification. *AJIL Unbound, 110,* 290–295. DOI: 10.1017/S2398772300009181

Scobell, A., & Harold, S. W. (2013). An "assertive" China? Insights from interviews. *Asian Security, 9*(2), 111–131. DOI: 10.1080/14799855.2013.795549

Scott, D. (2025). French maritime strategy: Carrier-led and Indo-Pacific focused. *Center for International Maritime Security.* https://cimsec.org/french-maritime-strategy-carrier-led-and-indo-pacific-focused/

Scott, M. (2024). When is the Northeast Passage open to ship traffic? *National Snow and Ice Data Center.* https://nsidc.org/learn/ask-scientist/when-northeast-passage-open-ship-trafc

Secretariat, A. S. E. A. N. (2017). *Declaration for a Decade of Coastal and Marine Environmental Protection in the South China Sea (2017-2027).* https://asean.org/wp-content/uploads/2017/11/Declaration-for-a-Decade-of-Coastal-and-Marine-Environmental-Protection-in-the-South-China-Sea-2017-2027.pdf

Secretariat, A. S. E. A. N. (2018). *Chairman's Statement of the ASEAN Post Ministerial Conference (PMC) 10+1 Sessions with the Dialogue Partners.* https://asean.org/chairmans-statement-of-the-asean-post-ministerial-conference-101-sessions-with-the-dialogue-partners-and-trilateral-meetings/

Secretariat, A. S. E. A. N. (2019). *Chairman's Statement of the 22nd ASEAN-China Summit.* https://asean.org/chairmans-statement-of-the-22nd-asean-china-summit-2/

Seil, C. (2024). Pragmatic offensive realism in the SCS. *European Guanxi*. https://www.europeanguanxi.com/post/pragmatic-offensive-realism-in-the-south-china-sea

Senate of the Philippines. (2023). *Senate condemns continued harassment of Pinoy fishermen, illegal Chinese incursion in WPS*. https://legacy.senate.gov.ph/press_release/2023/0801_zubiri1.asp

Shaka Tribe. (n.d.). *The art of Polynesian navigation: Exploring ancient seafaring techniques*. https://shakatribeshop.com/pages/the-art-of-polynesian-navigation-exploring-ancient-seafaring-techniques

Shalal, A. (2016). US says it will not recognize South China Sea exclusion zone. *Reuters*. https://www.reuters.com/article/world/u-s-says-it-will-not-recognize-south-china-sea-exclusion-zone-idUSKCN0WW1QB/

Sharma, A. (2010). The QUADrilateral Initiative: An evaluation. *South Asian Survey, 17*(2), 237–253. DOI: 10.1177/097152311201700204

Shekhar, V. (2022). Rise of QUAD as a 'premier regional grouping.'. *Journal of Global Strategic Studies, 2*(2), 37–60. DOI: 10.36859/jgss.v2i2.1287

Sherwin, S. L. (2017). Can international law make a difference? UNCLOS and the South China Sea. *Defense Technical Information Center*. https://apps.dtic.mil/sti/pdfs/AD1037983.pdf

Shi, X. (2022). Beyond AUKUS: The emerging grand maritime alliance. *China International Strategy Review, 4*(2), 248–267. DOI: 10.1007/s42533-022-00123-0

Silver, L., Devin, K., & Huang, C. (2020). Americans fault China for its role in the spread of COVID-19. *Pew Research Center*. https://www.pewresearch.org/global/2020/07/30/americans-fault-china-for-its-role-in-the-spread-of-covid-19/

Sim, D. (2024). How could a hawkish Donald Trump White House team shape US–China ties? *South China Morning Post*. https://www.scmp.com/news/china/diplomacy/article/3285848/how-could-hawkish-donald-trump-white-house-team-shape-us-china-ties

Simon, S. (2011). US–Southeast Asia relations: Deep in South China Sea diplomacy. *Comparative Connections: A Quarterly E-Journal on East Asian Bilateral Relations, 13*(2), 164-165.

Singh, M. (2025). India, Vietnam expand defense ties across land, sea, air domains. *Indo-Pacific Defense Forum*. https://ipdefenseforum.com/2025/05/india-vietnam-expand-defense-ties-across-land-sea-air-domains/

Singh, R. (2020). The fiasco that never ends: SCS. *World Press*. https://ecozhdc.wordpress.com/2020/08/30/the-fiasco-that-never-ends-south-china-sea/

Singh, A. K. (2022). UNCLOS: Facilitating ocean governance and maritime security. *Maritime Affairs*, *18*(1), 72–90. DOI: 10.1080/09733159.2022.2097643

Son, B. T. (2025). Vietnam's foreign affairs in 2024: Actively and proactively contribute to creating momentum to bring the country into a new era. *People's Police Newspaper.* https://cadn.com.vn/tich-cuc-chu-dong-gop-phan-tao-da-dua-dat-nuoc-buoc-vao-ky-nguyen-moi-post306975.html

Son, T. D. A. (Ed.). (2016). *Tu lieu ve chu quyen Viet Nam doi voi quan dao Hoang Sa* [Documents on Vietnam's sovereignty over the Hoang Sa archipelago]. Culture and Arts Publishing House.

Spinetta, L. (2006). Cutting China's "string of pearls". *U.S. Naval Institute Proceedings*. https://www.usni.org/magazines/proceedings/2006/october/cutting-chinas-string-pearls

Spirlet, T. (2024). Trump's first term avoided a fight in the SCS. It's only getting harder. *Business Insider*. https://www.businessinsider.com/trump-harder-time-countering-china-south-china-sea-2024-11

Staalesen, A. (2017). Murmansk counts on Chinese investors. *The Barents Observer*. https://www.thebarentsobserver.com/industry-and-energy/murmansk-counts-on-chinese-investors/135263

State Council Information Office of the People's Republic of China. (2015). *China's military strategy.* http://eng.mod.gov.cn/xb/Publications/WhitePapers/4887928.html

State Council Information Office of the People's Republic of China. (2019). *China's national defense in the new era*. https://english.www.gov.cn/archive/whitepaper/201907/24/content_WS5d3941ddc6d08408f502283d.html

Statista. (2022). *Leading countries by R&D spending worldwide 2022*. https://www.statista.com/statistics/732247/worldwide-research-and-development-gross-expenditure-top-countries/

Stevenson, K., & Envall, H. D. P. (2019). The "QUAD" and disaster management: An Australian perspective. In *Regional Security Cooperation* (pp. 13–23). Stimson Center. DOI: 10.26181/6005120FAB69E

Stewart, P., & Blanchard, B. (2018). Xi tells Mattis China won't give up "even one inch" of territory. *Reuters*. https://www.reuters.com/article/world/xi-tells-mattis-china-wont-give-up-even-one-inch-of-territory-idUSKBN1JN06N/

Stockholm International Peace Research Institute. (n.d.). *SIPRI military expenditure database*. https://www.sipri.org/databases/milex

Stone, M. (2019). US to sell 34 surveillance drones to allies in South China Sea region. *Reuters*. https://www.reuters.com/article/world/us-to-sell-34-surveillance-drones-to-allies-in-south-china-sea-region-idUSKCN1T42SS/

Storey, I. (2009). Maritime security in Southeast Asia: Two cheers for regional cooperation. *Southeast Asian Affairs*, 36–58. https://www.jstor.org/stable/27913377

Storey, I. (2020). Malaysia and the South China Sea Dispute: Policy Continuity amid Domestic Political Change. *ISEAS Perspective, 10*. https://www.iseas.edu.sg/wp-content/uploads/2020/02/ISEAS_Perspective_2020_18.pdf

Storey, I. (2020). *Southeast Asia and the COVID-19 pandemic: Impact and response*. ISEAS Yusof Ishak Institute.

Sumer, M. (2025). The rule of law at sea and the challenge of non-compliance: A decade after the South China Sea arbitration. *The Boğaziçi Law Review*, *3*(2), 190–211. DOI: 10.69800/blr.1780335

Sun, Y. (2018). The Northern Sea Route: The myth of Sino-Russian cooperation. *Stimson Center*. https://www.stimson.org/2018/northern-sea-route/

Suri, M. (2023). *Explaining EU maritime security cooperation through the Coordinated Maritime Presences tool*. FINABEL – The European Army Interoperability Centre.

Sutter, R. (2021). Vietnam-China relations in the new context. *Asia Policy*, *16*(2), 221–240.

Swaine, M. D., & Fravel, M. T. (2011). China's assertive behavior part two: The maritime periphery. *China Leadership Monitor*, *35*, 1–29.

Swenson, A., & Wacker, G. (2023). *South Korea's evolving Indo-Pacific strategy (SWP Research Paper 2/2023)*. Stiftung Wissenschaft und Politik.

Taffer, A. (2024). The puzzle of Chinese escalation vs. restraint in the South China Sea. *War on the Rocks*. https://warontherocks.com/2024/07/the-puzzle-of-chinese-escalation-vs-restraint-in-the-south-china-sea/

Tahir, H., & Amin, F. (2023). Assessing the effectiveness of QUAD in maritime containment of China in the Indo-Pacific region. *South Asian Economic Studies and Research*, *6*(4), 1–6. DOI: 10.36902/sjesr-vol6-iss4-2023(1-6)

Tan, Y. (2022). Chinese 'spy ship' Yuan Wang 5 docks in Sri Lanka despite Indian concern. *BBC.* https://www.bbc.com/news/world-asia-62558767

Ta, N. T., Pham, T. D., & Doan, M. H. (Eds.). (2015). *Non-traditional security: Theoretical and practical issues.* Political Theory Publishing House.

Tana, L. (1998). *Nguyen Cochinchina: Southern Vietnam in the seventeenth and eighteenth centuries.* Cornell University Southeast Asia Program. DOI: 10.7591/9781501732577

Tana, L. (1999). *Xu Dang Trong: Lich su kinh te-xa hoi Viet Nam the ki 17 va 18* [Cochinchina: Economic and social history of Vietnam in the 17th and 18th centuries]. (Nghi, N., Trans.). Tre Publishing House.

Tana, L. (2024). *A maritime Vietnam: From earliest times to the nineteenth century.* Cambridge University Press.

TASS. (2017). Arkhangelsk governor names China as key partner in Arctic projects. https://tass.com/economy/981893

Tatad, R., Despi, D., & Paculba, M. (2020). Navigating China's gray zone strategy in the South China Sea. *OSSSM Digest*, *25*(4), 1–31.

Teo, S. (2018). Middle power identities of Australia and South Korea. *The Pacific Review*, *31*(2), 159–177. DOI: 10.1080/09512748.2017.1371210

Tertia, J., & Perwita, A. A. B. (2018). Maritime security in Indo-Pacific: Issues, challenges, and prospects. *Journal of International Relations*, *14*(1), 77–95. DOI: 10.26593/jihi.v14i1.2795.77-95

Thang, N. Q. (2002). *Hoang Sa, Truong Sa lanh tho Viet Nam nhin tu cong phap quoc te* [Hoang Sa, Truong Sa as Vietnamese territory viewed from international public law]. Knowledge Publishing House.

Thao, T. T. (2025). Maritime security and Vietnamese perspective. *Science Council of Japan.* https://www.scj.go.jp/en/sca/activities/conferences/conf_5_programs/pdf/5thsecuritythao.pdf

That, V. V., Van, T. T. T., & Kiet, L. H. (2025). How China's Digital Silk Road Penetrates Vietnam Through M&A Activities: Evidence From E-commerce and Logistics. *SAGE Open*, *15*(4), 1–23. DOI: 10.1177/21582440251399749

Thayer, C. (2024). Australia-Vietnam comprehensive strategic partnership: The defence dimension. *The Strategist.* https://www.aspistrategist.org.au/australia-vietnam-comprehensive-strategic-partnership-the-defence-dimension/

Thayer, C. A. (2018b). A closer look at the ASEAN-China single draft South China Sea Code of Conduct. *The Diplomat*. https://thediplomat.com/2018/03/a-closer-look-at-the-asean-china-single-draft-south-china-sea-code-of-conduct

Thayer, C. A. (2011). Chinese assertiveness in the South China Sea and Southeast Asian responses. *Journal of Current Southeast Asian Affairs, 30*(2), 77–104. DOI: 10.1177/186810341103000205

Thayer, C. A. (2012). ASEAN's Code of Conduct in the South China Sea: A Litmus Test for Commumty-Building? *Asia-Pacific Journal, 10*(34), e4. DOI: 10.1017/S1557466012032998

The Asahi Shimbun. (2024). *Malaysia says it won't bow to China's demands to halt oil exploration in the South China Sea.* https://www.asahi.com/ajw/articles/15416756

The Ministry of Finance of the Socialist Republic of Vietnam. (2022). *Vietnam and ROK Take Ties to Comprehensive Strategic Partnership*. https://trial.mof.gov.vn/webcenter/portal/btcen

The State Council Information Office of the People's Republic of China. (2018). *China's Arctic policy*. https://english.www.gov.cn/archive/white_paper/2018/01/26/content_281476026660336.htm

The State Council of the People's Republic of China. (2025). *China, Vietnam Agree to Build All-round Cooperation Pattern*. https://english.www.gov.cn/news/202504/16/content_WS67fef369c6d0868f4e8f1bac.html

The Telegraph. (2025). *'We support freedom of navigation': India reaffirms South China Sea stance amid Beijing's objection*. https://www.telegraphindia.com/gallery/we-support-freedom-of-navigation-india-reaffirms-south-china-sea-stance-amid-beijings-objection-photogallery/cid/2116566?slide=3

The United States. (2022). The United States, Australia, and the United Kingdom Announce "AUKUS" Alliance Focused on Indo-Pacific Security. *The American Journal of International Law, 116*(1), 164–170. DOI: 10.1017/ajil.2021.69

Till, G. (2009). *Sea power: A guide for the twenty-first century*. Routledge. DOI: 10.4324/9780203880487

Ton, S. T. (2023). The world in 2023 and prospects for 2024. *Dan Tri Newspaper*. https://dantri.com.vn/the-gioi/buc-tranh-the-gioi-nam-2023-va-trien-vong-nam-2024-20231219182349296.htm

Tran, B. (2023). Vietnam's quest for enhanced maritime domain awareness. *ISEAS – Yusof Ishak Institute.* https://www.iseas.edu.sg/wp-content/uploads/2024/01/ISEAS_Perspective_2023_96.pdf

Tran, X. H., & Nguyen, M. G. (2024). Looking back at 50 years of Vietnam - Australia relations (1973 - 2023). In Institute of Southeast Asian Studies (Vietnam Academy of Social Sciences). *Proceedings of the International Conference: 50 years of Vietnam - Australia relations: Looking back and looking forward* (pp. 79-98). Social Sciences Publishing House.

Tran, N. T. (2012). Asia in Australia's foreign policy - history and present. *Journal of Social Sciences and Humanities, 53*, 16–23. https://www.thuvientailieu.vn/tai-lieu/chau-a-trong-chinh-sach-doi-ngoai-cuaaustralia-lich-su-va-hien-tai-tran-nam-tien-55151

Tran, V. T. (2017). Belt and Road: Towards the "Chinese Dream". *Communication Review, 895*, 100–105.

Trinh, V. D. (2025). Vietnam's nuanced securitization of China's assertiveness in the South China Sea. *The Pacific Review*, •••, 1–30. DOI: 10.1080/09512748.2025.2532614

Trong, N. P. (2021). Full text of General Secretary Nguyen Phu Trong's speech at the National Foreign Affairs Conference. *Government Newspaper.* https://baochinhphu.vn/toan-van-phat-bieu-cua-tong-bi-thu-nguyen-phu-trong-tai-hoi-nghi-doi-ngoai-toan-quoc-102305526.htm

Trung, H. (2023). After 50 years of rise, how does China challenge the power of the US and Japan? Voice of Vietnam. https://vov.vn/the-gioi/ho-so/sau-50-nam-troi-day-trung-quoc-hien-thach-thuc-suc-manh-my-va-nhat-ban-ra-sao-post1020596.vov

Trung, N. T., & Vu, T. M. (2018). The 2014 Oil Rig Crisis and its Implications for Vietnam–China Relations. In Le, H. H., & Tsvetov, A. (Eds.), *Vietnam's Foreign Policy under Doi Moi* (pp. 72–95). ISEAS–Yusof Ishak Institute. DOI: 10.1355/9789814818155-009

Truong, N. N. (2012). ASEAN-China and the East Sea 2002—A moment of cooperation. *To Quoc Newspaper*. https://toquoc.vn/aseantrung-quoc-va-bien-dong-2002-mot-khoanh-khac-hop-tac-99112664.htm

U.S. Department of Commerce, International Trade Administration. (2024). *Vietnam Country Commercial Guide: Defense and Security Sector.* https://www.trade.gov/country-commercial-guides/vietnam-defense-and-security-sector

U.S. Department of State. Bureau of East Asian and Pacific Affairs. (2025). *Bilateral Relations Fact Sheet: Relations with Vietnam.* https://2021-2025.state.gov/bureau-of-east-asian-and-pacific-affairs/releases/2025/01/u-s-relations-with-vietnam/

U.S. Embassy and Consulate in Vietnam. (2024). *Fact Sheet: One-year Anniversary of the U.S.-Vietnam Comprehensive Strategic Partnership.* https://vn.usembassy.gov/fact-sheet-one-year-anniversary-of-the-u-s-vietnam-comprehensive-strategic-partnership/

U.S. Energy Information Administration. (2016). *Algeria energy profile: Leading natural gas producer in Africa – Analysis.* Eurasia Review. https://www.eurasiareview.com/15032016-algeria-energy-profile-leading-natural-gas-producer-in-africa-analysis/

U.S. Energy Information Administration. (2024a). *World oil transit chokepoints.* https://www.eia.gov/international/analysis/special-topics/World_Oil_Transit_Chokepoints

U.S. Energy Information Administration. (2024b). *Amid regional conflict, the Strait of Hormuz remains critical oil chokepoint.* https://www.eia.gov/todayinenergy/detail.php?id=65504

U.S.-China Economic and Security Review Commission. (2018). Hearing on China's Belt and Road Initiative: Five years later. *USCC.* https://www.uscc.gov/sites/default/files/transcripts/Hearing%20Transcript%20-%20January%2025%2C%202018_0.pdf

Udah, J., Sonne, P., & Troianovski, A. (2025). Secret Russian intelligence document shows deep suspicion of China. *The New York Times.* https://www.nytimes.com/2025/06/07/world/europe/china-russiaspies-documents-putin-war.html

Ulis, P. (2022). QUAD HADR strategy for the Indo-Pacific. In *Humanitarian Assistance and Disaster Relief in the Indo-Pacific* (pp. 124–135). Routledge., DOI: 10.4324/9781003278719-11

Ungerer, C. (2007). The concept of "middle power" in Australian foreign policy. *The Australian Journal of Politics and History, 53*(4), 538–551. DOI: 10.1111/j.1467-8497.2007.00473.x

United Nations. (1982). *United Nations Convention on the Law of the Sea (UNCLOS).* https://www.un.org/depts/los/convention_agreements/texts/unclos/unclos_e.pdf

United Nations. (1982). *United Nations Convention on the Law of the Sea.* https://www.un.org/Depts/los/convention_agreements/convention_overview_convention.htm

United Nations. (2019). *Commission on the Limits of the Continental Shelf (CLCS) outer limits of the continental shelf beyond 200 nautical miles from the baselines: Submissions to the Commission: Partial submission by Malaysia in the South China Sea.* https://www.un.org/depts/los/clcs_new/submissions_files/submission_mysvnm_33_2009.htm

United Nations. (2020a). *Note verbale No. 126/POL-703/V/20.* https://www.un.org/Depts/los/clcs_new/submissions_files/mys_12_12_2019/2020_05_26_IDN_NV_UN_001_English.pdf

United Nations. (2020b). *Note verbale No. 324/2020.* https://www.un.org/Depts/los/clcs_new/submissions_files/mys_12_12_2019/2020_09_16_DEU_NV_UN_001.pdf

United States Energy Information Administration. (2024). *World oil transit chokepoints.* https://www.eia.gov/international/analysis/special-topics/World_Oil_Transit_Chokepoints

US Department of Defense. (2023). *Military and security developments involving the People's Republic of China.* https://media.defense.gov/2023/Oct/19/2003323409/-1/-1/1/2023-MILITARY-AND-SECURITY-DEVELOPMENTS-INVOLVING-THE-PEOPLES-REPUBLIC-OF-CHINA.PDF

US Trade Representative. (2018). *Findings of the investigation into China's acts, policies, and practices related to technology transfer, intellectual property, and innovation under Section 301 of the Trade Act of 1974, March 22.* USTR. https://ustr.gov/sites/default/files/Section%20301%20FINAL.PDF

US Trade Representative. (2018a). *Update concerning China's acts, policies and practices related to technology transfer, intellectual property, and innovation.* https://ustr.gov/sites/default/files/enforcement/301Investigations/301%20Report%20Update.pdf

Valori, G. E. (2025). Le rôle croissant de la marine française dans l'Indo-Pacifique [The growing role of the French Navy in the Indo-Pacific]. *World Geostrategic Insights.* https://www.wgi.world/le-role-croissant-de-la-marine-francaise-dans-lindo-pacifique/?lang=fr

Van, N. T., & Ngoc, M. P. (2009). Quan he thuong mai cua Dang Trong voi nguoi Hoa the ky XVI-XVIII [Trade relations between Dang Trong and the Chinese in the 16th-18th centuries.]. *Journal of Historical Studies, 9*, 40–45.

Vanttinen, P. (2021). Finland denied China airbase in the Arctic. *Euractiv.* https://www.euractiv.com/short_news/finland-denied-china-airbase-in-the-arctic/

Viet Nam News. (2024). *Vietnam modernizes military, strengthens national defense.* https://vietnamnews.vn/politics-laws/1689314/viet-nam-modernises-military-strengthens-national-defence.html

Viet Nam News. (2025). *Vietnam calls for respect for international law to ensure maritime* security. https://vietnamnews.vn/politics-laws/1723311/viet-nam-calls-for-respect-for-international-law-to-ensure-maritime-security.html

Vietnam Government Portal. (2016). *Overall Strategy for International Integration through 2020, vision to 2030.* http://news.chinhphu.vn/Home/Overall-strategy-for-international-integration-through-2020-vision-to-2030/20161/29060.vgp

Vietnam Journal of Science and Technology. (2021). *The regional structure of the Asia–Pacific by 2025 and Vietnam's policy.* https://vjst.vn/vn/tin-tuc/4544/cau-truc-khu-vuc-chau-a---thai-binh-duong-den-nam-2025-va-chinh-sach-cua-viet-nam.aspx

Vietnam News Agency. (n.d.). *Freedom of navigation in the South China Sea.* https://vietnam.vnanet.vn/vietnamese/long-form/tu-do-hang-hai-tren-bien-dong-343073.html

VietnamPlus. (2017). *ASEAN and China officially adopt COC framework draft.* https://www.vietnamplus.vn/asean-va-trung-quoc-chinh-thuc-thong-qua-du-thao-khung-coc-post459670.vnp

Vinh, T. T. (Ed.). (2007). *Lich su Viet Nam, Tap IV: The ky XVII-XVIII* [History of Vietnam, Volume IV: 17th-18th centuries]. Social Sciences Publishing House.

Vitous, C. A. (2023). Dynamics of environmental security in the Indo-Pacific. In *Environmental Security in Asia* (pp. 222–247). Routledge., DOI: 10.4324/9781003336143-15

Voice of Vietnam. (2019). *Why does China have to push the 'cow's tongue line' claim?* https://vov.gov.vn/vi-sao-trung-quoc-phai-thuc-day-bang-duoc-yeu-sach-duong-luoi-bo-dtnew-122636

Vo, X. V. (Ed.). (2019). *Non-traditional maritime security cooperation in Southeast Asia and suggestions for Vietnam's policy.* Social Sciences Publishing House.

Vu, M. P. (2024). Sitting in silence or standing in protests: Endogenous dynamics behind Vietnam foreign policy and the 2014 oil rig crisis. *The Pacific Review, 37*(2), 388–418. DOI: 10.1080/09512748.2023.2175897

Vuving, A. (2017). Tracking Vietnam's force build-up in the South China Sea. *Asia Maritime Transparency Initiative.* https://amti.csis.org/tracking-vietnams-force-build-south-china-sea/

Vuving, A. L. (2006). Strategy and evolution of Vietnam's China policy: A changing mixture of pathways. *Asian Survey*, *46*(6), 805–824. https://papers.ssrn.com/sol3/papers.cfm?abstract_id=1695196. DOI: 10.1525/as.2006.46.6.805

Vy, T. T. (1961). *Ngoai thuong Viet Nam hoi the ky XVII-XVIII va dau the ky XIX* [Vietnam's foreign trade in the 17th-18th and early 19th centuries]. Historical Studies Publishing House.

Wade, G. (2009). An early age of commerce in Southeast Asia, 900-1300 CE. *Journal of Southeast Asian Studies*, *40*(2), 221–265. DOI: 10.1017/S0022463409000149

Wang, C. N. (2025). China Belt and Road Initiative (BRI) investment report 2024. *Green Finance & Development Center.* https://greenfdc.org/china-belt-and-road-initiative-bri-investment-report-2024/

Wang, G. (2018). Digging into the roots of "peace disease". *Ministry of National Defense of the People's Republic of China.* http://www.mod.gov.cn/gfbw/jmsd/4815790.html

Wangsh, L. (2024). Chinese Coast Guard conduct joint patrol in Arctic Ocean. *China Daily*. https://global.chinadaily.com.cn/a/202410/02/WS66fce050a310f1265a1c5f6c.html

Weissmann, M. (2010). The South China Sea conflict and Sino-ASEAN relations: A study in conflict prevention and peace building. *Asian Perspective*, *34*(3), 35–69. DOI: 10.1353/apr.2010.0013

Wei, Z. (2022). The evolution of the 'QUAD': Driving forces, impacts, and prospects. *China International Strategy Review*, *4*(2), 288–304. DOI: 10.1007/s42533-022-00119-w

Wheeler, C. (2006). Re-thinking the sea in Vietnamese history: Littoral society in the integration of Thuan-Quang, seventeenth-eighteenth centuries. *Journal of Southeast Asian Studies*, *37*(1), 123–153. DOI: 10.1017/S0022463405000445

White House. (2018). *Prepared remarks for Vice President Pence at the East Asia Summit Plenary Session.* https://trumpwhitehouse.archives.gov/briefings-statements/prepared-remarks-vice-president-pence-east-asia-summit-plenary-session/

White House. (2023). *Quad Leaders' Joint Statement.* https://bidenwhitehouse.archives.gov/briefing-room/statements-releases/2023/05/20/quad-leaders-joint-statement/

White House. (2025). *United States-India Joint Leaders' Statement.* https://www.whitehouse.gov/briefings-statements/2025/02/united-states-india-joint-leaders-statement/

White, H. (2011). Power Shift: Australia's Future between Washington and Beijing. *Quarterly Essay.* https://www.quarterlyessay.com.au/essay/2010/08/power-shift/extract

Whomersley, C. (2017). The Award on the Merits in the Case Brought by the Philippines against China Relating to the South China Sea: A Critique. *Chinese Journal of International Law, 16*(3), 387–423. DOI: 10.1093/chinesejil/jmx023

Williams, H., Bingen, K. A., & MacKenzie, L. (2024). Why did China and Russia stage a joint bomber exercise near Alaska? *Center for Strategic and International Studies.* https://www.csis.org/analysis/why-did-china-and-russia-stage-joint-bomber-exercise-near-alaska

Williams, P. D., & Ali, H. Y. (2020). *The European Union training mission in Somalia: An assessment* (SIPRI Background Paper). Stockholm International Peace Research Institute. https://www.sipri.org/sites/default/files/2020-11/bp_2011_eutm_somalia_0.pdf

Wilson, J. L. (2002). Strategic partners: Russian-Chinese relations and the July 2001 friendship treaty. *Problems of Post-Communism, 49*(3), 3–13. DOI: 10.1080/10758216.2002.11655984

Wirth, C. (2021). Securing the seas, securing the state: The inside/outside of "Indo-Pacific" geopolitics. *The Asia-Pacific Journal, 19*(3), 137–173. https://apjjf.org/2021/3/Wirth

Wishnick, E. (2025). The Sino-Russian partnership: Cooperation without coordination. *China Leadership Monitor.* https://www.prcleader.org/post/the-sino-russian-partnership-cooperation-without-coordination

Womack, B. (2006). *China and Vietnam: The politics of asymmetry.* Cambridge University Press. DOI: 10.1017/CBO9780511610790

Wortzel, L. M. (2013). Cyber espionage and the theft of U.S. intellectual property and technology. *USCC.* https://www.uscc.gov/sites/default/files/Wortzel-OI-Cyber-Espionage-Intellectual-Property-Theft-2013-7-9.pdf

Wueger, D. (2016). India's Nuclear-Armed Submarines: Deterrence or Danger? *The Washington Quarterly, 39*(3), 77–90. DOI: 10.1080/0163660X.2016.1232636

Xia, Y., & Han, W. (2024). China's debt-to-GDP ratio climbs to record 287.8% in 2023. *Nikkei Asia.* https://asia.nikkei.com/Spotlight/Caixin/China-s-debt-to-GDP-ratio-climbs-to-record-287.8-in-2023

Xuanzum, L. (2023). Russian warships visit China following joint naval patrol in Pacific Ocean. *Global Times.* https://www.globaltimes.cn/page/202308/1296785.shtml

Xueren, L. (2025). Xi's visit to strengthen China-Vietnam bond, regional growth. *Xinhua.* https://english.cctv.com/2025/04/15/ARTIlLYpl3PF3RPLHDiluXxD250415.shtml

Yamaguchi, M. (2025). Pacifist Japan has slowly transformed from exclusively self-defense to a military buildup. *AP News.* https://apnews.com/article/japan-military-buildup-defense-constitution-us-china-4986b7e36b9bb86355898c6d762084e7

Yearbook, S. I. P. R. I. (2024). Armaments, disarmament and international security. *Stockholm International Peace Research Institute.* https://www.sipri.org/databases/milex

Yeo, J.-Y. (2023). *Indo-Pacific concept and Korea–ASEAN Solidarity Initiative: Regional perspectives (East Asian Institute Policy Brief).* National University of Singapore.

Yoon, S.-J. (2021). South Korea and the South China Sea: A middle-power model for practical policies? In G. Houlden, S. N. Romaniuk, & N. Hong (Eds.), *Security, strategy, and military dynamics in the South China Sea: Cross-national perspectives* (pp. 347–366). Bristol University Press. DOI: 10.2307/j.ctv1t4m1qr.24

Yoon, S. (2015). Implications of Xi Jinping's "true maritime power": Its context, significance, and impact on the region. *Naval War College Review, 68*(3), 40–63.

Yoon, S.-J. (2015). Maritime Asia: A South Korean perspective. In Till, G. (Ed.), *The changing maritime scene in Asia: Rising tensions and future strategic stability* (pp. 92–113). Springer.

York, M. (2015). ASEAN's ambiguous role in resolving South China Sea disputes. *Indonesian Journal of International Law, 12*(3), 325–346. DOI: 10.17304/ijil.vol12.3.607

Yoshihara, T. (2015). Maritime multilateral security cooperation in East and Southeast Asia. *Asia-Pacific Review, 22*(1), 24–47.

Yoshimatsu, H. (2022). ASEAN and Great Power Rivalry in Regionalism: From East Asia to the Indo-Pacific. *Journal of Current Southeast Asian Affairs, 42*(1), 25–44. DOI: 10.1177/18681034221139297

Young, R. R., & Gordon, G. A. (2020). Intermodal maritime supply chains: Assessing factors for resiliency and security. *Journal of Transportation Security, 13*(3), 231–244. DOI: 10.1007/s12198-020-00224-0

Yuste, P., Campbell, J. R., Canyon, D. V., Childers, M., & Ryan, B. J. (2019). Synchronized humanitarian, military and commercial logistics: An evolving synergistic partnership. *Safety (Basel, Switzerland), 5*(4), 67. DOI: 10.3390/safety5040067

Zeng, X., & Zhang, S. (2021). From "Asia Pacific" to "Indo Pacific": The adjustment of American Asia Pacific strategy from the perspective of critical geopolitics. *East Asian Affairs, 1*(2), 2150009. Advance online publication. DOI: 10.1142/S2737557921500091

Zhang J. (2023). Rebuilding strategic autonomy: ASEAN's response to US–China strategic competition. *China International Strategy Review,* 1–17. DOI: 10.1007/s42533-023-00128-3

Zhang, Z. (2021). US–China rivalry: Who has the stronger military? *South China Morning Post*. https://www.scmp.com/news/china/military/article/3140681/us-china-rivalry-who-has-stronger-military

Zhang, D., Tao, J., Wan, C., Huang, L., & Yang, M. (2024). Resilience analysis of maritime transportation networks: A systematic review. *Transportation Safety and Environment, 6*(4), tde009. Advance online publication. DOI: 10.1093/tse/tdae009

Zhang, K. (2022). Signals, deterrence, and the QUAD. *Asia Policy, 29*(4), 43–48. DOI: 10.1353/asp.2022.0069

Zhang, T., Zhang, X., & Ke, X. (2021). Quad-FPN: A novel quad feature pyramid network for SAR ship detection. *Remote Sensing (Basel), 13*(14), 2771. Advance online publication. DOI: 10.3390/rs13142771

Zhao, X. (2016). Authorities working on plan to delay retirements. *China Daily*. https://www.chinadaily.com.cn/china/2016-07/23/content_26192140.htm

Zhou, L., & Zhou, V. (2017). Donald Trump's early East Asia Summit exit casts doubt over US ties to Asia. *South China Morning Post*. https://www.scmp.com/news/china/diplomacy-defence/article/2119926/donald-trumps-early-summit-exit-casts-doubt-over-us

Zhu, F. (2012). *US rebalancing in the Asia-Pacific: China's response and the future regional order* (Discussion Paper No. 12). Victoria University of Wellington, Center for Strategic Studies.

Zhuo, C. (n.d.). Coast Guard, Russia Security Service sign joint MoE. *Ministry of National Defence of the People's Republic of China*. http://eng.mod.gov.cn/xb/MilitaryServices/News_213106/16220829.html

Zulqarnain, D., Shehwar, D., & Nizamani, S. A. (2024). Power dynamics in Indian Ocean: US Indo-Pacific strategic report and prospects for Pakistan's national security. *Government: Research Journal of Political Science*, *13*, 1–11.

About the Contributors

Kiet Hoang Le (Lê Hoàng Ki t) is a Ph.D Candidate at the Faculty of International Studies, University of Social Sciences and Humanities, Vietnam National University, Hanoi, Vietnam. His scholarly focus encompasses the exploration of power rivalry dynamics and security conflicts in the international arena. With approximately 30 publications indexed in prestigious Scopus and Web of Science databases, he has established a strong research profile in his field. His scholarly work has appeared in prominent international relations journals including China Quarterly of International Strategic Studies, Australian Journal of Maritime and Ocean Affairs, Journal of Liberty and International Affairs, Contemporary Chinese Political Economy and Strategic Relations, and Janus.Net, among others.

Hiep Xuan Tran (Tr n Xuân Hi p) is an Associate Professor and Ph.D holder who serves as a lecturer at The University of Da Nang, University of Science and Education, Vietnam. His principal research interests encompass general political and international relations issues, the Southeast Asian region, and Vietnam's international integration. He has published extensively on these themes in prestigious journals including India Quarterly: A Journal of International Affairs, International Journal of China Studies, Journal of Educational and Social Research, Contemporary Chinese Political Economy and Strategic Relations, Academic Journal of Interdisciplinary Studies, Journal of Asian Finance, Economics and Business, Cogent Arts and Humanities, Vestnik of Saint Petersburg University, and Asian and African Studies.

***

Hammad Ahsan, Assistant Professor of Political Science in the Government of Punjab, Pakistan. He holds an MPhil in International Relations and is currently pursuing a Ph.D in International Relations with a focus on the Indian Ocean Region. His academic interests encompass maritime security in the Indo-Pacific, energy geopolitics, the Indian Ocean Region (IOR), and strategic studies. Since beginning his teaching career in 2012, he has taught a wide range of courses in political science and international relations and has authored multiple research papers. He maintains an active interest in policy research, academic writing, and contributing to debates on Pakistan's strategic environment. His current research engagements include maritime security, nuclear deterrence at sea, and the strategic transformation of Azerbaijan's energy sector.

Judith Anne Lal is an Assistant Professor from the Department of Political Science and International Studies at Christ (Deemed to be University), Delhi NCR.

Thao Thi Bui (Bùi Th Th o), Associate Professor, Ph.D, is a Lecturer University at the Faculty of History, University of Education, Hue University, Vietnam. She earned her Bachelor's degree in History Education (2001) and Master's degree in History Education (2004) from Hue University of Education, and her Ph.D in History (2012) from Hue University of Sciences. Appointed Associate Professor in 2017, her research and teaching expertise focuses on modern and contemporary world history. She has published over 40 research articles, authored or co-authored 7 books and textbooks, and led 13 research projects, contributing significantly to historical scholarship in Vietnam.

Tridib Chakraborti, Professor Emeritus and Dean of the School of Liberal Arts and Culture Studies at Adamas University, Kolkata. He previously served as Professor and Head of the Department of International Relations at Jadavpur University, Kolkata, where he made significant contributions to academic scholarship and institutional development. His extensive expertise encompasses South Asian, Southeast Asian, and Asia-Pacific affairs, Indian political thought, foreign policy analysis, and strategic studies. Throughout his distinguished academic career, he has been recognized as a leading authority on regional geopolitics and India's engagement with its neighboring regions, contributing substantially to the field through research, teaching, and mentorship of emerging scholars in international relations.

Mohor Chakraborty, Assistant Professor in Political Science at South Calcutta Girls' College (affiliated with the University of Calcutta), Kolkata, India. Her research focuses on International Relations and Area Studies (South Asia, Southeast Asia, and the Indo-Pacific), as well as Peace and Conflict Studies. She has co-authored three books and has contributed numerous articles and chapters to peer-reviewed journals and edited volumes published by Springer, Palgrave Macmillan, Routledge, Wiley, IGI Global, Asian Vision Institute, Indian Council of

World Affairs, Pentagon Press, Gyan Publishing House, and Readers Service, among others. She has presented papers at various national and international conferences.

Duc Dang Minh (Đ ng Minh Đ c), Associate Professor, Ph.D, is a Senior Researcher at the Institute for European and American Studies, Vietnam Academy of Social Sciences (VASS), a position he has held since 2000. He currently serves as Deputy Director of the Institute for European and American Studies, VASS. He also teaches at the Faculty of Law, Hung Vuong University, Ho Chi Minh City. He earned his Bachelor's degree in Oriental Studies in 1997 from Hanoi Law University, a Master's degree in Law in 2006 from the Faculty of Law, Vietnam National University, Hanoi, and a Ph.D in Law in 2013 from the Graduate Academy of Social Sciences, VASS. His research interests focus on political and legal systems, comparative law, European regional integration and regionalism, as well as Vietnam's foreign policy and Vietnam's relations with European and American countries.

Hoang Thi Van Anh is pursuing a Master's degree in International Relations at the University of Warsaw, Poland, with a focus on Asian Regional Studies within the Faculty of Political Science and International Studies. She holds a Bachelor's degree in International Relations from Duy Tan University, Vietnam.

Le Ngo Huyen Trang holds a Bachelor's degree in International Relations from the School of International Studies, Hue University. Her research interests include migration conflicts, international human rights law, panda diplomacy, soft power, and public diplomacy with a particular focus on the Chinese model.

Ngoc Phuong Mai (Mai Phương Ng c), Ph.D, is a lecturer and researcher at Vinh University, Vietnam. Her scholarly work specializes in Vietnamese history and Vietnamese culture, exploring the intricate connections between historical developments and contemporary cultural practices. Through her research, Dr. Mai examines how historical events have shaped national identity, social structures, and cultural traditions in Vietnam. Her interdisciplinary approach combines historical analysis with cultural studies, investigating the evolution of Vietnamese society across different periods and the preservation of cultural heritage in modern contexts. Dr. Mai's work contributes to deeper understanding of Vietnam's rich historical narrative and its influence on present-day cultural dynamics, offering valuable insights into the nation's transformation and the enduring significance of traditional values in contemporary Vietnamese life.

Jamal Mokhtari, Ph.D, is a Post-Doctoral Researcher in the Department of Political Sciences at Ferdowsi University of Mashhad, Iran. His research expertise encompasses democracy, political theory, Iranian political thought, and international relations with focus on diplomacy and the Global South. He has contributed chapters to edited volumes on 21st-century diplomacy and strategic relations in Asia and the Middle East. His scholarly work explores political philosophy, comparing Western and Islamic political thought, and analyzing Iran's strategic partnerships in the evolving global order.

Nam Tien Tran (Tr n Nam Ti n), Associate Professor, Ph.D, is an Associate Professor of World History at the Faculty of History and International Relations, University of Social Sciences and Humanities, Vietnam National University - Ho Chi Minh City, Vietnam. He has extensive experience in teaching and research in the fields of international relations, foreign policy, Vietnam–United States relations, and regional security issues. His research interests focus on Vietnam's foreign policy, post-war reconciliation, international cooperation, and contemporary strategic dynamics in Southeast Asia. He has supervised numerous undergraduate, master's, and doctoral theses and has published widely in academic journals and edited volumes. He has also been actively involved in academic conferences, policy-oriented research projects, and international academic exchanges, contributing significantly to the advancement of international studies in Vietnam.

M.A. Nguyen Thi Phuong Dung has been a researcher of the Institute of European and Americas Studies, Vietnam Academy of Social Sciences (VASS) since 2014. She graduated B.A in International Relations in 2012 from the Diplomatic Academy of Vietnam; an MA in International Relations in 2016 from the University of Social Sciences and Humanities. Her research interests focus on the foreign and defense policies of the EU, France, Germany, and the French, German and European approaches to the Indo-Pacific

Nguyen Minh Giang, as the primary author of 2 SCOPUS journal articles, 6 international journal articles, 18 international conference papers, and 23 domestic conference papers, and a co-author of 4 SCOPUS journal articles and 2 domestic conference papers published at the Vietnam Academy of Social Sciences, University of Social Sciences and Humanities Ho Chi Minh City, Hanoi National University of Education, and Vietnam National University Hanoi, Nguyen Minh Giang mainly researches Australian foreign policy, international relations in the Asia-Pacific region, Vietnamese cultural history, and Indian culture, politics, and foreign policy.

Nguyen Thi Khanh Ly holds a Bachelor's degree in International Relations from the School of International Studies, Hue University. Her research interests include Chinese foreign policy, sea power, sustainable development, cultural diplomacy, and public diplomacy.

Nguyen Le Phuc Uyen is currently enrolled in the Master's program in International Relations at the University of Warsaw, Poland. Her academic concentration is in Asian Regional Studies, offered by the Faculty of Political Science and International Studies.

Thu Thi Anh Phan (Phan Th Anh Thư), Ph.D, is a scholar of international relations at the University of Social Sciences and Humanities, Vietnam National University Ho Chi Minh City, Vietnam. Her research focuses on foreign policy analysis, middle-power diplomacy, and non-traditional forms of international engagement. She has authored four scholarly monographs on the Republic of Korea, examining state–society relations, regional strategy, and diplomatic adaptation under structural constraints. Building on her sustained work on informal diplomacy, soft power, and network-based influence, her recent research advances the theorization of non-recognition diplomacy, including Taiwan's strategic engagement in Africa, where influence is generated through aid, civil society, and people-centered cooperation rather than formal diplomatic recognition.

Hoa Le Quynh Phan (Phan Lê Quỳnh Hoa), Ph.D, is a Senior Lecturer at Dong A University, Vietnam. Her research specializes in political science and intercultural studies, focusing on governance, human development, and education within contemporary socio-political contexts. She examines how social events and cultural transformations influence educational policy and capacity building. Through her interdisciplinary approach, Dr. Phan investigates the dynamic relationship between contemporary political developments and educational outcomes, contributing valuable insights to improve governance frameworks and development strategies. Her work bridges theoretical analysis with practical applications, advancing understanding of how cultural factors shape policy implementation and institutional effectiveness in diverse educational settings.

Shruti Rathore is a research scholar from the Department of International Studies at Christ (Deemed to be University), Delhi NCR. Having completed her bachelors and masters in Political Science from University of Delhi, she is currently specializing in the Indo-Pacific region, with a particular focus on maritime security, naval diplomacy, great power competition, and India's strategic positioning within the evolving regional order. She has published in several peer-reviewed journals and edited volumes, and her scholarly and analytical writings have appeared in platforms such as The Diplomat, The Diplomatist, The Geopolitics, and The Leaflet. In addition, she has teaching experience as Guest Faculty at University of Delhi, reflecting her engagement with both academic research and contemporary debates in international politics.

Trang Thu Nguyen (Nguy n Thu Trang), Ph.D, is Head of the Department of International Studies at the Faculty of History and International Relations, University of Social Sciences and Humanities, Vietnam National University – Ho Chi Minh City. She holds a Ph.D in International Studies and has extensive experience in teaching and research in international studies and global affairs. Her research interests include international relations theory, global governance, non-traditional security, sustainable development, and contemporary international affairs. She has participated in and coordinated various academic research projects, supervised undergraduate and graduate theses, and published in academic journals and conference proceedings. She is actively involved in academic conferences, curriculum development, and interdisciplinary teaching, contributing significantly to the advancement of international studies education and research in Vietnam.

Tran Thi Minh Ha holds a Bachelor's degree in International Relations from the School of International Studies, Hue University. Her academic interests include diplomatic history, ethnic conflicts, sociology, and development studies.

Hieu Bach Tran (Tr n Bách Hi u), Ph.D, is Head of the Faculty of Laws, International Relations and Politics at Thai Binh University, Vietnam. His scholarly work concentrates on international relations dynamics in the Asia-Pacific region, contemporary global issues, and comparative political systems. Dr. Tran's research examines regional security architecture, transnational governance challenges, and political development across diverse national contexts. Through rigorous analysis of geopolitical trends and institutional frameworks, he explores how emerging powers shape regional order and how states navigate complex multilateral relationships. His interdisciplinary approach integrates legal perspectives with political analysis, contributing theoretical and empirical insights to debates on sovereignty, cooperation mechanisms, and policy coordination in an increasingly interconnected world. Dr. Tran's work advances understanding of how nations balance domestic imperatives with international commitments while addressing shared challenges in governance, development, and security.

Vo Duong Anh Phuong holds a Bachelor's degree in International Relations from the International School, Hue University, Vietnam. Vo's research focuses on niche diplomacy in Southeast Asia and international relations in the context of sustainable development.

Index

Symbols

N

P

Q

R

S

U

V

X

www.ingramcontent.com/pod-product-compliance
Lightning Source LLC
LaVergne TN
LVHW061526290926
849162LV00004B/679